MW01283497

# Bulletproof TLS and PKI
## Second Edition

Ivan Ristić

**Feisty Duck**

LONDON

# Bulletproof TLS and PKI

by Ivan Ristić

Second edition (build 1090). Published in January 2022.
Copyright © 2022 Feisty Duck Limited. All rights reserved.

ISBN: 978-1907117091

First edition published in August 2014.

**Feisty Duck Limited**
*www.feistyduck.com*
*contact@feistyduck.com*

**Copyeditor:** Melinda Rankin

**Cover illustration:** Michael Lester

**Production editor:** Jelena Girić-Ristić

**Proofreader**: Sue Boshers

**Technical reviewers:** Emily Stark and Matt Caswell

All rights reserved. No part of this publication may be reproduced, stored in a retrieval system, or transmitted, in any form or by any means, without the prior permission in writing of the publisher.

The author and publisher have taken care in preparation of this book, but make no expressed or implied warranty of any kind and assume no responsibility for errors or omissions. No liability is assumed for incidental or consequential damages in connection with or arising out of the use of the information or programs contained herein.

# Table of Contents

# Preface

You are about to undertake a journey into the mysterious world of cryptography. If you are like me, and you find the experience equal parts challenging and rewarding, you may stay on this journey long after you finish reading this book. I am writing this in late 2021, seven years after the publication of the first edition, and my own journey is still very much ongoing. I don't think it's going to end any time soon.

Although I'd been a user of SSL since its early years, I developed a deep interest in it around 2004, when I worked on my first book, *Apache Security*. That book had a chapter dedicated to transport security; back then I thought that would be enough. About five years later, in 2009, I was looking for something new to do; I decided to spend more time on SSL and TLS, and I've stayed in the field ever since. The result is this book, now in its second edition more than a decade later.

My main reason for going back to SSL (it was still just SSL then) was the thought that I could improve things. I saw an important technology hampered by a lack of tools and documentation. Cryptography is a fascinating subject: it's a field in which, the more you know, the more you discover how much you don't know. I can't count how many times I've had the experience of reaching a new level of understanding of a complex topic only to have yet another layer of complexity open up to me; that's what makes the subject amazing.

I spent about two years writing the first edition of this book. At first, I thought I'd be able to spread the effort so that I wouldn't have to dedicate my life to it, but that didn't work. At some point, I realized that things are changing so quickly that I constantly need to go back and rewrite the "finished" chapters. Toward the end, I had to spend every spare moment writing to keep up. I am now working on the second edition, and the situation is very similar. Since the first edition's publication, TLS 1.3 was released, and that's a brand-new protocol that has led to many other changes elsewhere. It's not surprising that I needed to write a new chapter for TLS 1.3. But in the next three chapters I worked on, I found there were deep changes and a great deal of new content throughout there as well. More work followed. In the end, it took another two years to complete the second edition.

I wrote this book to save you time. I've spent many years learning everything I could about SSL/TLS and PKI and I know that only a few can afford to do the same. I thought that if I put the most important parts of what I've learned into a book, others might be able to achieve a similar level of understanding in a fraction of the time—and here we are.

This book has the word "bulletproof" in the title, but that doesn't mean that TLS is unbreakable. It does mean that if you follow the advice from this book you'll be able to get the most out of TLS and deploy it as securely as anyone else in the world. It's not always going to be easy—especially with web applications—but if you persist, you'll have the same or better security than 99% of deployments out there.

Broadly speaking, there are two paths you can take to read this book. One is to start from the beginning. If you have time, this is going to be the more enjoyable approach. I made sure to make the book approachable even if you have little experience with cryptography. You can also read the book from the end, so to speak, by starting with the configuration guide, which will give you practical advice you can use immediately. After that, use the rest of the book as a reference guide as needed.

## Scope and Audience

This book exists to document everything you need to know about SSL/TLS and PKI for practical, daily work. I aimed for just the right mix of theory, protocol detail, vulnerability and weakness information, and deployment advice to help you get your job done.

As I was writing the book, I imagined representatives of three diverse groups looking over my shoulder and asking me questions:

**System administrators**
Always pressed for time and forced to deal with an ever-increasing number of security issues on their systems, system administrators need reliable advice about TLS so that they can deal with its configuration quickly and efficiently. Turning to the Web for information on this subject is counterproductive, because there's so much incorrect and obsolete documentation out there.

**Developers**
Although SSL initially promised to provide security transparently for any TCP-based protocol, in reality developers play a significant part in ensuring that applications remain secure. This is particularly true for web applications, which evolved around SSL and TLS and incorporated features that can subvert them. In theory, you "just enable encryption"; in practice, you enable encryption but also pay attention to a dozen or so issues, ranging from small to big, that can break your security. In this book, I made a special effort to document every single one of those issues.

**Managers**

Last but not least, I wrote the book for managers who, even though not necessarily involved with the implementation, still have to understand what's going on and make decisions. The security space is getting increasingly complicated, so understanding the attacks and threats is often a job in itself. Often, there isn't any one way to deal with the situation, and the best way often depends on the context.

Overall, you will find very good coverage of HTTP and web applications here but little to no mention of other protocols. This is largely because HTTP is unique in the way it uses encryption, powered by browsers, which have become the most popular application-delivery platform we've ever had. With that power come many problems, which is why there is so much space dedicated to HTTP.

But don't let that deceive you; if you take away the HTTP chapters, the remaining content (about two-thirds of the book) provides generic advice that can be applied to any protocol that uses TLS.

# Contents

This book has 13 chapters, which can be grouped into several parts. The parts build on one another to provide a complete picture, starting with theory and ending with practical advice.

The first part, chapters 1 through 4, is the foundation of the book and discusses cryptography, SSL, TLS, and PKI:

- Chapter 1, *SSL, TLS, and Cryptography*, begins with an introduction to SSL and TLS and discusses where these secure protocols fit in the Internet infrastructure. The remainder of the chapter provides an introduction to cryptography and discusses the classic threat model of the active network attacker.

- Chapter 2, *TLS 1.3*, discusses TLS 1.3, the most recent protocol revision. At the time of writing, TLS 1.3 is well supported by both clients and servers, and widely used. This is the chapter you should read to understand how things work today.

- Chapter 3, *TLS 1.2*, discusses TLS 1.2, which is still very much relevant and needed in practice. Understanding this protocol is also very useful to understand what improvements were made in TLS 1.3 and why. Information about earlier protocol revisions is provided where appropriate. An overview of the protocol evolution from SSL 3 onward is included at the end for reference.

- Chapter 4, *Public Key Infrastructure*, is an introduction to Internet PKI, which is the predominant trust model used on the Internet today. The focus is on the standards and organizations as well as governance, ecosystem weaknesses and possible future improvements. This chapter now includes coverage of Certificate Transparency.

---

The second part, chapters 5 through 8, details the various problems with trust infrastructure, our security protocols, and their implementations in libraries and programs:

- Chapter 5, *Attacks against PKI*, deals with attacks on the trust ecosystem. It covers all the major CA compromises, detailing the weaknesses, attacks, and consequences. This chapter gives a thorough historical perspective on the security of the PKI ecosystem, which is important for understanding its evolution.

- Chapter 6, *HTTP and Browser Issues*, is all about the relationship between HTTP and TLS, the problems arising from the organic growth of the Web, and the messy interactions between different pieces of the web ecosystem.

- Chapter 7, *Implementation Issues*, deals with issues arising from design and programming mistakes related to random number generation, certificate validation, and other key TLS and PKI functionality. In addition, it discusses voluntary protocol downgrade and truncation attacks, as well as high-profile issues, such as Heartbleed, FREAK, and Logjam.

- Chapter 8, *Protocol Attacks*, is the longest chapter in the book. It covers all the major protocol flaws discovered in recent years: insecure renegotiation, BEAST, CRIME, Lucky 13, POODLE and POODLE TLS, RC4, TIME and BREACH, and Triple Handshake Attack. The newer ROBOT and Raccoon attacks are also there, among others. A brief discussion of Bullrun and its impact on the security of TLS is also included.

The third part, chapters 9 through 11, provides comprehensive advice about deploying TLS in a secure and efficient fashion:

- Chapter 9, *Performance*, focuses on the speed of TLS, going into great detail about various performance improvement techniques for those who want to squeeze every bit of speed out of their servers.

- Chapter 10, *HSTS, CSP, and Pinning*, covers some advanced topics that strengthen web applications, such as HTTP Strict Transport Security and Content Security Policy. It also covers pinning, which is an effective way of reducing the large attack surface imposed by our current PKI model.

- Chapter 11, *Configuration Guide*, is the map for the entire book and provides step-by-step instructions on how to deploy secure and well-performing TLS servers and web applications. This chapter has effectively been rewritten for the second edition.

The fourth and final part consists of chapters 12 and 13, which focus on OpenSSL, the de facto standard for everyday TLS and PKI work on the command line:

- Chapter 12, *OpenSSL Command Line*, describes the most frequently used OpenSSL functionality, with a focus on installation, configuration, and key and certificate management. The last section in this chapter provides instructions on how to construct and manage a private certification authority.

- Chapter 13, *Testing TLS with OpenSSL*, continues with OpenSSL and explains how to use its command-line tools to test server configuration. Even though it's often much easier to use an automated tool for testing, OpenSSL remains the tool you turn to when you want to be sure about what's going on.

## SSL versus TLS

It is unfortunate that we have two names for essentially the same protocol. In my experience, most people are familiar with the name SSL and use it in the context of transport layer encryption. You will also hear SSL in the context of "SSL certificates." Some people, usually those who spend more time with the protocols, use or try to make themselves use the correct name, whichever is right in the given context. It's probably a lost cause. Despite that, I tried to do the same. It was a bit cumbersome at times, but I think I managed to achieve it by (1) avoiding either name where possible, (2) mentioning where advice applies to all protocol versions, and (3) using TLS in all other cases. You probably won't notice, and that's fine.

For the second edition, however, I decided to drop the word "SSL" from the title, calling the book *Bulletproof TLS and PKI*. The world has left SSL behind, and it's time that we leave it behind as well.

## Online Resources

This book doesn't have an online companion, but it does have an online file repository that contains the files referenced in the text. The repository is available at *github.com/ivanr/bulletproof-tls*.

To be notified of events and news as they happen, follow @ivanristic on Twitter. TLS is all I do these days, and I try to highlight everything that's relevant. There's hardly any noise. In addition, my Twitter account is where I will mention improvements to the book as they happen.

You may also want to keep an eye on my blog, which is at *blog.ivanristic.com*. To be honest, I don't publish much these days, probably because if I am not working on this book, I am spending all of my time on my startup, called Hardenize, which is all about making the best of the available security standards. If you like this book, I suspect you will like Hardenize as well; check it out at *www.hardenize.com*. It has a very heavy focus on both TLS and PKI.

If you have access to this book in digital form, you may periodically log into your account on the Feisty Duck web site to download the most recent version. Your access includes unlimited updates of the same edition. If you'd like to stay up to date with events, consider subscribing to our monthly TLS Newsletter. Initially, the newsletter was just a mailing list we used to let our readers know when updates were made available, but later we decided to keep it as a useful no-fluff service.

# Feedback

I am fortunate that I can update this book whenever I want to. It's not a coincidence; I worked hard to make it that way. I published my first book with a traditional publisher and didn't enjoy the fact that your book is set in stone once it's out. So, for my other books, I built a platform for continuous publishing. If I make a change today, it will be available to you tomorrow, after an automated daily build takes place. It's a tad more difficult to update paper books, but with print on demand we're able to publish new revisions whenever there is need.

Therefore, unlike with many other books that might never see a new edition, your feedback matters. If you find an error, it will be fixed in a few days. The same is true for minor improvements, such as language changes or clarifications. If one of the platforms changes in some way or there's a new development, I can cover it. My aim with this book is to keep it up-to-date for as long as there's interest in it.

Please write to me at ivanr@webkreator.com.

# About the Author

In this section, I get to write about myself in third person; here are a few words about me:

> *Ivan Ristić writes computer security books and builds security products. His book Bulletproof TLS and PKI, the result of more than a decade of research and study, is widely recognized as the de facto reference manual for SSL/TLS and PKI. His work on SSL Labs made hundreds of thousands of web sites more secure. He also created ModSecurity, a leading open source web application firewall.*

> *More recently, Ivan founded Hardenize, a platform for automated discovery and continuous network security monitoring. He also serves as a member of Let's Encrypt's technical advisory board.*

# About the Technical Reviewers

In working on the second edition, I was joined by my technical reviewers, who helped me write a much better book than I would have otherwise been able to. They were my safety net in tackling complex topics.

**Emily Stark** is a technical lead and manager on the Chrome Security team, where she focuses on secure transport. Her team works on HTTPS adoption, certificate verification and policies, Certificate Transparency, the TLS stack, and connection security UX. She also works on usable security in the browser, with a research-driven approach. She holds degrees in computer science from Stanford University and MIT.

**Matt Caswell** is a programmer and open source enthusiast. He has been actively contributing to the OpenSSL Project for many years. He is currently a committer to the project, a member of the OpenSSL Technical Committee and a member of the OpenSSL Management Committee. Since becoming a full-time fellow on the project in 2014, he has made many significant contributions. Most recently, he developed most of OpenSSL's TLS 1.3 implementation and has been one of the primary developers of OpenSSL 3.0.

# Acknowledgments

Although I wrote all of the words in this book, I am not the sole author. My work builds on an incredible wealth of information about cryptography and computer security scattered among books, standards, research papers, conference talks, and blog posts—and even tweets. There are hundreds of people whose work made this book what it is.

Over the years, I have been fortunate to correspond about computer security with many people who have enriched my own knowledge of this subject. Many of them lent me a hand by reviewing parts of the manuscript. I am grateful for their help. It's been particularly comforting to have the key parts of the book reviewed by those who either designed the standards or broke them and by those who wrote the programs I talk about.

It's been comforting to work on the OpenSSL chapters with Matt Caswell, who is a member of the core OpenSSL development team. Matt joined me as a technical reviewer for the second edition of this book and provided me with detail and insights only someone deeply familiar with the subject matter can give.

Emily Stark also joined me for the second edition in the technical reviewer capacity and provided me with similarly deep insights that came from her years of involvement with Internet security, PKI, and browser development.

Kenny Paterson was tremendously helpful with his thorough review of the protocol attacks chapter, which is easily the longest and the most complicated part of the book. I suspect he gave me the same treatment his students get, and my writing is much better because of it. It took me an entire week to update the chapter in response to Kenny's comments.

Benne de Weger reviewed the chapters about cryptography and the PKI attacks. Nasko Oskov reviewed the key chapters about the protocol and Microsoft's implementation. Rick Andrews and his colleagues from Symantec helped with the chapters on PKI attacks and browser issues, as did Adam Langley. Marc Stevens wrote to me about PKI attacks and especially about chosen-prefix attacks against MD5 and SHA1. Nadhem AlFardan, Thai Duong, and Juliano Rizzo reviewed the protocol attacks chapter and were very helpful answering my questions about their work. Robert Merget helped me not miss some recent developments in writing the second edition. Ilya Grigorik's review of the performance chapter was thorough and his comments very useful. Jakob Schlyter reviewed the chapter about advanced topics (HSTS and CSP), with a special focus on DANE. Pascal Knecht reviewed the TLS 1.3 chapter. Jeremy Rowley helped me understand the challenges of public key pinning through the eyes of a CA. Alban Diquet shared his thoughts on the same from his perspective of pinning library writer. Viktor Dukhovni shared his insights on DNSSEC and DANE. I should also mention Ryan Hurst and Ryan Sleevi, with whom I've had many conversations about PKI over the years.

Vincent Bernat's microbenchmarking tool was very useful in working on the performance chapter.

Eric Lawrence sent me hundreds of notes and questions. I never thought I would see a review that thorough. Eric is every author's dream reviewer, and I am incredibly grateful for his attention.

Also, a big thanks to my readers who sent me great feedback: Pascal Cuoq, Joost van Dijk, Daniël van Eeden, Dr. Stephen N. Henson, Brian Howson, Rainer Jung, Saravanan Musuwathi Kesavan, Brian King, Hendrik Klinge, Olivier Levillain, Colm MacCárthaigh, Dave Novick, Pascal Messerli, and Christian Sage.

My special thanks goes to my copyeditor, Melinda Rankin, who was always quick to respond to my questions and even adapted to my DocBook workflow. Her quick and endlessly enthusiastic emails have been a breath of fresh air. More important, her edits made an otherwise complex topic easier to follow.

# 1 SSL, TLS, and Cryptography

We live in an increasingly connected world. During the last decade of the 20th century, the Internet rose to popularity and forever changed how we live our lives. Today we rely on our phones and computers to communicate, buy goods, pay bills, travel, work, and so on. Many of us, with *always-on* devices in our pockets, don't connect to the Internet, we *are* the Internet. There are already more phones than people. The number of smart phones is measured in billions and increases at a fast pace. In the meantime, plans are under way to connect all sorts of devices to the same network. Clearly, we're just getting started.

All devices connected to the Internet have one thing in common: to protect information in transit, they rely on cryptography and a protocol called *Transport Layer Security* (TLS). This chapter is a light introduction to the art and science of protecting network communication. My goal here is to provide just enough information to enable you to read the rest of the book without having to seek additional reading material unless you really want to.

## Transport Layer Security

When the Internet was originally designed, little thought was given to security as we understand it today. As a result, the core communication protocols are inherently insecure and rely on the honest behavior of all involved parties. That might have worked back in the day, when the Internet consisted of a small number of nodes—mostly at universities—but falls apart completely today when everyone is online.

TLS is a cryptographic protocol designed to provide secure communication over insecure infrastructure. What this means is that if TLS is properly deployed, you can open a communication channel to an arbitrary service on the Internet, be reasonably sure that you're talking to the correct server, and exchange information safe in knowing that your data won't fall into someone else's hands and that it will be received intact. These protocols protect the communication link or *transport layer*, which is where the name TLS comes from.

Security is not the only goal of TLS. It actually has four main goals, listed here in the order of priority:

**Cryptographic security**

> This is the main issue: enable secure communication between any two parties who wish to exchange information.

**Interoperability**

> Independent programmers should be able to develop programs and libraries that are able to communicate with one another using common cryptographic parameters.

**Extensibility**

> As you will soon see, TLS is effectively a framework for the development and deployment of cryptographic protocols. Its important goal is to be independent of the actual cryptographic primitives (e.g., ciphers and hashing functions) used, allowing migration from one primitive to another without needing to create new protocols.

**Efficiency**

> The final goal is to achieve all of the previous goals at an acceptable performance cost, reducing costly cryptographic operations down to the minimum and providing a session caching scheme to avoid them on subsequent connections.

> **Note**
>
> TLS is designed to work on top of a reliable stream network protocol such as TCP. There is also a variant of TLS called *Datagram Transport Layer Security* (DTLS), which is designed to work with potentially unreliable and lossy protocols, such as UDP.

# Networking Layers

At its core, the Internet is built on top of protocols called IP (*Internet Protocol*) and TCP (*Transmission Control Protocol*), which are used to package data into small packets for transport. As these packets travel thousands of miles across the world, they cross many computer systems (called *hops*) in many countries. Because the core protocols don't provide any security by themselves, anyone with access to the communication links can gain full access to the data as well as change the traffic without detection.

IP and TCP aren't the only vulnerable protocols. There's a range of other protocols that are used for *routing*—helping computers find other computers on the network. DNS and BGP are two such protocols. They, too, are insecure and can be hijacked in a variety of ways. If that happens, a connection intended for one computer might be answered by the attacker instead.

When encryption is deployed, the attacker might be able to gain access to the encrypted data, but she wouldn't be able to decrypt it or modify it. To prevent impersonation attacks, TLS relies on another important technology called *Public Key Infrastructure* (PKI), which ensures that the traffic is sent to the correct recipient.

To understand where TLS fits, we're going to take a look at the *Open Systems Interconnection* (OSI) model, which is a conceptual model that can be used to discuss network communication. In short, all functionality is mapped into seven layers. The bottom layer is the closest to the physical communication link; subsequent layers build on top of one another and provide higher levels of abstraction. At the top is the application layer, which carries application data.

> **Note**
>
> It's not always possible to neatly organize real-life protocols into the OSI model. For example, we could place HTTP/2 in the session layer because it deals with connection management, but it operates after encryption, not before as in the model. QUIC and HTTP/3 make this even more complicated: they build on UDP to take control of the transport, session, and presentation layers.

Table 1.1. OSI model layers

| # | OSI Layer | Description | Example protocols |
|---|-----------|-------------|-------------------|
| 7 | Application | Application data | HTTP, SMTP, IMAP |
| 6 | Presentation | Data representation, conversion, encryption | SSL/TLS |
| 5 | Session | Management of multiple connections | - |
| 4 | Transport | Reliable delivery of packets and streams | TCP, UDP |
| 3 | Network | Routing and delivery of datagrams between network nodes | IP, IPSec |
| 2 | Data link | Reliable local data connection (LAN) | Ethernet |
| 1 | Physical | Direct physical data connection (cables) | CAT5 |

Arranging communication in this way provides clean separation of concerns; protocols don't need to worry about the functionality implemented by lower layers. Further, protocols at different layers can be added and removed; a protocol at a lower layer can be used for many protocols from higher levels.

TLS is a great example of how this principle works in practice. It sits above TCP but below higher-level protocols such as HTTP. When encryption is not necessary, we can remove TLS from our model, but that doesn't affect the higher-level protocols, which continue to work directly with TCP. When you do want encryption, you can use it to encrypt HTTP, but also any other TCP protocol, such as SMTP, IMAP, and so on.

# Protocol History

TLS began its life under a different name; it used to be called *Secure Sockets Layer* (SSL). Even though hardly anyone uses SSL today because it's no longer considered secure, the name is still commonly used to refer to transport layer encryption. The first version of SSL came from Netscape, back when the original web browser, Netscape Navigator, ruled the Internet.[1] The first version of the protocol never saw the light of day, but the next—version 2—was released in November 1994. The first deployment was in Netscape Navigator 1.1, which was released in March 1995.

Developed with little to no consultation with security experts outside Netscape, SSL 2 ended up being a poor protocol with serious weaknesses. This forced Netscape to work on SSL 3, which was released in late 1995. Despite sharing the name with earlier protocol versions, SSL 3 was a brand new protocol design that established the design we know today.

In May 1996, the TLS working group was formed to migrate SSL from Netscape to IETF. The process was painfully slow because of the political fights between Microsoft and Netscape, a consequence of the larger fight to dominate the Web. TLS 1.0 was finally released in January 1999, as RFC 2246. Although the differences from SSL 3 were not big, the name was changed to please Microsoft.[2]

The next version, TLS 1.1, wasn't released until April 2006 and contained essentially only security fixes. However, a major change to the protocol was incorporation of *TLS extensions*, which were released a couple of years earlier, in June 2003.

TLS 1.2 was released in August 2008. It added support for authenticated encryption and generally removed all hard-coded security primitives from the specification, making the protocol fully flexible.

The next protocol version, TLS 1.3, spent a lot of time in development, with the work starting in late 2013 and the final RFC released in August 2018. Although initially it seemed that this update would only incorporate small incremental improvements, over time it turned into a complete protocol rewrite that kept backward compatibility, simplified the design, improved performance, and removed old and weak features. QUIC, an important new network protocol released in 2021, adapted TLS 1.3 as its core encryption engine.

# Cryptography

*Cryptography* is the science and art of secure communication. Although we associate encryption with the modern age, we've actually been using cryptography for thousands of years. The first mention of a *scytale*, an encryption tool, dates to the seventh century BC. Cryptography as we know it today was largely born in the 20th century for military use. Now it's part of our everyday lives.

---

[1] For a much more detailed history of the early years of the SSL protocol, I recommend Eric Rescorla's book *SSL and TLS: Designing and Building Secure Systems* (Addison-Wesley, 2001), pages 47–51.

[2] Security Standards and Name Changes in the Browser Wars [fsty.uk/t1] (Tim Dierks, 23 May 2014)

---

When cryptography is correctly deployed, it addresses the three core requirements of security: keeping secrets (*confidentiality*), verifying identities (*authenticity*), and ensuring safe transport (*integrity*).

In the rest of this chapter, I will discuss the basic building blocks of cryptography, with the goal of showing where additional security comes from. I will also discuss how cryptography is commonly attacked. Cryptography is a very diverse field and has a strong basis in mathematics, but I will keep my overview at a high level, with the aim of giving you a foundation that will enable you to follow the discussion in the rest of the text. Elsewhere in the book, where the topic demands, I will discuss some parts of cryptography in more detail.

> **Note**
>
> If you want to spend more time learning about cryptography, there's plenty of good literature available, although it can sometimes be challenging to find a resource that covers what you care about at the right level of depth. Two recent books that you might enjoy are *Serious Cryptography*, written by Jean-Philippe Aumasson (No Starch Press, 2017) and *Real-World Cryptography*, written by David Wong (Manning, 2021).

# Building Blocks

At the lowest level, cryptography relies on various *cryptographic primitives*. Each primitive is designed with a particular useful functionality in mind. For example, we might use one primitive for encryption and another for integrity checking. The primitives alone are not very useful, but we can combine them into *schemes* and *protocols* to provide robust security.

---

## Who Are Alice and Bob?

*Alice* and *Bob* are names commonly used for convenience when discussing cryptography. They make the otherwise often dry subject matter more interesting. Ron Rivest is credited for the first use of these names in the 1977 paper that introduced the RSA cryptosystem. Since then, a number of other names have entered cryptographic literature. In this chapter, I use the name *Eve* for an attacker with an eavesdropping ability and *Mallory* for an active attacker who can interfere with network traffic.

---

## Symmetric Encryption

*Symmetric encryption* (or *private-key cryptography*) is a method for obfuscation that enables secure transport of data over insecure communication channels. To communicate securely, Alice and Bob first agree on the encryption algorithm and a secret key. Later on, when Alice

Figure 1.1. Symmetric encryption

wants to send some data to Bob, she uses the secret key to encrypt the data. Bob uses the same key to decrypt it. Eve, who has access to the communication channel and can see the encrypted data, doesn't have the key and thus can't access the original data. Alice and Bob can continue to communicate securely for as long as they keep the secret key safe. Symmetric encryption is illustrated in Figure 1.1, "Symmetric encryption".

> **Note**
>
> Three terms are commonly used when discussing encryption: *plaintext* is the data in its original form, *cipher* is the algorithm used for encryption, and *ciphertext* is the data after encryption.

Symmetric encryption goes back thousands of years. For example, to encrypt with a *substitution cipher*, you replace each letter in the alphabet with some other letter; to decrypt, you reverse the process. In this case, there is no key; the security depends on keeping the method itself secret. That was the case with most early ciphers. Over time, we adopted a different approach, following the observation of a nineteenth-century cryptographer named *Auguste Kerckhoffs:*[3]

> *A cryptosystem should be secure even if the attacker knows everything about the system, except the secret key.*

Although it might seem strange at first, Kerckhoffs's principle—as it has come to be known—makes sense if you consider the following:

- For an encryption algorithm to be useful, it must be shared with others. As the number of people with access to the algorithm increases, the likelihood that the algorithm will fall into the enemy's hands increases too.

- A single algorithm without a key is very inconvenient to use in large groups; everyone can decrypt everyone's communication.

---

[3] la cryptographie militaire [fsty.uk/t2] (Fabien Petitcolas, retrieved 4 September 2021)

Chapter 1: SSL, TLS, and Cryptography

- It's very difficult to design good encryption algorithms. The more exposure and scrutiny an algorithm gets, the more secure it can be. Cryptographers recommend a conservative approach when adopting new algorithms; it usually takes years of breaking attempts until a cipher is considered secure.

A good encryption algorithm is one that produces seemingly random ciphertext, which can't be analyzed by the attacker to reveal any information about plaintext. For example, the substitution cipher is not a good algorithm, because the attacker could determine the frequency of each letter of ciphertext and compare it with the frequency of the letters in the English language. Because some letters appear more often than others, the attacker could use his observations to recover the plaintext. If a cipher is good, the only option for the attacker should be to try all possible decryption keys, otherwise known as an *exhaustive key search*.

At this point, the security of ciphertext depends entirely on the key. If the key is selected from a large *keyspace* and breaking the encryption requires iterating through a prohibitively large number of possible keys, then we say that a cipher is *computationally secure*.

### Note

The common way to measure encryption strength is via key length; the assumption is that keys are essentially random, which means that the keyspace is defined by the number of bits in a key. As an example, a 128-bit key (which is considered very secure) is one of 340 billion billion billion billion possible combinations.

Ciphers can be divided into two groups: stream and block ciphers.

## Stream Ciphers

Conceptually, *stream ciphers* operate in a way that matches how we tend to imagine encryption. You feed one byte of plaintext to the encryption algorithm, and out comes one byte of ciphertext. The reverse happens at the other end. The process is repeated for as long as there is data to process.

At its core, a stream cipher produces an infinite stream of seemingly random data called a *keystream*. To perform encryption, one byte of keystream is combined with one byte of plaintext using the XOR logical operation. Because XOR is reversible, to decrypt you perform XOR of ciphertext with the same keystream byte. This process is illustrated in Figure 1.2, "RC4 encryption".

An encryption process is considered secure if the attacker can't predict which keystream bytes are at which positions. For this reason, it is vital that stream ciphers are never used with the same key more than once. This is because, in practice, attackers know or can predict plaintext at certain locations (think of HTTP requests being encrypted; things such as request method, protocol version, and header names are the same across many requests).

Figure 1.2. RC4 encryption

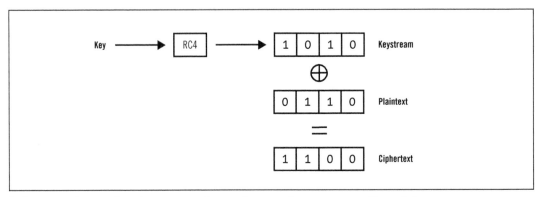

When you know the plaintext and can observe the corresponding ciphertext, you uncover parts of the keystream. You can use that information to uncover the same parts of future ciphertexts if the same key is used. To work around this problem, stream algorithms are used with one-time keys derived from long-term keys.

RC4 is one of the oldest stream ciphers. It became popular due to its speed and simplicity, but it's no longer considered secure. I discuss its weaknesses at some length in the section called "RC4 Weaknesses" in Chapter 8. For an example of a modern stream cipher, consider ChaCha20, designed by cryptographer D. J. Bernstein.

## Block Ciphers

*Block ciphers* encrypt blocks of data at a time; modern block ciphers tend to use a block size of 128 bits (16 bytes). A block cipher is a transformation function: it takes some input and produces output that appears random. For every possible input combination, there is exactly one output, as long as the key stays the same. A key property of block ciphers is that a small variation in input (e.g., a change of one bit anywhere) produces a large variation in output.

On their own, block ciphers are not very useful because of several limitations. First, you can only use them to encrypt data lengths equal to the size of the encryption block. To use a block cipher in practice, you need a scheme to handle data of arbitrary length. Another problem is that block ciphers are *deterministic*; they always produce the same output for the same input. This property opens up a number of attacks and needs to be dealt with.

In practice, block ciphers are used via encryption schemes called *block cipher modes*, which smooth over the limitations and sometimes add authentication to the mix. Block ciphers can also be used as the basis for other cryptographic primitives, such as hash functions, message authentication codes, pseudorandom generators, and even stream ciphers.

The world's most popular block cipher is AES (short for *Advanced Encryption Standard*), which is available in strengths of 128, 192, and 256 bits.

## Padding

One of the challenges with block ciphers is figuring out how to handle encryption of data lengths smaller than the encryption block size. For example, 128-bit AES requires 16 bytes of input data and produces the same amount as output. This is fine if you have all of your data in 16-byte blocks, but what do you do when you have less than that? One approach is to append some extra data to the end of your plaintext. This extra data is known as *padding*.

The padding can't consist of just any random data. It must follow some format that allows the receiver to see the padding for what it is and know exactly how many bytes to discard. In TLS, the last byte of an encryption block contains padding length, which indicates how many bytes of padding (excluding the padding length byte) there are. All padding bytes are set to the same value as the padding length byte. This approach enables the receiver to check that the padding is correct.

Figure 1.3. Example of TLS padding

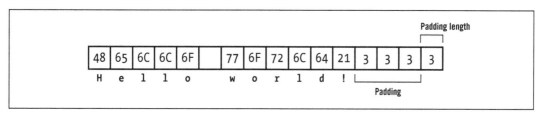

To discard the padding after decryption, the receiver examines the last byte in the data block and removes it. After that, he removes the indicated number of bytes while checking that they all have the same value.

# Hash Functions

A *hash function* is an algorithm that converts input of arbitrary length into small, fixed-size output. The result of a hash function is often called simply a *hash*. Hash functions are commonly used in programming, but not all hash functions are suitable for use in cryptography. *Cryptographic hash functions* are hash functions that have several additional properties:

**Preimage resistance**

Given a hash, it's computationally unfeasible to find or construct a message that produces it.

**Second preimage resistance**

Given a message and its hash, it's computationally unfeasible to find a different message with the same hash.

**Collision resistance**

It's computationally unfeasible to find two messages that have the same hash.

Hash functions are most commonly used as a compact way to represent and compare large amounts of data. For example, rather than compare two files directly (which might be difficult, for example, if they are stored in different parts of the world), you can compare their hashes. Hash functions are often called *fingerprints*, *message digests*, or simply *digests*.

Today, hash functions from the SHA2 and SHA3 families are examples of secure hash functions. Others—for example, SHA1 and MD5—are now considered insecure and shouldn't be used. Unlike with ciphers, the strength of a hash function doesn't equal the hash length. Because of the *birthday paradox* (a well-known problem in probability theory), the strength of a hash function is at most one half of the hash length.

## Message Authentication Codes

A hash function could be used to verify data integrity, but only if the hash of the data is transported separately from the data itself. Otherwise, an attacker could modify both the message and the hash, easily avoiding detection. A *message authentication code* (MAC) or a *keyed-hash* is a cryptographic function that extends hashing with authentication. Only those in possession of the *hashing key* can produce a valid MAC.

MACs are commonly used in combination with encryption. Even though Mallory can't decrypt ciphertext, she can modify it in transit if there is no MAC; *encryption provides confidentiality but not integrity*. If Mallory is smart about how she's modifying ciphertext, she could trick Bob into accepting a forged message as authentic. When a MAC is sent along with ciphertext, Bob (who shares the hashing key with Alice) can be sure that the message has not been tampered with.

Any hash function can be used as the basis for a MAC using a construction known as HMAC (short for *Hash-based Message Authentication Code*).[4] In essence, HMAC works by interleaving the hashing key with the message in a secure way.

## Block Cipher Modes

*Block cipher modes* are cryptographic schemes designed to extend block ciphers to encrypt data of arbitrary length. All block cipher modes support confidentiality, but some combine it with authentication. Some modes transform block ciphers to produce stream ciphers.

There are many output modes, and they are usually referred to by their acronyms: ECB, CBC, CFB, OFB, CTR, GCM, and so forth. (Don't worry about what the acronyms stand for.) I will discuss only ECB and CBC here: ECB as an example of how not to design a block cipher mode and CBC because it was used heavily in TLS until version 1.3. Authenticated cipher suites (e.g., GCM) first appeared in TLS 1.2; they provide confidentiality and integrity in the same package and avoid the design problem inherent in CBC suites.

---

[4] RFC 2104: HMAC: Keyed-Hashing for Message Authentication [fsty.uk/t3] (Krawczyk et al., February 1997)

Chapter 1: SSL, TLS, and Cryptography

## Electronic Codebook Mode

*Electronic Code Book* (ECB) mode is the simplest possible block cipher mode. It supports only data lengths that are the exact multiples of the block size; if you have data of different length, then you need to apply padding beforehand. To perform encryption, you split the data into chunks that match the block size and encrypt each block individually.

The simplicity of ECB is its downside. Because block ciphers are deterministic (i.e., they always produce the same result when the input is the same), so is ECB. This has serious consequences: (1) patterns in ciphertext will appear that match patterns in plaintext; (2) the attacker can detect when a message is repeated; and (3) an attacker who can observe ciphertext and submit arbitrary plaintext for encryption (commonly possible with HTTP and in many other situations) can, given enough attempts, *guess* the plaintext. This is what the BEAST attack against TLS was about; I discuss it in the section called "BEAST" in Chapter 8.

## Cipher Block Chaining Mode

*Cipher Block Chaining* (CBC), illustrated in Figure 1.4, "CBC mode encryption", is the next step up from ECB. To address the deterministic nature of ECB, CBC introduces the concept of the *initialization vector* (IV), which makes output different every time, even when input is the same.

Figure 1.4. CBC mode encryption

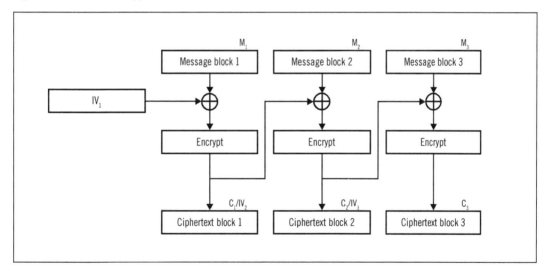

The process starts by generating a random (and thus unpredictable) IV, which is the same length as the encryption block size. Before encryption, the first block of plaintext is combined with the IV using XOR. This masks the plaintext and ensures that the ciphertext is always different. For the next encryption block, the ciphertext of the previous block is used as the IV, and so forth. As a result, all of the individual encryption operations are part of the same *chain*, which is where the mode name comes from. Crucially, the IV is transmitted on the wire to the receiving party, who needs it to perform decryption successfully.

## Asymmetric Encryption

Symmetric encryption does a great job at handling large amounts of data at great speeds, but it leaves a lot to be desired as soon as the number of parties involved increases:

- Members of the same group must share the same key. The more people join a group, the more exposed the group becomes to the key compromise.

- For better security, you could use a different key for every two people, but this approach doesn't scale. Although three people need only three keys, ten people would need 45 (9 + 8 + . . . + 1) keys. A thousand people would need 499,500 keys!

- Symmetric encryption can't be used on unattended systems to secure data. Because the process can be reversed by using the same key, a compromise of such a system leads to the compromise of all data stored in the system.

*Asymmetric encryption* (also known as *public key cryptography*) is a different approach to encryption that uses two keys instead of one. One of the keys is *private*; the other is *public*. As the names suggest, one of these keys is intended to be private, and the other is intended to be shared with everyone. There's a special mathematical relationship between these keys that enables some useful features. If you encrypt data using someone's public key, only their corresponding private key can decrypt it. On the other hand, if data is encrypted with the private key anyone can use the public key to unlock the message. The latter operation doesn't provide confidentiality, but it does function as a digital signature.

Figure 1.5. Asymmetric encryption

Asymmetric encryption makes secure communication in large groups much easier. Assuming that you can securely share your public key widely (a job for PKI, which I discuss in

Chapter 4, *Public Key Infrastructure*), anyone can send you a message that only you can read. If they also sign that message using their private key, you know exactly whom it is from.

Despite its interesting properties, public key cryptography is slow and thus unsuitable for use with large quantities of data. For this reason, it's usually used for authentication and negotiation of shared secrets, which are then used for fast symmetric encryption.

*RSA* (named from the initials of Ron Rivest, Adi Shamir, and Leonard Adleman) is the most popular asymmetric encryption method deployed today. The recommended strength for RSA today is 2,048 bits, which is equivalent to about 112 symmetric bits. RSA is slowly losing ground to a different family of algorithms based on *elliptic curves*, which promise better security at faster speeds.

## Digital Signatures

A *digital signature* is a cryptographic scheme that allows us to verify the authenticity of a digital message or document. The MAC, which I described earlier, is a type of digital signature; it can be used to verify authenticity provided that the secret hashing key is securely exchanged ahead of time. Although this type of verification is very useful in certain situations, it's inherently limited because it still relies on a shared secret key.

Digital signatures similar to the real-life handwritten ones are possible with the help of public key cryptography; we can exploit its asymmetric nature to devise an algorithm that allows a message signed by a private key to be verified with the corresponding public key.

The exact approach depends on the selected public key cryptosystem. For example, RSA can be used for encryption and decryption. If something is encrypted with a private RSA key, only the corresponding public key can decrypt it. We can use this property for digital signing if we combine it with hash functions:

1. Calculate a hash of the document you wish to sign; no matter the size of the input document, the output will always be fixed, for example, 256 bits for SHA256.

2. Encode the resulting hash and some additional metadata. For example, the receiver will need to know the hashing algorithm you used before she can process the signature.

3. Encrypt the encoded hash using the private key; the result will be the signature, which you can append to the document as proof of authenticity.

To verify the signature, the receiver takes the document and calculates the hash independently using the same algorithm. Then, she uses your public key to decrypt the message and recover the hash, confirm that the correct algorithms were used, and compare the decrypted hash with the one she calculated. The strength of this signature scheme depends on the individual strengths of the encryption, hashing, and encoding components.

> **Note**
>
> Not all digital signature algorithms function in the same way as RSA. In fact, RSA is an exception, because it can be used for both encryption and digital signing. Other popular public key algorithms, such as DSA and ECDSA, can't be used for encryption and rely on different approaches for signing.

## Random Number Generation

In cryptography, all security depends on the quality of random number generation. You've already seen in this chapter that security relies on known encryption algorithms and secret keys. Those keys are simply very long random numbers.

The problem with random numbers is that computers tend to be very predictable. They follow instructions to the letter. If you tell them to generate a random number, they probably won't do a very good job.[5] This is because true random numbers can be obtained only by observing certain physical processes. In absence of that, computers focus on collecting small amounts of *entropy*. This usually means monitoring keystrokes and mouse movements and the interaction with various peripheral devices, such as hard disks.

Entropy collected in this way is a type of *true random number generator* (TRNG), but the approach is not reliable enough to use directly. For example, you might need to generate a 4,096-bit key, but the system might have only a couple of hundreds of bits of entropy available. If there are no reliable external events to collect enough entropy, the system might stall.

For this reason, in practice we rely on *pseudorandom number generators* (PRNGs), which use small amounts of true random data to get them going. This process is known as *seeding*. From the seed, PRNGs produce unlimited amounts of pseudorandom data on demand. General-purpose PRNGs are often used in programming, but they are not appropriate for cryptography, even if their output is statistically random. *Cryptographically secure pseudorandom number generators* (CSPRNGs) are PRNGs that are also unpredictable. This attribute is crucial for security; an adversary mustn't be able to reverse-engineer the internal state of a CSPRNG by observing its output.

# Protocols

Cryptographic primitives such as encryption and hashing algorithms are seldom useful by themselves. We combine them into *schemes* and *protocols* so that we can satisfy complex security requirements. To illustrate how we might do that, let's consider a simplistic crypto-

---

[5] Some newer processors have built-in random number generators that are suitable for use in cryptography. There are also specialized external devices (e.g., in the form of USB sticks) that can be added to feed additional entropy to the operating system.

graphic protocol that allows Alice and Bob to communicate securely. We'll aim for all three main requirements: confidentiality, integrity, and authentication.

Let's assume that our protocol allows exchange of an arbitrary number of messages. Because symmetric encryption is very good at encrypting bulk data, we might select our favorite algorithm to use for this purpose, say, AES. With AES, Alice and Bob can exchange secure messages, and Mallory won't be able to recover the contents. But that's not quite enough, because Mallory can do other things, for example, modify the messages without being detected. To fix this problem, we can calculate a MAC of each message using a hashing key known only to Alice and Bob. When we send a message, we send along the MAC as well.

Now, Mallory can't modify the messages any longer. However, she could still drop or replay arbitrary messages. To deal with this, we extend our protocol to assign a sequence number to each message; crucially, we make the sequences part of the MAC calculation. If we see a gap in the sequence numbers, then we know that there's a message missing. If we see a sequence number duplicate, we detect a replay attack. For best results, we should also use a special message to mark the end of the conversation. Without such a message, Mallory would be able to end (truncate) the conversation undetected.

With all of these measures in place, the best Mallory can do is prevent Alice and Bob from talking to one another. There's nothing we can do about that.

So far, so good, but we're still missing a big piece: how are Alice and Bob going to negotiate the two needed keys (one for encryption and the other for integrity validation) in the presence of Mallory? We can solve this problem by adding two additional steps to the protocol.

First, we use public key cryptography to authenticate each party at the beginning of the conversation. For example, Alice could generate a random number and ask Bob to sign it to prove that it's really him. Bob could ask Alice to do the same.

With authentication out of the way, we can use a *key-exchange scheme* to negotiate encryption keys securely. For example, Alice could generate all the keys and send them to Bob by encrypting them with his public key; this is how the RSA key exchange works. Alternatively, we could have also used a protocol known as *Diffie-Hellman* (DH) key exchange for this purpose. The latter is slower, but it has better security properties.

In the end, we end up with a protocol that (1) starts with a handshake phase that includes authentication and key exchange, (2) follows with the data exchange phase with confidentiality and integrity, and (3) ends with a shutdown sequence. At a high level, our protocol is similar to the work done by SSL and TLS.

## Attacking Cryptography

Complex systems can usually be attacked in a variety of ways, and cryptography is no exception. First, you can attack the cryptographic primitives themselves. If a key is small, the adversary can use brute force to recover it. Such attacks usually require a lot of processing power as well as time. It's easier (for the attacker) if the used primitive has known vulnerabilities, in which case she can use analytic attacks to achieve the goal faster.

Cryptographic primitives are generally well understood, because they are relatively straightforward and do only one thing. Schemes are often easier to attack because they introduce additional complexity. In some cases, even cryptographers argue about the right way to perform certain operations. But both are relatively safe compared to protocols, which tend to introduce far more complexity and have a much larger attack surface.

Then, there are attacks against protocol *implementation*; in other words, exploitation of software bugs. For example, most cryptographic libraries are written in low-level languages such as C and even assembly, and that makes it very easy to introduce catastrophic programming errors. Even in the absence of bugs, sometimes great skill is needed to implement the primitives, schemes, and protocols in such a way that they can't be abused. For example, naïve implementations of certain algorithms can be exploited in *timing attacks*, in which the attacker breaks encryption by observing how long certain operations take.

It is also common that programmers with little experience in cryptography nevertheless attempt to implement—and even design—cryptographic protocols and schemes, with predictably insecure results.

For this reason, it is often said that cryptography is bypassed, not attacked. What this means is that the primitives are solid, but the rest of the software ecosystem isn't. Further, the keys are an attractive target: why spend months to brute-force a key when it might be much easier to break into a server to obtain it? Many cryptographic failures can be prevented by following simple rules such as these: (1) use well-established protocols and never design your own schemes; (2) use high-level libraries and never write code that deals with cryptography directly; and (3) use well-established primitives with sufficiently strong key sizes.

## Measuring Strength

We measure the strength of cryptography using the number of operations that need to be performed to break a particular primitive, presented as *bits* of security. Deploying with strong key sizes is the easiest thing to get right, and the rules are simple: 128 bits of security ($2^{128}$ operations) is sufficient for most deployments; use 256 bits if you need very long-term security or a big safety margin.

**Note**

The strength of symmetric cryptographic operations increases exponentially as more bits are added. This means that adding just another bit makes a key twice as strong.

In practice, the situation is somewhat more complicated, because not all operations are equivalent in terms of security. As a result, different bit values are used for symmetric operations, asymmetric operations, elliptic curve cryptography, and so on. You can use the information in the following table to convert from one size to another.

Table 1.2. Security levels and equivalent strength in bits, adapted from ECRYPT2 (2012)

| # | Protection | Sym-metric | Asym-metric | DH | Elliptic Curve | Hash |
|---|---|---|---|---|---|---|
| 1 | Attacks in real time by individuals | 32 | - | - | - | - |
| 2 | Very short-term protection against small organizations | 64 | 816 | 816 | 128 | 128 |
| 3 | Short-term protection against medium organizations | 72 | 1,008 | 1,008 | 144 | 144 |
| 4 | Very short-term protection against agencies | 80 | 1,248 | 1,248 | 160 | 160 |
| 5 | Short-term protection (10 years) | 96 | 1,776 | 1,776 | 192 | 192 |
| 6 | Medium-term protection (20 years) | 112 | 2,432 | 2,432 | 224 | 224 |
| 7 | Long-term protection (30 years) | 128 | 3,248 | 3,248 | 256 | 256 |
| 8 | Long-term protection and increased defense from quantum computers | 256 | 15,424 | 15,424 | 512 | 512 |

The data, which I adapted from a 2012 report on key and algorithm strength,[6] shows rough mappings from bits of one type to bits of another, but it also defines strength in relation to attacker capabilities and time. Although we tend to discuss whether an asset is secure (assuming *now*), in reality security is also a function of time. The strength of encryption changes, because as time goes by computers get faster and cheaper. Security is also a function of resources. A key of a small size might be impossible for an individual to break, but doing so could be within the reach of an agency. For this reason, when discussing security it's more useful to ask questions such as "secure against whom?" and "secure for how long?"

**Note**

The strength of cryptography can't be measured accurately, which is why you will find many different recommendations. Most of them are very similar, with small

---

[6] ECRYPT2 Yearly Report on Algorithms and Keysizes [fsty.uk/t4] (European Network of Excellence for Cryptology II, 30 September 2012)

differences. To view and compare other recommendations, visit *keylength.com*, which provides an overview of a variety of sources.[7]

Although the previous table provides a lot of useful information, you might find it difficult to use because the values don't correspond to commonly used key sizes. In practice, you'll find the following table adapted from NIST's recommendations more useful to convert from one set of bits to another:[8]

Table 1.3. Encryption strength mapping for commonly used key sizes

| Symmetric | RSA / DSA / DH | Elliptic curve crypto | Hash functions |
|---|---|---|---|
| 80 | 1,024 | 160 | 160 |
| 112 | 2,048 | 224 | 224 |
| 128 | 3,072 | 256 | 256 |
| 256 | 15,360 | 512 | 512 |

The fact that measuring and comparing different security approaches is difficult hasn't escaped cryptographers. In 2013, Lenstra published a fun paper in which he "proposed" that we stop using bits to represent security strength; instead, he offered intuitive security levels, such as how much energy is needed to boil all the water in a swimming pool ("pool security"), boiling the lake of Geneva ("lake security"), and so on.[9]

# Active and Passive Network Attacks

The traditional Internet threat model is that of a network attacker, which intercepts communication as it travels from one party to another. Traditionally, this type of attack is known as a *man-in-the-middle* (MITM) attack. If the attacker is just listening in on the conversation, we're talking about a *passive network attack*. If the attacker is actively modifying the traffic or influencing the conversation in some other way, we're talking about an *active network attack*. For fun, we'll call these attackers Eve and Mallory, respectively. Both attack types require access to the network, which can be achieved in several ways, as illustrated in Figure 1.6, "Conceptual SSL/TLS threat model".

## Gaining Access

In many cases, attacks require proximity either to the victim or the server, or access to the global network infrastructure. Whoever has access to the undersea cables and intermediary

---

[7] Cryptographic Key Length Recommendation [fsty.uk/t5] (BlueKrypt, retrieved 4 September 2021)

[8] NIST Special Publication 800-57: Recommendation for Key Management—Part 1: General, Revision 5 [fsty.uk/t6] (NIST, May 2020)

[9] Universal security; from bits and mips to pools, lakes—and beyond [fsty.uk/t7] (Lenstra et al., October 2013)

Chapter 1: SSL, TLS, and Cryptography

Figure 1.6. Conceptual SSL/TLS threat model

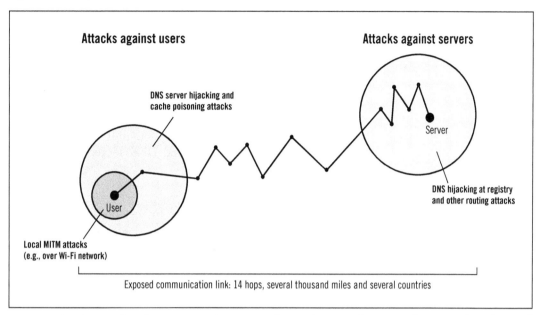

communication nodes (e.g., routers) can see the packets as they travel across the wire and interfere with them. Access can be obtained by tapping the cables,[10] in collaboration with telecoms,[11] or by hacking the equipment.[12]

Conceptually, the easiest way to carry out a network attack is to be close to the victim and reroute their traffic through a malicious node. Wireless networks without authentication, which so many people use these days, are particularly vulnerable because anyone in the vicinity can access them.

Other ways to attack include interfering with the routing infrastructure for domain name resolution, IP address routing, and so on.

**ARP spoofing**

*Address Resolution Protocol* (ARP) is used on local networks to associate network MAC addresses[13] with IP addresses. An attacker with access to the network can claim any IP address and effectively reroute traffic.

**WPAD hijacking**

*Web Proxy Auto-Discovery Protocol* (WPAD) is used by browsers to automatically retrieve HTTP proxy configuration. WPAD uses several methods, including DHCP

---

[10] The Creepy, Long-Standing Practice of Undersea Cable Tapping [fsty.uk/t8] (The Atlantic, 16 July 2013)

[11] New Details About NSA's Collaborative Relationships With America's Biggest Telecom Companies From Snowden Docs [fsty.uk/t9] (Washington Post, 30 August 2013)

[12] Photos of an NSA "upgrade" factory show Cisco router getting implant [fsty.uk/t10] (Ars Technica, 14 May 2014)

[13] In this case, MAC stands for *media access control*. It's a unique identifier assigned to networking cards by the manufacturer.

and DNS. To attack WPAD, an attacker starts a proxy on the local network and announces it to the local clients who look for it.

**DNS hijacking**

By hijacking a domain name with the registrar or changing the DNS configuration, an attacker can hijack all traffic intended for that domain name.

**DNS cache poisoning**

*DNS cache poisoning* is a type of attack that exploits weaknesses in caching DNS servers and enables the attacker to inject invalid domain name information into the cache. After a successful attack, all users of the affected DNS server will be given invalid information.

**BGP route hijacking**

*Border Gateway Protocol* (BGP) is a routing protocol used by the core Internet routers to discover where exactly IP address blocks are located. If an invalid route is accepted by one or more routers, all traffic for a particular IP address block can be redirected elsewhere, that is, to the attacker.

## Passive Attacks

Passive attacks are most useful against unencrypted traffic. During 2013, it became apparent that government agencies around the world routinely monitor and store large amounts of Internet traffic. For example, it was alleged then that GCHQ, the British spy agency, recorded all UK Internet traffic and kept it for three days.[14] Your email messages, photos, Internet chats, and other data could be sitting in a database somewhere, waiting to be cross-referenced and correlated for whatever purpose. If bulk traffic is handled like this, it's reasonable to expect that specific traffic is stored for much longer and perhaps indefinitely. In response to this and similar discoveries, the IETF declared that "pervasive monitoring is an attack" and should be defended against by using encryption whenever possible.[15]

Even against encrypted traffic, passive attacks can be useful as an element in the overall strategy. For example, you could store captured encrypted traffic until such a time when you can break the encryption. Just because some things are difficult to do today doesn't mean that they'll be difficult ten years from now, as computers get more powerful and cheaper and as weaknesses in cryptographic primitives are discovered.

To make things worse, computer systems often contain a critical configuration weakness that allows for retroactive decryption of recorded traffic. Before TLS 1.3, a very common key-exchange mechanism in TLS used to be based on the RSA algorithm; on the systems that use this approach, the configured server RSA key could be used to decrypt all previous

---

[14] GCHQ taps fibre-optic cables for secret access to world's communications [fsty.uk/t11] (The Guardian, 21 June 2013)

[15] RFC 7258: Pervasive Monitoring Is an Attack [fsty.uk/t12] (S. Farrell and H. Tschofenig, May 2014)

conversations. Other key-exchange mechanisms don't suffer from this problem and are said to support *forward secrecy*. Unfortunately, even though better mechanisms were available, many stayed with the RSA key exchange. For example, Lavabit—the encrypted email service famously used by Edward Snowden—didn't support forward secrecy on its web servers. Using a court order, the FBI compelled Lavabit to disclose its encryption key. With the key in its possession, the FBI could decrypt any recorded traffic (if it had any, of course).

Passive attacks work very well, because there is still so much unencrypted traffic and because bulk traffic collection can be fully automated. Google's Transparency Report provides a good way to observe the deployment of encryption over time.[16]

## Active Attacks

When someone talks about network attacks, they most commonly refer to active attacks in which Mallory interferes with the traffic in some way. Traditionally, the focus is on breaking authentication in order to trick Alice into thinking she's talking to Bob. If the attack is successful, Mallory receives messages from Alice and forwards them to Bob. Although Alice encrypts the messages, she encrypts them *for* Mallory, who has no trouble decrypting them. She can then reencrypt them to forward to Bob, who thinks he got them directly from Alice.

When it comes to TLS, the ideal case for Mallory is when she can present a certificate that Alice will accept as valid. In that case, the attack is seamless and almost impossible to detect.[17] A valid certificate could be obtained by abusing the public certificate infrastructure. There have been many such attacks over the years; in Chapter 5, *Attacks against PKI*, I document the ones that are publicly known. A certificate that *seems* valid could be constructed if there are bugs in the validation code that could be exploited. Historically, this is an area in which bugs are common. I discuss several examples in Chapter 7, *Implementation Issues*. Finally, if everything else fails, Mallory could present an invalid certificate and hope that Alice overrides the certificate warning. This happened in Syria in 2011.[18]

The rise of browsers as a powerful application-delivery platform created additional attack vectors that can be exploited in active network attacks. In this case, authentication is not attacked, but the victims' browsers are instrumented by the attacker to submit specially crafted requests that are used to subvert encryption. These attack vectors have been exploited in recent years to attack TLS in novel ways; you can find more information about them in Chapter 8, *Protocol Attacks*.

Active attacks can be very powerful, but they're difficult to scale. Whereas passive attacks only need to make copies of observed packets (which is a simple operation), active attacks require much more processing and effort to track individual connections. As a result, they

---

[16] Transparency Report [fsty.uk/t13] (Google, retrieved 4 September 2021)

[17] Unless you're very, very paranoid, and keeping track of all the certificates you encounter.

[18] A Syrian Man-in-the-Middle Attack against Facebook [fsty.uk/t14] (The Electronic Frontier Foundation, 5 May 2011)

require much more software and hardware. Rerouting large amounts of traffic is difficult to do without being noticed. Similarly, fraudulent certificates are difficult to use successfully for large-scale attacks because there are so many individuals and organizations who are keeping track of certificates used by various web sites. The approach with the best chance of success is exploitation of implementation bugs that can be used to bypass authentication, but such bugs, devastating as they are, are relatively rare.

For these reasons, active attacks are most likely to be used against individual, high-value targets. Such attacks can't be automated, which means that they require extra work, cost a lot, and are thus more difficult to justify. Also, in almost all cases it's much easier to attack the software itself, usually from a ready-made exploit arsenal.

There are some indications that the NSA deployed extensive infrastructure that enables them to attack almost arbitrary computers on the Internet, under the program called *QuantumInsert*.[19]

This program, which is a variation on the network attack theme, doesn't appear to target encryption; instead, it's used to deliver browser exploits against selected individuals. By placing special packet-injection nodes at important points in the communication infrastructure, the NSA is able to respond to connection requests faster than the real servers and redirect some traffic to the exploitation servers instead.

---

[19] Attacking Tor: How the NSA Targets Users' Online Anonymity [fsty.uk/t15] (Bruce Schneier, 4 October 2013)

# 2 TLS 1.3

TLS 1.3 is the most recent version of the TLS protocol. After many problems with the earlier versions of TLS, the authors of version 1.3 took their time to design a next-generation protocol that combines security with performance and backward compatibility. They also involved a wider cryptographic community to help them with protocol analysis and validation long before the final TLS 1.3 was released.

This chapter provides a high-level overview of TLS 1.3. I focus on the most important parts and discuss how they work together to provide the desired security properties. Everything you need to use this protocol on a daily basis is right here. After you're done, if you want to go further, read the rest of the book to understand the context in which TLS 1.3 was born; after that, you can dive into the protocol specification.

At the time of writing, TLS 1.3 is already widely used, but TLS 1.2 remains the better-supported protocol, especially with the long tail of properties that have very long upgrade cycles. Because of that, this book retains the TLS 1.2 protocol coverage from the first edition. You'll find it in the next chapter. Because so much of TLS 1.3's design was influenced by what came before it, you'll likely find that understanding TLS 1.2 is necessary to fully understand TLS 1.3.

## Record Protocol

From the outside, we can describe TLS as an intermediate layer that sits between an application layer and a lower, reliable network layer, such as TCP.[1] The role of TLS is to provide integrity and encryption for application data that would otherwise be transported in plaintext. When we peer inside the protocol, however, we can see that it consists of two layers. The *record protocol* is the outer shell in TLS, designed to carry, encrypt, and protect messages containing opaque data. You can think of it as the workhorse of the protocol.

---

[1] TLS is not suitable for direct use with UDP, but there is an adapted version of the protocol called DTLS (short for *Datagram Transport Layer Security*) that works around the issues inherent in operating in an unreliable environment. More recently, the new QUIC protocol relies on the cryptography as implemented in TLS 1.3 but doesn't use all other parts of the design.

For the record protocol to be able to do any work, we need to dig deeper. TLS delegates cryptographic negotiation, signaling, and in fact all other work to *subprotocols*. From the wire-level perspective, each subprotocol is a separate stream of messages carried by the record protocol. Each subprotocol is designed with a particular specific purpose in mind. This design of the record protocol introduces a useful abstraction, adds support for extensibility, and simplifies the individual parts.

In fact, the same design approach can be observed elsewhere and at the subprotocol layers. In a way, it's useful to think about TLS as a framework for implementation of cryptographic protocols. Core TLS provides a number of useful tools that support combining cryptographic primitives, as well as extension points to include additional functionality when it's needed.

> **Note**
>
> This chapter contains fragments of TLS structure using the same syntax as in the protocol specification. TLS uses its own presentation language, which is similar in style to C code. I expect that the fragments will be easy to follow. If you're not sure about what something means, refer to section 3 in the TLS 1.3. RFC.[2]

## Record Structure

At a glance, TLS 1.3 continues to use the same record layer format as previous versions. When I initially came across the record layer in the earlier protocol versions, I thought it was easy to understand. This is not quite the case anymore, as the format has had to evolve to fix some design issues and preserve backward compatibility at the same time.

Figure 2.1. TLS record

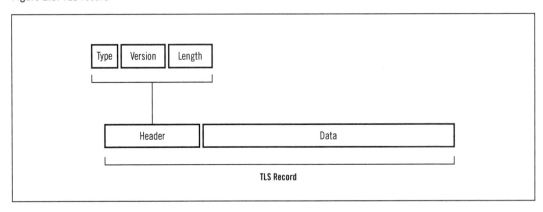

The record layer consists of series of *records* that are exchanged between client and server. Each record has a header that carries the subprotocol type, the TLS protocol version, and

---

[2] RFC 8446: The Transport Layer Security Protocol Version 1.3 [fsty.uk/t16] (E. Rescorla, August 2018)

the payload length. The remainder of the record is the transported payload. The payload is a fragment of data that belongs to one of the subprotocols.

```
struct {
    ContentType type;
    ProtocolVersion legacy_record_version;
    uint16 length;
    opaque fragment[TLSPlaintext.length];
} TLSPlaintext;

enum {
    invalid(0),
    change_cipher_spec(20),
    alert(21),
    handshake(22),
    application_data(23),
    (255)
} ContentType;
```

However, when you take a closer look, you notice that the protocol version has been de facto removed, as indicated by the field name, legacy_record_version. TLS 1.2 and earlier versions communicate the protocol version in two locations: in ClientHello messages during handshake and also in every record protocol message. Historically, that caused many interoperability problems. The biggest problems were caused by *middleboxes*, network devices such as firewalls, which are commonly configured to drop traffic they don't understand. Because record protocol messages don't really need to carry protocol information (the version is negotiated during the handshake and doesn't change afterward), TLS 1.3 doesn't use it. However, to avoid breaking the wire format, record protocol messages continue to carry a dummy version number as a placeholder. For compatibility reasons, the initial ClientHello message can use 0x0301 (TLS 1.0) as the record protocol version, but all subsequent messages must use 0x0303 (TLS 1.2).

Record protocol operates in two modes: it starts in plaintext, with a switch to encryption as soon as the necessary parameters are negotiated. Once the payload protection is activated, the structure of record protocol messages changes to hide the message types going forward.

```
struct {
    ContentType opaque_type = application_data;       /* 23 */
    ProtocolVersion legacy_record_version = 0x0303;   /* TLS 1.2 */
    uint16 length;
    opaque encrypted_record[TLSCiphertext.length];
} TLSCiphertext;
```

Looking at the structure of the protected message, you will notice that the type field has been replaced with opaque_type. Why this change? Leaving the subprotocol type unencrypted (as done in TLS 1.2 and earlier) leaks information, not only providing an adversary with potentially important information that could be used for profiling and attacks, but also giving data that middleboxes could use to filter traffic based on the values they observe. For this reason, what remains in plaintext is only a deprecated placeholder, the value of which is not used. The real type is encrypted, together with the content and padding.

```
struct {
    opaque content[TLSPlaintext.length];
    ContentType type;
    uint8 zeros[length_of_padding];
} TLSInnerPlaintext;
```

Because the length of the content is not supplied, the receiving side first decrypts to plaintext, then processes the result from the end, working backward. It starts by removing the padding, which consists of only NUL bytes (zeroes). This operation reveals the subprotocol type, which is only one byte, and what remains is the content itself. There is no danger of confusing the subprotocol type for padding because its value cannot be a zero.

## Encryption

One of the key goals of the record protocol is payload protection, which provides both confidentiality and integrity. For this, TLS 1.3 relies on *authenticated encryption*, also known as *authenticated encryption with associated data* (AEAD).

This encryption approach combines confidentiality and integrity in the same package, meaning that at the TLS layer, we don't need to be concerned with how that work is done. We can treat the operation as a reliable black box. But this is not the only approach that could provide the same result. In fact, previous protocol versions included support for non-authenticated encryption, which made the designs more complex as they needed to provide integrity checking at the protocol level. To make things worse, the approach taken had a variety of weaknesses.

Authenticated encryption works from an encryption key, a *nonce* (a number used once), and *plaintext*, as well as additional data that doesn't need to be encrypted but must be included in the integrity checking. The output of the encryption operation is an opaque blob of data we call *ciphertext*. The reverse operation takes the same parameters, except that it uses ciphertext as input instead of plaintext.

```
AEADEncrypted = AEAD-Encrypt(write_key, nonce, plaintext, additional_data)
```

The nonce is used to ensure that no two encryption operations are the same, even when they operate on the same plaintext. It is usually very important to ensure that the nonce is not repeated. Failure to do so is a critical failure that could lead to the compromise of the encryption keys. To support creation of nonces, TLS operates two 64-bit message counters—one for each direction of traffic. These counters are not transmitted on the network.

Instead, each side keeps track of the values and uses them in the encryption operations. Because each transmitted message is associated with a unique value, these counters also provide protection against replay attacks or processing of messages in incorrect order.

The *associated data* component of encryption includes all other data that is sent in a TLS message but is not encrypted. Almost all of the remaining fields are now obsolete, but including them in the AEAD encryption ensures they cannot be tampered with.

```
additional_data = TLSCiphertext.opaque_type ||
                  TLSCiphertext.legacy_record_version ||
                  TLSCiphertext.length
```

---

### Limits on Key Usage

Although TLS 1.3 treats encryption as a black box, in practice there are some aspects of the process that need to be monitored and restricted. For example, there is a limit to how much data can be safely encrypted using the same keys. The limit, which differs depending on the encryption primitive, is not small but could be reached in some cases if the connections are particularly long-lived. To deal with these situations, TLS 1.3 supports a key update mechanism, which resets the encryption parameters. The same method could be used should the nonces come close to wrapping.

---

# Length Hiding

Out of the box, TLS doesn't provide *length hiding*, meaning that the attacker who is able to observe the encrypted information can deduce the size of the plaintext based on the size of the encrypted messages. For example, if you were using TLS to secure transport of a user password, observing the length of the exchanged record might reveal the password size. Length hiding is not easy to implement robustly in a commercial environment wherein bandwidth increases may be prohibitively expensive. If costs were not an issue, you could just transmit continuously, even when you didn't have anything meaningful to send. Interactive protocols are especially vulnerable because they may be able to be influenced to generate network traffic under command of the attacker. This is certainly true of HTTP because browsers are happy to follow any link given.

However, TLS 1.3 does improve upon earlier protocol versions and provides facilities that could be used to implement length hiding if desired.

**Protected plaintext length**

You've already seen in this section that the length of plaintext is now encrypted. Before, the length was out in the open and fully exposed. Now, the length has to be deduced from what can be observed on the network.

### Message padding

Record messages provide support for padding of arbitrary length, leading to the increase of size of protocol messages. It is up to the implementations to use this facility. For example, one approach might be to make all protocol messages the same length, in an attempt to defeat profiling.

### Zero-length protocol messages

Further, it's also possible to send messages that don't contain any data, expanding them with padding so that they appear as real messages. Doing this makes traffic profiling more difficult, which may be especially useful for interactive protocols (anything that transports voice, keystrokes, and so on).

## Subprotocols

As mentioned earlier, the record protocol operates as a shell and delegates the bulk of the work to subprotocols. TLS 1.3 defines four subprotocols, each of which deals with one aspect of secure communication. They remain largely the same as the previous protocol versions, with some small changes.

### Alert protocol

Used for signaling and exceptional situations—for example, an inability to complete a handshake and informing the other side that the connection is about to close.

### Application data protocol

Transport of application data. It's the simplest of all subprotocols because it has only one message, which carries the data, as opaque bytes, from one side to the other.

### Change cipher spec protocol

Deprecated. In previous versions of TLS, the *change cipher spec protocol* was used to signal a switch to encryption after connection secrets are negotiated. Although not obviously insecure, the use of a separate subprotocol for signaling created a usability problem and led to vulnerabilities in popular implementations. This protocol remains in TLS 1.3 only to preserve backward compatibility. As with the design choices related to the record protocol, the goal was to have TLS 1.3 appear as earlier protocol versions on the wire. Thus, messages belonging to this protocol can still be sent by both client and server, but they're ignored on receipt.

### Handshake protocol

Arguably the most important subprotocol, the *handshake protocol* is in charge of negotiating connection security parameters. It implements a number of messages, which we will examine in great detail in the next section.

## Message Fragmentation

Although the record protocol limits the size of the data payload to 16,384 bytes, the record layer doesn't particularly care about what the subprotocol data looks like. One protocol record can carry several subprotocol messages, and, via fragmentation, subprotocol messages can span protocol records. It is also possible to mix subprotocol messages of different types within the same record.

In practice, every subprotocol has its own requirements that control how its data is handled. For application data, for example, there are no restrictions. However, handshake messages are not allowed to mix with messages of other protocol types, and the alert protocol mustn't be fragmented.

# Handshake Protocol

TLS connections start off unencrypted; it's the job of the *handshake protocol* (or subprotocol, if you prefer) to negotiate security parameters acceptable to both sides. During that process, several shared secrets are negotiated and used to generate the necessary encryption keys. The handshake protocol must balance interoperability, performance, and security so that all pieces fall into place.

If you recall, there are four key tasks that need to be accomplished:

1. Exchange capabilities and agree on common security parameters
2. Validate server identity and, optionally, client identity
3. Construct a variety of encryption keys
4. Verify that the handshake hasn't been modified by an active network attacker

A handshake consists of a series of messages that are exchanged until both sides are satisfied with the security parameters. As mentioned earlier, the messages are transported by the record protocol and may have been fragmented by the sender and then reassembled by the receiver.

The handshake protocol uses a simple wrapper to support multiple message types: first is the message type (one byte), followed by the message length (three bytes), then followed by the message itself.

```
struct {
    HandshakeType msg_type;
    uint24 length;
    HandshakeMessage message;
} Handshake;
```

However, the format alone doesn't tell the full story. Every handshake and TLS connection also has a state that influences what messages can be sent and received at that point in time. Receiving any other message leads to immediate connection termination.

## Key Exchange

If you have worked with the handshake from earlier protocol versions, you will find the TLS 1.3 handshake familiar, yet completely different. Although this new TLS version removes much of the cruft and complexity that accumulated over the years, the handshake itself ended up being more complicated. You can probably guess the reason for that: it's the tension between wanting to design a strong protocol that's fit for the future and the need to preserve the wire compatibility so that the new protocol has a chance to work in practice.

**Client speaks first**

The most impactful change, in terms of performance, is that the client begins the key exchange immediately, which means not being 100% sure about which features the server will want to negotiate. In earlier protocol versions, the server selects the type of key exchange, at the cost of an additional network round trip (because the client must first request a new connection and wait to hear from the server). In TLS 1.3, the client proposes one or more different key exchange approaches and sends the required parameters for all of them. This is expected to work in virtually all situations, and the end result is the reduction of handshake network latency by half.

**0-RTT mode**

There is then another performance-related change, and one that is more dramatic. A TLS 1.3 client that has communicated with the server before is able to submit encrypted application data in the first flight, in a message that immediately follows ClientHello. If this feature is used, the server receives it in the first message and can immediately process it. The net result is no latency increase over a plaintext TCP connection. This change is controversial because it trades security for an increase in network performance. We will examine it in more detail later in this chapter.

**Encrypted server extensions**

If the server is happy with the proposed connection parameters, it responds with a ServerHello message, which selects the security parameters for the connection and provides the other half of the necessary key exchange material. In previous TLS versions, this message included all server extensions, meaning that a lot of interesting data was exposed unencrypted. In TLS 1.3, only the necessary extensions are included in the first response. Everything else is sent encrypted, using the new EncryptedExtensions message. In fact, all the server's remaining handshake messages are encrypted from this point.

### Post-handshake messages

In an effort to encrypt more of the exchanged data, some further protocol messages are now exchanged after the handshake has taken place. This includes session resumption and client certificate authentication.

Figure 2.2. Typical full TLS 1.3 handshake with server authentication

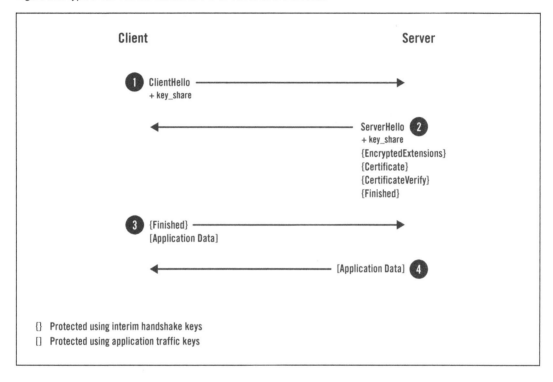

## Cryptographic Negotiation

The sections that follow focus on the format of handshake messages. To understand how the key exchange in TLS 1.3 actually works, it's useful to put aside the convoluted wire format and instead focus on what is exchanged and why. At a high level, each handshake has to select the encryption algorithm and hash function, perform key exchange, and authenticate the other party and the handshake itself.

### Encryption algorithm

The encryption algorithm and hash function are decided from the negotiated cipher suite. Clients indicate their supported cipher suites by placing them in the ClientHello message. Servers pick one suite from that list.

### Key exchange shares

In TLS 1.3, clients propose one or more key exchange algorithms at the very beginning of the conversation, without knowing which algorithms may be supported by the server. They also provide all the necessary information (*shares*, in the key_share extension) for the server to pick one algorithm and complete the key exchange immediately, without the need for further communication.

**Supported key exchange groups**

Clients will typically support several key exchange groups and algorithms but will propose to use only one or two main ones by default. For the situations in which the server is not able to accept their initial options, they also communicate all their supported groups using the supported_groups extension. This same extension is used for DHE and ECDHE groups.

**Signature algorithms**

The signature_algorithms extension communicates which algorithms the server is able to use during the handshake. By default, this extension covers both the TLS protocol signatures and the certificate signatures. Optionally, the signature_algorithms_cert extension can be used to specify different algorithms for the latter.

**Pre-shared keys**

For authentication, TLS 1.3 connections can use certificates or *pre-shared keys* (PSKs). The latter mechanism is most useful for session resumption, as you will see later in this chapter. If a client has one or more PSKs that it wishes to use, it will advertise its intent using the psk_key_exchange_modes extension and specify the identity of the actual keys using the pre_shared_key extension.

## ClientHello

The ClientHello message in TLS 1.3 resembles the same message in earlier protocol versions: the body of the message carries information about proposed security parameters and the list of desired cipher suites, and it ends with an extension block.

```
uint16 ProtocolVersion;
opaque Random[32];

uint8 CipherSuite[2];     /* Cryptographic suite selector */

struct {
    ProtocolVersion legacy_version = 0x0303;     /* TLS 1.2 */
    Random random;
    opaque legacy_session_id<0..32>;
    CipherSuite cipher_suites<2..2^16-2>;
    opaque legacy_compression_methods<1..2^8-1>;
    Extension extensions<8..2^16-1>;
} ClientHello;
```

A closer look will tell you that many of the fields have deprecated. In fact, only three fields remain in use, with most of the functionality moved into the extensions. There were two motivating factors for preserving the handshake in its historical format. First, it enables interoperability and allows TLS 1.3 clients to fall back to earlier TLS versions with older servers. Second, it fools middleboxes into letting this new protocol through because it looks like something they know.

**Protocol version**

The early drafts of TLS 1.3 attempted to retain the already-established mechanism for protocol version negotiation, but it soon became evident that there is a widespread problem causing interoperability issues. Simply put, too many server installations out there would panic upon encountering an unknown protocol version number. The biggest problem was the version in the record layer, but even the version in the ClientHello led to substantial issues, significant enough to derail TLS 1.3 altogether.[3] The solution was to deprecate the old protocol version fields and instead use extensions as the new protocol version negotiation mechanism.

**Random**

The random field remains in use and carries 32 bytes of cryptographically random data. The client and server contribute 32 bytes of randomness each so that, at the binary level, every handshake will be statistically unique.

**Session identifier**

The session resumption mechanism in TLS 1.3 is completely different, which means that the old session identifier is no longer needed.

**Cipher suites**

The cipher section remains in use and carries the cipher suites that the client is willing to negotiate, in the order of preference. A suite is represented via its two-byte identifier.

**Compression method**

Even before TLS 1.3, compression was found to be insecure due to information leakage. This is because attackers can typically influence what traffic is sent while observing encrypted communication on the wire. By modifying what is encrypted, the attacker can learn some information about parts of data they can't otherwise see. In TLS 1.3, the compression method field is set to zero (no compression).

Because so much of ClientHello is now hidden in the extensions, it's useful to examine a real-life handshake request to better understand what is communicated. The following is an overview of the ClientHello message sent by OpenSSL 1.1.1d after traces of earlier protocol versions are removed:

---

[3] TLS Version Intolerance in SSL Pulse [fsty.uk/t17] (Ivan Ristić, 2 August 2016)

---

```
Handshake protocol: ClientHello
    Version: TLS 1.2
    Random: 3ba9897c573fbe311d8b77f2d2b13c8b4b1322308787f921db0daf0b5ea8b4bc
    Session ID: 6565c4c660f83f4638e2e0b942fd6cb8fb0ec2b1113a992f3234479ea7096c1c
    Cipher Suites
        Suite: TLS_AES_256_GCM_SHA384
        Suite: TLS_CHACHA20_POLY1305_SHA256
        Suite: TLS_AES_128_GCM_SHA256
    Compression Methods
        Method: null
    Extensions
        Extension: server_name
            Name: example.com
        Extension: supported_groups
            Group: x25519
            Group: secp256r1
            Group: x448
            Group: secp521r1
            Group: secp384r1
        Extension: signature_algorithms
            Algorithm: ecdsa_secp256r1_sha256
            Algorithm: ecdsa_secp384r1_sha384
            Algorithm: ecdsa_secp521r1_sha512
            Algorithm: ed25519
            Algorithm: ed448
            Algorithm: rsa_pss_pss_sha256
            Algorithm: rsa_pss_pss_sha384
            Algorithm: rsa_pss_pss_sha512
            Algorithm: rsa_pss_rsae_sha256
            Algorithm: rsa_pss_rsae_sha384
            Algorithm: rsa_pss_rsae_sha512
            Algorithm: rsa_pkcs1_sha256
            Algorithm: rsa_pkcs1_sha384
            Algorithm: rsa_pkcs1_sha512
        Extension: supported_versions
            Version: TLS 1.3
        Extension: psk_key_exchange_modes
            Mode: psk_dhe_ke
        Extension: key_share
            Key Share Entry
                Group: x25519
                Key Exchange: c047a27d406ae731bc201deefc0a32a8df331be0ab161373ed208↵
e9e1a14f873
```

# ServerHello

Servers respond with a ServerHello message when they're willing to negotiate a secure connection. The main purpose of this message is to communicate the selected protocol version and cipher suite, along with additional information necessary to complete the handshake.

```
struct {
    ProtocolVersion legacy_version = 0x0303;     /* TLS 1.2 */
    Random random;
    opaque legacy_session_id_echo<0..32>;
    CipherSuite cipher_suite;
    uint8 legacy_compression_method = 0;
    Extension extensions<6..2^16-1>;
} ServerHello;
```

Originally, the random field in this message was only intended to carry the server's contribution to making each handshake unique. Over time, however, this field was overloaded to support additional functionality without changing the message structure. For one example, a special random value is used to build the HelloRetryRequest message, which I cover in the next section. It's also used in the normal handshake flow for *downgrade protection*. In the case that a TLS 1.3 server is negotiating TLS 1.2, the last eight bytes of random data must contain a special value, as follows:

```
44 4F 57 4E 47 52 44 01
```

This is a signal to the client that the server supports TLS 1.3. The same approach is used when TLS 1.1 or earlier are negotiated, except that the signaling bytes are different:[4]

```
44 4F 57 4E 47 52 44 00
```

For the downgrade protection to work, a TLS 1.3 client receiving a ServerHello must check the last bytes of the random field and abort the handshake if any of the two special values are detected.

The following ServerHello example is the response to the ClientHello from the previous section. As you can see, this response is much simpler, with the server deciding the connection parameters and communicating them back to the client.

```
Handshake Protocol: Server Hello
    Version: TLS 1.2
    Random: 7b8235fb3688f78f268402f7576036ec5a572ee623209f28216d201b343e286c
    Session ID: 6565c4c660f83f4638e2e0b942fd6cb8fb0ec2b1113a992f3234479ea7096c1c
    Cipher Suite: TLS_AES_256_GCM_SHA384
```

---

[4] In this place, TLS 1.3 also updates the TLS 1.2 protocol, recommending that TLS 1.2 servers use the same mechanism for downgrade protection when agreeing to use TLS 1.1.

---

```
            Compression Method: null
            Extensions
                Extension: key_share
                    Key Share Entry
                        Group: x25519
                        Key Exchange: 0ad9f9e59ed1fded4312a0ed0174635217270b022caf9cdcef480↵
    57a92224343
                Extension: supported_versions
                    Version: TLS 1.3
```

The ServerHello message in TLS 1.3 is also slimmer than in previous versions because some information has been moved into the following messages so that it can be encrypted. For example, notice how there is no session resumption data. Don't be fooled by the session ID field included in the body of the message; its real name is legacy_session_id_echo and it's just a mirror of the value sent by the client, used to preserve the wire format. Similarly, the negotiated version in the main body is a fake; the real version number is in the supported_versions extension.

## HelloRetryRequest

Because in TLS 1.3 clients have to guess what key exchange algorithms each server will like, there also needs to exist a mechanism for the server to communicate failures back. When the server is not able to accept a handshake, it sends a HelloRetryRequest message back to the client to describe the failure and provide guidance on how the problem can be resolved. Interestingly, this message actually reuses the entire structure of a ServerHello with a special value selected for the random bytes. This is another example of a design decision influenced by the need to preserve the wire protocol.

```
CF 21 AD 74 E5 9A 61 11 BE 1D 8C 02 1E 65 B8 91
C2 A2 11 16 7A BB 8C 5E 07 9E 09 E2 C8 A8 33 9C
```

For this to work, after receiving what appears to be a ServerHello message, the client must check the random field to see if it contains the special value. If it does, it's a HelloRetryRequest; otherwise, it's a genuine ServerHello.

# Authentication

Authentication in TLS 1.3 is generally done via a unified set of protocol messages, which is a welcome change from earlier protocol versions.[5] Certificate authentication involves two messages: first, an appropriate certificate is sent in the Certificate message, followed by

---

[5] In TLS 1.2 and earlier, server authentication and key exchange are combined, making it difficult to understand what processes are used to provide security.

CertificateVerify to provide proof of private key possession. The process is the same for both server and client, although client authentication is optional and done only if the server requests it. Separately, handshake integrity is verified via the Finished message, which both sides send when the handshake is complete.

## The Transcript Hash

The *transcript hash* concept is central to authentication in TLS. Its purpose is to bind all authentication activities to the unique set of messages exchanged between the parties and thus to the exact handshake. The hashing is done over the content produced by concatenating the specified handshake messages together:

```
Transcript-Hash(M1, M2, ... Mn) = Hash(M1 || M2 || ... || Mn)
```

Record layer headers are not included. A special transcript hash calculation is used when the server responds to a ClientHello with a HelloRetryRequest message, wherein the aim is to make it possible for the server to handle this situation without keeping state. To do this, the server sends the hash of the initial ClientHello message back to the client in the cookie extension that's part of the HelloRetryRequest message.

## Certificate

The Certificate message is used to send one or more certificates to the other party. Each certificate is wrapped in a holding structure that supports attaching arbitrary extensions to the certificates. In TLS 1.3, these extensions can be used to include OCSP revocation information, as well as *Certificate Transparency* (CT) logging proofs called *Signed Certificate Timestamps* (SCTs).[6]

```
enum {
    X509(0),
    RawPublicKey(2),
    (255)
} CertificateType;

struct {
    select (certificate_type) {
        case RawPublicKey:
            /* From RFC 7250 ASN.1_subjectPublicKeyInfo */
            opaque ASN1_subjectPublicKeyInfo<1..2^24-1>;
```

---

[6] In TLS 1.2 and earlier, OCSP revocation information is included in a separate handshake message, CertificateStatus. The change in TLS 1.3 now moves it close to the certificate, where it makes more sense. The main issue with the old mechanism is that it supports including revocation information only for the leaf certificates. A separate extension, status_request_v2, had to be developed to support providing revocation information for other certificates in the chain. In TLS 1.3, this extension is deprecated and must not be used.

```
        case X509:
            opaque cert_data<1..2^24-1>;
    };
    Extension extensions<0..2^16-1>;
} CertificateEntry;

struct {
    opaque certificate_request_context<0..2^8-1>;
    CertificateEntry certificate_list<0..2^24-1>;
} Certificate;
```

Unlike in earlier protocol versions, in TLS 1.3 the provided certificate chains don't have to be in the correct order. The server (leaf) certificate must still be first, but there are no order requirements on the rest of the chain. This is the recognition of the fact that, in the wild, many certificate chains are misconfigured, and clients already do what they can to build correct certificate chains working from the information they have.

Clients and servers use this same message for certificate transport. In TLS 1.3, servers can use only one certificate within the same connection, but clients potentially can use multiple certificates, authenticating themselves more than once. The certificate_request_context field, sent in the CertificateRequest message from the server, is used to make every subsequent client authentication different.

## CertificateVerify

The CertificateVerify message is used to prove possession of the private key corresponding to the certificate sent earlier in the handshake. This message is sent immediately after the certificate and must be followed by the Finished message. CertificateVerify contains an indication of the signature algorithm and a digital signature that binds the handshake and the certificate.

```
struct {
    SignatureScheme algorithm;
    opaque signature<0..2^16-1>;
} CertificateVerify;
```

The signature must be produced by the private key matching the certificate. The content to be signed consists of the following elements:

1.  A total of 64 spaces (0x20 octets), to defend against the fact that in earlier TLS versions an attacker could obtain the signature of a message with a chosen 32-byte

prefix (the contents of the `random` field in `ClientHello`).[7] This 64-byte prefix clears both the client and server random data.

2. A context that uniquely identifies the signature purpose; this is "TLS 1.3, server CertificateVerify" for server signatures and "TLS 1.3, client CertificateVerify" for clients.

3. A single zero-byte separator.

4. The transcript hash.

## CertificateRequest

The `CertificateRequest` message is sent by a server that requires client authentication. It includes an optional context field, the purpose of which is to make certificate requests, as well as one or more additional extensions.

```
struct {
    opaque certificate_request_context<0..2^8-1>;
    Extension extensions<2..2^16-1>;
} CertificateRequest;
```

**Certificate request context**

The `certificate_request_context` field is used to uniquely identify a specific certificate request. The server selects a value that is unique within the same connection, as well as unpredictable. The client is expected to mirror back the context value in its corresponding `CertificateVerify`. The context is used only when post-handshake client authentication is used; otherwise, the field is left empty.

**Extensions**

Every certificate request must include the `signature_algorithms` extension to specify which signature algorithms the server will accept. Optionally, the `certificate_authorities` extension could be used to specify which CAs are supported.

## Finished

The `Finished` message is the last message sent in every handshake. To verify the handshake integrity, the client and server both send cryptographic signatures of the exchanged data. The handshake proceeds only if the signatures can be verified. Any other result would imply a modification of the network traffic by a third party.

---

[7] Section 7.4.3 in RFC 5246

---

```
struct {
    opaque verify_data[Hash.length];
} Finished;
```

The only field in the message, verify_data, is an HMAC of the transcript hash.

```
verify_data = HMAC(finished_key,
    Transcript-Hash(Handshake Context, Certificate*, CertificateVerify*))
```

The Certificate and CertificateVerify messages are included in the hash only when they were part of the handshake. The signing key is generated as part of the key schedule, which I will cover in detail later in this chapter.

# Post-Handshake Authentication

Post-handshake authentication may take place with clients that indicate support for it via the post_handshake_auth extension. In this case, servers may ask a client to authenticate by sending a CertificateRequest message at any point after the initial handshake takes place.

# Authentication Using Pre-Shared Keys

Although certificates are usually seen as the primary authentication method, TLS 1.3 also supports authentication using PSKs. In this case, the client and server authenticate each other using a previously established shared secret; certificates are not needed. Although PSK authentication sounds like an optional feature, it's actually an important part of TLS 1.3 because session resumption depends on it. In a nutshell, once a handshake completes successfully (using certificates for authentication), the server can issue one or more PSKs to the client. The client can then use these PSKs on subsequent connections to bypass certificate authentication, resulting in better handshake performance.

The client uses the psk_key_exchange_modes extension to indicate support for PSK authentication. Two options are available, one that provides forward security (psk_dhe_ke) and one that doesn't (psk_ke). Although the name indicates otherwise, the psk_dhe_ke option includes both DHE and ECDHE key exchanges.

```
struct {
    PskKeyExchangeMode ke_modes<1..255>;
} PskKeyExchangeModes;

enum { psk_ke(0), psk_dhe_ke(1), (255) } PskKeyExchangeMode;
```

The actual authentication information is transported using the pre_shared_key extension, which clients can use to offer one or more PSK identities. Within each identity, the obfuscated_ticket_age field is populated for a PSK used for session resumption, but set to zero otherwise. This field is used to determine how fresh a `ClientHello` is from the client perspective, which is necessary as a defense against replay attacks. When early data is used, it must be encrypted using the first offered PSK. Binders are HMAC values that are used to demonstrate proof of PSK possession.

```
struct {
    PskIdentity identities<7..2^16-1>;
    PskBinderEntry binders<33..2^16-1>;
} OfferedPsks;

struct {
    opaque identity<1..2^16-1>;
    uint32 obfuscated_ticket_age;
} PskIdentity;

opaque PskBinderEntry<32..255>;
```

If PSK authentication is accepted, the server indicates the selected identity and the handshake can proceed. The selected PSK is used by both parties to generate the connection key material and complete the handshake.

A peculiar aspect of the PSK design is that the identity field is an opaque value that can be used in one of two ways, depending on how the server implements session resumption. In the simpler case, in which session data is stored server-side, PSK identity is an identifier that uniquely identifies the PSK and enables the server to retrieve the corresponding data from its storage. However, the same field can also be used to store the entire session state. In this case, the PSK identity must be properly secured by the server in order to prevent tampering.

## Session Resumption

In TLS 1.3, session resumption is implemented via pre-shared keys, as we discussed in the previous section. Servers that wish to support session resumption wait until the handshake is complete, then issue one or more tickets using the `NewSessionTicket` message.

```
struct {
    uint32 ticket_lifetime;
    uint32 ticket_age_add;
    opaque ticket_nonce<0..255>;
    opaque ticket<1..2^16-1>;
    Extension extensions<0..2^16-2>;
} NewSessionTicket;
```

The handshake and the nonce from the ticket together enable the client and server to calculate the PSK. The key used for the calculation, `resumption_master_secret`, is one of the keys created at the end of the key schedule (discussed later in this chapter).

```
HKDF-Expand-Label(resumption_master_secret,
                  "resumption", ticket_nonce, Hash.length)
```

The remaining fields in each ticket are used for bookkeeping and additional signaling:

**Ticket lifetime**

Indicates the lifetime of the ticket, in seconds. Tickets are allowed a lifetime of only up to seven days.

**Ticket age add**

Although the ticket age is initially securely transmitted to the client, it gets exposed in plaintext later on. The ticket age add is used to randomize the ticket age, as a way of preventing it from being used for passive network fingerprinting.

**Ticket nonce**

A number that must be unique within the same connection. It's used to support generation of multiple PSKs from a single handshake.

**Ticket**

The ticket itself is an opaque array of bytes. Depending on how the server implements session resumption, this value can be either a unique identifier (that the server looks up in a database) or an encrypted blob that contains all the information necessary to resume this session (after decryption, of course).

**Extensions**

Ticket extensions are used to transport additional data that may be necessary to correctly use the tickets. The TLS 1.3 specification documents only one extension, called early_data. If this extension is specified, the ticket is allowed to be used for the no-latency (0-RTT) mode. This extension also indicates how much data can be transported using 0-RTT mode.

# Alert Protocol

In TLS 1.3, as in previous protocol versions, the *alert protocol* is used to communicate errors and indicate connection closure. This protocol can be used with or without encryption, depending on the connection state. There is only one protocol message that consists of two bytes. Out of the two bytes, only one is used to carry the AlertDescription field, which uses one of the predefined values to indicate the type of message that is being communicated.

The other field is AlertLevel, which in previous protocol versions contained message severity. The field has been deprecated and remains in TLS 1.3 to preserve the wire format; message severity is implicit in the message type. All the defined TLS 1.3 alert messages are considered to be fatal and require connection termination.

Alert protocol messages are not allowed to be fragmented. This was possible in earlier protocol versions and led to possibly exploitable weaknesses in several popular protocol implementations.

```
enum {
    warning(1),
    fatal(2),
    (255)
} AlertLevel;

enum {
    close_notify(0),
    unexpected_message(10),
    bad_record_mac(20),
    record_overflow(22),
    handshake_failure(40),
    bad_certificate(42),
    unsupported_certificate(43),
    certificate_revoked(44),
    certificate_expired(45),
    certificate_unknown(46),
    illegal_parameter(47),
    unknown_ca(48),
    access_denied(49),
    decode_error(50),
    decrypt_error(51),
    protocol_version(70),
    insufficient_security(71),
    internal_error(80),
    inappropriate_fallback(86),
    user_canceled(90),
    missing_extension(109),
    unsupported_extension(110),
    unrecognized_name(112),
    bad_certificate_status_response(113),
    unknown_psk_identity(115),
    certificate_required(116),
    no_application_protocol(120),
    (255)
} AlertDescription;

struct {
    AlertLevel level;
    AlertDescription description;
} Alert;
```

## Connection Closure

In cryptography, orderly connection shutdown is necessary to ensure detection of truncation attacks, in which an active network attacker takes over the communication channel and stops the message flow. This could lead to processing of incomplete information, which could be used to the attacker's advantage.

TLS 1.3 supports two alerts for this purpose: user_canceled should be used for connection closure that happens before the handshake is complete, and close_notify should be used when encryption is already negotiated.

# Cryptographic Computations

To achieve security, a protocol needs robust encryption algorithms and strong encryption keys. Earlier in this chapter, we discussed how encryption is done, so let's now take a closer look at how the keys are generated. This is a process that happens during the handshake phase of every connection.

To satisfy the cryptographic principle that one key should be used only for one purpose, TLS 1.3 defines many encryption keys in a process that ensures that security is improved whenever information becomes available.

Table 2.1. TLS 1.3 encryption keys and secrets

| Key Purpose | Keys | Description |
| --- | --- | --- |
| Binder key (client) | 1 | Proof of PSK possession. |
| Early traffic secret (client) | 1 | Encryption of early data, client only. |
| Early exporter master secret | 1 | Early exporter master secret, intended for use outside TLS.[a] |
| Handshake traffic secrets (client, server) | 2 | Encryption of handshake traffic, one each for client and server. |
| Application traffic secret (client, server) | 2+ | Encryption of application traffic, one each for client and server. TLS initially generates two of these encryption keys, with an optional mechanism for the keys to be incrementally changed for the same connection. |
| Exporter master secret | 1 | Exporter master secret, intended for use outside TLS. |
| Resumption master secret | 1 | Generation of secrets (PSKs) that are used for session resumption. |

[a] *Exporters* make keying material available for external use—for example, by applications and other protocols that integrate with TLS.

## Key Derivation

Generation of cryptographic keys is implemented in a process called *key derivation* and it usually relies on a specific *key derivation function* (KDF) as a building block. The purpose of a KDF is to make it possible to use input that contains some useful entropy, but the structure and statistical properties of which might make it not suitable for direct use in cryptographic operations. A good example of such an input is a password, which could be prone to brute-force attacks or may be partially known to the attacker.

In TLS 1.3, key derivation is based on *HMAC-based key derivation function* (HKDF), which is standardized in RFC 5869. Earlier TLS revisions rely on a custom key derivation function, but, even though that construction is not considered insecure, in TLS 1.3 the decision was made to prefer a standardized and well-known cryptographic primitive instead.

HKDF consists of two phases. The first phase is called *extraction* and its goal is to extract useful entropy from the provided input, producing one strong pseudorandom key as a result. HKDF is designed to use an optional salt value:

```
HKDF-Extract(salt, input) -> extracted_key
```

The second phase is called *expansion*. It builds on the extraction output to support the generation of any number of derived pseudorandom keys of arbitrary length. The optional context value is used when multiple keys need to be generated:

```
HKDF-Expand(extracted_key, context, length) -> expanded_key
```

# Key Schedule

At a high level, two sides that want to communicate securely need only establish one sufficiently strong secret that the adversary doesn't know. For a brand-new connection, this is typically achieved using the Diffie-Hellman (DH) key exchange, backed by authentication to ensure that the exchange is taking place with the right party. Most TLS connections rely on server certificates for authentication, but there are also other methods—for example, session resumption or password-based authentication. In fact, there are situations when multiple secrets are available, and TLS 1.3 has been designed to take advantage of all of them.

The extraction function of HKDF is used directly, but for the expansion part TLS 1.3 specifies additional wrapper functions. The first such function is called `HKDF-Expand-Label`, and its purpose is to enable the generation of multiple keys for different purposes based on the same input; this is done via *labels*.

```
# Structure used as input for HKDF; it combines the
# context with a text label to generate a unique key.
struct {
    uint16 length = Length;
    opaque label<7..255> = "tls13 " + Label;
    opaque context<0..255> = Context;
} HkdfLabel;

# This wrapper function packages the context and
```

```
# the label together and invokes HKDF.
HKDF-Expand-Label(Secret, Label, Context, Length) =
    HKDF-Expand(Secret, HkdfLabel, Length)
```

The second function, `Derive-Secret`, is more interesting. Its purpose is to bind the key derivation process to the exact handshake for which the keys are being generated. This is done via a *transcript hash*, which is a hash of the exchanged handshake messages.

```
Derive-Secret(Secret, Label, Messages) =
    HKDF-Expand-Label(Secret, Label, Transcript-Hash(Messages), Hash.length)
```

During the handshake, the client and server each provide a strong random number with the goal of making every handshake unique, even if all other content in the handshake is the same. Because this randomness is propagated into the key derivation process via the wrapper functions, encryption keys are also unique, even if the same secrets are used as input (which would happen if the same input secret is used more than once). The actual key derivation operates in blocks, each of which is designed to produce a family of keys.

The first block in the key schedule builds from the PSK, which typically happens when an earlier session is resumed. The PSK may not be available, in which case a zero-length string is used instead, the same as for the salt. The extraction step produces the *Early Secret*, which is an intermediary value from which three working keys are expanded. The block ends with another expansion in order to prevent state reuse.

Figure 2.3. TLS 1.3 key schedule, part 1: Early secret

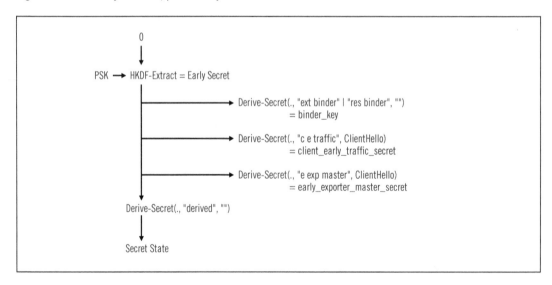

For its secret, the second block uses the ECDHE or DHE key exchange output if it's available and a zero-length string otherwise. The other input (HKDF salt) is the final state of the first block (*Secret State*). The extraction step produces *Handshake Secret*, from which two working keys are expanded.

Figure 2.4. TLS 1.3 key schedule, part 2: Handshake secret

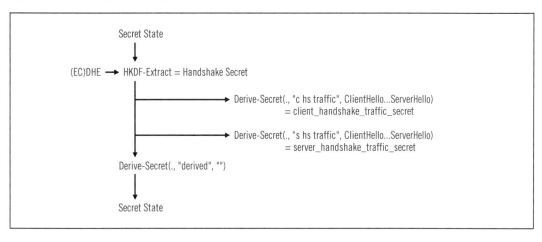

Finally, the third block operates without a secret, using the state from the previous block as HKDF salt, and produces the *Master Secret*, from which four working keys can be expanded as needed.

Figure 2.5. TLS 1.3 key schedule, part 3: Master secret

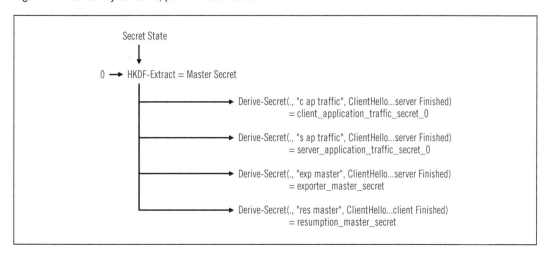

> ### Note
>
> You may recall that the Derive-Secret function relies on the transcript hash. Although we may think about the transcript hash as a fingerprint of a completed handshake, key derivation happens during the handshake while the communica-

> tion is still happening. Every subsequent key expansion will therefore use a poten-
> tially different transcript hash value.

You may notice in the diagrams that the names of the application traffic keys end with zeros. This is because these are only the initial encryption keys. TLS allows either side involved in the communication to update its sending encryption keys, signaled using the KeyUpdate message. This could happen at any point after the initial handshake is complete. The next iterations of the encryption keys are generated using the HKDF-Expand-Label function.

```
application_traffic_secret_N+1 =
    HKDF-Expand-Label(application_traffic_secret_N,
                      "traffic upd", "", Hash.length)
```

Another key that's needed is finished_key, which is used in Finished messages to support handshake integrity validation. This key is generated via a HKDF expansion from the current traffic key, which the specification refers to as the *Base Key*:

```
finished_key = HKDF-Expand-Label(BaseKey, "finished", "", Hash.length)
```

# Extensions

Extensions are so-called *tag-length-value* (TLV) structures designed to carry arbitrary data. They appeared first unofficially in TLS 1.0, then later officially in TLS 1.1. The principal idea behind extensions was to make it possible to extend the protocol with new features without requiring new protocol releases. They are now more powerful in TLS 1.3, with most of the fields in the original handshake protocol messages migrated to extensions. A good example is TLS protocol version negotiation, for which the supported_versions extension is now used. This move is largely in response to the realization that fixed fields don't work well from the perspective of protocol evolution.

Extensions are typically part of the main protocol messages—in particular, ClientHello and ServerHello—but they are also used in other places. For example, tickets support extensions and define the early_data extension to enable servers to indicate support for 0-RTT mode.

Throughout this chapter, I mention extensions when they are necessary for the understanding of the protocol, but I largely gloss over their contents. This is because I don't think the content is necessary to achieve a good understanding of TLS at a high level. If you'd like to understand the extensions better, you'll find many of them in the body of the TLS 1.3 specification. However, as they are part of a general-purpose extension mechanism, they are really scattered across many other documents. At the time of writing, IANA maintains a list of about 50 extensions and provides pointers to where they are defined.[8] If you care about that sort of thing, you'll enjoy using Wireshark to observe browser TLS handshakes and looking into which extensions are used and why. To get you started, the following table lists the most commonly seen extensions that are defined outside TLS 1.3.

Table 2.2. Commonly used extensions that are not part of the core TLS protocol

| Extension Name | Purpose | RFC |
|---|---|---|
| ALPN | Negotiates what application-layer protocol (e.g., HTTP/2) will be used after the TLS handshake. | RFC 7301 |
| Certificate Transparency | Carries proof of certificates being recorded in Certificate Transparency logs. | RFC 6962 |
| GREASE | Injects various protocol values at random to support early discovery of intolerant implementations. | RFC 8701 |
| OCSP | Requests and communicates certificate revocation status. | RFC 6066 |
| Padding | Works around a bug in the F5 load balancers that may otherwise result in handshake failure. | RFC 7685 |
| Server Name Indication | Indicates the hostname of the server to which connection is intended. | RFC 6066 |

# Cipher Suites

Cipher suites in TLS 1.3 are a very straightforward affair compared to earlier protocol versions. Whereas previously you had to navigate a maze of more than 300 cipher suites to understand everything that TLS had to offer, in TLS 1.3 there are only five cipher suites.

Table 2.3. TLS 1.3 cipher suites

| Cipher Suite Name | AEAD Algorithm | HKDF Hash |
|---|---|---|
| TLS_AES_128_CCM_SHA256 | AES-128-CCM | SHA256 |
| TLS_AES_128_CCM_8_SHA256 | AES-256-CCM-8 | SHA256 |
| TLS_AES_128_GCM_SHA256[a] | AES-128-GCM | SHA256 |
| TLS_AES_256_GCM_SHA384 | AES-256-GCM | SHA384 |
| TLS_CHACHA20_POLY1305_SHA256 | ChaCha20-Poly1305 | SHA256 |

[a] Must be supported by every implementation.

These five suites are designed to support a variety of operating environments:

- TLS_AES_128_GCM_SHA256 is fast on a variety of computer systems, such as desktops and laptops that normally support hardware acceleration. This cipher suite is the only one that's mandatory to implement.

---

[8] IANA: Transport Layer Security (TLS) Extensions [fsty.uk/t18] (retrieved 4 September 2021)

- The 256-bit AES-GCM variant provides an additional margin of safety, should you be concerned about quantum computers, for example.

- The ChaCha20 suite is faster on platforms that don't have hardware acceleration for AES-GCM, such as mobile devices.

- The two CCM suites are optimized for platforms that are severely constrained—for example, IoT devices. The first, TLS_AES_128_CCM_SHA256, provides better performance than either AES-GCM or ChaCha20. The second, TLS_AES_128_CCM_8_SHA256, further reduces bandwidth requirements.

The reduced number of suites in TLS 1.3 is great news for operators everywhere. The main advantage is that all options support forward secrecy and authenticated encryption, which means that you can't get it wrong, no matter what you choose. Moreover, with fewer choices, our ability to understand server configuration has greatly improved. Admittedly, TLS 1.3 is brand-new and we may see the number of suites grow over time, but it's not likely to get as bad as before; the current thinking in cryptography engineering is that less is more.

Figure 2.6. Cipher suite name construction in TLS 1.3

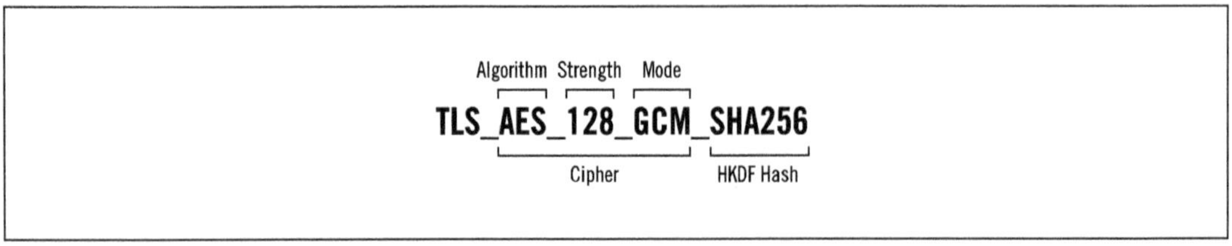

You may also notice that the names of the suites are now much simpler. That's because cipher suites have fewer responsibilities in TLS 1.3 than they had previously, with authentication and key exchange moved into the protocol itself. As a result, two out of three name components are now no longer needed. What remains is the cipher and the HKDF hash function.

# 0-RTT

0-RTT is a new protocol feature in TLS 1.3 that enables encrypted communication with no additional network latency compared to plaintext TCP—hence the name *zero round-trip time* mode. The original design of SSL, and later TLS, incurs network latency of two round trips, making TLS quite heavy over long distances. The changed handshake in TLS 1.3 reduces the default network latency to only one round trip and provides an optional zero-latency mode. Depending on your perspective, this feature is either a great performance improvement in TLS 1.3 or a security setback. The reason for this is simple: before version 1.3, TLS was a network encryption protocol that was separate from the application protocols it's used with. The 0-RTT mode improves performance by making security compromises, which means that we now have portions of TLS that have to be used *very carefully* to achieve reasonable security. Traditionally, features like that have always been the ones that fall first. On the positive side, 0-RTT is optional, so if you don't like it, you don't have to use it.

## Implementation Details

Conceptually, 0-RTT mode is straightforward and builds on PSK authentication, which we covered earlier in this chapter. After a handshake is complete, the server can issue one or more tickets. If the server wishes to use 0-RTT mode, it will indicate so by attaching the early_data extension to the ticket. Inside, it will further specify how much data can be transported using this mode.

A client that's in possession of a ticket enabled for 0-RTT can therefore use this feature on subsequent connections to the server. If it does, the ClientHello will specify the PSK that corresponds to the ticket and include an empty early_data extension as a signal that early data is coming. The data itself will be encrypted using a key derived from the PSK.

On the receiving end, the server has an option to accept such early data (and forward it immediately to the application layer for processing) or to ignore it and fall back to the standard handshake. I said 0-RTT mode was *conceptually* simple; in practice, there are many rules that govern its use so that it can be implemented with a reasonable margin of safety. This complexity is one more reason to be very careful when using this feature in practice.

There are two principal issues in regard to 0-RTT mode: loss of forward secrecy and replay attacks.

## 0-RTT and Forward Secrecy

If 0-RTT mode is not used, PSKs can be considered to be secure, or at least can be *made* secure. This is because they support two types of key exchange, one that supports forward secrecy (psk_dhe_ke) and one that doesn't (psk_ke). If the former type is used on a resumption, the resumed connections will be encrypted under different keys, providing forward security.

The 0-RTT mode cannot use the Diffie-Hellman key exchange for security because the data is encrypted by the client and sent immediately; there's no server input. To understand if 0-RTT can provide forward security, we need to dig deeper. It's possible in theory, but it depends on the alignment of a number of aspects.

Forward secrecy as a concept implies that data is not encrypted using a long-term encryption key or a key that can be derived from a long-term key. This is always true when the DH key exchange is used; every session uses different encryption keys that are separate from the authentication method. If we're not going to use DH, then we need to pay more attention to exactly how security is provided. To do that, we need to look more closely at how session resumption is implemented.

**PSK longevity**

With 0-RTT, early data is encrypted using a key derived from the PSK. Crucially, one ticket can be reused, which potentially means that a lot of data can be encrypted under the same key. This weakness can be avoided if servers allow only a short ticket lifetime in combination with new tickets being made available to clients after each successful handshake. The assumption here is that clients will prefer more recent tickets, rather than the old ones.

**Ticket encryption**

Session resumption is typically implemented using one of two approaches. Traditionally, servers store session information locally. No session data is transported on the network; clients are sent a unique identifier that is used to find the correct session, which is then retrieved from storage. This approach is safe, but doesn't scale well. If you have a cluster of servers that serve the same web site, it's a lot of work to make the same session information available to all of them. As a result, another session resumption mechanism evolved, one that is akin to HTTP cookies. In this second approach, there is no session storage server-side; instead, session data is encrypted with a special ticket key and sent back to the clients as an opaque blob. To make clusters work, they only need to share the same ticket key.

The security of ticket keys traditionally has been a neglected area, with little visibility into what various implementations are doing. In the context of 0-RTT mode, if the ticket key is not rotated in short intervals, 0-RTT cannot be considered to possess forward security. Actually, all previous protocol versions have this weakness; TLS 1.3 fixed it by supporting DH key exchange on resumption. Ironically, it also reintroduced the same problem with support for 0-RTT.

In the context of forward security, the verdict is that 0-RTT mode can be secure, but we've lost verifiability. Whereas without 0-RTT, we know that TLS 1.3 is forward-secure (because it supports only suites that provide this feature), with 0-RTT mode, we need to go through a lot of trouble to analyze the actual implementations and configurations to determine if the security is satisfactory.

# 0-RTT and Replay Attacks

A bigger problem with 0-RTT is that it's vulnerable to *replay attacks*. Without it, every TLS handshake is unique. There is a client that wants to talk to a server. Each side chooses a cryptographically strong random number, and the result is what makes the handshake unique. When 0-RTT mode is used, the server is not involved, and that's what enables the attacks. An active network attacker can capture the initial network flight and send it to the server multiple times. From the server perspective, all such attacker-submitted connection requests appear genuine and early data should be processed.

The desire for better network performance makes replay attacks possible; there are things you can do to make the attack difficult, but it cannot be eliminated in its entirety.

The TLS 1.3 specification provides some features to counter replay attacks. For example, the `obfuscated_ticket_age` field that's part of PSK authentication enables servers to determine ticket freshness, thus preventing active network attackers from reusing the same data indefinitely. There is also advice about some possible additional countermeasures—for example, keeping track of already-processed early data and refusing it if it's observed again. These countermeasures may be reasonable when there is only one server, but they get exponentially more complex when there is a cluster, or even servers that are spread geographically.

## Is 0-RTT Safe?

0-RTT may or may not be safe; the answer depends on your perspective, as well as how much effort you are willing to invest into ensuring its security. This feature comes with many drawbacks and should not be used by default. It should be used only after a careful analysis of browser and server implementations, server configuration, and application behavior. Alternatively, you could argue that 0-RTT is safe to use in situations that do not demand serious security. After all, exploiting the weaknesses of this feature is not trivial and requires significant resources.

The obvious users for 0-RTT mode are browsers. There is a dedicated RFC that covers some of the nuances of using this mode with HTTP.[9] Web sites always want better performance, and using 0-RTT mode is one way to get it. In chasing better responsiveness, web sites potentially allow the data transmitted in the first network flight to be compromised. But what is this data? It's likely that browsers will use 0-RTT only for GET requests and thus not to request any changes (which is usually achieved using other HTTP methods—for example, POST, PUT, and DELETE). So maybe that would be safe? Maybe, but there are two issues even with that restriction.

One is that some applications are poorly written and use GET requests to request changes. In this case, there would be damage if such requests were replayed. Usually, when replay attacks are discussed, we use bank transfers as an example. If you request some money to be transferred from your account to someone else's, you don't want your request to be reused many times until your account is empty.

---

[9] RFC 8470: Using Early Data in HTTP [fsty.uk/t19] (Thomson et al., September 2018)

The other problem is that most HTTP requests carry some authentication information, be it session cookies or HTTP Basic Authentication credentials. This is the type of data that would be transmitted as early data, encrypted (depending on the implementation) without forward secrecy. If this data is compromised, that would lead to user account compromise and potentially much more damage.

# Summary

Despite the small increase in the version number, TLS 1.3 is essentially a brand-new protocol. Every corner of TLS 1.2 has been examined, taken apart, and put together again while making it much better. The dusty corners have been cleaned up and old garbage thrown away. For that reason, it's difficult to talk about what has been improved—because everything has been. In a way, this entire chapter is one very long overview of the changes made in TLS 1.3. Still, let's take a quick look at the most important improvements at a high level.

**Reduced network latency**

The redesigned handshake reduces network latency down to only one round trip, thus significantly improving the performance of all connections. Resumed connections can be even faster if 0-RTT mode is enabled, although this mode comes with security drawbacks and must be reviewed carefully.

**Forward security**

The refresh of exchange modes resulted in all cipher suites supporting forward security. The RSA key exchange is no more. Historically, even though strong forward secrecy can be achieved with TLS 1.2, careful server configuration is required. Further, session resumption supports use the DH key exchange, which means that even resumed connections can have forward security. This is not quite true for 0-RTT mode, but it's still not as bad as it was previously.

**Reduction of information transported unencrypted**

TLS 1.3 has added protection, via encryption, to many parts that were previously exposed in plaintext. In a nutshell, there is now protection for almost everything that can be encrypted. This includes most of the handshake and both the client and server certificates. Previously exposed bits of information at the record layer have been deprecated, enforcing full encryption of exchanged data. The one crucial bit of information that remains unprotected is the server hostname, which is still exposed via SNI, but work continues outside the TLS protocol to close this hole.

**Refresh of cryptographic primitives**

The list of improvements at the cryptography level is very long and includes removal of obsolete primitives (e.g., RC4 and friends), added support for modern primitives (e.g., X25519 and ChaCha20), and removal of homegrown mechanisms in favor of standards (e.g., authenticated encryption and HKDF). Digital signatures have been tightened and key exchange parameter negotiation streamlined. Other dubious features such as compression and renegotiation have been removed. It is difficult to understate how much better TLS 1.3 is because the changes have been so extensive and touched every part of the protocol.

To sum it up in a sentence: TLS 1.3 is a modern cryptographic protocol, faster and substantially more secure than its predecessors.

# 3 TLS 1.2

TLS is a cryptographic protocol designed to secure connection-oriented network traffic, irrespective of what actual higher-level communication protocol is used. The focus of this chapter is TLS 1.2, with an occasional mention of earlier protocol versions where that makes sense.

As with the previous TLS 1.3 chapter, my goal is to give you a high-level overview that will enable you to understand what's going on without being distracted by implementation details. Wherever possible, I use message content examples, rather than definitions, which can sometimes be dry. The definitions in this chapter use the syntax that's the same as in the TLS specification, albeit with some minor simplifications. For more information on the syntax and the complete protocol reference, start with RFC 5246, which is where TLS 1.2 lives.[1] However, that one document doesn't tell the whole story. There are also many other relevant RFCs, which I reference throughout this chapter.

The best way to learn about TLS is to observe real-life traffic. My favorite approach is to use the network-capture tool Wireshark,[2] which comes with a TLS protocol parser: point your favorite browser at a secure web site, tell Wireshark to monitor the connection (it's best to restrict the capture to just one hostname and port 443), and observe the protocol messages.

After you're reasonably happy with your understanding of TLS (don't try too hard to learn it all; it's very hard to understand every feature, because there are so many of them), you'll be free to roam the various RFCs and even lurk on the key mailing lists. My two favorite places are the TLS Working Group document page,[3] where you can find the list of key documents and new proposals, and the TLS Working Group mailing list,[4] where you can follow the discussions about the future direction of TLS.

---

[1] RFC 5246: The Transport Layer Security Protocol Version 1.2 [fsty.uk/t20] (T. Dierks and E. Rescorla, August 2008)

[2] Wireshark [fsty.uk/t21] (retrieved 4 September 2021)

[3] TLS Working Group documents [fsty.uk/t22] (IETF, retrieved 4 September 2021)

[4] TLS Working Group mailing list archives [fsty.uk/t23] (IETF, retrieved 4 September 2021)

# Record Protocol

At a high level, TLS is implemented via the *record protocol*, which is in charge of transporting—and optionally encrypting—all lower-level messages exchanged over a connection. Each *TLS record* starts with a short header, which contains information about the record content type (or subprotocol), protocol version, and length. Message data follows immediately after the header.

Figure 3.1. TLS record

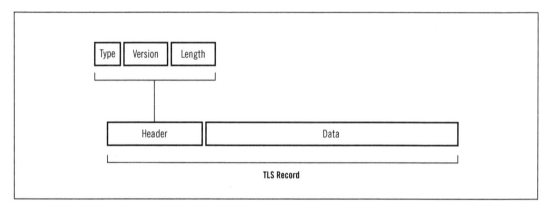

More formally, the TLS record fields are defined as follows:

```
struct {
    uint8 major;
    uint8 minor;
} ProtocolVersion;

enum {
    change_cipher_spec (20),
    alert (21),
    handshake (22),
    application_data (23)
} ContentType;

struct {
    ContentType type;
    ProtocolVersion version;
    uint16 length; /* Maximum length is 2^14 (16,384) bytes. */
    opaque fragment[TLSPlaintext.length];
} TLSPlaintext;
```

In addition to the visible fields, each TLS record is also assigned a unique 64-bit sequence number, which is not sent over the wire. Each side has its own sequence number and keeps track of the number of records sent by the other side. These values are used as part of the defense against replay attacks. You'll see how that works later on.

The record protocol is a useful protocol abstraction that takes care of several important, high-level aspects of the communication.

**Message transport**

The record protocol transports opaque data buffers submitted to it by other protocol layers. If a buffer is longer than the record length limit (16,384 bytes), the record protocol fragments it into smaller chunks. The opposite is also possible; smaller buffers belonging to the same subprotocol can be combined in a single record.

**Encryption and integrity validation**

Initially, on a brand new connection, messages are transported without any protection. (Technically, the TLS_NULL_WITH_NULL_NULL cipher suite is used.) This is necessary so that the first negotiation can take place. However, once the handshake is complete, the record layer starts to apply encryption and integrity validation according to the negotiated connection parameters.[5]

**Compression**

Transparent compression of data prior to encryption sounds nice in theory, but it was never very common in practice, mainly because everyone was already compressing their outbound traffic at the HTTP level. This feature suffered a fatal blow in 2012, when the CRIME attack exposed it as insecure.[6] It's now no longer used.

**Extensibility**

The record protocol takes care of data transport and encryption, but delegates all other features to subprotocols. This approach makes TLS extensible, because new subprotocols can be added easily. With encryption handled by the record protocol, all subprotocols are automatically protected using the negotiated connection parameters.

The main TLS specification defines four core subprotocols: *handshake protocol*, *change cipher spec protocol*, *application data protocol*, and *alert protocol*.

# Handshake Protocol

The handshake is the most elaborate part of the TLS protocol, during which the sides negotiate connection parameters and perform authentication. This phase usually requires six to ten messages, depending on which features are used. There can be many variations

---

[5] In most cases, this means that further traffic is encrypted and its integrity validated. But there's a small number of suites that don't use encryption; they use integrity validation only.

[6] I discuss the CRIME attack and various other compression-related weaknesses in the section called "Compression Side Channel Attacks" in Chapter 8.

in the exchange, depending on the configuration and supported protocol extensions. In practice, we see three common flows: (1) full handshake with server authentication, (2) abbreviated handshake that resumes an earlier session, and (3) handshake with client and server authentication.

Handshake protocol messages start with a header that carries the message type (one byte) and length (three bytes). The remainder of the message depends on the message type:

```
struct {
    HandshakeType msg_type;
    uint24 length;
    HandshakeMessage message;
} Handshake;
```

## Full Handshake

Every TLS connection begins with a handshake. If the client hasn't previously established a session with the server, the two sides will execute a *full handshake* in order to negotiate a *TLS session*. During this handshake, the client and the server will perform four main activities:

1. Exchange capabilities and agree on desired connection parameters.

2. Validate the presented certificate(s) or authenticate using other means.

3. Agree on a shared *master secret* that will be used to protect the session.

4. Verify that the handshake messages haven't been modified by a third party.

> ### Note
>
> In practice, steps 2 and 3 are part of a single step called *key exchange* (or, more generally, *key establishment*). I prefer to keep them separate in order to emphasize that the security of the protocol depends on correct authentication, which effectively sits outside TLS. Without authentication, an active network attacker can interject herself into the conversation and pose as the other side.

In this section, I discuss the most commonly seen TLS handshake, one between a client that's not authenticated and a server that is. The subsequent sections handle alternative protocol flows: client authentication and session resumption.

Figure 3.2. Full handshake with server authentication

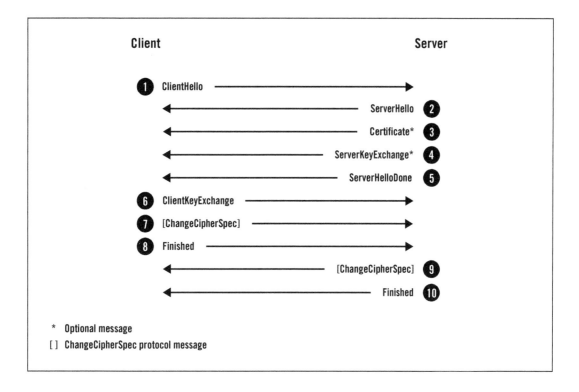

1. Client begins a new handshake and submits its capabilities to the server.

2. Server selects connection parameters.

3. Server sends its certificate chain (only if server authentication is required).

4. Depending on the selected key exchange, the server sends additional information required to generate the master secret.

5. Server indicates completion of its side of the negotiation.

6. Client sends additional information required to generate the master secret.

7. Client switches to encryption and informs the server.

8. Client sends a MAC of the handshake messages it sent and received.

9. Server switches to encryption and informs the client.

10. Server sends a MAC of the handshake messages it received and sent.

At this point—assuming there were no errors—the connection is established and the parties can begin to send application data. Now let's look at the handshake messages in more detail.

## ClientHello

The ClientHello message is always the first message sent in a new handshake. It's used to communicate client capabilities and preferences to the server. Clients send this message at the beginning of a new connection, when they wish to renegotiate, or in response to a server's renegotiation request (indicated by a HelloRequest message).

In the following example, you can see what a ClientHello message could look like. I reduced the amount of information presented for the sake of brevity, but all of the key elements are included.

```
Handshake protocol: ClientHello
    Version: TLS 1.2
    Random
        Client time: May 22, 2030 02:43:46 GMT
        Random bytes: b76b0e61829557eb4c611adfd2d36eb232dc1332fe29802e321ee871
    Session ID: (empty)
    Cipher Suites
        Suite: TLS_ECDHE_RSA_WITH_AES_128_GCM_SHA256
        Suite: TLS_DHE_RSA_WITH_AES_128_GCM_SHA256
        Suite: TLS_RSA_WITH_AES_128_GCM_SHA256
        Suite: TLS_ECDHE_RSA_WITH_AES_128_CBC_SHA
        Suite: TLS_DHE_RSA_WITH_AES_128_CBC_SHA
        Suite: TLS_RSA_WITH_AES_128_CBC_SHA
        Suite: TLS_RSA_WITH_3DES_EDE_CBC_SHA
        Suite: TLS_RSA_WITH_RC4_128_SHA
    Compression methods
        Method: null
    Extensions
        Extension: server_name
            Hostname: www.feistyduck.com
        Extension: renegotiation_info
        Extension: elliptic_curves
            Named curve: secp256r1
            Named curve: secp384r1
        Extension: signature_algorithms
            Algorithm: sha1/rsa
            Algorithm: sha256/rsa
            Algorithm: sha1/ecdsa
            Algorithm: sha256/ecdsa
```

As you can see, the structure of this message is easy to understand, with most data fields easy to understand from the names alone.

### Protocol version

Protocol version indicates the best protocol version the client supports.

### Random

The random field contains 32 bytes of data. Of those, 28 bytes are randomly generated. The remaining four bytes carry additional information influenced by the client's clock. Client time is not actually relevant for the protocol, and the specification is clear on this ("Clocks are not required to be set correctly by the basic TLS protocol, higher-level or application protocols may define additional requirements."); the field was included as a defense against weak random number generators, after just such a critical failure was discovered in Netscape Navigator in 1994.[7] Although this field used to contain the actual time, there are fears that client time could be used for large-scale browser fingerprinting.[8] As a result, some browsers add random clock skew to their time (as you can see in the example) or simply send four random bytes instead.

Both client and server contribute random data during the handshake. The randomness makes each handshake unique and plays a key role in authentication by preventing replay attacks and verifying the integrity of the initial data exchange.

### Session ID

On the first connection, the session ID field is empty, indicating that the client doesn't wish to resume an existing session. On subsequent connections, the ID field can contain the session's unique identifier, enabling the server to locate the correct session state in its cache. The session ID typically contains 32 bytes of randomly generated data and isn't valuable in itself.

### Cipher suites

The cipher suite block is a list of all cipher suites supported by the client in order of preference.

### Compression

Clients can submit one or more supported compression methods. The default compression method `null` indicates no compression.

### Extensions

The extension block contains an arbitrary number of extensions that carry additional data. I discuss the most commonly seen extensions later in this chapter.

## ServerHello

The purpose of the `ServerHello` message is for the server to communicate the selected connection parameters back to the client. This message is similar in structure to `ClientHello` but contains only one option per field:

---

[7] For more information about this problem, refer to the section called "Netscape Navigator (1994)" in Chapter 7.

[8] Deprecating gmt_unix_time in TLS [fsty.uk/t24] (N. Mathewson and B. Laurie, December 2013)

```
Handshake protocol: ServerHello
    Version: TLS 1.2
    Random
        Server time: Mar 10, 2059 02:35:57 GMT
        Random bytes: 8469b09b480c1978182ce1b59290487609f41132312ca22aacaf5012
    Session ID: 4cae75c91cf5adf55f93c9fb5dd36d19903b1182029af3d527b7a42ef1c32c80
    Cipher Suite: TLS_ECDHE_RSA_WITH_AES_128_GCM_SHA256
    Compression method: null
    Extensions
        Extension: server_name
        Extension: renegotiation_info
```

The server isn't required to support the same best version supported by the client. If it doesn't, it offers some other protocol version in the hope that the client will accept it.

## Certificate

The Certificate message is typically used to carry the server's X.509 certificate chain. Certificates are provided one after another, in ASN.1 DER encoding. The main certificate must be sent first, with all of the intermediary certificates following in the correct order. The root can and should be omitted, because it serves no purpose in this context.

The server must ensure that it sends a certificate appropriate for the selected cipher suite. For example, the public key algorithm must match that used in the suite. In addition, some key exchange mechanisms depend upon certain data being embedded in the certificate, and the certificates must be signed with algorithms supported by the client. All of this implies that the server could be configured with multiple certificates (each with a potentially different chain).

This Certificate message is optional, because not all suites use authentication and because there are some authentication methods that don't require certificates. Furthermore, although the default is to use X.509 certificates other forms of identification can be carried in this message; some suites rely on PGP keys.[9]

## ServerKeyExchange

The purpose of the ServerKeyExchange message is to carry additional data needed for key exchange. Its contents vary and depend on the negotiated cipher suite. In some cases, the server is not required to send anything, which means that the ServerKeyExchange message is not sent at all.

---

[9] RFC 5081: Using OpenPGP Keys for TLS Authentication [fsty.uk/t25] (N. Mavrogiannopoulos, November 2007)

## ServerHelloDone

ServerHelloDone is a signal that the server has sent all intended handshake messages. After this, the server waits for further messages from the client.

## ClientKeyExchange

The ClientKeyExchange message carries the client's contribution to the key exchange. It's a mandatory message whose contents depend on the negotiated cipher suite.

## ChangeCipherSpec

The ChangeCipherSpec message is a signal that the sending side obtained enough information to manufacture the connection parameters, generated the encryption keys, and is switching to encryption. Client and server both send this message when the time is right.

> ### Note
>
> ChangeCipherSpec is not a handshake message. Rather, it's implemented as the only message in its own subprotocol. One consequence of this decision is that this message is not part of the handshake integrity validation mechanism. This makes TLS more difficult to implement correctly; in June 2014 OpenSSL disclosed that it had been incorrectly handling ChangeCipherSpec messages, leaving it open to active network attacks.[10]
>
> The same problem exists with all other subprotocols. An active network attacker can send unauthenticated alert messages during the first handshake and, by exploiting the buffering mechanism, even subvert genuine alerts sent after encryption commences.[11] To avoid more serious problems, application data protocol messages aren't allowed before the first handshake is complete.

## Finished

The Finished message is the signal that the handshake is complete. Its contents are encrypted, which allows both sides to securely exchange the data required to verify the integrity of the entire handshake.

This message carries the verify_data field, which is a hash of all handshake messages as each side saw them mixed in with the newly negotiated master secret. This is done via a *pseudorandom function* (PRF), which is designed to produce an arbitrary amount of pseudorandom data. I describe the PRF later in this chapter. The Hash function is the same as in the PRF unless the negotiated suite specifies a different algorithm. The calculations are

---

[10] You'll find more information about this flaw in the section called "Library and Platform Validation Failures" in Chapter 7.

[11] The Alert attack [fsty.uk/t26] (miTLS, February 2012)

the same in both cases, although each side uses a different label: "client finished" for the client and "server finished" for the server:

```
verify_data = PRF(master_secret, finished_label, Hash(handshake_messages))
```

Because the Finished messages are encrypted and their integrity guaranteed by the negotiated MAC algorithm, an active network attacker can't change the handshake messages and then forge the correct verify_data values.

The attacker could also try to find a set of forged handshake messages that have exactly the same verify_data values as the genuine messages. That's not an easy attack in itself, but because the hashes are mixed in with the master secret (which the attacker doesn't know) she can't even attempt that approach.

In TLS 1.2, the Finished message is 12 bytes (96 bits) long by default, but cipher suites are allowed to use larger sizes. Earlier protocol versions also use a fixed length of 12 bytes, except for SSL 3, which uses 36 bytes.

## Client Authentication

Although authentication of either side is optional, server authentication is almost universally required. If the server selects a suite that isn't anonymous, it's required to follow up with its certificate chain in the Certificate message.

In contrast, the server requests client authentication by sending a CertificateRequest message that lists acceptable client certificates. In response, the client sends the certificate in its own Certificate message (in the same format used by the server for its certificates) and then proves possession of the corresponding private key with a CertificateVerify message.

Only an authenticated server is allowed to request client authentication. For this reason, this option is known as *mutual authentication*.

### CertificateRequest

With the CertificateRequest message, the server requests client authentication and communicates acceptable certificate public key and signature algorithms to the client. Optionally, it can also send its list of acceptable issuing certification authorities, indicated by using their distinguished names:

```
struct {
    ClientCertificateType certificate_types;
    SignatureAndHashAlgorithm supported_signature_algorithms;
    DistinguishedName certificate_authorities;
} CertificateRequest;
```

## CertificateVerify

The client uses the CertificateVerify message to prove the possession of the private key corresponding to the public key in the previously sent client certificate. This message contains a signature of all the handshake messages exchanged until this point:

```
struct {
    Signature handshake_messages_signature;
} CertificateVerify;
```

Figure 3.3. Full handshake, during which both client and server are authenticated

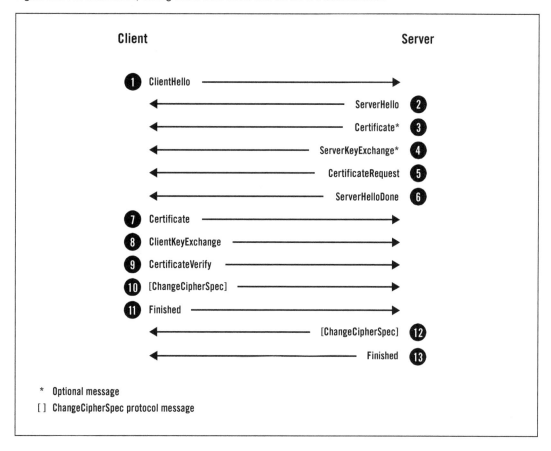

## Session Resumption

The full handshake is an elaborate protocol that requires many handshake messages and two network round trips before the client can start sending application data. In addition, the cryptographic operations carried out during the handshake often require intensive CPU processing. Authentication, usually in the form of client and server certificate validation (and revocation checking), requires even more effort. Much of this overhead can be avoided with an abbreviated handshake.

The original *session resumption* mechanism is based on both the client and the server keeping session security parameters for a period of time after a fully negotiated connection is terminated. A server that wishes to use session resumption assigns it a unique identifier called the *session ID*. The server then sends the session ID back to the client in the ServerHello message. (You can see this in the example in the previous section.)

A client that wishes to resume an earlier session submits the appropriate session ID in its ClientHello. If the server is willing to resume that session, it returns the same session ID in the ServerHello, generates a new set of keys using the previously negotiated master secret, switches to encryption, and sends its Finished message. The client, when it sees that the session is being resumed, does the same. The result is a short handshake that requires only one network round trip.

Figure 3.4. Abbreviated handshake—used to resume an already established session

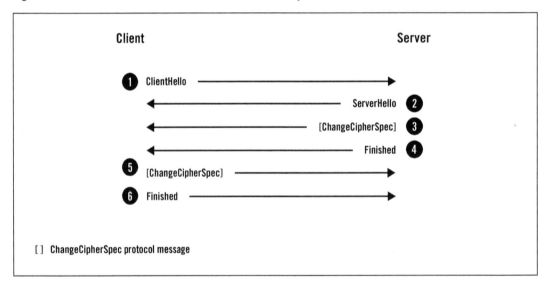

The alternative to server-side session caching and resumption is to use *session tickets*, introduced by RFC 4507 in 2006 and subsequently updated by RFC 5077 in 2008. In this case, all state is kept by the client (the mechanism is similar to HTTP cookies), but the message flow is otherwise the same.

# Key Exchange

The key exchange is easily the most interesting part of the handshake. In TLS, the security of the session depends on a 48-byte shared key called the *master secret*. The goal of key exchange is to generate another value, the *premaster secret*, which is the value from which the master secret is constructed.

TLS supports many key exchange algorithms in order to support various certificate types, public key algorithms, and key establishment protocols. Some are defined in the main TLS protocol specification, but many more are defined elsewhere. You can see the most commonly used algorithms in the following table.

Table 3.1. Overview of the most commonly used key exchange algorithms

| Key Exchange | Description |
|---|---|
| dh_anon | Diffie-Hellman (DH) key exchange without authentication |
| dhe_rsa | Ephemeral DH key exchange with RSA authentication |
| ecdh_anon | Ephemeral Elliptic Curve DH (ECDH) key exchange without authentication (RFC 4492) |
| ecdhe_rsa | Ephemeral ECDH key exchange with RSA authentication (RFC 4492) |
| ecdhe_ecdsa | Ephemeral ECDH key exchange with ECDSA authentication (RFC 4492) |
| krb5 | Kerberos key exchange (RFC 2712) |
| rsa | RSA key exchange and authentication |
| psk | Pre-Shared Key (PSK) key exchange and authentication (RFC 4279) |
| dhe_psk | Ephemeral DH key exchange with PSK authentication (RFC 4279) |
| rsa_psk | PSK key exchange and RSA authentication (RFC 4279) |
| srp | Secure Remote Password (SRP) key exchange and authentication (RFC 5054) |

Which key exchange is used depends on the negotiated suite. Once the suite is known, both sides know which algorithm to follow. In practice, there are four main key exchange algorithms:

**RSA**

RSA is effectively the standard key exchange algorithm. It's universally supported but suffers from one serious problem: its design allows a passive attacker to decrypt all encrypted data, provided she has access to the server's private key. Because of this, the RSA key exchange is being slowly replaced with other algorithms, those that support *forward secrecy*. The RSA key exchange is a *key transport* algorithm; the client generates the premaster secret and transports it to the server, encrypted with the server's public key.

**DHE_RSA**

*Ephemeral Diffie-Hellman* (DHE) key exchange is a well-established algorithm. It's liked because it provides forward secrecy but disliked because it's slow. DHE is a *key agreement* algorithm; the negotiating parties both contribute to the process and agree on a common key. In TLS, DHE is commonly used with RSA authentication.

### ECDHE_RSA and ECDHE_ECDSA

*Ephemeral Elliptic Curve Diffie-Hellman* (ECDHE) key exchange is based on elliptic curve cryptography, which is relatively new. It's liked because it's fast *and* provides forward secrecy. It's well supported only by modern clients. ECDHE is a key agreement algorithm conceptually similar to DHE. In TLS, ECDHE can be used with either RSA or ECDSA authentication.

No matter which key exchange is used, the server has the opportunity to speak first by sending its ServerKeyExchange message:

```
struct {
    select (KeyExchangeAlgorithm) {
        case dh_anon:
            ServerDHParams      params;
        case dhe_rsa:
            ServerDHParams      params;
            Signature           params_signature;
        case ecdh_anon:
            ServerECDHParams    params;
        case ecdhe_rsa:
        case ecdhe_ecdsa:
            ServerECDHParams    params;
            Signature           params_signature;
        case rsa:
        case dh_rsa:
            /* no message */
    };
} ServerKeyExchange;
```

As you can see in the message definition, there are several algorithms for which there is nothing for the server to send. This will be the case when all the required information is already available elsewhere. Otherwise, the server sends its key exchange parameters. Crucially, the server also sends a signature of the parameters, which is used for authentication. Using the signature, the client is able to verify that it's talking to the party that holds the private key corresponding to the public key from the certificate.

The ClientKeyExchange message is always required; the client uses it to send its key exchange parameters:

```
struct {
    select (KeyExchangeAlgorithm) {
        case rsa:
            EncryptedPreMasterSecret;
        case dhe_dss:
        case dhe_rsa:
        case dh_dss:
        case dh_rsa:
```

```
        case dh_anon:
            ClientDiffieHellmanPublic;
        case ecdhe:
            ClientECDiffieHellmanPublic;
    } exchange_keys;
} ClientKeyExchange;
```

# RSA Key Exchange

The RSA key exchange is quite straightforward; the client generates a premaster secret of 48 bytes,[12] encrypts it with the server's public key, and sends it in the ClientKeyExchange message. To obtain the premaster secret, the server only needs to decrypt the message. TLS uses the RSAES-PKCS1-v1_5 encryption scheme, which is defined in RFC 3447.[13]

> **Note**
>
> The RSA key exchange can operate in this way because the RSA algorithm can be used for encryption and digital signing. Other popular key types, such as DSA and ECDSA, can be used only for signing.

The simplicity of the RSA key exchange is also its principal weakness. The premaster secret is encrypted with the server's public key, which usually remains in use for several years. Anyone with access to the corresponding private key can recover the premaster secret and construct the same master secret, compromising session security.

The attack doesn't have to happen in real time. A powerful adversary could establish a long-term operation to record all encrypted traffic and wait patiently until she obtains the key. For example, advances in computer power could make it possible to brute-force the key. Alternatively, the key could be obtained using legal powers, coercion, bribery, or by breaking into a server that uses it. After the key compromise, it's possible to decrypt all previously recorded traffic.

The other common key exchange mechanisms used in TLS don't suffer from this problem and are said to support forward secrecy. When they are used, each connection uses an independent master secret. A compromised server key could be used to impersonate the server but couldn't be used to retroactively decrypt any traffic.

---

[12] The first two bytes in the premaster secret contain the newest protocol version supported by the client; they are used to prevent rollback attacks. The remaining 46 bytes are random and are used to establish a strong session key.

[13] RFC 3447: RSA Cryptography Specifications Version 2.1 [fsty.uk/t27] (Jonsson and Kaliski, February 2003)

---

# Diffie-Hellman Key Exchange

The *Diffie-Hellman* (DH) key exchange is a key agreement protocol that allows two parties to establish a shared secret over an insecure communication channel.

> **Note**
>
> The shared secret negotiated in this way is safe from passive attacks, but an active attacker could hijack the communication channel and pretend to be the other party. This is why the DH key exchange is commonly used with authentication.

Without going into the details of the algorithm, the trick is to use a mathematical function that's easy to calculate in one direction but very difficult to reverse, even when some of the aspects of the exchange are known. The best analogy is that of color mixing: if you have two colors, you can easily mix them to get a third color, but it's very difficult to determine the *exact* color shades that contributed to the mix.[14]

The DH key exchange requires six parameters; two (dh_p and dh_g) are called *domain parameters* and are selected by the server. During the negotiation, the client and server each generate two additional parameters. Each side sends one of its parameters (dh_Ys and dh_Yc) to the other end, and, with some calculation, they arrive at the shared key.

*Ephemeral Diffie-Hellman* (DHE) key exchange takes place when none of the parameters are reused. In contrast, there are some DH key exchange approaches in which some of the parameters are static and embedded in the server and client certificates. In this case, the result of the key exchange is always the same shared key, which means that there is no forward secrecy.

TLS supports static DH key exchanges, but they're used only very rarely, if ever. When a DHE suite is negotiated, the server sends all of its parameters in the ServerDHParams block:

```
struct {
    opaque dh_p;
    opaque dh_g;
    opaque dh_Ys;
} ServerDHParams;
```

The client, in response, sends its public parameter (dh_Yc):

```
struct {
    select (PublicValueEncoding) {
        case implicit:
            /* empty; used when the client's public
                parameter is embedded in its certificate */
        case explicit:
```

---

[14] Public Key Cryptography: Diffie-Hellman Key Exchange [fsty.uk/t28] (YouTube, retrieved 26 June 2014)

```
                opaque dh_Yc;
        } dh_public;
    } ClientDiffieHellmanPublic;
```

There are some practical problems with the DH exchange as it's currently used:

**DH parameter security**

The security of the DH key exchange depends on the quality of the domain parameters. A server could send weak or insecure parameters and compromise the security of the session. This issue was highlighted in the *Triple Handshake Attack* research paper, which covered weak DH parameters used as one of the attack vectors.[15]

**DH parameter negotiation**

TLS doesn't provide facilities for the client to communicate the strength of DH parameters it's willing to use. For example, some clients might want to avoid using weak parameters, or alternately, they might not be able to support stronger parameters. Because of this, a server that chooses a DHE suite can effectively only "hope" that the DH parameters will be acceptable to the client.

**Insufficient parameter strength**

Historically speaking, DH parameters have been largely ignored and their security neglected. Many libraries and servers use weak DH parameters by default and often don't provide a means to configure DH parameter strength. For this reason, it's not uncommon to see servers using weak 1,024-bit parameters and insecure 768- and even 512-bit parameters. More recently, some platforms have started using strong (2,048 bits and higher) parameters.

The Logjam attack, revealed in May 2015, showed that 512-bit DH parameters can be successfully exploited in real time by an attacker with modest resources and speculated that a strong attacker might even be able to exploit 768-bit parameters. The same research also highlighted the possibility that a very strong attacker could also break the small number of very widely used 1,024-bit standard groups to passively exploit millions of Internet servers. To find out more about this problem, head to the section called "Logjam" in Chapter 7, *Implementation Issues*.

These problems could be addressed by standardizing a set of domain parameters of varying strengths and extending TLS to enable clients to communicate their preferences.[16]

---

[15] For more information on the Triple Handshake Attack, head to the section called "Triple Handshake Attack" in Chapter 8.

[16] Negotiated Finite Field Diffie-Hellman Ephemeral Parameters for TLS [fsty.uk/t29] (D. Gillmor, June 2015)

---

# Elliptic Curve Diffie-Hellman Key Exchange

The ephemeral *Elliptic Curve Diffie-Hellman* (ECDH) key exchange is conceptually similar to DH, but it uses a different mathematical foundation at the core. As the name implies, ECDHE is based on elliptic curve (EC) cryptography.

An ECDH key exchange takes place over a specific elliptic curve, which is for the server to define. The curve takes the role of domain parameters in DH. In theory, static ECDH key exchange is supported, but in practice only the ephemeral variant (ECDHE) is used.

The server starts the key exchange by submitting its selected elliptic curve and public parameter (EC point):

```
struct {
    ECParameters curve_params;
    ECPoint public;
} ServerECDHParams;
```

The server can specify an arbitrary (explicit) curve for the key exchange, but this facility is not used in TLS. Instead, the server will specify a *named curve*, which is a reference to one of the possible predefined parameters:

```
struct {
    ECCurveType curve_type;
    select (curve_type) {
        case explicit_prime:
            /* omitted for clarity */
        case explicit_char2:
            /* omitted for clarity */
        case named_curve:
            NamedCurve namedcurve;
    };
} ECParameters;
```

The client then submits its own public parameter. After that, the calculations take place to arrive at the premaster secret:

```
struct {
    select (PublicValueEncoding) {
        case implicit:
            /* empty */
        case explicit:
            ECPoint ecdh_Yc;
    } ecdh_public;
} ClientECDiffieHellmanPublic;
```

The use of predefined parameters, along with the `elliptic_curve` extension that clients can use to submit supported curves, enables the server to select a curve that both sides support. You'll find more information on the available named curves later in the section called "Elliptic Curve Capabilities".

# Authentication

In TLS, authentication is tightly coupled with key exchange in order to avoid repetition of costly cryptographic operations. In most cases, the basis for authentication will be public key cryptography (most commonly RSA, but sometimes ECDSA) supported by certificates. Once the certificate is validated, the client has a known public key to work with. After that, it's down to the particular key exchange method to use the public key in some way to authenticate the other side.

During the RSA key exchange, the client generates a random value as the premaster secret and sends it encrypted with the server's public key. The authentication is implicit: it is assumed that only the server in possession of the corresponding private key can decrypt the message to obtain the premaster secret and use it to produce the correct Finished message.

During the DHE and ECDHE exchanges, the server contributes to the key exchange with its parameters. The parameters are signed with its private key. The client, which is in possession of the corresponding public key (obtained from the validated certificate), can verify that the parameters genuinely arrived from the intended server.

> **Note**
>
> Server parameters are signed concatenated with client and server random values that are unique to the handshake. Thus, although the signature is sent in the clear it's only valid for the current handshake, which means that the attacker can't reuse it. The Logjam attack showed that this way of binding signatures to handshakes is weak; an active network attacker can synchronize the random values and reuse server signatures under some circumstances.

# Encryption

TLS can encrypt data in a variety of ways, using ciphers such as 3DES, AES, ARIA, ChaCha20, CAMELLIA, RC4, and SEED. These ciphers provide different performance and security characteristics, with AES being by far the most popular choice in practice. Three types of encryption are supported: *stream*, *block*, and *authenticated* encryption. In TLS, integrity validation is part of the encryption process; it's handled either explicitly at the protocol level or implicitly by the negotiated cipher.

## Stream Encryption

When a stream cipher is used, encryption consists of two steps. In the first step, a MAC of the record sequence number, header, and plaintext is calculated. The inclusion of the header

---

in the MAC ensures that the unencrypted data in the header can't be tampered with. The inclusion of the sequence number in the MAC ensures that the messages can't be replayed. In the second step, the plaintext and the MAC are encrypted to form ciphertext.

Figure 3.5. Stream encryption

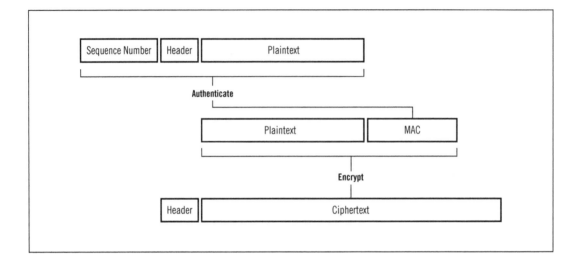

## Note

A suite that uses integrity validation but no encryption is implemented in the same way as encryption using a stream cipher. The plaintext is simply copied to the TLS record, but the MAC is calculated as described here.

## Block Encryption

When block ciphers are used, encryption is somewhat more involved, because it's necessary to work around the properties of block encryption. The following steps are required:

1. Calculate a MAC of the sequence number, header, and plaintext.

2. Construct padding to ensure that the length of data prior to encryption is a multiple of the cipher block size (usually 16 bytes).

3. Generate an unpredictable *initialization vector* (IV) of the same length as the cipher block size. The IV is used to ensure that the encryption is not deterministic.

4. Use the CBC block mode to encrypt plaintext, MAC, and padding.

5. Send the IV and ciphertext together.

Figure 3.6. Block encryption

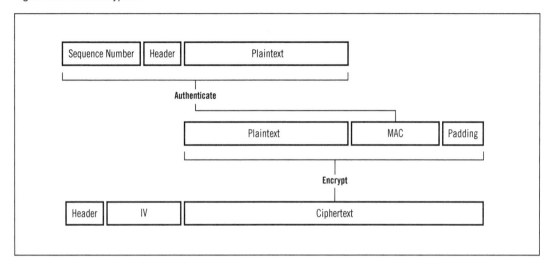

### Note

You'll find further information on the CBC block mode, padding, and initialization vectors in the section called "Building Blocks" in Chapter 1.

This process is known as *MAC-then-encrypt*, and it has been a source of many problems. In TLS 1.1 and newer versions, each record includes an explicit IV. TLS 1.0 and older versions use implicit IVs (the encrypted block from the previous TLS record is used as the IV for the next), but that approach was found to be insecure in 2011.[17]

The other problem is that the MAC calculation doesn't include padding, leaving an opportunity for an active network attacker to attempt *padding oracle attacks*, which were also successfully demonstrated against TLS.[18] The issue here is that the protocol specifies a block encryption approach that's difficult to implement securely in practice. As far as we know, current implementations are not obviously vulnerable, but this is a weak spot in the protocol that leaves many uneasy.

In September 2014, a TLS protocol extension was published to support a different arrangement to block encryption called *encrypt-then-MAC*.[19] In this alternative approach, plaintext and padding are first encrypted and then fed to the MAC algorithm. This ensures that the active network attacker can't manipulate any of the encrypted data.

---

[17] This problem was first exploited in the so-called BEAST attack, which I discuss in the section called "BEAST" in Chapter 8.

[18] I discuss padding oracle attacks in the section called "Lucky 13" in Chapter 8.

[19] RFC 7366: Encrypt-then-MAC for TLS and DTLS [fsty.uk/t30] (Peter Gutmann, September 2014)

## Authenticated Encryption

Authenticated ciphers combine encryption and integrity validation in one algorithm. Their full name is *authenticated encryption with associated data* (AEAD). On the surface, they appear to be a cross between stream ciphers and block ciphers. They don't use padding[20] and initialization vectors, but they do use a special value called *nonce*, which must be unique. The encryption process is somewhat simpler than with block ciphers:

1. Generate a unique 64-bit nonce.

2. Encrypt plaintext with the authenticated encryption algorithm; at the same time feed it the sequence number and record header for it to take into account as additional data for purposes of integrity validation.

3. Send the nonce and ciphertext together.

Figure 3.7. Authenticated encryption in TLS 1.2

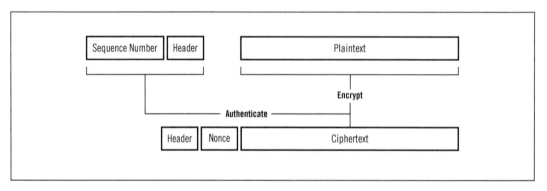

Authenticated encryption is currently favored as the best encryption mode available in TLS, because it avoids the issues inherent with the MAC-then-encrypt approach. Although TLS currently defines authenticated suites based on GCM and CCM block modes, only GCM suites are supported in practice. New authenticated suites based on the ChaCha20 stream ciphers are currently being standardized.[21]

## Renegotiation

Most TLS connections start with a handshake, proceed to exchange application data, and shutdown the conversation at the end. When *renegotiation* is requested, a new handshake takes place to agree on new connection security parameters. There are several cases in which this feature might be useful:

---

[20] Actually, they might use padding, but if they do, it's an implementation detail that's not exposed to the TLS protocol.

[21] RFC 7905: ChaCha20-Poly1305 Cipher Suites for TLS [fsty.uk/t31] (Langley et al., June 2016)

### Client certificates

Client certificates are not used often, but some sites use them because they provide two-factor authentication. There are two ways to deploy client certificates. You can require them for all connections to a site, but this approach is not very friendly to those who don't (yet) have a certificate; without a successful connection, you can't send them any information and instructions. Handling error conditions is equally impossible. For this reason, many operators prefer to allow connections to the root of the web site without a certificate and designate a subsection in which a client certificate is required. When a user attempts to navigate to the subsection, the server issues a request to renegotiate and then requests a client certificate.

### Information hiding

Such a two-step approach to enabling client certificates has an additional advantage: the second handshake is encrypted, which means that a passive attacker can't monitor the negotiation and, crucially, can't observe the client certificates. This addresses a potentially significant privacy issue, because client certificates usually contain identifying information. For example, the Tor protocol can use renegotiation in this way.[22]

### Change of encryption strength

Back in the day, when web site encryption was brand new (and very CPU intensive) it was common to see sites split their encryption configuration into two levels. You would use weaker encryption by default but require strong encryption in certain areas.[23] As with client certificates, this feature is implemented via renegotiation. When you attempt to cross into the more secure subsection of the web site, the server requests stronger security.

In addition, there are two situations in which renegotiation is required by the protocol, although neither is likely to occur in practice:

### Server-Gated Crypto

Back in the 1990s, when the United States did not allow export of strong cryptography, a feature called *Server-Gated Cryptography* (SGC) was used to enable US vendors to ship strong cryptography worldwide but enable it only for selected (mostly financial) US web sites. Browsers would use weak cryptography by default, upgrading to strong cryptography after encountering a special certificate. This upgrade was entirely client controlled, and it was implemented via renegotiation. Only a few selected CAs were allowed to issue the special certificates. Cryptography export restrictions were relaxed in 2000, making SGC obsolete.

---

[22] Tor Protocol Specification [fsty.uk/t32] (Dingledine and Mathewson, retrieved 11 November 2017)

[23] This thinking is flawed; your encryption is either sufficiently secure or it isn't. If your adversaries can break the weaker configuration, they can take full control of the victim's browser. With that, they can trick the victim into revealing all of their secrets (e.g., passwords).

---

### TLS record counter overflow

Internally, TLS packages data into records. Each record is assigned a unique 64-bit sequence number, which grows over time as records are exchanged. Client and server use one sequence number each for the records they send. The protocol mandates renegotiation if a sequence number is close to overflowing. However, because the counter is a very large number, overflows are unlikely in practice.

The protocol allows the client to request renegotiation at any time simply by sending a new ClientHello message, exactly as when starting a brand-new connection. This is known as *client-initiated renegotiation*.

If the server wishes to renegotiate, it sends a HelloRequest protocol message to the client; that's a signal to the client to stop sending application data and initiate a new handshake. This is known as *server-initiated renegotiation*.

Renegotiation, as originally designed, is insecure and can be abused by an active network attacker in many ways. The weakness was discovered in 2009[24] and corrected with the introduction of the renegotiation_info extension, which I discuss later in this chapter.

## Application Data Protocol

The application data protocol carries application messages, which are just buffers of data as far as TLS is concerned. These messages are packaged, fragmented, and encrypted by the record layer, using the current connection security parameters.

## Alert Protocol

*Alerts* are intended to use a simple notification mechanism to inform the other side in the communication of exceptional circumstances. They're generally used for error messages, with the exception of close_notify, which is used during connection shutdown. Alerts are very simple and contain only two fields:

```
struct {
    AlertLevel level;
    AlertDescription description;
} Alert;
```

The AlertLevel field carries the alert severity, which can be either warning or fatal. The AlertDescription is simply an alert code; for better or worse, there are no facilities to convey arbitrary information, for example, an actual error message.

Fatal messages result in an immediate termination of the current connection and invalidation of the session (ongoing connections of the same session may continue, but the session

---

[24] For more information, head to the section called "Insecure Renegotiation" in Chapter 8.

can no longer be resumed). The side sending a warning notification doesn't terminate the connection, but the receiving side is free to react to the warning by sending a fatal alert of its own.

# Connection Closure

*Closure alerts* are used to shutdown a TLS connection in an orderly fashion. Once one side decides that it wants to close the connection, it sends a `close_notify` alert. The other side, upon receiving the alert, discards any pending writes and sends a `close_notify` alert of its own. If any messages arrive after the alerts, they are ignored.

This simple shutdown protocol is necessary in order to avoid truncation attacks, in which an active network attacker interrupts a conversation midway and blocks all further messages. Without the shutdown protocol, the two sides can't determine if they are under attack or if the conversation is genuinely over.

> ### Note
>
> Although the protocol itself is not vulnerable to truncation attacks, there are many *implementations* that are, because violations of the connection shutdown protocol are widespread. I discuss this problem at length in the section called "Truncation Attacks" in Chapter 7.

# Cryptographic Operations

This section contains a brief discussion of several important aspects of the protocol: the pseudorandom function, master secret construction, and the generation of connection keys.

## Pseudorandom Function

In TLS, a *pseudorandom function* (PRF) is used to generate arbitrary amounts of pseudorandom data. The PRF takes a secret, a seed, and a unique label. From TLS 1.2 onward, all cipher suites are required to explicitly specify their PRF. All TLS 1.2 suites use a PRF based on HMAC and SHA256; the same PRF is used with older suites when they are negotiated with TLS 1.2.

TLS 1.2 defines a PRF based on a data expansion function P_hash, which uses HMAC and any hash function:

```
P_hash(secret, seed) = HMAC_hash(secret, A(1) + seed) +
                       HMAC_hash(secret, A(2) + seed) +
                       HMAC_hash(secret, A(3) + seed) + ...
```

The A(i) function is defined as follows:

```
A(1) = HMAC_hash(secret, seed)
A(2) = HMAC_hash(secret, A(1))
...
A(i) = HMAC_hash(secret, A(i-1))
```

The PRF is a wrapper around P_hash that combines the label with the seed:

```
PRF(secret, label, seed) = P_hash(secret, label + seed)
```

The introduction of a seed and a label allows the same secret to be reused in different contexts to produce different outputs (because the label and the seed are different).

## Master Secret

As you saw earlier, the output from the key exchange process is the premaster secret. This value is further processed, using the PRF, to produce a 48-byte (384-bit) master secret:

```
master_secret = PRF(pre_master_secret, "master secret",
                    client_random + server_random)
```

The processing occurs because the premaster secret might differ in size depending on the key exchange method used. Also, because the client and server random fields are used as the seed, the master secret is also effectively random[25] and bound to the negotiated handshake.

> **Note**
>
> The binding between the master secret and the handshake has been shown to be insufficient because it relies only on the exchanged random values. An attacker can observe and replicate these values to create multiple sessions that share the same master key. This weakness has been exploited by the Triple Handshake Attack mentioned earlier.[15]

## Key Generation

The key material needed for a connection is generated in a single PRF invocation based on the master secret and seeded with the client and server random values:

```
key_block = PRF(master_secret, "key expansion",
                server_random + client_random)
```

The key block, which varies in size depending on the negotiated parameters, is divided into up to six keys: two MAC keys, two encryption keys, and two initialization vectors (only

---

[25] Although the most commonly used key exchange mechanisms generate a different premaster secret every time, there are some mechanisms that rely on long-term authentication keys and thus reuse the same premaster secret. Randomization is essential to ensure that the session keys are not repeated.

when needed; stream ciphers don't use IV). AEAD suites don't use MAC keys. Different keys are used for different operations, which is recommended to prevent unforeseen interactions between cryptographic primitives when the key is shared. Also, because the client and the server have their own sets of keys, a message produced by one can't be interpreted to have been produced by the other. This design decision makes the protocol more robust.

> **Note**
>
> When resuming a session, the same session master key is used during the key block generation. However, the PRF is seeded with the client and server random values from the *current* handshake. Because these random values are different in every handshake, the keys are also different every time.

# Cipher Suites

As you have seen, TLS allows for a great deal of flexibility in implementing the desired security properties. It's effectively a framework for creating actual cryptographic protocols. Although previous versions hardcoded some cryptographic primitives into the protocol, TLS 1.2 is fully configurable. A *cipher suite* is a selection of cryptographic primitives and other parameters that define exactly how security will be implemented. A suite is defined roughly by the following attributes:

- Authentication method

- Key exchange method

- Encryption algorithm

- Encryption key size

- Cipher mode (when applicable)

- MAC algorithm (when applicable)

- PRF (TLS 1.2)

- Hash function used for the Finished message (TLS 1.2)

- Length of the verify_data structure (TLS 1.2)

Cipher suite names tend to be long and descriptive and pretty consistent: they are made from the names of the key exchange method, authentication method, cipher definition, and optional MAC or PRF algorithm.[26]

---

[26] TLS suites use the TLS_ prefix, SSL 3 suites use the SSL_ prefix, and SSL 2 suites use the SSL_CK_ prefix. In all cases, the approach to naming is roughly the same. However, not all vendors use the standard suite names. OpenSSL and GnuTLS use different names. Microsoft largely uses the standard names but sometimes extends them with suffixes that are used to indicate the strength of the ECDHE key exchange.

Figure 3.8. Cipher suite name construction before TLS 1.3

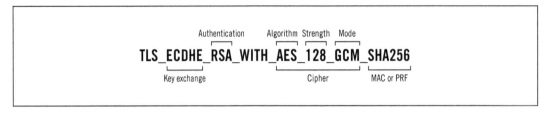

Although a suite name is not sufficient to convey all security parameters, the most important ones are easy to deduce. The information on the remaining parameters can be found in the RFC that carries the suite definition. You can see the security properties of a few selected suites in the following table. At the time of writing, there are more than 300 official cipher suites, which is too many to list here. For the complete list, head to the official TLS page over at IANA.[27]

Table 3.2. Examples of cipher suite names and their security properties

| Cipher Suite Name | Auth | KX | Cipher | MAC | PRF |
|---|---|---|---|---|---|
| TLS_ECDHE_RSA_WITH_AES_128_GCM_SHA256 | RSA | ECDHE | AES-128-GCM | - | SHA256 |
| TLS_ECDHE_ECDSA_WITH_AES_256_GCM_SHA384 | ECDSA | ECDHE | AES-256-GCM | - | SHA384 |
| TLS_DHE_RSA_WITH_3DES_EDE_CBC_SHA | RSA | DHE | 3DES-EDE-CBC | SHA1 | Protocol |
| TLS_RSA_WITH_AES_128_CBC_SHA | RSA | RSA | AES-128-CBC | SHA1 | Protocol |
| TLS_ECDHE_ECDSA_WITH_AES_128_CCM | ECDSA | ECDHE | AES-128-CCM | - | SHA256 |

With the introduction of TLS 1.2—which allows for additional custom parameters (e.g., PRF)—and authenticated suites, some level of understanding of the implementation is required to fully decode cipher suite names:

- Authenticated suites combine authentication and encryption in the cipher, which means that integrity validation need not be performed at the TLS level. GCM and ChaCha20-Poly1305 suites use the last segment to indicate the PRF instead of the MAC algorithm. CCM suites omit this last segment completely.

- TLS 1.2 is the only protocol that allows suites to define their PRFs. This means that for the suites defined before TLS 1.2 the negotiated protocol version dictates the PRF. For example, the TLS_RSA_WITH_AES_128_CBC_SHA suite uses a PRF based on HMAC-SHA256 when negotiated with TLS 1.2 but a PRF based on a HMAC-MD5/ HMAC-SHA1 combination when used with TLS 1.0. On the other hand, SHA384 GCM suites (which can be used only with TLS 1.2 and newer) will always use HMAC-SHA384 for the PRF.

---

[27] TLS Parameters [fsty.uk/t33] (IANA, retrieved 14 March 2017)

Chapter 3: TLS 1.2

> **Note**
>
> Cipher suite names use a shorthand notation to indicate the MAC algorithm that specifies only the hashing function. This often leads to confusion when the hashing functions have weaknesses. For example, although SHA1 is known to be weak to chosen-prefix attacks, it's not weak in the way it's used in TLS, which is in an HMAC construction. There are no significant known attacks against HMAC-SHA1.

Cipher suites don't have full control over their security parameters. Crucially, they only specify the required authentication and key exchange algorithms, but they don't have control over their strength.

> **Note**
>
> Cipher suites can be used only with the specific authentication mechanism they are intended for. For example, suites with ECDSA in the name require ECDSA keys. A server that has only an RSA key won't support any of the ECDSA suites.

When it comes to authentication, the strength typically depends on the certificate or, more specifically, on the key length and the signature algorithm. The strength of the RSA key exchange also depends on the certificate. DHE and ECDHE key exchanges can be configured with varying strengths, and this is usually done at the server level. Some servers expose this configuration to end users, but others don't. I discuss these aspects in more detail in Chapter 11, *Configuration Guide* and in the following technology-specific chapters.

# Extensions

*TLS extensions* are a general-purpose extension mechanism that's used to add functionality to the TLS protocol without changing the protocol itself. They first appeared in 2003 as a separate specification (RFC 3456) but have since been added to TLS 1.2.

Extensions are added in the form of an extension block that's placed at the end of `ClientHello` and `ServerHello` messages:

```
Extension extensions;
```

The block consists of a desired number of extensions placed one after another. Each extension begins with a two-byte extension type (unique identifier) and is followed by the extension data:

```
struct {
    ExtensionType extension_type;
    opaque extension_data;
} Extension;
```

It's up to each extension specification to determine the extension format and the desired behavior. In practice, extensions are used to signal support for some new functionality (thus changing the protocol) and to carry additional data needed during the handshake. Since their introduction, they have become the main vehicle for protocol evolution.

In this section, I will discuss the most commonly seen TLS extensions. Because IANA keeps track of extension types, the official list of extensions can be obtained from their web site.[28]

Table 3.3. A selection of commonly seen TLS extensions

| Type | Name | Description |
|------|------|-------------|
| 0 | server_name | Contains the intended secure virtual host for the connection |
| 5 | status_request | Indicates support for OCSP stapling |
| 13 (0x0d) | signature_algorithms | Contains supported signature algorithm/hash function pairs |
| 15 (0x0f) | heartbeat | Indicates support for the Heartbeat protocol |
| 16 (0x10) | application_layer_protocol_ negotiation | Contains supported application-layer protocols that the client is willing to negotiate |
| 18 (0x12) | signed_certificate_timestamp | Used by servers to submit the proof that the certificate had been shared with the public; part of Certificate Transparency |
| 21 (0x15) | padding | Used as a workaround for certain bugs in the F5 load balancers[a] |
| 35 (0x23) | session_ticket | Indicates support for stateless session resumption |
| 13172 (0x3374) | next_protocol_negotiation | Indicates support for Next Protocol Negotiation |
| 65281 (0xff01) | renegotiation_info | Indicates support for secure renegotiation |

[a] RFC 7685: A TLS ClientHello Padding Extension [fsty.uk/t34] (A. Langley, October 2015)

## Application Layer Protocol Negotiation

*Application-Layer Protocol Negotiation* (ALPN) is a protocol extension that enables the negotiation of different application-layer protocols over a TLS connection.[29] With ALPN, a server on port 443 could offer HTTP 1.1 by default but allow the negotiation of other protocols, such as SPDY or HTTP/2.

A client that supports ALPN uses the application_layer_protocol_negotiation extension to submit a list of supported application-layer protocols to the server. A compliant server decides on the protocol and uses the same extension to inform the client of its decision.

ALPN provides the same primary functionality as its older relative, NPN (discussed later on in this section), but they differ in secondary properties. Whereas NPN prefers to hide

---

[28] TLS Extensions [fsty.uk/t18] (IANA, retrieved 30 June 2014)

[29] RFC 7301: TLS Application-Layer Protocol Negotiation Extension [fsty.uk/t35] (Friedl et al., July 2014)

protocol decisions behind encryption, ALPN carries them in plaintext, allowing intermediary devices to inspect them and route traffic based on the observed information.

# Certificate Transparency

*Certificate Transparency*[30] is a proposal to improve Internet PKI by keeping a record of all public server certificates. The basic idea is that the CAs will submit their public certificates to public *log servers*. Each log server will return a proof of submission called a *Signed Certificate Timestamp* (SCT), which eventually will need to be inspected by end users (or their tools). There are several options for the transport of the SCT, and one of them is the new TLS extension called signed_certificate_timestamp.

# Elliptic Curve Capabilities

RFC 4492 specifies two extensions that are used to communicate client EC capabilities during the handshake. The elliptic_curves extension is used in ClientHello to list supported named curves, allowing the server to select one that's supported by both sides.

```
struct {
    NamedCurve elliptic_curve_list
} EllipticCurveList;
```

The main curves are specified in RFC 4492[31] based on the parameters defined by standards bodies, such as NIST:[32]

```
enum {
    sect163k1 (1), sect163r1 (2), sect163r2 (3),
    sect193r1 (4), sect193r2 (5), sect233k1 (6),
    sect233r1 (7), sect239k1 (8), sect283k1 (9),
    sect283r1 (10), sect409k1 (11), sect409r1 (12),
    sect571k1 (13), sect571r1 (14), secp160k1 (15),
    secp160r1 (16), secp160r2 (17), secp192k1 (18),
    secp192r1 (19), secp224k1 (20), secp224r1 (21),
    secp256k1 (22), secp256r1 (23), secp384r1 (24),
    secp521r1 (25),
    reserved (0xFE00..0xFEFF),
    arbitrary_explicit_prime_curves(0xFF01),
    arbitrary_explicit_char2_curves(0xFF02)
} NamedCurve;
```

---

[30] Certificate Transparency [fsty.uk/t36] (Google, retrieved 4 September 2021)

[31] RFC 4492: ECC Cipher Suites for TLS [fsty.uk/t37] (S. Blake-Wilson et al., May 2006)

[32] FIPS 186-3: Digital Signature Standard [fsty.uk/t38] (NIST, June 2009)

Brainpool curves were defined later, in RFC 7027.[33] Two additional curves, Curve25519 and Curve448, are currently being standardized for use in TLS.[34]

At this time, there is wide support for only two NIST curves: `secp256r1` and `secp384r1`. Arbitrary curves are generally not supported at all.[35]

---

### NIST Elliptic Curves

NIST's elliptic curves are sometimes considered suspicious, because there is no explanation of how the parameters were selected.[36] Especially after the Dual EC DRBG backdoor came to light, anything that cannot be explained has been seen by some as suspicious. The fear is that those named curves have weaknesses that are known to the designers but not to the general public. As a result, Curve25519 and Curve448 have been standardized to serve as long-term replacements.

---

The second defined extension is `ec_point_formats`, which enables negotiation of optional elliptic curve point compression. In theory, the use of compressed point formats can save precious bandwidth in constrained environments. In practice, the savings are small (e.g., about 64 bytes for a 256-bit curve), and the compressed formats generally are not used.

## Heartbeat

*Heartbeat*[37] is a protocol extension that adds support for keep-alive functionality (checking that the other party in the conversation is still available) and *path maximum transmission unit* (PMTU)[38] discovery to TLS and DTLS. Although TLS is commonly used over TCP, which does have keep-alive functionality already, Heartbeat is targeted at DTLS, which is deployed over unreliable protocols, such as UDP.

> **Note**
>
> Some have suggested that zero-length TLS records, which are explicitly allowed by the protocol, could be used for the keep-alive functionality. In practice, attempts to mitigate the BEAST attack showed that many applications can't tolerate records

---

[33] RFC 7027: ECC Brainpool Curves for TLS [fsty.uk/t39] (J. Merkle and M. Lochter, October 2013)

[34] ECC Cipher Suites for TLS 1.2 and Earlier [fsty.uk/t40] (Nir et al., March 2017)

[35] The generation of good, arbitrary elliptic curves is a complex and error-prone task that most developers choose to avoid. In addition, named curves can be optimized to run much faster.

[36] SafeCurves: choosing safe curves for elliptic-curve cryptography [fsty.uk/t41] (D. J. Bernstein, retrieved 4 September 2021)

[37] RFC 6520: TLS and DTLS Heartbeat Extension [fsty.uk/t42] (R. Seggelmann et al., February 2012)

[38] *Maximum transmission unit* (MTU) is the size of the largest data unit that can be sent whole. When two sides communicate directly, they can exchange their MTUs. However, when communication goes over many hops it is sometimes necessary to discover the effective path MTU by sending progressively larger packets.

without any data. In any case, zero-length TLS records wouldn't help with PMTU discovery, which needs payloads of varying sizes.

Initially, support for Heartbeat is advertised by both the client and the server via the heartbeat extension. During the negotiation, parties give each other permission to send heartbeat requests with the `HeartbeatMode` parameter:

```
struct {
    HeartbeatMode mode;
} HeartbeatExtension;

enum {
    peer_allowed_to_send (1),
    peer_not_allowed_to_send (2)
} HeartbeatMode;
```

Heartbeat is implemented as a TLS subprotocol, which means that heartbeat messages can be interleaved with application data and even other protocol messages. According to the RFC, heartbeat messages are allowed only once the handshake completes, but in practice OpenSSL allows them as soon as TLS extensions are exchanged.

It is not clear if Heartbeat is used in practice. Virtually no one knew what Heartbeat was until April 2014, when it was discovered that the OpenSSL implementation suffered from a fatal flaw that allowed the extraction of sensitive data from the server's process memory. At the time, OpenSSL had Heartbeat enabled by default. The attack that exploits this vulnerability, called *Heartbleed*, was arguably the worst thing to happen to TLS. You can read more about it in the section called "Heartbleed" in Chapter 7.

# Next Protocol Negotiation

When Google set out to design SPDY, a protocol intended to improve on HTTP, it needed a reliable protocol negotiation mechanism that would work with strict firewalls and in the presence of faulty proxies. Because SPDY was intended to always use TLS anyway, they decided to extend TLS with application-layer protocol negotiation. The result was *Next Protocol Negotiation* (NPN).

> **Note**
>
> If you research NPN, you might come across many different specification versions. Some of those versions were produced for the TLS working group during the standardization discussions. An older version of the specification is used in production.[39]

---

[39] Google Technical Note: TLS Next Protocol Negotiation Extension [fsty.uk/t43] (Adam Langley, May 2012)

A SPDY-enabled client submits a TLS handshake that incorporates an empty next_protocol_negotiation extension, but only if it also includes a server_name extension to indicate the desired hostname. In return, a compliant server responds with the next_protocol_negotiation extension, but one that contains a list of the supported application-layer protocols.

The client indicates the desired application-layer protocol by using a new handshake message called NextProtocol:

```
struct {
    opaque selected_protocol;
    opaque padding;
} NextProtocol;
```

In order to hide the client's choice from passive attackers, this message is submitted encrypted, which means that the client must send it after the ChangeCipherSpec message but before Finished. This is a deviation from the standard handshake message flow. The desired protocol name can be selected from the list provided by the server, but the client is also free to submit a protocol that is not advertised. The padding is used to hide the true length of the extension so that the adversary can't guess the selected protocol by looking at the size of the encrypted message.

NPN was submitted to the TLS working group for standardization[40] but, despite wide support in production (e.g., Chrome, Firefox, and OpenSSL), failed to win acceptance. The introduction of a new handshake message, which changes the usual handshake flow, was deemed disruptive and more complex than necessary. There were also concerns that the inability of intermediary devices to see what protocol is being negotiated might be problematic in practice. In the end, the group adopted the competing ALPN proposal.[41]

## Secure Renegotiation

The renegotiation_info extension improves TLS with verification that renegotiation is being carried out between the same two parties that negotiated the previous handshake.

Initially (during the first handshake on a connection), this extension is used by both parties to inform each other that they support secure renegotiation; for this, they simply send the extension without any data. To secure SSL 3, which doesn't support extensions, clients can instead use a special signaling suite, TLS_EMPTY_RENEGOTIATION_INFO_SCSV (0xff).

On subsequent handshakes, the extension is used to submit proof of knowledge of the previous handshake. Clients send the verify_data value from their previous Finished message.

---

[40] Next Protocol Negotiation 03 [fsty.uk/t44] (Adam Langley, 24 April 2012)

[41] Some missing context (was: Confirming consensus for ALPN) [fsty.uk/t45] (Yoav Nir, 15 March 2013)

Servers send two values: first the client's verify_data and then their own. The attacker couldn't have obtained these values, because the Finished message is always encrypted.

# Server Name Indication

*Server Name Indication* (SNI), implemented using the server_name extension,[42] provides a mechanism for a client to specify the name of the server it wishes to connect to. In other words, this extension provides support for *virtual secure servers*, giving servers enough information to look for a matching certificate among the available virtual secure hosts. Without this mechanism, only one certificate can be deployed per IP address.[43] Because SNI was a late addition to TLS (2006), many popular older products (e.g., Windows XP and some early Android versions) don't support it. This problem significantly slowed down the wide adoption of encryption.

# Session Tickets

*Session tickets* introduce a new session resumption mechanism that doesn't require any server-side storage.[44] The idea is that the server can take all of its session data (state), encrypt it with a special *ticket key*, and send it back to the client in the form of a *ticket*. On subsequent connections, the client submits the ticket back to the server; the server checks the ticket integrity, decrypts the contents, and uses the information in it to resume the session. This approach potentially makes it easier to scale web server clusters, which would otherwise need to synchronize session state among the nodes.

> ### Warning
>
> Session tickets break the TLS security model. They expose session state on the wire encrypted with a ticket key. Depending on the implementation, the ticket key might be weaker than the cipher used for the connection. For example, OpenSSL uses 128-bit AES keys for this purpose. Also, the *same* ticket key is reused across many sessions. This is similar to the situation with the RSA key exchange and breaks forward secrecy; if the ticket key is compromised it can be used to decrypt full connection data. For this reason, if session tickets are used, the ticket keys must be rotated frequently.

The client indicates support for this resumption mechanism with an empty session_ticket extension. If it wishes to resume an earlier session, then it should instead place the ticket in the extension. A compliant server that wishes to issue a new ticket includes an empty

---

[42] RFC 6066: TLS Extensions: Extension Definitions [fsty.uk/t46] (D. Eastlake 3rd, January 2011)

[43] Although HTTP has the facility to send host information via the Host request header, this is sent at the application protocol layer, which can be communicated to the server only after a successful TLS handshake.

[44] RFC 5077: TLS Session Resumption without Server-Side State [fsty.uk/t47] (Salowey et al., January 2008)

session_ticket extension in its ServerHello. It then waits for the client's Finished message, verifies it, and sends back the ticket in the NewSessionTicket handshake message. If the server wishes to resume an earlier session, then it responds with an abbreviated handshake, as with standard resumption.

> ### Note
>
> When a server decides to use session tickets for session resumption, it sends back an empty session ID field (in its ServerHello message). At this point, the session does not have a unique identifier. However, the ticket specification allows the *client* to select and submit a session ID (in its ClientHello) in a subsequent handshake that uses the ticket. A server that accepts the ticket must also respond with the same session ID. This is why the session ID appears in the TLS web server logs even when session tickets are used as the session-resumption mechanism.

## Signature Algorithms

The signature_algorithms extension, which is defined in TLS 1.2, enables clients to communicate support for various signature and hash algorithms. The TLS specification lists RSA, DSA, and ECDSA signature algorithms and MD5, SHA1, SHA224, SHA256, SHA384, and SHA512 hash functions. By using the signature_algorithm extension, clients submit the *signature–hash* algorithm pairs they support.

This extension is optional; if it's not present, the server infers the supported signature algorithms from the client's offered cipher suites (e.g., RSA suites indicate support for RSA signatures, ECDSA suites indicate support for ECDSA, and so on) and assumes support for SHA1.

## OCSP Stapling

The status_request extension[42] is used by clients to indicate support for *OCSP stapling*, which is a feature that a server can use to send fresh certificate revocation information to the client. (I discuss revocation at length in the section called "Certificate Revocation" in Chapter 6.) A server that supports stapling returns an empty status_request extension in its ServerHello and provides an OCSP response (in DER format) in the CertificateStatus handshake message immediately after the Certificate message.

OCSP stapling supports only one OCSP response and can be used to check the revocation status of the server certificate only. This limitation is addressed by RFC 6961,[45] which adds support for multiple OCSP responses (and uses the status_request_v2 extension to indicate

---

[45] RFC 6961: TLS Multiple Certificate Status Request Extension [fsty.uk/t48] (Y. Pettersen, June 2013)

support for it). However, at this time, this improved version is not well supported in either client or server software.

# Protocol Limitations

In addition to unintentional weaknesses, which I will discuss at length in subsequent chapters, TLS is known to currently have several limitations influenced by its positioning in the OSI layer and certain design decisions:

- Encryption protects the contents of a TCP connection, but the metadata of TCP and all other lower layers remains in plaintext. Thus, a passive observer can determine the IP addresses of the source and the destination. Information leakage of this type isn't the fault of TLS but a limitation inherent in our current layered networking model.

- Even at the TLS layer, a lot of the information is exposed as plaintext. The first handshake is never encrypted, allowing the passive observer to (1) learn about client capabilities and use them for fingerprinting, (2) examine the SNI information to determine the intended virtual host, (3) examine the host's certificate, and, when client certificates are used, (4) potentially obtain enough information to identify the user. There are workarounds to avoid these issues, but they're not used by mainstream implementations.

- After encryption is activated, some protocol information remains in the clear: the observer can see the subprotocol and length of each message. Depending on the protocol, the length might reveal useful clues about the underlying communication. For example, there have been several studies that have tried to infer what resources are being accessed over HTTP based on the indicated request and response sizes. Without length hiding, it's not possible to safely use compression before encryption (a common practice today).

The leakage of metadata at lower network layers is something that can't be addressed by TLS. The other limitations could be fixed, and, indeed, there are proposals and discussions about addressing them. You'll learn more about them later in the book.

# Differences between Protocol Versions

This section describes the major differences between various SSL and TLS protocol versions. There haven't been many changes to the core protocol since SSL 3. TLS 1.0 made limited changes only to justify a different name, and TLS 1.1 was primarily released to fix a few security problems. TLS 1.2 introduced authenticated encryption, cleaned up the hashing, and otherwise made the protocol free of any hardcoded primitives.

# SSL 3

SSL 3 was released in late 1995. Starting from scratch to address the many weaknesses of the previous protocol version, SSL 3 established the design that still remains in the latest versions of TLS. If you want to gain a better understanding of what SSL 3 changed and why, I recommend the protocol analysis paper by Wagner and Schneier.[46]

# TLS 1.0

TLS 1.0 was released in January 1999. It includes the following changes from SSL 3:

- This is the first version to specify a PRF based on the standard HMAC and implemented as a combination (XOR) of HMAC-MD5 and HMAC-SHA.

- Master secret generation now uses the PRF instead of a custom construction.

- The `verify_data` value is now based on the PRF instead of a custom construction.

- Integrity validation (MAC) uses the official HMAC. SSL 3 used an earlier, obsolete HMAC version.

- The format of the padding changed, making it more robust. In October 2014, the so-called POODLE attack exposed SSL 3 padding as insecure.

- FORTEZZA suites were removed.

As a practical matter, the result of the protocol cleanup was that TLS 1.0 was given FIPS approval, allowing its use by US government agencies.

If you want to study TLS 1.0 and earlier protocol versions, I recommend Eric Rescorla's book *SSL and TLS: Designing and Building Secure Systems*, published by Addison-Wesley in 2001. I have found this book to be invaluable for understanding the reasoning behind certain design decisions and for following the evolution of the early protocol versions.

# TLS 1.1

TLS 1.1 was released in April 2006. It includes the following major changes from TLS 1.0:

- CBC encryption now uses explicit IVs that are included in every TLS record. This addresses the predictable IV weakness, which was later exploited in the BEAST attack.

- Implementations are now required to use the `bad_record_mac` alert in response to padding problems to defend against padding attacks. The `decryption_failed` alert is deprecated.

---

[46] Analysis of the SSL 3.0 protocol [fsty.uk/t49] (David Wagner and Bruce Schneier, Proceedings of the Second USENIX Workshop on Electronic Commerce, 1996)

- This version includes TLS extensions (RFC 3546) by reference.

# TLS 1.2

TLS 1.2 was released in August 2008. It includes the following major changes from TLS 1.1:

- Support for authenticated encryption was added.
- Support for HMAC-SHA256 cipher suites was added.
- IDEA and DES cipher suites were removed.
- TLS extensions were incorporated in the main protocol specification, although most actual extensions remain documented elsewhere.
- A new extension, signature_algorithms, can be used by clients to communicate what hash and signature algorithms they are willing to accept.
- The MD5/SHA1 combination used in the PRF was replaced with SHA256 for the TLS 1.2 suites and all earlier suites when negotiated with this protocol version.
- Cipher suites are now allowed to specify their own PRFs.
- The MD5/SHA1 combination used for digital signatures was replaced with a single hash. By default, SHA256 is used, but cipher suites can specify their own. Before, the signature hash algorithm was mandated by the protocol; now the hash function is part of the signature structure, and implementations can choose the best algorithm.
- The length of the verify_data element in the Finished message can now be explicitly specified by cipher suites.

# 4 Public Key Infrastructure

Thanks to public key cryptography, we are able to communicate safely with people whose public keys we have, but there are many other problems that remain unsolved. For example, how can we communicate with people we've never met? How do we store public keys and revoke them? Most importantly, how do we do that at world scale, with millions of servers and billions of people and devices? It's a tall order, but it's what *Public Key Infrastructure* (PKI) was created to solve.

## Internet PKI

For most people, PKI is about the public key infrastructure as used on the Internet. But the real meaning of PKI is much wider because it was originally developed for other uses. Thus, it's more accurate to talk about *Internet PKI*, the term that was introduced by the PKIX Working Group that adapted PKI for use on the Internet. Another term that's recently been used is *Web PKI*, in which the focus is on how browsers consume and validate certificates. In this book, I'll generally use the name PKI to refer to Internet PKI, except maybe in a few cases in which the distinction is important. The lines between the different types of PKI are often blurred. For example, browser vendors wield a lot of power, and through Web PKI some of their influences spread to other ecosystems.

The goal of PKI is to enable secure communication among parties who have never met before. The model we use today relies on trusted third parties called *certification authorities* (CAs) to issue certificates that we unreservedly trust. Let's look at the various parties involved in making this model work.

**Subscriber**
> The *subscriber* (or *end entity*) is the party that wishes to provide secure services, which require a certificate.

**Registration authority**
> The *registration authority* (RA) carries out certain management functions related to certificate issuance. For example, an RA might perform the necessary identity validation before requesting a CA to issue a certificate. In some cases, RAs are also

Figure 4.1. Internet PKI certificate lifecycle

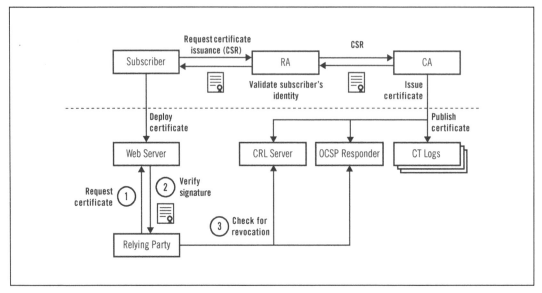

called *local registration authorities* (LRAs), for example, when a CA wants to establish a branch that is close to its users (such as one in a different country). In practice, many CAs also perform RA duties.

**Certification authority**

The *certification authority* (CA) is a party we trust to issue certificates that confirm subscriber identities. They are also required to provide up-to-date revocation information online so that relying parties can verify that certificates are still valid.

**Relying party**

The *relying party* is the certificate consumer. Technically, these are web browsers, other programs, and operating systems that perform certificate validation. They do this by relying on *root trust stores* that contain the ultimately trusted certificates (*trust anchors*) of selected CAs. In a wider sense, relying parties are end users who depend on certificates for secure communication on the Internet.

**Certificate Transparency Log**

*Certificate Transparency logs* (or *CT logs*) are services designed to support monitoring of activity in the entire PKI ecosystem. CAs that participate in the ecosystem publish certificates to CT logs, which, in turn, make them available to the public for auditing purposes.

## What Is Trust?

Discussions about PKI usually use words such as *identity*, *authority*, and *trust*. Because they rarely mean what we think they mean, these words often cause confusion and create a mismatch between our expectations and what exists in real life.

With most certificates, we get only limited assurances that we're talking to the right server. Some types of certificates provide a binding with an offline identity, but that doesn't mean much for security, which depends on too many other factors.

In PKI, *trust* is used only in a very technical sense of the word; it means that a certificate can be validated by a CA we have in the trust store. But it doesn't mean that we *trust* the subscriber for anything. Think about this: for years millions of people visited Amazon's web sites every day and made purchases, even though the homepage operated without encryption. Why did we do that? Ultimately, because they had earned our (real) trust.

# Standards

Internet PKI has its roots in X.509, an international standard for public key infrastructure that was originally designed to support X.500, a standard for electronic directory services. X.500 never took off, but X.509 was subsequently adapted for use on the Internet by the PKIX working group.[1]

From the charter:

> The PKIX Working Group was established in the fall of 1995 with the goal of developing Internet standards to support X.509-based Public Key Infrastructures (PKIs). Initially PKIX pursued this goal by profiling X.509 standards developed by the CCITT (later the ITU-T). Later, PKIX initiated the development of standards that are not profiles of ITU-T work, but rather are independent initiatives designed to address X.509-based PKI needs in the Internet. Over time this latter category of work has become the major focus of PKIX work, i.e., most PKIX-generated RFCs are no longer profiles of ITU-T X.509 documents.

The main document produced by the PKIX working group is RFC 5280, which documents the certificate format and trust path building as well as the format of *Certificate Revocation Lists* (CRLs).[2] The PKIX working group concluded in October 2013.

---

[1] PKIX Working Group [fsty.uk/t50] (IETF, retrieved 1 May 2021)

[2] RFC 5280: Internet X.509 Public Key Infrastructure Certificate and CRL Profile [fsty.uk/t51] (Cooper et al., May 2008)

> **Note**
>
> There's often a disconnect between standards and real life, and PKIX is a good example of this. This is in part because standards can be vague and fail to address real needs, but also because implementers often take matters into their hands. Sometimes, wrong decisions and bugs in widely deployed implementations restrict what we can do in practice. You will find many such instances documented in this book.

The *CA/Browser Forum* (or *CAB Forum*) is an industry group of CAs, browser vendors, and other interested parties whose goal is to establish and enforce standards for certificate issuance and processing.[3] The CA/Browser Forum was initially created to define standards for issuance of EV certificates, which came out in 2007.[4] Although initially a loose working group of CAs, the CA/Browser Forum changed its focus and restructured in 2012.[5] The same year, they released *Baseline Requirements for the Issuance and Management of Publicly-Trusted Certificates*, or *Baseline Requirements* for short.[6]

Although CAB Forum lists only about 50 CAs as members, Baseline Requirements effectively apply to all CAs; the document is incorporated into the WebTrust audit program for CAs[7] and explicitly required by some root store operators (e.g., Mozilla).

# Certificates

In X.509, a certificate is a digital document that contains a public key, some information about the entity associated with it, and one or more digital signatures that are used to verify its authenticity. In other words, it's a public key holder that enables us to exchange, store, and use public keys. That makes certificates the main building block of PKI.

---

[3] The CA/Browser Forum [fsty.uk/t52] (retrieved 1 May 2021)

[4] EV SSL Certificate Guidelines [fsty.uk/t53] (The CA/Browser Forum, retrieved 1 May 2021)

[5] The change of focus came from the realization that there were many burning security questions that were not being addressed. During 2011, there were several small and big CA failures, and the general feeling was that the PKI ecosystem was terribly insecure. Some even questioned the ecosystem's survival. With Baseline Requirements, the CA/Browser Forum addressed many of these issues.

[6] Baseline Requirements [fsty.uk/t54] (The CA/Browser Forum, retrieved 1 May 2021)

[7] WebTrust seal program [fsty.uk/t55] (CPA, retrieved 3 October 2021)

## ASN.1, BER, DER, and PEM

*Abstract Syntax Notation One* (ASN.1) is a set of rules that support definition, transport, and exchange of complex data structures and objects. ASN.1 was designed to support network communication between diverse platforms in a way that's independent of machine architecture and implementation language. ASN.1 is a standard originally defined in 1988 in X.208 and defined more recently in the X.680 series of documents published by ITU.[8]

ASN.1 defines data in an abstract way; separate standards exist to specify how data is encoded. *Basic Encoding Rules* (BER) is the first such standard. X.509 relies on *Distinguished Encoding Rules* (DER), which are a subset of BER that allow only one way to encode ASN.1 values. This is critical for use in cryptography, especially digital signatures. PEM (short for *Privacy-Enhanced Mail*, which has no meaning in this context) is an ASCII encoding of DER using Base64 encoding. ASN.1 is complicated, but, unless you're a developer dealing with cryptography, you probably won't have to work with it directly.

Most certificates are supplied in PEM format (because it's easy to email, copy, and paste), but you might sometimes encounter DER, too. If you need to convert from one format to another, use the OpenSSL x509 command.

If you're curious about what ASN.1 looks like, download any certificate and look inside. You can do this with OpenSSL's asn1parse command or, even better, with an online ASN.1 decoder.[9] If you want to learn more, it's not difficult to find good documentation online.[10]

The der-ascii project by David Benjamin makes experimenting very easy by providing a toolkit for disassembly and reassembly of DER structures.[11]

# Certificate Fields

An X.509 certificate is a data structure that consists of a set of predefined fields and—in version 3—a set of extensions. On the surface, the structure is flat and linear, although some fields can contain other structures. Extensions support adding arbitrary new data to certificates without having to define new format versions.

### Version

There are three certificate versions: 1, 2, and 3, encoded as values 0, 1, and 2. Version 1 supports only basic fields; version 2 adds unique identifiers (two additional fields); and version 3 adds extensions. Most certificates used today are in v3 format.

---

[8] X.680: Information technology - ASN.1 [fsty.uk/t56] (ITU, retrieved 1 May 2021)

[9] ASN.1 JavaScript decoder [fsty.uk/t57] (Lapo Luchini, retrieved 1 May 2021)

[10] A Warm Welcome to ASN.1 and DER [fsty.uk/t58] (Let's Encrypt, retrieved 1 May 2021)

[11] der-ascii [fsty.uk/t59] (GitHub, retrieved 2 October 2021)

---

**Serial Number**

Initially, serial numbers were specified as positive integers that uniquely identify a certificate issued by a given CA. Additional requirements were added later as a second layer of defense from chosen prefix attacks against certificate signatures (find out more in the next chapter, in the section called "RapidSSL Rogue CA Certificate"); serial numbers are now required to be nonsequential (unpredictable) and contain at least 20 bits of entropy.

**Signature Algorithm**

This field specifies the algorithm used for the certificate signature. It's placed here, inside the certificate, so that it can be protected by the signature.

**Issuer**

The *Issuer* field contains the *distinguished name* (DN) of the certificate issuer. It's a complex field that can contain many components depending on the represented entity. This, for example, is the DN used for one of Verisign's root certificates: / C=US/O=VeriSign, Inc./OU=Class 3 Public Primary Certification Authority; it contains three components, one each for country, organization, and organizational unit.

**Validity**

The certificate validity period is the time interval during which the certificate is valid. It's represented with two values: the starting date and the ending date. The range is inclusive; a certificate with the same starting and ending time has a lifetime of one second.

**Subject**

The *Subject* field contains the distinguished name of the entity associated with the public key for which the certificate is issued. Self-signed certificates have the same DN in their *Subject* and *Issuer* fields and they're signed with their own key pair. Initially, the *common name* (CN) component of the DN was used for server hostnames (e.g., /CN=www.example.com would be used for a certificate valid for *www.example.com*). Unfortunately, that caused some confusion about how to issue certificates that are valid for multiple hostnames. Today, the *Subject* field is deprecated in favor of the *Subject Alternative Name* extension.

**Public key**

This field contains the *Subject Public-Key Info* structure, which consists of the algorithm ID, optional parameters, and then the public key itself. For public certificates, RSA and ECDSA algorithms are currently allowed by Baseline Requirements. EdDSA is a new algorithm making its way into the standards and libraries, but it's not yet widely supported.

**Note**

Two additional certificate fields were added in version 2: *Issuer Unique ID* and *Subject Unique ID*. They were subsequently deprecated in version 3 in favor of the *Authority Key Identifier* and *Subject Key Identifier* extensions.

Figure 4.2. X.509 certificate fields

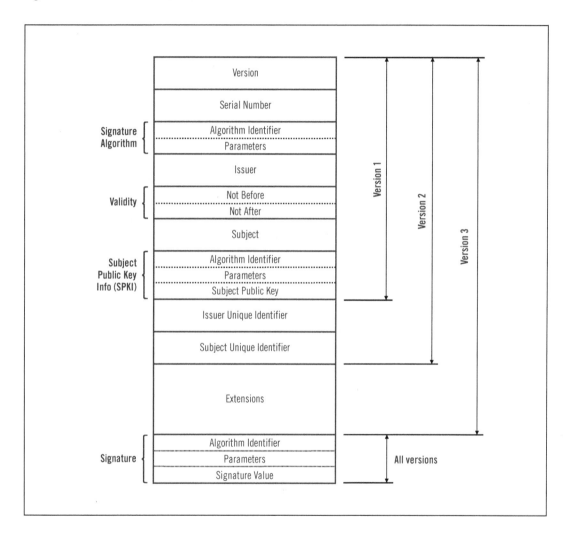

# Certificate Extensions

Certificate extensions were introduced in version 3 in order to add flexibility to the previously rigid certificate format. Each extension consists of a unique *object identifier* (OID), criticality indicator, and value, which is an ASN.1 structure. An extension marked as critical

---

must be understood and successfully processed; otherwise the entire certificate must be rejected.

**Authority Information Access**

The *Authority Information Access* (AIA) extension indicates how to access certain additional information and services provided by the issuing CA. One such piece of information is the location of the OCSP responder, provided as an HTTP URI. Relying parties can use the responder to check for revocation information in real time. In addition, some certificates also include the URI at which the issuing certificate can be found. That information is very useful for reconstruction of an incomplete certificate chain.

**Authority Key Identifier**

The content of this extension uniquely identifies the key that signed the certificate. It can be used during certificate path building to identify the parent certificate.

**Basic Constraints**

The *Basic Constraints* extension is used to indicate a CA certificate and, via the *path length constraint* field, control the depth of the subordinate CA certificate path (i.e., whether the CA certificate can issue further nested CA certificates and how deep). In theory, all CA certificates must include this extension; in practice, some root certificates issued as version 1 certificates are still used despite the fact that they contain no extensions.

**Certificate Policies**

This extension contains a list of one or more policies. A policy consists of an OID and an optional qualifier. When present, the qualifier usually contains the URI at which the full text of the policy can be obtained. Baseline Requirements establish that an end-entity certificate must always include at least one policy to indicate the terms under which the certificate was issued. The extension can be optionally used to indicate certificate validation type.

**CRL Distribution Points**

This extension is used to determine the location of the *Certificate Revocation List* (CRL) information, usually provided as an LDAP or HTTP URI. According to Baseline Requirements, a certificate must provide either CRL or OCSP revocation information.

**CT Poison**

CAs that wish to issue certificates that are CT compliant most commonly employ a two-step issuance process. In the first step they create a *precertificate*, which is an X.509 structure that contains substantially the same information as the certificate they wish to issue. Precertificates represent an intent to issue. In the second step, CAs issue a matching certificate, which includes a number of CT log signatures (of the corresponding precertificate). The *CT poison extension*, which is marked as critical, is used to prevent precertificates from being mistaken for actual certificates.

**CT Signed Certificate Timestamps**

*Signed Certificate Timestamps* (SCTs) are proofs of inclusion of a certificate in CT logs. They are signatures of precertificates or certificates. Clients that enforce a CT policy need to have a way of discovering the SCTs in order to verify the signatures and consider the certificates trusted. The most popular delivery mechanism is embedding the SCTs in the certificates themselves, and that's what this extension is used for. Other (less popular) mechanisms are transport via OCSP responses and a special TLS extension.

**Key Usage**

This extension defines the possible uses of the key contained in the certificate. There is a fixed number of uses, any of which can be set on a particular certificate. For example, a CA certificate could have the *Certificate Signer* and *CRL Signer* bits set.

**Extended Key Usage**

For more flexibility in determining or restricting public key usage, this extension allows arbitrary additional purposes to be specified, indicated by their OIDs. For example, end-entity certificates typically carry the `id-kp-serverAuth` and `id-kp-clientAuth` OIDs; code-signing certificates use the `id-kp-codeSigning` OID, and so on.

Although RFC 5280 indicates that *Extended Key Usage* (EKU) should be used only on end-entity certificates, in practice this extension is used on intermediate CA certificates to constrain the usage of the certificates issued from them.[12] Baseline Requirements, in particular, require the use of the EKU and Name Constraints extensions to consider an intermediate certificate to be *technically constrained*, meaning it can issue certificates only for a small number of hardcoded domain names. Because technically constrained intermediate certificates cannot issue arbitrary public certificates, their operators are not required to follow the same strict transparency requirements.

**Name Constraints**

The *Name Constraints* extension can be used to constrain the identities for which a CA can issue certificates. Identity namespaces can be explicitly excluded or permitted. This is a very useful feature that could, for example, allow an organization to obtain a subordinate CA that can issue certificates only for the company-owned domain names. With the namespaces constrained, such a CA certificate poses no danger to the entire ecosystem (i.e., a CA can't issue certificates for arbitrary sites).

RFC 5280 requires this extension to be marked as critical, but noncritical name constraints are used in practice. This is done to avoid rejection of certificates by

---

[12] Bug 725451: Support enforcing nested EKU constraints, do so by default [fsty.uk/t60] (Bugzilla@Mozilla, reported 8 February 2014)

some very widely deployed products and platforms that don't understand the *Name Constraints* extension, which would inevitably happen if the criticality flag was set.

### Subject Alternative Name

Traditionally, the *Subject* certificate field (more specifically, only its CN component) was used to create a binding between an identity and a public key. In practice, that approach is not flexible enough; it supports only hostnames and does not specify how multiple identities are handled. The *Subject Alternative Name* extension replaces the *Subject* field; it supports bindings to multiple identities specified by a DNS name, IP address, URI, and other types of identifier.

### Subject Key Identifier

This extension contains a unique value that can be used to identify certificates that contain a particular public key. It is recommended that the identifier be derived from the public key itself (e.g., by hashing). All CA certificates must include this extension and use the same identifier in the *Authority Key Identifier* extension of all issued certificates.

RFC 5280 defines several other extensions that are rarely used in public certificates; they are *Delta CRL Distribution Point*, *Inhibit anyPolicy*, *Issuer Alternative Name*, *Policy Constraints*, *Policy Mappings*, *Subject Directory Attributes*, and *Subject Information Access*.

# Certificate Chains

In the majority of cases, an end-entity certificate alone is insufficient for a successful validation. In practice, each server must provide a *chain of certificates* that leads to a trusted root. Certificate chains are used for security, technical, and administrative reasons.

Figure 4.3. Certificate chain

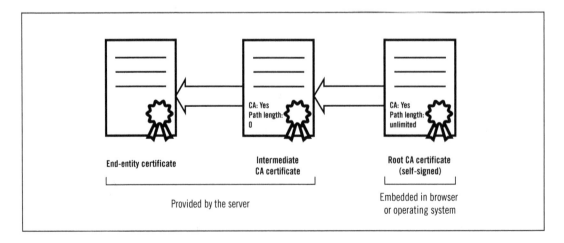

## Keeping the root safe

The root CA key is of great importance not only to the organization that owns it but also to the entire ecosystem. First, it has great financial value. Older and widely distributed keys are effectively irreplaceable because it takes many years to distribute a root certificate widely enough so that it becomes feasible on its own. Further, many root stores are not being updated any more. Second, if the key is compromised it can be used to issue fraudulent certificates for any domain name. If compromised, the associated certificates would have to be revoked, bringing down all the sites that depend on it.

Although in the past there were CAs issuing end-entity certificates directly from their roots, this practice is seen as too dangerous today. Baseline Requirements require that the root key is used only by issuing a direct command (i.e., automation is not allowed), implying that the root must be kept offline.

## Cross-certification

Cross-certification is the only way for new CAs to start operating. Because it takes a very long time for new roots to be widely distributed, a new root must initially be signed by some other well-established root. Over time, as old devices fade away, the new root will eventually become useful on its own. Consider studying Let's Encrypt's certificate hierarchy as a recent example of how cross-certification works in practice,[13] as well as its challenges with migration to its own root.[14]

## Compartmentalization

Unlike roots, subordinate CAs typically are placed online and used in automated systems. By splitting its operations across many subordinate CA certificates, a CA can spread the risk of exposure. For example, different subordinate CAs could be used for different certificate classes, or for different business units. Even within the same class of certificates, CAs might limit the total number of leaf certificates issued from a subordinate.

## Delegation

In some cases, a CA might want to issue a subordinate CA to another organization that is not affiliated with it. For example, a large company might want to issue their own certificates for the domain names they control. (That is often much cheaper than running a private CA and ensuring that the root certificate is distributed to all devices.) Sometimes, organizations might want to have full control, in which case the subordinate CA might be technically constrained to certain namespaces. In other cases, the CA remains in control over the certificates issued from the subordinate CA.

---

[13] Chain of Trust [fsty.uk/t61] (Let's Encrypt, retrieved 1 May 2021)

[14] Standing on Our Own Two Feet [fsty.uk/t62] (Jacob Hoffman-Andrews, 6 November 2020)

---

Although servers provide only one certificate chain on any one TLS connection, in practice there are often many paths leading from the leaf to various roots. In fact, there is no such thing as a canonical path. For example, in the case of cross-certification, one trust path will lead to the main CA's root and another to the alternative root. In addition, CAs themselves sometimes issue multiple certificates for the same keys. Each such additional certificate creates another trust path.

Path building often is poorly understood and implemented, leading to various problems in practice. Servers are expected to provide certificate chains that are complete and valid, but that often doesn't happen due to human error and various usability issues.

As a result, clients must often work to obtain certificates necessary to complete a trust path. Some clients may attempt to download them from the issuing CAs (using the information in the AIA X.509 extension). Some other clients keep a local cache of intermediates or even preload all of them.[15]

Path building and validation is a cause of many security issues in client software. This is not surprising, given vague, incomplete, and competing standards. Historically, many validation libraries had failed with simple tasks, such as validating that the issuing certificate belongs to a CA. The most commonly used libraries today are battle tested and secure only because they patched the worst problems, not because they were secure from the start. For many examples, refer to the section called "Certificate Validation Flaws" in Chapter 7.

# Relying Parties

For relying parties to be able to validate subscriber certificates, they must keep a collection of root CA certificates they trust. Most applications defer to the underlying operating system for encryption and certificate operations. There is a small number of exceptions by organizations—for example, Mozilla—that have enough in-house expertise to control the entire process. This is usually done so that the application behavior is the same across many different operating systems.

### Apple

Apple operates a root certificate program that is used on the iOS and OS X platforms.[16] To be considered for inclusion, a CA must pass an audit and demonstrate that it provides broad business value to Apple's customers.[17]

---

### Chrome

Historically, Chrome used to rely on the underlying operating system for certificate operations, except on Linux, where it relied on Mozilla's root store. Because Chrome has some very specific requirements when it comes to PKI, over time it added further layers of policies that it managed. For illustration, some of those layers included the following: (1) a blacklist of roots and other certificates that aren't trusted; (2) a list of CAs that can issue EV certificates; and (3) further *Certificate Transparency* requirements for some or all certificates. In 2020, Google announced that it would create and manage its own root store to use with Chrome on all platforms, except on iOS, where custom root stores are not supported.[18]

### Microsoft

Microsoft operates a root certificate program that is used on the Windows desktop, server, and mobile phone platforms.[19] Broadly, inclusion requires a yearly audit and a demonstration of business value to the Microsoft user base.

### Mozilla

Mozilla operates a uniquely transparent root certificate program,[20] which it uses for its products. Its root store is often used as the basis for the root stores of various Linux distributions. Heated discussions about policy decisions often take place on its security policy mailing list[21] and on Mozilla's bug tracking system.

All root certificate programs require CAs to satisfy a number of technical requirements, as well as undergo continuous independent audits designed for certification authorities. You'll find the details in each program's documentation.

# Certification Authorities

*Certification authorities* (CAs) are the most important part of the current Internet trust model. They can issue a certificate for any domain name, which means that anything they say goes. At the surface, it sounds like easy money, provided you can get your roots into a wide range of devices. But what exactly do you have to do to become a public CA?

1. Build out a competent CA organization:

    a. Establish strong expertise in PKI and CA operations.

    b. Design a robust, secure, and compartmentalized network to enable business operations yet protect the highly sensitive root and subordinate keys.

---

[18] Chrome Root Program [fsty.uk/t66] (Chromium, retrieved 3 October 2021)

[19] Program Requirements - Microsoft Trusted Root Program [fsty.uk/t67] (Microsoft, retrieved 1 May 2021)

[20] Mozilla CA Certificate Policy [fsty.uk/t68] (Mozilla, retrieved 1 May 2021)

[21] dev-security-policy [fsty.uk/t69] (Mozilla, retrieved 1 May 2021)

---

c.  Support the certificate lifecycle workflow.

d.  Comply with Baseline Requirements.

e.  Comply with EV SSL Certificate Guidelines.

f.  Comply with CT requirements of various relying parties.

g.  Provide a global CRL and OCSP infrastructure.

2. Comply with local laws; depending on the jurisdiction, this might mean obtaining a license.

3. Pass the audits required by the root programs.

4. Place your roots into a wide range of root programs.

5. Cross-certify your roots to bootstrap the operations.

For a long time, selling certificates was a relatively easy job for those who got in early. These days there's much less money to be made selling DV certificates, given that their price has been driven down by strong competition. This has been especially true since late 2015, when Let's Encrypt launched, offering free certificates to everyone.

# Certificate Lifecycle

The certificate lifecycle begins when a subscriber prepares a *Certificate Signing Request* (CSR) and submits it to the CA of their choice. A CSR will normally carry the list of hosts that should appear in the certificate, along with a public key and proof of possession of the corresponding private key (via a digital signature). CSRs can carry additional metadata, but not all of it is used in practice. CAs will often override the CSR values and use other sources for the information they embed in certificates.

The CA then follows the validation procedure, using different steps depending on the type of certificate requested:

**Domain validation**

*Domain-validated* (DV) certificates are issued based on proof of control over a domain name. Traditionally, that meant sending a confirmation email to one of the approved email addresses. If the recipient approves (i.e., follows the link in the email), then the certificate is issued. If confirmation via email is not possible, then any other means of communication (e.g., phone or snail mail) and practical demonstration of control are allowed. A similar procedure is followed when issuing certificates for IP addresses.

**Organization validation**

*Organization-validated* (OV) certificates require identity and authenticity verification. It wasn't until Baseline Requirements were adopted that the procedures for OV certificates were standardized. Before, there was a lot of inconsistency in how OV certificates were issued, but that's improved over the years.

**Extended validation**

*Extended Validation* (EV) certificates also require identity and authenticity verification, but with very strict requirements. They were introduced to address the lack of consistency in OV certificates, so it's no surprise that the validation procedures are extensively documented, leaving much less room for inconsistencies.

For a full list of validation methods, refer to Baseline Requirements, section 3.2. Issuance of DV certificates is typically fully automated. When proof of control is used, a new certificate is issued pretty much immediately. On the other end of the spectrum, it can take days or even weeks to obtain an EV certificate.

> **Note**
>
> When fraudulent certificate requests are submitted, attackers usually go after high-profile domain names. For this reason, CAs tend to maintain a list of such high-risk names and refuse to issue certificates for them without manual confirmation. This practice is required by Baseline Requirements.

After successful validation, the CA issues the certificate. In addition to the certificate itself, the CA will provide all of the intermediary certificates required to chain to their root. They also usually provide configuration instructions for major platforms.

The subscriber can now use the certificate in production, where it will hopefully stay until it expires. If the corresponding private key is compromised, the certificate is revoked. The procedure in this case is similar to that used for certificate issuance. There is often talk about certificate *reissuance*, but there is no such thing in PKI. After a certificate is permanently revoked,[22] an entirely new certificate is created to replace it.

---

[22] Interestingly, a certificate can be temporarily revoked by putting it *on hold*. After the hold is removed, the certificate is as good as new.

---

### Certificate Lifetimes

Initially, there were no restrictions imposed on certificate lifetimes. That changed with the EV certificates in 2007, which were limited to two years. In 2012, Baseline Requirements declared a limit of five years for all certificates. A further reduction to 39 months came in 2015, then 825 days in 2018. Finally, in September 2020, certificate lifetime was restricted to 398 days.

There is an argument to be made that even one year is too long. From the end user perspective, frequent rotation of certificates and their backing keys reduces the attack surface, especially in the light of lacking revocation mechanisms. Further, frequent certificate rotation effectively demands automation, which minimizes the effort and reduces mistakes in the long term.

From the ecosystem perspective, reduced lifetimes help make continuous improvements without paralysis due to backward compatibility issues.

---

# Revocation

Certificates are revoked when the associated private keys are compromised or no longer needed. In both cases, there is a risk of misuse if certificates continue to be seen as valid. The revocation protocols and procedures are designed to ensure certificate freshness and otherwise communicate revocation to relying parties. There are two standards for certificate revocation:

**Certificate Revocation List**

A *Certificate Revocation List* (CRL) is a list of all serial numbers belonging to revoked certificates that have not yet expired. CAs maintain one or more such lists. Every certificate should contain the location of the corresponding CRL in the *CRL Distribution Points* certificate extension. The main problem with CRLs is that they may grow large, making real-time lookups slow. They're also not updated very frequently.

**Online Certificate Status Protocol**

*Online Certificate Status Protocol* (OCSP) allows relying parties to obtain the revocation status of a single certificate. OCSP responses are special trust tokens that are issued and signed by the same CAs that issued the certificates. The location of the CA's OCSP server (also known as the *OCSP responder*) is encoded in the AIA certificate extension. OCSP allows for real-time lookups and addresses the main CRL deficiency, but it doesn't solve all revocation problems: the use of OCSP responders leads to performance and privacy issues and introduces a new point of failure.

Some of these issues can be addressed with a technique called *OCSP stapling*, which allows each server to embed an OCSP response directly into the TLS handshake. No further network communication is needed to establish certificate validity because the signature on the OCSP response can be verified.

Unfortunately, implementation of OCSP stapling in server software has traditionally been flawed, leading to a variety of issues, some very subtle.[23] This became especially evident with the introduction of a feature colloquially known as *must-staple*,[24] which, when enabled, requires that a certificate must always be accompanied by a fresh OCSP response to prove continued validity. The idea of this approach is that if a key is compromised and certificate revoked, it can be abused only for the duration of the validity of the OCSP response. With must-staple, failure to staple renders the certificate invalid. Lack of robustness of stapling implementations meant that this approach cannot be easily used or recommended.

Despite the wide availability of CRL and OCSP information, revocation remains an unsolved problem. Must-staple could potentially provide a better safety margin, but it's still not widely implemented. Another approach might be to avoid the need for revocation checking by relying on short-lived certificates, although this approach is still far off for a variety of reasons.[25]

# Certificate Transparency

*Certificate Transparency* (CT) is an extension of the public PKI that adds support for reliable and verifiable logging of all certificates. It was designed by Google in the aftermath of the DigiNotar incident that demonstrated how easy it was for a single actor to compromise the security of the entire ecosystem. The thinking was that if we were going to continue to use a system in which any one CA can issue a certificate for any property, we should at least have full visibility into its operations.

The principal idea is that with transparency, we force all activity out into the open, making it possible to detect malicious activity. The system acts as a deterrent, but there is no way to prevent misissuance. As for how things would work, I like this succinct description of CT from Ben Laurie's very first blog post about this topic:[26]

> Certificates are registered in a public audit log. Servers present proofs that their certificate is registered, along with the certificate itself. Clients check these proofs and domain owners monitor the logs. If a CA mis-issues a certificate then either
>
> - There is no proof of registration, so the browser rejects the certificate, or
> - There is a proof of registration and the certificate is published in the log, in which case the domain owner notices and complains, or

[23] ocsp-stapling.md [fsty.uk/t70] (Ryan Sleevi, retrieved 26 September 2021)

[24] X.509v3 TLS Feature Extension [fsty.uk/t71] (P. Hallam-Baker, October 2015)

[25] Improving Revocation: OCSP Must-Staple and Short-lived Certificates [fsty.uk/t72] (Mozilla Security Blog, 23 November 2015)

[26] Fixing CAs [fsty.uk/t73] (Ben Laurie, 29 November 2011)

- *There is a proof of registration but the certificate does not appear in the log, in which case the proof is now proof that the log misbehaved and should be struck off.*

---

### Certificate Transparency Timeline

- **Late 2011:** Adam Langley[27] and Ben Laurie begin to explore the concepts behind CT. The early discussions were hosted on The Right Key mailing list[28] and the CT development mailing list. The first active CT log is named Pilot.[29]

- **June 2013:** Certificate Transparency RFC 6962 is published in the Experimental category.

- **September 2013:** Google begins to plan requiring CT for EV certificates.[30]

- **March 2015:** Chrome 41 starts to require CT for all EV certificates issued in 2015. The ecosystem is powered by three geographically dispersed CT logs provided by Google: Pilot, Aviator, and Rocketeer.

- **June 2016:** Google requires Symantec to log all its certificates on account of discovered issuance irregularities.[31]

- **October 2016:** Google announces that CT will be required for all certificates starting in October 2017.[32] The actual enforcement was later postponed to give the ecosystem more time to prepare.[33]

- **September 2017:** Chrome 61 is released with support for the Expect-CT HTTP header, making it possible for anyone to opt-in to mandatory CT for their web sites.[34]

- **July 2018:** Chrome starts to require CT for all newly issued certificates.

- **October 2018:** Apple also begins to enforce CT as a requirement for all certificates.[35]

- **February 2021:** The ecosystem consists of CT logs run by six organizations: Cloudflare, DigiCert, Google, Let's Encrypt, Sectigo, and Trust Asia.

---

Certificate transparency progressed from being an idea in 2011, to an experiment around 2015, and finally to production in July 2018, when Chrome started to require it for all newly issued certificates. Apple joined in October of the same year. Together these two technology

---

[27] Certificate Transparency [fsty.uk/t74] (Adam Langley, 29 November 2011)

[28] The Right Key mailing list [fsty.uk/t75] (retrieved 30 December 2020)

[29] certificate-transparency mailing list [fsty.uk/t76] (retrieved 30 December 2020)

[30] Extended Validation in Chrome [fsty.uk/t77] (Certificate Transparency web site, retrieved 30 December 2020)

[31] Sustaining Digital Certificate Security [fsty.uk/t78] (Google Security Blog, 28 October 2015)

[32] Announcement: Requiring Certificate Transparency in 2017 [fsty.uk/t79] (Ryan Sleevi, 25 October 2016)

[33] Certificate Transparency in Chrome - Change to Enforcement Date [fsty.uk/t80] (Ryan Sleevi, 21 April 2017)

[34] Issue 679012: Expect-CT HTTP header [fsty.uk/t81] (Chromium bug tracker, 6 January 2017)

[35] Apple's Certificate Transparency policy [fsty.uk/t82] (Apple, retrieved 30 December 2020)

giants, via their grasp on browsers and operating systems, made CT de facto required for the entire ecosystem.

Microsoft adopted CT in its new Edge browser, which is based on Chromium; the requirements are the same as Google's. Firefox doesn't support CT and it's not clear if it will, given Mozilla's critique of the design in 2017.[36]

Technically, CT continues to be optional, with the caveat that certificates issued outside it won't function with the clients that require it. There are other use cases in which CT is not required and CAs continue to issue certificates that are not being logged. There is a lot of complexity involved with running CT infrastructure, but thankfully, end users need not worry about any of it.

In fact, all end users need to do is reap the benefits of certificate transparency, making it very easy for them to not only monitor issuance of their own certificates (not an easy feat for large organizations) but also keep an eye open for unexpected and potentially misissued certificates.

# How CT Works

The best way to understand CT is to approach it from the threat model perspective, then understand how each design decision mitigates certain problems. Let's break it down one aspect at a time.

## Public Certificates Must Be Logged

In the DigiNotar incident, the attacker achieved a full compromise of a CA and issued many certificates for a number of high-value properties. Because the compromise was so complete, there was no record of what had been issued. It's easy to see that this sort of problem is unacceptable, but the truth is that back then, CAs were issuing certificates without any technical oversight.

The only way to defend against this problem is to make all certificates public, which would then enable us to either detect misissuances or reject certificates that have not been published. CT changes the traditional PKI model, where trust is conveyed with a single digital signature on a certificate. With CT, additional signatures—proofs of logging—are required for a certificate to be accepted as valid.

Having a full record of all public certificates is also beneficial to make it possible to monitor the correctness of the issued certificates. In the public PKI space, it is not unusual to uncover a small or even a large number of incorrect certificates. Complete transparency makes auditing much easier.

---

[36] [Trans] WGLC comments on draft-ietf-trans-6962-bis-24 [fsty.uk/t83] (Richard Barnes, 16 January 2017)

## Multiple Logs

We have so far established that we will need some sort of log to hold public certificates. Adding logging as a requirement complicates CAs' operations. Suddenly there is a third party in the workflow, and one whose operation is critical for the process. So from the availability perspective, we need to support multiple log operators so that CAs' operations are not interrupted when one CT log is down.

Actually, the logging infrastructure of CT is now a point of failure for the entire world. Whereas before CAs operated independently, now all of them have to depend on the logs and no public certificates can be issued without them. Thus, what we ideally want is a level of diversity in CT log operators and software, providing a robust and resilient platform whose cost would be born by many organizations.

## CT Log Diversity

We also need log operator diversity at the certificate level. Absent strong technical controls (which is where we are at the moment), it wouldn't make sense for the same CA to issue a certificate and also to vouch that the certificate had been logged. But that's not the only reason; let's consider all of them.

**CT log operators**
From an architectural point of view, it makes sense to separate certificate issuance from logging; different functions should be implemented by separate systems. Further, certificate issuance is a critical and time-sensitive function, so we want to have a choice of CT log operators and infrastructure in order to improve availability. Logging one certificate to multiple logs increases both its security (it's less likely that all CT logs will misbehave) and its longevity (redundant CT logs in case some are distrusted during the certificate lifetime).

**Legal jurisdictions**
When multiple CT logs are supported, an ideal technical policy would require spreading them across multiple jurisdictions in order to reduce the chances of legal interference.

**CT log software implementations**
At a technical level, we might also want to have multiple independent CT log software implementations, ensuring that the same weakness is not exploited in all CT log installations.

At this time, only CT log operator diversity is enforced. Google's policy requires one Google log, whereas Apple's policy requires any two distinct operators. This is one area where it would be useful to see further improvements in the future.

## User Agent Policies

A *user agent CT policy* is a set of CT requirements that are enforced at the point of certificate consumption. The design of CT doesn't prescribe any specific policy, leaving it to the adopters to decide on the details. A complete policy consists of two parts. One part is maintaining a list of trustworthy CT logs whose SCTs are recognized. The other part is detailing how many SCTs are necessary and from which logs.

## Monitoring of CT Logs

So far we've arrived at a very complex trust system where instead of trusting one CA, we trust a bunch of CT log operators. But who's going to watch the watchers? For all we know, an operator could show one set of data to one party and something else to another, or completely change the contents of their log the next day. To account for this we need another security layer in the form of *monitors*, whose job is to keep the log operators honest.

Given that more than a billion certificates are published every year, monitors can't just reread the logs every day to verify their integrity, but there is an interesting cryptographic construction that helps with this task; it's called *Merkle trees*. Without going into a great level of detail just now, Merkle trees enable us to store a number of entries in a tree structure while using cryptographic hashing to ensure that new entries build on top of the ones that came before. When a tree is constructed, its entire state can be reduced to a single hash that acts as a fingerprint. Crucially, if anything about the tree changes, then the fingerprint will change as well. A comparison to a house of cards is appropriate here; move any card at the bottom and the entire house collapses.

The addition of Merkle trees to the design makes monitoring feasible. Monitors continuously follow log activity and watch as the house of cards is built. They read all new data added to the logs and, in fact, build parts of the monitored Merkle trees independently, verifying that the log's hashes match their own.

## Monitoring of Certificates

We also use the name *monitor* in the context of domain name operators wanting to have visibility into all certificates issued for their properties. This is a much simpler form of monitoring, where it's only necessary to consume all published certificates to find the ones that you're interested in. This, of course, is only easy because we're relying on other parties to ensure the correct operations of the logs.

## Delayed Publishing

Our decision to support log monitoring and integrity validation comes with a drawback, which is that it becomes impossible to instantly publish new certificates. Doing so would require serialization of all publishing operations, which wouldn't scale or support other requirements for availability and performance. So instead what happens is that CAs submit their logs and in return receive proofs of logging, which are called *Signed Certificate Timestamps* (SCTs). SCTs are essentially digitally signed promises to publish the certificates within a deadline, or *maximum merge delay* (MMD). In the CT ecosystem as it is deployed today, all logs use an MMD of 24 hours.

## Precertificates

Now we need to figure out how to distinguish logged certificates from those that haven't been. We don't want to have to check every certificate individually as that would both vastly complicate the infrastructure and introduce massive performance penalties. The only alternative is to make SCTs available to clients at the point of certificate consumption. One option would be to embed the SCTs in the certificates, but we can also consider extending the TLS protocol or incorporating the necessary data into OCSP. The TLS approach isn't feasible as it would require everyone in the entire world to update their server software, which would never happen. The OCSP approach isn't feasible at scale either: because OCSP revocation checking is widely ignored in the current landscape, the only approach would be to use OCSP stapling, and then we have the same problem—that everyone would have to update. Thus the only feasible approach is to embed SCTs in the certificates.

Wanting to embed SCTs in certificates leads to a chicken and egg situation: What should CAs submit to CAs? They can't submit certificates because they first need to obtain the SCTs, and they can't get those without the certificates. This is solved by an introduction of a new type of object, called a *precertificate*. In the first design of CT, precertificates are essentially the same as certificates without the SCTs, but they include a special *poison extension*.[37] The process is now as follows: (1) a CA creates a precertificate, which it then (2) submits to a number of CT logs to obtain SCTs, after which it (3) builds the matching certificates with the embedded SCTs. In terms of the information they carry, precertificates and certificates are identical and must be. They are also considered equivalent for compliance purposes: issuing a precertificate is the same as issuing an actual certificate.

Precertificates are an optional part of CT. Operators who are content with delivering SCTs using other means (via OCSP or TLS) log certificates directly, and only at the point in time when they wish to obtain the SCTs. Although it's not required to log certificates that have embedded SCTs, some CAs log them as well and thus create a fully public record of their activity.

---

[37] This extension is necessary to prevent precertificates from being interpreted as certificates.

## Auditing

To complete the design, we need to be able to answer this question: Are all public certificates actually being published? Without further work, we only have promises to publish, but what if some SCTs are issued but never followed up on? What we can do, and what is being done, is to submit certificates and then observe if they appear in the logs within the allocated time, but that only verifies the correct log operation in the nonadversarial case. How do we detect when a CA and a couple of CT log operators collude to issue a stealth certificate? Or if someone exploits the same software bug in a variety of CT logs and achieves the same effect? In CT terminology, this process is called *auditing*, and it is possibly the most complicated aspect of CT.

Auditing is a process in which SCTs observed in real life are continuously verified to be included in CT logs. Merkle trees support this operation via *inclusion proofs*. In theory, every client can look up the certificates directly, assuming the MMD has passed. In practice, that would require an entirely different type of infrastructure (one that scales), so instead we'll go with a network of auditors that act as proxies and provide auditing as a service. Some tricky aspects related to privacy need to be resolved, but we are otherwise able to complete the design, as least in theory. Another relevant concept is the ability for monitors to compare their views of CT logs to ensure that they are identical. This is known as *gossiping* and is still a work in progress at this time.[38]

# State of CT

CT has been a resounding success. After years of guessing what the PKI ecosystem looked like, we now have full and easy access to all public certificates. CT has not only enabled us to trust the public PKI once again, but it's helped bring it into shape with constant monitoring and refinement of issuance policies.

Google has put a substantial amount of resources into designing and bootstrapping the ecosystem and continues to prop it up. A handful of companies have joined Google's effort and support the ecosystem.[39] Google's reference implementation of CT log software, Trillian,[40] is actually a generic platform on top of which CT is implemented as a feature. Other functionality is being developed to support other types of transparency—for example, that of software artifacts.[41]

---

[38] How will Certificate Transparency Logs be Audited in Practice? [fsty.uk/t84] (Andrew Ayer, 10 January 2018)

[39] Certificate Transparency [fsty.uk/t36] (Google, retrieved 26 August 2021)

[40] Trillian [fsty.uk/t85] (Google @ GitHub, retrieved 26 August 2021)

[41] Tamper-Evident Logs [fsty.uk/t86] (Google, retrieved 26 August 2021)

Despite this, CT is not yet complete. Lessons are being learned, and Google continues to make improvements. Some parts of the design such as auditing are difficult to implement in a performant and privacy-preserving way, but progress is being made.[42]

The current CT ecosystem is designed around RFC 6962 from 2013,[43] but by late 2021, the design of CT version 2 will be complete.[44] The second iteration makes a number of improvements that simplify CT and make it a better protocol but otherwise don't substantially change the design. The only exception may be the added support for communicating inclusion proofs to clients at runtime. Time will tell if there will be a desire or need to upgrade to this version, given few differences and in the light of high implementation costs.

A potential problem with CT as it's currently implemented is that there are multiple CT policies to comply with—currently, one from Google[45] and another from Apple.[46] These policies, which were initially very similar, started to deviate in 2021.

Google made it difficult for other organizations to adopt its policy because it embedded itself in the requirements. In the early days of CT, there was no SCT auditing, and even in late 2021 SCT auditing is still in its early days. To account for this weakness, Google mandated in its policy that every certificate must have a SCT from one of its logs. This aspect of Google's policy remains a point of contention as it's made Google into a single point of failure for certificate issuance worldwide. Google has indicated that it will remove the "one Google log" requirement after SCT auditing becomes operational. In its 2021 policy, Apple instead adopted log operator diversity in a generic way.

The reduction of certificate lifetimes to 398 days made it easier to understand how to comply with the CT requirements. At the time of writing, certificates need two SCTs if they're issued for 180 days or less, or three SCTs otherwise. In addition, at least two distinct log operators must be used, one of which must be Google.

# Certification Authority Authorization

*Certification Authority Authorization* (CAA)[47] provides a way for domain name owners to control which CAs are allowed to issue certificates for their properties. It is intended as a defense-in-depth measure against attacks on the validation process during certificate issuance.

---

[42] Certificate Transparency: SCT Auditing [fsty.uk/t87] (Ivan Ristić, 30 March 2021)

[43] RFC 6962: Certificate Transparency [fsty.uk/t88] (Laurie et al., June 2013)

[44] Certificate Transparency Version 2.0 [fsty.uk/t89] (Laurie et al., last updated 31 August 2021)

[45] Chromium Certificate Transparency Policy [fsty.uk/t90] (Google, retrieved 26 August 2021)

[46] Apple's Certificate Transparency policy [fsty.uk/t82] (Apple, retrieved 26 August 2021)

[47] RFC 8659: DNS CAA Resource Record [fsty.uk/t91] (Hallam-Baker et al., November 2019)

Behind the scenes, CAA relies on DNS for policy distribution. It extends DNS by adding the *CAA Resource Record* (CAA RR), which is used to create authorization entries. Each record contains a *property tag* and an instruction to CAs.

For example, the `issue` tag can be used to allow a CA (identified by its domain name) to issue a certificate for a particular host:

```
certs.example.com      CAA 0 issue "letsencrypt.org"
```

It's possible to specify multiple `issue` tags and give permission for certificate issuance to a number of CAs. The same tag, when it stands alone for a particular hostname and specifies no domain name, can be used to forbid certificate issuance:

```
nocerts.example.com    CAA 0 issue ";"
```

Other tags include `issuewild`, which concerns itself only with wildcard certificates. In tandem with `issue`, it is possible (but not required) to have separate policies for issuance of standard and wildcard certificates. The standard also specifies the `iodef` tag, which defines a communication channel (e.g., an email address) for CAs to report invalid certificate issuance requests back to site owners.

True success of CAA requires wide adoption by CAs because otherwise attackers could always target the noncompliant CAs and get fraudulent certificates from them. In March 2017, the CA/Browser Forum voted to mandate use of CAA by all compliant CAs, effective as of 8 September 2017.[48] Over the years, the CA/Browser Forum provided additional clarifications as to exactly how CAA should be used. This is in line with all other IETF documents, where RFCs focus on technical aspects of a problem, not policy.

Adoption of CAA was made difficult by the fact that it relies on a new DNS RR, which meant that users generally needed to wait for server software to add support for it. Users who outsourced their DNS delivery had to wait until their vendors offered support, and that took a while as well.[49]

Although CAA is easy to write by hand, you may also look at SSL Mate's CAA Record Generator, which may help minimize configuration mistakes and also provides instructions for DNS software that doesn't yet support CAA natively.[50]

SSL Mate also maintains a CAA Test Suite, which can be used verify correct operation of CAA check implementations.[51]

---

[48] Ballot 181—Make CAA Checking Mandatory [fsty.uk/t92] (CA/Browser Forum, March 2017)

[49] Who Supports CAA? [fsty.uk/t93] (SSL Mate, retrieved 1 May 2021)

[50] CAA Record Generator [fsty.uk/t94] (SSL Mate, retrieved 1 May 2021)

[51] CAA Test Suite [fsty.uk/t95] (SSL Mate, retrieved 1 May 2021)

**CAA and DNSSEC**

Like DANE, CAA works best with DNSSEC. Without it, CAs must take special care not to expose themselves to DNS spoofing attacks, which can be avoided by checking CAA records from multiple vantage positions. CAA strongly recommends DNSSEC but doesn't require it. By its nature, DNSSEC makes it easy to implement auditing because valid digital signatures can be retained and used to conclusively prove the instructions provided by domain name owners.

The presence of DNSSEC alters how CAA lookup failures are processed. Normally, after at least one retry, CAs are allowed to proceed with issuance if a CAA lookup fails. With DNSSEC in place, lookup failures prevent issuance.

## CAA Extensions

CAA has been designed to support extensions, enabling other parties and RFCs to introduce custom functionality. It is possible to create new tags but also to extend the existing standardized tags. There is also a facility to support protocol evolution by indicating tag criticality. As with X.509 extensions, a critical tag must be understood by the processor; otherwise, the processing must fail.

### CAA contact extensions

The CA/Browser Forum's Baseline Requirements document two CAA tags to enable domain owners to specify how they wish to be contacted in relation to matters related to certificate issuance. The `contactemail` property tag can be used to publish an email address, while the `contactphone` property tag can be used to publish a phone number.

These extensions came in response to the removal of domain owner information from WHOIS data. With the introduction of GDPR in 2018, WHOIS records became redacted, making it more difficult for CAs to reliably communicate with domain name owners. These new extensions can be used to maintain a reliable communication channel.

### Account URI and domain control validation parameters

The ACME Working Group added two parameters for the existing `issue` and `issuewild` property tags.[52] The `accounturi` parameter supports issuance control at a granularity that's finer than a single CA. Large organizations that consist of many departments may operate multiple accounts served by the same CA and may not wish one department to be able to obtain certificates for properties for which another department is responsible. The `validationmethods` property is directly related to ACME and can be used to restrict which validation methods can be used for certificate validation purposes.

---

[52] RFC 8657: CAA Record Extensions for Account URI and ACME Method Binding [fsty.uk/t96] (November 2019)

# Deploying CAA

Deploying CAA is straightforward, with some caveats. The main challenge comes from the fact that once CAA is deployed, it becomes a hard fail for all CAs that are not authorized. A CAA configuration that unexpectedly prevents issuance will create friction and could possibly lead to availability issues, depending on your environment. Here are some steps you can follow to deploy CAA in a smooth fashion:

1. CAA is best configured at the domain name level, from where it will apply to the entire namespace, including all subdomains. Before you start making DNS changes, you first need to understand the existing issuance patterns. In large organizations, this is often easier said then done. A good CT monitoring solution—one that can provide you with a complete list of certificates for the domain name—is essential here.

2. Armed with a good understanding of the existing arrangements, you can proceed to build the list of authorized CAs. The list should include several organizations you're comfortable working with. For critical properties, you should use at least two reliable vendors. Even if you're planning to predominantly work with only one vendor, allowing two in your CAA configuration means you won't have to scramble even if you need to use an alternative source of certificates in a pinch.

3. Next, procure the CAA identifiers you'll need for the configuration, usually the CAs' main domain names. It's a good idea to create a test subdomain and deploy your future CAA configuration on it first. Then, request a test certificate from each of your allowed CAs.

4. Everyone involved with certificate issuance will need to understand that, from some point in the future on, not all CAs will be accepted. Before making any changes to the DNS, communicate your plans to everyone who may be impacted and ask them to switch to using the authorized CAs. Then spend some time monitoring certificate issuance and ensure that there are no violations.

5. If third parties are in charge of some of your DNS configuration, you need to check if they also handle certificate issuance for the subdomains over which they have control. If they do, they will need to either conform to your CAA policy or configure an overriding CAA configuration at the subdomains to allow issuance from their preferred CAs.

6. Once you're satisfied that your new policy is being followed, make the changes to the CAA configuration. Given the all or nothing nature of CAA, consider having a plan for an emergency rollback or deployment to override CAA configuration for specific situations.

# CAA in Practice

CAA is a welcome addition because it puts control over certificate issuance back in the hands of domain owners. With CAA deployed, the attack surface of a domain name is reduced to just the CAs allowed by policy. After a couple of years of ambiguities and slow rollout, CAA can now be considered to be fully operational and practically useful. But that doesn't mean that there aren't any challenges to deal with.

**Operating CAA at scale**

At scale, CAA may be difficult to operate. In complex environments, many departments share ownership of subdomains on the same domain name, along with possibly difficult issuance practices. By its nature, CAA mismatch is a hard fail that prevents issuance, and that also possibly makes rollouts difficult. An organization needs to first achieve a good level of control over its issuance practices before it can consider deploying CAA. In some situations, deploying CT monitoring alone is sufficient to achieve good visibility of issued certificates and CAA is not necessarily needed.

**Delegation loophole**

CAA is a technical mechanism that is delegated to a third party when the underlying DNS infrastructure is delegated. For example, if a subdomain is delegated to a CDN via a CNAME record, the CDN provider has control over the CAA records for the subdomain and can therefore control what CAs are used for it. This makes sense from a technical perspective as otherwise it would be very difficult to automate certificate issuance. But it also makes it impossible to have full policy control from a central location.

**CAs do not communicate with domain owners**

Support for the `iodef` property tag is not mandated by the CA/Browser Forum. As a result, CAs don't currently inform domain owners of their CAA processing. Such information would be invaluable as an early warning mechanism for subdomain takeover attacks. It would be even better if there were a form of CAA transparency, similar to CT, where all CAA operations are recorded and made available to the public. This would enable large-scale monitors to observe and verify the correct implementation of CAA by all CAs allowed to issue public certificates.

**Opaque implementation at CA level**

The nature of CAA and the CA business is such that CAs must implement their own validation code. Given the state of software development, this is an obvious weakness of the approach. Lack of transparency means that the only way to verify a CA's implementation is to attempt to get a certificate from it while deploying an incompatible issuance policy. Historically, CAA validation issues have been a frequent source of CA issues.[53]

**Monitoring woes**

On the surface, it may seem that CAA can be used to complement CT monitoring—for example, by double-checking the CAA configuration every time a new certificate is observed. In practice, this may be possible in some environments, but not in others. To implement this type of monitoring, one would have to have a full record of all DNS changes for a given host. Otherwise, it's possible that CAA configuration is updated immediately before and after an issuance, making it a change that cannot be easily detected from outside.[54] This type of CAA change is especially common when DNS is delegated to a third party. Despite this problem, CAA is useful as an indicator, but it must be interpreted in the context of the associated DNS infrastructure.

If you'd like to gain a better understanding of how CAA is used and enforced in practice, I recommend reading a deep dive published by Scheitle et al.[55]

Their data is available on *caastudy.github.io*.[56]

# Certificate Lifecycle Automation

When it comes to certificate lifecycle automation, we can talk about two distinct fields of operation. The first field concerns enterprise environments, machine-to-machine communication, and other types of behind-the-scenes operation. The second field is more recent and focuses on end user certificates.

# Enterprise Protocols

The protocols from this group are used, for example, when a network device is deployed for the first time and needs to bootstrap trust. Or if a mobile device needs to become part of an enterprise network. It's something you may have used as an end user, but you're unlikely to have heard about otherwise unless you actually worked on one of these systems.

---

[53] CAA incidents in Mozilla's issue tracker [fsty.uk/t97] (retrieved 2 October 2021)

[54] Hardenize—a startup I built to help organizations take control of their PKI operations—provides comprehensive certificate monitoring that detects new certificates as soon as they are published to CT logs. For every new certificate we see, we immediately run a CAA configuration check. We also maintain CAA configuration history. Despite all this, we occasionally still come across a CAA false positive.

[55] A First Look at Certification Authority Authorization [fsty.uk/t98] (Scheitle et al., April 2018)

[56] CAA Study [fsty.uk/t99] (Scheitle at al., retrieved 1 May 2021)

### Simple Certificate Enrollment Protocol

*Simple Certificate Enrollment Protocol* (SCEP)[57] is an enrollment protocol used by many network operators and platforms—for example, Apple, Cisco, and Microsoft. Although the RFC for it came out in September 2020, by then the protocol had been in service for over two decades with many interoperable implementations.

### Enrollment over Secure Transport

*Enrollment over Secure Transport* (EST)[58] followed SCEP about a decade later. It focuses on the same functionality, but simplifies the protocol by relying on HTTP and TLS for transport.

### Certificate Management Protocol

*Certificate Management Protocol* (CMP)[59] is a more complex protocol that supports a variety of operations related to the X.509 certificate lifecycle. It is often used as the communication channel among end users, registration authorities, and certification authorities.

## Automated Certificate Management Environment

*Automated Certificate Management Environment* (ACME) is a protocol for certificate life-cycle automation designed primarily for use by users that are not closely connected to CAs. This approach is in contrast to other (earlier) protocols that favored enterprise environments. Let's Encrypt,[60] a free and nonprofit CA, designed the first version of ACME for its own use. ACME was subsequently adopted by IETF and continues to grow.[61] As of the time of writing, ACME is in its second version, released in March 2019.[62]

Although ACME is now growing in complexity because it's being extended to support a variety of ancillary use cases, automated issuance is based on a conceptually simple proof of control. For example, to prove ownership of a domain name, an end user may be asked to put a special random number on the associated web site. Another commonly used approach is to put the same number somewhere in the DNS configuration of the domain name.

## Weaknesses

Observed from a strict security perspective, Internet PKI suffers from many weaknesses, some big and some small; I will outline both kinds in this section. However, before we

---

[57] Simple Certificate Enrolment Protocol [fsty.uk/t100] (P. Gutmann, September 2020)

[58] Enrollment over Secure Transport [fsty.uk/t101] (Pritikin et al., October 2013)

[59] Internet X.509 PKI Certificate Management Protocol [fsty.uk/t102] (Adams et al., September 2005)

[60] Let's Encrypt [fsty.uk/t103] (retrieved 16 February 2021)

[61] ACME Working Group [fsty.uk/t104] (IETF, retrieved 1 May 2021)

[62] RFC 8555: Automatic Certificate Management Environment [fsty.uk/t105] (Barnes et al., March 2019)

move to the problems, we must establish the context. In 1995, when the secure Web was just taking off, the Internet was a much different place and much less important than it is now. Back then, we needed encryption mainly to support the new ecommerce economy. Today, ecommerce is well established, but we need and want much more. With the rise of the Internet, for some groups of people, encryption is genuinely a matter of life and death.

But what we have today is a system that does what it was originally designed to do: provide enough security for online shopping. In a wider sense, the system provides us with what I like to call *commercial security*. It's a sort of security that can be achieved with relatively little money, makes web sites go fast, tolerates insecure practices, and does not annoy users too much. The system is controlled by CAs, commercial entities in pursuit of profit, and browser vendors, who are primarily interested in increasing their market share. Although there is some overlap between the interests of these groups and those of end users, there is often a mismatch.

CAs, in particular, just can't win. There are dozens of CAs that together issue more than a billion certificates every year and generally make the world go round. Error rates are very small. Certainly, the security could be improved, but the whole system just works. Despite that, there's a strong resentment from many subscribers because for a long time the only way to get certificates was to pay for them. Most don't want to pay. Those who do pay want to pay as little as possible while still demanding flawless security.

In truth, anyone looking for real security (for whatever meaning of that word) is ultimately not going to get it from an ecosystem that's—for better or worse—afraid to break things for security. That said, problems are being fixed, as you will see later on. Now onto the flaws.

### Permission of domain owners not required for certificate issuance

The biggest problem we have is conceptual: by default, any CA can issue a certificate for any domain name without explicit permission. The key issue here is that there are no technical measures in place to protect us from CAs' omissions and security lapses. This might not have seemed like a big problem early on, when only a few CAs existed, but it's a huge issue today now that there are a great many. It's been said many times: the security of the entire PKI system today is as good as the weakest link, and we have many potentially weak links. All CAs are required to undergo audits, but the quality of those audits is uncertain. For example, DigiNotar, the Dutch CA whose security was completely compromised in 2011, had been audited.

Starting with late 2017, all CAs are required to check CAA policies before certificate issuance, effectively seeking permission. With the introduction of this technology, domain name owners are able to restrict which CAs are allowed to issue certificates for their domain names. Although CAA reduces the problem, its enforcement is administrative rather than technical. Owners can publish their policies, but each individual CA must ensure that they are being followed.

There is a separate question of whether CAs themselves can be trusted to do their jobs well and for the public benefit: Who are those hundreds of organizations that we allow to issue our certificates with relatively little supervision? The fear that they might put their commercial interests above our security needs is sometimes justified. For example, in 2012 Trustwave admitted to issuing a subordinate certificate that would be used for traffic inspection, forging certificates for any web site on the fly.[63] Although Trustwave is the only CA to publicly admit to issuing such certificates, there were rumors that such behavior was not uncommon.

Many fear that governments abuse the system to allow themselves to forge certificates for arbitrary domain names. Can we really be sure that some of the CAs are not just fronts for government operations? And, even if they are not, can we be sure that they can't be compelled to do whatever their governments tell them to? We can't. The only unknown is the extent to which governments will interfere with the operation of commercial CAs.

### No trust agility

Another conceptual problem is lack of trust agility. Relying parties operate root stores that contain a number of CA certificates. A CA thus either is or isn't trusted; there isn't a middle ground. A relying party can remove a CA from the store, but the process is very disruptive and happens only in case of gross incompetence or if a CA is small.

This is not to say that slaps on the wrist or even outright removal of CAs is not possible. For example, there have been relying parties using various types of penalty, like revoking EV privileges from a CA or restricting certificate issuance only to certain top-level domain names. In 2017, browsers stopped trusting new certificates from the WoSign and StartCom certification authorities while continuing to support their already-existing certificates. And in 2018 we saw a complete distrust of all certificates issued by Symantec, one of the biggest CAs at that time.

### Weak domain validation

Issuance of DV certificates that relies on email is based on domain name ownership information retrieved via the insecure WHOIS protocol that is easily spoofed by an active network attack. Furthermore, the interaction is most commonly carried out using email, which in itself can be insecure. It's easy to obtain a fraudulent DV certificate if a domain name is hijacked or if access to the key mailbox is obtained. In recent years, there's been a significant rise of issuance in which validation is done via proof of control. This type of validation is more secure, but attacks such as DNS and BGP route hijacking have been observed.[64] It's possible to attack the implementation

---

[63] Clarifying The Trustwave CA Policy Update [fsty.uk/t106] (Trustwave, 4 February 2012)

[64] Bamboozling Certificate Authorities with BGP [fsty.uk/t107] (Birge-Lee et al., August 2018)

of the validation process at the CA by intercepting network traffic at its end. Some CAs have recently started employing validation from multiple vantage locations as a precautionary measure.

**Revocation does not work**

It is generally seen that revocation does not work in practice. We saw several CA failures in 2011, and, in every case, browsers had to issue patches or use their proprietary blacklisting channels to reliably revoke the misissued certificates.

There are two reasons why that was necessary. First, there's a delay in propagating revocation information to each system. Baseline Requirements allow CRL and OCSP information to stay valid for up to 10 days (12 months for intermediate certificates). This means that it takes at least 10 days for the revocation information to fully propagate. The second problem is the *soft-fail* policy implemented in all browsers in use at the time; they would attempt to obtain revocation information but ignore all failures. An active network attacker can easily suppress OCSP requests, for example, allowing them to use a fraudulent certificate indefinitely.

These problems have caused browser vendors to abandon revocation checking. CRL was the first to suffer, but OCSP followed. The current trend is to use proprietary mechanisms for reliable revocation of intermediate and selected high-value leaf certificates, forgoing revocation checking in all other cases. A possible future solution to this problem is to provide mechanisms for web sites to require revocation checking in one way or another, but there's been little progress so far.

The battle for revocation is largely fought entirely in the browser space; you'll find complete coverage of this topic in the section called "Certificate Revocation" in Chapter 6.

**Interception via custom-installed certificates**

The security of each PKI client depends on the integrity of its root store. Custom roots can be added to operating systems, clients, and devices. In some cases, users are requested or prompted to install these roots. In others, their devices come preinstalled with additional roots or they are added by antivirus software and malware. In corporate environments, interception is frequently mandatory and the intermediates create additional security problems.[65] Even countries have made attempts to mandate installation of custom roots to support large-scale interception. All these practices break the promise of end-to-end encryption.[66]

**Certificate warnings defeat the purpose of encryption**

Possibly the biggest failure of PKI is its lax approach to certificate validation. Many libraries and applications skip validation altogether. Browsers check certificates, but

---

[65] The Security Impact of HTTPS Interception [fsty.uk/t108] (Durumeric et al., February 2017)

[66] You can read much more about these and other PKI problems in the next chapter.

---

when an invalid certificate is encountered, they present their users with warnings that can be bypassed. Early on, studies indicated that anywhere from 30% to 70% of users clicked through certificate warnings, completely defeating security. Improvements were made and came from two directions. One is introduction of a new standard called *HTTP Strict Transport Security*, which, when deployed, instructs compliant browsers to replace warnings with errors that cannot be bypassed. The other direction was continuous refinement of browser user interfaces, which made the warnings more scary and bypass controls more difficult to find.

## Improvement Attempts

Over the years, there have been successful and unsuccessful attempts to improve the security of public PKI. In the former group, we have incremental improvements such as CT and CAA. In the latter group, we see mainly attempts to completely redefine PKI and start from scratch. These ideas failed for two principal reasons, one being that technical security leads to complexity and low usability, and the other that success of any new technology today requires the backing of one of the big players.

### Perspectives

*Perspectives*[67] was the first project to introduce the concept of independent notaries to assist with TLS authentication. Rather than make a decision about certification authenticity alone, clients consult *trusted notaries*. Accessing the same server from different vantage points can defeat attacks that take place close to the client. Notaries can also keep track of a server over a period of time to defeat more advanced attacks. Perspectives launched in 2008 and continues to operate.

### Convergence

*Convergence*[68] was an interesting, but short-lived, conceptual fork of Perspectives with some aspects of the implementation improved. To improve privacy, requests to notaries are proxied through several servers so that the notary that knows the identity of the client does not know the contents of the request. To improve performance, site certificates are cached for extended periods of time. Convergence had momentum when it launched in 2011, but it hasn't seen any activity since 2013.

### Sovereign Keys

The *Sovereign Keys* proposal[69] extends the existing security infrastructure (either CAs or DNSSEC) with additional security guarantees. The main idea is that a domain name can be claimed using a *sovereign key*, which is recorded in publicly verifiable logs. Once a name is claimed, its certificates can be valid only if they are signed by the

---

[67] Perspectives Project [fsty.uk/t109] (retrieved 3 October 2021)

[68] Convergence [fsty.uk/t110] (retrieved 27 May 2014)

[69] The Sovereign Keys Project [fsty.uk/t111] (The EFF, retrieved 27 May 2014)

sovereign key. On the negative side, there seem to be no provisions to recover from the loss of a sovereign key, which makes this proposal very risky. Sovereign Keys was announced in 2011, but it hasn't progressed past the idea stage.

**MECAI**

*MECAI* (which stands for *Mutually Endorsing CA Infrastructure*)[70] is a variation of the notary concept in which the CAs run the infrastructure. Servers do all the hard work and obtain freshness vouchers to deliver to clients. The fact that most of the process happens behind the scenes improves privacy and performance.

# PKI Ecosystem Measurements

Before 2010, there weren't many attempts to research the world's certificates. You could say that in 2010, the era of active scanning and monitoring of the PKI ecosystem began. At Black Hat USA in July of that year, I published a survey of about 120 million domain names (covering all the main TLDs), with an analysis of the observed certificates and the security of the TLS servers.[71] Just a couple of days later, at DEFCON, the Electronic Frontier Foundation (EFF) announced *SSL Observatory*, a similar survey of the entire IPv4 address space.[72] The EFF's most important contribution was making all collected certificate data available to the public, sparking the imagination of many and leading to other scanning efforts. For a while there was a talk of an automated and continuous monitoring effort under the name *Distributed SSL Observatory*,[73] but the project never materialized.

In 2011, Holz et al. published a proper study using a combination of a third-party scan of the entire IPv4 space, their own scanning of secure servers in the Alexa top one million list, and passive monitoring of traffic on their research network.[74] They, too, published their data sets. This was the first time that a rigorous academic analysis of Internet PKI was carried out.

In April 2012, as part of SSL Labs I started a project called *SSL Pulse*, which continues to perform monthly scans of about 150,000 of the most popular secure sites obtained by crawling the Alexa top one million list.[75]

---

[70] Mutually Endorsing CA Infrastructure version 2 [fsty.uk/t112] (Kai Engert, 24 February 2012)

[71] Internet SSL Survey 2010 is here! [fsty.uk/t113] (Ivan Ristić, 29 July 2010)

[72] The EFF SSL Observatory [fsty.uk/t114] (Electronic Frontier Foundation, retrieved 26 May 2014)

[73] HTTPS Everywhere & the Decentralized SSL Observatory [fsty.uk/t115] (Peter Eckersley, 29 February 2012)

[74] The SSL Landscape - A Thorough Analysis of the X.509 PKI Using Active and Passive Measurements [fsty.uk/t116] (Holz et al., Internet Measurement Conference, November 2011)

[75] SSL Pulse [fsty.uk/t117] (SSL Labs, retrieved 2 October 2021)

Also in 2012, the International Computer Science Institute (ICSI) announced their *ICSI Certificate Notary* project, which monitors live network traffic of 10 partner organizations.[76] Their reports were of particular interest because they showed real-life certificates and encryption parameters. The project stopped updating its public web page at some point in 2018. ICSI also used to maintain a visualization of the entire PKI ecosystem and the relationships among CAs in its *Tree of Trust*.[77]

The most comprehensive study to come out so far was published in 2013 by Durumeric et al., who performed 110 Internet-wide scans over a period of 14 months.[78] To carry out their project, they developed a specialized tool called ZMap, which is now open source.[79] If raw data is what you're after, there's no better place to turn to than Rapid7, which offers multiple years' worth of data via its web site.[80]

In February 2014, Microsoft announced that they are extending the telemetry collected by Internet Explorer 11 to include certificate data.[81] The goal was to use the collected information to quickly detect attacks against the users of this browser.

That same month, Delignat-Lavaud et al. published an evaluation of adherence to the CAB Forum guidelines over time.[82] The results showed very good adherence for EV certificates, which always had the benefit of strict requirements, as well as improvements after the introduction of Baseline Requirements.

In 2015, Comodo launched a certificate search engine called crt.sh (pronounced "search") that primarily feeds off Certificate Transparency logs.[83] Comodo also focused on certificate quality and uncovered large numbers of incorrectly constructed certificates.

The University of Michigan continued to expand its research; in late 2015, it launched Censys,[84] then a search engine focused on network security (now a cybersecurity company). Censys continuously crawls the Internet and makes its data freely available to security researchers.

There weren't any fatal flaws or smoking guns discovered, but these efforts provided great visibility into the PKI ecosystem and highlighted a number of important problems that needed fixing. For example, the public was generally unaware that CAs regularly issue certificates for private IP addresses (that anyone can use on their internal networks) and

---

[76] The ICSI Certificate Notary [fsty.uk/t118] (ICSI, retrieved 1 May 2021)

[77] The ICSI SSL Notary: CA Certificates [fsty.uk/t119] (ICSI, retrieved 1 May 2021)

[78] Analysis of the HTTPS Certificate Ecosystem [fsty.uk/t120] (Durumeric et al., Internet Measurement Conference, October 2013)

[79] zmap [fsty.uk/t121] (GitHub, retrieved 1 May 2021)

[80] Open Data [fsty.uk/t122] (Rapid7, retrieved 1 May 2021)

[81] A novel method in IE11 for dealing with fraudulent digital certificates [fsty.uk/t123] (Windows PKI Blog, 21 February 2014)

[82] Web PKI: Closing the Gap between Guidelines and Practices [fsty.uk/t124] (Delignat-Lavaud et al., NDSS, February 2014)

[83] crt.sh [fsty.uk/t125] (Comodo, retrieved 1 May 2021)

[84] Censys [fsty.uk/t126] (University of Michigan, retrieved 1 May 2021)

domain names that are not fully qualified (e.g., *localhost*, *mail*, *intranet*, and such). Further, a great number of misissuances and technical violations were uncovered.

The introduction of mandatory CT via Chrome in 2018 completely changed how we see the PKI ecosystem. Since then, rather than having to waste a lot effort chasing public certificates, we can obtain them with relatively little effort by talking to a handful of CT logs. This is opening new possibilities for monitoring certificate construction[85] and issuance practices.[86]

---

[85] Tracking Certificate Misissuance in the Wild [fsty.uk/t127] (Kumar et al., May 2018)

[86] The Rise of Certificate Transparency and Its Implications on the Internet Ecosystem [fsty.uk/t128] (Scheitle et al., October 2018)

# 5 Attacks against PKI

There's an inherent flaw in how *Public key Infrastructure* (PKI) currently operates: any CA can issue a certificate for any hostname without having to seek approval from the domain name owner. It seems incredible that this system, which has been in use for decades, essentially relies on everyone—hundreds of entities and thousands of people—doing the right thing every time.

There are several attack vectors that could be exploited. In many cases, the validation process is the target. If you can convince a CA that you are the legitimate owner of a domain name, they will issue you a certificate. In other cases, the target is the security of the CAs themselves; if a CA is compromised the attacker can generate certificates for any web site. And in some cases it has come to light that certain CAs issued subordinate certificates that were then used to issue certificates representing web sites at large.

This chapter documents the most interesting incidents and attacks against PKI, starting with the first widely reported incident from 2001 and continuing to the present day.

## Verisign Microsoft Code-Signing Certificate

In January 2001, Verisign got tricked into issuing two code-signing certificates to someone claiming to represent Microsoft. To pull off something like that, the attacker needed to establish a false identity, convince one or more people at Verisign that the request was authentic, and pay the certificate fees of about $400 per certificate. In other words, it required deep knowledge of the system, skill, and determination. The problem was uncovered several weeks later, during a routine audit. The public found out about the incident in late March, after Microsoft put mitigation measures in place.

These fraudulent certificates were not afforded any special level of trust by the operating system, and the code signed by them wouldn't run without warning. Still, they were thought to represent a danger to the users of all Windows operating systems. Because they had been issued under the name "Microsoft Corporation," it was reasonable to believe that most people would approve the installation of the code signed by them. In Microsoft's own words:[1]

> *Programs signed using these certificates would not be able to run automatically or bypass any normal security restrictions. However, the warning dialogue that appears before such programs could run would claim that they had been digitally signed by Microsoft. Clearly, this would be a significant aid in persuading a user to run the program.*

Upon discovering the mistake, Verisign promptly revoked the certificates, but that was not enough to protect the users, because the fraudulent certificates had not included any revocation information. Because of that, in late March 2001, Microsoft was forced to release an emergency software update to explicitly blacklist the offending certificates. This apparently caused a lively debate about the implementation of certificate revocation in Microsoft Windows.[2] One of Microsoft's Knowledge Base articles posted at the time also provided instructions for how to remove a trusted certification authority from the operating system.

# Thawte login.live.com

In the summer of 2008, security researcher Mike Zusman tricked Thawte's certificate validation process to obtain a certificate for *login.live.com*, which was (and still is) Microsoft's single sign-on authentication hub, used by millions.

Mike exploited two facts: first, that Thawte uses email for domain name authentication and second, that Microsoft allows anyone to register `@live.com` email addresses. The most obvious email aliases (e.g., `hostmaster` or `webmaster`) were either reserved or already registered, but as it happened Thawte allowed a particularly wide range of aliases for confirmation purposes. One of the email addresses Thawte accepted for authentication was `sslcertificates@live.com`, and that one was available for registration. As soon as Mike obtained access to this email address, obtaining a certificate was trivial.

Although Mike disclosed the problem in August of 2008,[3] he revealed the name of the exploited CA only later in the year.[4] Exploit details were revealed the following year, in his DEFCON 17 talk.[8]

Seven years later, in 2015, the exact same thing happened to Microsoft again, but on the *live.fi* domain name.[5]

---

[1] Erroneous VeriSign-Issued Digital Certificates Pose Spoofing Hazard [fsty.uk/t129] (Microsoft Security Bulletin MS01-017, 22 March 2001)

[2] Microsoft, VeriSign, and Certificate Revocation [fsty.uk/t130] (Gregory L. Guerin, 20 April 2001)

[3] DNS vuln + SSL cert = FAIL [fsty.uk/t131] (Intrepidus Group's blog, 30 July 2008)

[4] Mike's Thawte tweet [fsty.uk/t132] (31 December 2008)

[5] A Finnish man created this simple email account - and received Microsoft's security certificate [fsty.uk/t133] (Tivi, 18 March 2015)

# StartCom Breach (2008)

On December 19, 2008, Mike Zusman managed to bypass StartCom's domain name validation by exploiting a flaw in StartCom's web site.[6] The flaw in the web application that controlled certificate issuance allowed him to obtain validation for any domain name. (StartCom operates a two-step process: in the first step you prove that you have control over a domain name, and in the second you request a certificate.) Using his discovery, Mike requested and obtained two certificates for domain names he had no authorization for.

His attack was detected very quickly, but only because he proceeded to obtain authorization and request certificates for *paypal.com* and *verisign.com*. As it turned out, StartCom had a secondary control mechanism in the form of a blacklist of high-profile web sites. This defense-in-depth measure flagged Mike's activity and caused all fraudulently issued certificates to be revoked within minutes.

StartCom published a detailed report documenting the attack and events that took place.[7] Mike discussed the events in more detail at his DEFCON 17 talk.[8]

# CertStar (Comodo) Mozilla Certificate

Only a couple of days after Mike Zusman's attack on StartCom, their CTO and COO Eddy Nigg discovered a similar problem with another CA.[9] Following a trail left by some email spam that was trying to mislead him into "renewing" his certificates with another company,[10] Eddy Nigg came across CertStar, a Comodo partner based in Denmark who would happily issue certificates without performing *any* domain name validation. Eddy first obtained a certificate for *startcom.org* and then for *mozilla.org*. Unsurprisingly, a fraudulent certificate for Mozilla's high-profile domain name made a big splash in the press and prompted a lively discussion on the `mozilla.dev.tech.crypto` mailing list.[11]

After verifying all 111 certificates issued by CertStar, Comodo revoked 11 (on top of the two ordered by Eddy Nigg) for which it could not verify authenticity and said that there was no reason to suspect that any of them actually were fraudulent.[12]

---

[6] Nobody is perfect [fsty.uk/t134] (Mike Zusman, 1 January 2009)

[7] Full Disclosure [fsty.uk/t135] (Eddy Nigg, 3 January 2009)

[8] Criminal charges are not pursued: Hacking PKI (Mike Zusman, DEFCON 17, 31 July 2009): slides [fsty.uk/t136] and video [fsty.uk/t137].

[9] (Un)trusted Certificates [fsty.uk/t138] (Eddy Nigg, 23 December 2008)

[10] SSL Certificate for Mozilla.com Issued Without Validation [fsty.uk/t139] (SSL Shopper, 23 December 2008)

[11] Unbelievable! [fsty.uk/t140] (mozilla.dev.tech.crypto, 22 December 2008)

[12] Re: Unbelievable! [fsty.uk/t141](Robin Alden, 25 December 2008)

---

# RapidSSL Rogue CA Certificate

In 2008, a group of researchers led by Alex Sotirov and Marc Stevens carried out a spectacular proof-of-concept attack against Internet PKI in which they managed to obtain a rogue CA certificate that could be used to sign a certificate for any web site in the world.[13]

To fully appreciate this attack, you need to understand the long history of attacks against MD5, shown in the sidebar. You will find that this final blow was the last one in a long line of improving attacks, which started at some point after MD5 had been broken in 2004. In other words, a result of a persistent and sustained effort.

After releasing their work on colliding certificates for different identities in 2006, Marc Stevens and other researchers from his team continued to improve the chosen-prefix collision technique in 2007. They were able to freely generate colliding certificates in a simulation with their own (private) certification authority in an environment they fully controlled. In real life, however, there were several constraints that were preventing exploitation.

## Chosen-Prefix Collision Attack

The goal of the attacker is to create two documents with the same MD5 signature. Most digital signature techniques sign hashes of data (instead of the data directly). If you can construct two documents that both have the same MD5 hash, then a signature for one is also valid for the other. All you now need to do is send one of the two documents (the innocent one) to a trust authority for signing and subsequently copy over the signature to the second document (the forgery).

When it comes to certificates, there's another problem: you can't just send your own certificate to a CA to sign. Instead, you send them some information (e.g., domain name and your public key), and *they* generate the certificate. This is a significant constraint, but it can be overcome.

A collision attack can be carried out using two specially constructed collision blocks that manipulate the hashing algorithm, with the goal of bringing it to the same state for two different inputs. Taking into account both inputs (one in the innocent document and the other in the forgery), the collision blocks undo the differences as far as the hashing algorithm is concerned. This means two things: (1) you must know the prefix of the innocent document in advance—this is where the name *chosen-prefix* comes from—and (2) you must be able to put one of the collision blocks into it.

In practice, it's not possible to put the collision blocks right at the end, which is why the resulting files must also have identical suffixes. In other words, once you get the collision right, you don't want any differences in the files to make the hash different again.

---

[13] MD5 considered harmful today [fsty.uk/t142] (Sotirov et al., 30 December 2008)

---

Chapter 5: Attacks against PKI

# MD5 and PKI Attacks Timeline

- **1991**: Ronald Rivest designs MD5 as a replacement for MD4.

- **1991–1996**: MD5 becomes very popular and is deployed in a wide range of applications. In the meantime, early signs of weaknesses in MD5[14] lead researchers to start recommending that new applications use other, more secure hash functions.[15]

- **2004**: Wang et al. demonstrate a full collision.[16] MD5 is now considered properly broken, but the attacks are not yet sophisticated enough to use in practice.

- **2005**: Lenstra, Wang, and de Weger demonstrate a practical collision,[17] showing two different certificates with the same MD5 hash and thus the same signature. The two certificates differ in the RSA key space, but the remaining information (i.e., the certificate identity) is the same.

- **2006**: Stevens, Lenstra, and de Weger present a new technique,[18] initially called *target collision* but later renamed to *chosen-prefix collision*, which allows for creation of two certificates that have the same MD5 hash but different identities. MD5 is now fully broken, with meaningful attacks practical.

- **2008**: Despite the fact that MD5 has been considered weak for more than a decade and the fact that a meaningful attack was demonstrated in 2006, some certification authorities are still using it to sign new certificates. A group of researchers led by Sotirov and Stevens use an MD5 collision to carry out an attack against PKI and obtain a "rogue" CA certificate, which they can use to generate a valid certificate for any web site.[19]

- **2012**: A very sophisticated malware nicknamed *Flame* (also known as *Flamer* or *Sky-wiper*) is discovered infecting networks in the Middle East.[20] The malware, which is thought to be government sponsored, is later discovered to have used an MD5 collision against a Microsoft CA certificate in order to carry out attacks against the Windows Update code-signing mechanism. After analyzing the evidence, Marc Stevens concludes that the attack had been carried out using a previously unknown attack variant.[21] No one knows how long Flame had been operating, but it is thought that it was active for anywhere from two to five years.

---

[14] Collisions for the compression function of MD5 [fsty.uk/t143] (B. den Boer and A. Bosselaers, *Advances in Cryptology*, 1993)

[15] Cryptanalysis of MD5 Compress [fsty.uk/t144] (H. Dobbertin, May 1996)

[16] Collisions for hash functions MD4, MD5, HAVAL-128, and RIPEMD [fsty.uk/t145] (Wang et al., 2004)

[17] Colliding X.509 Certificates based on MD5-collisions [fsty.uk/t146] (Lenstra, Wang, de Weger, 1 March 2005)

[18] Colliding X.509 Certificates for Different Identities [fsty.uk/t147] (Stevens, Lenstra, de Weger, 23 October 2006)

[19] MD5 considered harmful today [fsty.uk/t142] (Sotirov et al., 30 December 2008)

[20] What is Flame? [fsty.uk/t148] (Kaspersky Lab)

[21] CWI cryptanalyst discovers new cryptographic attack variant in Flame spy malware [fsty.uk/t149] (CWI, 7 June 2012)

---

# Construction of Colliding Certificates

To use the chosen-prefix technique in real life requires that we carry out the attack under constraints imposed by the structure of the document we wish to forge and the constraints imposed by the process in which the document is created and digitally signed.

In the context of digital signatures, those constraints are as follows:

1. Certificates are created by certification authorities, using the information submitted in a CSR.

2. The overall structure of a certificate is determined by the X.509v3 specification. The attacker cannot influence the structure but *can* predict it.

3. Some information that ends up in the certificate is copied over from the CSR. The attacker fully controls that part. Crucially, a certificate will always have a public key that is copied verbatim from the CSR. The key is "random" by design, which means that a specially crafted random-looking collision block won't raise any alarms.

4. Some further information will be added to the certificate by the certification authority. The attacker may be able to influence some parts (e.g., the certificate expiration time), but in general, the best they can do here is predict what the content will be.

From this information, it's clear that the collision prefix will include all the certificate fields that appear before the public key (which is where the collision block will be stored). Because the contents of the collision block depends on the prefix, the entire prefix must be known before the collision data can be created and subsequently sent to the certification authority. Looking at the certificate fields in the prefix, most of them are either known (e.g., the issuer information can be obtained from another certificate issued by the same CA) or provided by the attacker in the CSR (e.g., common name). However, there are two fields controlled by the CA and not known in advance: the certificate serial number and the expiration date. For the time being, we'll assume that the attacker will be able to predict the contents of these two fields; later, we'll examine how that can be achieved.

We also have to figure out what to do with the part that comes after the public key (the suffix). As it turns out, this part consists of several X.509 extensions, all of them known in advance. With proper alignment (MD5 operates on blocks of data), the suffix is simply the same in both certificates.

Thus, the attack process is as follows:

1. Determine what the prefix of the CA-generated certificate will look like and determine what some of the CSR fields need to be.

2. Construct a desired prefix for the rogue certificate.

3. Determine the suffix.

4. Construct collision blocks using the data from the previous three steps.

5. Build a CSR and submit it to the certification authority.

6. Build a rogue certificate by combining the rogue prefix, the second collision block, the suffix, and the signature taken from the real certificate.

> **Note**
>
> The second collision block and the suffix must be part of the forged certificate for the attack to work, but they must be hidden in some way so as not to create problems when the certificate is used. In the RapidSSL attack, the *tumor* was placed into an unimportant X.509v3 comment extension, which is ignored during processing. Someone knowledgeable would be able to spot the anomaly, but virtually no one examines certificates at this level.

## Predicting the Prefix

Now let's go back to discuss how the researchers managed to predict the contents of the two fields (expiration time and serial number) that changed with every certificate. As it turns out, it was a combination of luck and "help" from the CA. Here's how it played out:

- RapidSSL's certificate-issuance process was fully automated, and it always took exactly six seconds from the time a CSR was submitted until the certificate was generated. This meant that it was possible to reliably predict the certificate expiration time down to a second, which was sufficient.

- Rather than randomize the serial number (which is considered best practice), RapidSSL's serial number had been a simple counter incremented by one for every new certificate. This meant that if you obtained two certificates in quick succession you could predict the serial number of the second certificate.

There were six CAs issuing MD5-signed certificates at the time, but it was these two facts about RapidSSL and lack of any other prevention measures[22] that eventually made everything click. However, a big complication was the fact that when using the team's special computing cluster consisting of 200 PlayStation 3 consoles they needed about a day to generate one collision. Thus, they not only had to choose the exact moment in time during which to submit a CSR but also predict the serial number that would be assigned to the certificate.

---

[22] PKI is obviously a tricky business to be in, which is why in cryptography there are all sorts of best practices and defense-in-depth measures designed to kick in when everything else fails. A certificate designed to sign other certificates incorporates a special X.509v3 extension called *Basic Constraints*, with the CA bit set to `true`. This extension also has a parameter called `pathlen`, which can be used to restrict the depth of subsequent CA certificates. If the `pathlen` parameter in RapidSSL's CA certificate had been set to zero (which means that no further subordinate CA certificates are allowed), the rogue CA certificate would have been useless.

---

**Genuine certificate (left):**

- header
- version number "3"
- serial number "643015"
- signature algorithm "MD5 with RSA"
- issuer
  - country "US"
  - organization "Equifax Secure Inc."
  - common name "Equifax Secure Global eBusiness CA-1"
- validity "from 3 Nov. 2008 7:52:02 to 4 Nov. 2009 7:52:02"
- subject
  - country "US"
  - organization "i.broke.the.internet.and.all.i.got.was.this.t-shirt.phreedom.org"
  - organizational unit "GT11029001"
  - organizational unit "See www.rapidssl.com/resources/cps (c)08"
  - organizational unit "Domain Control Validated - RapidSSL(R)"
  - common name "i.broke.the.internet.and.all.i.got.was.this.t-shirt.phreedom.org"
- public key
  - public key algorithm "RSA"
  - modulus (2048 bits) header

```
          B2D3 2581AA28E878B1E5
0AD53C0F36576EA9 5F06410E6BB4CB07
17000000         5BFD6B1C7B9CE8A9

A3C5450B36BB01D1 53AAC3088F6FF84F
3E87874411DC60E0 DF9255F9B8731B54
93C59FD046C460B6 3562CDB9AF1CA86B
1AC95B3C9637C0ED 67EFBBFEC08B9C50

2F29BD83229E8E08 FAAC1370A2587F62
628A11F789F6DFB6 6759731 6FB63168A
B49138CE2EF5B6BE 4CA49449E46510A
4215C9C130E269D5 457DA526BBB961EC

6264F039E1E7BC68 D850519E1D60D3D1
A3A70AF80320A170 011791364F027031
8683DDF70FD8071D 11B31304A5DAF0AE
50B1280E63692A0C 826F8F4733DF6CA2

0692F14F45BED930 36A32B8CD677AE35
637F4E4C9A934836 D99F
```

- extensions
  - public exponent "65537"
  - key usage "..."
  - subject key identifier "..."
  - crl distribution points "..."
  - authority key identifier "..."
  - extended key usage "..."
  - basic constraints "CA = FALSE"
- signature algorithm "MD5 with RSA"
- signature

```
A721028DD10EA280 7725FD4360158FEC
EF9047D484421526 111CCDC23C1029A9
B6DFAB577591DAE5 2BB390451C306356
3F8AD950FAED586C C065AC6657DE1CC6
763BF5000E8E45CE 7F4C90EC2BC6CDB3
B48F62D0FEB7C526 7244EDF6985BAECB
D195F5DA08BE6846 B175C8EC1D8F1E7A
94F1AA5378A245AE 54EAD19E74C87667
```

**Collision blocks (middle):**

block 1, block 2, block 3, block 4, block 5, block 6, block 7, block 8

birthday bits (96)

block 9 — 1st near collision block

block 10 — 2nd near collision block

block 11 — 3rd near collision block

block 12 (identical), block 13 (identical), block 14 (identical), block 15 (identical)

(identical)

Byte offsets: 4, 9, 14, 29, 31, 44, 74, 121, 153, 157, 170, 245, 266, 317, 366, 441, 445, 460, 474, 500, 512, 576, 640, 704, 730, 735, 741, 757, 788, 832, 849, 882, 896, 913, 927 (left); 0, 64, 102, 128, 266, 320, 384, 448, 477, 500 (middle); 4, 9, 12, 27, 29, 42, 72, 119, 151, 153, 213, 216, 231, 238, 370, 375, 379, 396, 413, 444 (right)

**Collided certificate (right):**

- header
- version number "3"
- serial number "65"
- signature algorithm "MD5 with RSA"
- issuer
  - country "US"
  - organization "Equifax Secure Inc."
  - common name "Equifax Secure Global eBusiness CA-1"
- validity "from 31 Jul. 2004 0:00:00 to 2 Sep. 2004 0:00:00"
- subject
  - common name "MD5 Collisions Inc. (http://www.phreedom.org/md5)"
- public key
  - public key algorithm "RSA"
  - header
  - modulus (1024 bits)

```
BAA659C92C28D62A B0F8ED9F46A4A437
EE0E196859D1B303 9951D6169A5E376B
15E00E4BF58464F8 A3DB416F35D59B15
1FDBC4385270B197 5E8FA0B5F77E39F0
32AC1EAD44D2B3FA 48C3CE919B8CF49C
7CE15AF5C837689A 83DEE7CA20973142
73159168F488AFF9 2828C5E90F73B017
4B134C9975D044E6 7E086C1AF24F1B41
```

  - public exponent "65537"
  - key usage "..."
  - basic constraints "CA = TRUE"
  - subject key identifier "..."
- authority key identifier "..."
- header
- extensions
  - tumor (Netscape comment)

```
33000000         275E39E089610F4E

A3C5450B36BB01D1 53AAC3088F6FF84F
3E87874411DC60E0 DF9255F9B8731B54
93C59FD046C460B6 3562CDB9AF1CA869
1AC95B3C9637C0ED 67EFBBFEC08B9C50

2F29BD83229E8E08 FAAC1370A2587F62
628A11F789F6DFB6 67593716FB63168A
B49138CE2EF5B6BE 4CA49449E46510A
4215C9C130E269D5 457DA526BBB961EC

6264F039E1E7BC68 D850519E1D60D3D1
A3A70AF80320A170 011791364F027031
8683DDF70FD8071D 11B31304A5DCF0AE
50B1280E63692A0C 826F8F4733DF6CA2

0692F14F45BED930 36A32B8CD677AE35
637F4E4C9A934836 D99F0203010001A3
81BD3081BA300E06 03551D0F0101FF04
04030204F0301D06 03551D0E04160414

CDA683FAA56037F7 96371729DE4178F1
878955E7303B0603 551D1F0434303230
30A02BAA02C862A68 7474703A2F2F6372
6C2E6765 6F747275 73742E636F6D2F63

726C732F676C6F6F62 616C6361312E6372
6C301F0603551D23 041830168014EEA8
A07472506B44B7C9 23D8FBA8FFB3576B
686C301D0603551D 250416301406082B

0601050507030106 082B060105050703
02300C0603551D13 0101FF04023000 "
```

- signature algorithm "MD5 with RSA"
- signature

```
A721028DD10EA280 7725FD4360158FEC
EF9047D484421526 111CCDC23C1029A9
B6DFAB577591DAE5 2BB390451C306356
3F8AD950FAED586C C065AC6657DE1CC6
763BF5000E8E45CE 7F4C90EC2BC6CDB3
B48F62D0FEB7C526 7244EDF6985BAECB
D195F5DA08BE6846 B175C8EC1D8F1E7A
94F1AA5378A245AE 54EAD19E74C87667
```

Their approach was to carry out the attack on Sunday evenings, during the CA's least busy period. They would obtain the value of the serial number counter on a Friday and aim to submit a CSR so that the resulting serial number would be higher by 1,000. As the time of the attack approached, they would push the counter up by requesting new certificates, aiming to get as close to the 1,000 mark as possible. During each weekend, they had enough time to submit three attempts. After three unsuccessful weekends, they succeeded on the fourth.

## What Happened Next

While planning the attack, the researchers took measures to minimize any potential fallout. For example, the rogue certificate had been created with an expiration date in the past, which meant that even if the private key behind it was leaked the certificate would have been useless. The key parties in charge of browser trust stores (e.g., Microsoft, Mozilla, etc.) were contacted prior to the publication of the attack, which allowed them to preemptively blacklist the rogue CA certificate. RapidSSL had also been given an advance warning,[23] and that caused them to speed up their migration to SHA1. They upgraded to SHA1 very quickly, within hours of the public announcement.[24] Full details of the chosen-prefix collision technique were released only later, after the researchers had been satisfied that it was safe to do so.

In the end, the attack cost only the $657 in certificate costs,[25] but the researchers had access to a cluster of 200 PS3 computers. Equivalent CPU power on EC2 would have cost about $20,000. When the attack was announced, the researchers estimated that with an improved approach they could repeat the attack in a day for only $2,000.

## Comodo Resellers Breaches

A series of incidents unfolded in 2011, starting with another Comodo breach in March. The first attack took place on March 15th, when one of Comodo's registration authorities (RAs) was "thoroughly compromised" (in the words of Robin Alden, then the CTO of Comodo), leading to the issuance of nine certificates for seven web sites.[26] The sites in question were:

- *addons.mozilla.org*
- *global trustee*
- *google.com*

---

[23] Verisign and responsible disclosure [fsty.uk/t150] (Alexander Sotirov, 6 January 2009)

[24] This morning's MD5 attack - resolved [fsty.uk/t151] (Tim Callan, 30 December 2008)

[25] Even though they requested a large number of certificates, most of them were reissued, which RapidSSL allowed for free.

[26] Comodo Report of Incident [fsty.uk/t152] (Comodo, 22 March 2011)

---

- *login.live.com*
- *login.skype.com*
- *login.yahoo.com*
- *mail.google.com*

Clearly, with exception of the "global trustee" certificate whose purpose is unclear, all the certificates were for key web sites that hundreds of millions of users visit every day. Fortunately, the attack was detected very quickly and all the fraudulent certificates revoked within hours. It wasn't even clear if all of these certificates were retrieved by the attacker. Comodo saw only the Yahoo certificate hit their OCSP responder (and only twice) and none of the other certificates.[27]

The next day, Comodo started to inform various other relevant parties, and the patching process began.[28] Although Comodo didn't disclose the identity of the compromised RA, it was later alleged by the attacker that it was an Italian company, Instant SSL. The attacks were disclosed to the public on March 22nd by Comodo, Mozilla, Microsoft, and others.

An interesting fact is that some people learned about the attacks several days earlier from clues in the Chrome source code (which is publicly available). Jacob Appelbaum wrote about his discovery on the Tor blog.[29]

Comodo went on to disclose two further reseller compromises on March 26th, although one of them later turned out to be a false report. The other report was genuine but didn't result in any fraudulent certificates being issued. Apparently, the security measures introduced after the March 15th incident were effective and prevented the attacker from issuing further certificates.[30]

Also on March 26th, the attacker himself started to communicate with the public,[31] and that's when we learned about ComodoHacker (the name he chose for himself), which later turned out to be a much bigger story, spanning months of activity, many CAs, and many incidents. You can read more about him in the sidebar later in this chapter.

In May, Comodo was again in the news because one of their resellers, ComodoBR, was found to have an SQL injection vulnerability on their web site.[32] The attacker used the vulnerability to retrieve private customer data (including certificate signing requests), but there were no other PKI-related consequences.

---

[27] Strictly speaking, this is not an entirely reliable indicator of certificate use, because an active network attacker can suppress all OCSP traffic from the victim.

[28] Bug 642395: Deal with bogus certs issued by Comodo partner [fsty.uk/t153] (Bugzilla@Mozilla, reported 17 March 2011)

[29] Detecting Certificate Authority compromises and web browser collusion [fsty.uk/t154] (Jacob Appelbaum, 22 March 2011)

[30] RE: Web Browsers and Comodo Announce A Successful Certificate Authority Attack, Perhaps From Iran [fsty.uk/t155] (Robin Alden, 29 March 2011)

[31] A message from Comodo Hacker [fsty.uk/t156] (ComodoHacker, 26 March 2011)

[32] New hack on Comodo reseller exposes private data [fsty.uk/t157] (The Register, 24 May 2011)

---

In the end, this series of incidents exposed how operating a large network of partners on a trust basis alone is entirely unfeasible, especially in a complex ecosystem such as PKI. Comodo claimed that after the 2008 incident only 9% of their partners were left with the ability to fully control certificate issuing, but that was clearly still too many. After the first 2011 incident, no resellers were left able to issue certificates without further validation from Comodo.

More importantly, these incidents showed how Comodo (and possibly other CAs) had not been maintaining a realistic threat model. This was acknowledged by Robin Alden in a post on `mozilla.dev.security.policy` (emphasis mine):

> *We were dealing with the threat model that the RA could be Underperforming [sic] with, or trying to avoid doing, their validation duty (neither of which were the case for this RA),* **but what we had not done was adequately consider the new (to us) threat model of the RA being the subject of a targeted attack and entirely compromised.**

# StartCom Breach (2011)

In the summer of 2011, StartCom was again targeted, supposedly by the same person who had previously attacked Comodo.[33] Because of the incident, which took place on June 15th, StartCom stopped issuing new certificates for about a week. The following message appeared on their web site:

> *Due to an attack on our systems and a security breach that occurred at the 15th of June, issuance of digital certificates and related services has been suspended. Our services will remain offline until further notice. Subscribers and holders of valid certificates are not affected in any form. Visitors to web sites and other parties relying on valid certificates are not affected. We apologize for the temporary inconvenience and thank you for your understanding.*

Apparently, no fraudulent certificates were issued and the attacker—who might have gained access to some sensitive data and come very close to the company's precious root key[34]—did not cause any significant long-term damage. The company never followed up with an official report about the incident, acknowledging the incident only via a post on Eddy Nigg's blog.[35]

# DigiNotar

DigiNotar was a Dutch CA that was in the business of issuing certificates to the general public as well as handling the PKI aspects of the Dutch e-government program PKIoverheid

---

[33] Another status update message [fsty.uk/t158] (ComodoHacker, 6 September 2011)

[34] Response to some comments [fsty.uk/t159] (ComodoHacker, 7 September 2011)

[35] Cyber War [fsty.uk/t160] (Eddy Nigg, 9 September 2011)

(*overheid* means government in Dutch). In 2011, DigiNotar became the first CA to be completely compromised, with fraudulent certificates used in real, and possibly very serious, active network attacks. Needless to say, DigiNotar's root certificates were all revoked and the company went out of business, declaring voluntary bankruptcy in September 2011.

Table 5.1. Common names used in rogue certificates issued by the DigiNotar attacker

| | | |
|---|---|---|
| *.*.com | *.*.org | *.10million.org (2) |
| *.android.com | *.aol.com | *.azadegi.com (2) |
| *.balatarin.com (3) | *.comodo.com (3) | *.digicert.com (2) |
| *.globalsign.com (7) | *.google.com (26) | *.JanamFadayeRahbar.com |
| *.logmein.com | *.microsoft.com (3) | *.mossad.gov.il (2) |
| *.mozilla.org | *.RamzShekaneBozorg.com | *.SahebeDonyayeDigital.com |
| *.skype.com (22) | *.startssl.com | *.thawte.com (6) |
| *.torproject.org (14) | *.walla.co.il (2) | *.windowsupdate.com (3) |
| *.wordpress.com (14) | addons.mozilla.org (17) | azadegi.com (16) |
| Comodo Root CA (20) | CyberTrust Root CA (20) | DigiCert Root CA (21) |
| Equifax Root CA (40) | friends.walla.co.il (8) | GlobalSign Root CA (20) |
| login.live.com (17) | login.yahoo.com (19) | my.screenname.aol.com |
| secure.logmein.com (17) | Thawte Root CA (45) | twitter.com (18) |
| VeriSign Root CA (21) | wordpress.com (12) | www.10million.org (8) |
| www.balatarin.com (16) | www.cia.gov (25) | www.cybertrust.com |
| www.Equifax.com | www.facebook.com (14) | www.globalsign.com |
| www.google.com (12) | www.hamdami.com | www.mossad.gov.il (5) |
| www.sis.gov.uk (10) | www.update.microsoft.com (4) | |

## Public Discovery

The incident came to light on August 27th, when an Iranian Gmail user reported intermittent problems when accessing his email account.[36] According to the testimony, there were daily "downtime" periods of 30 to 60 minutes, during which access was impossible due to an unusual certificate warning message. As it turned out, the downtime described by the user was caused by an active network attack that Chrome detected and prevented using its proprietary public key pinning mechanism.

In the days that followed, we learned that the reported problem was actually part of a very large attack on a scale previously unheard of, affecting an estimated 300,000 IP addresses. Virtually all of the IP addresses were in Iran. The intercepting certificates were all issued by DigiNotar. But how was that possible?

[36] Is This MITM Attack to Gmail's SSL ? [fsty.uk/t161] (alibo, 27 August 2011)

# Fall of a Certification Authority

Faced with a huge security incident that affected its digital infrastructure, the Dutch government immediately took control of DigiNotar and hired an external security consultancy, Fox-IT, to investigate. Fox-IT published their initial report[37] one week later, on September 5th. Here is the most relevant part of the report:

> The most critical servers contain malicious software that can normally be detected by anti-virus software. The separation of critical components was not functioning or was not in place. We have strong indications that the CA-servers, although physically very securely placed in a tempest proof environment, were accessible over the network from the management LAN.

> The network has been severely breached. All CA servers were members of one Windows domain, which made it possible to access them all using one obtained user/password combination. The password was not very strong and could easily be brute-forced.

> The software installed on the public web servers was outdated and not patched.

> No antivirus protection was present on the investigated servers.

> An intrusion prevention system is operational. It is not clear at the moment why it didn't block some of the outside web server attacks. No secure central network logging is in place.

The full report was released one year later, in August 2012; at 100 pages, it provides the most detailed report of a CA breach ever seen.[38] From the report, we learned that the initial attack occurred on June 17th, when a public-facing web server running a vulnerable content-management application was breached. From there, it took the attacker until July 1st to break into the most secure network segment, where the root material was placed. This network segment was not connected to the Internet directly, but the attacker was able to tunnel into it from less important systems.

The first batch of 128 rogue certificates was issued on July 10th, roughly a week from when the attacker first had access to the CA servers themselves. Several other batches followed, arriving at a total of at least 531 certificates for 53 unique identities. Due to the scale of the breach, the actual number of rogue certificates is not known; the logs were tampered with, and many of the certificates later discovered in the wild could not be found in the appropriate databases.

---

[37] DigiNotar public report version 1 [fsty.uk/t162] (Fox-IT, 5 September 2011)

[38] Black Tulip Update [fsty.uk/t163] (Dutch government, 13 August 2012)

Some of the certificates were not intended for well-known web sites but were used to carry various messages instead. The phrases in the following table were seen in various places in the certificates.

Table 5.2. Messages seen embedded in the rogue certificates (it's not clear if the translations are accurate)

| Original message | Translation |
| --- | --- |
| Daneshmande Bi nazir | Peerless scientist |
| Hameye Ramzaro Mishkanam | Will break all cyphers |
| Janam Fadaye Rahbar | I will sacrifice my life for my leader |
| Ramz Shekane Bozorg | Great cryptanalyst |
| Sahebe Donyaye | Possessor of the world (God) |
| Sare Toro Ham Mishkanam | I will break Tor too |
| Sarbaze Gomnam | Unknown soldier |

It also transpired that DigiNotar had discovered the intrusion on July 19th and, with the help of an outside consultancy (not Fox-IT), cleaned up their systems by the end of July. Unfortunately, the damage had already been done. Presumably under the impression that the incident had been contained, DigiNotar quietly revoked a small number of fraudulent certificates (the ones they knew about), and—recklessly—failed to inform anyone.

# Man-in-the-Middle Attacks

Given the scale of the compromise, it is doubtful that a prompt disclosure would have saved DigiNotar, but it would have definitely stopped the attackers from using the rogue certificates. We know this because the rogue certificates were generated with embedded OCSP information, and the investigators were able to track the certificate deployment by examining the logs of DigiNotar's OCSP responder.[39]

Initially, after the certificates were generated the logs showed few requests: most likely a result of testing by the attacker. The first signs of mass deployment were starting to show on August 4th, with continuous increases in volume until August 29th, which was the day on which browsers revoked the DigiNotar root certification and killed all rogue certificates. We know from attacked users that the attack was not constant but occurred in bursts. Perhaps there was a reason for such behavior, such as limitations of the attack method (DNS cache

---

[39] When a TLS client encounters a certificate that contains OCSP information, it contacts the designated OCSP server to determine if the certificate has been revoked. This method of tracking is not foolproof, because the MITM attacker can suppress all traffic to the OCSP server. Browsers tend to fail quietly when they encounter OCSP communication failures.

Chapter 5: Attacks against PKI

poisoning was mentioned as the likely approach[40] used) or simply an inability to cope with a large amount of traffic at any one time.

Figure 5.2. DigiNotar OCSP activity in August 2011 [Source: Fox-IT]

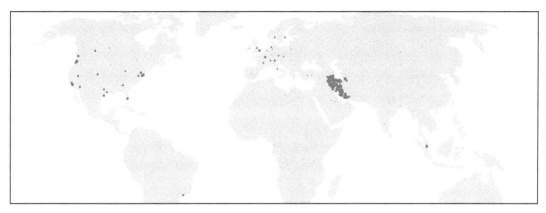

Besides, the attackers were likely only interested in collecting Gmail passwords, and—assuming their capacity was limited—once they saw a password from one IP address they could move on to intercept another. With a password cache, they could abuse the accounts at their leisure (people rarely change their passwords) by connecting to Gmail directly.

All in all, there were exactly 654,313 OCSP requests to check the revocation status of the rogue Google certificate, submitted from 298,140 unique IP addresses. About 95% of those were within Iran, with the remaining IP addresses identified as the Tor exit nodes, proxies, and virtual private networks from around the world.

## ComodoHacker Claims Responsibility

ComodoHacker claimed responsibility for the DigiNotar breach, posting from his Pastebin account on September 5th.[41] He followed up with three further posts, as well as the calc.exe binary signed with one of the certificates, thus offering definitive proof that he was involved in the incident. The posts contain some details about the attacks, which match the information in the official report (which was released to the public only much later).

> *How I got access to 6 layer network behind internet servers of DigiNotar, how I found passwords, how I got SYSTEM privilage [sic] in fully patched and up-*

---

[40] DNS cache poisoning is an attack against DNS infrastructure in which the attacker exploits weaknesses in the DNS protocol as well as some implementations. Using clever tricks along with packet flooding, it might be possible to trick a caching DNS server into delegating domain name decisions from the actual owner to the attacker. If that happens, the attacker determines what IP addresses are returned for domain names in the attacking space. A successful attack will impact all users connecting to the caching DNS server. During the DigiNotar MITM attacks in Iran, some users reported that changing their DNS configuration from their ISP's servers to other servers (e.g., Google's) stopped the attacks.

[41] Striking Back... [fsty.uk/t164] (ComodoHacker, 5 September 2011)

---

*to-date system, how I bypassed their nCipher NetHSM, their hardware keys, their RSA certificate manager, their 6th layer internal "CERT NETWORK" which have no ANY connection to internet, how I got full remote desktop connection when there was firewalls that blocked all ports except 80 and 443 and doesn't allow Reverse or direct VNC connections, more and more and more...*

---

## Who Is ComodoHacker?

ComodoHacker made his public appearance in 2011 and left a mark on the PKI with a string of attacks against several certification authorities. The first batch of attacks came in March 2011, when several Comodo partners were breached. Rogue certificates were issued but also quickly discovered, which prevented their exploitation.

StartCom appears to have been attacked in June, and the attacker appears to have had some success, but, according to both parties, no fraudulent certificates were issued. StartCom stopped issuing certificates but never provided any substantial details about the incident.

Then there was the DigiNotar attack, which resulted in a full compromise of the DigiNotar certification authority and shook up the entire PKI ecosystem.

After being mentioned as a successful target in one of ComodoHacker's messages, GlobalSign felt it prudent to halt certificate issuance for a period of time and investigate. They subsequently found that their public-facing web server, which is not part of the CA infrastructure, had been breached.[42] The only casualty was the private key for the *www.globalsign.com* domain name.

Immediately after the Comodo incidents, the hacker started communicating with the public via the ComodoHacker account on Pastebin[43] and left 10 messages in total. After the DigiNotar incident, he also had a brief period during which he was posting on Twitter, under the name *ich sun* and handle *ichsunx2*.[44] Although he appeared to have initially enjoyed the attention and even gave interviews, his last communication was via Twitter in September 2011.

---

It's not clear if ComodoHacker was actually involved with the attacks in Iran, however. Although he was happy to claim responsibility for the CA hacks, ComodoHacker distanced himself from the MITM attacks. His second DigiNotar post contained the following sentence:

*I'm single person, do not AGAIN try to make an ARMY out of me in Iran. If someone in Iran used certs I have generated, I'm not one who should explain.*

---

[42] September 2011 Security Incident Report [fsty.uk/t165] (GlobalSign, 13 December 2011)

[43] ComodoHacker's Pastebin [fsty.uk/t166] (retrieved 7 August 2014)

[44] ich sun on Twitter [fsty.uk/t167] (retrieved 7 August 2014)

In a subsequent post, he repeated that statement:

> [...] I'm the only hacker, just I have shared some certs with some people in Iran, that's all... Hacker is single, just know it

# DigiCert Sdn. Bhd.

In November 2011, a Malaysian certification authority, DigiCert Sdn. Bhd., was found to be issuing dangerously weak certificates. This company, which is not related to the better known and US-based DigiCert, Inc., was operating as an intermediate certification authority on a contract with Entrust and, before that, CyberTrust (Verizon). Twenty-two certificates were found to be not only weak but lacking in other critical aspects:

**Weak 512-bit keys**

A key that is only 512 bits long can be relatively easily refactored using only brute force.[45] With the key in hand, a malicious party can impersonate the victim web site without triggering certificate warnings.

**Missing usage restrictions**

Certificates are expected to carry usage restrictions in the *Extended Key Usage* (EKU) extension. Even though DigiCert Sdn. Bhd. had been contractually restricted to issuing only web site certificates, because some of their certificates were missing the usage restrictions they could be used for any purpose: for example, code signing.

**Missing revocation information**

None of the 22 certificates contained revocation information. This meant that after the invalid certificates were discovered there was no way to reliably revoke them.

As it turned out, the problem was discovered only after one of the public keys was found to have been broken by brute force and used to sign malware.[46] After finding out about the problem, Entrust revoked the intermediate certificate[47] and informed the browser vendors. Within a week, both Entrust and CyberTrust revoked their respective intermediate certificates, Mozilla informed the public via a post on their blog,[48] and browser vendors released updates to explicitly blacklist the intermediate certificates and the known weak server certificates. In the aftermath, DigiCert, Inc. was left having to explain the name confusion to their customers.[49]

---

[45] But not brute force in the sense that all possible numbers are tried. It's more efficient to use one of the integer factorization methods, for example, the *general number field sieve* (GNFS).

[46] Bug #698753: Entrust SubCA: 512-bit key issuance and other CPS violations; malware in the wild [fsty.uk/t168] (Bugzilla@Mozilla, 1 November 2011)

[47] Entrust Bulletin on Certificates Issued with Weak 512-bit RSA Keys by Digicert Malaysia [fsty.uk/t169] (Entrust, retrieved 3 July 2014)

[48] Revoking Trust in DigiCert Sdn. Bhd Intermediate Certificate Authority [fsty.uk/t170] (Mozilla Security Blog, 3 November 2011)

[49] DigiCert, Inc. Of No Relation to Recent "Digi" Insecure Certificates [fsty.uk/t171] (DigiCert, Inc., 1 November 2011)

# Flame

In May 2012, security researchers began analyzing a new strand of malware that was making rounds chiefly in the Middle East. The malware in question, called *Flame*[20] (also known as *Flamer* or *Skywiper*), turned out to be the most advanced yet: over 20 MB in size, over 20 attack modules (the usual malware stuff, such as network sniffing, microphone activation, file retrieval, and so on), and built using components such as a lightweight relational database (SQLite) and a scripting language (Lua). It was all done in such a way that it remained undetected for a very long time (which meant low or undetectable failures; it was clearly not an average software development job).

Overall, Flame was discovered on about 1,000 systems in what seemed to be very targeted attacks.[50] Soon thereafter, the creators of the Flame malware issued a suicide command, with the intention that all instances would delete themselves. Still, many instances of the malware and several instances of the command and control servers were captured and analyzed.[51]

Figure 5.3. Flame activity [Source: Kaspersky Lab]

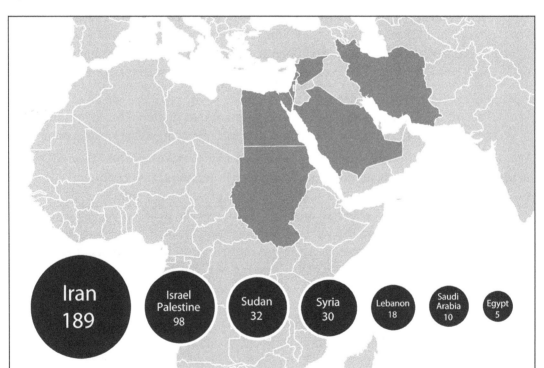

---

[50] Identification of a New Targeted Cyber-Attack [fsty.uk/t172] (MAHER, 28 May 2012)

[51] Flame / Skywiper / Flamer reports [fsty.uk/t173] (CrySyS Lab, 31 May 2012)

---

Chapter 5: Attacks against PKI

# Flame against Windows Update

What happened next stunned everyone. It transpired that one of the functions of the Flame malware was an attack against the Windows Update mechanism, which could be used to propagate to Windows installations on the local network. The surprising part was the fact that Flame used a cryptographic attack to achieve it.[52] On top of that, the specific cryptographic technique wasn't previously known.

Once on a local network, subverting Windows Update turned out to be simple. Internet Explorer supports *Web Proxy Auto-Discovery* (WPAD), which is a protocol that programs can use to find HTTP proxies on the local network. An adversary with access to the local network can advertise as a proxy and gain access to the victim's HTTP(S) traffic. Flame did exactly this and included a simple web server that posed as a Windows Update server to advertise available "updates" laced with malicious code.[53]

Windows Update does not appear to use TLS (a simple test on my desktop showed all update traffic in plaintext), but Microsoft does use code signing for their updates, which means that no one should be able to create binaries that would be accepted as originating from Microsoft. The twist in the story was that Flame was somehow able to sign all its binaries as Microsoft.

# Flame against Windows Terminal Services

When Microsoft started talking about the weaknesses attacked by Flame, a story of deep incompetence unfolded. In order to operate Terminal Services licensing, upon activation each Terminal Server installation would receive a special subordinate CA certificate. The sub-CA would then be used to create end-user licenses. Microsoft made several critical errors when designing this system:

1. The main Terminal Services CA certificate (which was used to issue subordinate CAs allocated to individual customers) was issued from the same trusted root as the Windows Update CA.

2. The parent Terminal Services CA was allowed to be used for licensing and—for some unexplained reason—code signing.

3. Subordinate CA certificates had no usage restrictions, which meant that they inherited the restrictions of the parent certificate.

What this meant was that every single Terminal Server customer was given an unrestricted subordinate CA certificate they could use to sign Windows Update binaries, *with no hacking required*.

---

[52] Analyzing the MD5 collision in Flame [fsty.uk/t174] (Alex Sotirov, 11 June 2012)

[53] Snack Attack: Analyzing Flame's Replication Pattern [fsty.uk/t175] (Alexander Gostev, 7 June 2012)

Fortunately for Microsoft, such certificates could "only" be used against Windows XP machines. The subordinate CA certificates contained a proprietary X.509 extension called Hydra, and it was marked critical.[54]

The Windows XP code for certificate checking ignores critical extensions, but Windows Vista (released worldwide on 30 January 2007) and subsequent Windows versions understand critical extensions and handle them properly. This meant that the Flame authors had to find a way to obtain a certificate without the Hydra extension.

## Flame against MD5

The other critical mistake made by Microsoft when designing the Terminal Server licensing scheme was using MD5 signatures for the certificates. The other errors (discussed in the previous section) were relatively subtle and required a good understanding of PKI to detect, but at the time that Microsoft's system was designed, MD5 was widely known to be insecure. There had been a very effective demonstration of the insecurity of MD5 in 2008, with the generation of the rogue CA certificate in the RapidSSL attack. To put it into perspective, Microsoft wouldn't even allow MD5 certificates in their own root certificate program at that time, but they were used for Terminal Server licensing.

If you've read the earlier section describing the RapidSSL attack and the generation of a rogue CA certificate, you probably know what happened next: Flame used a chosen-prefix collision attack against MD5 in order to generate a rogue CA certificate. The attack was conceptually the same as the RapidSSL attack described earlier. Here's what we know:

1.  Insecure MD5 signatures were used, which opened up the system to cryptographic attacks.

2.  Certificate issuance was automated and the timing controlled by the attacker. All fields except certificate validity and certificate serial number were known in advance.

3.  Certificate validity was predictable, requiring second precision.

4.  Serial numbers were not serial as in the RapidSSL case, but they were predictable (number of milliseconds since boot, followed by two fixed bytes, followed by a serial certificate number) and required millisecond precision.

The millisecond precision required probably made the task much more difficult and required a good network connection in order to minimize jitter. Access to a high-powered computing cluster would have sped up collision search and improved accuracy. We do not know how many attempts were needed (perhaps Microsoft knows, if they're keeping good records of the licensing activity), but the attackers were obviously successful in the end.

---

[54] In PKI, when an extension is marked critical, certificate chain validation can be successful only if the client (performing the validation) understands the extension. Otherwise, validation fails. The idea behind this feature is that a critical extension might contain some information of which understanding is required for robust validation.

Marc Stevens, the principal force behind the previously published chosen-prefix collision attack technique, analyzed the rogue certificate and determined that:[55]

> *Flame used a chosen-prefix collision attack. [...] Flame used a birthday search followed by 4 near-collision blocks to obtain a collision.*
>
> *These collision bits were hidden inside the RSA modulus in the original cert and inside the issuerUniqueID field in the evil cert. Using my forensic tool I was able to retrieve the near-collision blocks of the original cert (that is not available and might never be) and the chaining value before the first near-collision block. Using this information I was able to reconstruct the 4 differential paths. These differential paths clearly show that a new variant chosen-prefix collision attack was used as well as a new differential path construction algorithm that are not in the literature.*

Whoever designed Flame and carried out the attacks against Microsoft obviously had at their disposal serious hardware, a capable team of developers, and access to world-class cryptographers.

---

## Counter Cryptanalysis

Collision attacks against hash functions used for signatures are a real danger. Even though MD5 troubles are largely behind us, SHA1, which is still very widely used, is also known to be weak. In an ideal world, we would have stopped using it by now. In reality, it will stay in use for a couple more years, because we have to deal with a massive ecosystem and huge inertia.

In response to this problem, Marc Stevens invented *counter-cryptanalysis*,[56] a system of looking for traces of successful collision attacks in certificates, as described in the abstract of the research paper:

> *We introduce counter-cryptanalysis as a new paradigm for strengthening weak cryptographic primitives against cryptanalytic attacks. Redesigning a weak primitive to more strongly resist cryptanalytic techniques will unavoidably break backwards compatibility. Instead, counter-cryptanalysis exploits unavoidable anomalies introduced by cryptanalytic attacks to detect and block cryptanalytic attacks while maintaining full backwards compatibility.*

---

[55] Microsoft Sub-CA used in malware signing [fsty.uk/t176] (Marc Stevens, 12 June 2012)

[56] Counter-cryptanalysis [fsty.uk/t177] (Marc Stevens, CRYPTO 2013)

# TURKTRUST

In December 2012, Google uncovered another serious PKI problem thanks to the public key pinning mechanism supported by the Chrome browser. Pinning is a mechanism that allows user agents to check that only authorized CAs are issuing certificates for specific web sites. Chrome ships with a small, hardcoded list of sites, but they are some of the most visible sites in the world.[57]

In December 2012, when a Chrome user encountered a certificate that did not match with the hardcoded built-in list, their browser communicated the entire offending certificate chain back to Google. With access to the chain, they were able to link the rogue certificate to TURKTRUST, a Turkish certification authority.[58]

The invalid subordinate certificates were promptly revoked by all parties. TURKTRUST published a detailed report only a couple of days later and continued to provide regular updates.[59] We learned that a mistake had been made in August 2011 at TURKTRUST during a transition between two system installations, causing two certificates issued on that day to be marked as CA certificates. The mistake remained undetected for about 15 months, during which time the certificates were used as humble server certificates.

At some point in December 2012, a firewall with MITM capabilities was installed at EGO, one of the two organizations in possession of a misissued subordinate CA certificate. A contractor imported the certificate into the firewall, which started to perform its MITM function by generating fake web site certificates on demand. In the process, a clone of one of Google's certificates was made and used and subsequently detected by Chrome.

It's not clear if the contractor knew that the certificate in question was a CA certificate. If you're troubleshooting a MITM device and you are not familiar with PKI, importing any valid certificate you have sitting around seems like a thing that you might try.

The browser root store operators accepted TURKTRUST's position that the incident was the result of an administrative error. There was no evidence of attack against the CA; fake certificates were not seen outside EGO's own network. Mozilla asked TURKTRUST to undergo an out-of-order audit, and Google and Opera decided to stop recognizing TURKTRUST's EV certificates.

# ANSSI

In December 2013, Google announced that Chrome was revoking trust in a subordinate CA certificate issued by ANSSI (*Agence nationale de la sécurité des systèmes d'information*),

---

[57] I discuss public key pinning in the section called "Pinning" in Chapter 10.

[58] Enhancing digital certificate security [fsty.uk/t178] (Google Online Security Blog, 3 January 2013)

[59] Public Announcements [fsty.uk/t179] (TURKTRUST, 7 January 2013)

a French network and information security agency. A few days later, the trust in the parent ANSSI certification authority was restricted to allow only certificates issued for the domain names corresponding to French territories (.fr being the main such top-level domain name).[60]

The reason for the revocation was the discovery that the subordinate CA certificate had been used in a transparent interception device running on the agency's network. As a result, certificates for various domain names were generated, some of which belonged to Google. Once again, Chrome's pinning of Google's certificate detected a misuse of the PKI.

Mozilla[61] and Microsoft[62] also disabled the offending CA certificate. The agency issued a brief statement blaming human error for the problem. There's been no evidence that the inappropriate certificate was used anywhere outside the network of the French Treasury.[63]

As is usually the case, a discussion followed on `mozilla.dev.security.policy`.[64]

In addition to more details of the incident being provided, various other problems with how ANSSI used the CA certificate were uncovered. For example, many of their certificates did not include any revocation information. Unusual activity was detected on their CRLs, with thousands of certificates suddenly appearing on previously empty lists. It's not clear if and how the incident concluded. According to their own admission, ANSSI will be unable to comply with Baseline Requirements until at least December 2015, which is two years after Mozilla's deadline.[65]

# National Informatics Centre of India

In July 2014, Google detected misissued certificates for several of their domain names and tracked them down to the intermediate certificates belonging to the National Information Centre (NIC) of India, which were issued by the Indian Controller of Certifying Authorities (CCA). It later transpired that the subordinate CA (NIC Certifying Authority or NICCA) had been compromised, with fraudulent certificates issued for Google's and Yahoo's domain names. The intermediate certificates in question were subsequently revoked, and NICCA stopped issuing certificates altogether. In Chrome, the root CCA authority was limited to only accept certificates for a number of Indian (.in) subdomains.[66]

---

[60] Further improving digital certificate security [fsty.uk/t180] (Google Online Security Blog, 7 December 2013)

[61] Revoking Trust in one ANSSI Certificate [fsty.uk/t181] (Mozilla Security blog, 9 December 2013)

[62] Improperly Issued Digital Certificates Could Allow Spoofing [fsty.uk/t182] (Microsoft Security Advisory 2916652, 9 December 2013)

[63] Revocation of an IGC/A branch [fsty.uk/t183] (ANSSI, 7 December 2013)

[64] Revoking Trust in one ANSSI Certificate [fsty.uk/t184] (mozilla.dev.security.policy, 9 December 2013)

[65] Announcing Version 2.1 of Mozilla CA Certificate Policy [fsty.uk/t185] (Mozilla Security Blog, 15 February 2013)

[66] Maintaining digital certificate security [fsty.uk/t186] (Google Online Security Blog, 8 July 2014)

# Widespread SSL Interception

Despite many PKI weaknesses, the biggest danger to the ecosystem proved to be widespread SSL interception carried out by locally installed software, employers, and network providers. Over time, such interception became common, even though we usually don't hear about it. Those directly affected are usually not aware of what's happening and don't report the incidents. Once in a while, we get lucky, the incidents do get reported, and our awareness of these problems raises by a bit. A research paper from Durumeric et al., published in 2017, highlighted that interception is common and has a significant negative security impact.[67]

In 2020, X. de Carné de Carnavalet and P. C. van Oorschot conducted a systematic analysis of how TLS can be intentionally subverted to break its security guarantees.[68]

## Gogo

In January 2015, Adrienne Porter Felt (a member of the Google Chrome security team) reported that in-flight Internet connectivity company Gogo is intercepting all encrypted traffic and serving invalid certificates bearing hostnames of legitimate web sites.[69]

Gogo didn't have a way of magically producing valid certificates, which meant that all its users had to click through certificate warnings in order to reach their desired web sites. That's why the certificates were invalid. However, that doesn't change the fact that Gogo potentially had unrestricted access to users' sensitive information.

Adrienne's tweet hit a nerve with the community. Massively retweeted, the fact that a commercial entity is routinely executing network attacks against its users became widely reported in the media. Gogo subsequently issued a statement "blaming" its actions on their need to control in-flight bandwidth usage.[70] The claim is bogus, although the company might have genuinely believed that the interception was necessary. Some days later, they stopped with the interception altogether.[71]

## Superfish and Friends

Just one month later, in February 2015, Adrienne sparked another public disclosure, which was that Lenovo had been shipping ad-injector software (some would say malware) called

---

[67] The Security Impact of HTTPS Interception [fsty.uk/t108] (Durumeric et al., February 2017)

[68] A survey and analysis of TLS interception mechanisms and motivations [fsty.uk/t187] (X. de Carné de Carnavalet and P. C. van Oorschot, 30 October 2020)

[69] hey @Gogo, why are you issuing *.google.com certificates on your planes? [fsty.uk/t188] (Adrienne Porter Felt, 2 January 2015)

[70] Our Technology Statement from Gogo regarding our streaming video policy [fsty.uk/t189] (Gogo, 5 January 2015)

[71] Gogo no longer issuing fake Google SSL certificates [fsty.uk/t190] (Runway Girl Network, 13 January 2015)

*Superfish* preinstalled on some of its systems.[72] Interesting for us is that this software performed interception of all user traffic, including that destined for secure web sites. To avoid certificate warnings, Superfish used an unwanted "trusted" root certificate that was added to the operating system root store without user consent. With the root in place, Superfish redirected all browser traffic to a local proxy process. That process, in turn, retrieved from the Internet whatever content was requested, with whatever modifications it wanted to make.

Not only were these actions morally questionable (the ad-injector software was able to observe all traffic, no matter how private or sensitive it was), they were also deeply incompetent. The correct way to perform this type of interception is to generate a unique root for each user. Superfish used one and the *same* root certificate for all systems, meaning that any affected Lenovo user could extract the corresponding private root key and use it to attack all other similarly affected users. Unsurprisingly, the root in question was extracted promptly after the public discovery.[73] (Perhaps also before, but we don't have any information about that.)

There were other problems: the proxy software running on each user's laptop had weaker TLS capabilities than the browsers the users would be running; it supported TLS 1.1, but not the most recent TLS 1.2. It also offered many weak suites and effectively downgraded the users' security. Even worse, it failed to properly validate invalid certificates, effectively legitimizing self-signed certificates and MITM attacks equally. This is worth saying again: users with Superfish effectively didn't see certificate warnings, no matter what sites they were visiting.[74]

> ### Note
>
> By design, locally installed roots are allowed to bypass strict security measures such as pinning. This approach allows enterprises to perform (possibly legitimate) SSL interception. That's why Superfish could even intercept traffic to Google, despite Google's heavy security measures.

Analysis done by Facebook showed that Superfish affected many users across the world. In Kazakhstan, Superfish accounted for as much as 4.5% of Facebook connections.[75]

Lenovo initially tried to defend their actions, but eventually accepted the inevitable. The company subsequently worked with Microsoft to remove Superfish and the unwanted roots

---

[72] #Superfish Round-Up [fsty.uk/t191] (Chris Palmer, 22 February 2015)

[73] Extracting the SuperFish certificate [fsty.uk/t192] (Robert Graham, 19 February 2015)

[74] Komodia/Superfish SSL Validation is broken [fsty.uk/t193] (Filippo Valsorda, 20 February 2015)

[75] Windows SSL Interception Gone Wild [fsty.uk/t194] (Facebook, 20 February 2015)

---

from the affected systems. Microsoft released statistics showing Superfish removed from roughly 250,000 systems in just a couple of days.[76]

> **Note**
>
> As is usually the case, an online test was produced. Filippo Valsorda published a test for Superfish, Komodia, and PrivDog.[77] Hanno Böck implemented a wider test for a number of similar products.[78]

Further research uncovered that Superfish was built using an SSL interception SDK provided by a company called Komodia. From Komodia's web site:

> *Our advanced SSL hijacker SDK is a brand new technology that allows you to access data that was encrypted using SSL and perform on the fly SSL decryption. The hijacker uses Komodia's Redirector platform to allow you easy access to the data and the ability to modify, redirect, block, and record the data without triggering the target browser's certification warning.*

Superfish is not the only SSL-interception product and apparently not the only one with security flaws. Although Comodo's product PrivDog (in version 3.0.96.0) uses a per-user interception root, it also fails to perform proper certificate validation, effectively facilitating MITM attacks as well.[79]

Komodia, Superfish, and PrivDog came to our attention first, but there are many similar products. As the security researchers started to take notice, dozens of other similar products surfaced and became publicly known. Among them are some very well-known names among security products.[80]

# CNNIC

In March 2015, a company called Mideast Communication Systems (MCS) received a test intermediate certificate from CNNIC (China Internet Network Information Center), the agency in charge of the Internet in China. MCS's intention was to start offering certificates and related services on the Egyptian market. Unfortunately, during testing, the intermediate certificate was imported into a device that was capable of performing transparent SSL interception, and that eventually led to the creation of at least one misissued certificate. The

---

[76] MSRT March: Superfish cleanup [fsty.uk/t195] (Microsoft Malware Protection Center, 10 March 2015)

[77] Superfish, Komodia, PrivDog vulnerability test [fsty.uk/t196] (Filippo Valsorda, retrieved 22 March 2015)

[78] Check for bad certs from Komodia / Superfish [fsty.uk/t197] (Hanno Böck, retrieved 22 March 2015)

[79] Comodo ships Adware Privdog worse than Superfish [fsty.uk/t198] (Hanno Böck, 23 February 2015)

[80] The Risks of SSL Inspection [fsty.uk/t199] (Will Dormann, 13 March 2015)

Chrome browser used by one of the engineers duly reported the certificate sighting back to Google.[81]

After an investigation, Google decided to revoke trust in CNNIC's roots, and so did Mozilla.[82] Both organizations continued to recognize all valid certificates issued from them until the moment of revocation, implemented using a whitelist that was supplied by CNNIC. Even though MCS's actions resulted in misissued certificates, ultimately CNNIC was considered at fault for issuing an unrestricted globally valid intermediate CA certificate to an organization that was not equipped to handle it.[83]

# Root Key Compromise

One of the best ways to attack PKI is to go after the root certificates directly. For government agencies, one approach might be to simply request the private keys from the CAs in their countries. If that's seen as possibly controversial and dangerous, anyone with a modest budget (say, a million dollars or so) could start a brand new CA and get their roots embedded in trust stores everywhere. They might or might not feel the need to run a proper CA as a cover; there are many roots that have never been seen issuing end-entity certificates.

This approach to attacking Internet PKI would have been viable for many years, but at some point a couple of years ago people started paying attention to what's happening in the ecosystem. Browser plug-ins for certificate tracking were built; they alert users whenever a new certificate is encountered. Google implemented public key pinning in Chrome, now a very popular browser. And the Electronic Frontier Foundation extended its HTTPS Everywhere browser plug-in to monitor root certificate usage.[84]

A far less messy approach (both then and now) would be to break the existing root and intermediate certificates. If you have access to the key belonging to an intermediate certificate, you can issue arbitrary certificates. For best results (the smallest chance of being discovered), fraudulent certificates should be issued from the same CA as the genuine ones. Many sites, especially the big ones, operate multiple certificates at the same time. If the issuing CA is the same, how are you going to differentiate a fraudulent certificate from a genuine one?

In 2003 (more than ten years ago!), Shamir and Tromer estimated that a $10 million purpose-built machine (plus $20 million for the initial design and development) could

---

[81] Maintaining digital certificate security [fsty.uk/t200] (Google Online Security Blog, 23 March 2015)

[82] Distrusting New CNNIC Certificates [fsty.uk/t201] (Mozilla Security Blog, 2 April 2015)

[83] Consequences of mis-issuance under CNNIC [fsty.uk/t202] (mozilla.dev.security.policy discussion thread, started on 23 March 2015)

[84] HTTPS Everywhere [fsty.uk/t203] (The Electronic Frontier Foundation, retrieved 3 July 2014)

break a 1,024-bit key in about a year.[85] For state agencies, that's very cheap, considering the possibilities that rogue certificates open. These agencies routinely spend billions of dollars on various projects of interest. More recently, in 2013, Tromer reduced the estimate to only $1 million.[86]

In that light, it's reasonable to assume that all 1,024-bit keys of relevance are already broken by multiple government agencies from countries around the world.

In some cases, it might also be reasonable to expect that end-entity certificates have been targeted. For example, Google transitioned away from 1,024-bit certificates only in 2013.[87]

Given the small cost of breaking those weak keys, it's surprising that they remained in use for such a long time. Mozilla originally planned to remove weak roots by the end of 2013,[88] but it managed to complete the process only in late 2015.[89]

## Symantec Test Certificates

In September 2015, Google published a blog post disclosing its discovery that Symantec had issued a certificate for *google.com* without authorization.[90]

On the same day Symantec issued a blog post (no longer available online or in the archives) claiming that three certificates had been issued without authorization; Symantec blamed the mistake on two of its employees, who were then dismissed in a bid to demonstrate a decisive action. The three certificates were of the *Extended Validation* variety; they were found in the *Certificate Transparency* (CT) logs because, earlier that year, Chrome mandated CT for all EV certificates. For a time it seemed that the incident had been resolved, but there was more activity behind the scenes; Google employees started to comb the CT logs and discovered more problems.

After further research and several incident report updates from Symantec, the end result was a total of 2,645 misissued certificates, all generated by Symantec for test purposes.[91]

Google, unhappy that Symantec was unable to produce a comprehensive incident report after being alerted about the first certificates discovered, decided to punish Symantec by requiring that all its certificates be published to CT starting in June 2016.[92]

---

[85] On the Cost of Factoring RSA-1024 [fsty.uk/t204] (Shamir and Tromer, 2003)

[86] Facebook's outmoded Web crypto opens door to NSA spying [fsty.uk/t205] (CNET, 28 June 2013)

[87] Google certificates upgrade in progress [fsty.uk/t206] (Google Developers Blog, 30 July 2013)

[88] Dates for phasing out MD5-based signatures and 1024-bit moduli [fsty.uk/t207] (MozillaWiki, retrieved 3 July 2014)

[89] Bug #1156844 - Turn off trust bits for Equifax Secure Certificate Authority 1024-bit root certificate [fsty.uk/t208] (Bugzilla@Mozilla, closed 21 December 2015)

[90] Improved Digital Certificate Security [fsty.uk/t209] (Google Security Blog, 18 September 2015)

[91] Add Symantec Test Certs to OneCRL [fsty.uk/t210] (Bugzilla@Mozilla, retrieved 2 May 2017)

[92] Sustaining Digital Certificate Security [fsty.uk/t78] (Google Security Blog, 28 October 2015)

# Kazakhstan Interception Attacks

In November 2015, Kazakhtelecom JSC—Kazakhstan's dominant telecom provider—issued a press release announcing that its users would be expected to install a special *national security certificate* to enable interception and monitoring of encrypted traffic.[93] The press release was removed quickly after media attention.

The second attempt followed in 2019, when Kazakhstan's ISPs were being requested to instruct their customers to install a "Qaznet Trust Network" root certificate designed for large-scale interception. Kazakhstan's government said that the installation of the interception certificate was voluntary.[94]

Apple,[95] Google,[96] and Mozilla[97] all said that they would modify their browsers to ignore the certificate, even if it is manually added to be trusted. A team of researchers investigated the interception in detail and discovered that it had been aimed at 37 unique domain names, mostly social media and communication services.[98]

Again in early December 2020, Kazakhstan's ISPs started redirecting access to foreign Internet services by users from Nur-Sultan (Kazakhstan's capital). Instead of the requested traffic, they were being shown a page with instructions to install another interception certificate. Kazakhstan called this initiative a cybersecurity training exercise.[99]At the time of writing (the end of December 2020), the offending certificate has been added to Mozilla's blocklist via an entry in its proprietary OneCRL revocation mechanism. Censored Planet has a dedicated page showing the interception activities in real time.[100]

# WoSign and StartCom

Until late 2016, many thought that there was little to no trust agility in the Internet PKI ecosystem. The thinking was that any CA with a substantial user base couldn't be removed without causing too much disruption. Until then the only CA ever to die was DigiNotar—not a small CA, but not a significant player globally. Then the unthinkable happened: Apple, Google, and Mozilla decided to kill off not one, but two CAs at the same time. Others (most notably Microsoft) didn't act, but their silence didn't and couldn't change anything.

---

[93] Kazakhtelecom JSC notifies on introduction of National security certificate from 1 January 2016 [fsty.uk/t211] (30 November 2015)

[94] Vice Minister: Installing a "security certificate" is up to users [fsty.uk/t212] (Radio Azattyk, 19 July 2019)

[95] Google and Mozilla block Kazakhstan root CA certificate from Chrome and Firefox [fsty.uk/t213] (VentureBeat, 21 August 2019)

[96] Protecting Chrome users in Kazakhstan [fsty.uk/t214] (Google Security Blog, 21 August 2019)

[97] Protecting our Users in Kazakhstan [fsty.uk/t215] (Mozilla Security Blog, 21 August 2019)

[98] Kazakhstan's HTTPS Interception [fsty.uk/t216] (Raman et al., October 2020)

[99] Kazakhstan government is intercepting HTTPS traffic in its capital [fsty.uk/t217] (ZDNet; 6 December 2020)

[100] Kazakhstan's HTTPS Interception Live (Again) [fsty.uk/t218] (Censored Planet, retrieved 6 January 2021)

In this story the WoSign CA was the lead character; StartCom was collateral damage. WoSign was a young and aggressive Chinese CA that first became known globally for their free certificates, before Let's Encrypt became popular. A big player in China, WoSign wanted to expand and used free certificates as a way of gaining market share and becoming relevant. It subsequently acquired StartCom, an Israeli CA that had been issuing free certificates similarly for years. Unfortunately, WoSign's operations were marred by problems, and at some point in the second half of 2016 Mozilla began to seriously investigate its activities. The investigation uncovered WoSign's history of operational problems and less-than-transparent communication with its root stores, from January 2015 onward.[101]

Perhaps the final blow was the discovery that WoSign had purchased StartCom but failed to disclose the transaction, even though this was a requirement of Mozilla's root store policy. To make things worse, WoSign continued to deny the transaction until finally faced with enough evidence. As a result, Mozilla[102] and Google[103] decided that WoSign couldn't be trusted. Apple followed soon thereafter. In Mozilla's own words, it decided to act because "the levels of deception demonstrated by representatives of the combined company have led to Mozilla's decision to distrust future certificates chaining up to the currently-included WoSign and StartCom root certificates."

Although StartCom had its own history of security issues, well documented in this chapter, it faced the same fate as WoSign largely only because the organizational hierarchies of the two companies had been unified and much of the infrastructure was being shared.

So, how do you remove a CA from a root store without too much disruption? The answer was to continue to serve the existing user base but refuse to accept certificates issued after a certain date. In the case of WoSign and StartCom, Google and Mozilla settled on 21 October 2016. The root stores announced their decisions in late October, but started to enforce them in January 2017. The blog posts made it clear that the end goal is full distrust of all existing certificates belonging to the offending CAs. In subsequent releases, Chrome started to distrust even existing certificates, working based on Alexa's top 1 million list of most popular web sites. This caused much confusion because their actions were not widely announced ahead of time.

WoSign and StartCom continued to operate, although obviously they couldn't issue their own trusted certificates any longer. Instead, they acted as resellers for other CAs while they worked to reestablish themselves as fully trusted CAs.

[101] CA:WoSign Issues [fsty.uk/t219] (Mozilla Wiki, retrieved 2 May 2017)

[102] Distrusting New WoSign and StartCom Certificates [fsty.uk/t220] (Mozilla Security Blog, 24 October 2016)

[103] Distrusting WoSign and StartCom Certificates [fsty.uk/t221] (Google Security Blog, 31 October 2016)

# SHA1 Finally Falls

In February 2017, to no one's surprise and after several years of "any day now" speculations, came an announcement that SHA1 had been broken.[104] The research was a collaboration between the Cryptology Group at Centrum Wiskunde & Informatica (CWI) and Google. The web site launched just for this purpose[105] begins as follows:

> *We have broken SHA-1 in practice.*

And that's all you need to know. Just a month prior, after three years of planning, major browsers started considering SHA1 certificates unsafe. Unlike in the MD5 debacle (discussed at length earlier in this chapter), the security community did the right thing this time and retired an aging cryptographic primitive before it was too late. Google's effort to break SHA1 took more than 6,500 CPU and 110 years of GPU computation combined. In addition to the computing power, the two-year project was a team effort, summed up by this paragraph from the announcement blog post:

> *Marc Stevens and Elie Bursztein started collaborating on making Marc's cryptanalytic attacks against SHA-1 practical using Google infrastructure. Ange Albertini developed the PDF attack, Pierre Karpman worked on the cryptanalysis and the GPU implementation, Yarik Markov took care of the distributed GPU code, Alex Petit Bianco implemented the collision detector to protect Google users and Clement Baisse oversaw the reliability of the computations.*

The team's proof of concept was the release of two different PDF documents that share the same SHA1 signature. More interestingly, the same collision could be reused by anyone to produce other document forgeries, possibly even in formats other than PDF. According to Marc Stevens:[106]

> *Our single expensive SHA-1 collision can be reused to craft many colliding file pairs by anyone for free.*

To amusement of many, both Subversion and Git version control systems broke when developers tried to check collision proof-of-concept PDFs into their repositories. Linus Torvalds in particular was left red-faced for refusing to acknowledge the problem with SHA1 and abandon it—back in 2005.[107]

---

104 Announcing the first SHA1 collision [fsty.uk/t222] (Google Security Blog, 23 February 2017)

105 SHAttered [fsty.uk/t223] (retrieved 3 May 2017)

106 Tweet about SHA1 collision reuse [fsty.uk/t224] (Marc Stevens, 26 February 2017)

107 SHA1 collisions make Git vulnerable to attacks by third-parties, not just repo maintainers [fsty.uk/t225] (John Gilmore, 26 February 2017)

Marc Stevens subsequently released a drop-in SHA1 library that incorporates detection of chosen-prefix attacks.[108]

## Identical-Prefix Attack: SHAttered

SHAttered is an *identical-prefix attack* against SHA1. Stevens had described this attack earlier, but it took further years of work to put it in practice.[109] In cryptography, this type of attack is also known as a *classical collision*. SHA1 is a hash function that produces 160-bit output from input of arbitrary length. Internally, input is divided into 512-bit blocks. The attack works by crafting two *near-collision block pairs* to manipulate the internal state of the SHA1 function so that it works for the selected prefix P and *any* suffix S:

$$\text{SHA1}(P||M_1^{(1)}||M_2^{(1)}||S) = \text{SHA1}(P||M_1^{(2)}||M_2^{(2)}||S)$$

In essence, two near-collision blocks are needed because achieving a full collision requires more work than can be achieved within only one 512-bit block. Thus, the first near collision does part of the work, but the second collision finishes the job.

## Chosen-Prefix Attack: Shambles

In 2019 came an improved attack against SHA1, under the name Shambles.[110] This later work is a *chosen-prefix attack*, which is more difficult to carry out. This is the same attack that was used to break MD5 in the attacks carried out by Flame and against RapidSSL, both described earlier in this chapter.

In the classical collision, the attacker is able to choose the prefix, which is the same in the original and the forgery. In the chosen-prefix attack, the attacker has to work with a prefix that's already been decided. As a result, this attack is much more difficult to pull off. On the other hand, chosen-prefix attacks are more useful in practice to subvert digital signature schemes.

The researchers behind Shambles used about 150 GPU years of computation power for their work. They estimated a cost of about $100K. The end result was generation of two PGP public keys with the same SHA1 hash. The Shambles attack didn't have a practical impact at the time it came out, thanks to the earlier initiatives to deprecate SHA1. CAs stopped issuing SHA1 certificates at the beginning of 2016 and browsers stopped accepting them at the beginning of 2017.

---

[108] sha1collisiondetection [fsty.uk/t226] (Marc Stevens, retrieved 3 May 2017)

[109] New collision attacks on SHA-1 based on optimal joint local-collision analysis [fsty.uk/t227] (Marc Stevens, May 2013)

[110] SHA-1 is a Shambles [fsty.uk/t228] (7 January 2020)

# Demise of Symantec PKI

For a long time it was thought that there are some CAs that are so embedded in the Internet PKI that they are too big to fail, but 2017 proved otherwise. In March 2017, after many years of being dissatisfied with Symantec's PKI practices, Google announced that it would remove trust in all existing Symantec certificates.[111] The announcement followed an investigation that started in January 2017 and initially had a scope of about 127 certificates suspected to have been misissued.[112]

In the course of the investigation, Symantec's responses revealed further information that, in the words of Google, created a fatal uncertainty about the entirety of the CA's certificates:[113]

> *In effect, each of these parties were able to effect issuance by validating information improperly. At least 30,000 certificates were issued by these parties, with no independent way to assess the compliance of these parties to the expected standards.*
>
> *Further, these certificates cannot be technically identified or distinguished from certificates where Symantec performed the validation role. As a consequence, the insufficient demonstration of compliance, along with the inability to distinguish such certificates, combined with the incomplete identification of the scope of the issues, create a degree of uncertainty related to the entire corpus of certificates.*

In essence, the decision came down to the fact that Symantec had delegated certificate issuance to four parties without proper oversight and scrutiny.

Google's initial plan was a de facto termination of Symantec's PKI activities. It included a gradual distrust of existing certificates across seven Chrome releases, as well as setting a limit of only seven months for the validity of new certificates. The combination of these two actions could have put Symantec under very unfavorable market conditions.

Fortunately, a different course of action emerged over time. Rather than face the original plan, Symantec instead agreed to delegate all its PKI operations to another CA and selected DigiCert for the role. In return, Google agreed to a deprecation plan that wouldn't kill off the entire business.[114] In the end, Symantec sold its entire certificate business to DigiCert.[115]

---

[111] Intent to Deprecate and Remove: Trust in existing Symantec-issued Certificates [fsty.uk/t229] (Ryan Sleevi, 23 March 2017)

[112] Symantec: Mis-issued test certificates by CrossCert [fsty.uk/t230] (Mozilla's Bugzilla; 26 January 2017)

[113] Re: Intent to Deprecate and Remove: Trust in existing Symantec-issued Certificates [fsty.uk/t231] (Ryan Sleevi; 24 March 2017)

[114] Chrome's Plan to Distrust Symantec Certificates [fsty.uk/t232] (Google Security Blog; 11 September 2017)

[115] DigiCert to Acquire Symantec's Website Security Business [fsty.uk/t233] (DigiCert, 2 August 2017)

As of December 2017, DigiCert was able to issue "Symantec" certificates from a brand new hierarchy under its control. The existing Symantec certificates, issued from the legacy PKI hierarchy, were deprecated in two waves, first in March 2018 with Chrome 66 and then again in September 2018 with Chrome 70. DigiCert had to work frantically to replace many of these certificates before they were deprecated. Symantec had also issued a number of intermediates that were independently managed; those were exempted from the deprecations.

## Assorted Validation Incidents

Domain name ownership validation is a tricky business. Failures, small and big, happen all the time. CAs are under constant pressure to do it cheaper and faster; they operate in the same competitive environment as everybody else, with the exception that their mistakes sometimes can be costly. In this section I will describe several incidents representative of CAs' real-life challenges.

### StartEncrypt validation failures

In early June 2016, StartCom launched StartEncrypt, a new protocol and accompanying tools to support automated certificate issuance. This was the company's response to the rising popularity of Let's Encrypt (an unconditionally free CA) and its ACME protocol. On the surface, StartEncrypt offered some interesting capabilities not available elsewhere—for example, automated certificate validation *and* installation, as well as support for OV and EV certificates, which Let's Encrypt didn't offer. Unfortunately, StartCom made serious errors during the design and implementation of this new offering, and fatal flaws were disclosed before the month was over.[116] Two flaws stood out: (1) the protocol allowed the attacker to choose the path of the validation response, which meant that the protocol could be used to obtain a fraudulent certificate for any web site that hosted user content; and (2) the verification part followed redirections, which meant that it could be used to obtain a certificate for any web site that allowed arbitrary redirections. StartCom subsequently abandoned the protocol and said that it would implement ACME instead.

### Comodo issues certificates for the *sb* and *tc* top-level domains

In September 2016, Comodo mistakenly issued a certificate valid for both *sb* and *www.sb* hostnames after validating only the latter variant. This was a mistake because the two hostnames had different owners. This misissuance followed an earlier similar problem with a certificate for the *tb* top-level domain name, but in that case both hostname variants had the same owner.[117]

---

[116] StartEncrypt considered harmful today [fsty.uk/t234] (Computest, 30 June 2017)

[117] Incident Report—certificate with 'sb' as a SAN:dnsName [fsty.uk/t235] (Robin Alden, 26 September 2016)

### Comodo uses OCR as part of the validation process

In October 2016, security researchers Florian Heinz and Martin Kluge discovered a flaw in Comodo's certificate validation process, exposing the use of optical character recognition (OCR) as a potentially vulnerable component.[118] It's well known that the WHOIS system, which is used to determine domain name ownership, is a mess, and yet CAs often have to use it for certificate validation. One particular problem is that some WHOIS providers (in this case, *.eu* and *.be* registrars) do not offer machine-readable email addresses but show them as images. Although this helps reduce spam, it also represents a headache for CAs, who need domain name owners' email addresses for legitimate reasons. To get around the problem of only having access to images of email addresses, Comodo deployed an automated OCR system to recover the email addresses. Unfortunately, the OCR was prone to errors, confusing certain similar characters—for example, l and 1. When the security researchers discovered this, they were able to trick Comodo into issuing a certificate for an unauthorized domain name. Comodo subsequently discontinued use of OCR for domain name ownership validation.

### GoDaddy accepts 404 responses as proof of ownership

In January 2017, GoDaddy disclosed a bug in its validation process that resulted in 8,850 certificates being issued without authorization.[119]

In one of its variation approaches, GoDaddy would send a random number to a web site and require the web site operator to output the same random number in response to prove ownership. This superficially agreeable approach is flawed because many sites are configured to display the requested URL on their 404 (Page Not Found) responses.[120] In such cases GoDaddy would accept a 404 page as proof of ownership. After discovering this problem, GoDaddy stopped using this particular validation technique. Interestingly, this problem had been identified and resolved in CA/B Forum's Ballot 169.[121] Technically, GoDaddy wasn't in the wrong, because the effective date of Ballot 169 was March 1, 2017.

### ACME's TLS-SNI-01 challenge type found to be broken

At the very beginning of 2018, ACME's TLS-SNI-01 challenge type was found to be broken and Let's Encrypt had to disable it.[122] This validation method was a special-purpose mechanism intended for situations in which validation needed to be done at the TLS layer, rather than the plaintext HTTP-01. Security researcher Frans

---

[118] Incident Report—OCR [fsty.uk/t236] (Robin Alden, 19 October 2016)

[119] Incident Report—Certificates issued without proper domain validation [fsty.uk/t237] (Wayne Thayer, 10 January 2017)

[120] Re: Incident Report—Certificates issued without proper domain validation [fsty.uk/t238] (Patrick Figel, 11 January 2017)

[121] Ballot 169—Revised Validation Requirements [fsty.uk/t239] (CA/B Forum, 5 August 2017)

[122] Issue with TLS-SNI-01 and Shared Hosting Infrastructure [fsty.uk/t240] (Let's Encrypt, 9 January 2018)

Rosén discovered that TLS-SNI-01 could be abused to get certificates for properties hosted with "vulnerable" large infrastructure providers such as AWS and Heroku.[123]

The root cause was the fact that those providers used internal routing systems that enabled the attacker to provide the correct response to the challenge, despite the fact that they didn't control the property for which the certificate was being requested. In essence, this was a confusion-style attack that exploited differences in how the validation request was being understood by Let's Encrypt and the providers. TLS-ALPN-01 was later designed to support the same goals as TLS-SNI-01, but in a safe way.[124]

### Trustico found to hold 23,000 private keys

In March 2018, it transpired that Trustico, a certificate reseller that had a relationship with Symantec at the time, held about 23,000 private certificate keys. This became known after Trustico wanted to accelerate its phasing out of Symantec certificates and attempted to get all existing certificates revoked. It disclosed the existence of the private key collection to DigiCert, which subsequently brought up the issue for discussion on Mozilla's policy mailing list.[125]

Trustico definitely succeeded in its quest to revoke the certificates after sending all the collected keys to DigiCert via email. In its statement, the company indicated it was holding private keys in cold storage.[126] Trustico's web site was later apparently found to have easily exploitable security problems.[127] According to Baseline Requirements (Section 6.1.2), parties other than end users are not allowed to archive private keys without explicit authorization.

### Let's Encrypt botches CAA verification

In February 2020, Let's Encrypt disclosed a problem in its CAA verification code[128] affecting about three million out of its 116 million active certificates (2.6%). The company subsequently announced that it would revoke all the affected certificates, giving the web site operators only a day to react.[129]

The short deadline was dictated by Baseline Requirements. About 1.7 million certificates were replaced in the next couple of days, and in the end Let's Encrypt decided not to proceed with the revocations of the remaining certificates. Because it only issues certificates that are valid for up to 90 days, all affected certificates expired by the end of May 2020.[130]

---

[123] How I exploited ACME TLS-SNI-01 [fsty.uk/t241] (Detectify Labs, 12 January 2018)

[124] RFC 8737: ACME TLS ALPN Challenge Extension [fsty.uk/t242] (R. B. Shoemaker, February 2020)

[125] How do you handle mass revocation requests? [fsty.uk/t243] (Jeremy Rowley, 28 February 2018)

[126] Distrusted Symantec® SSL Replacement [fsty.uk/t244] (Trustico, 28 February 2018)

[127] @cujanovic's tweet [fsty.uk/t245] (Twitter; 1 March 2018)

[128] Let's Encrypt: CAA Rechecking bug [fsty.uk/t246] (Mozilla's Bugzilla, 28 February 2020)

[129] Revoking certain certificates on March 4 (Let's Encrypt, 3 March 2020)

[130] Let's Encrypt: Incomplete revocation for CAA rechecking bug [fsty.uk/t247] (Mozilla's Bugzilla, 1 March 2020)

# 6 HTTP and Browser Issues

In this chapter, we focus on the relationship between TLS and HTTP. TLS was designed to secure TCP connections, but there is so much more going on in today's browsers. In many cases, the problems that arise come from the browser vendors' struggle to deal with legacy web sites; they're afraid to "break" the Web. Nevertheless, we continue to make progress toward better security. Many of the problems documented in this chapter are now a thing of the past if modern browsers are assumed. They will remain a problem in the long tail of older and less popular software applications.

## Sidejacking

*Sidejacking* is a special case of web application session hijacking in which session tokens[1] are retrieved from an unencrypted traffic stream. This type of attack is very easy to perform on a wireless or local network. In the case of a web site that does not use encryption, all the attacker needs to do is observe the unencrypted traffic and extract the session token from it. If a site uses encryption only partially, two types of mistakes are possible:

**Session leakage by design**
> Back in the days of SSL, many sites used encryption to protect account passwords but revert to plaintext as soon as authentication is complete. This approach does result in a slight improvement of security, but effectively only replaces leakage of one type of credentials (passwords) with the leakage of another type (session tokens). Session tokens are indeed somewhat less valuable because they are valid only for a limited period of time (assuming session management is correctly implemented), but they are much easier to capture and almost as easy to abuse by a motivated attacker.

---

[1] In web applications, as soon as a user connects to a web site a new *session* is created. Each session is assigned a secret token (also known as a *session ID*), which is used to identify ownership. This token is similar to a one-time password. If the attacker discovers the token that belongs to an authenticated session, she can gain full access to the web site under the identity of the victim.

---

### Session leakage by mistake

Even when you try very hard to use encryption on an entire site, it is easy to make a mistake and leave one or more resources to be retrieved over plaintext. Even when most pages are protected, a single plaintext resource retrieved from the same domain name may lead to session token compromise.[2] This is known as a *mixed content* problem. It is almost entirely mitigated in today's modern browsers, either because mixing plaintext and encrypted content within the same page is no longer allowed or because plaintext cookies are now kept separately from those that are encrypted.

Figure 6.1. Wireshark network capture showing a session cookie in the clear

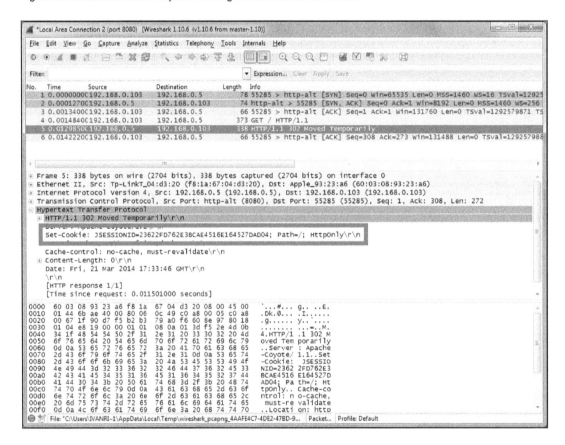

Sidejacking works well against any type of session token transport, because the attacker has full access to the communication between a user and the target web site. Thus, this attack can be used to obtain not only session tokens placed in cookies (the most common

---

[2] This is because session tokens are typically transported using cookies, which are sent with every request to the web site that issued them. As you will see later in this chapter, cookies *can* be secured, but most sites don't do so consistently.

---

transport mechanism) but also those placed in URLs (request path or parameters).[3] Once a session token is obtained, the attacker can reuse the captured value to communicate directly with the web site and assume the identity of the victim.

In the security community, sidejacking became better known in August 2007, when Robert Graham and David Maynor discussed it at Black Hat USA and released the accompanying Ferret and Hamster tools[4] that automate the attack.

A couple of years later, a Firefox add-on called Firesheep,[5] written by Eric Butler, made a much bigger splash because it made sidejacking trivially easy to carry out. Firesheep became very widely known and even caused several high-profile web sites to switch to full encryption. Firesheep was quickly followed by a detection tool called BlackSheep[6] and a counterattack tool called FireShepherd.[7] In addition, a tool called Idiocy[8] was released to automatically post warnings to compromised accounts.

# Cookie Stealing

Sidejacking, in the form discussed in the previous section, cannot be used against web sites that use encryption consistently, with 100% coverage. In such situations, the session tokens are securely hidden behind a layer of encryption. You may think that such complete implementation of TLS also means that sidejacking is not possible, but that's not the case. A common mistake made by programmers is to forget to properly configure (secure) application cookies for use with encryption. When this happens, an attacker can use a clever technique called *cookie stealing* to obtain the session tokens after all.

Historically, cookies operate across both insecure and secure transports on ports 80 and 443. When you deploy TLS on a web site, you are also expected to mark all cookies as secure, letting the browsers know how to handle them. If you don't, it may seem that your users are protected, but they're not. The appearance of security comes from that fact that browsers won't normally submit any plaintext requests on port 80. However, if an attacker can find a way to force them to, the cookies will be revealed.

Conceptually, the attack is simple: the attacker is an active *man in the middle* (MITM) observing a victim's network communication. The attacker cannot attack the encrypted traffic to the target web site, but she can wait for the victim to submit an unencrypted HTTP request to *any other* web site. At that point, she steps in, hijacks the insecure connection,

---

[3] Sidejacking aside, using URLs for transport of session tokens is never a good idea. URLs are commonly recorded in web server logs and inspected by antivirus tools and various other types of gateways that are prevalent.

[4] SideJacking with Hamster [fsty.uk/t248] (Robert Graham, 5 August 2007)

[5] Firesheep announcement [fsty.uk/t249] (Eric Butler, 24 October 2010)

[6] BlackSheep [fsty.uk/t250] (Zscaler, retrieved 15 July 2014)

[7] FireShepherd [fsty.uk/t251] (Gunnar Atli Sigurdsson, retrieved 15 July 2014)

[8] Idiocy [fsty.uk/t252] (Jonty Wareing, retrieved 15 July 2014)

and responds to one of the victim's plaintext HTTP requests by redirecting the browser to the target web site on port 80. Because any site can issue a redirection to any other site, the browser happily follows.

The end result is a plaintext connection to the target web site, which includes all nonsecure cookies in the browser's possession. Against a typical web application that doesn't mark cookies secure, the attacker now has the victim's session tokens and can hijack the session.

The attack works even if the target web site is not actually responding on port 80. Because the attacker is in the middle, she can impersonate any plaintext server on any port.

Another approach that could be used by the attacker is to redirect the victim to the same hostname and port 443 (which is always open for a secure site) but force plaintext with *http://www.example.com:443*. Even though this request fails because the browser is attempting to speak plaintext HTTP on an encrypted port, the attempted request contains all the insecure cookies and thus all the information the attacker wants to obtain.

Figure 6.2. Active network attacker stealing unsecured cookies

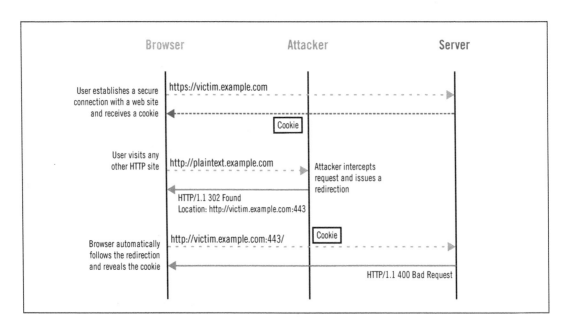

Mike Perry was the first to bring up this problem in public, shortly after sidejacking itself was publicized. But his email to the Bugtraq mailing list[9] went largely unnoticed. He

---

[9] Active Gmail "Sidejacking" - https is NOT ENOUGH [fsty.uk/t253] (Mike Perry, 5 August 2007)

Chapter 6: HTTP and Browser Issues

persisted with a talk[10] at DEFCON 16 the following year as well as a proof-of-concept tool called CookieMonster.[11]

# Cookie Manipulation

Cookie manipulation attacks are employed in situations in which the attacker can't access the existing cookies because they are properly secured. By exploiting the weaknesses in the cookie specification, she is able to inject new cookies and overwrite and delete existing application cookies. The main message in this section is that the integrity of an application's cookies can't always be guaranteed, even when the application is fully encrypted.

## Understanding HTTP Cookies

HTTP cookies are an extension mechanism designed to enable client-side persistence of small amounts of data. For each cookie they wish to create, servers specify a name and value pair along with some metadata to describe the scope and lifetime. Cookies are created using the Set-Cookie HTTP response header:

```
Set-Cookie: SID=31d4d96e407aad42; Domain=www.example.com; Path=/; Secure; HttpOnly
Set-Cookie: lang=en-US; Expires=Wed, 09 Jun 2021 10:18:14 GMT
```

User agents store cookies in so-called *cookie jars*. On every HTTP transaction, they look into their jars for applicable cookies and submit all of them using the Cookie HTTP request header:

```
Cookie: SID=31d4d96e407aad42; lang=en-US
```

From the start, cookies had been very poorly specified, and they remained so for a very long time. As a result, implementations are inconsistent and contain loopholes. As you will see in this chapter, many of the loopholes can be exploited for attacks. Proper documentation became available only in 2011, in RFC 6265.[12] A new effort is currently underway to update the cookie specification and make it more secure. Many improvements in the new specification have already been implemented in modern browsers.[13]

From the security point of view, the problem with cookies is twofold: (1) they were poorly designed to begin with, allowing behavior that encourages security weaknesses, and (2) they are not in sync with the main security mechanism browsers use today, the *Same-Origin Policy* (SOP).

---

[10] HTTPS Cookie Stealing [fsty.uk/t254] (Mike Perry, 4 August 2008)

[11] CookieMonster [fsty.uk/t255] (Mike Perry, retrieved 15 July 2014)

[12] RFC 6265: HTTP State Management Mechanism [fsty.uk/t256] (A. Barth, April 2011)

[13] Cookies: HTTP State Management Mechanism [fsty.uk/t257] (West et al., retrieved 5 September 2021)

---

### Loose hostname scoping

Cookies are designed for sharing among all hostnames of a particular domain name as well as across protocols and ports. A cookie destined for *example.com* will work on all subdomains (e.g., *www.example.com* and *secure.example.com*). Similarly, a hostname such as *blog.example.com* emits cookies only for *blog.example.com* by default (when the Domain parameter is not specified) but can also explicitly expand the scope to the parent *example.com*. As a result, a rogue server is able to inject cookies into other sites and applications installed on hostnames that are sharing the same domain name. I'll call them *related hostnames* or *related sites*.

This loose approach to scoping is in contrast with SOP rules, which generally define a security context with an exact match of protocol, hostname, and port.

### Servers do not see metadata

Servers receive only cookie names and values, but not any other information. Crucially, they don't know the origin of the cookies. If this information were available, servers would be able to reject cookies that they themselves didn't issue.

### Lack of integrity of security cookies

The fact that cookies work seamlessly across both HTTP and HTTPS protocols is a major worry. Although you can use the secure attribute to denote a cookie that is allowed to be submitted only over an encrypted channel, insecure and secure cookies are stored within the same namespace. What's even worse, the security flag is not part of the cookie identity; if the cookie name, domain, and path match, then an insecure cookie will overwrite a previously set secure one.

In a nutshell, the major flaw of HTTP cookies is that their integrity is not guaranteed. In the remainder of this section, I focus on the security implications of the cookie design on TLS; for wider coverage of the history of various security issues in browsers, I recommend Michal Zalewski's book *The Tangled Web*, published by No Starch Press in 2011.

## Cookie Manipulation Attacks

There are three types of cookie manipulation attacks. Two of them can result in the creation of new cookies and so fall under *cookie injection*. The third one allows cookies to be deleted. As is customary in application security, the attacks bear somewhat unusual and dramatic names.

Various researchers have rediscovered these problems over the years, giving them different names. Although I prefer cookie injection, because it accurately describes what is going on, other names you might come across are *cross-site cooking*,[14] *cookie fixation, cookie forcing*,[15] and *cookie tossing*.[16]

Cookie manipulation attacks have had a good run, but they're slowly going away as browsers continue to improve their handling of insecure cookies. For example, Chrome 58, released in May 2017, made changes to prevent insecure contexts from accessing existing secure cookies.[17]

Chrome 88 is making further changes to introduce Schemeful Same-Site cookies, in which plaintext and encrypted origins are in entirely separate namespaces. With this change, insecure contexts won't even be able to create cookies that are stored in the secure jars.[18]

## Cookie Eviction

*Cookie eviction* is an attack on the browser's cookie store. If for some reason the attacker does not like the cookies that are in the browser's store, he might attempt to exploit the fact that cookie stores limit individual cookie size, the number of cookies per domain name, and the combined cookie size. By submitting a large number of dummy cookies, the attacker eventually causes the browser to purge all the real cookies, leaving only the forced ones in the store.

Browser cookie jars are restricted in various ways. The overall number of cookies is limited, and so is the storage space. There is also a per-host limit (usually of several dozen), which is imposed in order to prevent a single host from taking over the entire jar. Individual cookies are usually limited to around four kilobytes. Thus, a cookie eviction attack might require the use of multiple domain names to fully overflow a cookie jar.

## Direct Cookie Injection

When performing direct cookie injection, the attacker is faced with a site that uses secure cookies. Because of that, she is not able to read the cookies (without breaking encryption), but she can always create new cookies and sometimes overwrite the existing ones. This attack exploits the fact that, historically, insecure and secure cookies lived in the same namespace,[19] although some browsers are now fighting back with *strict secure cookies*.[20]

The attack is conceptually similar to the one used for cookie stealing in the previous section: the attacker intercepts any plaintext HTTP transaction initiated by the victim and uses it

---

[14] Cross-Site Cooking [fsty.uk/t258] (Michal Zalewski, 29 January 2006)

[15] Cookie forcing [fsty.uk/t259] (Chris Evans, 24 November 2008)

[16] New Ways I'm Going to Hack Your Web App [fsty.uk/t260] (Lundeen et al., August 2011)

[17] Feature: Strict Secure Cookies [fsty.uk/t261] (Chrome Platform Status, retrieved 8 February 2021)

[18] Feature: Schemeful same-site [fsty.uk/t262] (Chrome Platform Status, retrieved 9 February 2021)

[19] Multiple Browser Cookie Injection Vulnerabilities [fsty.uk/t263] (Paul Johnston and Richard Moore, 15 September 2004)

[20] Deprecate modification of 'secure' cookies from non-secure origins [fsty.uk/t264] (M. West, January 2016)

---

to force a plaintext HTTP request to the target web site. He then intercepts that request and replies with an HTTP response that includes arbitrary cookies. The attack could be as simple as:

```
Set-Cookie: JSESSIONID=06D10C8B946311BEE81037A5493574D2
```

In practice, for the overwriting to work, the forced cookie's name, domain, and path must match that of the original. The attacker must observe what metadata values are used by the target web site and replicate them in the attack. For example, the session cookies issued by Tomcat always have the path set to the web site root:

```
Set-Cookie: JSESSIONID=06D10C8B946311BEE81037A5493574D2; Path=/
```

## Cookie Injection from Related Hostnames

When direct cookie injection is not possible (i.e., it's not possible to impersonate the target web site), the attacker might attack the fact that cookies are shared among related hostnames. If the attacker can compromise some other site on a related hostname, he might be able to inject a cookie from there.[21]

For example, you might be running a strongly secured *www.example.com* but also have a blogging site, installed at *blog.example.com* and hosted by a third-party with lesser focus on security. If the attacker can find a *Cross-Site Scripting* (XSS) vulnerability in the blogging application, he will be able to manipulate the cookies of the main application. The attack is the same as in the previous section: the victim is forced to submit an HTTP request to the vulnerable site, where arbitrary cookies can be set.

> **Note**
>
> Of course, any situation in which there are sites run by separate entities or departments should be a cause for caution. Not only are the members of the other groups a potential weak link, but they can be threats themselves.

If the victim does not already hold any cookies from the target web site, the attacker is in luck. Whatever cookies he sets will be used by the victim. Assuming XSS, attacking is as simple as executing the following code (from a page on *blog.example.com*):

```
document.cookie = 'JSESSIONID=FORCED_ID; domain=example.com';
```

Notice how the attacker must use the `domain` attribute to expand the scope of the cookie from the default *blog.example.com* to *example.com*, which will then be valid for the intended target, *www.example.com*.

---

[21] Hacking Github with Webkit [fsty.uk/t265] (Egor Homakov, 8 March 2013)

## Getting the First Cookie

More often than not, the victim will already hold some genuine cookies. If the attacker injects another cookie with the same name (as in the previous example), the browser will accept both cookies and send them with every request to the target web site:

```
Cookie: JSESSIONID=REAL_ID; JSESSIONID=FORCED_ID
```

This happens because the browser sees these two values as separate cookies; their name, domain, and path attributes do not match exactly. But although the attacker has successfully injected a cookie, the attack cannot proceed; when there are multiple cookies with the same name, typically only the first one is "seen" by web applications.

From here, the attacker can attempt to evict all genuine cookies from the store by using a large amount of dummy cookies. That might work, but it's tricky to pull off.

Alternatively, he may try to tweak cookie metadata to push the forced cookie into the first position. One such trick is to use the path attribute,[22] which exploits the fact that browsers submit more specific cookies first:

```
document.cookie = 'JSESSIONID=SECOND_FORCED_ID; domain=example.com; path=/admin';
```

Assuming the browser is accessing a URL at or below */admin/*, it will submit the cookies in the following order:

```
Cookie: JSESSIONID=SECOND_FORCED_ID; JSESSIONID=REAL_ID; JSESSIONID=FORCED_ID
```

If there are multiple sections that need to be targeted, the attacker can issue multiple cookies, one for each path. But there's still one situation in which forcing a cookie from a related hostname might overwrite the original cookie: when the target web site explicitly sets the cookie domain to the root hostname (e.g., *example.com*).

## Overwriting Cookies Using Related Hostnames

Overwriting a cookie from a related hostname does not always work because most sites set cookies without explicitly specifying the domain. These cookies are marked as *host-only*. When injecting from a related domain name, you have to specify a domain, which means that such a cookie will never match the original one even if the hostnames are the same.

There is another reason overwriting a cookie from a related hostname sometimes fails: you are not allowed to issue cookies for a sibling hostname. From *blog.example.com*, you can issue a cookie for *example.com* and *www.blog.example.com* but not for *www.example.com*.

This brings me to two cases in which overwriting is possible:

---

[22] Understanding Cookie Security [fsty.uk/t266] (Alex kuza55, 22 February 2008)

- For sites that explicitly "upgrade" the cookie domain to their root (e.g., *example.com*). I tested this case using Firefox 28, but most other browsers should follow the same behavior.

- For Internet Explorer (tested with version 11), which does not make a distinction between explicitly and implicitly set domains. However, because the names still have to match, this attack will work only against sites that issue cookies from the root (e.g., *example.com*).

### Overwriting Cookies Using Fake Related Hostnames

There is one more case in which the attacker will be able to overwrite the original cookie value: the web site is explicitly setting the cookie domain, but it does not have to be the root (as in the previous case).

That's because the MITM attacker can choose which related hostnames he attacks. The core of the Internet runs on unauthenticated DNS, which means that the attacker can take control of the DNS and make up arbitrary hostnames. For example, if he needs to attack *www.example.com*, he can make up a subdomain, say, *www.www.example.com*. From *that* name, he can then issue a cookie for *www.example.com*.

## Impact

Anecdotally, many web sites are designed under the assumption that the attacker can't discover or influence what's in the cookies. Because that's not always true, things can break, but exactly how will depend on the particular application. For example:

**XSS**

If developers don't expect cookies to change, they might use them in insecure ways. For example, they might output them to HTML directly, in which case a compromise can lead to a XSS vulnerability.

**CSRF defense bypass**

Some web site designs rely on *Cross-Site Request Forgery* (CSRF) defenses, which require that a token placed in the page parameters matches that in the cookie. Being able to force a particular cookie value onto a client defeats this approach.

**Application state change**

Developers quite often treat cookies as secure storage resistant to tampering. It might happen that there is some part of the application that relies on a cookie value for decision making. If the cookie can be manipulated, so can the application. For example, there might be a cookie named admin set to 1 if the user is an administrator. Clearly, users can always manipulate their own cookies and thus attack the application, so this is not necessarily a TLS issue. However, it can still be an attack vector used by a

MITM attacker. The proposed mitigation techniques (discussed later in this section) defend against all attacks of this type.

**Session fixation**

*Session fixation* is a reverse session hijacking attack. Rather than obtaining the victim's session ID, the attacker connects to the target web site to obtain a session ID of his own and tricks the victim into reusing it. For example, with session fixation, a victim could be tricked into uploading some sensitive information into an account under an attacker's control. This attack is not as powerful as session hijacking, but it could have serious consequences depending on the features of the target site.

# Mitigation

Cookie manipulation attacks can generally be addressed with appropriate mitigation steps that focus on preventing the attacker from forging cookies and checking that received cookies are genuine:

**Deploy HTTP Strict Transport Security with subdomain coverage**

*HTTP Strict Transport Security* (HSTS)[23] is a standard that enforces encryption on the hostname for which it is enabled. Optionally, it can enforce encryption on all subdomains of the main host. With this approach, an MITM attacker cannot inject any cookies using DNS trickery without breaking encryption.

HSTS significantly reduces the attack surface but is not in itself a complete solution. For example, it does not handle cases in which genuine (encrypted) related sites are compromised or run by different, untrusted entities. I discuss HSTS at length in the section called "HTTP Strict Transport Security" in Chapter 10.

**Use cookie name prefixes**

Some of the problems inherent in the cookie specification can be addressed with a new class of "super-secure" cookies. That's the idea behind *cookie prefixes*, which were initially a separate specification[24] but now live in the updated main cookie specification. Cookie name prefixes are a backward-compatible hack that uses special cookie names to opt-in into a better security model. For example, a cookie whose name starts with "__Secure-" must also have the "secure" attribute set. A cookie whose name starts with "__Host-" must be marked as secure but also issued for the root path ("/") and without a set domain, making it a cookie that's valid only for the issuing host. This new breed of super-secure cookies is already supported by modern browsers. They have several important properties: (1) they can be issued only by encrypted contexts, (2) they provide strong isolation between plaintext and encrypted contexts, and (3) they provide strong isolation between related hosts.

---

[23] RFC 6797: HTTP Strict Transport Security [fsty.uk/t267] (Hodges et al., November 2012)

[24] Cookie Prefixes [fsty.uk/t268] (M. West, retrieved 18 March 2017)

### Validate cookie integrity

If we start from the position that cookie injection is a valid attack vector that is not yet properly mitigated, then the best defense you can employ is to use integrity validation—ensuring that the cookie you receive from a client originated from your web site. This can be achieved with a *Hash-based Message Authentication Code* (better known by its acronym, HMAC).[25]

HMAC is a type of digital signature that enables you to validate that the content has not been tampered with. A cookie with an HMAC signature attached to it can't be modified without the changes being detected. That's a nice improvement. However, it is still possible to inject the cookie issued to one user into another user's account. Thus, for best security, it is critical that the integrity validation scheme is designed in such a way that cookies issued to one user are not valid for another. In practice, this translates to using different HMAC secrets for different user accounts.

Cookies that don't need to be accessed from JavaScript can be encrypted and integrity-validated. The integrity validation and encryption techniques can be used only for cookies that transport some data but can't be used to protect session cookies.

Even with an integrity validation and encryption scheme in place, cookies can still be stolen (e.g., via XSS) and potentially used by the attacker. For example, if session cookies are stolen, an attacker can use them to impersonate her victim.

# SSL Stripping

*SSL stripping* (or, more accurately, *HTTPS stripping*) exploits the fact that most users begin their browsing session on a plaintext portion of a web site or type addresses without explicitly specifying the *https://* prefix (browsers generally try plaintext access first).[26] Because the plaintext traffic of these users is fully visible and vulnerable, it can be modified at will by an active network attacker.

For example, if a web site normally contains a link to the secure server, the attacker can rewrite the content to replace the secure link with a plaintext one. Without a secure link to click on, the victim is forever prevented from entering the secure area. In the meantime, the attacker is responding to those plaintext links by proxying the genuine web site content (possibly obtained over TLS). At this point, the attacker can not only observe sensitive information but can also modify the requests and responses at will.

---

[25] RFC 2014: HMAC: Keyed-Hashing for Message Authentication [fsty.uk/t3] (Krawczyk et al., February 1997)

[26] Browser vendors would love to default to trying the secure scheme first, but this is another case of doing things that provide a better user experience. It's an area where continuous improvements are made. For example, Chrome now sometimes defaults to HTTPS if there is evidence in the user's browsing history that the web site redirects to HTTPS anyway. From Firefox 91 on, HTTPS is used by default in Private Browsing mode.

Figure 6.3. Active network attack variations

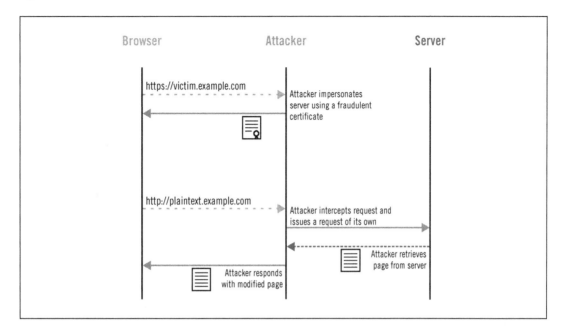

HTTPS stripping attacks rely on the fact that most users can not tell the difference between insecure and secure browsing. Faced with a user who can spot the difference, the attacker can attempt a tricky alternative and redirect the user to a secure web site that's under the attacker's full control but the name of which is very similar to that of the target web site. Common tricks include very long addresses that contain the entire target address within (e.g., *https://victim.com.example.com*) or addresses that differ from the real ones only by one character or that use similar Unicode characters.

Behind the scenes, the attacker may or may not actually be using a secure connection to the target web site, but that's little consolation for the victim because the attacker can not only observe the supposedly secure content but can also modify it at will.

From the attacker's point of view, HTTPS stripping attacks are very interesting because they can be easily automated using tools that are readily available. A well-known tool in this category is sslstrip.[27]

# MITM Certificates

HTTPS stripping is likely to work well against most users, but there are some users who can resist it. They will notice the difference between secure and insecure sites and even actively

---

[27] sslstrip [fsty.uk/t269] (Moxie Marlinspike, retrieved 10 February 2021)

check the security indicators. Some users also use bookmarks for navigation, going straight to the secure area from their first request.

The active network attacker is still able to redirect all traffic to go through them, but exploitation requires much more effort. Here are some possible alternative attack methods:

**Exploitation of validation flaws**

The security of TLS depends on the client correctly validating the credentials presented to it. If the validation is not implemented correctly, it might be possible to use a special invalid certificate or a certificate chain that can't be distinguished from a valid one.

**Rogue certificates**

*Rogue certificates* are fraudulent certificates that are, for all intents and purposes, as good as genuine. In 2021, they are largely a historical threat, thanks to stricter validation practices and the ecosystem transparency provided by Certificate Transparency. But history is full of examples of various attacks against CAs. For example, an attack on RapidSSL in 2008 resulted in the creation of a globally valid intermediate certificate. You can read more about it in the section called "RapidSSL Rogue CA Certificate" in Chapter 5. Another attack vector was suspected exploitation of very weak 1,024-bit private keys belonging to some CAs, which were still trusted as recently as a couple of years ago. According to some estimates, breaking a 1,024-bit key was thought to be fairly inexpensive, at only about $1 million and about a year to execute.[28]

With a rogue certificate in hand, the attacker will be invisible to everyone except the most paranoid user. Combined with the fact that the MITM can interfere with OCSP revocation checks and that most browsers ignore OCSP failures, if the attacker can maintain full control over a victim's Internet connection over an extended period of time it might also be effectively impossible to revoke a rogue certificate.

**Valid certificate controlled by attacker**

If the attacker is somehow able to obtain a certificate valid for the web site that they wish to attack, there is little to differentiate them from the real thing. In combination with broken revocation checking, this attack vector is a real threat. Attackers may obtain a valid certificate by breaking into the victim's servers, or by abusing other parts of the infrastructure, such as hijacking DNS or BGP.[29]

**Self-signed certificates**

If everything else fails, the attacker may try the least sophisticated approach, which is to present the victim with a self-signed certificate that has most fields copied from the

---

[28] Facebook's outmoded Web crypto opens door to NSA spying [fsty.uk/t205] (CNET, 28 June 2013)

[29] Bamboozling Certificate Authorities with BGP [fsty.uk/t107] (Birge-Lee et al., August 2018)

---

real one. Such a certificate is guaranteed to generate a warning, but users sometimes click through such warnings. More about that in the next section.

Two well-known tools in this category are sslsniff[30] and SSLsplit.[31]

# Certificate Warnings

For proper security, cryptography needs authentication. If you can't tell that you're talking to the right party, then all bets are off. Someone could be hijacking the communication channel to impersonate your intended recipient, and you wouldn't be able to tell. It's a situation similar to picking up the phone and talking to someone on the other end without knowing if they are who they claim they are.

In the context of TLS, we use certificates for authentication. (TLS supports other authentication methods, but they are rarely used.) When you connect to a server, you have a particular hostname in mind, and the expectation is that the server will present a certificate that proves that they have the right to handle traffic for that hostname.

If you receive an invalid certificate, the right thing to do is to abandon the connection attempt. Unfortunately, browsers don't do that. Because the Web is full of invalid certificates, it's almost guaranteed that none of the invalid certificates you encounter will be malicious. Faced with this problem, browser vendors decided a long time ago not to enforce strict TLS connection security, instead pushing the problem down to their users in the form of *certificate warnings*.

Which brings me to one of the ugliest truths about TLS: its sole purpose is to protect you from active network attacks, but when the attack comes all you will get is a certificate warning from your browser. Then it will be down to *you* to determine if you are under attack.

## Why So Many Invalid Certificates?

There's plenty of anecdotal evidence about the prevalence of invalid certificates. It's hard to actually find someone who has not been exposed to them. Here are some of the root causes:

**Misconfigured virtual hosting**
Many web sites continue to run only on port 80 and don't use encryption. A common configuration mistake is to host these plaintext sites on the same IP address as some other site that uses encryption on port 443. As a result, users who attempt to access the plaintext sites via an *https* prefix end up in the wrong place; the certificate they get doesn't match the intended name.

---

[30] sslsniff [fsty.uk/t270] (Moxie Marlinspike, retrieved 8 February 2021)

[31] SSLsplit - transparent and scalable SSL/TLS interception [fsty.uk/t271] (Daniel Roethlisberger, retrieved 8 February 2021)

Part of the problem is that at the technical level, we don't really have a mechanism for web sites to state if they support encryption. In that light, the correct way to deploy a plaintext site is to put it on an IP address on which port 443 is closed. That way, there won't be room for confusion.

This used to be a much bigger problem in the past. In 2010, I scanned about 119 million domain names, searching for secure sites.[32] The lists included all .com, .net, and .org domain names that existed at the time. I found 22.65 million (19%) sites that responded on port 443, hosted on roughly two million IP addresses. From those, only about 720,000 (3.2%) had certificates whose names matched the intended hostname.

Having a certificate with the right name is a good start, but it's not enough. Roughly 30% of the name-matched certificates in my 2010 survey could not be trusted due to other problems.

**Insufficient name coverage**

In a small number of cases, certificates are purchased and deployed, but the site operator fails to specify all required hostnames. For example, if you're hosting a site at *www.example.com*, the certificate should include that name but also the plain *example.com*. If you have other domain names pointing to your web site, the certificates should include them, too.

**Self-signed certificates and private CAs**

Certificates that are self-signed or issued by private CAs are not appropriate for use with the general public. Such certificates can't be easily and reliably distinguished from certificates used in MITM attacks.

Why are people using these certificates, then? There are many reasons, including: (1) purchasing, configuring, and renewing certificates is additional work and requires continuous effort; (2) up until a few years ago, certificates used to be expensive; and (3) some people believe that publicly trusted certificates should be free and refuse to buy them. However, the simple truth is that only publicly trusted certificates are appropriate for public web sites. We don't have an alternative at this time.

**Certificates used by appliances**

These days, most appliances have web-based administrative user interfaces and require secure communication. When these devices are manufactured, the hostname and IP address they will use is not known, which means that the manufacturers cannot install valid certificates onto them. In theory, end users could install valid certificates themselves, but many of these appliances are seldom used and are hardly worth the effort. In addition, many of the user interfaces do not allow user-provided certificates to be used.

---

[32] Internet SSL Survey 2010 is here! [fsty.uk/t113] (Ivan Ristić, 29 July 2010)

### Expired certificates

The other substantial reason for invalid certificates is expiration. In my survey, 57% of the failures fell into this category. In many cases, site owners forget to renew their certificates. Or, they give up on having valid certificates altogether but don't take the old ones down.

### Misconfiguration

Another frequent problem is misconfiguration. For a certificate to be trusted, a user agent needs to establish a chain of trust from the server certificate to a trusted root. Servers are required to provide a complete working chain, but many fail to do so. Browsers will often try to reconstruct incomplete chains, but they are not guaranteed to succeed. Other user agent types typically don't try.

### Other problems

Although many issues are the result of server problems, often there are significant client-side problems. One study from 2017 looked at Chrome certificate errors and found a variety of problems, with client clock skew a major contributing factor.[33]

When it comes to what users are experiencing, one study from 2013 looked at about 3.9 billion public TLS connections (made by real people from their devices) and found that 1.54% resulted in certificate warnings.[34] But that's only on the public Internet, where sites generally try to avoid warnings. In certain environments (e.g., intranets and internal applications), you might be expected to click through certificate warnings every single day as you're accessing web applications required for your work.

# Effectiveness of Certificate Warnings

The world would be much better without certificate warnings, but the truth is that browser vendors are balancing on a fine line between improving security and keeping their users happy. In 2008, I made a halfhearted attempt to convince Mozilla to hide the ability to add exceptions for invalid certificates in Firefox. I wanted to make it very difficult to bypass certificate warnings. Unsurprisingly, my bug submission was rejected.[35] Their response (in the form of a link to an earlier blog post),[36] was that they had tried, but the push-back from their users had been too strong. This is a reflection of a wider problem of misaligned priorities; browser vendors want increased market share, but increasing security usually has the opposite effect. As a result, browser vendors implement as much security as they can while trying to keep their most vocal users reasonably happy. Very occasionally, users

---

[33] Where the Wild Warnings Are: Root Causes of Chrome Certificate Errors [fsty.uk/t272] (Acer et al., October 2017)

[34] Here's My Cert, So Trust Me, Maybe? Understanding TLS Errors on the Web [fsty.uk/t273] (Akhawe et al., WWW Conference, 2013)

[35] Bug 431827: Exceptions for invalid SSL certificates are too easy to add [fsty.uk/t274] (Bugzilla@Mozilla, reported 2 May 2008)

[36] TODO: Break Internet [fsty.uk/t275] (Johnathan Nightingale, 11 October 2007)

complain about certificate warnings that come from genuine MITM attacks, and that reminds everyone what these warnings are for.[37] Perhaps the biggest problem with MITM attacks is that users are not aware of them (after all, certificate warnings are a "normal" part of life) and do not report them.

Still, the fact remains that the harder you make it for your users to override certificate warnings, the better security you will get. Today, major browsers generally rely on *interstitial* or *interruptive warnings*, which take over the entire browser content window. The old-style (native) dialog warnings are seen as ineffective; they look the same as all other prompts we get from our computers all the time. Most browsers allow users to click through the warnings. When only one click is required to get around the obstacle, the harsh language is all that stands between you and the web site. As it turns out, lots of people decide to go on.

Early studies of certificate warning effectiveness reported high click-through rates. But they largely relied on controlled environments (research labs), which was considered unreliable by some:[38]

> *Furthermore, our analysis also raised concerns about the limitations of laboratory studies for usable security research on human behaviors when ecological validity is important. [...] The observed reluctance of security concerned people to take part in our study raises concerns about the ability of such studies to accurately and reliably draw conclusions about security practices and user behavior of the general population.*

In the meantime, browser vendors started to use *telemetry* to monitor the usage of their products. That allowed for observation of users' behavior in their own environments, providing more accurate results. It turned out that Firefox had the best implementation, with only 33% of their users proceeding to the sites with invalid certificates. As a comparison, about 70% of Chrome users clicked through.[39] A later study reduced the click-through rate of Chrome users to 56% by mimicking the design used by Firefox.[40]

Chrome later continued to make improvements and switched to remembering user decisions for a period of time, leading to reduced click-through rates similar to those observed by Firefox.[41]

---

[37] Bug 460374: All certificates show not trusted - get error code (MITM in-the-wild) [fsty.uk/t276] (Bugzilla@Mozilla, reported 16 October 2008)

[38] On the Challenges in Usable Security Lab Studies: Lessons Learned from Replicating a Study on SSL Warnings [fsty.uk/t277] (Sotirakopoulos et al., Symposium on Usable Privacy and Security, 2011)

[39] Alice in Warningland: A Large-Scale Field Study of Browser Security Warning Effectiveness [fsty.uk/t278] (Akhawe and Felt; USENIX Security, 2013)

[40] Experimenting At Scale With Google Chrome's SSL Warning [fsty.uk/t279] (Felt at al., ACM CHI Conference on Human Factors in Computing Systems, 2014)

[41] A Week to Remember: The Impact of Browser Warning Storage Policies [fsty.uk/t280] (Joel Weinberger and Adrienne Porter Felt, June 2016)

## Mitigation

If you care about the security of your web site, you are probably going to be very worried about your users clicking through a genuine MITM attack. After all, you're going through all the trouble of using valid certificates, configuring your servers, and otherwise making sure everything is fine on your end for their protection.

Clearly, there's little you can do about the entire ecosystem, but you can protect your sites by supporting HSTS, which is a signal to the supporting browsers to adjust their behavior and adopt a stricter security posture when it comes to encryption. One of the features of HSTS is the suppression of certificate warnings. If there is an issue with the certificate on an HSTS site, all failures are fatal and cannot be overridden. With that, you are back in control of your own security.

## Security Indicators

Security indicators are user interface elements that relay additional information about security of the current page. They typically say things such as the following:

- "This page uses encryption"
- "We know what legal entity operates this web site"
- "This page uses an invalid certificate"
- "There is some sort of security problem with this page"

With the exception of *Extended Validation* (EV) certificates, which link legal entities to web sites, the other indicators exist largely because web site encryption is optional. In a world in which the Web was 100 percent encrypted and there were no certificate warnings and no mixed content, you wouldn't need to pay attention.

When I initially wrote this section, back in 2014, I spent a lot of time putting together screenshots to illustrate the diversity of security indicators. Even before my book went to print, the security indicators all changed, and they are quite different today as I work on the second edition of this book. The biggest change since 2014 is that EV certificates no longer get any special treatment.

Figure 6.4. Historical examples of browser security indicators (2014)

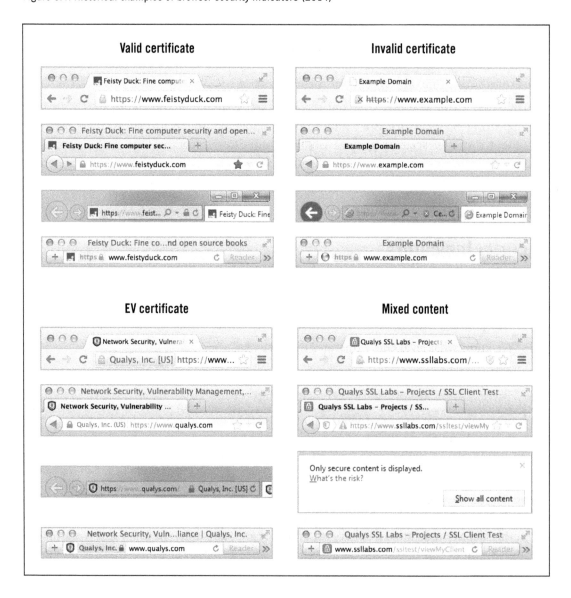

The biggest problem with security indicators is that most users don't pay attention to them and possibly don't even notice them. We know this from several studies that focused on security indicators. One study used eye tracking and determined that many users spend little time looking at browser chrome, focusing on the content instead.[42] In the same study, none of the participants even realized the EV indicators existed. This confirms the results of

---

[42] Exploring User Reactions to New Browser Cues for Extended Validation Certificates [fsty.uk/t281] (Sobey at al., ESORICS, 2008)

another study, whose authors arrived at the same conclusion.[43] A more recent study from 2019 arrived at the same conclusion: *EV indicators do not impact user behavior.*[44]

Perhaps one of the contributing factors to the confusion is the lack of consistency, both among different browsers and in different versions of the same browser. User interface guidelines exist,[45] but they are not specific enough.

In the early days of SSL there was a huge push to educate browser users about the meaning of the padlock ("If you see a padlock, you're safe."). A couple of years later, browser vendors started playing with the user interface. In some cases (e.g., Firefox), there were changes made with every new release.

At the same time, web sites started to use the padlock on their web pages, further diluting the message. Thus we went from having the padlock mean one specific thing (encryption is present) to using it as a generic security indicator. In many cases, its presence is meaningless. For example, there are many sites that prominently feature a padlock but use no encryption.

When it comes to mobile platforms, the situation seems to be worse. Due to much smaller screen sizes, browser vendors are trying to remove virtually all user interface elements, affecting security indicators in particular. With many mobile browsers, even security experts have a hard time distinguishing secure sites from insecure ones.[46]

This has led some researchers to conclude that mobile users are three times more vulnerable to phishing attacks.[47] In addition, the security of mobile (nonbrowser) applications in general is difficult to assess. Although all applications should use secure protocols for backend communication, we don't know if that's actually happening, because they provide no indications. And, even if they did, who is to say that they're not just displaying an image of a padlock without any security at all?

> **Note**
>
> All of this is not to say that browsers' security indicators serve no purpose. They do, but you could say that their primary goal these days is to motivate web site owners to improve the security of their web sites, out of fear that their users will be confused and scared away. As an example, browser security warnings played a significant, positive role during the migration away from SHA1 certificates. Over a period of about two years, starting in 2014, they helped raise user awareness

---

[43] An Evaluation of Extended Validation and Picture-in-Picture Phishing Attacks [fsty.uk/t282] (Jackson et al., Proceedings of Usable Security, 2007)

[44] The Web's Identity Crisis: Understanding the Effectiveness of Website Identity Indicators [fsty.uk/t283] (Thompson et al., August 2019)

[45] Web Security Context: User Interface Guidelines [fsty.uk/t284] (W3C Recommendation, 12 August 2010)

[46] Measuring SSL Indicators on Mobile Browsers: Extended Life, or End of the Road? [fsty.uk/t285] (Amrutkar et al., Information Security Conference, 2012)

[47] Mobile Users Three Times More Vulnerable to Phishing Attacks [fsty.uk/t286] (Mickey Boodaei, 4 January 2011)

and eventually helped the ecosystem hit the necessary milestones and smoothly transition to SHA256.

# Mixed Content

The TLS protocol concerns itself with a single network connection and focuses only on keeping the data secure at the network level. This separation of concerns works well for simpler protocols, for example, SMTP. However, there are some protocols, such as FTP and HTTP, that make use of multiple connections from the same security context. TLS doesn't provide any guidance for such situations; it's up to the developers to implement it securely.

When it comes to HTTPS, you'd struggle to find a page that uses only a single connection. On virtually all web sites, HTML markup, images, style sheets, JavaScript, and other page resources arrive not only over multiple connections but possibly from multiple servers and sites spread across the entire Internet. For a page to be properly encrypted, it's necessary that all the content is retrieved over HTTPS. In practice, that's very often not the case, leading to *mixed content* security problems.

### Note

This section covers only same-page mixed content, but the same problem exists at the web site level. Web sites that mix plaintext and secure pages are prone to development errors (e.g., use of insecure cookies or sensitive content available without encryption) and SSL stripping attacks. Traditionally, browsers used to show a warning when a form on an encrypted page attempted to send data without encryption. A similar problem can arise if insecure download is attempted,[48] either because the link itself is not secure or because there is an insecure redirection somewhere down the line.[49]

# Root Causes

To understand why mixed content issues are so pervasive, we have to go back to the origins of the Web and consider the breakneck pace of its evolution. The focus has always been on getting things done and overcoming the limits imposed by costs, technology, and security.

### Performance

In the early days of SSL, its performance on the Web was very poor compared to the performance of plaintext HTTP. Today, servers tend to have much faster processors and plenty of RAM, and yet we're still concerned about the speed of cryptographic operations. Back in the day, the only way to obtain good SSL performance was to use specialized hardware accelerators, which were terribly expensive.

---

[48] Protecting users from insecure downloads in Google Chrome [fsty.uk/t287] (Chromium Blog, 6 February 2020)

[49] Microsoft Edge and mixed content downloads [fsty.uk/t288] (Microsoft, 30 April 2020)

Because of the performance problems, everyone tried to stay away from SSL. There was no concept of providing 100% encryption coverage for web sites. You might even argue that such an approach was justifiable and that the choice was mostly between some security and no security at all.

Today, performance is still a concern, but it's predominantly about network latency. Because of the additional round trips required to establish a secure connection, there's a slight delay when accessing a secure web site. I talk more about performance issues in Chapter 9, *Performance*.

### Mashups

At some point, the Web really took off, and the concept of *mashups* was born. Web sites no longer provided all of the content themselves. Instead, they mixed and matched content from various sites and focused on the user experience, hiding away content origin. In some cases, the content was freely available. In others, mashups operated via commercial deals.

A special case of a mashup is the use of third-party code for web site analytics, made extremely popular by Google when it gave its analytics service away for free.[50]

Mashups are, generally speaking, a nightmare for security. They're mostly implemented by incorporating some JavaScript code from a third-party web site. Unfortunately, although this approach to site building reduces costs dramatically, it also gives the third-party web sites almost full control over all the sites that rely on them. It also creates a problem for web site users: with so many entities involved on the same site, it becomes difficult to understand what entities they're communicating with and where their data is stored.

In the context of encryption, the main issue is that in many cases third-party content and services are not available via a secure server. Sometimes, secure access is available but costs more. As a result, people simply resorted to including insecure (plaintext) content from their "secure" web sites.

To illustrate this problem, consider that Google's own ad platform, AdSense, added support for secure delivery only in September 2013.[51]

### Infrastructure costs

As competition among web sites grew, it became impossible to deliver a web site from a single geographic location and remain competitive. *Content delivery networks* (CDNs) rose in popularity to deliver content to visitors at the best possible performance. The idea is that by spreading a number of servers across the globe, site visitors can always talk to the fastest one.

---

[50] Google Analytics Usage Statistics [fsty.uk/t289] (BuiltWith, retrieved 13 February 2021)
[51] Use AdSense on your HTTPS sites [fsty.uk/t290] (Sandor Sas, 16 September 2013)

The problem with CDNs is that they are intended to serve huge amounts of (usually static) data files for many customers. Encryption not only increases CPU and RAM requirements but also might affect caching and adds the burden of certificate and key management.

On top of that, there's the issue of IP addresses. For plaintext HTTP, for which virtual web site hosting is widely supported, IP addresses don't matter; one address can host any number of plaintext web sites. This makes large-scale hosting and distribution easy. For a very long time, virtual hosting of secure web sites was not as easy, given that some older clients required that one dedicated IP address was used per site.

### Abandoned content and migration errors

Because the Web started out as plaintext, many web sites gradually adopted encryption. Even when encryption became available, many large properties continued to serve pages with plaintext links, sometimes intentionally and sometimes in error. This issue created a chicken-and-egg situation, where browsers couldn't address mixed content issues because they didn't want to break some very popular web sites, but the web sites wouldn't fix the problems because everything worked from their perspective.

Because of all this history, mixed content became deeply ingrained in web sites and with developers, which in turn forced browser vendors to only very slowly transition to enforcing encryption for all page content.

## Impact

The impact of mixed content issues depends on the nature of the resource that is left without encryption. Over the years, two terms emerged: *mixed passive content* (or *mixed display*) for resources that are lower risk, for example, images, and *mixed active content* (or *mixed scripting*) for higher-risk content, such as HTML markup and JavaScript. The Mixed Content specification prefers the terms *blockable* and *upgradeable*.[52]

Mixed active content is the really dangerous category. A single unprotected inclusion of a JavaScript file can be hijacked by an active network attacker and used to obtain full control over the page. The same can be said for other dangerous resource types, such as HTML markup (if included via a frame), style sheets, Flash and Java applications, and so on. When successful, the attacker can perform arbitrary actions on that web site using the victim's identity.

Mixed passive content is not as dangerous, but it still leads to page integrity and confidentiality issues. For example, the attacker could discover what parts of a web site are being visited. Or they could mess with the victim by sending them messages embedded in

---

[52] Mixed Content Level 2 Editor's Draft [fsty.uk/t291] (W3C, 20 November 2020)

images. This could lead to phishing. It's also possible to inject exploits into images, targeting browsers' image processing code.

In addition, in most browsers, an unencrypted resource delivered from the same hostname as the main page will expose the site's insecure session cookies over the network. As I discussed earlier in this chapter, cookies that are not properly secured can be retrieved by an active attacker, but with mixed content they can be retrieved by a passive attacker, too.

## Browser Treatment

Initially, mixed content was allowed by all browsers. The vendors expected web site designers and programmers to understand the potential security issues and make the right decisions. Over time, this attitude changed and the vendors started to become more interested in this problem and to restrict what was allowed.

Today, most browsers tend to implement a compromise between breakage and security: mixed passive content tends to be allowed, but mixed active content is not.

**Chrome**

Chrome changed its handling of mixed active content in version 14,[53] but considered the job done only with version 21.[54] Starting with version 38, Chrome began blocking all mixed active content.[55]

An announcement in October 2019 declared the end of all mixed content, boosted by autoupgrading plaintext links in an attempt to fix broken markup wherever possible.[56]

A series of changes took place over time and concluded with Chrome 86, released in October 2020.

**Firefox**

Firefox has a long history of being able to detect and warn about mixed content but, due to internal implementation issues, not being able to block it. The bug for this issue remained open for about 12 years.[57] With version 23, Firefox finally started to block all mixed active content.[58]

---

[53] Trying to end mixed scripting vulnerabilities [fsty.uk/t292] (Google Online Security blog, 16 June 2011)

[54] Ending mixed scripting vulnerabilities [fsty.uk/t293] (Google Online Security blog, 3 August 2012)

[55] PSA: Tightening Blink's mixed content behavior [fsty.uk/t294] (Mike West, 30 June 2014)

[56] No More Mixed Messages About HTTPS [fsty.uk/t295] (Chromium Blog, 3 October 2019)

[57] Bug 62178: Implement mechanism to prevent sending insecure requests from a secure context [fsty.uk/t296] (Bugzilla@Mozilla, reported 6 December 2000)

[58] Mixed Content Blocking Enabled in Firefox 23! [fsty.uk/t297] (Tanvi Vyas, 10 April 2013)

### Internet Explorer and Edge

Internet Explorer had mixed content detection since at least Internet Explorer 5 (1999). When detecting a combination of encrypted and plaintext resources on the same page, IE would prompt the user to decide how to handle the problem. Microsoft almost switched to blocking insecure content by default and even deployed that behavior in IE 7 beta,[59] but backed down due to user pressure. It made the change later, in IE 9.[60] At that time, Microsoft also started allowing passive mixed content by default.

In 2020, Microsoft released its second iteration of the Edge browser, this time built on the open source Chromium project. As a result, its features are closely aligned with Chrome's. This is true for the browser's mixed content handling, which is also blocking with autoupgrade where available.

### Safari

Safari was the last major browser to start blocking mixed content. Apple enacted this behavior in its browsers starting with version 9, released in the second half of 2015.

### Note

Mixed content vulnerabilities can be very deep. In most modern browsers, there are many ways in which insecure HTTP requests can originate from secure pages. For example, it is likely that browser plugins can make whatever requests they want irrespective of the encryption status of the host page. This is especially true for plug-ins such as Flash and Java, which are platforms in their own right. There's now a W3C effort to standardize browser handling of mixed content, which should help get a consistent behavior across all products.[61]

## Prevalence of Mixed Content

Anecdotally, mixed content is very common. At Qualys, we investigated this problem in 2011 along with several other application-level issues that result in full breakage of encryption in web applications.[62] We analyzed the homepages of about 250,000 secure web sites from the Alexa top one million list and determined that 22.41% of them used insecure content. If images are excluded, the number fell to 18.71%.

A different and more detailed study of 18,526 sites extracted from Alexa's top 100,000 took place in 2013.[63] For each site, up to 200 secure pages were analyzed, for a total of 481,656

---

[59] SSL, TLS and a Little ActiveX: How IE7 Strikes a Balance Between Security and Compatibility [fsty.uk/t298] (Rob Franco, 18 October 2006)

[60] Internet Explorer 9 Security Part 4: Protecting Consumers from Malicious Mixed Content [fsty.uk/t299] (Eric Lawrence, 23 June 2011)

[61] W3C: Mixed Content Level 2 [fsty.uk/t291] (Stark et al., retrieved 13 February 2021)

[62] A study of what really breaks SSL [fsty.uk/t300] (Michael Small and Ivan Ristić, May 2011)

[63] A Dangerous Mix: Large-scale analysis of mixed-content websites [fsty.uk/t301] (Chen et al., Information Security Conference, 2013)

Table 6.1. Mixed content in 481,656 secure pages from Alexa's top 100,000 sites [Source: Chen et al., 2013]

| Type | # Inclusions | % remote | # Files | # Webpages | % Websites |
|------|-------------|----------|---------|------------|------------|
| Image | 406,932 | 38% | 138,959 | 45,417 | 30% |
| Frame | 25,362 | 90% | 15,227 | 15,419 | 14% |
| CSS | 35,957 | 44% | 6,680 | 15,911 | 12% |
| JavaScript | 150,179 | 72% | 29,952 | 45,059 | 26% |
| Flash | 1,721 | 62% | 638 | 1,474 | 2% |
| Total | 620,151 | 47% | 191,456 | 74,946 | 43% |

pages. You can see the results in Table 6.1, "Mixed content in 481,656 secure pages from Alexa's top 100,000 sites [Source: Chen et al., 2013]".

The numbers have come down since. More recently, Chrome's own tracking of various types of behaviors across popular web sites shows mixed passive content on roughly 8.5% in early 2021.[64]

# Mitigation

The good news is that despite browsers' lax attitude to mixed content issues you are in full control of this problem. If you implement your sites correctly, you won't be vulnerable. There are two technologies that can help you minimize and, possibly, eliminate mixed content issues, even when it comes to incorrectly implemented applications:

**HTTP Strict Transport Security**

HSTS is a mechanism that enforces secure resource retrieval, even in the face of user mistakes (such as attempting to access your web site on port 80) and implementation errors (such as when your developers place an insecure link on a secure page). This feature effectively eliminates mixed content issues, but only when the resources are on the hostnames you control. That doesn't mean that you should leave the insecure resources as they are. In fact, because mixed content checks take place before HSTS is enforced, the security indicators will indicate the existence of the problem.

**Content Security Policy**

To reliably block insecure resource retrieval from third-party web sites, use *Content Security Policy* (CSP). This security feature allows blocking of all insecure resources on a page, no matter where they reside. Perhaps more interestingly, CSP has a reporting feature that could be used to detect insecure resources without blocking them. By doing so, over time, all insecure content can be removed. Finally, blocking isn't the only option; CSP can now also transparently rewrite insecure links to enable

---

[64] UpgradeInsecureRequestsEnabled [fsty.uk/t302] (Chrome Platform Status, retrieved 13 February 2021)

encryption. This, of course, works only if the same resource is available at the same address with and without encryption.

HSTS and CSP are both declarative measures, which means that they can be added at a web server level without having to change applications. In a way, you can think of them as safety nets, because they can enforce security even for incorrectly implemented web sites.

For example, a very frequent problem on secure web sites comes from the fact that many of them implement automatic redirection from port 80 to port 443. That makes sense, because if some user does arrive to your plaintext web site you want to send him to the right (secure) place. However, because redirection is automatic it is often invisible; a plaintext link for an image will be redirected to a secure one, and the browser will retrieve it without anyone noticing. Anyone except the attacker, maybe. For this reason, consider always redirecting to the same entry point on the secure web site. If you do this, any mistakes in how resources are referenced will be detected and corrected in the development phase.

## Toward a Fully Encrypted Web

The partially encrypted Web of today will never give us robust security because there are too many opportunities to do the wrong thing. The good news is that we are now in a transition period and have been for a number of years already. With the help of some key browser vendors and other organizations of all sizes, we are on our way to a fully encrypted Web.[65] Because browser vendors don't want to break anything big, the progress is slow, but the effort is paying off. In early 2017, both Google[66] and Mozilla[67] reported that the world is regularly getting over 50 percent of page loads over HTTPS. As I write this, in February 2021, it's closer to 90%. We're almost there.

Browser vendors generally prefer a combined carrot-and-stick approach. They tell web site operators off for having bad security, but they also offer operators advanced browser functionality only if encryption is available—features such as the following:

**Expanded scope of security warnings**
> Browser security indicators are gradually increasing their scope and are now warning browser users about HTTP being insecure. For example, in January 2017, Chrome (in version 56) and Firefox (in version 51) started warning users about HTTP pages that accept passwords or credit card numbers.[68]

---

[65] Marking HTTP As Non-Secure [fsty.uk/t303] (Chromium, retrieved 8 May 2017)

[66] Google Transparency Report: HTTPS [fsty.uk/t304] (Google, retrieved 8 May 2017)

[67] Percentage of Web Pages Loaded by Firefox Using HTTPS [fsty.uk/t305] (Let's Encrypt, retrieved 8 May 2017)

[68] Firefox and Chrome start warning about insecure login forms [fsty.uk/t306] (Feisty Duck, 31 January 2017)

Google subsequently increased the scope of the warnings to include all forms submitted over HTTP and all HTTP traffic when in incognito mode. In 2018 (in Chrome 68), Google again extended the warnings to all plaintext HTTP pages.[69]

**Powerful features available with encryption only**

In parallel, powerful features are being made available only to encrypted pages. This is especially true for features that transmit data that could be considered valuable by active network attackers—for example, users' geographic locations, which was the first to be restricted.[70]

# Extended Validation Certificates

*Extended Validation* (EV) certificates are designed to establish a link between a domain name and the legal entity behind it. Individuals and nonincorporated entities can't get EV certificates. In the early days of SSL, all certificates required strict verification, similar to how EV certificates are issued today. Later on, certificate price wars led to the wide adoption of *domain-validated* (DV) certificates, which relied on email validation, which could be automated. That was possible because there were no formal regulations of the certificate validation procedures. EV certificates were defined in 2007 by the CA/Browser Forum to bring back strict issuance standards.[71]

EV certificates offer two advantages: (1) the identity of the domain owner is known and encoded in the certificate and (2) the manual verification process makes certificate forgery more difficult. As far as I am aware, there's never been a fraudulent or a misissued EV certificate.

On the other hand, it's questionable if those advantages translate into any practical benefits, at least when the general user population is concerned. As we've seen in earlier sections in this chapter, users rarely notice security indicators, even the prominent ones used for EV certificates. For this reason, end users are going to miss the link to the domain name owner. Further, fraudulent DV certificates can be used to attack EV sites. The only way to prevent these attacks is for end users to understand what EV certificates mean, remember that a site uses them, notice the absence of the appropriate security indicators, and decide not to proceed. This seems unlikely, given the percentage of users who proceed to a web site even after shown a scary certificate warning.

Separately, there is also a question about the value of the additional information provided, especially given the possibility of name collisions. This was neatly demonstrated first by James Burton in September 2017 when he incorporated a legal entity with the name "Iden-

---

[69] A milestone for Chrome security: marking HTTP as "not secure" [fsty.uk/t307] (Chrome, 24 July 2018)

[70] Deprecating Powerful Features on Insecure Origins [fsty.uk/t308] (Chromium, retrieved 8 May 2017)

[71] EV SSL Certificate Guidelines [fsty.uk/t53] (CA/Browser Forum, retrieved 15 July 2014)

---

tify Verified."[72] When he obtained an EV certificate for this entity, the misleading name appeared in the URL bar. Shortly after, Ian Carroll went one step further and incorporated Stripe, Inc. in Kentucky, intentionally using the same name as the more famous Stripe, Inc. incorporated in Delaware. He then got an EV certificate for his new legal entity, all of which was perfectly in line with the issuance requirements.[73] Amusingly, Comodo first revoked Ian's EV certificate, then admitted error, apologized, and offered a replacement.[74]

In theory, it's possible that the treatment of EV certificates could be improved. For example, browsers could add features to allow site operators to always require EV certificates on their web sites, similar to how you can use HSTS to always require encryption today. That would be a form of pinning and would raise the effort required to impersonate a web site. In practice, it's not likely to happen because the browser vendors have little incentive to invest development time to help EV certificates succeed. In fact, browser vendors have been sending negative signals about EV indicators for years. Apple removed the EV indicators from Safari in 2018.[75] In 2019, both Chrome[76] and Firefox[77] decided to remove these indicators from their user interfaces.

The topic of certificates, user agents, and trust is a complex one and continues to evolve. If you want to see how things may develop in the future, keep an eye on *Brand Indicators for Message Identification* (BIMI), which is being designed to regulate the use of (trademarked) brand logos in email clients.[78]

Another problem is that EV certificates are detected and indicated on the page level without taking into account what type of certificate is used by the resources (e.g., scripts). Given the high cost of EV certificates, it is not unusual that complex sites often rely on DV certificates for the largely invisible subdomains.[79]

This means that a careful network attacker can use a DV certificate against an EV site, potentially without affecting the green security indicators. Zusman and Sotirov demonstrated several interesting attack vectors:[80]

**Resources delivered from other domain names**

In many cases, sites will use an EV certificate on the main domain name but retrieve resources from many other hostnames, all of which will typically use DV certificates.

---

[72] First part of phishing with EV [fsty.uk/t309] (James Burton, 13 September 2017)

[73] Extended Validation Is Broken [fsty.uk/t310] (Ian Carroll, 12 December 2017)

[74] On Comodo CA's Recent Revocation of an SSL Certificate for Kentucky-based Stripe, Inc. [fsty.uk/t311] (Comodo CA, May 2018)

[75] Minutes for CA/Browser Forum F2F Meeting 44 [fsty.uk/t312] (CA/Browser forum, 6 June 2018)

[76] Upcoming Change to Chrome's Identity Indicators [fsty.uk/t313] (Chrome developers, 9 August 2019)

[77] Improved Security and Privacy Indicators in Firefox 70 [fsty.uk/t314] (Mozilla Security Blog, 15 October 2019)

[78] BIMI [fsty.uk/t315] (AuthIndicators Working Group, retrieved 7 February 2021)

[79] Beware of Finer-Grained Origins [fsty.uk/t316] (Jackson and Barth, Web 2.0 Security and Privacy, 2008)

[80] Sub-Prime PKI: Attacking Extended Validation SSL [fsty.uk/t317] (Zusman and Sotirov, Black Hat USA, 2009)

---

Browser connections for these other names can be intercepted with a fraudulent DV certificate, leading to malware injection.

**Cookie theft**

Because browsers do not enforce certificate continuity, it's possible to use a DV certificate to intercept a connection for the main domain name, steal existing or set new cookies, and redirect back to the real server. The attack happens quickly and won't be noticed by most users.

**Persistent malware injection**

If caching is enforced (the attacker can essentially say that a resource is never refreshed), injected malware can persist in the browser file cache and stay active for long periods of time, even on subsequent site visits.

# Certificate Revocation

When it comes to the certificate validity period, there is a tension between wanting to reduce administrative burden and needing to provide reasonably fresh information during verification. In theory, the idea is that every certificate should be checked for revocation before it is considered trusted. In practice, there are a number of issues that make revocation checking difficult.

## Inadequate Client-Side Support

Arguably the biggest problem with revocation checking is that client-side support is inadequate. Making things worse is the fact that revocation is something you never need—until you need it badly. As such, it's always something that can be dealt with "later."

It's genuinely quite difficult to understand what browsers do about revocation, when they do it, and how. Because there is no documentation, you have to rely on reading obscure mailing lists, bug reports, and source code to understand what's happening. For example, for a long time, it wasn't clear that CRLs aren't used by many browsers. Support for new features, such as OCSP stapling, was slow to arrive. Testing can provide some answers, but only at a point in time; there are no guarantees that the next version of a product will continue to behave in the same manner.

Outside the browser world, command-line tools still struggle with certificate validation, let alone revocation. And because most libraries do not use revocation checks by default, developers generally don't bother either.

The overall conclusion is that revocation does not work as designed, for one reason or another. This became painfully clear during 2011, after several CAs had been compromised. In each case, the only way to reliably revoke fraudulent certificates was to use blacklisting, but not via CRL or OCSP. Instead, all vendors resorted to issuing patch releases, which contained hardcoded information about the fraudulent certificates. Chrome, Firefox, and Microsoft subsequently built proprietary mechanisms to allow them to push new blacklisted certificates to their users without forcing a software upgrade.

## Key Issues with Revocation-Checking Standards

At a high level, there are some design flaws in both CRL and OCSP that limit their usefulness. There are three main problems:

**Disconnect between certificates and queries**

CRL and OCSP refer to certificates using their serial numbers, which are just arbitrary numbers assigned by CAs. This is unfortunate, because it's impossible to be completely certain that the certificate you have is the same one the CA is referring to. This fact could be exploited during a CA compromise by creating a forged certificate that reuses a serial number of an existing and valid certificate.

**Blocking certificates instead of endorsing them**

CRL is, by definition, a block list, and cannot be anything else. OCSP suffered from coming after CRLs and was probably designed to be easy to use on top of the existing CRL infrastructure. In the early days, OCSP responders operated largely by feeding from the information available in CRLs. That was a missed opportunity to change from sending negative signals about (revoked) certificates to sending positive signals about certificates that are valid.

The focus on blocking was amplified by the practice of treating the "good" OCSP response status as "not revoked," even when the server actually had *no knowledge* of the serial number in question. As of August 2013, the CA/Browser Forum forbids this practice.

It might seem like nitpicking, but this design flaw came up as a real problem during the DigiNotar incident. Because this CA had been completely compromised, there was no record of what fraudulent certificates had been issued. As a result, they could not be revoked individually. Although DigiNotar's root certificates were eventually removed from all browsers, as a short-term measure their OCSP responders were configured to return "revoked" for all their certificates.

**Privacy**

Both CRL and OCSP suffer from privacy issues: when you communicate with a CA to obtain revocation information, you disclose to it some information about your browsing habits. The leakage is smaller in the case of CRLs as they usually cover a large number of certificates.

With OCSP, the privacy issue is real, making many unhappy. If a powerful adversary wishes to monitor everyone's browsing habits, it's much easier to monitor the traffic flowing to a dozen or so major OCSP responders than to eavesdrop on the actual traffic of the entire world.

To address this problem, site operators should deploy *OCSP stapling*, which is a mechanism that allows them to deliver OCSP responses directly to their users along with their certificates. With this change, users no longer need to talk to CAs, and there is no information leakage.

# Certificate Revocation Lists

Initially, *Certificate Revocation Lists* (CRLs) were the only mechanism for revocation checking. The idea was that every CA would make a list of revoked certificates available for download at a location specified in all their certificates. Clients would consult the appropriate list before trusting a certificate. This approach proved difficult to scale, leading to the creation of OCSP for real-time checks.

## Issues with CRL Size

CRLs might have seemed like a good idea initially, when the number of revocations was small. But when the number of revocations exploded, so did the size of the CRLs. For example, GoDaddy's revocation information grew from 158 KB in 2007 to 41 MB in 2013.[81]

To reduce the size of CRLs, over time CAs started to split their revocation information across many smaller individual files. This makes the CRL size problem less visible; if you're an active web user you're likely to need many of the CRLs, which means that you will have to download large quantities of data on an ongoing basis. It might not be an issue for desktop users, but it's definitely unacceptable for mobile users. Even if bandwidth consumption does not worry you, the CPU power required for processing such large files might be prohibitive.

> ## Note
>
> The problem with CRL size could have been solved by using *delta CRLs*, which contain only the differences from a previously known full CRL. However, this feature, even though supported on all Windows platforms, has found little use in Internet PKI.

---

[81] NIST Workshop: Improving Trust in the Online Marketplace [fsty.uk/t318] (Ryan Koski, 10 April 2013)

## CRL Freshness

CRL size is not the only problem. Long validity periods pose a significant problem and reduce CRL effectiveness. For example, in May 2013 Netcraft reported how a revoked intermediary certificate on a popular web site went unnoticed (until they reported on it).[82]

The certificate in question did not have any OCSP information, but the CRL was correct. What happened? A part of the explanation could be that no client used the CRL to check the intermediate certificates, which reflects the sad state of CRL support. However, even assuming that clients use CRLs correctly (e.g., Internet Explorer), the fact remains that the CA industry currently allows unreasonably long validity periods for intermediate certificates. Here's the relevant quote from Baseline Requirements[83] (emphasis mine):

> *The CA SHALL update and reissue CRLs at least (i) once every twelve months and (ii) within 24 hours after revoking a Subordinate CA Certificate, and **the value of the nextUpdate field MUST NOT be more than twelve months beyond the value of the thisUpdate field.***

Thus, a CRL for an intermediate certificate is going to be considered fresh for 12 months, whereas a critical revocation can be added at any day of the year. Allowing such a long period was probably partially motivated by the desire to cache the CRLs for as long as possible, because intermediate certificates are often used by millions of sites. In addition, CRLs are signed by root keys, which are kept offline for safety; frequent issuance of CRLs would impact the security. Still, long freshness periods of CRLs negatively impact the effectiveness of revocation. This is especially true for intermediate certificates, which, if compromised, could be used to impersonate any web site. By comparison, CRLs for server certificates mustn't be older than 10 days.

# Online Certificate Status Protocol

*Online Certificate Status Protocol* (OCSP) came after CRL to provide real-time access to certificate revocation information. The idea was that without the burden of having to download a large CRL you can afford to use OCSP on every visit to a web site.

## OCSP Replay Attacks

In cryptography, a well-understood attack against secure communication is the *replay attack*, in which the attacker captures and reuses a genuine message, possibly in a different

---

[82] How certificate revocation (doesn't) work in practice [fsty.uk/t319] (Netcraft, 13 May 2013)

[83] Baseline Requirements [fsty.uk/t54] (CA/Browser Forum, retrieved 11 September 2021)

context. OCSP, as originally designed,[84] is not vulnerable to replay attacks; clients are invited to submit a one-time token (*nonce*) with every request, and servers are expected to include that same value in their signed response. The attacker cannot replay responses because the nonce is different every time.

This secure-by-default approach ended up being difficult to scale and, at some point, gave way to a lightweight approach that is less secure but easier to support in high-volume environments. The *Lightweight OCSP Profile*[85] introduced a series of recommendations designed to allow for batch generation of OCSP responses and their caching. In order to support the caching, the replay protection had to go. Without the nonce, an OCSP response is just a file that you can generate once, keep for a while, and deliver using a CDN.

As a result, clients generally don't even try to use nonces with OCSP requests. If they do, servers usually ignore them. Thus, the only defense against replay attacks is the built-in time limit: attackers can reuse OCSP responses until they expire. That window of opportunity will depend on the CA in question and on the type of certificate (e.g., responses for EV certificates might have a short life, but those for DV certificates might have a much longer one), but it's usually about a week.

As is the case with CRLs, Baseline Requirements allow OCSP responses that are valid for up to 10 days or up to 12 months for intermediate certificates. As with CRLs, when an intermediate certificate is revoked, an OCSP response must be updated within 24 hours.

## OCSP Response Suppression

The *OCSP response suppression* attack relies on the fact that many clients that use OCSP ignore failures; they submit OCSP requests in good faith but carry on when things go wrong. Thus, an active attacker can suppress revocation checks by forcing all OCSP requests to fail. The easiest way to do this is to drop all connections to OCSP responders. It is also possible to impersonate the responders and return HTTP errors. Adam Langley did this once and concluded that "revocation doesn't work."[86]

Prior to Adam's experiment, in 2009 Moxie Marlinspike highlighted a flaw in the OCSP protocol that allows for suppression without network-level failures. In OCSP, successful responses are digitally signed, which means that even an active attacker cannot forge them. However, there are several unauthenticated response types dealing with failures. If all you need is to make a response fail, you simply return one of the unauthenticated error codes.[87]

---

[84] RFC 6960: X.509 Internet PKI Online Certificate Status Protocol [fsty.uk/t320] (S. Santesson et al., June 2013)

[85] RFC 5019: The Lightweight OCSP Profile for High-Volume Environments [fsty.uk/t321] (A. Deacon and R. Hurst, September 2007)

[86] Revocation doesn't work [fsty.uk/t322] (Adam Langley, 18 March 2011)

[87] Defeating OCSP With The Character '3' [fsty.uk/t323] (Moxie Marlinspike, 29 July 2009)

---

## Client-Side OCSP Support

In many cases, there is no need to attack OCSP revocation because user agents ignore it completely. Older platforms and browsers do not use OCSP or do not use it by default. For example, Windows XP and OS X before 10.7 fall into this category.

More important, however, is the fact that modern browsers choose not to use OCSP or use it only in special circumstances. For example, for a long time iOS used OCSP only for EV certificates.[88] Chrome largely stopped using OCSP in 2012,[89] replacing all standards-based revocation checks with a lightweight proprietary mechanism called *CRLSets*.[90] CRLSets improve revocation checking performance (all checks are local and thus fast) but decrease security because they cover only a subset of all revocations, mostly those related to CA certificates. Private CAs are especially vulnerable, because there is no way for them to be included in the CRLSets. In the most recent versions, OCSP revocation checking is attempted only for EV certificates and only if their CRLSets don't already cover the issuing CA.

In March 2015, Mozilla introduced OneCRL,[91] which is a proprietary mechanism for revocation checking of intermediate certificates and, possibly, a small number of important leaf certificates. Further information about Mozilla's plans is published on its wiki.[92]

In 2020, Mozilla added support for CRLite, an alternative mechanism for revocation checking whose main advantage is efficient transport and storage of revocation information that enables it to cover all certificates, not only the ones belonging to CAs.[93] CRLite was proposed in a 2017 research paper that demonstrated that 300 MB of revocation information can be efficiently packed to only one MB.[94] A significant challenge with CRLite is being able to collect all the necessary information, mainly because not all CAs support CRLs. Let's Encrypt doesn't, and as a result its certificates are not covered by Mozilla's CRLite implementation.

Even when OCSP is used, virtually all browsers implement *soft-fail*. They attempt OCSP requests and react properly to successful OCSP responses but ignore all failures. In practice, this provides protection only in a small number of use cases. As you've seen in the previous section, soft-fail clearly does not work against an active attacker who can simply suppress all OCSP traffic.

---

[88] CRL and OCSP behavior of iOS / Security.Framework? [fsty.uk/t324] (Stack Overflow, answered 2 March 2012)

[89] Revocation checking and Chrome's CRL [fsty.uk/t325] (Adam Langley, 05 February 2012)

[90] CRLSets [fsty.uk/t326] (Chromium Wiki, retrieved 15 July 2014)

[91] Revoking Intermediate Certificates: Introducing OneCRL [fsty.uk/t327] (Mozilla Security Blog, 3 March 2015)

[92] CA:Revocation Plan [fsty.uk/t328] (Mozilla Wiki, retrieved 7 February 2021)

[93] Introducing CRLite: All of the Web PKI's revocations, compressed [fsty.uk/t329] (Mozilla Security Blog, 9 January 2020)

[94] CRLite: A Scalable System for Pushing All TLS Revocations to All Browsers [fsty.uk/t330] (Larisch et al., May 2017)

Typically, the worst that can happen when revocation checking fails is that an EV site will lose its security status, leading to all EV indicators being stripped from the user interface. I am not sure we can expect anyone to actually notice such an event. And, if they do, how should they react to it?

## Responder Availability and Performance

From its beginnings and to this day, OCSP has had a reputation for being unreliable. The problems in the early days caused browsers to adopt the inadequate soft-fail approach, and OCSP never recovered. CAs are much better these days at making their responders available, but browser vendors don't want to put their reputation on the line for a matter they don't control. Thanks to Netcraft, we have visibility into the performance of OCSP responders of various CAs.[95]

There are three separate issues to consider:

Availability

OCSP responder availability is the biggest issue. If you're running a secure web site and your CA's OCSP responder is down, your site will suffer. If browsers implemented hard-fail, then your site would be down, too.[96]

Even with soft-fail, it's likely that you will experience severe performance issues in the case of the OCSP responder downtime. User agents that use OCSP will attempt to check for revocation, and they all have a network timeout after which they give up. This timeout is typically set at several seconds. As an illustration, the last time I looked at how Firefox behaved, I discovered that it used a timeout of three seconds by default, or 10 seconds in hard-fail mode.

There is also an additional problem with the *captive portals*, or situations when users don't have full access to the Internet (and thus to various OCSP responders) but still need to validate certificates in some way. In practice, this happens most often when you are required to authenticate on a Wi-Fi network. Although captive portals could take care to whitelist public OCSP responders, most don't do that.

Performance

By its nature, OCSP is slow. It requires user agents to first parse a certificate, then obtain the OCSP URL, open a separate TCP connection to the OCSP responder, wait for a response, and only then proceed to the original web site. A slow OCSP responder may add hundreds of milliseconds of latency to the first connection to your web site.[97]

---

[95] OCSP Uptime [fsty.uk/t331] (Netcraft, retrieved 7 February 2021)

[96] Certificate revocation and the performance of OCSP [fsty.uk/t332] (Netcraft, 16 April 2013)

[97] The Case for Prefetching and Prevalidating TLS Server Certificates [fsty.uk/t333] (Stark et al., February 2012)

---

OCSP responder performance is an often-neglected yet important technical differentiator among CAs. You basically want to select a CA that will provide minimal slowdown to your web site. For that, a fast and globally distributed OCSP responder network is required. Some CAs are using their own infrastructure, while others are opting for commercial CDNs.

Maintaining a robust OCSP responder is not a trivial task. Verisign (now Symantec) was known for operating a highly available OCSP responder service, serving billions of OCSP responses every day.

### Correctness

If an OCSP responder is available and fast, that does not mean that it is actually responding correctly. Some CAs do not synchronize their OCSP responders with changes in their main database. For example, some time ago I obtained a certificate from a public CA, installed it on my web site, and promptly discovered that all OCSP requests were failing.

After contacting the CA, I learned that they allow up to 40 minutes from the creation of a certificate until they update the OCSP responders. My suggestion to postpone certificate issuance until their entire infrastructure was ready was dismissed as "too complicated."

At this point, it's unlikely that OCSP revocation will ever be changed to a hard-fail system. CAs had a slow start initially, and when browsers adopted soft-fail they had little incentive to improve. Today, the likely scenario is that the availability and performance concerns will be addressed by a wider adoption of *OCSP stapling*, which allows servers to retrieve OCSP responses from the CAs once and deliver them directly to end users along with their certificates.

> **Note**
>
> While I was writing the first edition of this book, I had my Firefox browser configured to hard-fail (in about:config, set security.ocsp.require to true). In all of that time, I had OCSP responder availability issues only with one CA. Interestingly, it was the same CA that has the 40-minute delay on their OCSP responders.

## Client Clock Skew

Incorrect client time is a significant cause of communication errors, which we mostly talk about in the context of certificates. For example, it's a best practice to avoid deploying your new certificates immediately; if you allow some time to pass, you maximize the chances that the certificate will be considered valid by clients whose clocks are incorrect. According to one study, as many as 33% of certificate errors on Windows were observed to come from the incorrect time.[98]

OCSP responses have it much worse, given that they are only valid for about a week, making them much more likely to fail due to incorrect time. Unlike with a certificate, where you can wait for a month before it is deployed, with an OCSP response you could wait for only about three days, and by then it would have only about three days left on it.

To deal with this problem, some browsers are resorting to trying to figure out the correct time directly, bypassing the operating system.[99]

## OCSP Stapling

OCSP stapling aims to remove or minimize the performance and privacy issues involved with invoking OCSP responders directly. Instead of expecting every end user to check the revocation status of a certificate for themselves, the certificate's owner talks to the CA, obtains freshness proof, and relays it to the users. The OCSP response is the same, but the alternative delivery method avoids the need for additional network communication and all problems that go with it. OCSP stapling is implemented via a TLS feature called Status Request.[100]

Initially, OCSP stapling was designed to support only leaf certificates. A separate TLS extension was subsequently introduced to support stapling of intermediate certificates but hasn't gained much support.[101]

After the introduction of OCSP stapling, server software needed to be updated to support it. Not unexpectedly, support for this feature was slow to arrive. Open source web servers typically do not enable OCSP stapling by default, which in practice means that few deployments use it. In contrast, Microsoft's IIS web server supports OCSP stapling well and uses it by default. It's not surprising that Microsoft's web servers thus make up the majority of the OCSP stapling market share.

A bigger problem is that many server applications, even very popular ones, implement OCSP stapling in a poor way.[102] In the best case, such applications treat this feature as a performance optimization, meaning that they use only best effort to obtain and deliver stapled OCSP responses. In the worst case, enabling OCSP stapling creates new availability issues because web servers may sometimes return expired or otherwise invalid OCSP responses, confusing clients. Some servers, if they find themselves without an OCSP response

---

[98] Where the Wild Warnings Are: Root Causes of Chrome HTTPS Certificate Errors [fsty.uk/t334] (Acer et al., October 2017)

[99] Sane time [fsty.uk/t335] (Chromium, retrieved 7 February 2021)

[100] RFC 6066: TLS Extensions: Extension Definitions [fsty.uk/t336] (D. Eastlake 3rd, January 2011)

[101] RFC 6961: TLS Multiple Certificate Status Request Extension [fsty.uk/t48] (Y. Pettersen, June 2013)

[102] ocsp-stapling.md [fsty.uk/t70] (Ryan Sleevi, retrieved 8 May 2017)

they need, will stop responding to HTTP requests altogether. Coupled with a CA for which the OCSP responder is slow, such an approach may add service blackouts of tens of seconds. Clearly, OCSP stapling won't take off until we can rely on it to just work.[103]

## OCSP Must-Staple

At this point, it seems that the world has given up on revocation checking via direct out-of-band communication with issuing CAs. Both CRL and OCSP have problems that have caused them to be rejected by browser vendors and site operators who are in permanent pursuit of high availability and faster operation—but not everything is lost. There is a possibility that a new feature, called *must-staple*, could in theory provide the best of both worlds, performance and security in the same package.

At the core, the idea is to make use of OCSP stapling, in which web sites deliver evidence of certificate freshness with every TLS handshake. As of the time of writing, OCSP stapling improves privacy, availability, and performance. It doesn't provide any security benefits because it's not required and will be omitted by the attacker. However, if we make OCSP stapling mandatory (this feature is referred to as "must-staple"), a stolen certificate will be useful to the thief only for as long as she is able to staple it with a valid OCSP response; that's typically a matter of days, compared to possibly months until the certificate expires.

Mandatory OCSP stapling is supported by a relatively recent addition called the *TLS Feature Extension*.[104] Mozilla started supporting mandatory OCSP stapling for certificates as of Firefox 45, released in March 2016.[105] There's little information at this time from other browser vendors regarding their plans to support mandatory stapling. The biggest practical obstacles to a wider adoption of must-staple certificates are good server-side support in popular platforms, along with the ability of user agents to deal with client clock skew.[106]

---

[103] High-reliability OCSP stapling and why it matters [fsty.uk/t337] (Cloudflare, 10 July 2017)

[104] RFC 7633: X.509v3 TLS Feature Extension [fsty.uk/t338] (P. Hallam-Baker, October 2015)

[105] Improving Revocation: OCSP Must-Staple and Short-lived Certificates [fsty.uk/t72] (Mozilla Security Blog, 23 November 2015)

[106] Is the Web Ready for OCSP Must-Staple? [fsty.uk/t339] (Chung et al., October 2018)

---

Chapter 6: HTTP and Browser Issues

# 7 Implementation Issues

The software we write today is inherently insecure, for several reasons. First, the basic tools —programming languages and libraries—are not written with security in mind. Languages such as C and C++ are inherently unsafe and result in code that is fast but fragile. Often, a single coding mistake can crash the entire program. That is simply absurd. Libraries and APIs are virtually never designed to minimize errors and maximize security. Documentation and books are rife with code and designs that suffer from basic security issues.

The second reason goes much deeper and has to do with the economics of writing software. In today's world, emphasis is on getting work "done" by minimizing up-front costs (in both time and money), without fully considering the long-term effects of insecure code. Security—or, more generally, code quality—is not valued by end users, which is why companies tend not to invest in it.

As a result, you will often hear that cryptography is bypassed, not broken. The major cryptographic primitives are well understood and, given choice, no one attacks them first. But the primitives are seldom useful by themselves; they need to be combined into schemes and protocols and then implemented in code. These additional steps then become the main point of failure, which is why you will also often hear that only a fool implements their own crypto.

The history is full of major cryptographic protocols with critical design flaws, but there are even more examples of various implementation problems in well-known projects. The situation gets much worse when you start looking at projects developed without the necessary expertise in cryptography.

This chapter reviews the major implementation issues, both those historical and the ones still relevant.

## Certificate Validation Flaws

For a TLS connection to be trusted, every client must perform two basic checks: determine that the certificate applies to the intended hostname and determine that the certificate is valid and can be trusted. Sounds simple, but the devil is in the details. When certificate-checking code is developed, developers will test with the certificate chains they find in real life, but those will never be malicious and designed to subvert security. As a result, developers often miss some critical checks.

For example, the following is a list of some (but not all!) of the things that need to be checked for each certificate chain.

1. The end entity (server) certificate is valid for the intended hostname.

2. All chain certificates (including the end-entity one) must be checked to see that:

   - They have not expired.

   - Their signatures are valid.

3. An intermediate certificate might need to satisfy further requirements:

   - Can be used to sign other certificates for the intended purpose (e.g., an intermediate certificate might be allowed to sign web server certificates, but cannot be used for code signing).

   - Can be used to sign other CA certificates.[1]

   - Can be used to sign the hostname in the leaf certificate.

In addition, a robust implementation will check a number of other things, for example, that all the keys are strong and that weak signatures (e.g., MD2, MD5, and SHA1) are not used.

## Library and Platform Validation Failures

Certificate validation flaws in libraries are not very common, but their impact is usually significant, because all code that relies on them inherits the problems. Well-known validation flaws include the following:

**Basic Constraints check failure in Microsoft CryptoAPI (2002)[2]**
This is an early example of validation failure in probably the most widely used codebase, which affected all Microsoft platforms as well as some products running on other operating systems. Because of this flaw, any valid server certificate could be used to sign a fraudulent certificate that would then be trusted. The fraudulent certificate could then be used in active MITM attacks. Konqueror (the default browser of the KDE desktop) was also found to suffer from the same problem. Further variations of the flaw were later discovered in Microsoft's code, including some that could be used for code signing on the Windows platform.

---

[1] For security reasons, the CA certificate that issues the end-entity certificate shouldn't be allowed to issue subordinate CA certificates. All other intermediate certificates in the chain must have this privilege.

[2] Certificate Validation Flaw Could Enable Identity Spoofing [fsty.uk/t340] (Microsoft Security Bulletin MS02-050, 4 September 2002)

This problem was discovered by Moxie Marlinspike in August 2002. Later, Moxie went on to write sslsniff,[3] a MITM attack tool, for the sole purpose of demonstrating that this problem can be exploited. In 2009, Moxie also reported that OpenSSL (around version 0.9.6) had been vulnerable to the same problem, but no further details are available.

### Chain validation failure in GnuTLS (2008)[4]

A flaw in the certificate chain validation code allowed invalid chains to be recognized as valid by simply appending any trusted root certificate to the end of any nontrusted chain. The error was that the appended certificate, which caused the entire chain to be trusted, was removed prior to checking that all certificates are part of a single chain.

### DSA and ECDSA signature validation failures in OpenSSL (2009)[5]

In 2009, the Google Security Team discovered that, due to insufficient error checking in OpenSSL code, DSA and ECDSA signature failures could not be detected. The practical impact of this problem was that any MITM attacker could present a fraudulent certificate chain that would be seen as valid.

### Basic Constraints check failure in iOS (2011)[6]

Almost a decade later, Apple was discovered to have made the same mistake in the chain validation as Microsoft and others before. The iOS platforms before 4.2.10 and 4.3.5 were not checking if certificates are allowed to act as subordinate CAs, making it possible for any leaf certificate to sign any other certificate.

### Connection authentication failure in iOS and OS X (2014)

On 21 February 2014, Apple released updates for iOS 6.x and 7.x in order to fix a bug in TLS connection authentication.[7] Although Apple didn't provide any details (they never do), the description caught everyone's attention and sparked a large-scale hunt for the bug. It turned out that a devastating slip in the connection authentication code allowed any DHE and ECDHE connection to be silently hijacked by an active MITM.[8] The bug was also found to exist in the latest version of OS X (10.9), which had been released in October 2013. Unfortunately, a fix was not immediately available; it's not clear why Apple would choose not to synchronize releases for such a significant security issue. Possibly because of a strong backlash, the fix (OS X 10.9.2) came only a couple of days later, on February 25th.

---

[3] sslsniff [fsty.uk/t270] (Moxie Marlinspike, retrieved 12 September 2021)

[4] Analysis of vulnerability GNUTLS-SA-2008-3 CVE-2008-4989 [fsty.uk/t341] (Martin von Gagern, 10 November 2008)

[5] Incorrect checks for malformed signatures [fsty.uk/t342] (OpenSSL, 7 January 2009)

[6] TWSL2011-007: iOS SSL Implementation Does Not Validate Certificate Chain [fsty.uk/t343] (Trustwave SpiderLabs, 25 July 2011)

[7] About the security content of iOS 7.0.6 [fsty.uk/t344] (Apple, 21 February 2014)

[8] Apple's SSL/TLS bug [fsty.uk/t345] (Adam Langley, 22 February 2014)

---

In the context of TLS authentication, this bug is as bad as they get. The weakness is in a transient part of the handshake that is never logged. (If you were to attack certificate authentication, for example, you would need to provide a fraudulent certificate chain, which might be recorded and reported.) If proper care is taken to use it only against vulnerable clients (which should be possible, given that the TLS handshake exposes enough information to allow for pretty reliable fingerprinting), an attack could be reliable, silent, and effective without leaving any trace.

All applications running on the vulnerable operating systems were exposed to this problem. The only exceptions were cross-platform applications (for example, Chrome and Firefox) that rely on their own TLS stack.

### Chain validation failures in GnuTLS (2014)

In early 2014, GnuTLS disclosed two separate vulnerabilities related to certificate chain validation.[9] The first bug caused GnuTLS to treat any X.509 certificate in version 1 format as an intermediary CA certificate. If someone could obtain a valid server certificate in v1 format (not very likely, given that this is an obsolete format), they could use it to impersonate any server when GnuTLS is used for access. This vulnerability had been introduced in GnuTLS 2.11.5.

As for the second vulnerability, shortly after Apple's TLS authentication bug had been revealed, GnuTLS disclosed a similar bug of their own: a malformed certificate could short-circuit the validation process and appear as valid.[10] It is probable that the maintainers, after learning about Apple's bug, decided to review their code in search of similar problems. Although GnuTLS isn't used by major browsers and isn't as popular as OpenSSL on the server side, it still has some major users. For example, many of the packages shipped by Debian use it. Thus, this vulnerability might have had a significant impact. This vulnerability had been present in the code for a very long time, possibly from the very first versions of GnuTLS.

### OpenSSL ChangeCipherSpec injection (2014)

In June 2014, the OpenSSL project disclosed a long-standing vulnerability that allowed an active network attacker to inject ChangeCipherSpec messages into handshakes between two OpenSSL endpoints and force negotiation of a predictable master secret.[11] This problem existed in virtually every version of OpenSSL, but—as far as we know—it's not exploitable unless a vulnerable version from the OpenSSL 1.0.1 branch is running on the server. The root cause is that, during a TLS handshake, the ChangeCipherSpec message is used by each side to signal the end of negotiation and a switch to encryption, but this message is not authenticated because it's not part of the

---

[9] Advisories [fsty.uk/t346] (GnuTLS, retrieved 17 July 2014)

[10] Dissecting the GnuTLS Bug [fsty.uk/t347] (Johanna, 5 March 2014)

[11] OpenSSL Security Advisory CVE-2014-0224 [fsty.uk/t348] (OpenSSL, 5 June 2014)

handshake protocol. If the attacker sends the message early (which OpenSSL should have caught), the vulnerable sides construct encryption keys too early and with the information the attacker knows.[12]

This vulnerability is quite serious and easy to exploit, but its impact is reduced, because OpenSSL is required on both sides of the communication, and yet OpenSSL is rarely used on the client side. The most prominent platform that uses OpenSSL in this way is Android 4.4 (KitKat), which was subsequently fixed. According to SSL Pulse, immediately after the vulnerability was released, there were about 14% of servers running the exploitable versions of OpenSSL.

### OpenSSL alternative chains certificate forgery (2015)

OpenSSL suffered another authentication vulnerability in July 2015. A bug in the certificate chain validation code allowed network attackers to use a leaf certificate as a valid intermediate (CA).[13] Fortunately, the impact of this problem was low because the flaw had only been introduced the month prior; most deployments don't follow OpenSSL that closely. Following the publication of a test case for this problem,[14] an exploitation module for Metasploit was added.[15]

In 2014, a group of researchers published the results of comprehensive adversarial testing of certificate validation in several libraries.[16] They developed a concept of "mutated" certificates, or *frankencerts*, built from real certificates.[17] Although the widely used libraries and browsers passed the tests, the lesser-used libraries, such as PolarSSL, GnuTLS, CyaSSL, and MatrixSSL, were all found to have serious flaws.

## Application Validation Failures

If major platforms and libraries can have serious validation vulnerabilities, we can intuitively expect that other software will fare much worse. After all, for most developers security is something that stands in the way between them and shipping their project. There's been ample anecdotal evidence of certificate validation failures in end-user code, but the scale of the problem became more clear after a research paper on the topic was published in 2012.[18] From the abstract (emphasis mine):

---

[12] Early ChangeCipherSpec Attack [fsty.uk/t349] (Adam Langley, 5 June 2014)

[13] Alternative chains certificate forgery [fsty.uk/t350] (CVE-2015-1793) (OpenSSL Security Advisory, 9 July 2015)

[14] Add test for CVE-2015-1793 [fsty.uk/t351] (OpenSSL commit, 2 July 2015)

[15] Add openssl_altchainsforgery_mitm_proxy.rb [fsty.uk/t352] (Metasploit pull request, 16 July 2015)

[16] Using Frankencerts for Automated Adversarial Testing of Certificate Validation in SSL/TLS Implementations [fsty.uk/t353] (Brubaker et al., S&P, 2014)

[17] Frankencert [fsty.uk/t354] (sumanj, GitHub, retrieved 17 July 2014)

[18] The most dangerous code in the world: validating SSL certificates in non-browser software [fsty.uk/t355] (Georgiev et al., CCS, 2012)

---

> *We demonstrate that SSL certificate validation is completely broken in many security-critical applications and libraries. Vulnerable software includes Amazon's EC2 Java library and all cloud clients based on it; Amazon's and PayPal's merchant SDKs responsible for transmitting payment details from e-commerce sites to payment gateways; integrated shopping carts such as osCommerce, ZenCart, Ubercart, and PrestaShop; AdMob code used by mobile websites; Chase mobile banking and several other Android apps and libraries; Java Web-services middleware—including Apache Axis, Axis 2, Codehaus XFire, and Pusher library for Android—and all applications employing this middleware. **Any SSL connection from any of these programs is insecure against a man-in-the-middle attack.***

If this is not cause for alarm, then I don't know what is. Clearly, there are some major components of the Internet infrastructure mentioned in the report. According to the team behind the research, the chief problems are the badly designed APIs. Not only are the libraries often insecure by default (no certificate validation at all), but they make it difficult to write code that is secure. Most libraries are simply too low level and expect too much from their users. For example, OpenSSL expects developers to provide their own code to perform hostname validation.

The report very accurately describes a major problem with our entire development stacks, affecting all code and security, not only SSL and TLS. Yes, there are libraries that are insecure and difficult to use, but the real problem is that we keep on using them. No wonder we keep on repeating the same mistakes.

To be fair, there are some platforms that behave correctly. Java's SSL/TLS implementation (JSSE), for example, performs all necessary validation by default, much to the annoyance of many developers who don't want to bother to set up a trusted development infrastructure. Anecdotal evidence suggests that most developers, in development, disable all validation in their code. We can only wonder how often checks are re-enabled in production.

## Hostname Validation Issues

Speaking of hostname validation—how difficult can it be to verify if a certificate is valid for the intended hostname? As it turns out, the verification is often incorrectly implemented, as several vulnerabilities show. At Black Hat USA in 2009, Dan Kaminsky[19] and Moxie Marlinspike[20] independently detailed how to perform MITM attacks entirely silently, without any warnings experienced by the victims.

---

[19] PKI Layer Cake: New Collision Attacks Against the Global X.509 Infrastructure [fsty.uk/t356] (Kaminsky et al., Black Hat USA, 2009)

[20] More Tricks For Defeating SSL In Practice [fsty.uk/t357] (Moxie Marlinspike, Black Hat USA, 2009)

Several flaws were needed to pull the attacks off, but in both cases the key was the NUL byte, which is used in C and C++ for string termination. In this context, the NUL byte is not part of the data but only indicates that the data is ending. This way of representing textual data is handy, because you only need to carry a pointer to your data. Then, as you're processing the text, whenever you see the NUL byte, you know that you've reached the end.

Figure 7.1. Representation of a C string in memory

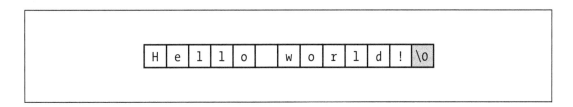

Certificate structures, which rely on the ASN.1 notation standard, use a different approach, in which all structures are stored with their length. Problems arise when these different approaches to handling strings meet: certificates are encoded in one way (ASN.1) but processed in another (C code).

The attack is this: construct a certificate that has a NUL byte in the hostname, and bet that (1) most clients will think that that's where the hostname ends and that (2) the NUL byte will thwart a CA's validation process.

Here's how Moxie executed the attack:

1. Construct a special hostname with a NUL byte in it. Moxie used the following: *www.paypal.com\0.thoughtcrime.org* (the NUL byte is indicated with \0, but is normally "invisible"). The rules are to:

   - Place the hostname you wish to impersonate before the NUL byte.

   - Put some domain name you control after the NUL byte.

2. For CAs, the NUL byte is nothing special.[21] They issue certificates based on the validation of the hostname suffix, which maps to some top-level domain name. In the previous attack example, the domain name is *thoughtcrime.org*, which belongs to Moxie. He will naturally approve the certificate request.

3. The resulting certificate can now be used against vulnerable clients with a modified version of sslsniff.

---

[21] Actually, that's not strictly true. Some CAs were found to incorrectly process the NUL byte and mistake it for a string terminator. These days, it's very likely that CAs perform all sorts of checks on the submitted hostnames.

Figure 7.2. The domain name used by Moxie Marlinspike in his proof-of-concept attack

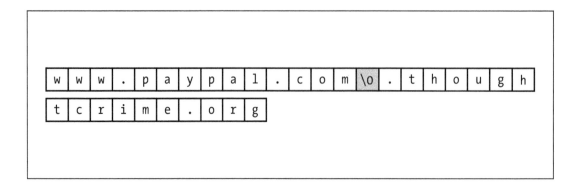

Microsoft's CryptoAPI, GnuTLS, and NSS libraries were all found to be vulnerable to the NUL byte attack, affecting Firefox, Internet Explorer, and many other user agents. And when you add to the mix the PKI feature that allows for wildcards in hostnames you may end up with a certificate issued to *\0thoughtcrime.org, which worked as a universal interception certificate.

## Insecure Encryption Activation

There are typically two ways to use TLS; one is to use an *always-on* approach, where a conversation starts immediately with the TLS handshake, after which an application layer protocol takes over. Sometimes, when backward compatibility with an older plaintext protocol is required, communication starts as plaintext and has to be explicitly upgraded to TLS. In SMTP, the command that does this is called STARTTLS, and this same name is commonly used to refer to the upgrade request in a variety of protocols. This optionality opens up several attack vectors that can be exploited if there are omissions in the application code.

**Lack of STARTTLS enforcement**

When a protocol can be used with or without encryption, it's up to client software to enforce the desired minimum security standard. It's a common implementation flaw to request encryption but to proceed without it if it's not offered. To exploit this problem, an active network attacker hijacks the plaintext connection and removes the STARTTLS request. All communication proceeds as plaintext.

**Buffering of insecure plaintext**

Another common flaw is omitting resetting the protocol state after encryption starts, enabling the attacker to influence the conversation they don't actually have access to. In some situations, attackers can inject commands into the plaintext part of the conversation only for them to be processed afterward.

Chapter 7: Implementation Issues

Problems like this are easy to create and difficult to find because every single client and server has to do the right thing. For illustration, a survey released in August 2021 found more than 40 vulnerabilities in STARTTLS implementations.[22]

It's worth highlighting that these flaws do not affect server-to-server SMTP, where it is in fact acceptable to deliver email via plaintext if encryption is not available. By default, email delivery as currently in use today defends only against passive attacks. Defending against active attacks requires either strict configuration of the sending MTA or support for modern standards such as MTA-STS.

# Random Number Generation

All cryptography relies on random number generation, making this functionality the essential building block of secure communication.[23] For example, you need random numbers whenever you are generating a new key. Keep in mind that key generation is not something you do only once in a while (e.g., if you're installing a new server) but something that protocols (e.g., TLS) do behind the scenes on every single connection.

With a good *random number generator* (RNG), for example, a 256-bit symmetric key will provide 256 bits of security (when used with a strong algorithm). But if the RNG is flawed, rather than having a random number from that large 256-bit space you may end up with one from a much smaller space, say, 32 bits. The smaller the effective space, the worse the security. If the effective size of the key is too small, even brute-force attacks against it may be possible.

## Netscape Navigator (1994)

One of the early examples of random number generation failure was in Netscape Navigator, the flagship product of the company that designed SSL itself. This browser used a simplistic algorithm for random number generation that relied on the time since boot in microseconds and the IDs of the underlying operating system process and its parent. The problem was revealed in 1995, when two researchers reverse engineered the code of the RNG[24] and wrote a program that uncovers the master encryption key.[25]

In the best case for the attacker, having an account on the same Unix machine as the victim meant that he could determine the process and parent process IDs. The attacker would

---

[22] Why TLS is better without STARTTLS [fsty.uk/t358] (Poddebniak et al., August 2021)

[23] True random number generation is not possible unless specialized hardware components are used. In practice, we rely on *pseudorandom number generators* (PRNGs). Most PRNGs use a small amount of entropy as a seed, after which they can produce a large quantity of pseudorandom numbers. In this section, I use RNG and PRNG interchangeably.

[24] Randomness and the Netscape Browser [fsty.uk/t359] (Ian Goldberg and David Wagner, January 1996)

[25] unssl.c [fsty.uk/t360] (Ian Goldberg and David Wagner, September 1995)

then determine the time in seconds from observing packets as they travel on the network, reducing the problem to guessing the microseconds value—which is only about 20 bits of security. To break through that required only 25 seconds on the hardware they had at hand.

In the more realistic case of an attacker with no knowledge of process IDs, the size of the problem would be reduced to 47 bits—still within reach of brute-force attacks, even at that time.

## Debian (2006)

In May 2008, Luciano Bello discovered[26] that a catastrophic programming error concerning the RNG used in the OpenSSL system libraries had been made by the Debian Project in September 2006 and that the bug consequently ended up in the project's stable release (Debian *etch*) in April 2007. Debian is not only a very popular Linux distribution but also a starting point from which many other distributions are built (most notably, Ubuntu), which meant that the problem affected a great number of servers in the world.

The programming error had been the accidental removal (commenting out) of a single line of code, which fed entropy to the random number generator. With that line removed, the only entropy left was some auxiliary input from the process ID, which meant that there were only 16 (!) bits of entropy for all cryptographic operations. With so few bits, all crypto on the affected installations was effectively nonexistent. All private keys generated on vulnerable servers could be easily guessed.

This was the affected fragment of the code:

```
/*
 * Don't add uninitialised data.
        MD_Update(&m,buf,j);
 */
        MD_Update(&m,(unsigned char *)&(md_c[0]),sizeof(md_c));
        MD_Final(&m,local_md);
        md_c[1]++;
```

The biggest security exposure came from weak OpenSSH keys,[27] but that was largely mitigated by the fact that these keys are stored in well-known locations and could be easily checked. The Debian project built a blacklist of vulnerable keys as well as tools to look for them.

Replacing vulnerable TLS keys was more difficult, because the process could not be implemented as part of the automated patching process. Scripts were built to scan all files and detect weak keys. Because the problem can be detected from a server's public key,

---

[26] DSA-1571-1: openssl — predictable random number generator [fsty.uk/t361] (Debian, 13 May 2008)

[27] Working exploit for Debian generated SSH Keys [fsty.uk/t362] (Markus Müller, 15 May 2008)

remote-testing tools were made available; for example, I added one to the SSL Labs web site. In addition, because most server certificates last only for a year or two, CAs were able to apply tests (against public keys, which are embedded in certificate signing requests) and refuse to issue certificates for vulnerable private keys. Overall, however, there was a great sense of confusion, and many people reported that the detection tools were not correctly flagging vulnerable keys even though they had been generated on vulnerable systems.

The discovery of the Debian RNG issue highlighted the fact that open source projects are often touched—for whatever reason—by those who are not very familiar with the code. There is often very little quality assurance even for critical system components such as OpenSSL. And yet millions rely on that code afterward.

Tension between project developers and packagers is a well-known problem in open source circles.[28] Distributions often fork open source projects and change their behavior in significant ways but keep the names the same. As a result, there is often confusion regarding which versions are affected by problems and who is responsible for fixing them. The underlying root cause is friction between developers and packagers, which results from different development schedules and different priorities and development goals.[29]

> ### Note
>
> Debian is not the only operating system that has suffered problems with random number generation. In 2007, three researchers published a paper discussing RNG weaknesses in Windows 2000.[30] It was later discovered that Windows XP was also affected. Then, in March 2013, the NetBSD project announced that NetBSD 6.0, first released in October 2012, had a bug in the kernel RNG that impacted security.[31]

## Insufficient Entropy on Embedded Devices

In February 2012, a group of researchers published the results of an extensive study of the quality of RSA and DSA keys found on the Internet.[32] The results indicated that at least 0.5% of the seen RSA keys (used for SSL/TLS) were insecure and could easily be compromised. The results for DSA (used for SSH) were worse, with 1.03% of the keys considered insecure.

The large majority of the discovered problems could be attributed to issues with random number generation. The study concluded:

---

[28] Vendors Are Bad For Security [fsty.uk/t363] (Ben Laurie, 13 May 2008)

[29] Debian and OpenSSL: The Aftermath [fsty.uk/t364] (Ben Laurie, 14 May 2008)

[30] Microsoft confirms that XP contains random number generator bug [fsty.uk/t365] (Computer World, 21 November 2007)

[31] RNG Bug May Result in Weak Cryptographic Keys [fsty.uk/t366] (NetBSD, 29 March 2013)

[32] Widespread Weak Keys in Network Devices [fsty.uk/t367] (factorable.net, retrieved 17 July 2014)

---

*Ultimately, the results of our study should serve as a wake-up call that secure random number generation continues to be an unsolved problem in important areas of practice.*

On the positive side, virtually all of the discovered problems were on headless and embedded devices, and the study concluded that nearly all keys used on nonembedded servers are secure. Just a fraction of the discovered certificates were signed by public CAs. The main problems identified were the following:

**Default keys**

Some manufacturers are shipping their products with default encryption keys. Clearly, this practice defeats the purpose, because all product users end up using the same keys and can compromise one another after extracting the private keys (from the hardware or software). Furthermore, those keys will inevitably be shared with the world.[33]

**Repeated keys due to low entropy**

Some devices generate keys on first boot, when there is little entropy available. Such keys are generally predictable. The paper describes the experiment of a simulated headless first boot running Linux, which clearly demonstrates the weaknesses of the Linux entropy-gathering code in the first seconds after first boot.

**Factorable keys**

Most interestingly, for RSA keys it was discovered that many share one of the two primes that make the modulus, a condition that allows the keys to be compromised. Given that the primes should be randomly generated, the same primes should not occur. According to the research, the root cause is a particular pattern in the OpenSSL code that generates RSA keys coupled with low-entropy conditions.

The summary of the TLS-related findings can be seen in Table 7.1, "Summary of vulnerable private keys [Source: factorable.net]".

Clearly, there are failures at every level (e.g., manufacturers could have checked for these issues and worked around them), but ultimately the study uncovered what is really a usability problem: cryptographic applications rely on the underlying operating system to provide them with enough randomness, but that often does not happen. And when it does not, there is no way to detect failures directly (e.g., Linux will never block on /dev/urandom reads). Few applications use defense-in-depth measures and use statistical tests to verify that their random data is indeed random.

This inability to rely on system-provided randomness may force some developers to take matters into their own hands and use their own RNGs instead. This approach is unlikely to

---

[33] LittleBlackBox [fsty.uk/t368] (Database of private SSL/SSH keys of embedded devices, retrieved 17 July 2014)

Table 7.1. Summary of vulnerable private keys [Source: factorable.net]

| | | |
|---|---:|---:|
| Number of live hosts | 12,828,613 | (100.00%) |
| . . . using repeated keys | 7,770,232 | (60.50%) |
| . . . using vulnerable repeated keys | 714,243 | (5.57%) |
| . . . using default certificates or default keys | 670,391 | (5.23%) |
| . . . using low-entropy repeated keys | 43,852 | (0.34%) |
| . . . using RSA keys we could factor | 64,081 | (0.50%) |
| . . . using Debian weak keys | 4,147 | (0.03%) |
| . . . using 512-bit RSA keys | 123,038 | (0.96%) |
| . . . identified as a vulnerable device model | 985,031 | (7.68%) |
| . . . using low-entropy repeated keys | 314,640 | (2.45%) |

be successful, however, because random number generation is a difficult task that's easy to get wrong.

Since 2012, there's been a steady stream of new research in this field. It's easy to see why: certificates are easy to collect from the Internet and relatively easy to break in an automated fashion. A report published at DEF CON 29 in 2021 looked into additional root causes of insecurity and found poorly written software APIs and otherwise poor coding practices.[34]

# Heartbleed

*Heartbleed*, a devastating vulnerability in OpenSSL, was disclosed to the public in April 2014. This attack exploits a flaw in the implementation of the *Heartbeat* protocol, which is a little-used TLS protocol extension (more about it in the section called "Heartbeat" in Chapter 3).

Heartbleed is arguably the worst thing to happen to TLS, which is ironic, given that it's not a cryptographic failure. Rather, it's a testament to the poor state of software development and quality of open source in general.

In the fallout after Heartbleed, everyone's eyes were on OpenSSL. Although the lack of funding for the project and its poor code quality had been known for a very long time, it took a massive vulnerability for the community to take action. The results were good and bad, depending on your point of view. The Linux Foundation announced a three-year project called Core Infrastructure Initiative, which aims to distribute $3.9 million to underfunded open source projects,[35] OpenSSL published a roadmap to identify and fix the problems with the project,[36] and, in the meantime, the OpenBSD Project forked OpenSSL into a new

---

[34] You're Doing IoT RNG [fsty.uk/t369] (Petro and Cecil, 5 August 2021)

[35] Tech giants, chastened by Heartbleed, finally agree to fund OpenSSL [fsty.uk/t370] (Jon Brodkin, Ars Technica, 24 April 2014)

[36] OpenSSL Project Roadmap [fsty.uk/t371] (OpenSSL, retrieved 17 July 2014)

project called LibreSSL and started to make rapid changes with a goal to improve the code quality.[37]

## Impact

Because of a missing length check in the code, a remote attacker is able to retrieve more data than she sends; up to 64 KB of server process memory in a single heartbeat request. By submitting multiple requests, the attacker can retrieve an unlimited number of memory snapshots. If there is any sensitive data in the server memory—and there always is—the attacker can probably retrieve it. Because OpenSSL deals with encryption, the most likely extraction target is the server's private key, but there are many other interesting assets: session ticket keys, TLS session keys, and passwords come to mind.

Heartbleed affects OpenSSL versions 1.0.1 through 1.0.1f. Versions from the earlier branches, 0.9.x and 1.0.0, are not vulnerable. Unsurprisingly, vast numbers of servers were impacted. Netcraft estimated that 17% of the servers (or about half a million) worldwide were susceptible.[38]

Remarkably, most of the servers have been patched already. The combination of the seriousness of the problem, freely available testing tools, and media attention resulted in the fastest patching rate TLS has ever seen. One Internet-wide scan suggested that about 1.36% of devices listening on port 443 were vulnerable a month after the vulnerability disclosure.[39] At about the same time, the SSL Pulse dataset (popular web sites, according to the Alexa list) showed only 0.8% of sites vulnerable.

Immediately after the disclosure, most commentators recommended changing private keys as a precaution, but there was no proof that private key extraction was possible. It's likely that everyone was initially too busy testing for the vulnerability and patching. Later, when the attention turned back to exploitation, retrieving server private keys turned out to be straightforward.[40] In some cases, the keys would fall after many requests—in others, after few. More advanced exploitation techniques were subsequently developed.[41]

In the days immediately after the disclosure, exploitation of vulnerable sites was rampant. Private keys were not the only target. For example, Mandiant reported detecting a successful

---

[37] LibreSSL [fsty.uk/t372] (OpenBSD, retrieved 17 July 2014)

[38] Half a million widely trusted websites vulnerable to Heartbleed bug [fsty.uk/t373] (Netcraft, 8 April 2014)

[39] 300k servers vulnerable to Heartbleed one month later [fsty.uk/t374] (Robert Graham, 8 May 2014)

[40] The Results of the CloudFlare Challenge [fsty.uk/t375] (Nick Sullivan, 11 April 2014)

[41] Searching for The Prime Suspect: How Heartbleed Leaked Private Keys [fsty.uk/t376] (John Graham-Cumming, 28 April 2014)

attack on a VPN server that resulted in a bypass of multifactor authentication. The attackers extracted TLS session keys from server memory.[42]

Social insurance numbers were stolen from the Canadian tax authority and passwords extracted from the Mumsnet web site (a popular site for parents in the UK).[43]

Heartbleed was easy to exploit to begin with, but now, with so many tools publicly available, anyone can exploit a vulnerable server in minutes. Some tools are quite advanced and provide full automation of private key discovery.

> **Note**
>
> If you'd like to learn more about the bug itself and how to test for vulnerable servers, head to the section called "Testing for Heartbleed" in Chapter 13, *Testing TLS with OpenSSL*.

# Mitigation

Patching is the best way to start to address Heartbleed. If you're relying on a system-provided version of OpenSSL, your vendor will have hopefully provided the patches by now. If you're compiling from source, use the most recent OpenSSL 1.0.1 version available. In that case, you can also configure OpenSSL to remove support for the Heartbeat protocol, using the OPENSSL_NO_HEARTBEATS flag. For example:

```
$ ./config -DOPENSSL_NO_HEARTBEATS
$ make
```

After this you'll probably need to recompile all other software packages that depend on your version of OpenSSL.

Many products (e.g., appliances) embed OpenSSL and might be vulnerable. Because they had no advanced warning about Heartbleed, none of them were ready with patches on the day of the disclosure. Vendors with many products probably struggled to issue patches for all of them.

After the vulnerability is fixed, turn your attention to the sensitive data that might have leaked from the server. At the very least, you'll need to replace the server private keys, obtain new certificates, and revoke the old certificates. According to Netcraft, which is monitoring the status of Heartbleed remediation activities worldwide, sites often omit performing one or more of these steps.[44]

---

[42] Attackers Exploit the Heartbleed OpenSSL Vulnerability to Circumvent Multi-factor Authentication on VPNs [fsty.uk/t377] (Christopher Glyer, 18 April 2014)

[43] Heartbleed hacks hit Mumsnet and Canada's tax agency [fsty.uk/t378] (BBC, 14 April 2014)

[44] Keys left unchanged in many Heartbleed replacement certificates! [fsty.uk/t379] (Netcraft, 9 May 2014)

After the private keys and certificates are dealt with, focus on what else might have been in the server memory. Session ticket keys are the obvious next target. Replace them. After that, consider other secrets, for example, user passwords. Depending on your risk profile, it might be necessary to advise or ask your users to change their passwords, as some web sites have done.

Heartbleed could not be used to gain access to your data stores, at least not directly. Indirectly, it could have been possible to obtain some information that is as useful. For example, on a database-driven web site, the database password is used on every request and thus resides in memory. Replacing all internal passwords is the best way to remain safe.

Sites who had forward secrecy deployed before the attack are in the best situation: their past communication can't be decrypted following a compromise of the server private key. If you're in the other group, consider deploying forward secrecy now. This is exactly why this feature is so important.

> ### Warning
>
> Although we focus on servers, clients using vulnerable versions of OpenSSL are vulnerable too. Heartbeat is a two-way protocol. If a vulnerable client connects to a rogue server, the server can extract the client's process memory.[45]

---

### Ticketbleed

In February 2017, Filippo Valsorda disclosed a Heartbleed-like vulnerability in some F5 products.[46] *Ticketbleed* is a software vulnerability in F5's code that handles session tickets. Due to the incorrect expectation that session IDs are fixed in length to 32 bytes, an attacker was able to send a shorter session ID (e.g., just one byte) and get up to 31 bytes of process memory back.

---

# FREAK

In January 2015, a low-severity advisory was published by the OpenSSL project, warning that its clients happily accepted a weak export RSA key from a server during a *full-strength* RSA handshake. Crucially, the vulnerability existed even if the client didn't offer to use any export-grade RSA suites. The issue was classified as CVE-2015-0204 and didn't initially attract a lot of attention.

Some researchers grasped the potential of the original disclosure and started to work on a powerful proof-of-concept attack. In early March, they announced that they had successful-

---

[45] Pacemaker [fsty.uk/t380] (Heartbleed client exploit, retrieved 19 May 2014)

[46] Ticketbleed [fsty.uk/t381] (Filippo Valsorda, February 2017)

ly exploited CVE-2015-0204 to attack (their own) communication with the *www.nsa.gov* web site with a MITM attack. They also gave the attack a name: FREAK, short for *Factoring RSA Export Keys*.

The point of the exercise was to show that large numbers of servers are vulnerable to practical MITM attacks. As a result of the researchers' work, the original discovery was reclassified as *high* severity.

## Export Cryptography

To properly discuss FREAK, we need to go back in time, to the late 1990s, and understand *export-strength* suites. Before September 1998, the United States used to restrict export of strong encryption, limiting cipher strength to 40 bits and key exchange strength to 512 bits. Export suites were designed specifically to stay under these limits.

However, it wasn't enough to just define weaker cipher suites: for better performance, pure RSA suites combine authentication and key exchange. Although strong authentication was generally allowed, with RSA suites you couldn't separate authorization from key exchange. The solution was to extend the protocol to produce intentionally weak RSA keys to use in concert with export cipher suites. Thus, a server with a strong RSA can continue to use it for authentication. For the key exchange, it will generate a weak 512-bit key whenever it wants to negotiate an export suite.[47]

Export cipher suites went into obsolescence after the United States relaxed export control of cryptography in January 2000, but the code remained in many (most?) SSL/TLS libraries. As it happens, some of that old code could be triggered by manipulation of protocol messages.

## Attack

During the normal RSA key exchange, a client generates a random premaster secret and sends it to the server encrypted with the server's public RSA key. If the RSA key is strong, the key exchange is also strong. When an export suite is negotiated, the server generates a *weak* RSA key, signs it with its strong key, and sends the weak key to the client in the ServerKeyExchange message. The client then uses that weak key to encrypt a premaster secret in order to comply with export regulations. Even though the key is weak, a network attacker can't exploit it for an active attack because the signature is still strong (assuming a strong server key, of course).

---

[47] Another feature, called *Server-Gated Cryptography* (SGC), was added in order to allow only selected servers to enable strong encryption with clients that would use weak cryptography with everyone else. The idea was to embed special signals in certificates issued only to US companies. After noticing the signal, a client would transparently renegotiate to upgrade to stronger encryption.

> **Note**
>
> To fully follow the discussion in this section, you need to have an understanding of some protocol details. If you haven't already, before proceeding further read about the protocol and the handshake in Chapter 3, *TLS 1.2*.

Today, export cipher suites are hopelessly weak. If negotiated, a weak key is used for the key exchange. Although the network attacker can't interfere with the handshake itself, she can record the entire conversation, then later brute-force the weak key, recover the premaster secret, and decrypt everything. A powerful attacker can do this in minutes or maybe even faster; virtually anyone can do it in hours.

Fortunately, modern clients don't support export suites any more, but FREAK is powerful because it doesn't need them. During the normal RSA key exchange, the ServerKeyExchange message is not allowed. Unexpectedly, vulnerable libraries still process this message and subsequently use the supplied weak RSA key for the key exchange.[48]

To exploit FREAK, the attacker must somehow force the ServerKeyExchange onto the victim. Doing this will downgrade the strength of the connection to only 512 bits. However, there are two obstacles: (1) the injected signature must still be signed by the strong RSA key used on the target server, and (2) having interfered with the TLS handshake, the attacker must find a way to also forge the correct Finished message to legitimize the changes, even though that's something only the real server should be able to do. The attack is illustrated in Figure 7.3, "FREAK attack".

Because of the first obstacle, the attack works only against servers that support export suites. The attacker connects to the server directly, offering to use only export suites. This triggers an export suite negotiation, during which the server sends a ServerKeyExchange message. The trick here is to reuse this message against the victim. Although TLS does defend against signature replay attacks, the defense relies on the client and server random numbers, sent in ClientHello and ServerHello, respectively. However, an active network attacker can wait for the client to connect first, then copy the original random numbers in a separate connection to the target server. The end result is a ServerKeyExchange message that passes the victim's validation.

The bigger problem is producing the correct Finished message. If you recall, this message is encrypted and effectively contains a hash of all handshake messages. For a TLS handshake to complete successfully, each side must receive the correct message from the other side. The

---

[48] Ironically, OpenSSL implemented this behavior as a *feature*. (For reference, look for the documentation for the SSL_OP_EPHEMERAL_RSA configuration option.) The RSA key exchange doesn't provide forward secrecy, because the server key is used to protect all premaster secrets. Because the key stays the same for a long time, whoever gets it can decrypt all previously recorded conversations. However, if you generate a fresh RSA key during every handshake, each connection is encrypted using a different (albeit weaker) key. Back then, using 512-bit keys for this purpose probably didn't seem as bad as it does today—or perhaps they didn't expect that some implementations would reuse such weak keys.

Figure 7.3. FREAK attack

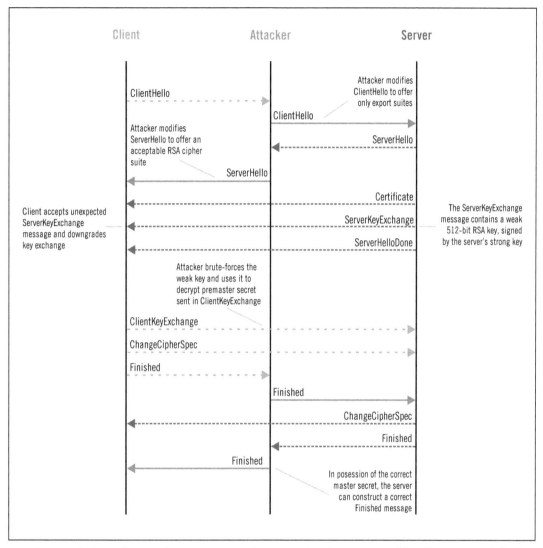

attacker can't just change these messages because they're protected by the protocol (using both encryption and integrity validation). However, by now, the attacker has succeeded in reducing the strength of the key exchange to 512 bits. If she has access to powerful computational capacities, she can brute-force this weak key in real time, decrypt the premaster secret sent by the client, and gain full control of the connection. That also means being able to send the correct Finished messages.

Now, 512-bit keys are weak, but they're not that weak. Certainly, we should expect that some organizations are capable of breaking such keys in real time, but this is not something everyone should need to worry about. It gets worse, however. For performance reasons, rather than generate weak keys for every new connection, some servers generate only one weak key and reuse it over a period of time. Sometimes, it's used for a long time, enough for even a modestly equipped attacker to break it. That's what the researchers did. They identified a server that reused keys, spent about $100 on cloud computing resources (EC2), and broke the key in about seven hours.[49] With the key, the researchers could trivially execute MITM attacks against all vulnerable clients for as long as the key stayed the same. Brilliant!

## Impact and Mitigation

Initially, it was thought that only OpenSSL had been vulnerable to the FREAK attack. Although not many browsers use OpenSSL for client operations, one big user is the Android platform, which meant that billions of phones were potentially vulnerable. This problem affects not only browsers, but probably also all applications running on the vulnerable platforms.[50]

The attack surface exploded when it was discovered that Secure Transport (Apple's SSL/TLS library) and Schannel (Microsoft's library) are vulnerable to the same problem.[51] Other, less widely used platforms were also affected. Of the major browsers, only Firefox was not impacted.

Secure Transport[52] and Schannel[53] were fixed soon after the discovery, but because there is such a diversity of deployments, it's difficult to say exactly which products are no longer vulnerable. For example, at the time of writing, the Secure Transport fix is available only for OS X v10.8.x and newer and iOS 8.2; earlier versions remain vulnerable.[54]

> **Note**
>
> The FREAK attack is an excellent reminder that it is prudent to remove old and otherwise unneeded functionality. Doing so reduces the attack surface and therefore reduces the risk.

The advice for server operators is to remove export cipher suites, because they are necessary to carry out the attack. No servers should have been running these weak suites in the first place, but many operators are carelessly conservative when removing older protocol features. According to the web site that was set up to track the FREAK vulnerability, before

---

[49] Attack of the week: FREAK (or 'factoring the NSA for fun and profit') [fsty.uk/t382] (Matthew Green, 3 March 2015)

[50] HTTPS-crippling FREAK exploit affects thousands of Android and iOS apps [fsty.uk/t383] (Ars Technica, 17 March 2015)

[51] Stop the presses: HTTPS-crippling "FREAK" bug affects Windows after all [fsty.uk/t384] (Ars Technica, 6 March 2015)

[52] About Security Update 2015-002 [fsty.uk/t385] (Apple, 9 March 2015)

[53] Security Advisory 3046015: Vulnerability in Schannel Could Allow Security Feature Bypass [fsty.uk/t386] (Microsoft, 5 March 2015)

[54] About the security content of iOS 8.2 [fsty.uk/t387] (Apple, 9 March 2015)

the disclosure about a quarter of secure servers on the Internet offered weak suites and were potentially vulnerable.

Not all of those servers were equally vulnerable. It is estimated that about two-thirds of those reused weak keys, whereas the remainder would generate a new key for every connection.[55]

---

### State Machine Attacks against SSL and TLS

FREAK is one of the problems identified by miTLS, a project run by Microsoft Research-Inria Joint Centre.[56] miTLS is a verified reference implementation of the TLS protocol.[57] In developing miTLS, its authors research and improve TLS security. FREAK was included in their larger work that covers attacks against the TLS state machine, which found many implementations vulnerable to one attack or the other.[58] You can find more information on their web site, *www.smacktls.com*.

---

# Logjam

After the FREAK attack came out in January 2015, those with a good understanding of the SSL and TLS protocols knew that it was only a matter of time before a similar attack against the ephemeral Diffie-Hellman (DHE) key exchange would be announced. FREAK attacked the RSA key exchange, but export suites require a similar downgrade mechanism (to only 512 bits of security) for DHE. If you can attack one weak key exchange mechanism, surely you can also attack the other? However, when a new vulnerability called *Logjam* was announced by a 14-author team in May 2015, we got not only what was expected, but also much more.[59] The name of the attack is a pun; it's a reference to the *discrete logarithm problem* (DLP), a one-way function on which the DH key exchange is built.

## Active Attack against Insecure DHE Key Exchange

The first announced attack centers on an active network attacker (let's call her Mallory) who intercepts a victim's TLS connections and forces the use of weak DHE key exchange that can be broken in real time. This attack conceptually mirrors the approach taken with the FREAK attack. Because of the similarities, I am not going to spend a lot of time discussing

---

[55] GitHub Gist: Temporary RSA 512 Bit Keylife for FREAK attack [fsty.uk/t388] (ValdikSS, retrieved 21 March 2015)

[56] It's a collaboration between Microsoft Research and Inria, a public research organization dedicated to computational sciences. You can find out more about it at *www.msr-inria.fr*.

[57] miTLS [fsty.uk/t389] (Microsoft Research-Inria Joint Centre, retrieved 21 March 2015)

[58] A Messy State of the Union: Taming the Composite State Machines of TLS [fsty.uk/t390] (Beurdouche at al., March 2015)

[59] The Logjam Attack [fsty.uk/t391] (Adrian et al., published on 20 May 2015)

the details of the new attack; instead, I will assume that you're already familiar with FREAK and highlight only the differences from it, as follows:

**Servers willing to use insecure DH parameters**

During the DHE key exchange, servers generate ephemeral keys and sign them with their private key for authentication purposes. For Logjam to exist, a server must be willing to use weak (e.g., 512-bit) ephemeral keys. This most commonly happens with servers that use export DHE cipher suites, which are limited to 512 bits. If the circumstances are right, Mallory can execute an attack to force and then break the weak DHE key exchange, in exactly the same approach used with FREAK.

In some cases, insecure servers can even be exploited passively when servers naturally negotiate insecure DH parameters. However, this is generally rare; most clients don't support export suites, which represent the biggest attack surface. In addition, most servers prefer the faster ECDHE and RSA key exchanges, meaning the chances of DHE negotiation are small.

**Servers caching ephemeral DH keys**

For an active attack to succeed, Mallory must intercept the original TLS handshake, interfere with it to force insecure encryption, and then produce the correct Finished message to avoid detection. This means that she must break 512 bits of security in about one minute; that's roughly how long modern browsers wait before giving up on a handshake. Under these constraints, attacks are very difficult to execute, even for a well-equipped attacker.

However, it turns out that some servers unwisely cache their "ephemeral" keys. With a server that does this, Mallory can break the ephemeral key ahead of time and use the result to execute real-time attacks for as long as the server's key stays the same. When the key is eventually changed, Mallory can break it again if she needs to continue with her attacks.

According to the paper, about 15% of servers cache their keys, but only about 0.1% use 512-bit DH parameters that are immediately exploitable. Most notably, Microsoft IIS caches its ephemeral keys for up to two hours. OpenSSL has a switch to enable this behavior, but the most popular web servers—Apache and Nginx—don't use it.

**Clients willing to accept weak DH parameters**

The Logjam attack can be used only against clients that are willing to accept insecure DH parameters. Unfortunately, at the time the attack was announced, all major browsers accepted insecure 512-bit key exchanges. The attack works even against clients that don't support export DHE suites; this is because DH suites (export or not) don't specify how strong the key exchange should be. In practice, it's the servers that decide.

We could say that browsers (and other clients) made Logjam possible by accepting insecure DH parameters, but the attack also highlighted a flaw in the TLS protocol. If you recall, FREAK exploits client-side TLS implementation flaws that allow ServerKeyExchange messages where they are forbidden by the protocol. Logjam doesn't need an implementation flaw because it uses a protocol weakness: server signatures (of DH parameters) can be replayed. TLS does include replay protection in the signature design, but the protection mechanism relies only on the unique client and server random values. The problem is that an active attacker can synchronize these values by observing the value offered by a client and reusing it with the server in a *different* handshake. Critically, this flaw enables the attacker to force negotiation of a cipher suite that wouldn't have been selected otherwise.

## Precomputation Attack against Insecure DHE Key Exchange

The active attack against insecure DH key exchange described in the previous section is very clever, but it is limited to servers that allow insecure DH parameter strengths of 512 bits and cache their ephemeral values. Attacks against higher strengths are not feasible. At the time of the announcement, servers that used 768-bit DH parameters could be found, but most deployed with 1,024 bits. Attacking these strengths directly is out of reach, even for government agencies. However, this is where the *precomputation attack* comes in.

The key to understanding precomputation attacks is knowing that the DH key exchange always operates on agreed-upon *domain parameters*. They consist of two values: one is the *prime* (p) and the other is the *generator* (g). Practically speaking, these parameters are used to obscure the key exchange and make certain mathematical operations very difficult for the attacker. Mallory knows the domain parameters because they're public (for example, in TLS before version 1.3 they are sent over the network by the server), but that in itself does not help her. To break the key exchange, she must discover either of the two secret ephemeral keys generated during the key exchange. In the remainder of this discussion, I'll assume that she chooses to target the server's key (y).

The best currently known way to attack the DH key exchange is to use something called a *number field sieve* (NFS). The breakthrough highlighted by the Logjam research is that NFS can be split into two major steps. The first step is where most of the effort is, but, crucially, the computation in it depends only on the value of the prime. This means that, once the results of this first step are available, they can be used to quickly discover the secret keys of *any* key exchange that uses the same prime. For illustration, in the experiment carried out by the paper authors, the precomputation attack against a 512-bit prime took one week. After that, the authors could carry out attacks against individual key exchanges (that used the same prime) in under 60 seconds.

With precomputation taken into account, it's clear that active attacks against 512-bit DH parameters are within reach of virtually anyone. But how safe are 768- and 1,024-bit strengths?

## State-Level Threats against Weak DH Key Exchange

Using their own experience with breaking 512-bit DH parameters, together with experimentation and additional information available from other sources, the researchers estimated how long it would take them to break 768- and 1,024-bit parameters. You can see the estimates in Table 7.2, "Estimated costs of attacks against weak DH parameters [Source: Adrian et al.]". Clearly, attacker costs increase dramatically once larger strengths are targeted.

Table 7.2. Estimated costs of attacks against weak DH parameters [Source: Adrian et al.]

| DH Parameters | Precomputation (core years) | Individual attacks (core time) |
|---|---|---|
| DH-512 | 10 | 10 minutes |
| DH-768 | 36,500 | 2 days |
| DH-1024 | 45,000,000 | 30 days |

However, taking into account that the computations are largely highly parallelizable and that the attacks can be further optimized, they concluded that breaking 768-bit parameters is within reach of academic researchers. As for 1,024-bit parameters, the researchers estimated that the cost of specialized hardware that could get the job done is in the order of hundreds of millions of dollars; an attack would then take about a year to complete.

At this point, you might be thinking that hundreds of millions is a lot of money to spend just for breaking a single set of 1,024-bit parameters, and you'd be right. Unfortunately, the attacker's job is made much easier by the fact that many applications rely on standardized DH parameters, known as *standard groups*. What that means is that there are many servers out there that use the same prime. Because of that, results from a single precomputation can be used against hundreds and thousands of servers.

### Note

In the light of the Logjam attack, it might seem that the practice of using standard groups is insecure, but there are actually good reasons to continue to follow it. Recent experience with security protocols has shown that designers should themselves do as much work as possible. With less for implementers to do, there's less chance that they will make mistakes. For example, even in the Logjam paper there are two sections dedicated to exploiting insecurely generated DH parameters. These problems go away if standardized parameters are used. The real problem exploited by Logjam is that the standard groups currently in use are too weak.

## Impact

The impact of Logjam differs depending on which attacks you look at. In the worst category are servers that naturally negotiate DHE suites and use insecure (e.g., 512-bit) parameters.

Their traffic can be easily decrypted passively by an attacker who can record the encrypted conversation. In the next step up are servers that use insecure parameters but normally prefer RSA or ECDHE key exchanges. Those servers can be attacked via an active attack but have to be important enough to be targeted. If those servers use a common DH prime, the cost of an active MITM attack is much smaller because of the precomputation attack.

According to the research authors, about 6.56% of the trusted HTTPS servers could be exploited passively by an attacker who broke one 1,024-bit group and about 10% by an attacker who broke 10 such groups. An active attacker could break 12.8% and 23.8% of servers, respectively.

### Note

For an active attack to be successful, Mallory must be able to break the key exchange within one minute at the most. However, modern browsers support a feature called *False Start*, which compromises security in exchange for better performance. Such browsers send HTTP requests early and before they verify TLS handshake integrity. Against a browser that does this, Mallory might not need to break the key exchange in real time. Because HTTP requests often contain sensitive information—for example, cookies and passwords—breaking the key exchange later can be as useful. For more information, head to the section called "False Start" in Chapter 9, *Performance*.

Passive attacks on protocols other than TLS are much more interesting. Protocols such as SSH and IPsec handle a lot of traffic; they also tend to use 1,024-bit DH parameters, often standard groups. For SSH, for example, the authors estimated that an attacker who breaks only one standard group (1,024-bit Oakley Group 2) is able to passively decrypt traffic to 25.7% (3.6 million) servers. The situation is much worse for IPsec, where the same attacker can passively listen to over 60% of servers.

## Mitigation

Despite the potential for damage, Logjam is easy to mitigate. Disabling export cipher suites, a relic of a bygone era, is usually sufficient to address the immediate (easily exploitable) problem. In the second step, if you have any DHE suites in your configuration, make sure they're using 2,048-bit parameters. Don't use parameters below 1,024 bits.

Depending on your target audience, increasing DH parameter strength to 2,048 bits might not be straightforward. The main problem is that Java 6 clients don't support strengths above 1,024 bits.[60]

---

[60] Neither do Java 7 clients. However, they do support the ECDHE key exchange out of the box, which means that you can configure your servers to always use ECDHE with them and never attempt DHE.

---

If you are torn between a need to support Java 6 clients and desire to offer strong security, you have two choices. One is to stay with 1,024-bit DH parameters but make sure that you're not using a standard group: generate unique DH parameters for each server in production.

The other choice is to disable DHE altogether. The fact is that DHE is not a popular key exchange algorithm. Many dislike it because it's much slower than the alternatives, RSA and ECDHE. (If you're curious about the performance differences, look at my analysis in Chapter 9, *Performance*.) Although you shouldn't use the RSA key exchange because it doesn't offer forward secrecy, ECDHE is a clear winner when it comes to both security and performance. Because virtually all modern clients support ECDHE, chances are that disabling DHE wouldn't greatly impact your security. Probably the only impact will be that a small percentage of your traffic will lose forward secrecy.

Browser vendors, caught supporting too-short DH parameters, reacted by increasing the minimum strength to stronger values—either 768 or 1,024 bits. Longer term, we can expect that support for DH will be completely removed in favor of ECDHE.

### Is NSA Breaking 1,024-bit Diffie-Hellman Key Exchange?

The Logjam paper authors believe the NSA is capable of breaking at least a small number of 1,024-bit DH groups—but is the agency actually doing it? With the NSA's yearly budget that exceeds $10 billion, it's certainly within its financial abilities. The Logjam attack is a perfect match for an earlier discovery: the NSA is seemingly able to decrypt large amounts of VPN traffic. This information comes from the confidential documents leaked by Edward Snowden and published by Der Spiegel in December 2014.[61] Although the documents don't say how the encrypted communication is broken, they do show the system's architecture and input requirements. They are consistent with the possibility of an efficient break of a 1,024-bit Diffie-Hellman key exchange.

## Protocol Downgrade Attacks

*Protocol downgrade attacks* occur when an active MITM attempts to interfere with the TLS handshake in order to influence connection parameters; the idea is that they might want to force an inferior protocol or a weak cipher suite. In SSL 2, such attacks are easy, because this protocol doesn't provide handshake integrity. Subsequent protocol versions do provide handshake integrity as well as additional mechanisms to detect similar attacks.

However, the protocol designers failed to anticipate interoperability issues related to protocol evolution. Browsers try very hard to communicate successfully with every server.

---

[61] Prying Eyes: Inside the NSA's War on Internet Security [fsty.uk/t392] (Der Spiegel, 28 December 2014)

---

Unfortunately, when it comes to TLS, such attempts often result in security compromises because browsers will voluntarily downgrade their security capabilities, thus sacrificing security for interoperability.

## Rollback Protection in SSL 3

In SSL 2, there was no mechanism to ensure the integrity of the handshake, thus making that protocol version vulnerable to downgrade attacks. As a result, a MITM could always force a handshake to use the least secure parameters available. Handshake integrity validation was added in SSL 3, as part of a major protocol cleanup.

But in order to provide handshake integrity (as well as other improvements) SSL 3 had to change the format of the initial handshake request (ClientHello). Additionally, it was agreed that the servers that understood the new protocol would automatically upgrade to the new format with compatible clients. But several problems remained:

1. The SSL 3 handshake provides integrity protection, but you can't use that handshake format because most servers understand only SSL 2.

2. Even with an SSL 3 server, if there is an active MITM, he can always intercept the connection and pretend to be an SSL 2–only server that does not understand anything better.

3. If you subsequently attempt to use an SSL 2 handshake, there is no handshake integrity, and the MITM can interfere with the negotiation.

To address these loopholes, SSL 3 incorporates *protocol rollback protection*[62] that enables SSL 3–aware clients and servers to detect when they are under attack. When an SSL 3 client falls back to SSL 2 for compatibility reasons, it formats the PKCS #1 block of the RSA key exchange in a special way.[63] In SSL 2, the end of the block must contain at least eight bytes of random data; an SSL 3 client instead fills those eight bytes with 0x03. Thus, if an SSL 3 client is forced down to SSL 2 by a MITM attack, the SSL 3 server will notice the special formatting, detect the attack, and abort the handshake. A genuine SSL 2 server will not inspect the padding, and the handshake will proceed normally.

However, there is one loophole that can break the rollback protection.[64] In SSL 2, the length of the master key mirrors the length of the negotiated cipher suite; in the worst case, it's only 40 bits long. Furthermore, it's the client that selects the cipher suite from those supported by the server, generates the master key, and sends it to the server using public key encryption.

---

[62] RFC 6101: The SSL Protocol Version 3.0, Section E.2. [fsty.uk/t393] (Freier et al., August 2011)

[63] In SSL 2, RSA was the only authentication and key exchange mechanism. Thus, rollback protection implemented as a hack of this key exchange was sufficient to fully address the issue.

[64] *SSL and TLS: Designing and Building Secure Systems*, page 137 (Eric Rescorla, Addison-Wesley, October 2000)

The server decrypts the message using its private RSA key, obtains the master key, and proves ownership to the client.

For a MITM, brute-forcing the RSA key might be too much work, but he can attack the weak master key. He could pose as a server and offer only one 40-bit suite, uncover the master key by brute force, and complete the handshake successfully. This attack is easy to carry out given the computational power available today. This attack vector is largely obsolete by now, given that few clients continue to support SSL 2. Still, the conclusion is that SSL 2 does not provide more than 40 bits of security. Attackers who can execute brute-force attacks of that strength in real time can consistently break all SSL 2 connections.

## Interoperability Problems

With the release of the first follow-up version (SSL 3), interoperability problems started to appear. These problems, and attempts to overcome them, set the stage for what is to become a new class of security issues.

### Version Intolerance

The first problem encountered was *version intolerance*. SSL 2 did not consider protocol evolution and didn't provide instructions for how to handle unknown protocol versions. This excerpt from Eric Rescorla's SSL book illustrates the situation:[64]

> *Unfortunately, the SSLv2 specification wasn't very clear on how servers should handle CLIENT-HELLO messages with version numbers higher than they support. This problem was made worse by the fact that Netscape's SSLREF reference implementation simply rejected connections with higher version numbers. Thus, it's not guaranteed that all SSLv2 servers will respond correctly to the backward-compatible handshake, although the vast majority will.*

SSL 3 did not greatly improve in this respect, mentioning client version handling only in one sentence of the specification:

> server_version: *This field will contain the lower of that suggested by the client in the client hello and the highest supported by the server.*

Starting with TLS 1.0, there is more text to handle backward compatibility, but only TLS 1.2 provides clear guidance:

> *A TLS 1.2 client who wishes to negotiate with such older servers will send a normal TLS 1.2 ClientHello, containing {3,3} (TLS 1.2) in ClientHello.client_version. If the server does not support this version, it will respond with a ServerHello containing an older version number. If the*

*client agrees to use this version, the negotiation will proceed as appropriate for the negotiated protocol.*

As a result of these specification ambiguities, many servers refused handshakes if the offered protocol version was not to their liking. The result was a serious interoperability issue when browsers began to support TLS 1.2. For this reason, Internet Explorer, the first browser to implement TLS 1.2, launched with both TLS 1.1 and TLS 1.2 disabled by default.

The *Renegotiation Indication Extension* specification (released in 2010, two years after TLS 1.2) made an attempt to solve the problem, in the hope that developers will, while implementing the new renegotiation mechanism, also address version and extension intolerance. In Section 3.6., it says:

> *TLS servers implementing this specification MUST ignore any unknown extensions offered by the client and they MUST accept version numbers higher than their highest version number and negotiate the highest common version. These two requirements reiterate preexisting requirements in RFC 5246 and are merely stated here in the interest of forward compatibility.*

There is a similar intolerance problem related to the TLS version used at the record layer. In addition to the version number used in the ClientHello message, clients also have to decide what version to use at the TLS record layer in the first message sent to the server, at a time when they still don't know what versions the server supports. The confusion about the record layer version is even greater, and many servers show greater intolerance. In practice, some libraries always specify TLS 1.0, whereas others specify their best-supported version, as in their ClientHello (e.g., TLS 1.2).

This type of intolerance created a very serious problem for TLS 1.3. According to some rough tests I carried out in 2014, if this new version number were used at the record layer, a large number of servers (easily over 10 percent) would refuse the handshake. Using TLS 2.0 for the next version of the protocol is virtually impossible, because the intolerance would affect over 70 percent of all servers. To minimize this problem, the TLS 1.3 specification deprecated the record layer version number and froze it at TLS 1.0. However, even with that change it was evident that using a new version number would be difficult and probably impossible in practice. As a result, TLS 1.3 subsequently introduced an entirely new version negotiation mechanism that relies on extensions and allows the "visible" version number to remain at TLS 1.2.

## Extension Intolerance

Early versions of the protocol (SSL 3 and TLS 1.0) had no explicit mechanism for adding new functionality without introducing new protocol revisions. The only thing resembling forward compatibility is a provision that allows the ClientHello message to include extra data at the end. Implementations were instructed to ignore this extra data if they could not understand it. This vague extension mechanism was later replaced with *TLS Extensions*,[65] which added a generic extension mechanism to both ClientHello and ServerHello messages. In TLS 1.2, extensions were merged with the main protocol specification.

Given the vagueness of the early specifications, it's not surprising that a substantial number of SSL 3 and TLS 1.0 servers refuse handshakes with clients that specify extra data.

## Other Interoperability Problems

There are other interoperability problems, mostly arising due to a combination of specification vagueness and sloppy programming:

**Long handshake intolerance**
　　The size of the ClientHello message is not limited, but in the early days clients tended to support only a small number of cipher suites, which kept the length low. That changed with the OpenSSL 1.0.1 branch, which added support for a wide range of cipher suites. That, combined with the use of extensions to specify additional information (e.g., desired hostname and elliptic curve capabilities), caused the size of ClientHello to grow substantially. It then transpired that one product—F5's BIG IP load balancer—could not handle handshake messages over 255 bytes and under 512 bytes. Because of the popularity of BIG IP (especially among some of the largest web sites), this issue had a negative impact on the speed of TLS 1.2 adoption.

**Arbitrary extension intolerance**
　　Sometimes servers that understand TLS extensions fail, for no apparent reason, to negotiate connections that include extensions unknown to them. This usually happens with the *Server Name Indication* and *Status Request* (OCSP stapling) extensions.

**Failure to correctly handle fragmentation**
　　Historically, there were many issues related to message fragmentation. SSL and TLS protocols allow all higher-level messages to be fragmented and delivered via several (lower-level) record protocol messages. Most implementations handle fragmentation of application data messages (which are expected to be long) but fail when faced with fragmented messages of other types simply because such fragmentation almost never occurs in practice. Similarly, some products would fail when faced with zero-size records—which derailed initial attempts to mitigate the predictable IV problem in TLS 1.0 and earlier protocols. Early attempts to address the same problem using the 1/n-1 split (sending two records instead of just one, with the first record containing only one byte) were equally derailed, because some products could not handle an HTTP request split across two TLS messages.

---

[65] RFC 3546: TLS Extensions [fsty.uk/t394] (Blake-Wilson et al., June 2003)

Table 7.3. Voluntary protocol downgrade behavior of major browsers in July 2014

| Browser | First attempt | Second attempt | Third attempt | Fourth attempt |
|---|---|---|---|---|
| Chrome 33 | TLS 1.2 | TLS 1.1 | TLS 1.0 | SSL 3 |
| Firefox 27 | TLS 1.2 | TLS 1.1 | TLS 1.0 | SSL 3 |
| IE 6 | SSL 3 | SSL 2 | | |
| IE 7 (Vista) | TLS 1.0 | SSL 3 | | |
| IE 8 (XP) | TLS 1.0 (no ext.) | SSL 3 | | |
| IE 8-10 (Win 7) | TLS 1.0 | SSL 3 | | |
| IE 11 | TLS 1.2 | TLS 1.0 | SSL 3 | |
| Safari 7 | TLS 1.2 | TLS 1.0 | SSL 3 | |

# Voluntary Protocol Downgrade

When the interoperability issues started to appear, browsers responded by implementing *voluntary protocol downgrade*. The idea is that you first try your best version of TLS, with all options enabled, but if that fails you try again with fewer options and lower protocol versions; you continue in this manner until (hopefully) a connection is successful. When TLS 1.0 was the best supported protocol, voluntary protocol downgrade meant at least two connection attempts. Later, when browsers started to support TLS 1.2, three or four attempts were needed.

> **Note**
>
> Interoperability issues are not the only problem causing TLS handshakes to fail. There is ample anecdotal evidence that proxies, firewalls, and antivirus software often intercept and filter connections based on protocol version numbers and other handshake attributes.

To understand this behavior, I surveyed various versions of popular desktop browsers, back when the problem was at its peak. I used a custom TCP proxy designed to allow only SSL 3 connections. Everything else was rejected with a `handshake_failure` TLS alert. You can see the results in Table 7.3, "Voluntary protocol downgrade behavior of major browsers in July 2014".

My test results show that, in July 2014, it was possible to downgrade all major browsers to SSL 3.[66] In the case of Internet Explorer 6, you could actually go as low as SSL 2. Given that SSL 2 is vulnerable to brute-forcing of the master key, Internet Explorer 6 provided a maximum 40 bits of security.

---

[66] Even Opera, which had previously implemented protocol downgrade protection, lost that capability when its team abandoned their own engine and switched to Chrome's Blink for version 15.

---

As for SSL 3, this version was shown to be unambiguously insecure in October 2014 by the POODLE attack. A successful attack can exploit the weaknesses to retrieve small pieces of encrypted data (e.g., cookies). Even if you ignore the vulnerabilities, this old protocol version is significantly inferior to the latest TLS 1.2:

- No support for the GCM, SHA256 and SHA384 suites.

- No elliptic curve cryptography. When it comes to forward secrecy, very few sites support ephemeral Diffie-Hellman (DH) key exchange to use in absence of EC. Without EC, those sites lose forward secrecy.

- SSL 3 is vulnerable to the BEAST attack, but modern browsers implement countermeasures for it. However, some sites prefer to use RC4 with TLS 1.0 and earlier protocols. For such sites, the attacker can force the inferior RC4.

- Microsoft's SSL 3 stack does not support AES, which means that IE will offer only RC4 and 3DES suites.

From this list, I'd say the biggest problem was the loss of forward secrecy. A serious attack could downgrade someone's connections to force an RSA key exchange and then later recover the server's private key to recover the encrypted conversation.

> **Note**
>
> Depending on the exact nature of the communication failure, the fallback mechanism could be triggered even with servers that are not intolerant. For example, there were reports that Firefox sometimes, over unreliable connections, fell back to SSL 3, breaking sites that use virtual secure hosting. (That's because virtual secure hosting relies on TLS extensions, which are not supported in SSL 3.)[67]

Over the years, browsers made many security improvements. For example, after the discovery of the POODLE attack, they first stopped downgrading to SSL 3, then disabled this version altogether. The behavior is constantly changing, and the direction is toward no fallback at all. Firefox removed all downgrades in March 2015 and Chrome in April 2016. Consider the downgrade behavior documented here as an illustration of a past problem that has been remedied.

---

[67] Bug #450280: PSM sometimes falls back from TLS to SSL3 when holding F5 (which causes SNI to be disabled) [fsty.uk/t395] (Bugzilla@Mozilla, reported on 12 August 2008)

# Rollback Protection in TLS 1.0 and Better

Because SSL 3 and newer protocol versions provide handshake integrity, rollback attacks against parties that support only SSL 3 and better do not work.[68]

In case you're wondering, brute-forcing the master key, which was possible against SSL 2, no longer works either, because the master key is now fixed at 384 bits.

TLS 1.0 (and all subsequent protocol revisions up to TLS 1.2) continued with the SSL 3 tradition and included rollback protection in the RSA key exchange, using an additional version number sent by the client and protected with the server's private key. From section 7.4.7.1 of the TLS 1.2 specification:

> The version number in the PreMasterSecret is the version offered by the client in the ClientHello.client_version, not the version negotiated for the connection. This feature is designed to prevent rollback attacks.

As protection measures go, this isn't great, given that it doesn't apply to other key exchanges—namely, DHE and ECDHE. To make things worse, protocol implementers failed to use the right version numbers in the right places. Yngve Pettersen, who used to maintain the SSL/TLS stack for Opera (while they were using a separate stack), had this to say on the topic (emphasis mine):[69]

> Second, the RSA-based method for agreeing on the TLS encryption key is defined in such a way that the client also sends a copy of the version number it sent to the server and against which the server is then to check against the version number it received. This would protect the protocol version selection, even if the hash function security for a version is broken. **Unfortunately, a number of clients and servers have implemented this incorrectly, meaning that this method is not effective.**

There's a statement to the same effect in the TLS 1.2 specification:

> Unfortunately, some old implementations use the negotiated version instead, and therefore checking the version number may lead to failure to interoperate with such incorrect client implementations.

The same specification subsequently advises implementers to enforce rollback protection only with newer clients:

---

[68] The protection is provided by the Finished message, which is sent at the end of the handshake to verify its integrity. In SSL 3, this message is 388 bits long. Curiously, TLS 1.0 reduced the size of this message to only 96 bits. In TLS 1.2, the Finished message still uses only 96 bits by default, but the specification now allows cipher suites to increase its strength. Despite that, all cipher suites continue to use only 96 bits.

[69] Standards work update [fsty.uk/t396] (Yngve Nysæter Pettersen, 2 November 2012)

> *If `ClientHello.client_version` is TLS 1.1 or higher, server implementations MUST check the version number as described in the note below.*

But despite having two defense mechanisms rollback attacks are still possible, because of the voluntary protocol downgrade behavior discussed earlier.

## Attacking Voluntary Protocol Downgrade

The built-in protocol defenses against rollback attacks are effective at preventing an attacker from interfering with a single connection. However, when voluntary protocol downgrades are present, rollback attacks are still possible. This is because the MITM doesn't actually need to change any handshake data. Rather, they can block attempts to negotiate any protocol version greater than SSL 3, simply by closing such connections as they are attempted. To defend against this type of attack, a different defense is needed.

## Improved Rollback Defenses

Voluntary protocol downgrade behavior was a gaping hole in TLS security. Despite everyone's efforts to upgrade the infrastructure to TLS 1.2, an active attacker could still downgrade communication to TLS 1.0 or, sometimes, even SSL 3. This subject had been discussed on the TLS WG mailing list many times, but consensus was difficult to achieve. I have collected a series of links and pointers to mailing discussions, which are of interest not only to see how the thoughts about this problem evolved but also to observe the complexities involved with the working group operation.

The topic was first brought up in 2011,[70] when Eric Rescorla proposed to use special *signaling cipher suite values* (or SCSVs) to enable clients to communicate their best supported protocol version even when trying to negotiate a lower version. A server that detects version number discrepancy is required to terminate the connection. The assumption is that a server that supports this defense also won't be prone to any of the intolerance issues. The SCSV approach was chosen because it had been successfully deployed to signal support for secure renegotiation in combination with SSL 3 protocol.[71]

In 2012, Adam Langley proposed a system also based on signaling suites and keeping the attack detection on the server side.[72]

---

[70] One approach to rollback protection [fsty.uk/t397] (Eric Rescorla, 26 September 2011)

[71] With modern protocol versions, clients can use TLS extensions to signal their capabilities. But because SSL 3 does not support extensions, another mechanism was needed. The solution was to use signaling suites, which cannot be negotiated but can be used to pass small bits of information from clients to servers.

[72] Cipher suite values to indicate TLS capability [fsty.uk/t398] (Adam Langley, 5 June 2012)

After the discussion that followed, Yngve Pettersen submitted an alternative proposal,[73] preferring to implement detection in the client.[74] (That would make deployment much easier; rather than upgrading lots of servers, which would inevitably take a very long time, only the handful of user agents need to be upgraded.) His proposal built on RFC 5746 (Renegotiation Indication Extension), which specifically forbids compliant servers to be intolerant to future protocol version numbers. According to Yngve's measurements, only 0.14% of the servers implementing RFC 5746 showed signs of intolerance. He subsequently implemented this rollback protection in Opera 10.50.[75]

Another discussion followed in April 2013.[76] Finally, in September 2013, Bodo Moeller submitted a draft[77] that was subsequently refined[78] and eventually published as RFC 7507.[79] Bodo's proposal was to use a single signaling suite to indicate voluntary fallback activity. A server that understands the signal and supports a newer protocol version than the one client is attempting to negotiate is required to abort the negotiation. Chrome 33 was the first browser to implement this feature.[80]

How can we explain the lack of interest in Yngve's proposal? Probably because no matter how rare, there are still servers that implement secure renegotiation but are intolerant to higher protocol version numbers. I think that browser vendors simply don't want to go into a direction that would inevitably result in a backlash against them. On the other hand, a SCSV solution would be enforced server-side and trigger only on genuine attacks.

The problem with the SCSV approach is that it will take many years to spread widely. The few sites that care about their security could start using it quickly, but for the rest the changes would be too costly to justify. Google started using the fallback defense in February 2014, implementing support for it in Chrome and their web sites at the same time. OpenSSL 1.0.1j, released in October 2014, includes server-side support for this new standard. Mozilla started supporting the SCSV with Firefox 35, which was released in January 2015.[81]

In contrast, the Internet Explorer team stated that they had no plans to implement this defense mechanism.[82]

---

[73] Fwd: New Version Notification for draft-pettersen-tls-version-rollback-removal-00.txt [fsty.uk/t399] (Yngve Pettersen, 3 July 2012)

[74] Managing and removing automatic version rollback in TLS Clients [fsty.uk/t400] (Yngve Pettersen, February 2014)

[75] Starting with version 15, Opera switched to the Blink browser engine (Google's fork of WebKit), abandoning its own engine and the SSL/TLS stack. That probably meant also abandoning the rollback implementation as proposed by Yngve.

[76] SCSVs and SSLv3 fallback [fsty.uk/t401] (Trevor Perrin, 4 April 2013)

[77] TLS Fallback SCSV for Preventing Protocol Downgrade Attacks [fsty.uk/t402] (Bodo Moeller and Adam Langley, June 2014)

[78] An SCSV to stop TLS fallback. [fsty.uk/t403] (Adam Langley, 25 November 2013)

[79] RFC 7507: TLS Fallback SCSV for Preventing Protocol Downgrade Attacks [fsty.uk/t404] (Moeller et al., April 2015)

[80] TLS Symmetric Crypto [fsty.uk/t405] (Adam Langley, 27 February 2014)

[81] The POODLE Attack and the End of SSL 3.0 [fsty.uk/t406] (Mozilla Security Blog, 14 October 2014)

[82] Internet Explorer should send TLS_FALLBACK_SCSV [fsty.uk/t407] (IE Feedback Home, opened 16 October 2014)

In retrospect, it ended up being easier to just remove the voluntary downgrade behavior from browsers.

## GREASE: Preventing Future Interoperability Problems Today

The cause of most interoperability problems is that developers often don't spend enough time reading specifications and instead implement what works for them at the time of development. When interoperability issues are discovered, possibly years later, there's nothing that can be done because there's no way to force the flawed code to be updated.

Although we can't do anything about the problems we have today, we can stack odds in our favor for the problems of tomorrow. To that end, David Benjamin, a Chromium developer, implemented GREASE (*Generate Random Extensions And Sustain Extensibility*), a client behavior that continuously injects random invalid values into various parts of the TLS protocol.[83] Well-behaving servers ignore these values, so everything works fine. Servers that are intolerant will break immediately during development, forcing developers to fix the problems before they're propagated to end users. GREASE went into production with Chrome 55 in late 2016.

## Downgrade Protection in TLS 1.3

TLS 1.3, released in 2018, removed the RSA key exchange from the protocol and any associated downgrade defenses along with it. In their place, a new mechanism was devised and incorporated into the server's random value. The specified mechanism can be used to protect against downgrades from both TLS 1.3 and TLS 1.2. In the latter case, TLS 1.2 clients and servers need to be updated to take advantage of the mechanism.

If you recall, during a TLS handshake, the client and server exchange 32-byte random numbers. In TLS 1.3, the last eight bytes of the server's random value is used for downgrade protection.

When a TLS 1.3 server negotiates TLS 1.2, it must set the last eight bytes of their random value to the following:

```
44 4F 57 4E 47 52 44 01
```

When TLS 1.1 or earlier is negotiated, the last eight bytes of the random value must be set to the following:

```
44 4F 57 4E 47 52 44 00
```

In both cases, the first seven bytes of the string contain the word DOWNGRD. The last byte is used to differentiate between the two situations. On the receiving end, when TLS 1.3 and

---

[83] RFC 8701: Applying GREASE to TLS Extensibility [fsty.uk/t408] (David Benjamin, January 2020)

TLS 1.2 clients are seeing a server response that uses an inferior protocol version, they can check the server's random value for the special signaling value. When the appropriate value is observed, they will know that they are under attack and must abort the connection with an illegal_parameter alert.

When used with TLS 1.2, this downgrade protection applies when ephemeral key exchanges are used but doesn't work with the RSA key exchange. In the latter case, the earlier TLS 1.0 protection mechanism could be used.

# Truncation Attacks

In a *truncation attack*, an attacker is able to prematurely terminate a secure conversation, preventing one or more messages from being delivered. Normally, a secure protocol is expected to detect such attacks. SSL 2 is vulnerable to truncation attacks, but SSL 3 addressed the issue with the addition of the close_notify message. Subsequent protocol revisions kept the protection. For example, the following text is included in TLS 1.2 (Section 7.2.1):

> *Unless some other fatal alert has been transmitted, each party is required to send a close_notify alert before closing the write side of the connection. The other party MUST respond with a close_notify alert of its own and close down the connection immediately, discarding any pending writes.*

This works because close_notify is authenticated. If any of the preceding messages are missing, the integrity verification mechanisms built into TLS detect the problem.

Unfortunately, connection closure violations have always been widespread. Many clients and servers abruptly close connections and omit the shutdown procedure mandated by the standard. Internet Explorer is one such client, but there are many more.

Drowning in bogus warning messages about truncation attacks, well-behaved applications started to ignore this problem, effectively opening themselves up to real attacks.

Actually, the standards themselves encouraged such behavior by not actually requiring reliable connection termination. The following text appears in the SSL 3 specification:

> *It is not required for the initiator of the close to wait for the responding close_notify alert before closing the read side of the connection.*

In other words, don't bother confirming that the other side received all of the sent data. TLS, in version 1.1, made things worse by relaxing the rules about session resumption. Before, errors of any kind required TLS sessions to be dropped. In practice, this meant that the client would have to perform a full (CPU-intensive) handshake on the following connection. But TLS 1.1 removed this requirement for incorrectly terminated connections. From Section 7.2.1 (emphasis mine):

*Note that as of TLS 1.1, failure to properly close a connection no longer requires that a session not be resumed. **This is a change from TLS 1.0 to conform with widespread implementation practice.***

That's a shame, because the change removed the only real incentive to get the misbehaving user agents to improve. As a result, we are effectively without defense against truncation attacks.

## Truncation Attack History

Truncation attacks against SSL 3 and TLS were first discussed in 2007,[84] when Berbecaru and Lioy demonstrated these attacks against a variety of browsers. They focused on truncating responses. For example, the browser would show only a partial page or image delivered over TLS without any indication that the documents were incomplete.

The topic was revisited in 2013,[85] this time in more detail. In particular, Smyth and Pironti were able to show several compelling attacks, ranging from attacks against electronic voting systems (Helios) to attacks against web-based email accounts (Microsoft and Google) in public computer environments. In all cases, the trick was to prevent the user from logging out without him noticing. To do this, they exploited applications that told their users that they had logged off before they actually did. By using TLS truncation against HTTP requests, the researchers were able to keep the users logged in. After that, if the attacker could access the same computer he could assume the victim's application session and thus the user's identity.

> **Note**
>
> It is particularly interesting that truncation attacks work against HTTP, even though HTTP messages tend to include length information. This is another example of cutting corners just to make the Web "work."

## Cookie Cutting

In 2014, new and more effective techniques to perform truncation attacks came to light.[86] Researchers applied the ideas from earlier attacks on TLS (such as the BEAST attack), in which the attacker is able to control TLS record length by injecting data of arbitrary length into HTTP requests and responses. If you control TLS record length, then you can control the point at which records are split (due to size limits and other constraints). Combined

---

[84] On the Robustness of Applications Based on the SSL and TLS Security Protocols (Diana Berbecaru and Antonio Lioy, *Public Key Infrastructure*, *Lecture Notes in Computer Science*, volume 4582, pages 248–264; 2007)

[85] Truncating TLS Connections to Violate Beliefs in Web Applications [fsty.uk/t409] (Ben Smyth and Alfredo Pironti, Black Hat USA, 2013)

[86] Triple Handshakes and Cookie Cutters [fsty.uk/t410] (Bhargavan et al., March 2014)

with a truncation attack, you can split HTTP request or response headers, which has some interesting consequences.

One application of HTTP response header truncation is now known as a *cookie cutter* attack; it can be used to downgrade secure cookies into plain, insecure ones. Let's examine a set of HTTP response headers in which secure cookies are used:

```
HTTP/1.1 302 Moved Temporarily
Date: Fri, 28 Mar 2014 10:49:56 GMT
Server: Apache
Strict-Transport-Security: max-age=31536000; includeSubDomains
Cache-Control: no-cache, must-revalidate
Location: /account/login.html?redirected_from=/admin/
Content-Length: 0
Set-Cookie: JSESSIONID=9A83C2D6CCC2392D4C1A6C12FFFA4072; Path=/; Secure; HttpOnly
Keep-Alive: timeout=5, max=100
Connection: Keep-Alive
```

To make a cookie secure, you append the Secure attribute to the header line. But, because this attribute comes after the name and value, if you can truncate the HTTP response immediately after the Path attribute an insecure cookie will be created.

Clearly, if you truncate the response headers they become incomplete and thus invalid; the truncated header line will not be terminated with a newline (CRLF), and there won't be an empty line at the end. However, it turns out that some browsers ignore even such obviously malformed HTTP messages and process the headers anyway. Most browsers were vulnerable to one type of truncation attack or another, as the following table illustrates.

Table 7.4. TLS truncation in browsers [Source: Bhargavan et al.]

| Browser | In-header truncation | Content-Length ignored | Missing terminating chunk ignored |
|---|---|---|---|
| Android browser 4.2.2 | Yes | Yes | Yes |
| Android Chrome 27 | Yes | Yes | Yes |
| Android Chrome 28 | No | No | Yes |
| Android Firefox 24 | No | Yes | Yes |
| Safari Mobile 7.0.2 | Yes | Yes | Yes |
| Opera Classic 12.1 | Yes | Yes | Yes |
| Internet Explorer 10 | No | Yes | Yes |

The attack is quite elaborate, but if automated it seems reasonably practical. Here's how to do it:

1. **Attack a user that does not yet have an established session with the target web site.** The web site will not set a new cookie if an old one exists. This can be achieved

with some social engineering or, from an active network attacker perspective, by redirecting a plaintext request.

2. **Find an entry point that allows you to inject arbitrary data into the HTTP response.** This is key to the attack; it allows you to position the truncation location at the TLS record boundary. For example, on many web sites when you attempt to access a resource that requires authentication, the redirection includes the resource address. You can see this in the earlier example, which uses the redirected_from parameter for this purpose.

   Redirection responses are the ideal entry point because they don't have any content (response body). If you attempt to truncate any other response, the absence of content might make the user suspicious.

3. **Submit padding that splits response headers into two TLS records.** Normally, the entire HTTP redirection response is small and fits in a single TLS record. Your goal is to split this record into two. Because TLS records are limited to 16,384 bytes, if you submit a very long payload and push the size past this limit, the TLS stack will split the response into two records.

4. **Close the secure connection after the first TLS record.** This part of the attack is straightforward: observe the TLS communication and drop the connection (e.g., by sending an RST signal) immediately after the first TLS record.

5. **Extract the insecure cookie.** At this point, the partial cookie will have been consumed and all that remains is to extract it from the user agent. This is a *cookie stealing* attack.

Another target for the cookie cutter attack is the Strict-Transport-Security response header. If you truncate the header immediately after the first digit of the max-age parameter, the HSTS entry will expire after nine seconds at most. Additionally, the includeSubDomains parameter, if present, will be neutralized, too. With HSTS out of the way, you can proceed with an *HTTPS stripping* attack or manipulate the cookies in some other way, as discussed in Chapter 6, *HTTP and Browser Issues*.

It is expected that the cookie cutter attack will be addressed by implementing stricter checks and parsers at the browser level. Some vendors have already implemented fixes, but for most the current status is unknown.

# Deployment Weaknesses

Sometimes, weaknesses arise in deployment, when commonly used practices lead to exploitable weaknesses. The problems described in this section arise from the secure protocols defined in abstract, without clear guidance as to how they should be implemented by servers. As a result, subtle problems arise.

# Virtual Host Confusion

Certificate sharing is generally not recommended, unless it's used by closely related web sites. At one level, there's the issue that all sites that share the certificate must also share the private key. The sharing weakens security and reduces it to the strength of the weakest link. Also, you don't want multiple independent teams to all have access to the same private key.

However, all sites that share a certificate are also bound at the application level; if one site is compromised or otherwise exploited in some way, other sites that share the same certificate can also be attacked if the circumstances are right. The other sites could be running on a different port or IP address and be located anywhere on the Internet.

For example, let's suppose that an attacker gains control of a weak site that uses a multidomain certificate. Operating from an active network attack perspective, she observes users connecting to other sites configured with the same certificate. (I'll call them secure sites.) She then hijacks a TLS connection intended for one such secure site and sends it to the weak site under her control. Because the certificate is the same, the victim's browser won't detect anything unusual and the HTTP request will be processed by the web server. Because the attacker controls that web server, she can record the cookies included in the hijacked connection and use them to hijack the victim's application session. She can also respond with arbitrary JavaScript code that will be executed in the context of the *secure* site.

There's a catch: the web server on the weak site must ignore the fact that the HTTP Host headers reference a site that isn't hosted there. Depending on the level of control, the attacker might be able to reconfigure the server to ensure that's the case. However, it's also common that servers ignore invalid host information and always respond with a default site.

Robert Hansen was the first to highlight this problem when he successfully transferred a XSS vulnerability from *mxr.mozilla.org* to *addons.mozilla.org* because both used the same certificate.[87] In 2014, Delignat-Lavaud and Bhargavan highlighted this problem in a research paper and gave it the name *virtual host confusion*.[88] They also showed how to exploit the problem in several real-life scenarios and even uncovered a long-standing problem that could have been used to impersonate some of the most popular web sites in the world.

> **Note**
>
> The same attack can be applied to other protocols. Take SMTP servers, for example. Using the same traffic redirection trick, the attacker can break into one weak

---

[87] MitM DNS Rebinding SSL/TLS Wildcards and XSS [fsty.uk/t411] (Robert Hansen, 22 August 2010)

[88] Virtual Host Confusion: Weaknesses and Exploits [fsty.uk/t412] (Antoine Delignat-Lavaud and Karthikeyan Bhargavan, 6 August 2014)

> SMTP server and later redirect TLS connections to it. If the certificate is shared, email for some other secure sites will be effectively delivered to the attacker.

Confusion attacks that involve different protocols are usually known as *application layer content confusion attacks*. SSL and early TLS didn't have a way for a client and servers to communicate what application protocol should be used. This problem was eventually fixed with the introduction of the *Application Layer Protocol Negotiation* (ALPN) extension, which is now widely deployed because it was needed for HTTP/2 adoption. But even though this facility is now available, client and server enforcement is still lacking. In 2021, a group of researchers publicized this problem under the name ALPACA attack.[89]

## TLS Session Cache Sharing

Another problem highlighted by Delignat-Lavaud and Bhargavan is that TLS session cache sharing among unrelated servers and web sites, which is common, can be abused to bypass certificate authentication.[88] Once a TLS session is established, the client can resume it not only with the original server but also with any other server that shares the same session cache, even if it isn't intended to respond to the requested web site and doesn't have the correct certificate.

This weakness effectively creates a bond among all sites that share the cache (either via server session caching or session tickets) and allows the attacker who compromises one site to escalate access to the other sites. Traffic redirection, the same trick as discussed in the previous section, is the primary attack technique.

For server-side session caching, the flaw is in server applications that don't check that a session is resumed with the same host with which it was originally established. It's a similar situation with session tickets. However, in the latter case there is usually a workaround, because servers allow per-host ticket key configuration. It's therefore recommended to have each host use its own ticket key. Alternatively, ensure that the server-side session cache correctly uses partitioning to separate cache entries belonging to different hosts.

---

[89] ALPACA Attack [fsty.uk/t413] (Brinkmann et al., August 2021)

# 8 Protocol Attacks

Over the years, the security of SSL and TLS protocols has been going in and out of the focus of researchers. The very beginnings were quite shaky. At Netscape, internally, SSL version 1 was apparently considered to be so insecure that the company scrapped it and made version 2 the first public release instead. That was in late 1994. That version did well enough to kick off the ecommerce boom, but it didn't do very well as far as security is concerned. The next version, SSL 3, had to be released in 1996 to address the many security problems.

A long, quiet period followed. In 1999, SSL 3 was standardized as TLS 1.0, with almost no changes. TLS 1.1 and TLS 1.2 were released in 2006 and 2008, respectively, but virtually everyone stayed with TLS 1.0. At some point around 2008, we started to focus on security again. Ever since, there's been a constant pressure on TLS, scrutinizing every little feature and use case. TLS 1.3, released in 2018, is a substantial rewrite that addressed all known problems and retained backward compatibility.

In this chapter, I document the attacks that broke various aspects of TLS in recent years. In chronological order, they are insecure renegotiation in 2009; BEAST in 2011; CRIME in 2012; Lucky 13, RC4 biases, TIME, and BREACH in 2013; Triple Handshake Attack and POODLE in 2014; and SLOTH, DROWN, and Sweet32 in 2016. In the second edition, I have added coverage of ROBOT (2017) and Raccoon (2020) attacks. I conclude the chapter with a brief discussion of the possibility that some of the standards and cryptographic algorithms are being subverted by government agencies. If you're looking for FREAK and Logjam, which came out in 2015 but are mostly not protocol issues, you'll find them in Chapter 7, *Implementation Issues*.

## Insecure Renegotiation

*Insecure renegotiation* (also known as *TLS Authentication Gap*) is a protocol issue first discovered by Marsh Ray in August 2009. Ray also led an industry-wide effort to fix the protocol and coordinate public disclosure. Before that work was completed, the issue was independently discovered by Martin Rex (in November of the same year).[1] At that point, the information became public, prematurely.[2]

## Why Was Renegotiation Insecure?

The renegotiation vulnerability existed because there was no continuity between the old and new TLS streams even though both take place over the same TCP connection. In other words, the server does not verify that the same party is behind both conversations. As far as integrity is concerned, it is entirely possible that after each renegotiation a different client is talking to the server.

Application code typically has little interaction with the encryption layer. For example, if renegotiation occurs in the middle of an HTTP request, the application is not notified. Furthermore, web servers will sometimes buffer data that was received prior to renegotiation and forward it to the application together with the data received after renegotiation. Connection parameters may also change; for example, a different client certificate might be used after renegotiation. The end result is that there is a mismatch between what is happening at the TLS layer and what applications see.

An active network attacker can exploit this problem in three steps:

1. Intercept a TCP connection request from the victim (client) to the target server.

2. Open a new TLS connection to the server and send the attack payload.

3. From then on, continue to operate as a transparent proxy between the victim and the server. For the client, the connection has just begun; it will submit a new TLS handshake. The server, which has already seen a valid TLS connection (and the attack payload), will interpret the client's handshake as renegotiation. Once the renegotiation is complete, the client and the server will continue to exchange application data. The attacker's payload and the client's data will both be seen as part of the same data stream by the server, and the attack will have been successful.

---

[1] MITM attack on delayed TLS-client auth through renegotiation [fsty.uk/t414] (Martin Rex, 4 November 2009)

[2] Renegotiating TLS [fsty.uk/t415] (Marsh Ray and Steve Dispensa, 4 November 2009)

Figure 8.1. Active network attack against insecure renegotiation

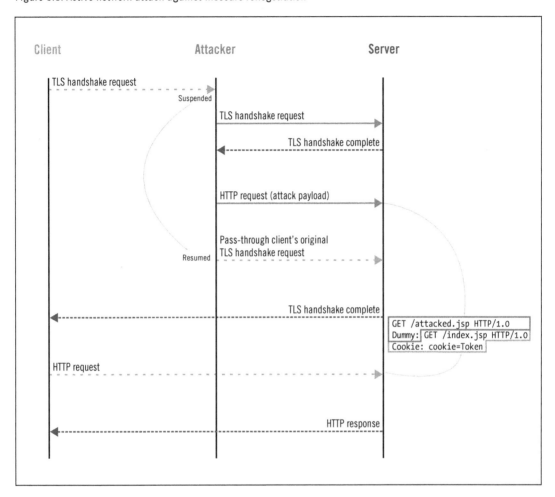

This scenario shows the attacker violating the integrity of application data, which TLS was designed to protect. The attacker was able to inject arbitrary plaintext into the beginning of the connection. The impact of the attack depends on the underlying protocol and server implementation and will be discussed in the following sections.

## Triggering the Weakness

Before he can exploit the insecure renegotiation vulnerability, the attacker needs to find a way to trigger renegotiation. Before this vulnerability was discovered, most servers were allowing client-initiated renegotiation, which meant that most were easy targets. A rare exception was Microsoft IIS, which, starting with version 6, would not accept client-initiated renegotiation at all.

But even without client-initiated renegotiation, sites using client certificates or supporting SGC might be equally easy to exploit. The attacker just needs to examine the web site to determine under what conditions renegotiation is required. If such a condition is easily triggered, the attacker may use it for the attack. Depending on the exact configuration of the server, the resulting attack vector may be as useful as client-initiated renegotiation.

# Attacks against HTTP

When it comes to insecure renegotiation, attacks against HTTP are the best understood. Many variants exist, with their feasibility depending on the design of the target web site and on the technical prowess (and the browser used) by the victim. Initially, only one attack was discussed, but the security community collaborated to come up with other possibilities. Thierry Zoller, in particular, spent considerable effort tracking down and documenting the attack vectors as well as designing proof-of-concept attacks.[3]

## Execution of Arbitrary GET Requests

The easiest attack to carry out is to perform arbitrary GET requests using the credentials of the victim. The effective request consisting of the attack payload (in bold) and the victim's request might look something like this:

```
GET /path/to/resource.jsp HTTP/1.0
X-Ignore: GET /index.jsp HTTP/1.0
Cookie: JSESSIONID=B3DF4B07AE33CA7DF207651CDB42136A
```

We already know that the attacker can prepend arbitrary plaintext to the victim's request. The attacker's challenge is to use this ability to control the attack vector, neutralize the parts of the genuine request that would break the attack (that's the victim's request line), and use the parts that contain key information (e.g., session cookies or HTTP Basic Authentication) to successfully authenticate.

The attacker can do that by starting the attack payload with a complete HTTP request line—thereby choosing the entry point of the attack—and then following with a *partial header line*; this header, which is purposefully left incomplete (no newline at the end), will neutralize the first line of the victim's request. All subsequent request headers submitted by the victim will become part of the request.

So what do we get with this? The attacker can choose where the request goes, and the victim's credentials are used. But the attacker cannot actually retrieve the credentials, and the HTTP response will go back to the victim. It appears that the effect of this attack is similar to that of a *Cross-Site Request Forgery* (abbreviated to CSRF or, sometimes,

---

[3] TLS/SSLv3 renegotiation vulnerability explained [fsty.uk/t416] (Thierry Zoller, 23 December 2011)

XSRF). Most sites that care about security will have already addressed this well-known web application security problem. Those sites that did not address CSRF are probably easier to attack in other ways.

This was the attack vector that was initially presented and, because of the similarity to CSRF, caused many to dismiss the insecure vulnerability as unimportant.

## Credentials Theft

In the days following the public disclosure, improved attacks started to appear. Just a couple of days later, Anil Kurmus improved the attack to retrieve encrypted data.[4]

In researching the possible attack vectors, most focused on trying to use the credentials included with hijacked requests (i.e., session cookies or Basic Authentication credentials). Anil realized that although he was not able to retrieve any data directly he was still able to submit it to the web site using a *different* identity, one that was under his control. (Reverse session hijacking, if you will.) From there, the challenge was to get the data back from the web site somehow.

His proof-of-concept attack was against Twitter. He managed to post the victim's credentials (which were in the headers of the victim's HTTP request) as a tweet of his own. This was the request (the attacker's payload in bold):

```
POST /statuses/update.xml HTTP/1.0
Authorization: Basic [attacker's credentials]
Content-Type: application/x-www-form-urlencoded
Content-Length: [estimated body length]

status=POST /statuses/update.xml HTTP/1.1
Authorization: Basic [victim's credentials]
```

In the improved version of the attack, the entire victim's request is submitted in the request body as the contents of the `status` parameter. As a result, Twitter treats it as the text of a tweet and publishes it in the attacker's tweet stream. On other sites, the attacker might post a new message on the forum, send an email message to himself, and so forth.

The only challenge here is getting the `Content-Length` header right. The attacker does not know the size of the request in advance, which is why he cannot use the correct length. But to succeed with the attack he only needs to use a large enough value to cover the part of the victim's request that contains sensitive data. Once the web server hits the limit specified in the `Content-Length` header, it will consider the request complete and process it. The rest of the data will be treated as another HTTP request on the same connection (and probably ignored, given that it's unlikely that it would be well formed).

---

[4] TLS renegotiation vulnerability: definitely not a full blown MITM, yet more than just a simple CSRF [fsty.uk/t417] (Anil Kurmus, 11 November 2009)

## User Redirection

If the attacker can find a resource on the target web site that responds with a redirection, he might be able to perform one of the following attacks:

**Send the user to a malicious web site**

> An open redirection point on the web site could be used to send the victim to the destination of the attacker's choice. This is ideal for phishing, because the attacker can build a replica of the target web site, possibly using a similar domain name to make the deception more effective. It's very easy to make up a name that feels related and "official" (e.g., *www.myfeistyduck.com*, when the real domain name is *www.feistyduck.com*). To finalize the deception, the attacker can get a proper certificate for the malicious web site.

**Downgrade connection to plaintext HTTP**

> If the attacker can find a redirection on the target web site that will send the user to (any) plaintext web site, then the TLS connection is effectively downgraded. From there, the attacker can use a tool such as `sslstrip` and establish full control over the victim's browsing.

**Capture credentials via redirected POST**

> If the site contains a redirection that uses the 307 status code—which requires that the redirection is carried out without changing the original request method—it may be possible to redirect the entire request (POST body included) to the location of the attacker's choice. All browsers support this, although some require user confirmation.[5] This attack is quite dangerous, because it allows the attacker to retrieve encrypted data without having to rely on the site's own functionality. In other words, it may not be necessary to have an account on the target web site. This is a big deal, because the really juicy targets make that step difficult (think banks and similar financial institutions).

A good discussion of the use of redirection to exploit insecure renegotiation is available in the research paper from Leviathan Security Group.[6]

---

[5] The last time I tested this feature, in July 2013, the latest versions of Chrome, Internet Explorer, and Safari were happy to redirect the request to an entirely different web site without any warning. Firefox and Opera asked for confirmation, but the prompts used by both could be improved. For example, Firefox provided no information about where the new request would be going. Opera provided the most information (the current address as well as the intended destination) along with options to cancel, proceed with the POST method, or convert to a GET method. Still, all that would probably be too confusing for the average user.

[6] Generalization of the TLS Renegotiation Flaw Using HTTP 300 Redirection to Effect Cryptographic Downgrade Attacks [fsty.uk/t418] (Frank Heidt and Mikhail Davidov, December 2009)

---

## Cross-Site Scripting

In some rare cases, the attacker might be able to inject HTML and JavaScript into the victim's browser and take full control of it via XSS. This could be done using the TRACE HTTP method, which requires servers to mirror the request in the response. Under attack, the reflected content would contain the attacker's payload.

This attack will not work against the major browsers, because TRACE responses usually use the message/http content type. But, according to Thierry Zoller, there were some less used Windows browsers that always handle responses as HTML; those were vulnerable.

# Attacks against Other Protocols

Although HTTP received most of the attention, we should assume that all protocols (that rely on TLS) are vulnerable to insecure renegotiation unless the opposite can be proven. Any protocol that does not reset state between renegotiations will be vulnerable.

**SMTP**

Wietse Venema, a member of the Postfix project, published an analysis of the insecure renegotiation impact on SMTP and the Postfix mail server.[7] According to the report, SMTP is vulnerable, but the exploitation might be tricky, because, unlike HTTP, one SMTP transaction consists of many commands and responses. He concluded that Postfix was not vulnerable—but only by luck, because of certain implementation decisions. The report suggested several client- and server-side improvements to defend against this problem.

Insecure renegotiation did not pose a significant threat to SMTP because, unfortunately, most SMTP servers do not use valid certificates and (possibly as a result) most SMTP clients do not actually validate certificates. In other words, active network attacks against SMTP are already easy to execute; no further tricks are required.

**FTPS**

Alun Jones, author of the WFTPD Server, published an analysis of the impact of the insecure renegotiation vulnerability on FTPS.[8] The main conclusion is that due to the way file transfer is implemented in some FTP servers, an active network attacker could use the renegotiation issue to tell the server to disable encryption of the command channel. As a result, the integrity of the transferred files could be compromised.

---

[7] Redirecting and modifying SMTP mail with TLS session renegotiation attacks [fsty.uk/t419] (Wietse Venema, 8 November 2009)

[8] My take on the SSL MITM Attacks – part 3 – the FTPS attacks [fsty.uk/t420] (Alun Jones, Tales from the Crypto, 18 November 2009)

# Insecure Renegotiation Issues Introduced by Architecture

System design and architecture decisions can sometimes introduce insecure renegotiation where it otherwise doesn't exist. Take *SSL offloading*, for example. This practice is often used to add encryption to services that otherwise do not support it or to improve the performance of a system by moving TLS handling away from the main service point. If insecure renegotiation is supported at the point of TLS termination, the system as a whole will be vulnerable even if the actual web servers are not.

## Impact

Insecure renegotiation is a serious vulnerability because it completely breaks the security guarantees promised by TLS. Not only is communication integrity compromised, but the attacker might also be able to retrieve the communicated data itself. There's a variety of attacks that can take place, ranging from CSRF to theft of credentials to sophisticated phishing. Because a good technical background and per-site research is required, this is a type of attack that requires a motivated attacker, likely against higher-value targets.

The ideal case for the attacker is one in which there are automated systems involved, because automated systems rarely scrutinize failures, have poor logging facilities, and retry requests indefinitely until they are successful. This scenario thus creates a large attack surface that is much easier to exploit than attacking end users (browsers) directly.

The attack against insecure renegotiation is well understood, and the tools needed to carry it out are widely available. The proof of concept for the Twitter attack can be found on the Internet, and only a slight modification to any of the widely available network attack tools would be needed to extend them to exploit the vulnerability.

The compromise of integrity has another side effect, which stems from the fact that the attacker can submit arbitrary requests under the identity of the victim. Even if the attacker is not able to retrieve any data or trick the victim, he can always forge his attack payloads to make it seem as if the victim was attacking the server. Because of inadequate logging facilities at most web sites, this type of attack (executed under the identity of the victim) would be extremely difficult to dispute, and yet it could have devastating consequences for the victim. For this reason alone, end users should configure their browsers to accept communication only with servers that support secure renegotiation.[9]

## Mitigation

Insecure renegotiation shouldn't be your problem in 2021 because TLS 1.3 should be your main security protocol, and this version does not support renegotiation. If you're using

---

[9] For example, in Firefox, on the about:config page, change the security.ssl.require_safe_negotiation setting to true.

earlier protocol versions still, there are several ways in which insecure renegotiation can be addressed, some better than others.

**Upgrade to support secure renegotiation**

In early 2010, the *Renegotiation Indication* extension was released to address the problem with renegotiation at the protocol level.[10] Today, years later, you should expect that all products can be upgraded to support secure renegotiation. If you're dealing with products that cannot be upgraded, it's probably an opportunity to consider if they're still worth using. That said, in 2017 it's acceptable to use a product that doesn't support secure renegotiation only if it doesn't support renegotiation at all.

**Disable renegotiation**

In the first several months after the discovery, disabling renegotiation was the only mitigation option. However, some tools did not support this feature (typically when deploying client certificate authentication), in which case secure renegotiation was the only secure option.

## Discovery and Remediation Timeline

The insecure renegotiation issue gave us a rare opportunity to examine and assess our collective ability to fix a vulnerable protocol. Clearly, in an ecosystem as complex as TLS, fixing any problem will require extensive collaboration and take years; but how many years, exactly? To find out, take a look at Figure 8.2, "Insecure renegotiation remediation timeline".

Roughly, what the timeline shows is that we need:

1. About six months to fix the protocol.

2. A further 12 months for libraries and operating systems to be fixed and patches issued.

3. A further 24 months for the majority to apply the patches (or recycle those old systems).

According to the measurements done by Opera, 50% of the servers they tracked had been patched to support secure renegotiation within one year of the official RFC release.[11]

The same data set, in February 2014, reported 83.3% patched servers.[12] The conclusion is that we need about four years to address flaws of this type.

---

[10] RFC 5746: TLS Renegotiation Indication Extension [fsty.uk/t421] (Rescorla et al., February 2010)

[11] Secure browsing like it's 1995 [fsty.uk/t422] (Audun Mathias Øygard, 17 March 2011)

[12] Re: Call for acceptance of draft-moeller-tls-downgrade-scsv [fsty.uk/t423] (Yngve N. Pettersen, 9 February 2014)

Figure 8.2. Insecure renegotiation remediation timeline

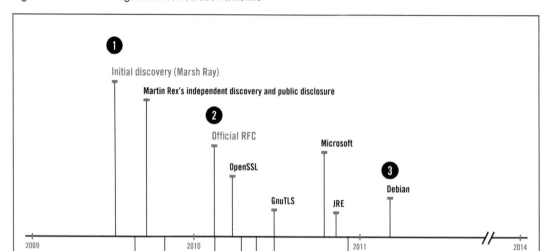

## BEAST

In the summer of 2011, Duong and Rizzo announced a new attack technique that could be used against TLS 1.0 and earlier protocols to extract small pieces of encrypted data.[13] Their work built on previously known weakness in the predictable *initialization vector* (IV) construction as used in TLS 1.0. The weakness, which was thought to be impractical to exploit, had been fixed in TLS 1.1, but at the time of discovery there was effectively no browser support for newer TLS versions.

In many ways, the so-called BEAST attack was a wake-up call for the ecosystem. First, it emphasized (again) that attacks only get better. As you will learn later in this section, this was a weakness that had been known for almost a decade and dismissed, but all it took was two motivated researchers to make it practical. Duong and Rizzo showed that we must not ignore small problems, because they eventually grow big.

---

[13] Here come the ⊕ Ninjas [fsty.uk/t424] (Duong and Rizzo, incomplete version, 13 May 2011)

Second, the disclosure and the surrounding fuss made it painfully clear how little attention browser vendors paid to the TLS protocol. They, along with most of the software industry, became too focused on exploitability. They didn't take into account that protocol issues, and other problems that require interoperability of large numbers of clients and servers, take years to address. They are much different from buffer overflows and similar flaws, which can be fixed relatively quickly.

Thai gave a candid account of how BEAST came together in his blog post,[14] and you can almost feel his frustration when he realizes that he is losing the attention of browser vendors because, even though he can demonstrate the attack in a simulation, he is unable to demonstrate it in a practical environment. But they persisted, managed to build a working proof of concept, demonstrated it, and finally got the attention they deserved.

# How the Attack Works

The BEAST attack is an exploit targeted at the *Cipher Block Chaining* (CBC) encryption as implemented in TLS 1.0 and earlier protocol versions. As mentioned earlier, the issue is that IVs are predictable, which allows the attacker to effectively reduce the CBC mode to *Electronic Code Book* (ECB) mode, which is inherently insecure.

## ECB Oracle

ECB is the simplest mode of operation: you split input data into blocks and encrypt each block individually. There are several security issues with this approach, but the one we're interested in here is that ECB does not hide the deterministic nature of block cipher encryption. What this means is that every time you encrypt the same piece of data the output is also the same. This is a very useful property for the attacker; if he is able to submit arbitrary data for encryption, he can use that to recover earlier encrypted data by guessing. It goes like this:

1. Observe a block of encrypted data that contains some secret. The size of the block will depend on the encryption algorithm, for example, 16 bytes for AES-128.

2. Submit 16 bytes of plaintext for encryption. Because of how block ciphers work (one bit of difference anywhere in input affects all output bytes), the attacker is only able to guess the entire block at once.

3. Observe the encrypted block and compare it to the ciphertext observed in step 1. If they are the same, the guess is correct. If the guess is incorrect, go back to step 2.

---

[14] BEAST [fsty.uk/t425] (Thai Duong, 5 September 2011)

---

Because the attacker can only guess the entire block at a time, this is not a great attack. To guess 16 bytes, the attacker would need to make $2^{128}$ guesses, or $2^{127}$ on average. But, as we shall see later, there are ways in which the attack can be improved.

## CBC with Predictable IV

The key difference between CBC and ECB is that CBC uses an IV to mask each message before encryption. The goal is to hide patterns in ciphertext. With proper masking in place, the ciphertext is always different even if the input is the same. As a result, CBC is not vulnerable to plaintext guessing in the way ECB is.

For the IV to be effective, it must be unpredictable for each message. One way to achieve this is to generate one block of random data for every block that we wish to encrypt. But that wouldn't be very practical, because it would double the size of output. In practice, CBC in SSL 3 and TLS 1.0 uses only one block of random data at the beginning. From there on, the encrypted version of the current block is used as the IV for the next block, hence the word *chaining* in the name.

The chaining approach is safe, but only if the attacker is not able to observe encrypted data and influence what will be encrypted in the immediately following block. Otherwise, simply by seeing one encrypted block he will know the IV used for the next. Unfortunately, TLS 1.0 and earlier treat the entire *connection* as a single message and use a random IV only for the first TLS record. All subsequent records use the last encryption block as their IV. Because the attacker can see all the encrypted data, he knows the IVs for all records from the second one onward. TLS 1.1 and 1.2 use per-record IVs and thus don't have the same weakness.

The TLS 1.0 approach fails catastrophically when faced with an active attacker who can submit arbitrary plaintext for encryption, observe the corresponding ciphertexts, and adapt the attacks based on the observations. In other words, the protocol is vulnerable to a *blockwise chosen-plaintext* attack. When the IV is predictable, CBC effectively downgrades to ECB.

Figure 8.3, "BEAST attack against CBC with predictable IV" illustrates the attack against CBC with predictable IV showing three encryption blocks: two blocks sent by the browser and one block sent (via the browser) by the attacker. For simplicity, I made it so that each message consumes exactly one encryption block; I also removed padding, which TLS would normally use.

The attacker's goal is to reveal the contents of the second block. He can't target the first block, because its IV value is never seen on the network. But after seeing the first block he knows the IV of the second ($IV_2$), and after seeing the second block he knows the IV of the third block ($IV_3$). He also knows the encrypted version of the second block ($C_2$).

After seeing the first two blocks, the attacker takes over and instruments the victim's browser to submit plaintext for encryption. For every guess, he can observe the encrypted version on the wire. Because he knows all the IVs, he can craft his guesses in such a way that the effects of IV are eliminated. When a guess is successful, the encrypted version of the guess ($C_3$) will be the same as the encrypted version of the secret ($C_2$).

Figure 8.3. BEAST attack against CBC with predictable IV

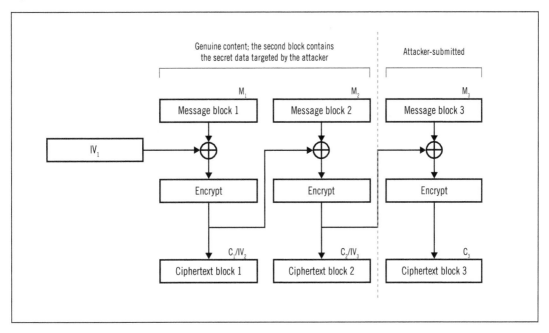

To understand how the IVs can be effectively eliminated, we have to look at some of the math involved. Let's examine the encryption of $M_2$, which contains some secret, and $M_3$, which is controlled by the attacker:

$$C_2 = E(M_2 \oplus IV_2) = E(M_2 \oplus C_1)$$
$$C_3 = E(M_3 \oplus IV_3) = E(M_3 \oplus C_2)$$

Messages are first XORed with their IV, then encrypted. Because different IVs are used each time, even if $M_2$ is the same as $M_3$ the corresponding encryptions, $C_2$ and $C_3$, will be different. However, because we know both IVs ($C_1$ and $C_2$), we can craft $M_3$ in such a way as to neutralize the masking. Assuming $M_g$ is the guess we wish to make:

$$M_3 = M_g \oplus C_1 \oplus C_2$$

The encryption of $M_3$ will thus be:

$$C_3 = E(M_3 \oplus C_2) = E(M_g \oplus C_1 \oplus C_2 \oplus C_2) = E(M_g \oplus C_1)$$

And if our guess is correct ($M_g = M_2$), then the encryption of our block will be the same as the encryption of the second block:

$$C_3 = E(M_g \oplus C_1) = E(M_2 \oplus C_1) = C_2$$

## Practical Attack

We now understand the weakness of predictable IVs, but exploiting it is still difficult due to the fact that we have to guess the entire block (typically 16 bytes) at a time. However, when applied to HTTP, there are some optimizations we can make.

- HTTP messages often contain small fragments of sensitive data, for example, passwords and session tokens. Sometimes guessing only 16 bytes is all we need.

- The sensitive data typically uses a restricted character set; for example, session tokens are often encoded as hexadecimal digits, which can have only 16 different values.

- The structure of HTTP messages is very predictable, which means that our sensitive data will often be mixed with some other content we know. For example, the string Cookie: will always be placed before the name of the first cookie in an HTTP request.

When all these factors are taken into account, the required number of guesses can be much lower, although still not low enough for practical use.

BEAST became possible when Duong and Rizzo realized that modern browsers can be instrumented by a skillful attacker, giving him an unprecedented level of control. Crucially, the attacker needs to be able to (1) influence the position of the secret in the request and (2) have full control over what is being encrypted and when it is sent.

The first condition is not difficult to fulfill; for example, to push a cookie value around you only need to add extra characters to the request URI. The second condition is problematic; that level of control is not available from JavaScript. However, Duong and Rizzo determined that they could use Java applets. They also needed to exploit a separate bug in order to get Java to send traffic to arbitrary web sites.[15] They needed to do this to make BEAST universal and able to attack any web site. Exploitation of this additional problem in Java is not always necessary. Web sites that allow user-uploaded content can be tricked into accepting Java applets. They then run in the context of the target web site and can send traffic to it.[16]

There is another condition, mentioned earlier, and that is to be able to observe encrypted network traffic, which is necessary in order to determine the next IV values. Further, the IVs need to be communicated to the code running in the browsers.

In practice, BEAST is an active network attack. Although social engineering could be used to send the victim to the web site that contains the rogue JavaScript code, it's much simpler to inject the code into any plaintext web site visited by the victim at the time of attack.

---

[15] Without permission, Java applets can only communicate with their parent web site. This restriction is known as the *same-origin policy* (SOP). Duong and Rizzo discovered a way to bypass that restriction. It's not entirely clear if the Java SOP bypass remains: when I reviewed the updated Java release in 2013, it was possible to exploit it with additional effort.

[16] The pitfalls of allowing file uploads on your website [fsty.uk/t426] (Mathias Karlsson and Frans Rosén, 20 May 2014)

If you can manage all of that, then implementing BEAST is easy. By changing the position of the secret within the HTTP request, you can align it with encryption blocks in such a way that a single block contains 15 bytes of known plaintext and only one byte of the secret. Guessing that one byte is much easier; you need $2^8$ (256) guesses in the worst case, and $2^7$ (128) guesses on average. Assuming low-entropy data (e.g., hexadecimal digits), you can get as low as eight (average) guesses per character. When time is of the essence, you can also submit multiple guesses in parallel.

---

### JavaScript Malware

*JavaScript malware* is a generic term used for malicious code running in a victim's browser. Most malware is designed to attack the browser itself, impersonate the user, or attack other web sites, often without being noticed. BEAST was the first exploit to use JavaScript malware to break cryptography, but many others followed. You'll find their details later in the chapter.

The use of JavaScript malware is a good example of the changing threat model. When SSL was first designed in 1994, browsers were only simple tools designed for HTML rendering. Today, they are powerful application-delivery platforms.

---

## Client-Side Mitigation

BEAST is a client-side vulnerability and requires that countermeasures are deployed at the user-agent level. In 2004, when the problem was originally discovered, OpenSSL tried to address it by injecting an empty (no data) TLS record before each real TLS record. With this change, even though the attacker can predict the next IV, that value is used for the zero-length TLS record that has no value. The application data follows in the next record, but it uses an IV that the attacker does not know *in advance* (at the time the attack payload is constructed), which means that there is no opportunity to execute an attack.

Unfortunately, this approach did not work, because some TLS clients (most notably, Internet Explorer) were found to react badly to zero-sized TLS records. Given that at the time there was no practical attack to worry about, OpenSSL dropped the mitigation technique. As far as we know, no other library tried to address the issue.

In 2011, browsers mitigated BEAST by using a variation of the empty fragment technique. The *1/n-1 split*, proposed by Xuelei Fan,[17] still sends two records instead of one but places one byte of application data in the first record and everything else in the second. This approach achieves an effectively random IV for the bulk of the data: whatever is in the second record is safe. One byte of the data is still exposed to the predictable IV, but because it sits in an encryption block with at least seven (more likely 15) other bytes that are

---

[17] Bug #665814, comment #59: Rizzo/Duong chosen plaintext attack (BEAST) on SSL/TLS 1.0 [fsty.uk/t427] (Xuelei Fan, 20 July 2011)

effectively random and different for every record (the MAC) the attacker cannot guess that byte easily.

The 1/n-1 split fared much better than the original approach, but the adoption still did not go smoothly. Chrome enabled the countermeasures first but had to revert the change because too many (big) sites broke.[18] The Chrome developers persisted, and soon other browser vendors joined, making the change inevitable.

Table 8.1. BEAST mitigation status of major libraries, platforms, and browsers

| Product | Version (Date) | Comments |
| --- | --- | --- |
| Apple | OS X v10.9 Mavericks (22 October 2013) and v10.8.5 Mountain Lion (25 February 2014) | The 1/n-1 split shipped in Mountain Lion (OS X v10.8), but it was disabled by default. The mitigation is supposed to be configurable, but there's a bug that prevents the defaults from being changed.[a] |
| Chrome | v16 (16 December 2011) | Initially enabled in v15, but backed off due to too many big sites not working. |
| Firefox | v10 (31 January 2012) | Almost made it to Firefox v9, but Mozilla changed their minds at the last moment to give the incompatible sites more time to upgrade.[b] |
| Microsoft | MS12-006[c] (10 January 2012) | The mitigation is enabled in Internet Explorer, but disabled by default for all other Schannel (Microsoft's TLS library) users. Microsoft recommended deployment of TLS 1.1 as a way of addressing BEAST for nonbrowser scenarios. The knowledge base article 2643584 discusses the various settings in detail.[d] |
| NSS | v3.13[e] (14 October 2011) | Enabled by default for all programs. |
| OpenSSL | Mitigated using empty fragments by applications that set the SSL_OP_ALL flag. | The issue is tracked under bug #2635.[f] |
| Opera | v11.60[g] (6 December 2011) | The comment "Fixed a low severity issue, as reported by Thai Duong and Juliano Rizzo; details will be disclosed at a later date" was in the release notes of v11.51 but was subsequently removed. |
| Oracle | JDK 6u28 and 7u1 (18 October 2011)[h] | |

[a] Apple enabled BEAST mitigations in OS X 10.9 Mavericks [fsty.uk/t429] (Ivan Ristić, 31 October 2013)

[b] Bug #702111: Servers intolerant to 1/n-1 record splitting. "The connection was reset" [fsty.uk/t430] (Bugzilla@Mozilla, 13 November 2011)

[c] Microsoft Security Bulletin MS12-006 [fsty.uk/t431] (10 January 2012)

[d] Microsoft Knowledge Base Article 2643584 [fsty.uk/t432] (10 January 2012)

[e] NSS 3.13 Release Notes [fsty.uk/t433] (14 October 2011)

[f] Bug #2635: 1/n-1 record splitting technique for CVE-2011-3389 [fsty.uk/t434] (Tomas Mraz, 31 October 2011)

[g] Opera 11.60 for Windows changelog [fsty.uk/t435] (6 December 2012)

[h] Oracle Java SE Critical Patch Update Advisory - October 2011 [fsty.uk/t436] (Oracle's web site)

---

[18] BEAST followup [fsty.uk/t428] (Adam Langley, 15 January 2012)

---

Chapter 8: Protocol Attacks

The cost of the 1/n-1 split is an additional 37 bytes that need to be sent with every burst of client application data.[19]

Many client-side tools (e.g., libraries and command-line applications) continue to lack the 1/n-1 split and are thus technically vulnerable, but they are not likely to be exploitable. Without the ability to inject arbitrary plaintext into the communication, there is nothing the attacker can do to exploit the weakness.

## Server-Side Mitigation

Although client-side mitigation produced good results, it was also necessary to consider server-side mitigation, given that there is no telling when all clients will be upgraded. Up until 2013, the recommended approach for BEAST mitigation server-side was to ensure RC4 suites are used by default. With CBC suites out of the picture, there was nothing for BEAST to exploit. But in early 2013 we learned about two new attacks, one against RC4 and another against the CBC construction in TLS. (Both are discussed in detail later in this chapter.) The RC4 weaknesses broke the only server-side mitigation strategy available for BEAST.

## History

The insecurity of predictable IVs has been known since at least 1995, when Phil Rogaway published a critique of cryptographic constructions in the IPsec standard drafts.[20] He said that:

> [...] it is essential that the IV be unpredictable by the adversary.

Clearly, this problem had not been widely understood, because predictable IVs made it into SSL 3 (1996) and later TLS 1.0 (1999).

In 2002, the problem was rediscovered in the SSH protocol[21] and was also found to apply to TLS.[22] Empty TLS record countermeasures were added to OpenSSL in May 2002,

---

[19] Some user agents (e.g., Java and OS X) chose not to use BEAST countermeasures for the first burst of data; they deployed it only from the second burst onward. This saves on bandwidth but provides less security. Application data is probably still safe, because to make a guess you need to see something encrypted first. However, before any application data is sent, TLS uses encryption for its own needs. In most cases, this will be the Finished message, which is not very interesting because it changes on every connection. However, as TLS is evolving, other bits and pieces are being encrypted in the first message. In theory, a future change might make TLS vulnerable again. In practice, because BEAST was fixed in TLS 1.1 it's very unlikely that TLS 1.0 servers will support these new features. In TLS 1.1, the cost is equal to the size of the encryption block, which is typically 16 bytes.

[20] Problems with Proposed IP Cryptography [fsty.uk/t437] (Phil Rogaway, 3 April 1995)

[21] An Attack Against SSH2 Protocol [fsty.uk/t438] (Wei Dai, 6 February 2002)

[22] Re: an attack against SSH2 protocol [fsty.uk/t439] (Bodo Moeller, 8 February 2002)

---

but disabled only two months later because of interoperability issues; they broke Internet Explorer and possibly other clients.[23]

Apparently no one thought this attack was worth pursuing further, and thus no one tried to find a mitigation technique that worked. It was a missed opportunity to address the problem almost a decade before the practical attack came to light. Still, two papers were published that year: one to discuss how to fix the SSH protocol[24] and the other to discuss blockwise-adaptive attacks against several encryption approaches, including CBC.[25]

In 2004, Gregory Bard showed how predictable IVs in TLS can be exploited to reveal fragments of sensitive information.[26] He spelled out the problem inherent in the CBC encryption as implemented in SSL 3.0 and TLS 1.0:

> *We show that this introduces a vulnerability in SSL which (potentially) enables easy recovery of low-entropy strings such as passwords or PINs that have been encrypted. Moreover, we argue that the open nature of web browsers provides a feasible "point of entry" for this attack via a corrupted plug-in [...]*

Bard didn't find a way to exploit the weakness, but later published another paper, this one describing a *blockwise-adaptive chosen-plaintext attack* on SSL, showing how the position of sensitive data within block boundaries significantly impacts the number of guesses required to recover it.[27]

The protocol weakness had been resolved in TLS 1.1 (2006) with a random IV for each TLS record. However, browsers didn't implement this (or later) versions and couldn't benefit from the fix. Only after BEAST made a big splash in 2011 did browser vendors start to think about supporting newer protocols.

In 2011, most libraries and browser vendors implemented the 1/n-1 split mitigation technique. After all the time spent researching the problem, the fix was almost trivial; for NSS, it took only about 30 lines of code.[28]

---

[23] But even if the countermeasures had remained they wouldn't have addressed the BEAST attack. TLS is a duplex protocol, with two separate streams of data, one sent by the client and the other sent by the server, each using separate IVs. An empty fragment mitigation technique implemented on the server wouldn't have fixed the same vulnerability in the client stream, which is where BEAST attacked. TLS stacks used by browsers (e.g, NSS and Schannel) had no countermeasures for predictable IVs.

[24] Breaking and Provably Repairing the SSH Authenticated Encryption Scheme: A Case Study of the Encode-then-Encrypt-and-MAC Paradigm [fsty.uk/t440] (Bellare, Kohno, and Namprempre, Ninth ACM Conference on Computer and Communication Security, 18 November 2002)

[25] Blockwise-Adaptive Attackers: Revisiting the (In)Security of Some Provably Secure Encryption Modes: CBC, GEM, IACBC [fsty.uk/t441] (Joux, Martinet, and Valette, pages 17–30, CRYPTO 2002)

[26] Vulnerability of SSL to Chosen-Plaintext Attack [fsty.uk/t442] (Gregory V. Bard, ESORICS, 2004)

[27] A Challenging but Feasible Blockwise-Adaptive Chosen-Plaintext Attack on SSL [fsty.uk/t443] (Gregory Bard, SECRYPT, 2006)

[28] cbcrandomiv.patch [fsty.uk/t444] (NSS 1/n-1 patch in Chromium, 18 August 2011)

---

Apple waited until late 2013 to implement BEAST mitigations in their TLS stack (and thus Safari). As for protocol support, it wasn't until late 2013 that major browsers started to support TLS 1.2 by default.

# Impact

If a BEAST attack is successful, the attacker will obtain the victim's session token, which will give him access to the entire web application session. He will be able to perform arbitrary actions on the web site, using the identity of the victim. Under the right conditions, BEAST is easy to execute; however, getting everything aligned (especially today) is difficult.

Because the vulnerability exploited by the BEAST attack is in the protocols, at the time of the announcement virtually all SSL and TLS clients were vulnerable. BEAST is a client-side vulnerability. TLS operates two data streams, one sent from the client to the server and the other sent from the server to the client. The BEAST attack targets the client data stream and requires the attacker to be able to control exactly what is sent to the target web server. The interactivity is key; without it, the attack cannot succeed. Thus, even though the server data stream suffers from the same problem of predictable IVs it is impossible to exploit it in practice because the attacker cannot have sufficient control of the server-sent data.

In addition to the interactivity requirement, two further server-controlled conditions are required:

**CBC suites have priority**

Because only CBC suites are vulnerable, those servers that prefer RC4 suites over CBC (or don't support CBC at all) are not vulnerable to the BEAST attack. Even if both sides support CBC suites, the attacker cannot influence the suite selection.

**TLS compression is disabled**

TLS has the ability to compress content prior to encryption. Compression does not protect against the BEAST attack, but it does make it more difficult. Normally, the bytes sent by the attacker are encrypted and sent over the wire. With compression enabled, the bytes are first compressed, which means that the attacker no longer knows what exactly is encrypted. To make the attack work, the attacker would also have to guess the compressed bytes, which may be very difficult. For this reason, the original BEAST exploit implemented by Duong and Rizzo could not attack compressed TLS connections. In my estimate, compression was enabled on about half of all web servers at the time BEAST was announced. However, client-side support for compression was very weak then and is nonexistent today.

Going back to the interactivity, native browser capabilities were not sufficient to carry out the attack, which is why the authors resorted to using third-party plug-ins. The final exploit was implemented in Java and used a previously unknown weakness in the Java plug-in. This meant that the presence of Java was yet another requirement for a successful attack.

To sum up:

1. The attacker must be able to execute an active network attack from a location close to the victim. For example, any Wi-Fi network or a LAN would probably do. Strong cryptography and programming skills are required to implement the exploit.

2. The victim must have the Java plug-in installed. Java was in those days virtually universally available (now not as much), so there wouldn't have been a shortage of candidates.

3. In addition to being authenticated to the target web site, the victim must also be browsing some other site controlled by the attacker. This could be achieved with social engineering, for example. Alternatively, the attacker can hijack any other plain-text HTTP web site. Because the majority of web sites are still not encrypted, this constraint was also easy to satisfy.

4. The server must use CBC suites by default and have compression disabled. Anecdotally, a large number of servers fit these criteria.

At the time it was announced, the BEAST attack was relatively easy to carry out by a determined attacker despite the long list of constraints.

# Compression Side Channel Attacks

*Compression side channel attacks* are a special case of *message length side channel attacks*. Let's assume that you can observe someone's encrypted communication while they are using their online banking application. To obtain the current balance of a savings account, the application might invoke a particular API call. Just seeing the size of that one response might be sufficient to approximate the value: the balance of a particularly wealthy victim will have many digits, making the response longer.

It turns out that when you add compression to the mix, and the attacker is able to submit his own data for compression, a *compression oracle* is created. In this section, I discuss a series of compression-related attacks on TLS, including CRIME, TIME, BREACH, Rupture, and HEIST.

## How the Compression Oracle Works

Compression is very interesting in this context because it changes the size of data, and the differences depend on the nature of the data itself. If all you can do is observe compression ratios, your attacks might not amount to much; there is only so much you can deduce from knowing if something compresses well. At best, you might be able to distinguish one type of traffic from another. For example, text usually compresses very well, but images not so much.

This attack gets far more interesting if you are able to submit your own data for compression and mix it with some other secret data (that you don't know but want to recover) while observing the results. In this case, your data influences the compression process; by varying your data you discover things about what else is compressed at the same time.

To understand why this attack is so powerful, we need to look at how compression works. In essence, all lossless compression algorithms work by eliminating redundancy. If a series of characters is repeated two or more times in input, the output will contain only one copy of such data along with instructions for where to place copies. For example, consider how a very popular LZ77 algorithm would compress a piece of text (see the following figure).

Figure 8.4. Compression reduces data size by identifying and removing repeated fragments

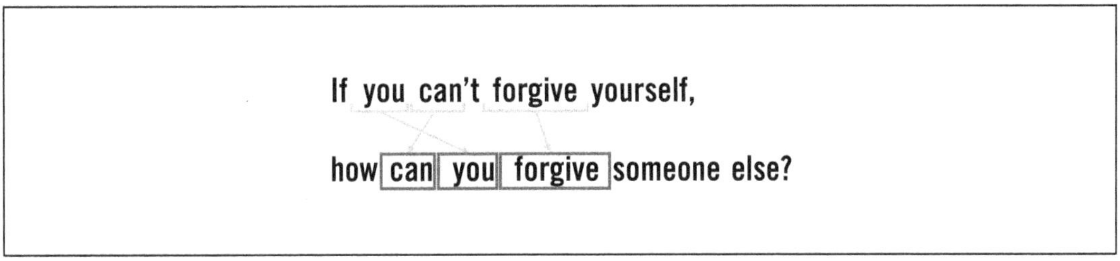

An *oracle* is said to exist if you can have your arbitrary data (guesses) compressed in the same context as some secret. By observing the size of the compressed output, you are able to tell if your guesses are correct. How? If you guess correctly, compression kicks in and reduces the size of the output, and you know that you are right. If you submit random content, there's no compression, and the size increases.

Figure 8.5. Illustration of a compression oracle: one correct and one incorrect guess

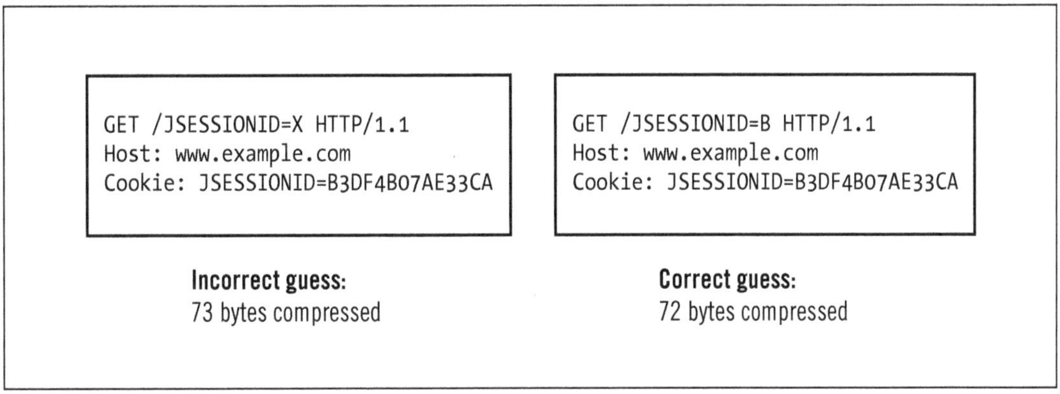

As you shall see in the following sections, there are many obstacles to deal with in order to make the attack practical, but conceptually it really is that simple.

## Is Information Leakage a Flaw in the TLS protocol?

It might seem that information leakage is a flaw in the SSL and TLS protocols, but it's actually a documented limitation. Here's the relevant part of TLS 1.2 (Section 6):

> *Any protocol designed for use over TLS must be carefully designed to deal with all possible attacks against it. As a practical matter, this means that the protocol designer must be aware of what security properties TLS does and does not provide and cannot safely rely on the latter.*
>
> *Note in particular that type and length of a record are not protected by encryption. If this information is itself sensitive, application designers may wish to take steps (padding, cover traffic) to minimize information leakage.*

TLS 1.3 later added an explicit mechanism to support *length hiding* but didn't specify any particular algorithm. Some might say that the real flaw is the fact that browsers allow adversaries unprecedented level of control of their victims' browsers—and that might be true. Adaptive plaintext attacks are a big deal in cryptography, but here we have TLS, designed with one set of capabilities in mind and used in scenarios that were outside the scope of the original design.

All browser-based attacks against encryption rely on the fact that the attacker can submit requests in the context of a *genuine user session*, which results in attacker-supplied data transported in the same request as the victim's confidential data. Few will argue that this is natural. If we accept that a random web page should be allowed to submit requests to arbitrary web sites, we should at least ensure that they do so from their own separate environment (i.e., a sandbox).

Sadly, the Web has evolved in such a way that everything is entangled, which means that enforcing strict separation in this way would break far too many web sites. In time, the solution will probably come in the form of elective separation, which will allow a site to declare its own security space.

As for length hiding, even if such a feature is ever implemented, there is always the question of its effectiveness. It most certainly won't work in all situations. Some highly secure systems address this problem by always communicating at a constant rate, using the full bandwidth provided by the underlying channel. However, that approach is prohibitively expensive for most deployments.

# History of Attacks

Compression as a side channel mechanism was first introduced by John Kelsey. In his 2002 paper,[29] he presented a series of attack scenarios, each varying in effectiveness. Among them was the extraction of fragments of sensitive data, the attack that was later going to be

---

[29] Compression and Information Leakage of Plaintext [fsty.uk/t445] (John Kelsey, FSE, 2002)

improved in the browser context. The world was a much different place in 2002, and the best attack was difficult to utilize in real life. Hence, the author concluded that:

> The string-extraction attacks are not likely to be practical against many systems, since they require such a specialized kind of partial chosen-plaintext access.

Compression side channel attacks were again in the news a couple of years later, although not against TLS. In 2007, a team of researchers first developed algorithms to identify the spoken language of an encrypted internet call[30] and later managed to identify spoken English phrases with an average accuracy of 50%, rising to 90% for some phrases.[31]

In the following years, browsers continued to evolve, making adaptive chosen-plaintext attacks not only possible but also practical against virtually everyone. In 2011, the BEAST attack showed how the attacker can take control of a victim's browser in order to execute a blended attack against encryption.

In August 2011, privacy issues stemming from compression side channel attacks were discussed on the SPDY[32] development mailing list.[33] In particular, this quote from Adam Langley describes how a compression side channel attack might work against browsers:

> The attacker is running script in evil.com. Concurrently, the same client has a compressed connection open to victim.com and is logged in, with a secret cookie. evil.com can induce requests to victim.com by, say, adding <img> tags with a src pointing to victim.com. [...] The attacker can watch the wire and measure the size of the requests that are sent. By altering the URL, the attacker could attempt to minimise the request size: i.e. when the URL matches the cookie.
>
> I've just tried this with an HTTP request for fun and it's pretty easy to get the first 5 characters in a base64 encoded cookie. [...] That's a practical attack and would make a great paper if someone has the time.

# CRIME

A practical compression side channel exploit came in 2012, under the name CRIME, developed by Duong and Rizzo, the authors behind BEAST. CRIME exploits the TLS compression side channel by using JavaScript malware to extract client cookies in an active

---

[30] Language identification of encrypted VoIP traffic: Alejandra y Roberto or Alice and Bob? [fsty.uk/t446] (Wright et al., USENIX Security, 2007)

[31] Uncovering Spoken Phrases in Encrypted Voice over IP Conversations [fsty.uk/t447] (Wright et al., ACM Transactions on Information and System Security, Vol. 13, No. 4, Article 35, December 2010)

[32] SPDY is a relatively new protocol designed by Google to speed up web browsing.

[33] Compression contexts and privacy considerations [fsty.uk/t448] (Adam Langley, 11 August 2011)

network attack. It was officially presented at the Ekoparty conference in September 2012.[34] Unofficially, early press briefings[35] leaked enough information to enable experts to correctly guess what the attack was about.[36]

A proof of concept, the collaboration of several speculators, was published.[37] With the cat out of the bag, further information and a video demonstration were revealed days before the conference.[38] The CRIME authors never released their code, but they claimed that their exploit was able to uncover one cookie character using only six requests.

The mechanics of the CRIME attack are the same as for BEAST: the attacker must instrument the victim's browser to submit many requests to the target server, while observing network packets as they travel on the wire. Each request is a guess, exactly as discussed in the earlier compression oracle section. Unlike BEAST, CRIME requires less control over request content and timing, making exploitation much easier and using only native browser functionality.

## TIME

After CRIME, we didn't have to wait long for the attacks to improve. In March 2013, Tal Be'ery presented TIME at Black Hat Europe 2013.[39] A significant constraint on CRIME is the fact that the attacker must have access to the local network in order to observe the network packets. Although TIME still uses compression as its principal weapon, the improved attack extends the JavaScript component to use I/O timing differences to measure the size of compressed records. The approach is straightforward, with <img> tags used to initiate requests from the victim's browser and onLoad and onReadyStateChange event handlers to take measurements. The entire attack takes place in the browser itself.

With this change, the attack can now be executed against anyone on the Internet, provided you can get them to run your JavaScript malware. In practice, this will require some form of social engineering.

One problem still remains, though. CRIME works by observing one-byte differences in compressed output; is it really possible to use timing to detect differences that small? As it turns out, it's possible, by playing tricks at the network layer.

In TCP, great care is taken not to overwhelm the other party by sending too much data. The problem is this: there's usually a significant distance between two sides engaged in a conversation. For example, it takes about 45 ms for a packet to travel between London and

---

[34] The CRIME attack [fsty.uk/t449] (Duong and Rizzo, Ekoparty Security Conference 9° edición, 2012)

[35] New Attack Uses SSL/TLS Information Leak to Hijack HTTPS Sessions [fsty.uk/t450] (Threatpost, 5 September 2012)

[36] CRIME - How to beat the BEAST successor? [fsty.uk/t451] (Thomas Pornin, 8 September 2012)

[37] It's not a crime to build a CRIME [fsty.uk/t452] (Krzysztof Kotowicz, 11 September 2012)

[38] Crack in Internet's foundation of trust allows HTTPS session hijacking [fsty.uk/t453] (Ars Technica, 13 September 2012)

[39] A Perfect CRIME? TIME Will Tell [fsty.uk/t454] (Tal Be'ery and Amichai Shulman, March 2013)

New York. If you send only one packet at a time and wait for a confirmation, you can send only one packet of data every 90 ms. To speed up the communication, TCP allows both sides to send many packets at once. However, to ensure that the other party is not overwhelmed, they have to stay within a prescribed limit, or the *congestion window*. The congestion window starts small and grows over time, an approach otherwise known as *slow start.*

Initial congestion window sizes vary. Older TCP stacks will use smaller windows of 5 to 6 KB, but there was recently a push to increase this to about 15 KB. The attack works equally well for all sizes. In the following example, I assume that the client uses an initial congestion window of 5 KB (three packets).

Figure 8.6. Using the TCP initial congestion window size as a timing oracle

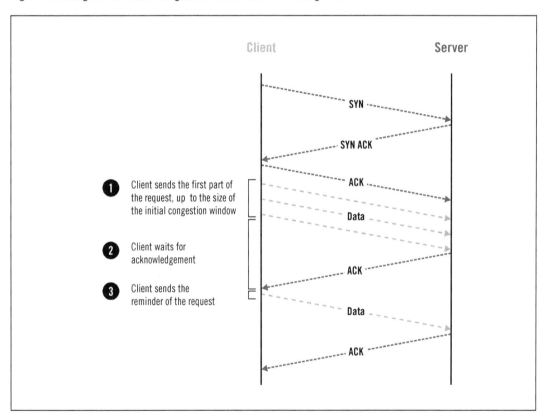

At the beginning of a connection, if the data you want to send fits into the congestion window, then you can send it all at once. But if you have too much data you will first have to send as much as you can, then wait for the server to confirm receipt, then send what you have remaining. That wait will add one *round-trip time* (RTT) to the operation. For the London–New York connection, that comes to about 90 ms of extra time. To use this behavior as a timing oracle, you increase the size of the data until you completely fill the initial congestion window. If you add just one more byte, the request will take one RTT longer, which is a delay you can measure from JavaScript. At this point you can start playing with compression; if you manipulate the data so that compression reduces the size by one byte, the request will take one RTT less. From here, exploitation continues as discussed in earlier sections.

Attacks against HTTP requests are easier because you have direct control over what is sent. They allow you to extract secrets that browsers have, for example, session cookies. If you want to extract secrets transported in HTTP responses, things get more complicated:

- Response compression takes place on the server, which means that you need to observe the server's initial congestion window, not the client's (as with HTTP requests).

- You must be able to inject your data into the page that contains the secret you wish to obtain. In practice, this means that the application must mirror some data you send to it.

- When timing responses, you must take into account that both the client's and the server's windows are likely to overflow, making it more difficult to know what caused a delay.

On the other hand, unlike TLS compression, HTTP-level response compression is very common. Compression side channel attacks work equally well against both.

As far as we know, TIME has not progressed beyond a proof of concept. In practice, there might be many obstacles to overcome in order to make the attack work in real life. For example, the authors mention that due to network jitter they need to repeat the same request several times to reliably detect boundaries. Furthermore, the congestion window size grows over the time of the connection, which means that you need to take your measurements with a fresh connection every time. However, most servers use persistent connections for performance reasons, and you don't have control over this from JavaScript. As a result, the attack might need to operate slowly, using one connection, then waiting for the browser to close it, then trying again. Overall, it might take quite a while for successful extraction of, say, a 16-character secret.

## BREACH

Another compression side channel attack focused on HTTP responses, called BREACH, followed in August 2013.[40] The authors focused on demonstrating that CRIME works equally well on HTTP response compression. They used the same attack position—that of an active man in the middle—and developed a working exploit. Their main contribution

---

[40] BREACH: Reviving the CRIME Attack [fsty.uk/t455] (Gluck et al., August 2013)

is in the analysis and the practical demonstration. For example, they used their exploit to attack Outlook Web Access (OWA), showing that they can retrieve CSRF tokens with 95% reliability and often in under 30 seconds.[41]

The BREACH authors put together a web site to publicize their work,[42] and the proof-of-concept source code is available at GitHub.[43]

## Attack Details

BREACH is conceptually identical to CRIME, requiring that the attacker has access to the victim's network traffic and ability to run JavaScript code in the victim's browser. The attack surface is different. HTTP response compression applies only to response bodies, which means that no secrets can be extracted from the response headers. However, response bodies often have interesting sensitive data. The authors focused on extracting CSRF tokens (their example is shown ahead), which would allow them to impersonate the victim in the attacked web application.

To bootstrap the attack, an injection point into the response body is needed. In OWA, the `id` parameter is reflected in output. Thus, if the attacker submits the following request with the attack payload:

```
GET /owa/?ae=Item&t=IPM.Note&a=New&id=INJECTED-VALUE
```

The response body will contain the injected value:

```
<span id=requestUrl>https://malbot.net:443/owa/forms/
basic/BasicEditMessage.aspx?ae=Item&amp;t=IPM.Note&
amp;a=New&amp;id=INJECTED-VALUE</span>
```

This is sufficient to begin to extract any secret placed elsewhere in the body, for example, a CSRF token:

```
<td nowrap id="tdErrLgf"><a href="logoff.owa?
canary=d634cda866f14c73ac135ae858c0d894">Log
Off</a></td>
```

To establish the baseline, the attacker submits `canary=` as the first payload. Because of the duplication, the compressed response body will be smaller, which can be detected on the network. From here, the attack continues as in CRIME.

Although the attack seems simple at first, in practice there are further issues that need to be dealt with:

---

[41] The authors presented BREACH at Black Hat USA 2013, in a session titled "SSL, Gone in 30 seconds."

[42] BREACH web site [fsty.uk/t456] (retrieved 16 July 2014)

[43] BREACH repository [fsty.uk/t457] (Neal Harris, retrieved 16 July 2014)

### Huffman encoding

Most of the Internet runs on DEFLATE compression, which is actually a combination of two algorithms: LZ77 and Huffman encoding. The former is what we use for the attacks, but the latter actually makes us work harder. Huffman encoding is a variable-length encoding that exploits the fact that, usually, some characters appear more often than others. Normally, we always use one byte to represent one character. To save space, we can represent more frequent characters with shorter symbols (fewer bits than in a byte) and less frequent characters with longer symbols (more bits than in a byte).

Huffman encoding can skew the resulting lengths of both successful and unsuccessful guesses. To deal with this problem, it's necessary to double the number of requests, using two for each guess.

### Block ciphers

The conceptual attack works great against encryption, but expects streaming ciphers, for which the size of data is directly reflected in ciphertext. When block ciphers are used, ciphertext grows only one block at a time, for example, 16 bytes for 128-bit AES. In such a case, further padding is needed to bring ciphertext to the edge of growing by another block. For this, several requests might be needed. Once you determine the size of the padding, you can make as many guesses as there are padding bytes. For every new guess, you remove one byte of the padding.

### Response content diversity

For the attacks that work against HTTP responses (TIME and BREACH), the "diverse" nature of markup formatting, coding practices, and encodings tends to make the attacks more difficult. For example, the attacks require a known prefix to bootstrap the attack, but the secret values are sometimes prefixed with characters that cannot be injected (e.g., quotes). Or, there might be variations in response size (in absence of attacks), which make guessing more difficult.

The CRIME authors used an interesting technique variation when attacking TLS compression. TLS record sizes are limited to 16 KB (16,384 bytes), which also means that this is the largest block on which compression can operate. This is interesting because the attacker is able to fully control the first 16 KB. It goes something like this:

1. For a GET request, the first 5 bytes are always going to be the same: the request method (GET) followed by a space and the first character in the URL (/). If you then add 16,379 bytes of random data to the URL, you fill the entire TLS record. You can submit this request and observe its compressed size.

2. You can now start reducing the amount of random data in the URL, one byte at a time, allowing bytes from the request back in the block. Some of the bytes will be predictable (e.g., HTTP/1.1, the protocol information that always follows the URL), but at some point you will encounter the first unknown byte.

3. Now you have a block of 16,383 bytes you know and one byte you don't. You submit that as a request. Then, without making further requests, you build a list of candidates for the unknown byte, simulate the first 16 KB as a request and compress it using the same compression method, and compare the compressed size to that of the size of the actual request. In the ideal case, there will be only one match, and it will disclose the unknown byte.

This technique is quite neat, because it requires a smaller number of requests. On the other hand, the compression library used by the attacker needs to produce the same output for the same input. In practice, different compression settings and different library versions might introduce variations.

## Further Attack Improvements

In the following years, security researchers continued to improve upon the original attacks. At Black Hat Asia in 2016, a group of researchers presented the Rupture framework, which made BREACH easier to execute.[44]

Later in 2016, the HEIST attack was published, improving TIME and other attacks by focusing on the exploitation of the browser and protocol features not available when the original attacks were published.[45]

## Impact against TLS Compression and SPDY

In this section, I discuss the various prerequisites necessary for a successful exploitation of a compression side channel attack against either TLS compression or SPDY. In both cases, CRIME attacks header compression, which makes session cookies the best target.

**Active network attack**

CRIME requires access to the victim's network traffic. It's a local attack, which can be performed with little effort against someone on the same LAN or Wi-Fi network. The attack can be either passive or active, but the latter gives the attacker more flexibility.

**Client-side control**

The attacker must also be able to assert enough control over the victim's browser to submit arbitrary requests to the target web site. You could do this with JavaScript malware, but it can be done much more simply with a series of <img> tags with specially crafted source URLs.

This could be achieved with social engineering or, more likely, by injecting HTML markup into any plaintext web site that the victim is interacting with at the time of attack.

---

[44] Rupture: A compression side-channel attack framework [fsty.uk/t458] (Karakostas et al., April 2016)
[45] HEIST [fsty.uk/t459] (Mathy Vanhoef and Tom Van Goethem, August 2016)

### Vulnerable protocols

As the authors of CRIME themselves said, compression is everywhere. They detailed attacks against TLS compression and the SPDY protocol. At the time of the announcement, I was able to use the SSL Pulse statistics and some of the other metrics obtained via the SSL Labs web site to estimate support for compression on both the client and server sides. For TLS compression, about 42% of the servers in the SSL Pulse data set supported it. Only about 2% of the servers supported SPDY, but those were some of the biggest sites (e.g., Google, Twitter, etc.).

That said, two sides are required to enable compression, and this is where the situation got better. Because TLS compression was never a high priority for browser vendors,[46] Chrome was the only browser that supported compression then. Firefox had compression implemented, but to my knowledge the code never went into a production release. Because both browser vendors had advance knowledge of the problem, they made sure that compression was disabled ahead of time. My measurements (from observing the visits to the SSL Labs web site) showed only 7% client-side support for compression.

In response to CRIME, most vendors patched their products and libraries to disable TLS compression altogether.

### Preparation

This is not an attack that can be blindly executed against just any web site. For example, to start the attack it's necessary to use a known prefix as a starting point. Because these things differ from site to site, some amount of research is necessary, but it's not a lot of effort for the attack against TLS compression.

### Outcome

In the best case, the attacker is able to obtain the password used for HTTP Basic Authentication. In practice, this authentication method is not often used, making session cookies the next best thing. A successful attack results in the attacker obtaining full control over the victim's session and everything that comes with it.

## Impact against HTTP Response Compression

Against HTTP compression, the impact of compression side channels is very different: (1) the attack surface is much larger and there is little chance that it will be reduced and (2) successful exploitation requires the attacker to do much more work upfront and their reward is smaller.

---

[46] Sites that care about performance will already compress HTTP responses, which is where the bulk of the bandwidth is. Trying to compress already compressed traffic increases CPU and RAM consumption but yields little improvement. It might be possible to move compression entirely to the TLS layer, but then it would try to compress images, which are not likely to compress well.

---

The prerequisites for attacks against HTTP compressions are the same as in the previous case; the attacker must be able to take control over the network communication and have limited control over the victim's browser. But there are differences when it comes to other factors:

**Attack surface**

> HTTP compression is also vulnerable to compression side attacks. (The CRIME authors did not spend much time on it, but others have since worked in this area.) Unlike TLS compression, HTTP compression exposes a huge attack surface and cannot be simply turned off. Many sites depend on it so heavily that they might not be able to operate (cost efficiently) without it.
>
> There is also an additional requirement that the attacker is able to inject arbitrary text into the HTTP response body, at the desired attack point. That's usually possible to achieve.

**Preparation**

> On the other side, much more work is needed to exploit HTTP compression. In fact, you could say that an intimate understanding of the target web site is required. Session cookies are generally not available in HTTP response bodies, which means that the attackers must look for some other secret information. And that information might be much more difficult to find.

**Outcome**

> The exact outcome will depend on the nature of the secret information. Any secret information can be extracted, provided the attacker knows it's there. For most applications, the most interesting target will be the CSRF protection tokens. If one such token is uncovered, the attacker might be able to carry out an arbitrary command on the target web site under the identity of the victim. There are some sites that use their session tokens for CSRF protection. In such cases, the outcome will be session hijacking.

## Mitigation of Attacks against TLS and SPDY

TLS compression is now dead, and it was CRIME that killed it. At the time of the disclosure, though, about 30% of all browser users were vulnerable. The exposure came through Chrome, the only browser that supported TLS compression at the time. The problem was quickly resolved thanks to Chrome's autoupdate feature, which enabled quick propagation of the fix to most users.

OpenSSL had support for compression, so it's possible to find old installations and user agents that still support it, but they are not likely to be attacked because they are not browsers (i.e., malware injection is not likely).

As for SPDY, header compression had been disabled in both Chrome and Firefox. Now that the problem is known, we can assume that the future versions of this protocol will not be vulnerable. HTTP/2, which succeeded SPDY, implements a special header compression algorithm called HPACK, which is not vulnerable to compression attacks.

## Mitigation of Attacks against HTTP Compression

Addressing the compression side channel inherent in HTTP compression is a much more difficult problem, even if the attack is not exactly easy to execute. The difficulty is twofold: (1) you probably can't afford to disable compression and (2) mitigation requires application changes, which are cost-prohibitive. Still, there are some hacks that just might work well enough. Here's a quick overview of the possibilities:

**Request rate control**

Both the authors of TIME and BREACH have commented on sometimes getting caught due to the excessive number of requests they had to submit. (The BREACH authors cited thousands of requests against OWA.) Enforcing a reasonable rate of requests for user sessions could detect similar attacks or, in the worst case, slow down the attacker significantly. This mitigation could be implemented at a web server, load-balancer, or web application firewall (WAF) layer, which means that it does not need to be very costly.

**Length hiding**

One possible defense measure is to hide the real response length. For example, we could deploy a response body filter to analyze HTML markup and inject random padding. Whitespace is largely ignored in HTML, yet variations in response size would make the attackers' job more difficult. According to the BREACH authors, random padding can be defeated using statistical analysis at the cost of a significant increase in the number of requests.

The best aspect of this approach is that it can be applied at the web server level, with no changes to deployed applications. For example, Paul Querna proposed to use variations in chunked HTTP encoding at a web server level for length hiding.[47] This approach does not change the markup at all, yet it changes the size of the packets on the wire.

**Token masking**

Threats against CSRF tokens can be mitigated by the use of *masking*, ensuring that the characters that appear in HTML markup are never the same. Here's how: (1) for every byte in the token, generate one random byte; (2) XOR the token byte with the random byte; and (3) include all the random bytes in the output. This process is

---

[47] breach attack [fsty.uk/t460] (Paul Querna, 6 August 2013)

reversible; by repeating the XOR operations on the server, you recover the original token value. This measure is ideally suited for implementation at the framework level.

**Partial compression disabling**

When I first thought about attacks against HTTP response bodies, my thoughts were to focus on the fact that the `Referer` header will never contain the name of the target web site. (If the attacker can do that, then she already has enough access to the site via XSS.) Initially, I proposed to drop cookies on such requests. Without the cookies, there is no user session, and no attack surface. Someone from the community had a better idea: for requests with the incorrect referrer information, simply disable response compression.[48] There would be a small performance penalty but only for the small number of users who don't supply any referrer information. More importantly, there wouldn't be any breakage, unlike with the cookie approach.

**Context hiding**

The best way to mitigate the CRIME family of attacks is to avoid compressing sensitive information in the same context with attacker-provided data. This is easier said than done. It's probably something that you should take into consideration when building new applications, but it's very difficult to retrofit existing applications to address the weakness. At Black Hat Europe 2016, a group of researchers provided a toolkit that employs data masking to support continued use of HTTP response compression but keep attacker-provided data in a separate context.[49]

# Lucky 13

In February 2013, AlFardan and Paterson released a paper detailing a variety of attacks that can be used to recover small portions of plaintext provided that a CBC suite is used.[50] Their work is commonly known as the *Lucky 13 attack*. As with BEAST and CRIME, in the web context small portions of plaintext virtually always refer to browser cookies or HTTP Basic Authentication. Outside HTTP, any protocol that uses password authentication is probably vulnerable.

The root cause of the problem is in the fact that the padding, which is used in the CBC mode, is not protected by the integrity validation mechanisms of TLS. This allows the attacker to modify the padding in transit and observe how the server behaves. If the attacker is able to detect the server reacting to the modified padding, information leaks out and leads to plaintext discovery.

---

[48] BREACH mitigation [fsty.uk/t461] (manu, 14 October 2013)

[49] CTX: Eliminating BREACH with Context Hiding [fsty.uk/t462] (Karakostas et al., November 2016)

[50] Lucky Thirteen: Breaking the TLS and DTLS Record Protocols [fsty.uk/t463] (AlFardan and Paterson, 4 February 2013)

This is one of the best attacks against TLS we saw in recent years. Using JavaScript malware injected into a victim's browser, the attack needs about 8,192 HTTP requests to discover one byte of plaintext (e.g., from a cookie or password).

## What Is a Padding Oracle?

There is a special class of attack that can be mounted against the receiving party if the padding can be manipulated. This might be possible if the encryption scheme does not authenticate ciphertext; for example, TLS doesn't in CBC mode. The attacker can't manipulate the padding directly, because it's encrypted. But she can make arbitrary changes to the ciphertext, where she thinks the padding might be. An *oracle* is said to exist if the attacker is able to tell which manipulations result in a correct padding after decryption and which do not.

But how do you get from there to plaintext recovery? At the end of the day, encryption is all about hiding (masking) plaintext using some secret seemingly random data. If the attacker can reveal the mask, she can effectively reverse the encryption process and reveal the plaintext, too.

Going back to the padding oracle, every time the attacker submits a guess that results in correct padding after decryption she discovers one byte of the mask that is used for decryption. She can now use that byte to decrypt one byte of plaintext. From here, she can continue to recover the next byte, and so on, until the entire plaintext is revealed.

The key to successful padding oracle exploitation is to (1) submit a lot of guesses and (2) find a way to determine if a guess was successful. Some badly designed protocols might fail to hide padding errors. More likely, the attacker will need to deduce the outcome by observing server behavior. For example, timing oracles observe the response latency, watching for timing differences when padding is correct and when it is not.

If you care to learn about the details behind padding oracle attacks, you can head to one of the tutorials available online[51] or review an online simulation that shows the process in detail.[52]

Padding oracle issues are best avoided by verifying the integrity of data before any of it is processed. Such checks prevent ciphertext manipulation and preempt all padding oracle attacks.

---

[51] Automated Padding Oracle Attacks with PadBuster [fsty.uk/t464] (Brian Holyfield, 14 September 2010)

[52] Padding oracle attack simulation [fsty.uk/t465] (Erlend Oftedal, retrieved 28 February 2014)

---

# Attacks against TLS

The *padding oracle attack* (against TLS and other protocols) was first identified by Serge Vaudenay in 2001 (formally published in 2002).[53] TLS 1.0 uses the decryption_failed alert for padding errors and bad_record_mac for MAC failures. This design, although insecure, was not practically exploitable because alerts are encrypted and the network attacker can't differentiate between the two types of failure.

In 2003, Canvel et al.[54] improved the attack to use a timing padding oracle and demonstrated a successful attack against OpenSSL. They exploited the fact that OpenSSL skipped the MAC calculation and responded slightly faster when the padding was incorrect. The researcher's proof-of-concept attack was against an IMAP server; situated close to the target, they could obtain the IMAP password in about one hour.

Padding oracles are exploited by repeatedly making guesses about which combinations of bytes might decrypt to valid padding. The attacker starts with some intercepted ciphertext, modifies it, and submits it to the server. Most guesses will naturally be incorrect. In TLS, every failed guess terminates the entire TLS session, which means that the same encrypted block cannot be modified and attempted again. For her next guess, the attacker needs to intercept another valid encrypted block. That is why Canvel et al. attacked IMAP; automated services that automatically retry after failure are the ideal case for this attack.

In order to improve the security of CBC, OpenSSL (and other TLS implementations) modified its code to minimize the information leakage.[55] TLS 1.1 deprecated the decryption_failed alert and added the following warning (emphasis mine):

> *Canvel et al. [CBCTIME] have demonstrated a timing attack on CBC padding based on the time required to compute the MAC. In order to defend against this attack, implementations MUST ensure that record processing time is essentially the same whether or not the padding is correct. In general, the best way to do this is to compute the MAC even if the padding is incorrect, and only then reject the packet. For instance, if the pad appears to be incorrect, the implementation might assume a zero-length pad and then compute the MAC.* **This leaves a small timing channel, since MAC performance depends to some extent on the size of the data fragment, but it is not believed to be large enough to be exploitable, due to the large block size of existing MACs and the small size of the timing signal.**

---

[53] Security Flaws Induced by CBC Padding - Applications to SSL, IPSEC, WTLS... [fsty.uk/t466] (Serge Vaudenay, pages 534–546, EUROCRYPT 2002)

[54] Password Interception in a SSL/TLS Channel [fsty.uk/t467] (Canvel et al., CRYPTO 2003)

[55] Security of CBC Ciphersuites in SSL/TLS: Problems and Countermeasures [fsty.uk/t468] (Moeller et al., last updated on 20 May 2004)

In February 2013, AlFardan and Paterson demonstrated that the remaining side channel is, in fact, exploitable, using new techniques to realize Vaudenay's padding oracle. They named their new attack Lucky 13 and showed that CBC—as implemented in TLS and DTLS—is too fragile and that it should have been abandoned a long time ago. Their work demonstrated how small problems, left unattended, can escalate later because technology evolves in unpredictable ways.

# Impact

For the padding oracle to be exploited, the adversary must be able to mount an active attack, which means that he must be able to intercept and modify encrypted traffic. Additionally, because the timing differences are subtle the attacker must be very close to the target server in order to detect them. The researchers performed their experiments when the attacker and the server were both on the same local network. Remote attacks do not appear to be feasible for TLS, although they are for DTLS, when used with timing amplification techniques developed by AlFardan and Paterson in 2012.[56]

**Attacks against automated systems**

> The classic full plaintext recovery padding oracle attack is carried out against automated systems, which are likely to communicate with the server often and have built-in resiliency mechanisms that makes them try again on failed connections. Because the attack is spanning many connections, it works only with protocols that always place sensitive data (e.g., passwords) in the same location. IMAP is a good candidate. This attack requires roughly 8.4 million connections to recover 16 bytes of data. Because each incorrect guess results in a TLS error and because TLS is designed to destroy sessions in such situations, every new connection is forced to use a full handshake with the server. As a result, this attack is slow. Still, it's not far from being feasible under certain circumstances if the attacker has months of time available and is able to influence the automated process to open connections at a faster rate.

**Attacks when some of the plaintext is known**

> A partial plaintext recovery attack, which can be performed if one byte at one of the last two positions in a block is known, allows each of the remaining bytes to be recovered with roughly 65,536 attempts.

**Attacks against browsers using JavaScript malware**

> AlFardan and Paterson's best attack uses JavaScript malware against the victim's browser, targeting HTTP cookies. Because the malware can influence the position of the cookie in a request, it is possible to arrange the encryption blocks in such a way that only one byte of the cookie is unknown. Because of the limited character range used by cookies, the researchers estimate that only 8,192 requests are needed

---

[56] Plaintext-Recovery Attacks Against Datagram TLS [fsty.uk/t469] (AlFardan and Paterson, NDSS, February 2012)

to uncover one byte of plaintext. The best aspect of this attack is the fact that the malware is submitting all the requests and that, even though they all fail, all the connection failures are invisible to the victim. Furthermore, no special plug-ins or cross-origin privileges are required.

## Mitigation

AlFardan and Paterson identified problems in a number of implementations, reported the problems to the developers, and coordinated the disclosure so that all libraries were already fixed at the time of announcement.

The writing was clearly on the wall for CBC, but in the world in which browsers didn't yet support TLS 1.2 and its authenticated GCM suites, for a while there were no alternatives. A wider adoption of TLS 1.2 enabled web sites to deploy better encryption and avoid padding oracle issues. Finally, TLS 1.3 removed CBC suites and solved the problem forever. In September 2014, a new TLS protocol extension was added to change how CBC suites work to authenticate ciphertext instead of plaintext, but its arrival was too late to make an impact.[57]

# RC4 Weaknesses

RC4, designed by Ron Rivest in 1987, was one of the first ciphers and probably also the most widely deployed for a great many years. Its popularity came not only from the fact that it had been around for a very long time but also due to it being simple to implement and running very fast in software and hardware. Over time, cracks in the security of RC4 started to appear, but the attacks never seemed to be serious enough and RC4 continued to be deployed for much longer than it should have been.

## Key Scheduling Weaknesses

For a very long time, the biggest known problem with RC4 was the weakness in the key scheduling algorithm, published in a paper by Fluhrer, Mantin, and Shamir in 2001.[58] The authors discovered that there are large classes of keys that have a weakness where a small part of the key determines a large number of initial outputs. In practice, this means that if even a part of a key is reused over a period of time the attacker could (1) uncover parts of the keystream (e.g., from known plaintext at certain locations) and then (2) uncover unknown plaintext bytes at those positions in all other streams. This discovery was used to

---

[57] RFC 7366: Encrypt-then-MAC for TLS and DTLS [fsty.uk/t470] (Peter Gutmann, September 2014)
[58] Weaknesses in the Key Scheduling Algorithm of RC4 [fsty.uk/t471] (Fluhrer, Mantin, and Shamir, 2001)

break the WEP protocol.[59] The initial attack implemented against WEP required 10 million messages for the key recovery. The technique was later improved to require only under 100,000 messages.

TLS is not vulnerable to this problem, because every connection uses a substantially different key. Thus, RC4 remained in wide use, because the known issues didn't apply to the way it was used in TLS.[60] Despite its known flaws, RC4 remained the most popular cipher used with TLS. My 2010 large-scale survey of SSL server configuration found that RC4 was the preferred cipher and supported by about 98% of surveyed servers.[61] People who understood the key scheduling weakness disliked RC4 because it was easy to misuse and, as a result, recommended against it for new systems.[62]

When the BEAST attack was announced in 2011, it instantly made all block cipher suites unsafe. (Even though BEAST works only against TLS 1.0 and earlier protocol versions, support for TLS 1.1 or better was nonexistent at the time.) Because RC4—a streaming cipher—was not vulnerable to BEAST, it suddenly became the only secure algorithm to use in TLS. In March 2013, when new flaws in RC4 were announced, the ICSI Certificate Notary project showed RC4 usage at about 50% of all traffic. By July 2014, the RC4 market share was about 26%.[63]

In February 2015, RFC 7465 was published to forbid further usage of RC4 in TLS.[64] Modern browsers removed RC4 altogether during 2016, firmly showing that RC4 belongs in the past.

## Early Single-Byte Biases

*Encryption biases* were another reason cryptographers were worried about RC4. As early as 2001, it was known that some values appear in the keystream more often than others.[65] In particular, the second keystream byte was known to be biased toward zero with a probability of 1/128 (twice as much as the expected 1/256).

To understand how biases can lead to the compromise of plaintext, we need to go back to how RC4 works. This cipher operates in a streaming fashion; after the initial setup phase, it produces an endless stream of data. This data, which was supposed to be effectively random looking from the outside, is then mixed with the plaintext, using a XOR operation against

---

[59] WEP didn't quite reuse its keys but derived new keys from a master key using concatenation, a method that resulted in the session keys that are similar to the master key. TLS, for example, uses hashing, which means that connection keys cannot be traced back to the master key.

[60] RSA Security Response to Weaknesses in Key Scheduling Algorithm of RC4 [fsty.uk/t472] (RSA Laboratories Technical Note, 1 September 2001)

[61] Internet SSL Survey 2010 is here! [fsty.uk/t113] (Ivan Ristić, 29 July 2010)

[62] What's the deal with RC4? [fsty.uk/t473] (Matthew Green, 15 December 2011)

[63] The ICSI Certificate Notary [fsty.uk/t474] (International Computer Science Institute, retrieved 16 July 2014)

[64] RFC 7465: Prohibiting RC4 Cipher Suites [fsty.uk/t475] (Andrei Popov, February 2015)

[65] A Practical Attack on Broadcast RC4 [fsty.uk/t476] (Mantin and Shamir, 2011)

one byte at a time. The XOR operation, when used with a sufficiently random data stream, changes plaintext into something that's effectively gibberish for everyone except those who know the RC4 key.

When we say that a bias exists, that means that some values appear more often than others. The worst case is the already mentioned bias toward zero. Why? Because a value XORed with a zero remains unchanged. Thus, because we know that the second byte of every RC4 data stream leans toward zero we also know that the second byte of encrypted output will tend to be the same as the original text!

To exploit this problem you need to obtain the same text encrypted with many different encryption keys. Against TLS, this means attacking many connections.[66] Then you look at all the bytes at position 2; the value that appears most often is most likely to be the same as in plaintext. Some amount of guessing is involved, but, the more different encryptions you obtain, the higher the chances that you will guess correctly.

Figure 8.7. The bias in the second byte of the RC4 keystream [Source: AlFardan et al., 2013]

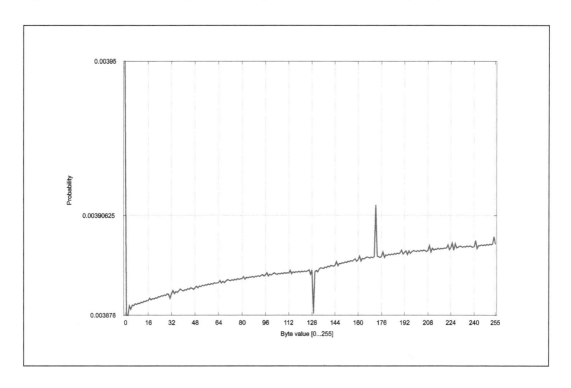

---

[66] In cryptography, this is known as a *multisession* attack. The name might be confusing in the context of TLS, because a *TLS session* is a set of cryptographic parameters that are used across multiple connections via the session reuse mechanism. Even with session reuse, TLS generates new encryption keys for every connection.

What can be achieved using these individual biases varies and depends on protocol design. The first requirement is that useful data actually exists at the given location. For example, in TLS the first 36 bytes are most commonly used by the Finished protocol message that changes with every connection and has no long-term value.[67] For TLS, the second-byte bias is not going to be useful.

The second requirement is to get the same application data in the same location every time across a great number of connections. For some protocols, this is not a problem. In HTTP, for example, cookies and passwords are in the same place on every request.

## Biases across the First 256 Bytes

In March 2013, AlFardan et al. published a paper describing newly discovered weaknesses in RC4 and two strong attacks against its use in TLS.[68]

One of the attacks was based on the fact that RC4 biases were not limited to a few bytes here and there. By producing and analyzing keystreams of $2^{44}$ different RC4 keys, the researchers uncovered multiple biases at every one of the first 256 positions. They further improved the recovery algorithms to deal with multiple biases at individual positions (e.g., a certain byte is more likely to have values 10 and 23, with all other values equally likely). The resulting attack requires $2^{32}$ data samples to recover all 256 bytes with a success rate close to 100%. With optimization that can be applied when the attacked data uses a reduced character set (e.g., passwords and HTTP cookies), the number of data samples can be reduced to about $2^{28}$. This is a far cry from the $2^{128}$ bits of security promised by RC4.

> **Note**
>
> How is it possible that the full scope of the bias issues remained undiscovered for so long after so many early warning signs? One theory I heard was that most cryptographers thought that RC4 had already been demonstrated to be insecure and that no further work was needed. In fact, many cryptographers were very surprised to learn how popular it was. It's likely that the lack of a strong attack against RC4 as used in TLS contributed to its continued use.

Despite the seriousness of the attack, it remains largely theoretical due to many constraints:

**Number of connections**

In the best case, this attack requires $2^{28}$ samples of encrypted plaintext. Put another way, that's 268,435,456 connections. Clearly, obtaining all those samples is going to take a lot of time and potentially utilize a lot of network traffic. Under controlled

---

[67] Some protocol extensions add additional messages that are also encrypted. For example, this is the case with the *Next Protocol Negotiation* (NPN) extension, which is used to negotiate SPDY. Unlike the Finished message, whose contents are effectively random, those other messages could be attacked using the RC4 biases.

[68] On the Security of RC4 in TLS and WPA [fsty.uk/t477] (AlFardan et al., 13 March 2013)

conditions, with two sides designed to produce as many RC4 connections as possible, and with session resumption enabled, the authors cite an experiment of about 16 hours using over 500 connections per second for a total of $2^{25}$ connections.

In a scenario closer to real life, a purely passive attack would take much longer. For example, assuming one connection per second (86,400 connections per day), it would take over eight years to obtain all the required samples.

The connection rate might be increased by controlling a victim's browser (using injected JavaScript), forcing it to submit many connections at the same time. This is the same approach taken by the BEAST exploit. In this case, additional effort is needed to defeat persistent connections (keep-alives) and prevent multiple requests over the same connection (the attack can use only the first 256 bytes of each connection). To do this, the active network attacker could reset every connection at the TCP level after the first response is observed. Because TLS is designed to throw away sessions that encounter errors, in this scenario every connection would require a full handshake. That would make the attack much slower.[69]

### Positioning

This is a man-in-the-middle attack. Per the previous discussion, a pure passive attack is very unlikely to produce results within a reasonable amount of time. An active attack would require a combination of JavaScript malware and active network attack ability.

### Scope

This attack works only against the first 256 bytes of plaintext. Because such a large number of samples is required, it's unlikely that the same meaningful secret data will be present throughout. This restricts the attack to protocols that use password authentication or, for HTTP, cookies. As it turns out, the HTTP use case is not very likely because all major browsers place cookies past the 220-byte boundary. (If you recall, the first 36 bytes are of little interest because they are always used by the TLS protocol.) HTTP Basic Authentication is vulnerable in Chrome, which places the password at around the 100-byte mark. All other browsers place passwords out of the reach of this attack.

---

[69] In theory. In practice, applications tend to be very tolerant of connections that are not properly shutdown, a fact that can be exploited for truncation attacks. You can find out more about this topic in the section called "Truncation Attacks" in Chapter 7.

---

## Double-Byte Biases

In addition to having single-byte biases, RC4 was known to also have biases involving consecutive bytes. These do not exist at only one position in the encrypted stream but show up continuously in the output at regular intervals.[70]

In their second attack, AlFardan et al. showed how to use the double-byte biases for plaintext recovery. The double-byte attack has an advantage in that it does not require samples to be obtained using different RC4 keys. This makes the attack much more efficient, because multiple samples can be obtained over the same connection. On the other hand, because it's still the case that the same plaintext needs to be encrypted over and over, the attacker must have near-complete control over the traffic. Passive attacks are not possible.

The double-byte bias attack can recover 16 bytes of plaintext from 13 x $2^{30}$ samples of encrypted plaintext. To collect one sample, a POST request of exactly 512 bytes is used. Assuming a response of similar size, the attack would consume about 3.25 TB of traffic in both directions. Under controlled conditions, that many samples would take about 2,000 hours (or 83 days) to collect at a speed of six million samples per hour.

Although much more practical than the first attack, this version is equally unlikely to be useful in practice.

## Subsequent Improved Attacks

In March 2015, Garman et al. released details of their improved attacks on RC4, designed specifically for the case in which this cipher is used to protect passwords.[71] According to the authors, their attacks achieve good success rates with around $2^{26}$ encryptions, compared to the previous best similar attacks that required $2^{34}$ encryptions to retrieve the contents of an HTTP session cookie.

Also in March 2015, Imperva highlighted the *Invariance Weakness* flaw of RC4, previously published in 2001.[72] This research focuses on the fact that RC4 is known to occasionally produce bad keys, leading to the possible compromise of about the first 64 bytes of plaintext in TLS.[73] Although the attacker can't influence the creation of bad RC4 keys, a passive attacker who can observe millions of TLS connections encrypted using RC4 will be able to reveal plaintext in a fraction of cases. About one in every $2^{24}$ connections could be compromised this way.

---

[70] Statistical Analysis of the Alleged RC4 Keystream Generator [fsty.uk/t478] (Fluhrer and McGrew, 2001)

[71] Attacks Only Get Better: Password Recovery Attacks Against RC4 in TLS [fsty.uk/t479] (Garman et al., March 2015)

[72] Attacking SSL when using RC4 [fsty.uk/t480] (Imperva, 26 March 2015)

[73] Technically, about 100 raw plaintext bytes are exposed, but the first 36 bytes of every TLS connection are used by the protocol itself, meaning that up to 64 bytes of application data could be exposed.

---

Chapter 8: Protocol Attacks

In July 2015, research by Vanhoef and Piessens further improved RC4 attacks by reducing the time to exploitation of a 16-character cookie to only about 75 hours (although they also note a success in only 52 hours in one case).[74] Their approach was to execute a BEAST-style attack in which JavaScript malware is injected into the victim's browser to speed up the attack. However, even this approved attack still requires the victim to execute about $9 \times 2^{27}$ requests, each carrying an encryption of the same secret. To execute the attack in 75 hours, the researchers had to submit about 4,450 requests per second; it's doubtful that so many requests and at such a large speed can be used in a real-life attack.

# Triple Handshake Attack

In 2009, after the TLS renegotiation mechanism had been found to be insecure, the protocols were fixed by creating a new method for *secure renegotiation*. (If you haven't already, read about insecure renegotiation earlier in this chapter, in the section called "Insecure Renegotiation".) But that effort hadn't been quite successful. In 2014, a group of researchers showed a so-called *Triple Handshake Attack*, which combined two separate TLS weaknesses to break renegotiation one more time.[75]

## The Attack

To understand how the attack works, you first need to know how renegotiation is secured. When renegotiation takes place, the server expects the client to supply its previous `verify_data` value (from the encrypted `Finished` message in the previous handshake). Because only the client can know that value, the server can be sure that it's the same client.

It might seem impossible for the attacker to know the correct value, given that it is always transmitted encrypted. And yet it was possible to uncover the "secret" value and break renegotiation; the attack works in three steps and exploits two weaknesses in TLS.

### Step 1: Unknown Key-Share Weakness

The first exploited weakness is in the RSA key exchange. The generation of the master secret, which is the cornerstone of TLS session security, is chiefly driven by the client:

1. Client generates a premaster key and a random value and sends them to the server

2. Server generates its own random value and sends it to the client

3. Client and server calculate the master secret from these three values

Both random values are transported in the clear, but to prevent just anyone from performing active network attacks on TLS, the premaster secret is protected; the client encrypts it

---

[74] RC4 No More [fsty.uk/t481] (Vanhoef and Piessens, retrieved 25 July 2015)

[75] Triple Handshakes Considered Harmful: Breaking and Fixing Authentication over TLS [fsty.uk/t410] (Bhargavan et al., March 2014)

with the server's public key, which means that the attacker can't get to it. Unless she has access to the server's private key, that is; therein lies the first twist.

The Triple Handshake Attack relies on a *malicious server*. In this variant, you somehow convince the victim to visit a seemingly innocent web site under your control. (The usual approach is to use social engineering.) On that web site, you have your own valid certificate.

This is where the fun begins. The client generates a premaster key and a random value and sends them to the malicious server.[76] The premaster secret is encrypted, but the malicious server is the intended recipient and has no trouble decrypting it. Before the handshake with the client is complete, the malicious server opens a separate connection to the target server and *mirrors* the premaster key and the client's random value. The malicious server then takes the target server's random value and forwards it to the client. When this exchange is complete, there are two separate TLS connections and three parties involved in the communication, but they all share the same connection parameters and thus also the same master key.

This weakness is called an *unknown key-share*,[77] and you can probably guess that it is not desirable. However, on its own it does not seem exploitable. The malicious server cannot really achieve anything sinister at this point. It has the same master key and can thus see all the communication, but it could do that anyway and without involving the other server. If the attacker attempted to do anything at this point, she would be performing a phishing attack; it's a real problem, but not one TLS can solve.

> **Note**
>
> The RSA key exchange is almost universally supported, but there is also an attack variant that works against the ephemeral Diffie-Hellman (DHE) key exchange. The researchers discovered that the mainstream TLS implementations accept insecure DH parameters that are not prime numbers. In the TLS protocol, it is the server that chooses DH parameters. Thus, a malicious server can choose them in such a way that the DHE key exchange can be easily broken. The ECDHE key exchange, an elliptic curve variant of DHE, cannot be broken because no TLS implementation supports arbitrary DH parameters (as is the case with DHE). Instead, ECDHE relies on *named curves*, which are known good sets of parameters.

---

[76] Because the malicious server is in the middle, it can always force the use of a suite that relies on the RSA key exchange for as long as there is one such suite supported by both sides that are being attacked. In TLS, servers choose suites. When opening a handshake to the target server, the malicious server offers only suites that use the RSA key exchange.

[77] Unknown key-share attacks on the station-to-station (STS) protocol [fsty.uk/t482] (S. Blake-Wilson and A. Menezes, pages 154–170, in *Public Key Cryptography*, 1999)

---

Figure 8.8. Triple Handshake Attack: Unknown key-share

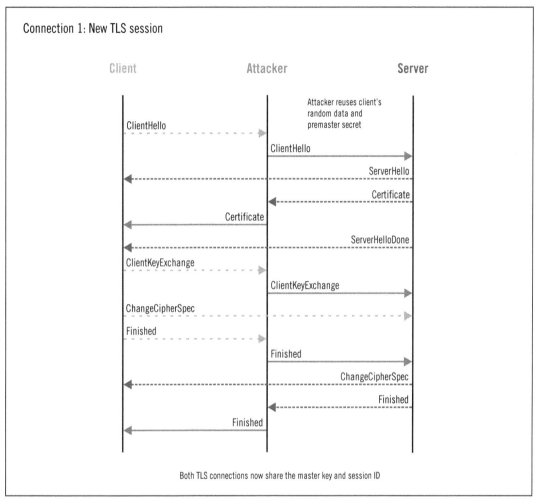

Step 2: Full Synchronization

The attacker can't attack renegotiation just yet because each connection has a different client `verify_data` value. Why? Because the server certificates differ: the first connection sees the attacking-hostname's certificate, whereas the second connection sees the certificate of the target web server.

There's nothing the attacker can do for that first connection, but in the next step she can take advantage of the session resumption mechanism and its abbreviated handshake. When a session is resumed, there is no authentication; the assumption is that the knowledge of the master key is sufficient to authenticate the two parties.

Figure 8.9. Triple Handshake Attack: Full TLS connection synchronization

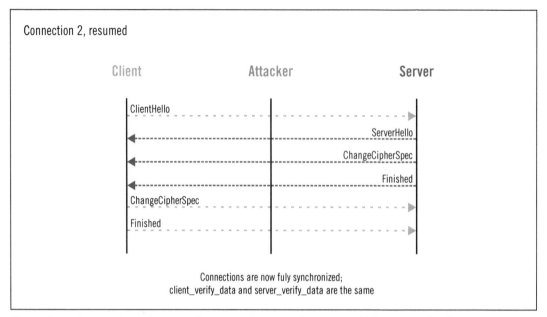

But, when the session resumes, the only elements that were different in the first connection (the certificates) are not required any more. Thus, when the handshake completes, the Finished messages on both connections will be the same!

## Step 3: Impersonation

The attacker can now proceed to trigger renegotiation in order to force the use of the victim's client certificate, leading to impersonation, as shown in Figure 8.10, "Triple Handshake Attack: Impersonation". She is in full control of both connections and can send arbitrary application data either way. On the target web server, she navigates to a resource that requires authentication. In response, the target server requests renegotiation and a client certificate during the subsequent handshake. Because the security parameters are now identical on both connections, the attacker can just mirror the protocol messages, leaving the victim and the target server to negotiate new connection parameters. Except that this time the client will authenticate with a client certificate. At that point, the attack is successful.

After renegotiation, the malicious server loses traffic visibility, although it still stays in the middle and continues to mirror encrypted data until either side terminates the connection.

## Impact

The Triple Handshake Attack demonstrates how a supposedly secure TLS connection can be compromised. Application data sent to the target server before renegotiation comes from

Figure 8.10. Triple Handshake Attack: Impersonation

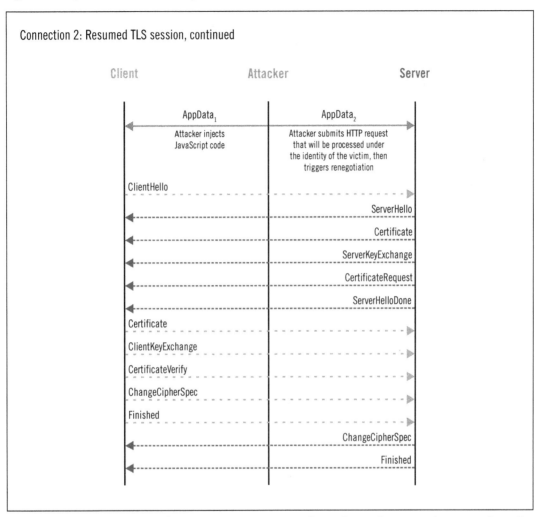

the attacker, the data sent after renegotiation comes from the authenticated user, and yet for the server there is no difference. The exploitation opportunities are similar to those of the original insecure renegotiation vulnerability (described at the beginning of this chapter in the section called "Insecure Renegotiation"). The easiest exploit is to execute a request on the target web server under the identity of the victim. Think money transfers, for example.

However, this attack vector is not very easy to use. First, the attacker has to find suitable entry points in the application and design specific payloads for each. Second, after renegotiation she loses traffic visibility and thus can't see the results of the attack or perform further attacks on the same connection. She can perform another attack, but doing so at the TLS level is going to be frustrating and slow.

There is another, potentially more dangerous, attack vector. Because the attacker can send arbitrary data to either connection before renegotiation, she has full control over the victim's browser. The victim is on *her web site*, after all. This allows the attacker to inject JavaScript malware into the browser. After renegotiation and authentication, the malware can submit unlimited background HTTP requests to the target server—all under the identity of the victim—and freely observe the responses.

Normally, browsers do not allow one web site to submit arbitrary requests to other sites. In this case, all communication is carried out in the context of the attacker's site. Behind the scenes they are routed to the target web site, but, as far as the browser is concerned, it's all one web site.

This second attack vector is effectively a form of phishing, with the triple handshake component required in order to subvert client certificate authentication. It's a much more powerful form of attack, limited only by the programming skills of the attacker and her ability to keep the victim on the web site for as long as possible.

## Prerequisites

The Triple Handshake Attack is quite complex and works only under some very specific circumstances. Two aspects need to align before the weaknesses can be exploited.

The first is that the attack can be used only against sites that use client certificates. Take away that and there can be no impersonation. The second aspect is more intriguing. The attack is a form of phishing; the victims must be willing to use their client certificates on a site where they are not normally used. I would love to say that this is unlikely to happen, but the opposite is probably true.

When it comes to getting the victim to the rogue web server, it's always possible to use social engineering or email, like all other phishing attacks. Given the attacker's position, he can also redirect any plaintext HTTP request to the site. However, that might create suspicions from the user, who will unexpectedly arrive at an unknown web site.

Given that few sites use client certificates, the applicability of the Triple Handshake Attack is not massive, unlike with the original insecure renegotiation problem. On the other hand, the sites that use client certificates are usually the more sensitive ones. This attack was never going to be used by petty criminals.

## Mitigation

The core vulnerabilities exploited by the Triple Handshake Attack are in the protocol, and that makes TLS the best place to address the issue. That was achieved with RFC 7627, published in September 2015.[78] There was initially another effort to further strengthen renegotiation, but that effort has been abandoned.[79]

In the short term, browser vendors reacted by tweaking their software to abort connections when they see a different certificate after renegotiation. Similarly, degenerate DH public keys are no longer accepted. Of course, these mitigations are generally available only in the more recent browser versions; older Internet Explorer versions should be safe too, because Microsoft patches the system-wide libraries, not just their browser.

The Triple Handshake Attack completely went away with the wider adoption of TLS 1.3, which not only excluded renegotiation but also incorporated other proposed defense mechanisms.

# POODLE

In October 2014, Google Security Team announced POODLE (*Padding Oracle On Downgraded Legacy Encryption*), a vulnerability in SSL 3 that allows network attackers to retrieve small portions of encrypted text.[80]

The root cause that makes this vulnerability possible is the flawed design of the CBC construction, which authenticates plaintext but leaves padding unprotected. This enables network attackers to make changes to the padding in transit and exploit padding oracles to reveal encrypted content. I discussed this type of attack earlier in this chapter. If you haven't already, I recommend that you read the section called "Lucky 13" before continuing to learn more about POODLE.

What makes POODLE possible is the loose padding construction and checking rules that exist in SSL 3, but have been fixed in TLS 1.0 and later protocol versions. You can see the differences between the two approaches in Figure 8.11, "Padding in SSL 3 and TLS 1.0+ side by side".

SSL 3 padding reserves the last byte in an encrypted block to hold padding length, but doesn't have any rules about what the actual padding bytes should contain. Crucially, there's no check to ensure that the padding bytes have not been tampered with. In other words, SSL 3 padding is not *deterministic*. In TLS 1.0 and better, the sender must set all padding bytes to the same value as the padding length byte. The recipient checks the padding immediately after decryption. If the padding length and all padding bytes are not the same, the entire encrypted block is rejected as invalid.

Attacking the POODLE vulnerability requires that the attacker is able to change the padding without affecting the MAC or any of the plaintext. This means arranging plaintext

---

[78] RFC 7627: TLS Session Hash and Extended Master Secret Extension [fsty.uk/t483] (Bhargavan et al., September 2015)

[79] TLS Resumption Indication Extension [fsty.uk/t484] (Bhargavan et al., April 2014)

[80] This POODLE bites: exploiting the SSL 3.0 fallback [fsty.uk/t485] (Google Security Team, 14 October 2014)

Figure 8.11. Padding in SSL 3 and TLS 1.0+ side by side

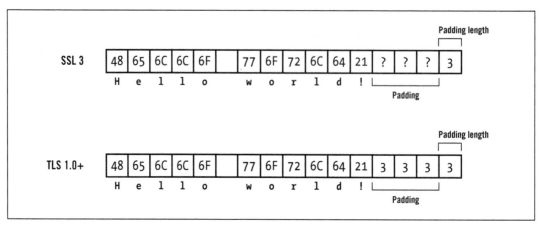

in such a way that the entire last block of encryption is used for the padding alone. This is necessary due to the fact that the attacker can't modify the padding directly, because she has access only to the encrypted version. Because of how block encryption works, even a single bit changed anywhere in ciphertext changes roughly half of the bits after decryption. However, if the entire last block is taken up by the padding, the attacker can make whatever changes she likes without triggering a failure in MAC validation.

Let's suppose the attacker does make a small change. Because that will trigger many changes after decryption, decrypted content will effectively be random. However, thanks to the loose padding specification in SSL 3, changes in the padding bytes won't be detected: the padding length is the only value that needs to be correct for the entire encryption block to be accepted. In practice, this means that one in every 256 changes will be accepted, no matter what the change is.

What can the attacker do with this? She can't recover any plaintext directly, but she does know that when her modification is accepted, the last byte *after* decryption has the correct padding length value. That value is equal to the maximum padding length, which is 15 for 16-byte blocks (e.g., AES) and 7 for 8-byte blocks (e.g., 3DES). Thus, she has an *oracle*; she just has to figure out how to exploit it. For that, she can examine the CBC construction in detail.

Before encryption takes place, a block of plaintext is XORed with a block of IV, which is essentially some random data. However, even though it's random, the IV is known to the attacker from the second block onward.[81]

For simplicity, I'll focus only on the plaintext byte that the attacker is targeting:

$$E(P_i[15] \oplus C_{i-1}[15]) = C_i[15]$$

---

[81] In SSL 3, the first IV block on a connection is derived from the master secret; the attacker doesn't know it. However, all subsequent IV blocks are known because of the chaining in CBC: the IV for the current block is the same as the previous encrypted block.

---

Chapter 8: Protocol Attacks

Figure 8.12. CBC encryption and decryption process

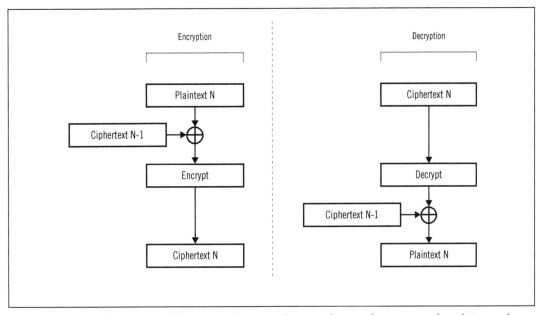

Even though both encrypted bytes are known, the attacker can't uncover the plaintext byte, because she doesn't have the encryption key.

Now, consider the reverse process. Decryption takes place first, after which the result is XORed with the correct IV block (the previous block of ciphertext). Again, the attacker knows both ciphertext bytes because she saw them on the wire. Because of the SSL 3 flaw, she also knows that the last byte in the block after the XOR operation is 15. That is sufficient for the attack:

$$D(C_i[15]) \oplus C_{n-1}[15] = 15$$
$$D(C_i[15]) = 15 \oplus C_{n-1}[15]$$
$$P_i[15] \oplus C_{i-1}[15] = 15 \oplus C_{n-1}[15]$$
$$P_i[15] = 15 \oplus C_{n-1}[15] \oplus C_{i-1}[15]$$

Thus, when a guess is correct, the attacker needs only two XOR operations to retrieve one byte of plaintext.

## Practical Attack

As is the case with other similar recent attacks against SSL and TLS, POODLE exploitation requires a complex setup: the attacker must be able to have enough control of the victim's browser to submit arbitrary requests to the target server. In addition, she must control the network and coordinate her activity with the in-browser component. This technique was pioneered by BEAST and used in other cryptographic attacks since.

Each attempt consists of the browser initiating a request and the attacker replacing the last encrypted block with one of her choosing. The process is repeated until a guess is correct and one byte of plaintext is recovered. The attacker then moves onto the next byte.

Within each request, the attacker must influence the position of the secret bytes she wishes to recover and control the padding so that it consumes the entire last encrypted block. This typically means being able to inject something before the secret and something after it. In practice, this can be achieved by using the POST request method and controlling the submitted URL and the request body.

The following example shows the contents of a TLS record just before encryption: application data is at the beginning, followed by the MAC (M), the padding (P), and padding length. The secret is the session identifier transported in the cookie JSESSIONID. As required for the attack, the first byte of the cookie value is the last byte in its block.

```
00000000  50 4f 53 54 20 2f 61 61  61 61 20 48 54 54 50 2f  |POST /aaaa HTTP/|
00000010  31 2e 30 0d 0a 48 6f 73  74 3a 20 65 78 61 6d 70  |1.0..Host: examp|
00000020  6c 65 2e 63 6f 6d 0d 0a  43 6f 6e 74 65 6e 74 2d  |le.com..Content-|
00000030  4c 65 6e 67 74 68 3a 20  31 32 0d 0a 43 6f 6f 6b  |Length: 12..Cook|
00000040  69 65 3a 20 4a 53 45 53  53 49 4f 4e 49 44 3d 42  |ie: JSESSIONID=B|
00000050  33 44 46 34 42 30 37 41  45 33 33 43 41 0d 0a 0d  |3DF4B07AE33CA...|
00000060  0a 30 31 32 33 34 35 36  37 38 39 41 4d 4d 4d 4d  |.0123456789AMMMM|
00000070  4d 4d 4d 4d 4d 4d 4d 4d  4d 4d 4d 4d 4d 4d 4d 4d  |MMMMMMMMMMMMMMMM|
00000080  50 50 50 50 50 50 50 50  50 50 50 50 50 50 50 0f  |PPPPPPPPPPPPPPP.|
```

Arriving at the correct URL and request body lengths for the first attempt requires some work, because padding hides the exact length of plaintext. This can be done by changing the payload length by one character and observing changes to the encrypted version. For example, assuming the submission as shown in the previous example, removing one byte from the URL would change padding length from 15 to zero, decreasing the overall ciphertext length by an entire block length of 16 bytes. Once this happens, the attacker knows the exact padding length.

From here, it gets easier. After a successful guess, decreasing the length of the URL by one and increasing the length of the request body by one will advance to the next cookie character while still satisfying the attack requirements.

Thus, the entire attack goes like this: (1) the attacker starts with a large URL and minimal request body; (2) she shortens the URL, one byte at a time, until she finds the correct padding length; (3) she submits enough guesses to uncover one encrypted byte; and (4) she iterates over the remaining secret bytes by changing the URL and request body lengths in sync.

A typical session identifier might consist of 16 to 32 characters, but let's assume that the attacker needs to guess between 100 and 200 characters because she doesn't know exactly where the cookie value begins. At 256 requests per character, this is one of the more efficient cryptographic attacks discussed in this chapter.

## Impact

Given that SSL 3 was roughly 20 years old when POODLE was announced and that virtually all servers supported TLS 1.0 and better, you wouldn't expect POODLE to have a serious impact on security. SSL 3 and newer protocol revisions have built-in defense against protocol downgrade attacks. Surely, everyone could just negotiate a better, secure protocol version? Unfortunately, that was only true in theory. In practice, all major browsers had been designed to downgrade their cryptographic abilities when TLS handshakes fail. As a result, when POODLE was announced, it was possible to get most browsers to use SSL 3, even with sites that support better versions. I wrote more about this problem in the section called "Protocol Downgrade Attacks" in Chapter 7).

---

### POODLE TLS

Although TLS 1.0 improved how padding is constructed, in December 2014 it was revealed that POODLE affected some applications and devices when they were using TLS.[82] The flaw was not in the protocol, but in the implementations. It appears that some developers missed the change to the padding construction when transitioning from SSL 3 to TLS, leaving their implementations vulnerable to the same attacks. In at least some of the cases, the vulnerability was discovered in a hardware acceleration card used by many appliance vendors.

According to SSL Pulse, about 10% of the monitored servers were vulnerable to POODLE TLS in December 2014. Months after the discovery of this attack variant, it's still not clear if we've learned about all the vulnerable products.[83]

Further problems in this space were discovered in the following years and given colorful names such as Sleeping POODLE, Zombie POODLE, and GOLDENDOODLE.[84]

---

Protocol downgrade aside, POODLE is a relatively easy attack to execute, but it requires a sophisticated attacker positioned close to the victim. As with other attacks using the same combination of in-browser and network capabilities, the goal is to retrieve something small yet valuable, typically a cookie value or password. This high barrier to entry ensures that POODLE, if attacked, is generally feasible only against high-value targets. A successful retrieval of a session cookie will enable the attacker to assume the victim's identity on the web site in question and get everything else that follows from it.

---

[82] Poodle Bites TLS [fsty.uk/t486] (Ivan Ristić, 8 December 2014)

[83] There are more POODLEs in the forest [fsty.uk/t487] (Yngve Pettersen, 14 July 2015)

[84] Zombie POODLE and GOLDENDOODLE Vulnerabilities [fsty.uk/t488] (Yash Sannegowda, 22 April 2019)

## Mitigation

Faced with a serious vulnerability in older protocol versions, browser vendors decided not to implement any mitigation measures and to instead use the opportunity to speed up the deprecation of SSL 3. The initial measure was to minimize the attack surface: Chrome, Firefox, and Internet Explorer disabled fallback to SSL 3. Safari kept the fallback, but instead disabled all CBC suites in that situation. After a short transition period, Chrome and Firefox moved to disable SSL 3 by default (in versions 40 and 34, respectively). In April 2015, an update for Internet Explorer 11 did the same.

> **Note**
>
> A new protocol downgrade defense was standardized in RFC 7507.[85] Using a special signaling suite value, `TLS_FALLBACK_SCSV`, a browser can signal to the server that it has downgraded. A server that understands this feature should then reject the connection, thus preventing the attack. Google has been using this defense in Chrome since version 33.[86] Firefox implemented it in version 35.[87]

RFC 7568, published in June 2015, finally deprecated SSL 3.[88]

# Key-Compromise Impersonation

All versions of TLS up to and including 1.2 are vulnerable to a *Key-Compromise Impersonation* (KCI, or sometimes K-CI) attack if certain conditions are met. An attacker who is able to convince a user to install a special client certificate can later impersonate vulnerable web sites by intercepting and modifying the user's network traffic.[89]

This is essentially an attack against the non-ephemeral Diffie-Hellman key exchange and both standard and elliptic variants. The role of the certificate is to force the use of a known private key for the key exchange. An attacker who is in possession of the private key can complete any DH key exchange in which the key is used. In the context of TLS, that enables them to also complete the TLS handshake. Although the core weakness is straightforward, a successful attack requires alignment of many different aspects:

1. The attacker must be able to get the victim to install a client certificate with a compromised private key.

2. The attack works only against static DH key exchange algorithms, which means that the victim's client has to support one of the matching cipher suites.

---

[85] RFC 7507: TLS Fallback SCSV for Preventing Protocol Downgrade Attacks [fsty.uk/t489] (Moeller et al., April 2015)

[86] TLS Symmetric Crypto [fsty.uk/t405] (Adam Langley, 27 February 2014)

[87] The POODLE Attack and the End of SSL 3.0 [fsty.uk/t406] (Mozilla Security Blog, 14 October 2014)

[88] RFC 7568: Deprecating Secure Sockets Layer Version 3.0 [fsty.uk/t490] (Barnes et al., June 2015)

[89] KCI Attacks against TLS [fsty.uk/t491] (ESSE, August 2015)

---

3. Similarly, the targeted server must be configured with a special certificate that enables static DH key exchanges. Although such certificates are virtually never used in practice, the researchers discovered that ECDSA certificates (which are very widely used) could be successfully repurposed for the attack, provided they have the KeyAgreement bit set in the X.509 Key Usage (KU) extension. This bit is not supposed to be set, but the researchers did find it on the certificate Facebook used at the time of the disclosure. Even if the bit is not set, the attack may still be possible if client software relies on a library that doesn't correctly check the KU extension.

4. Finally, the attackers must be able to intercept the victim's network communication to interfere with the TLS handshakes. Posing as the target server, they force the use of the static DH key exchange and request the compromised client certificate. With that, they are able to successfully handshake with the client, which believes it's talking to the real server.

Although intriguing, this attack exploited obsolete functionality in the older versions of the TLS protocol and, even then, it was only possible when further implementation and deployment issues were present. In the short term, the vulnerability in Facebook was resolved by removing the incorrectly configured certificate. Subsequently, clients and libraries were tightened with stricter checks, as well as removal of suites that support static DH key exchange. These suites are no longer supported in TLS 1.3.

# SLOTH

In January 2016, Karthikeyan Bhargavan and Gaëtan Leurent published a systematic analysis of the use of hashing functions in several widely used security protocols. They revealed many weaknesses that existed due to continued reliance on weak hash functions—namely, MD5 and SHA1.[90] In their research paper they presented a new class of *transcript collision attack*; for publicity they named their attack *SLOTH*, short for *Security Losses from Obsolete and Truncated Transcript Hashes*. Although none of their attacks had a very practical impact, they showed that slowness in removing obsolete cryptographic components can lead to significant reduction of security guarantees.

According to Bhargavan and Leurent, many cryptographers continue to believe that hash functions vulnerable to chosen-prefix attacks remain strong when they are not vulnerable to other attack types (e.g., preimage attacks). The researchers' main contribution was thus to show that modern security protocols can also be exploited using chosen-prefix collision attacks and that they can be exploited if they rely on weak hash functions.

---

[90] Security Losses from Obsolete and Truncated Transcript Hashes [fsty.uk/t492] (Karthikeyan Bhargavan and Gaëtan Leurent, January 2016)

## Note

Some of the key attacks shown by SLOTH rely on chosen-prefix collision attacks against MD5, which is the same technique used to create the rogue certification authority in 2008. This type of attack introduces a number of challenges that the attackers must overcome. Before you continue to study SLOTH I recommend that you reread the section called "RapidSSL Rogue CA Certificate" in Chapter 5. In addition, many of the attack concepts are the same as those for the Triple Handshake Attack, covered earlier in this chapter.

# Attacks against TLS

SLOTH attacked several protocols, such as TLS, IKE, SSH, and TLS channel bindings. For full coverage I recommend that you refer to the original paper, which naturally discusses all these attacks in detail. In this section I'll only cover the main attacks against TLS.

### Breaking TLS 1.2 client authentication

SLOTH's most interesting technique uses a chosen-prefix collision attack against client authentication in TLS 1.2. The authors exploit the fact that TLS is a flexible protocol that allows injection of arbitrary data into the protocol messages; this additional data is necessary to forge collisions and—crucially—will be ignored by clients and servers alike. If a successful collision is found (and we know how to do this against MD5), an active network attacker can hijack a genuine client connection attempt to create its own connection using the victim's client certificate. In this case, one collision block is injected into the server's `CertificateRequest` message (posing as a distinguished name of an allowed CA) and the other collision block is added to the `ClientHello` message as a made-up extension.

Now, this is all clear in theory, and we've seen it before in the Rogue CA attack and Flame malware. In practice, there are several other challenges to overcome. For one, impersonating the victim is not sufficient to fully break a TLS connection. Even though the active network attacker is now in the middle, the key exchange is still happening between the real client and the server. Because the attacker can't influence this negotiation, at the end of the TLS handshake she won't be able to produce the correct `Finished` message to prove that she is the real client. SLOTH solves this by breaking DH key exchange on the client side by sending invalid DH parameters to the server. This attack (a separate vulnerability) was previously explained by Logjam and relies on the fact that, in TLS, servers have full control over DH parameters whereas clients don't; clients can employ some checks, but usually don't.

Another challenge is forcing the use of MD5 for signatures. Ironically, this is where TLS 1.2 introduced an exploitable weakness. In TLS 1.1 and earlier, protocol messages are signed using a concatenation of MD5 and SHA1, which can be broken at a (high) cost of $2^{77}$ hashes. TLS 1.2 introduced negotiable signature algorithms and, crucially, continued to allow MD5 for this purpose. The cost of breaking MD5 in this context is only $2^{39}$. Even though MD5 is allowed by TLS 1.2, not all clients support it, but SLOTH authors found that popular Java clients and servers did.

In the end, their proof-of-concept attack took about an hour to break a single TLS connection, which is a great success. Even though this is not fast enough to attack real clients, unattended programs—which are usually happy to wait indefinitely—can be exploited.

### Breaking TLS 1.2 server authentication

Unlike in the previous case, chosen-prefix collision attacks can't be used against TLS servers because server signatures don't allow injection of free-form data blocks, which is necessary for a collision. (The only attack-controlled parameter is the client nonce, which is fixed to 32 bytes of data.) However, even for this situation, SLOTH described a largely theoretical attack that reduces the security guarantees of TLS.

To break the TLS server signature the attacker must produce a working hash, which is a $2^{128}$ effort, even when MD5 is used. SLOTH showed that by collecting $2^x$ server signatures beforehand, the effort required for the actual attack can be reduced to $2^{128-x}$.

This attack variant requires servers that continue to use MD5 for signatures, and SLOTH authors discovered that about 31 percent of the servers on Alexa's top 1 million list did so. Equally, the attack requires that clients also support MD5 for signatures, which isn't the case with modern browsers—or so we thought. The researchers made a crucial discovery that many clients (libraries) in fact support MD5 signatures if offered by a server, even though they aren't configured to do so. Most prominently, this was the case with NSS, the library used by Firefox and some versions of Chrome. GnuTLS and BouncyCastle libraries shared the same flaw.

### Breaking TLS 1.3 server authentication

TLS 1.3, the next version of the TLS protocol, is vastly different internally, so much so that it can be considered a completely different protocol. Interestingly for SLOTH, server signatures are implemented differently and do allow for chosen-prefix collision attacks. SLOTH authors examined TLS 1.3 draft revision 10, the latest at the time, and found that it still allowed MD5 use, making it theoretically vulnerable. In practice, it's almost certain that MD5 would have been removed before standardization; the designers simply hadn't reached that point yet.

### Downgrading TLS 1.0 and 1.1 handshakes

SLOTH also showed a chosen-prefix collision attack against TLS 1.0 and TLS 1.1 handshakes that requires a $2^{77}$ effort, enabling the attacker to downgrade connection security to the weakest algorithm supported by all parties. This attack is the least practical of all the findings, requiring not only a lot of work to execute the down-grade, but also further work to break the weakened connection.

## Impact

The SLOTH research pointed to many weak aspects of widely used security protocols, as well as some omissions in popular libraries. It also helped improve our understanding of how continued use of weak hash functions can be exploited. The end results were improvements all around, leading to a stronger ecosystem. In terms of immediate negative security impact, none of the attacks was practical and there was little end users could do to influence their security one way or another.

# DROWN

*DROWN* (*Decrypting RSA using Obsolete and Weakened eNcryption*) is a novel cross-protocol attack that exploits weaknesses in the SSL 2 protocol and transfers them to servers running TLS in the case that the key material is reused. The DROWN research was released in March 2016, long after SSL 2 had been deemed insecure, showing yet again how continued use of obsolete cryptography can backfire spectacularly.[91]

At the core of DROWN is a previously unknown SSL 2 flaw that enables attackers to decrypt RSA ciphertexts. With this capability in hand, the researchers were able to abuse passively recorded TLS handshakes based on the RSA key exchange and decrypt entire TLS sessions. Several attack variants were presented, ranging from attacking servers that reuse RSA keys to performing real-time active network attacks against servers that share only a certificate hostname (and not the key) with another server that runs SSL 2. A variant of the attack was applied to the QUIC protocol.

## Attacks against TLS

Of interest to us here are the practical attacks against TLS. DROWN comes in two flavors: one more general but more difficult to execute and another specific to certain configurations but feasible in practice.

### General DROWN

The first of the two attacks, called *general DROWN*, is a pure cryptographic attack that exploits a previously unknown SSL 2 protocol flaw, a variant of the Bleichenbacher padding-oracle attack. This flaw turns any SSL 2 server into an oracle that can be used to reveal information about RSA ciphertexts. This flaw in itself would probably be only of historic interest, given that properly maintained servers no longer

---

[91] The DROWN Attack [fsty.uk/t493] (DROWN web site, retrieved 26 June 2017)

run SSL 2. However, the researchers have been able to transfer the attack to TLS—more specifically, the RSA key exchange. (This wasn't going to be the last time the Bleichenbacher attack would be used in practice; the ROBOT attack that came in late 2017 is also based on it.)

If you recall, in the RSA key exchange clients effectively determine all encryption keys used in a TLS session. Early on they generate a random *premaster secret* and send it to the server encrypted with its public RSA key; perhaps you can see where this is heading. The researchers were able to take this encrypted secret and use the SSL 2 oracle to decrypt it. The attack requires about 1,000 passively collected TLS sessions, about 40,000 connections to the SSL 2 server, and about $2^{50}$ offline computations. One of the TLS sessions will be decrypted; the proof-of-concept attack took about eight hours on EC2. At the time of disclosure, about 79 percent of all HTTPS servers were vulnerable to this attack type.

### Special DROWN

The *special DROWN* attack is so named because it uses several OpenSSL flaws (CVE-2015-3197, CVE-2016-0703, and CVE-2016-0704) to speed up the attack so much that it becomes possible to use it in real time. This attack variant requires fewer than 8,000 connections and runs for under a minute on a single CPU core. At the time of disclosure, about 26 percent of all HTTPS servers were vulnerable to this attack type.

# Impact

DROWN is an often-misunderstood vulnerability. The main point of confusion comes from the fact that a perfectly configured server (i.e., one that doesn't support SSL 2) can be vulnerable if it shares some aspect of its configuration with some other directly vulnerable server. Overall, there are four cases to take into account:

### Direct general DROWN vulnerability

The first and most obvious case occurs when a server supports SSL 2. Such a server can always be attacked directly; it provides only minimal security because it's vulnerable to DROWN and other weaknesses inherent in SSL 2. Only passive attacks are feasible in this case. For the situation to be exploited, the TLS protocols must support and use the RSA key exchange.

### Direct special DROWN vulnerability

Servers that continue to use SSL 2 but also have a vulnerable version of OpenSSL are directly vulnerable, but also easier to exploit. In this case, both passive and active network attacks are possible. The latter can be run against TLS protocols even if the RSA key exchange isn't supported.

---

### Vulnerability transfer with RSA key reuse

Vulnerability transfer is the cross-protocol aspect of DROWN. A server that isn't vulnerable to DROWN directly (because it doesn't support SSL 2) can still be attacked if it uses the same RSA key as some other server that is directly vulnerable. What's particularly interesting is that the problem can be transferred from one server to another, and the ports can also be different. A common problem is to generate one RSA key for use with both SMTP and HTTPS. Because SSL 2 is more commonly enabled in email servers, this usage is often the root cause of vulnerability transfer.

### Vulnerability transfer with certificate hostname overlap

In the worst case, a server vulnerable to special DROWN can be used to transfer the vulnerability to any hostname that appears in the server's certificate. In this case, because the attack can be carried out in real time, the attacker can forge a seemingly secure TLS handshake by abusing the RSA key on the vulnerable server. Therefore, victims can't tell that the incorrect key is used.

## Mitigation

If you have full control over your infrastructure, mitigating DROWN is easy. Because the DROWN attack relies on the presence of an oracle exploited via SSL 2, as soon as you turn off this protocol version you're back to being secure. There is no memory effect. For best results, you should also ensure you're running a patched version of OpenSSL on all your servers.

Difficulties sometimes arise with outsourced infrastructure elements, if the vendors are not responsive to the requests to disable SSL 2. If they're vulnerable only to generic DROWN, you can resolve the situation yourself by regenerating the RSA keys you control. The vendor will continue to be vulnerable but won't be able to transfer the vulnerability to you. Unfortunately, if the vendor is vulnerable to special DROWN, which effectively exploits certificates, RSA key regeneration won't help. In this case your only option is to get the vendor either to disable SSL 2 or to remove your hostnames from its certificates. In general, it's a good idea to switch providers if you're dealing with a vendor that won't resolve vulnerabilities within a reasonable time frame. If you've already left the vendor but it still has your name on its certificate, then contact the issuing CA, which may be able to provide you recourse.

## Sweet32

In August 2016, researchers Karthikeyan Bhargavan and Gaëtan Leurent released a paper and coined the name *Sweet32* to highlight the problem of continued use of 64-bit block ciphers such as 3DES.[92] Discussions of block ciphers typically raise the concept of block operations (i.e., how block ciphers handle entire blocks of data at a time), but they often provide little if any information on how block size impacts overall security; the focus is usually on the key size alone. In some ways, this is appropriate, as it's more important to get the key size right. On the other hand, block size cannot be neglected; if it is, we end up in a situation in which a large portion of the Internet supports and uses ciphers that can be exploited in practice.

It's generally well known among cryptographers that block ciphers are only safe to use for encryption of up to $2^{n/2}$ messages (the *birthday bound*). According to the probability theory and the *birthday paradox*,[93] the chance of collision increases significantly as the birthday bound is approached. The birthday paradox (or *birthday attack*) is often mentioned in the context of hash functions and is the reason that 256-bit hash functions have only 128 bits of security.

For block ciphers, a collision on its own is not as dangerous as with hash functions, but it nevertheless can be exploited practically by a capable attacker. At the core is the fact that some information is revealed when two messages are encrypted to the same ciphertext. Let's take a look at the CBC block encryption mode; in it, a plaintext message is first XOR-ed with the previous block of ciphertext, then encrypted:

$C_i = E(P_i \oplus C_{i-1})$

Thus, if you see the same encrypted block twice, you learn something about the plaintext; you'll know that

$P_i \oplus C_{i-1} = P_j \oplus C_{j-1}$

Is the same as

$P_i \oplus P_j = C_{i-1} \oplus C_{j-1}$

An active network attacker will be able to observe $C_{i-1}$ and $C_{j-1}$ on the network, which means that, after a collision, the attacker will know the result of the XOR operation of the two plaintext blocks. Finally, if the attacker knows some or all of one of the plaintexts, she will be able to determine some or all of the other plaintext.

## Prerequisites

By now we've established that the attack is rather simple conceptually, but carrying it out isn't that easy. Successful attackers must be able to perform a chosen-plaintext attack over an extended period of time to encrypt a very large amount of data, creating one or more

---

[92] Sweet32: Birthday attacks on 64-bit block ciphers in TLS and OpenVPN [fsty.uk/t494] (Karthikeyan Bhargavan and Gaëtan Leurent, August 2016)

[93] According to the birthday paradox, the probability of two people in the room sharing a birthday is 50 percent with only 23 people and 99.9 percent with only 70 people. In other words, birthday "collisions" happen much faster than expected.

---

collisions until their goals are met. They must also be able to observe the encrypted data on the network; this is what we typically call an *active network attacker*. Consider the following aspects of server configuration and attack execution:

**Ciphers**

Modern block ciphers use blocks of at least 128 bits, but 64-bit blocks are used by 3DES and Blowfish.[94] The first of the two, 3DES, is very widely used in various protocols. When it comes to TLS, it's still commonly supported by browsers and servers, even though there's little reason to use it today. Some very big web companies might need to continue to support it for very wide backward compatibility. Even then, it should be used as a cipher of last resort. In any case, for an attack to be possible the client and server must naturally negotiate a 3DES suite, which isn't very common. The Sweet32 authors estimated that only between 1 and 2 percent of connections would end up with this obsolete cipher.

Blowfish has never been available for use with TLS, but it's used by default by OpenVPN, a very popular VPN server.

**Browser control**

Sweet32 is a chosen-plaintext attack, which means that the attacker must have significant control over what's being encrypted. In the HTTPS context this translates to an active network attack in which the victim's browser is hijacked and used to send HTTP connections to target web sites. Crucially, all those connections carry a secret (e.g., an HTTP session cookie) that the attacker wishes to uncover. The secret part of the traffic is mixed with plaintext that the attacker knows. For example, the attacker can force browsers to submit HTTP requests with extremely large URLs, all part of the known plaintext, thus making successful exploitation far more likely.

**Data volume**

For a 64-bit block cipher such as DES, the birthday bound is at $2^{32}$ messages, or 32 GB of data at eight bytes per message. HTTP session cookies are usually longer; in the proof of concept the authors assumed 16 bytes, or two blocks. Their faster attack used about 780 GB of data; their slower variant needed 280 GB of data, but took much longer.

Even with today's fast networks, Sweet32 takes a long time and submits many HTTP requests. The researchers carried out their attacks by sending between 1,500 and 2,000 requests per second over many hours. One of their successful attacks required about 30 hours of continuous network communication.

The data volume requirements significantly dampen the usefulness of the attack; for success, you need a well-positioned attacker targeting a browser left unattended

---

[94] In TLS there is also IDEA, but this cipher is very rarely seen in practice.

Chapter 8: Protocol Attacks

for an extended period of time. The browser must be on a high-speed Internet connection, and the targeted application must not limit the maximum duration of its HTTP sessions.

**Connection longevity**

A successful attack not only requires a very long time, it also must have all the data encrypted with the same key, which in practice means the same TLS (and TCP) connection. For HTTP, the most commonly used servers such as Apache and Nginx limit by default how many requests can be submitted over the same connection. On the other hand, the IIS, another very popular web server, imposes no limits.

For VPN software, the situation is different; such software typically operates long-lived connections, and some might do so without rotating the encryption keys to avoid the birthday bound.

# Impact

A successful Sweet32 attack will compromise a web application session ID, leading to session hijacking. Cookie-based session IDs are the main mechanism used today for session maintenance. HTTP Basic Authentication can also be attacked, but this authentication mechanism isn't often seen these days. In any case, the end result is the same: user impersonation.

# Mitigation

The best mitigation is to simply stop using obsolete 64-bit ciphers. The only such cipher of significance in the web context is 3DES, which you might need to support very old Windows XP clients, but chances are that you don't have many such clients. In practice, most servers that support or enforce 3DES just haven't been updated for a long time.

If you have good reasons to believe you can't stop using 3DES, enforce server cipher suite preference and put 3DES at the bottom of the list. That will ensure that this weak cipher will only ever be used with clients that can't negotiate anything else.

From here, consider other mitigation methods; most importantly, limit the maximum number of HTTP requests that can be submitted over the same TCP connection. Practically any sane number you choose will effectively mitigate the Sweet32 attack.

# The Bleichenbacher Attack

The Bleichenbacher vulnerability is an adaptive chosen ciphertext attack on the RSA PKCS #1 v1.5 padding scheme. An attacker can send different payloads to a server and observe its responses in order to extract parts of RSA-encrypted data. Bleichenbacher described this problem in a 1998 paper[95] and so it was known, although perhaps not sufficiently well. Over the years, many libraries were found to be insufficiently protected. Research on the *Return Of Bleichenbacher's Oracle Threat* (ROBOT), which came out in late 2017, is the first large-scale evaluation of the presence of Bleichenbacher vulnerabilities in the wild.[96]

The results were not encouraging, with about a third of the top 100 Alexa domains being affected, as well as many high-profile products from Cisco, Citrix, F5, IBM, and others. As a proof of concept, the team behind the research exploited the Bleichenbacher vulnerability to sign a message using a private key operated by one of Facebook's web servers. The key itself remained private, but the web server provided all the information necessary for the signing operation to take place.

Even after ROBOT, Bleichenbacher vulnerabilities continue to be discovered, and it's likely that we will continue to hear about this problem in the future. For example, in late 2018, the NCC Group released the results of their work that identified many vulnerabilities in various libraries, including some that could affect TLS 1.3, which nominally can't be vulnerable.[97]

## Understanding the Attack

To understand the attack, you need to begin with the implementation details of RSA encryption and decryption. At its core, RSA is about integer multiplication and division, but that *textbook approach* exhibits properties that make it insecure. For example, without some random element to feed into the process, RSA encryption is deterministic, meaning that the same plaintext always produces the same ciphertext. Thus, in practice, additional measures need to be used so that RSA operations can be said to be cryptographically safe.

Traditionally, RSA operations have used the approach known as RSA PKCS #1 v1.5, now documented in the historical RFC 2313.[98]

This approach specifies a transport structure that aids the encryption process, adding padding that enables encryption of data whose length is smaller than the key size. At the same time, the padding is randomly generated, which means that encryption is no longer deterministic.

It is the addition of this outer shell that creates new opportunities for attacks against poorly implemented decryption implementations. The root cause of the difficulties is an all-or-nothing property of RSA encryption that dictates that all bits of a ciphertext must be secure against the attacker; if there is a single bit that can be decrypted, the entire message falls.

---

[95] Chosen Ciphertext Attacks Against Protocols Based on the RSA Encryption Standard PKCS #1 [fsty.uk/t495] (Daniel Bleichenbacher, 1998)

[96] The ROBOT Attack [fsty.uk/t496] (Böck et al., December 2017)

[97] The 9 Lives of Bleichenbacher's CAT: New Cache ATtacks on TLS Implementations [fsty.uk/t497] (Ronen et al., November 2018)

[98] PKCS #1: RSA Encryption Version 1.5 [fsty.uk/t498] (B. Kaliski, March 1998)

---

If we look again at the RSA packaging and think about the process of decryption, it's clear that every implementation will need to incorporate a check of the resulting structure after decryption. This is necessary in order to discard the padding to get to the data. An implementation might check that the first two bytes are 0x00 and 0x02 and that there is at least one 0x00 byte after the padding. If some invalid input is fed to decryption, the result is not likely to be a valid PKCS #1 v1.5 structure. That decryption can fail is in itself not problematic, but the implementation must be careful not to reveal that the decryption failed. If the attacker can learn that the ciphertext they sent decrypted correctly (as far as the structure is concerned), they will have learned enough to start breaking the encryption, one chunk at a time.

In cryptographic terminology, an incorrect implementation leads to the existence of an *oracle* that can be queried. The key words "adaptive chosen-ciphertext" now make more sense and mean that the attacker (1) chooses the ciphertext that is fed to the decryption process and (2) can adapt to the results until they get the desired outcome.

Protocols that wish to use this type of RSA encryption must incorporate countermeasures that are specific to the protocol, all focused on not revealing key information to the attacker. One approach might be to perform an integrity validation check on the entire ciphertext before decryption is done. In TLS, the connection handshake continues even when decryption is unsuccessful, leading to the attacker being blocked later by another integrity check.

## Impact

When the conditions are right, the Bleichenbacher vulnerability is a serious weakness. To exploit it, tens of thousands of connections are required. Thus, it's not super fast, but it is achievable, as the ROBOT research team demonstrated by abusing Facebook's private web server key. When a server is vulnerable, attackers can use the oracle to perform operations using its private key. In practice, this means that recorded encrypted communication can be decrypted after the fact. There are various other vectors, but they're generally all useful only for specific targeted attacks against high-value targets.

In evaluating the possible impact of this problem, consider that a vulnerability in one server and protocol can possibly be transferred to any other server that uses the same RSA key. This is another reason to avoid key reuse across unrelated systems.

The problems with RSA PKCS #1 v1.5 have been known for a long time. For that reason and the fact that the RSA key exchange doesn't provide forward secrecy, protocol designers have generally been avoiding it for new designs. TLS 1.3, in particular, removed the RSA key exchange early on and switched to RSA-PSS for signatures.[99]

---

[99] RFC 8017: PKCS #1: RSA Cryptography Specifications Version 2.2 [fsty.uk/t499] (Moriarty et al., November 2016)

## Detection and Mitigation

The Bleichenbacher vulnerability exists at the library level, which means that it should be addressed with an update of the vulnerable components. If vendor patches aren't available, another approach is to reconfigure the TLS configuration of the affected devices to remove the suites that rely on the RSA key exchange. Switching to suites that use the ECDHE key exchange will significantly reduce the severity of the problem while a permanent solution is being sought.[100]

If you're not sure if you're affected, consider using the free tool provided by the researchers behind the ROBOT attack to help you determine the state of your servers.[101]

# The Raccoon Attack

Raccoon[102] is a time-based side channel vulnerability in TLS 1.2 and earlier protocol versions that came out in September 2020. More specifically, it's a timing vulnerability in the DH key exchange that creates an oracle that could be used to compromise encryption. The attacker starts by passively observing a network connection between a client and a server. They then use the information observed from the TLS handshake to craft a series of packets, send them to the same server, and very precisely measure its response times. With enough attempts, the attackers can uncover the negotiated premaster secret. A successful attack can lead to a full compromise of the initial connection as well as all session resumptions. Even if the captured traffic doesn't contain anything sensitive, most HTTP exchanges include passwords and session tokens that can be used to assume the victim's identity.

## Impact

This is a very interesting discovery, but as the authors themselves say, Raccoon is a complex timing attack that is very hard to exploit. To succeed, attackers require several conditions that are difficult to achieve:

- Server that supports and actively uses TLS 1.2 or earlier.

- Server that supports and actively uses the DH key exchange.

- Client that supports the DH key exchange.

- Server that reuses its DH parameters across key exchanges.

---

[100] The DHE key exchange, which is also resistant to the Bleichenbacher attack, is no longer suitable for use in a general case as browsers typically no longer support it.

[101] robot-detect [fsty.uk/t500] (GitHub, retrieved 27 December 2020)

[102] Raccoon Attack [fsty.uk/t501] (retrieved 27 December 2020)

---

Chapter 8: Protocol Attacks

- Attacker must be able to mount a passive network attack and capture encrypted communication.

- Attacker must be able to measure very slight differences in response times, which usually translates to being very close to the server where latency is very small and there isn't significant network jitter.

The combination of all of the above is difficult to achieve in practice. For example, many modern servers today prefer TLS 1.3. The DH key exchange is typically not supported by modern browsers. Most web servers generate fresh DH parameters for every subsequent key exchange.

## Mitigation

Servers with modern configuration will not be vulnerable to this attack, because they either will support TLS 1.3 or will not use the DH key exchange. If you do have a server that is vulnerable, chances are it's not going to work with a modern browser, but there may be other vulnerable clients out there. The easiest mitigation is to disable the DH cipher suites and replace them with ECDHE instead.

# Bullrun

*Bullrun* (or *BULLRUN*) is the codename for a classified program run by the United States *National Security Agency* (NSA). Its purpose is to break encrypted communication by any means possible. Probably the most successful approach taken is, simply, computer hacking. If you can obtain a server's private key by hacking into it, there is no reason to attack encryption. More interesting for us, however, is that one of the means is weakening of products and security standards. This is a statement from a budget proposal from a leaked confidential document:[103]

> *Influence policies, standards and specification for commercial public key technologies.*

According to *The New York Times*, the NSA has about $250 million a year to spend on these activities. British GCHQ apparently has its own program for similar activities, codenamed *Edgehill*.[104]

TLS, one of the major security protocols, is an obvious target of this program. The public disclosure of Bullrun has caused many to view standards development in a completely different light. How can we trust the standards if we don't trust the people who design them?

---

[103] Secret Documents Reveal N.S.A. Campaign Against Encryption [fsty.uk/t502] (The New York Times, 5 September 2013)

[104] Revealed: how US and UK spy agencies defeat internet privacy and security [fsty.uk/t503] (The Guardian, 6 September 2013)

# Dual Elliptic Curve Deterministic Random Bit Generator

*Dual Elliptic Curve Deterministic Random Bit Generator* (Dual EC DRBG) is a *pseudorandom number generator* (PRNG) algorithm standardized by the *International Organization for Standardization* (ISO) in ISO 18031 in 2005 and the United States *National Institute of Standards and Technology* (NIST) in 2006.

In 2007, two researchers discussed a possible backdoor in this algorithm,[105] but their discovery received little attention.

When the Bullrun program came to light in September 2013, Dual EC DRBG was implicated as an NSA backdoor. In the same month, NIST issued a bulletin denouncing their own algorithm:[106]

> *NIST strongly recommends that, pending the resolution of the security concerns and the re-issuance of SP 800-90A, the Dual_EC_DRBG, as specified in the January 2012 version of SP 800-90A, no longer be used.*

In 2013, Reuters wrote about a $10 million payment from the NSA to RSA Security, Inc., leading to the RSA adopting Dual EC DRBG as the default PRNG in their TLS implementation, BSAFE.[107] Many other TLS implementations offered Dual EC DRBG as an option (most likely because it was required for the FIPS 140-2 validation), but as far as we know none used it by default. The implementation in OpenSSL was found to be faulty and thus unusable.[108]

In 2015, Juniper Networks alerted its users about a security vulnerability in the NetScreen line of VPN products. It was subsequently discovered that it had also added support for Dual EC DRBG.[109] The discovered breach involved a third party breaking Juniper's security to alter NetScreen and hijack the backdoor for their own purposes.[110]

How does this affect TLS, you may ask? In cryptography, all security depends on the quality of the data produced by the PRNG in use. Historically, we've seen many implementations fail at this point, as discussed in the section called "Random Number Generation" in Chapter 7. If you can break someone's PRNG, chances are you can break everything else. The TLS protocol requires client and server to send about 28 bytes of random data each as part of the handshake; this data is used to generate the master secret, which is used to protect the entire TLS session. If you can backdoor the PRNG implementation, those 28 bytes might be

---

[105] On the Possibility of a Back Door in the NIST SP800-90 Dual Ec Prng [fsty.uk/t504] (Shumow and Ferguson, August 2007)

[106] SUPPLEMENTAL ITL BULLETIN FOR SEPTEMBER 2013 [fsty.uk/t505] (NIST, September 2013)

[107] Exclusive: Secret contract tied NSA and security industry pioneer [fsty.uk/t506] (Reuters, 20 December 2013)

[108] Flaw in Dual EC DRBG (no, not that one) (Steve Marquess, 19 December 2013)

[109] A Systematic Analysis of the Juniper Dual EC Incident [fsty.uk/t507] (Checkoway et al., October 2016)

[110] Juniper Breach Mystery Starts to Clear With New Details on Hackers and U.S. Role [fsty.uk/t508] (Bloomberg, 2 September 2021)

---

enough to reveal the internal state of the generator and thus help substantially with breaking the TLS session.

In 2014, researchers demonstrated that Dual EC DRBG could, indeed, be backdoored,[111] although they couldn't offer proof that a backdoor existed. At the same time, they discovered that a nonstandard TLS extension, written at the request of the NSA, had been implemented in BSAFE to expose more data from the PRNG on a TLS connection.[112]

With more random data exposed to the attacker, it becomes up to 65,000 times easier to break TLS connections.

---

[111] On the Practical Exploitability of Dual EC in TLS Implementations [fsty.uk/t509] (Checkoway et al., 2014)

[112] Extended Random [fsty.uk/t510] (projectbullrun.org, retrieved 16 July 2014)

# 9 Performance

People sometimes care about security, but they *always* care about speed; no one ever wanted their web site to be slower. Some of the motivation for increasing performance comes from our fascination with going faster. There is a lot of anecdotal evidence that programmers are obsessed with performance, often needlessly and at expense of code quality. On the other hand, it is well documented that speed improvements increase revenue. In 2006, Google said that adding 0.5 seconds to their search results caused a 20% drop in traffic.[1] And Amazon said that an increase of 100 ms in latency costs them 1% in revenue.[2]

There is no doubt that TLS has a reputation for being slow. Most of it comes from the early days, when CPUs were much slower and only a few big sites could afford encryption. Not so today; computing power is no longer a bottleneck for TLS. In 2010, after Google enabled encryption on their email service by default, they famously stated that SSL/TLS is not computationally expensive any more:[3]

> *On our production frontend machines, SSL/TLS accounts for less than 1% of the CPU load, less than 10KB of memory per connection and less than 2% of network overhead. Many people believe that SSL takes a lot of CPU time and we hope the above numbers (public for the first time) will help to dispel that.*

This chapter is all about getting as close as possible to Google's performance numbers. A large part of the discussion is about latency reduction. Most of the techniques apply to any protocol (even when encryption is not used) but are especially important for TLS because of its increased connection setup costs. The rest is about using the least amount of CPU power possible to achieve desired security and making sure that user agents need to do as little work as possible to validate your certificates.

---

[1] Marissa Mayer at Web 2.0 [fsty.uk/t511] (Greg Linden, 9 November 2006)

[2] Make Data Useful [fsty.uk/t512] (Greg Linden, 28 November 2006)

[3] Overclocking SSL [fsty.uk/t513] (Adam Langley, 25 Jun 2010)

# Latency and Connection Management

The speed of network communication is shaped by two main factors: bandwidth and latency. Bandwidth is a measure of how much data you can send in a unit of time. Latency describes the delay from when a message is sent until it is received on the other end. Of the two, bandwidth is the less interesting factor because you can generally always buy more of it. Latency can't be avoided because it's imposed on us by the speed limits at which data travels over network connections.

Latency is a big limiting factor whenever an interactive exchange of messages is required. In a typical request-response protocol, it takes some time for the request to reach its destination, and for the response to travel back. This measure, known as *round trip time* (RTT), is how we measure latency.

For example, every TCP connection begins a setup phase called the *three-way handshake*: (1) client sends a SYN message to request a new connection; (2) server accepts and responds with SYN ACK; (3) client confirms with ACK and starts sending data. It takes 1.5 round trips for this handshake to complete. In practice, with *client-speaks-first* protocols such as HTTP and TLS, the actual latency is one round trip, because the client can start sending data immediately after the ACK signal.

Latency has a particularly large impact on TLS, because it has its own elaborate handshake. TLS 1.2 and earlier protocols need two additional round trips to complete the first connection. When we add the latency of TCP, TLS 1.2, and HTTP together, we see that one complete request takes a total of four round trips.

Traditionally, SSL and TLS supported two types of handshake: full and abbreviated. On the first connection, client and server have to use the full handshake, but in addition to negotiating an encrypted connection, they also negotiate a *session*. Subsequent connections can use an abbreviated handshake that reuses an earlier session. In TLS 1.2, the abbreviated handshake requires only a single round trip, compared to two round trips of the full handshake.

Several attempts have been made to improve TLS handshake latency over the years. One of them is False Start, which reduces the latency of the full handshake by one round trip and which is still in use. (More about it in the next section.) Other efforts were unsuccessful, including TLS Snap Start[4] and Fast-Track Session Establishment for TLS.[5] On the TCP side, there is also TCP Fast Open,[6] which operates in a similar fashion to TLS session resumption and removes the latency of new TCP handshakes after one full connection is established.

---

[4] TLS Snap Start [fsty.uk/t514] (A. Langley, June 2010)

[5] Fast-Track Session Establishment for TLS [fsty.uk/t515] (Shacham and Boneh, September 2001)

[6] RFC 7413: TCP Fast Open [fsty.uk/t516] (Cheng et al., December 2014)

---

Figure 9.1. TCP , TLS 1.2, and HTTP network latencies

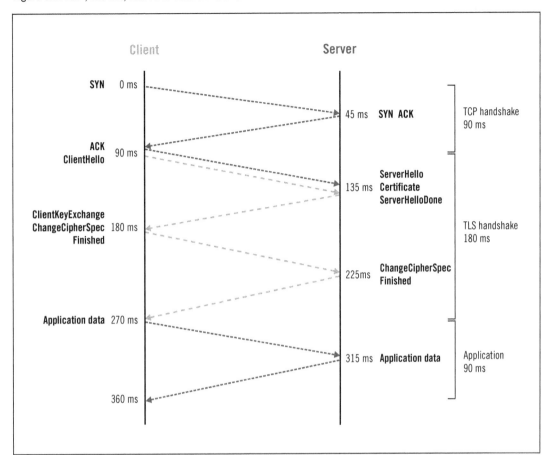

Despite the initial optimism and support for this effort added to many platforms,[7] it eventually fizzled out due to various incompatibilities at scale.[8]

TLS 1.3, released in 2018, redesigned the TLS handshake to reduce latency, bringing it down to just one round trip, and even to zero round trips in some circumstances. Although browsers were already able to achieve this with support for False Start, TLS 1.3 offered a more efficient and safer handshake to all clients and servers.

---

[7] Building a faster and more secure web with TCP Fast Open, TLS False Start, and TLS 1.3 [fsty.uk/t517] (Microsoft, 15 June 2016)

[8] The Sad Story of TCP Fast Open [fsty.uk/t518] (Craig Andrews, 11 April 2019)

# False Start

In 2010, Google proposed a modification to the TLS protocol in order to reduce the latency of the full handshake from two round trips to only one round trip.[9] Normally, a full TLS 1.2 handshake requires two round trips, consisting of four bursts of protocol messages (two for each client and server), and TLS allows sending of (encrypted) application data only after the handshake is fully complete. *False Start* proposes a tweak to the timing of protocol messages; rather than wait for the entire handshake to be complete, we can start sending application data earlier, *assuming* that the handshake will be successful.

With this change, it's possible to achieve much better performance. Google cited a 30% reduction in handshake latency, which is a big deal.[10] The downside of this change is that if attacked, the client will have sent some encrypted application data to the attacker, which wouldn't happen otherwise. Furthermore, because the integrity of the handshake is validated only after it is fully completed, the parameters used for the encryption could have been influenced by the attacker. This is a problem for HTTP, because such requests often contain user credentials.

To counter this attack vector, Google proposed to only ever use False Start with strong cryptography: sufficiently strong private keys, key exchanges that support forward secrecy, and 128-bit cipher suites. They left a loophole in not requiring a strong key exchange. Later, in May 2015, an attack called Logjam (I cover it in the section called "Logjam" in Chapter 7, *Implementation Issues*) showed that it was possible for an active attacker to force browsers that support False Start to send HTTP requests protected with as low as 512 bits of security.

Despite the performance improvements, Google declared False Start a failure in 2012—there were too many incompatible servers on the Internet.[11] But they didn't turn it off altogether; Chrome continued to use False Start with servers that implement the NPN extension (used to negotiate the SPDY protocol), which were deemed safe. Other browsers followed and adopted similar behaviors. Firefox supports False Start since version 28[12] and has the same requirements as Chrome. Apple added support in OS X 10.9, requiring strong cipher suites and forward security but not NPN.[13] Internet Explorer, starting with version 10, implements False Start as per the original proposal, but also uses a blacklist to disable this feature on sites that are known not to support it.[14]

Today, NPN and SPDY are a thing of the past. Although it's difficult to know what browsers do exactly over time, I verified that False Start is still used by Chrome with servers that

---

[9] Changing HTTPS [fsty.uk/t519] (Adam Langley, 5 September 2010)

[10] SSL FalseStart Performance Results [fsty.uk/t520] (Mike Belshe, The Chromium Blog, 18 May 2011)

[11] False Start's Failure [fsty.uk/t521] (Adam Langley, 11 Apr 2012)

[12] Re-enable TLS False Start [fsty.uk/t522] (Bugzilla@Mozilla, bug #942729)

[13] sslTransport.c [fsty.uk/t523] (Apple Secure Transport source code, retrieved 5 May 2014)

[14] Networking Improvements in IE10 and Windows 8 [fsty.uk/t524] (Eric Lawrence, IEInternals, 1 August 2012)

support the ALPN extension (which replaced NPN). False Start was eventually published as a historical RFC.[15]

# TCP Optimization

Although a complete discussion of TCP optimization is out of the scope of this book, there are two tweaks that are so important and easy to use that everyone should know about them. Both are related to the *congestion control* mechanism built into TCP. At the beginning of a new connection, you don't know how fast the other side can go. If there is ample bandwidth, you can send data at the fastest possible rate, but what if you're dealing with a slow mobile connection? If you send too much data, you will overwhelm the link, leading to the connection breakdown. For this reason, a speed limit—known as a *congestion window*—is built into every TCP connection. This window is initially small, but grows over time with evidence of good performance. This mechanism is known as *slow start*.

This brings us to the ugly truth: all TCP connections start slow and increase speed over time until they reach their full potential. This is bad news for HTTP connections, which are often short-lived; they almost always operate under suboptimal conditions.

The situation is even worse for TLS connections, which consume the precious initial connection bytes (when the congestion window is small) with TLS handshake messages. If the congestion window is big enough, then there will be no additional delay from slow start. If, however, it happens that there is a long handshake message that can't fit into the congestion window, the sender will have to split it into two chunks, send one chunk, wait for an acknowledgment (one round trip), increase the congestion window, and only then send the reminder. Later in this chapter, I will discuss several cases in which this situation can happen.

## Initial Congestion Window Tuning

The starting speed limit is known as the *initial congestion window* (initcwnd). If you are deploying on a modern platform, the limit will probably be already set at a high value. RFC 6928, which came out in April 2013,[16] recommended setting initcwnd to 10 network segments (about 15 KB) by default. The previous recommendation was to use two to four network segments as a starting point.

On older Linux platforms, you can change the initcwnd size for all your routes with:

```
# ip route | while read p; do ip route change $p initcwnd 10; done
```

---

[15] RFC 7918: TLS False Start [fsty.uk/t525] (Langley et al., August 2016)

[16] RFC 6928: Increasing TCP's Initial Window [fsty.uk/t526] (Chu et al., April 2013)

High-performance environments should probably investigate if there is some other initial congestion window that performs better for them. In situations like that, it's useful to observe what big companies do.[17]

## Preventing Slow Start When Idle

Another problem is that slow start can kick in on a connection that has not seen any traffic for some time, reducing its speed. And very quickly, too. The period of inactivity can be very small, for example, one second. This means that, by default, virtually every long-running connection (e.g., a HTTP connection that uses keep-alives) will be downgraded from fast to slow! For best results, this feature is best disabled.

On Linux, you can disable slow start due to inactivity with:

```
# sysctl -w net.ipv4.tcp_slow_start_after_idle=0
```

The setting can be made permanent by adding it to your /etc/sysctl.conf configuration.

# Connection Persistence

Most of the TLS performance impact is concentrated in the handshake, which takes place at the beginning of every connection. One important optimization technique is to reduce the number of connections used by keeping each connection open for as long as possible. With this, you minimize the TLS overhead and also improve the TCP performance. As we've seen in the previous section, the longer the TCP connection stays open, the faster it goes.

In HTTP, most transactions tend to be very short, translating to short-lived TCP connections. Although the standard originally didn't provide a way for a connection to stay open for a long time, *keep-alives* were added to HTTP/1.0 as an experimental feature and became enabled by default in HTTP/1.1.

Keeping many connections open for long periods of time can be challenging, because not all web servers are able to handle this situation well. For example, the Apache web server was initially designed to dedicate an entire *worker* (process or thread, depending on configuration) to each connection. The problem with this approach is that slow clients can use up all the available workers and block the web server. Also, it's very easy for an attacker to open a large number of connections and send data very slowly, performing a denial of service attack.[18]

More recently, the trend has been to use event-driven web servers, which handle all communication by using a fixed thread pool (or even a single execution thread), thus minimizing

---

[17] Initcwnd settings of major CDN providers [fsty.uk/t527] (CDN Planet, 13 February 2017)
[18] Slowloris HTTP DoS [fsty.uk/t528] (RSnake et al., 17 June 2009)

per-connection costs and reducing the chances of attack. Nginx is an example of a web server that was built from the start to operate in this way. Apache also later switched to using the event-driven model by default. The best approach is to front application servers with a reverse proxy layer that terminates TLS and performs connection management.

The disadvantage of long-lived connections is that, after the last HTTP connection is complete, the server waits for a certain time (the *keep-alive timeout*) before closing the connection. Although any one connection won't consume a lot of resources, keeping connections open reduces the overall scalability of the server. The best case for keep-alives is with a client that sends a large number of requests in a burst. The worst case is when the client sends only one request and leaves the connection open but never submits another request.

> **Warning**
>
> When deploying with long keep-alive timeouts, it's critical to limit the maximum number of concurrent connections so that the server is not overloaded. Tune the server by testing its operation at the edge of capacity. If TLS is handled by OpenSSL, make sure that the server is setting the SSL_MODE_RELEASE_BUFFERS flag correctly.[19]

It's difficult to recommend any one keep-alive timeout value because this is something that needs to be tuned on a per web site basis. On the one hand, you want to keep as many connections open as possible in order to maximize the chances that one of the clients will submit further requests. On the other hand, you don't want all of those idle connections to consume too much of the available capacity because that would mean that new clients wouldn't be able to connect.

# HTTP/2

There is only so much we can achieve by tuning TCP and HTTP connection persistence alone. Web sites have grown in complexity over the years and the number of required resources and their size have increased. Retrieving one request at a time became unsatisfactory. There was an attempt to extend HTTP with *pipelining*, which would allow many idempotent requests to be submitted in parallel (without waiting for responses), but this feature was difficult to get to work reliably across the entire ecosystem. Eventually, we ended up with browsers using multiple TCP connections to the same web site to improve performance.

---

[19] SSL_CTX_set_mode(3) [fsty.uk/t529] (OpenSSL, retrieved 3 October 2021)

To go further, in 2009 Google started to experiment with a new protocol called SPDY.[20] The idea was to introduce a new protocol layer between TCP and HTTP to speed things up. Positioned in the middle, SPDY could improve connection management without making any changes to HTTP itself.

With SPDY, multiple HTTP requests and responses are multiplexed, which means that a browser only ever needs one connection per server. A single long-lived connection allows for much better TCP utilization and reduced server load.

SPDY was a great success, showing performance improvements in a variety of situations. Perhaps most importantly, it led to an effort to design the next version of the HTTP protocol, which was released in 2015 as HTTP/2. In other words, SPDY woke HTTP from a deep sleep: the previous version, HTTP 1.1, had been released in 1999. By now, SPDY is only of historic interest as it's been fully superseded by HTTP/2.

HTTP/2 was very attractive for its performance improvements, and that led to fast adoption. Anticipating this, the protocol designers did something very interesting: they mandated use of TLS 1.2 with only a few selected and secure cipher suites. As a result, deployments of HTTP/2 also became secure, at least when it came to network transport security. Although the protocol didn't require encryption, major browsers all decided not to support HTTP/2 without it.

## QUIC and HTTP/3

Google also led the way with HTTP/3, the follow-up upgrade to HTTP. Although multiplexing at the TCP level brought many performance benefits, room for further improvements remained. One issue is that the TCP and TLS handshakes are carried out sequentially, meaning that TLS can't start until TCP has been negotiated. A single protocol that always supports encryption could unify the handshakes to make further latency reductions. Another problem is *head of line blocking*. HTTP/2 carries many multiplexed connections (called *streams*) over the same TCP connection. A loss of a single packet leads to the stalling of all streams.

After adopting SPDY for its own infrastructure and the Chrome browser, in 2013 Google continued to work on a new protocol called QUIC,[21] which, at the time, stood for *Quick UDP Internet Connections*.[22] This new protocol built on UDP, avoiding TCP and its limitations. The initial experiments proved promising and so QUIC underwent standardization at IETF over a five-year period until its release as four RFCs in May 2021. There are many additional RFCs that cover HTTP/3 and various QUIC extensions. More are to come.

---

[20] SPDY [fsty.uk/t530] (The Chromium Projects, retrieved 31 May 2015)

[21] Experimenting with QUIC [fsty.uk/t531] (Chromium Blog, 27 June 2013)

[22] The standardization process at IETF abolished the acronym and QUIC is now simply the name of the new protocol.

---

# Ossification

While reading about QUIC, you'll often come across the term *ossification*. This word has several definitions, one of which is the natural process of bone formation. In our context, it refers to the resistance to change in complex ecosystems. In particular, when it comes to networking, different participants have varying expectations of what network traffic and communication will look like. Developers tend to write code that's tested against what they can observe, often neglecting to study various standards and ignoring possible future changes. As a result, it becomes more and more difficult to introduce changes that work for everyone.

There have been several prominent cases of ossification in the TLS space. One example is a bug in F5 load balancers, which are very popular among some of the biggest companies in the world. Browser vendors had to work around this problem and this bug eventually led to an official TLS padding extension, whose entire purpose was to ensure that the ClientHello message isn't shorter than 512 bytes. More importantly, TLS 1.3 had to make a series of design decisions just to avoid standing out too much. Some devices would throw a fit at the mere sight of a new TLS version number. It took a lot of effort to make TLS 1.3 work for the majority of networks and devices out there. A mechanism called GREASE (*Generate Random Extensions And Sustain Extensibility*) was invented to help reduce ossification in TLS.[23]

Consider QUIC for a moment. Making improvements to TCP is not possible because it will be decades until all currently active servers are upgraded to take advantage of the improvements. At the same time, the Internet is full of *middleboxes*, which often refuse to accept traffic that they don't understand, even when it's perfectly valid.

In the end, QUIC decided to abandon TCP and build on UDP as the only feasible choice. The current direction in network design is thus to keep the network pipes as simple as possible, pushing new protocols outside operating systems and their kernels into user space where upgrades are possible, while encrypting as much of the traffic as possible so that the middleboxes can't get to it. This is a concept that will be familiar to programmers; it's often much easier to build something from scratch entirely rather than improve an existing complex system.

A notable change during the standardization process was that instead of specifying its own encryption, QUIC was changed to use TLS 1.3 instead. If you recall, TLS itself is designed as two collaborative layers. On the outside is the record layer, which takes care of encryption and provides transport protection for the second layer, which carries protocols that provide important functionality such as the protocol handshake and negotiation of encryption keys. QUIC assumes the role of the record layer: it encrypts application data directly but delegates all the cryptography decisions to the TLS 1.3 handshake subprotocol. In the end, as far as encryption is concerned, QUIC behaves just like TLS 1.3 and is configured in the same way.

---

[23] RFC 8701: Applying Generate Random Extensions And Sustain Extensibility (GREASE) to TLS Extensibility [fsty.uk/t532] (D. Benjamin, January 2020)

Covering QUIC in detail is outside the scope of this book, but a great starting point that explores various nuances and design decisions is Daniel Stenberg's *HTTP/3 Explained.*[24]

## QUIC Handshake Limitations

QUIC building on top of UDP makes some things easier but other things harder. Standalone TLS connections always operate on top of an established TCP connection, which means that servers can transmit at full speed within the allowed congestion window. This window is usually large enough by default, and can be increased up to roughly 64 KB. Because QUIC uses UDP, the first packet it gets contains an IP address that is not authenticated. In fact, the address may be spoofed in what's known as a *reflected DoS attack*. This type of attack is very effective if servers do not restrict how much data they're sending.

To deal with this problem, QUIC stipulates that a server may respond with only up to three times the amount of received traffic. QUIC clients are required to send at least 1,200 bytes in their first communication, which means that until the address of the client is validated, any server can expect to send only up to 3,600 bytes in its first flight. Crucially, if there is more data to send, the server must wait for the client to acknowledge the connection, which introduces a latency of one round trip.

What this means is that any QUIC operator must carefully monitor the size of the TLS handshake to ensure that it stays under the limit. When done well, the server side of the handshake can be kept at about 3,000 bytes, the bulk of which will be the certificate chain along with a stapled OCSP response. But if there are too many certificates sent, the handshake will go beyond that size, and all advantages of using QUIC for reduced latency disappear.

The concept of address validation is well explored in QUIC; resumed connections, and especially 0-RTT handshakes, are expected to provide *address validation tokens*, which then enables the server to respond with data at full speed.

## Handshake Latency Comparison across Protocols

As of 2021, we have at our disposal a variety of protocols that we can use for network communication and encryption. We have the default TCP transport with TLS 1.2 or TLS 1.3 for encryption, which we can combine with either HTTP/1 or HTTP/2. And in the opposite corner we have the brand new QUIC and TLS 1.3 combination. All these protocols and options offer a variety of handshakes with different security and performance characteristics. Let's examine them in more detail to understand what we can use and when, using the following table as a starting point. This one table summarizes the evolution of networking

---

[24] HTTP/3 explained [fsty.uk/t533] (Daniel Stenberg et al., retrieved 2 June 2021)

since the beginning of the Web, covering TCP, HTTP, TLS, and QUIC. Each row represents one typical approach to delivering HTTP services.

Table 9.1. Comparison of latency and connection management options across protocols

| Protocol | Full hand-shake latency | Resumed handshake la-tency | 0-RTT resump-tion latency | Multiplexing | Head of line blocking |
|---|---|---|---|---|---|
| TCP + TLS 1.2 + HTTP/1 | 4 (3)[a] | 3 | - | No | No |
| TCP + TLS 1.3 + HTTP/2 | 3 | 3 | 2 | Yes | Yes |
| QUIC + HTTP/3 | 2 | 2 | 1 | Yes | No |

[a] Three round trips when False Start is taken into account.

In the first column, we track how many round trips are required to establish the first connection. The worst result is when TCP is combined with TLS 1.2 in a nonbrowser environment, when four round trips are needed: one for TCP, two for TLS, and another one for HTTP. Browsers tend to support False Start, reducing the number of round trips to three. The best result is when QUIC is used, when only two round trips are needed: one for the encrypted connection and another for HTTP.

When it comes to the latency of resumed connections, here we see that there is little practical difference between TLS 1.2 and TLS 1.3, but QUIC maintains its lead. However, the modern options support 0-RTT resumption, which may offer better performance in some situations. Here we can also observe a terminology clash; 0-RTT with TLS 1.3 still requires a new TCP connection, whereas in QUIC the initial client communication handles connection, encryption, and HTTP all in one. The promise of super-fast resumptions is very tempting, but it works only in limited situations and with weaker security guarantees; refer to the section called "0-RTT and Forward Secrecy" in Chapter 2 for more information.

The last two protocols cover connection management. With the old-school HTTP/1, complex interactions require use of multiple connections that have to be managed individually. HTTP/2 and HTTP/3 protocols prefer multiplexing streams over a single connection. This will probably help; with fewer connections to keep open, servers can afford to keep them open for longer, thus maximizing the chances of reuse. HTTP/2 adds multiplexing but also introduces head of line blocking. HTTP/3 takes that away.

What conclusions can we make? First of all, TLS 1.3 is a clear winner because it offers better security and better performance without any drawbacks. HTTP/2 is also a winner because it simplifies connection management for browsers and other high-performance clients. It does so at the cost of head of line blocking, which may or may not be a problem depending on the client base. QUIC and HTTP/3 offer a different take on connection management and may lead to even better performance in some situations.

# Content Delivery Networks

If you maintain a web site that targets a global audience, you need to use a *content delivery network* (CDN) to achieve world-class performance. CDNs are geographically distributed servers that add value largely by offering edge caching and traffic optimization that reduces network latency (often also called *WAN optimization*).

Most times, when you need to scale a web site, throwing money at the problem helps. If your database is dying under heavy load, you can buy a bigger server. If your site can't run on a single server, you can deploy a cluster. However, no amount of money can eliminate network latency. The further away your users are from your servers, the slower your web site will be.

In such situations, connection setup is a big limiting factor. TCP connections start with a three-way handshake, which requires a round trip to complete. Then there's the TLS handshake, which requires one or two additional round trips. If you recall, one complete HTTP transaction requires three round trips if TLS 1.3 is used. That's about 90 ms for a nearby user who's about 30 ms RTT away, but may be much more for someone who is on the other side of the world.

CDNs typically operate large numbers of geographically distributed servers, with the idea being to have servers as close to end users as possible. With that proximity, they typically reduce latency in two ways—edge caching and connection management.

**Edge caching**

> Because CDNs place servers close to users, they can deliver your files to users as if your servers were right there. Some CDNs enable you to push your files to them; this approach offers the best control and performance, but it's more difficult to manage. Some other CDNs operate as reverse proxies (they retrieve files over HTTP when they need them and cache them locally for a period of time); they are not as optimized but are very easy to deploy.

**Connection management**

> Caching is the best-case scenario for CDN deployment, but it's not suitable for all sites. If your content is dynamic and user specific, your servers will need to do the actual work. But a good CDN should be able to help, even without any caching, via connection management. This seems counterintuitive at first: how can traffic go faster through a CDN than when it goes directly to the origin server? The answer is that a CDN can eliminate most of the connection setup cost by reusing connections over long periods of time.

> During connection setup, most of the time is spent waiting. You send a packet and wait for a response. When the other end is very far away, you wait for a long time. But when the other end is near, you get a quick response. To minimize the waiting, CDNs can route traffic through their own infrastructure, exiting at a point

closest to the destination. With full control over their own servers, CDNs can keep the internal connections open for a long time. If they use TCP, that means that there is no connection setup and that connections run at their maximum speed. But they can also use proprietary protocols and connection multiplexing for even better performance.

When a CDN is used, the user connects to the closest CDN node, which is only a short distance away. Because the distance is small, the network latency of the TLS 1.2 handshake will also be small—for example, 15 ms for a round trip time of 5 ms. In the ideal case for a new TLS connection, the CDN can reuse existing long-range connections that it keeps open, going from that node all the way to the final destination. That means that no further work is necessary; after the initial fast TLS handshake with the CDN, the user's connection with the server is effectively open and application data can begin to flow.

Of course, not all CDNs operate sophisticated internal networks that operate in this way; it's necessary to research the implementation details when deciding which CDN to use. Or, even better, test the actual performance.

Figure 9.2. TLS 1.2 connection setup time between London and New York

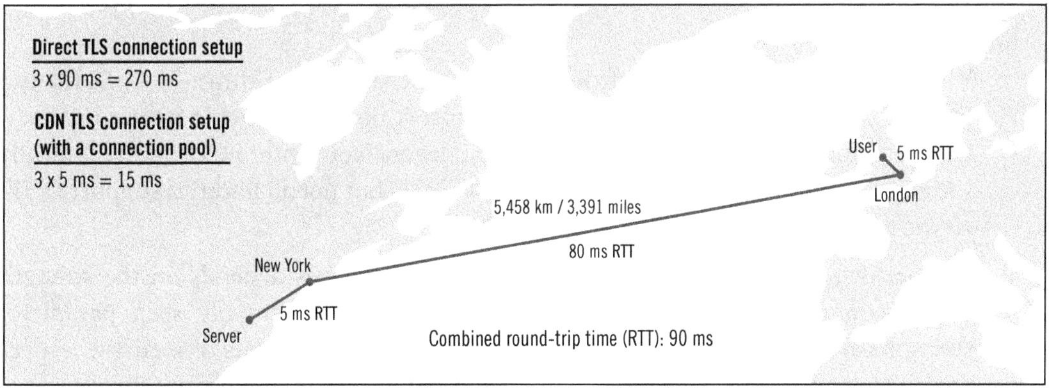

## TLS Protocol Optimization

With connection management out of the way, I'll now focus on the performance characteristics of TLS. The aim here is to understand how different aspects of TLS impact performance, which will equip you with the knowledge to tune the protocol for both security and speed.

## Key Exchange

After latency, the next biggest cost of using TLS comes from having to perform CPU-intensive cryptographic operations in order to securely agree on connection security parameters.

---

This part of the communication is known as *key exchange*. Its cost is largely determined by the choice of server private key algorithm, key size, and the key exchange algorithm.

### Key size

To achieve security, cryptography relies on processes that are relatively fast with access to relevant keys but hugely expensive and time consuming otherwise. The effort required to break an encryption key depends on its size; the bigger the key, the better the protection. However, a bigger key also requires more CPU to encrypt and decrypt and increases handshake size. For best results, select a key size that provides the appropriate level of security, but don't go beyond that.

### Key algorithm

There are two private key algorithms that you can use today: RSA and ECDSA.[25] RSA is still the dominating algorithm, largely because it was the only and best-supported choice for a very long time. But RSA is starting to be too slow now that 2,048 bits is the minimum strength and some are considering deploying 3,072 bits of security in the near future. ECDSA is much faster and thus increasingly appealing. At a modest size of 256 bits, ECDSA provides security equivalent to 3,072-bit RSA and better performance. By now, ECDSA is widely supported, making it even more difficult to make a case for using RSA.

### Key exchange

With TLS 1.2, you can choose from three key exchange algorithms: RSA, DHE, and ECDHE. But you don't want to use RSA because it does not provide forward secrecy. Of the remaining two, DHE is slow. That leaves you with ECDHE. Technically speaking, TLS 1.3 supports only DHE and ECDHE, but not all libraries support DHE, so you're left only with ECDHE.

The performance of the DHE and ECDHE key exchanges depends on the strength of the configured negotiation parameters. For DHE, commonly seen parameter strengths are 1,024 and 2,048 bits, which provide 80 and 112 bits of security, respectively. As for ECDHE, the security and performance are influenced by the choice of named curve. For a long time, the P-256 (secp256r1) curve was the de facto standard, but X25519 is well-supported today and offers better performance. Browsers also support P-384 (secp384r1), but this curve is significantly slower server-side and doesn't provide a meaningful increase in security.

In practice, you can't freely combine key and key exchange algorithms. In TLS 1.2 and earlier protocols, both algorithms are controlled by the negotiated cipher suites and only some combinations are available. For example, with an RSA private key you can choose either DHE or ECDHE, but ECDHE is the only option with ECDSA. In TLS 1.3, suites

---

[25] Although the protocol includes many DSA (DSS) suites, there isn't wide support for using DSA keys at 2,048 and higher strengths. The maximum is 1,024 bits, which is insecure.

no longer control the key exchange; it's negotiated using a separate mechanism that is not under your direct control.

To understand the performance differences among the handshake primitives, I ran a test using TLS 1.2 and four suites that you will likely encounter in practice. (If you're curious, the performance of TLS 1.3 is roughly the same when equivalent suites are used.) For the test, I used a dedicated Amazon EC2 m4.xlarge instance with four Intel Xeon E5-2686 v4 vCPUs running at 2.30 GHz. The test was run using a modification[26] of Vincent Bernat's tool for OpenSSL microbenchmarking.[27] I tested OpenSSL 1.1.1f that comes with Ubuntu 20.04 LTS. The tool runs on two threads (one for the client and another for the server), performs 1,000 TLS handshakes sequentially, and measures CPU consumption of each thread. You can see the results in the following graph.

Figure 9.3. Performance comparison of TLS key exchange algorithms (lower is better)

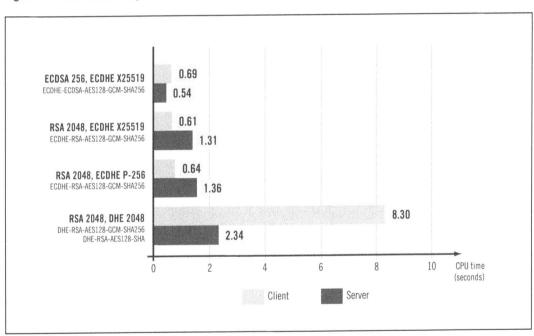

Looking at the results, it's obvious why the industry turned toward elliptic curve cryptography: it offers better security, as well as much better performance. The lesson is clear: prefer ECDSA and ECDHE, with RSA and DHE only for interoperability with older clients.

Should you chase the best possible performance and replace all your RSA server keys with ECDSA? Maybe. It depends. If performing 2.4x handshakes per second for the same

[26] ivanr / ssl-dos [fsty.uk/t534] (GitHub, retrieved 15 May 2021)

[27] SSL/TLS & Perfect Forward Secrecy [fsty.uk/t535] (Vincent Bernat, 28 November 2011)

CPU makes a difference in your environment, then you should. This may be the case, for example, if you have a dedicated reverse proxy layer that terminates TLS. Otherwise, switch to ECDSA when there is a convenient opportunity.

> **Note**
>
> The test results presented here should be used only as a guideline. They measure the performance of a particular version of OpenSSL that's used for both sides of the connection. In practice, TLS performance will vary across libraries, devices, and CPUs.

## Certificates

During a full TLS handshake, the server presents its certificate chain for inspection by the client. The size of the certificate chain and its correctness can have an impact on handshake performance.

**Use as few certificates as possible**

Each certificate in the chain adds to the size of the handshake. Too many certificates in the chain may cause overflow of the initial server allowance. In the early days of SSL, there were CAs that issued server certificates directly from their roots, but this practice is dangerous (the roots should be kept offline) and no longer allowed. Today, having two certificates in the chain is the best you can get: one certificate for the server and another for the issuing CA.

Size is not the only factor; each certificate in the chain must be validated by checking that the signature matches the public key in the issuing certificate. Depending on the user agent, the revocation status of each certificate might need to be checked, too.

Although I wouldn't recommend that you choose your CA based on the size of its trust chain, if performance matters to you, this is something you will need to take into account.

**Include only necessary certificates**

It's a frequent error to include unnecessary certificates in the chain. Each such certificate typically adds 1–2 KB to the overall size of the handshake.

Often, the root certificate is included, even though it serves no purpose there. User agents will either trust the root certificate (and thus already have a copy) or they won't. Having the root in the chain makes no difference. This is a common problem because even some CAs include their root certificates in the installation instructions.

In other cases, unnecessary certificates in the chain are a result of configuration error. It's not uncommon to see servers including intermediate certificates left over from a previous configuration. In some rare cases, servers send their entire collection of trusted certificates—hundreds of them.

## Provide a complete chain

For a TLS connection to be trusted, the server must provide a complete chain that terminates with a trusted root. A common error is to provide an incomplete certificate chain. Although some user agents are able to obtain the missing certificates, doing that might involve looking for them over HTTP, which is an activity that could take a long time. For best results, ensure that the chain is valid.

## Use EC certificate chains

Because ECDSA keys use fewer bits, ECDSA certificates take less space. Therefore it makes sense to use ECDSA for the server key, as well as select a CA that can provide a chain with ECDSA through to the root. Huang et al. observed that a 256-bit ECDSA certificate chain is about 1 KB shorter than a 2,048-bit RSA chain.[28]

## Be careful about having too many hostnames on the same certificate

Recently, it has become common practice to share one certificate among dozens and, in some cases, even hundreds of sites. Historically, this was necessary in order for many sites to share the same IP address, thus supporting clients that do not support *virtual secure sites* (via the *Server Name Indication* extension, or SNI). Each hostname added to the certificate increases its size. A few hostnames are not going to have any noticeable effect, but hundreds might.

There's a trick you can use if you want to keep handshake size down to a minimum but still have to host multiple sites on the same IP address: (1) get a separate certificate for each hostname you wish to run and configure your web server to serve these certificates to the clients that support SNI; (2) get one fallback certificate that contains all the hostnames you have on the same IP address and configure your web server to serve it to the clients that do not support SNI. If you do this, your SNI clients (the majority) will get small certificates for the sites they wish to access, and everyone else (a small number of legacy clients) will get the single long certificate.

## Certificate compression and caching

Realizing that certificates use a significant amount of every single first handshake, the TLS Working Group designed two protocol extensions that reduce handshake size. One of these extensions focuses on certificate compression,[29] while the other focuses on certificate caching, enabling servers to avoid sending certificate chains that clients already have.[30]At the time of writing, these extensions are not widely supported. BoringSSL and Chrome implement certificate compression using Brotli,[31] but there is little apparent activity related to certificate caching.

---

[28] An Experimental Study of TLS Forward Secrecy Deployments [fsty.uk/t536] (Huang et al., 2014)

[29] RFC 8879: TLS Certificate Compression [fsty.uk/t537] (Ghedini and Vasiliev, December 2020)

[30] RFC 7924: TLS Cached Information Extension [fsty.uk/t538] (Santesson and Tschofenig, July 2016)

[31] TLS 1.3 certificate compression with Brotli [fsty.uk/t539] (Chrome Status, retrieved 15 May 2021)

---

**Warning**

When client authentication is required, it's possible to configure your server to advertise which issuing CAs are acceptable for the client certificate. Each such CA is identified with its distinguished name. When there are too many CAs in the configuration, the size of the list can run into many kilobytes, which impedes performance. Because advertising acceptable CAs is optional, you can avoid it for performance reasons.

# Revocation Checking

The idea behind certificate checking is simple: we wish to notify users that a particular certificate is no longer to be trusted. In practice, the desire for security is pitted against desire to make web sites go faster. To perform a revocation check, clients have to do additional work, thus slowing down user interactions. In other words, enforcing revocation checking may make your web sites slower.

Browsers largely gave up on revocation checking, citing exactly performance as their main reason. Web site operators can choose to either side with the browser vendors and ignore revocation (relying on shorter-lived certificates is a good idea in this case) or delve into OCSP stapling, which comes with its own challenges. If you prefer the latter option, this section provides an overview of your options.

**Use certificates with OCSP information**

OCSP is designed for real-time lookups, which allow user agents to request revocation information only for the web site they are visiting. As a result, lookups are short and quick (one HTTP request). CRL, by comparison, is a list of many revoked certificates that is much larger. This is why TLS clients typically ignore CRLs.

**Use CAs with fast and reliable OCSP responders**

OCSP responder performance varies among CAs. This fact remained hidden for a long time, which is unusual given the potential for high performance degradation by slow and faulty OCSP responders. Before you commit to a CA, check their OCSP responder performance. Refer to the section called "Responder Availability and Performance" in Chapter 6 for more information. As a rule of thumb, the best performance is going to be with CAs who use CDNs to distribute revocation information.

**Use OCSP stapling**

*OCSP stapling* is a protocol feature that allows revocation information (the entire OCSP response) to be included in the TLS handshake. With OCSP stapling enabled, user agents are given all the information they need to perform revocation checking and don't need to communicate with third-party servers. On the one hand, this improves overall performance. On the other hand, stapled OCSP responses increase the size of every handshake.

OCSP responses vary in size, depending on the issuing CA's deployment practices. Short OCSP responses are signed by the same CA certificate that issued the end-entity certificate (the one that is being checked for revocation). Because the user agent will already have the issuing CA certificate, the OCSP response can contain only the revocation status and a signature.

Some CAs prefer to use a different certificate to sign their OCSP responses. Because user agents don't know about that other certificate in advance, the CAs must include it with every OCSP response. This practice adds slightly over 1 KB to the size of the OCSP response.

In theory, OCSP stapling enables you to take back control of the revocation of your own certificates. In theory, it's often not correctly implemented, which leads to a variety of availability issues. You will find more information about this in the section called "Revocation" in Chapter 4, *Public Key Infrastructure*.

# Session Resumption

TLS understands two types of handshakes: full and abbreviated. In theory, the full handshake is performed only once, after which the client establishes a *session* with the server. On subsequent connections, the two can use the faster abbreviated handshake and resume the previously negotiated session. The abbreviated handshake is faster because it doesn't require any costly cryptographic operations and uses one less round trip. The reduction of latency was a big deal, making session resumption an important optimization technique. This changed for browsers with the introduction of False Start because only one round trip was used for both handshakes. TLS 1.3, which always uses a single round trip, expanded this to all clients, not only browsers. Today, session resumption remains important for its reduced computational requirements.

TLS session resumption is controlled by both parties involved in the communication. On your side, you should aim to configure session caching so that individual sessions remain valid for about a day. After that, it will be up to clients to decide when to resume and when to start afresh. In 2010, Google reported a 50% resumption rate.[3] In 2017, Cloudflare reported 40%.[32]

# Transport Overhead

In TLS, the minimal unit of transport is a TLS record, which contains up to 16,384 bytes of data. Packaging, encryption, and integrity algorithms introduce additional overhead, which varies depending on the negotiated protocol and cipher suite. To understand these overheads, we have to study exactly how TLS records are assembled depending on what

---

[32] Introducing Zero Round Trip Time Resumption [fsty.uk/t540] (Nick Sullivan, 15 March 2017)

parameters are used. The two protocol chapters in this book provide enough material, but if you don't want to go back to them now, the following illustration will refresh your memory; it's an overview of all encryption methods supported in new and old protocol versions.

Figure 9.4. TLS record overhead for streaming, block, and authenticated cipher suites in TLS 1.2 and TLS 1.3

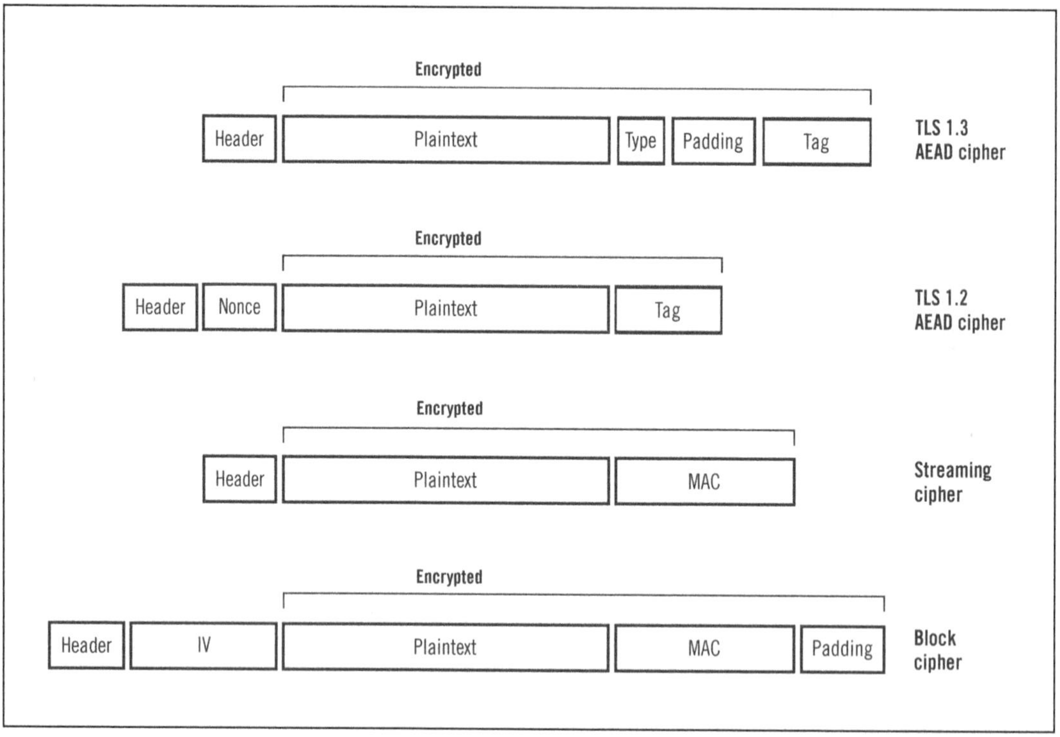

The illustration leads with the AEAD suites that are the workhorses of both TLS 1.3 and TLS 1.2, but includes the legacy and now-obsolete encryption methods of the early days of TLS for comparison. There's a variety of elements in play, so let's examine them in more detail:

**TLS record header**

Every TLS record starts with a five-byte header: one byte to indicate content type, two bytes for protocol version, and two bytes for data length. This overhead element is always the same, no matter which protocol is negotiated.

**Encrypted content type**

In TLS 1.3, the content type from the header is no longer used, but it stayed as a placeholder in order to preserve backward compatibility. There is therefore an additional content type byte inside each TLS record.

### Explicit nonce or IV

All protocol versions until and including TLS 1.2 allowed a per-record randomly generated value designed to prevent encryption from being deterministic when observed on the wire. An initialization vector (IV) was used with legacy block ciphers. AEAD suites use an explicit nonce component, although this doesn't apply to ChaCha20 suites. TLS 1.3 dispenses with explicit nonces altogether and delegates nonce construction to the AEAD algorithms.

### Integrity validation

Integrity validation is provided by a *tag* when AEAD encryption is used, or a *message authentication code* (MAC) in the case of legacy encryption. These fields require 16 bytes when modern cipher suites are used.

### Block cipher padding

Because block ciphers operate only on lengths that are multiples of their block size, plaintexts that don't satisfy this requirement must be padded with additional data. In the worst case, the size of the encrypted data is extended by one entire block. This usually means 16 bytes. Stream algorithms don't have this problem and don't require padding. All AEAD suites currently supported by TLS are effectively stream algorithms.

### TLS protocol padding

An innovation in TLS 1.3 was added support for length hiding, which is a technique that can be used to increase the size of ciphertext to hide the true length of plaintext. Length hiding is supported via optional TLS protocol padding. Although supported, this feature is typically not used.

Even with a good understanding of how things work under the hood, the only way to truly understand the overhead is to look at one combination of protocol and cipher suite at the time and dig deep into the specifications. In Table 9.2, "Transport overhead for each of the widely available ciphers" you can see the overhead calculations for the most commonly used suites.

As you can see, the overhead varies a lot among cipher suites. Streamlined encryption in TLS 1.3 and a focus on AEAD encryption makes things easy to understand because there is an effectively fixed overhead of 22 bytes per TLS record.

When it comes to TLS 1.2 (and earlier) cipher suites, there is great variety, with the overheads ranging from 21 bytes in case of ChaCha20 to 69 bytes for legacy CBC suites that use SHA256 for integrity checking. But if we stick with AEAD suites in TLS 1.2 (as we should), the maximum overhead is up to 29 bytes.

If we take a look at the TCP/IP layer, the overheads of modern TLS don't seem that bad: in the case of IPv4 the overhead is about 60 bytes, and in the case of IPv6 about 80 bytes. In

Table 9.2. Transport overhead for each of the widely available ciphers

| Cipher | Protocol | TLS Record | IV/Nonce | Padding | HMAC/Tag | Total |
|---|---|---|---|---|---|---|
| AES-128-GCM-SHA256 | TLS 1.3 | 6 | - | - | 16 | 22 |
| AES-256-GCM-SHA384 | TLS 1.3 | 6 | - | - | 16 | 22 |
| CHACHA20_POLY1305_SHA256 | TLS 1.3 | 6 | - | - | 16 | 22 |
| AES-128-CBC-SHA | TLS 1.2 | 5 | 16 | 16 | 20 | 57 |
| AES-128-CBC-SHA256 | TLS 1.2 | 5 | 16 | 16 | 32 | 69 |
| AES-128-GCM-SHA256 | TLS 1.2 | 5 | 8 | - | 16 | 29 |
| AES-256-CBC-SHA | TLS 1.2 | 5 | 16 | 16 | 20 | 57 |
| AES-256-CBC-SHA256 | TLS 1.2 | 5 | 16 | 16 | 32 | 69 |
| AES-256-GCM-SHA384 | TLS 1.2 | 5 | 8 | - | 16 | 29 |
| CHACHA20_POLY1305_SHA256 | TLS 1.2 | 5 | - | - | 16 | 21 |

addition, TCP packets tend to be smaller, whereas TLS records can grow in size up to 16 KB. It's likely that TCP will incur more overhead than TLS.

## Symmetric Encryption

When it comes to CPU consumption, the worst is over once a TLS handshake completes. Still, cryptographic operations used for symmetric encryption have a noticeable CPU cost, which depends on the choice of cipher, cipher mode, and integrity validation functions. With the decline in the number of available suites in TLS 1.3, this topic is not as interesting as it once was, but it's still useful to understand how your choices can impact performance.

To determine performance characteristics of various cipher suites, I conducted further tests using the same environment that I used earlier in this chapter. I made sure to select a processor that supports the AES-NI instruction set, which provides hardware acceleration for the AES cipher.[33] I expect most performance-sensitive web sites to operate on similar hardware. Each test run consisted of two threads—one for the client and the other for the server—sending about 1 GB of data to the other side, 16 KB at time. I tested all practical and secure cipher suites available today as well as some legacy suites for comparison. You can see the results in the following chart, in which I've ordered the suites with TLS 1.3 and the most frequently used ones at the top. Client and server performance is essentially the same, which is why I am not showing them separately.

Looking at the three TLS 1.3 suites at the top, AES is a clear winner, no doubt owing to hardware acceleration. The single ChaCha20 suite is slower, but not by much. Remember,

---

[33] If you're purchasing hardware, examine the CPU specifications to determine AES-NI support. In a cloud environment, you should be able to do the same by examining the vendor's documentation. On a server running Linux, look for the "aes" flag in /proc/cpuinfo.

Chapter 9: Performance

Figure 9.5. Performance comparison of various TLS 1.3 and TLS 1.2 cipher suites (lower is better)

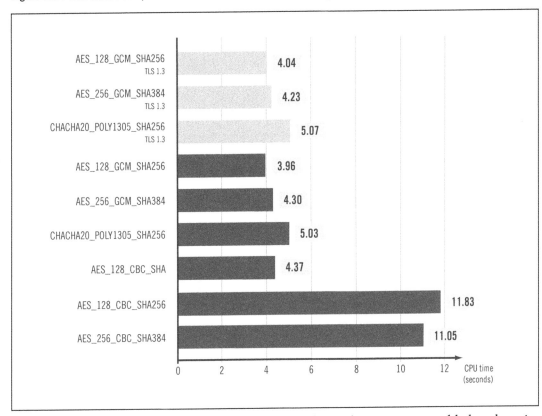

this is an isolated test of one aspect of encryption; when other aspects are added to the mix, there isn't likely to be a great performance difference.

The next three suites are TLS 1.2 equivalents and the performance differences mirror those of the TLS 1.3 suites. The last three suites are some legacy suites that are not going to be used often, if ever.

Although we tend to spend most of our time benchmarking servers, it's worth keeping an eye on client-side performance. Newer desktops and laptops support hardware-accelerated AES, but there are large numbers of underpowered mobile devices that don't. ChaCha20 suites may be slower than hardware-accelerated AES, but these suites are faster on mobile devices.[34] In practice, when security is otherwise equivalent or comparable, servers can actively detect which suites would be faster on a per-client basis and choose those for best performance. For this to be possible, clients need to indicate their preference for ChaCha20 suites by placing them ahead of AES in the initial request.

---

[34] ChaCha20 and Poly1305 for TLS [fsty.uk/t541] (Adam Langley, 7 October 2013)

# TLS Record Buffering

If you recall from an earlier discussion, TLS records are the smallest unit of data TLS can send and receive. Because there is mismatch between the size of TLS records and the size of the underlying TCP packets, a full-sized TLS record of 16 KB needs to be chopped up into smaller TCP packets, typically each under 1.5 KB.

Figure 9.6. Example fragmentation of 32 KB of application data for transport using TLS and TCP

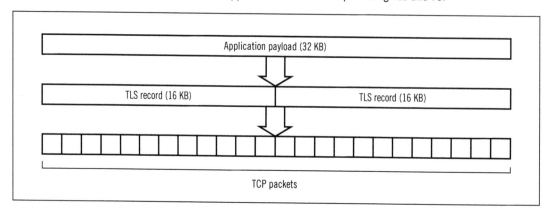

But there's a catch: even though some pieces of an entire record will arrive sooner and some later, no processing can be done until all of them are available. This is because a TLS record is also the smallest unit of data that can be safely decrypted. This buffering effect can sometimes result in an increase in latency.

**Packet loss and delay**

Although TCP can recover from lost and delayed packets, it does so at a cost of one round trip. Each additional round trip means a delay for the entire TLS record, not just the lost packet.

**Initial congestion window**

Another way to trigger an additional round trip delay is by sending large chunks of data early in a connection, overflowing the initial congestion window. Once the congestion window is full, the sender will need to wait for an acknowledgment (one round trip) before it can grow the congestion window and send more data.

Taking these factors into account, we can see how TLS record buffering can affect those first page loads, when you want browsers to start processing the data as soon as possible. If your web server supports TLS record tuning, you should consider changing the default value—which is historically set at about 16 KB—to something more reasonable. Finding the best size requires some experimentation because the correct value depends on the operating system (TCP) configuration and the overhead of TLS, which I discussed earlier in this chapter.

If you don't want to spend much time on this task, consider using about 4 KB as a reasonable default. If you want to match the size of TCP packets closely, you'll need to observe the overheads of TCP/IP by monitoring the packets your servers send. With that, and with the understanding of the TLS overheads, you can do your own calculations. For example, assuming that you have an application that can restrict maximum application data writes and that the IP *maximum transmission unit* (MTU) is 1,500 bytes, the calculation is as follows:

```
  1,500 bytes MTU
-    40 bytes IPv6 header
-    40 bytes TCP header
-    69 bytes TLS record
-------------------------
= 1,351 bytes of application data
```

If you know for a fact that your servers are never going to negotiate some of the cipher suites with very large overheads, you can increase your default TLS record size by about 40 bytes. The main thing is to avoid larger values that won't fit into a single TCP transmission.

## Interoperability

Interoperability issues can sometimes have a substantial negative performance impact, yet they often remain hidden unless you know exactly where to look. For example, if your server reacts poorly to handshakes that offer newer protocols and features, clients may need to work extra hard to establish the connection, typically by trying different approaches.[35] However, unless you experience this problem yourself and notice the performance degradation, it's unlikely that you will know about it. The best way to ensure good TLS performance is to run an up-to-date TLS stack with support for the most recent protocol versions and extensions.

## Hardware Acceleration

In the early days of SSL, public cryptography was too slow for the then-available hardware. As a result, the only way to achieve decent performance was by using hardware acceleration. Over time, as the speed of general-purpose CPUs increased, acceleration devices started to lose their market.[36]

---

[35] Multiple connection attempts are part of the voluntary protocol downgrade mechanism that used to be employed by modern browsers. I discuss it at length in the section called "Voluntary Protocol Downgrade" in Chapter 7.

[36] High Scalability for SSL and Apache [fsty.uk/t542] (Cox and Thorpe, July 2000)

Companies running the world's largest web sites are happy handling encryption in software. For example, Facebook had this to say on hardware acceleration:[37]

> *We have found that modern software-based TLS implementations running on commodity CPUs are fast enough to handle heavy HTTPS traffic load without needing to resort to dedicated cryptographic hardware. We serve all of our HTTPS traffic using software running on commodity hardware.*

Today, large deployments typically scale horizontally via separate reverse proxy layers that terminate encryption, as well as perform other duties, such as admission control. If hardware cryptographic devices are purchased, it's more for compliance reasons and their ability to store private keys safely (this type of product is known as *Hardware Security Module*, or HSM) and less for their ability to accelerate public key cryptography. With the popularity of cloud services, there are now cloud-powered HSMs that provide similar benefits but without having to purchase any hardware.

# Denial of Service Attacks

*Denial of Service* (DoS) attacks—for fun or for profit—are common on the Internet. Attacking is easy and cheap. Defending, on the other hand, is costly and time consuming. Any small web site can be quickly overwhelmed by pretty much anyone who wants to try. As for bigger sites, if they stay up, it's only because they spent a lot of money on defense and the attackers haven't tried hard enough.

The principal way of executing serious DoS attacks is using botnets, which are large networks of compromised computers. Servers are valued as botnet nodes because they tend to have access to ample bandwidth. Home computers are valued because there are so many of them; what they lack in power, they make up in numbers.

If someone is willing to use a botnet to attack you, chances are that your TLS configuration is not going to make a difference. With or without TLS, determined attackers can continuously increase the size of the botnet until they succeed, at little cost to them. DoS attacks remain a problem that has to be dealt with at the network level.

On your own, chances are you will only be able to defend against small DoS attacks. To counter them, you'll need to have monitoring in place to know when you're attacked, as well as some capability to block offending IP addresses at the network level. Being able to communicate with your upstream network provider helps a great deal because it may be willing to block the offending traffic on its end. In a cloud environment, being able to quickly add additional server resources might be of help. Ultimately, to defend against a serious attacker, you'll have to outsource defense to a third party, which usually means shielding your servers behind someone else's.

---

[37] HTTP2 Expression of Interest [fsty.uk/t543] (Doug Beaver, on the HTTP Working Group mailing list, 15 July 2012)

# Amplifying Attacks Using Client-Initiated Renegotiation

*Renegotiation* is an obsolete TLS protocol feature that allows either side to request a new handshake on the same TCP connection. This feature, now no longer supported in TLS 1.3, was rarely used, but it made it easier to execute DoS attacks.

In a "standard" TLS computational DoS attack, there's one handshake per connection. If you have connection throttling in place, you know that one connection to your TLS server costs you some amount in CPU processing power. If client-initiated renegotiation is allowed, attackers can perform many handshakes on the same connection, leaving you less able to detect the abuse. It's still possible to detect the attacks, but that would typically require deep traffic inspection, ideally by parsing the protocol messages. This ability is not as common as straightforward connection counting.[38] Using renegotiation as part of the attack also reduces the number of concurrent connections needed and thus improves overall attack latency.

In October 2011, a German hacker group, "The Hacker's Choice," released a tool called `thc-ssl-dos`, which uses renegotiation to amplify computational DoS attacks against TLS.[39]

Not all servers support client-initiated renegotiation. IIS stopped supporting it with IIS 6, Nginx never supported it, and Apache stopped supporting it in 2.2.15. But there is still a number of vendors who are reluctant to remove this feature. Some vendors who are keeping client-initiated renegotiation are looking to limit the number of renegotiations that take place on the same connection. Ideally, you shouldn't allow client-initiated renegotiation at all.

# Optimized TLS Denial of Service Attacks

Renegotiation makes TLS computational DoS attacks more difficult to detect, but tools that use it are not fundamentally different; they're still essentially sending a large number of virtual clients to a web site. In both cases, the handshake CPU processing asymmetry is what makes the attack possible. As it turns out, it is possible to improve the approach so that no cryptographic operations are needed on the client.

When the `thc-ssl-dos` tool was announced, it received a fair amount of media interest. Eric Rescorla, one of the TLS protocol designers, followed up with an analysis of the use of renegotiation as a DoS amplification technique.[40] His conclusion was that there is an easier way to execute computational TLS DoS. In his approach, clients use hardcoded handshake messages that require no cryptographic operations. In addition, they avoid parsing or otherwise validating any of the messages received from the server. Because the messages are

---

[38] SSL computational DoS mitigation [fsty.uk/t544] (Vincent Bernat, 1 November 2011)

[39] THC SSL DOS [fsty.uk/t545] (The Hacker's Choice, 24 October 2011)

[40] SSL/TLS and Computational DoS [fsty.uk/t546] (Eric Rescorla, 25 October 2011)

structurally correct, they appear valid to the server until the very end of the handshake. By that point, it's too late, because all the expensive work had been done.

Using Eric's blueprint, Michal Trojnara subsequently wrote a proof-of-concept tool called sslsqueeze.[41]

When I tested sslsqueeze, I found it very effective. A single-CPU attack server consumed all CPU resources on an eight-CPU target server in the same data center after only a couple of seconds. The TLS Working Group explored extending TLS with a mechanism to support requesting clients that are not malicious, but ultimately decided against it.[42]

---

[41] sslsqueeze on GitHub [fsty.uk/t547] (Michal Trojnara, retrieved 23 May 2021)

[42] TLS Client Puzzles Extension [fsty.uk/t548] (E. Nygren et al., December 2016)

# 10 HSTS, CSP, and Pinning

This chapter discusses several technologies that can substantially improve the security of the SSL/TLS and PKI ecosystem. They fall into two groups. In the first group, we have *HTTP Strict Transport Security* (HSTS) and *Content Security Policy* (CSP), which are HTTP-specific and widely supported by browsers. They are not only practical today but also fundamental for the security of your web sites.

The technologies in the second group implement *pinning*, which is a technique that improves TLS server authentication. There are several competing approaches to pinning, at varying levels of maturity. For native applications, for which the same developer controls both client and server communication, pinning is under your full control. When it comes to browsers, pinning is generally not recommended anymore, but it may still be possible with a lot of planning and coordination with browser vendors.

## HTTP Strict Transport Security

*HTTP Strict Transport Security* (HSTS), released in November 2012 as RFC 6797,[1] is a standard that describes a strict approach to the handling of web site encryption. It is designed to mitigate several critical weaknesses in how TLS was historically implemented in browsers:

**No way of knowing if a site supports TLS**

Because HTTP initially didn't support encryption, a browser could connect only to port 80. Later, support for encrypted web sites on port 443 was added, but, given just a domain name, browsers have to choose between HTTP and HTTPS protocols. Traditionally, browsers were defaulting to port 80, although this is now changing. Still, for as long as browsers are willing to send unencrypted traffic, various active network attacks will remain possible.

---

[1] RFC 6797: HTTP Strict Transport Security (HSTS) [fsty.uk/t267] (Hodges and Jackson, November 2012)

**Tolerance of certificate problems**

Since the very beginning of the Web, browsers have been sidestepping the problem of TLS connection authenticity. Rather than abandon connections to sites with invalid certificates, browsers display warnings and allow their users to click through. Studies of older browsers showed that many users ignored the warnings and exposed themselves to active attacks. Modern certificate warnings are more robust, but some users will still click through.

**Mixed content issues**

Another possible point of failure is allowing insecure (plaintext) resources to participate in the building of an otherwise encrypted page. Historically, this used to be a much bigger problem because browsers would allow so-called active content (e.g., JavaScript) to be retrieved insecurely. More recently, improvements have been made, but passive mixed content (e.g., images and videos) is still possible in some browsers.

**Cookie security issues**

There are a variety of problems related to cookie security. For example, a common implementation error is to forget to indicate that a cookie should be secure. If that happens, even when a web site is available only under TLS, an active network attacker can tease the cookies out from the victim's browser. Other problems may enable active network attackers to inject cookies into an otherwise secure application.

When HSTS is deployed on a web site, it addresses all of these issues via two mechanisms: (1) plaintext URLs are transparently rewritten to use encryption and (2) all certificate errors are considered final, with users not allowed to click through. In this way, HSTS significantly reduces the attack surface and makes the job of secure web site deployment much easier.

HSTS has its origins in the work of Jackson and Barth, who, in 2008, designed Force-HTTPS,[2] a cookie-based mechanism to allow "sophisticated users to transparently retrofit security onto some insecure sites that support HTTPS." Along with their paper, they provided a proof of concept in the form of a Firefox extension.

> **Note**
>
> Although HSTS is today considered to be a best practice, there are other efforts to help us solve the same problem. One such effort is a new standard for *HTTPS DNS resource records*, which can be used for a variety of useful things, including communicating a preference for encrypted network communication over plaintext.[3]

---

[2] ForceHTTPS: Protecting High-Security Web Sites from Network Attacks [fsty.uk/t549] (Jackson and Barth, 2008)

[3] Service binding and parameter specification via the DNS [fsty.uk/t550] (dnsop WG, retrieved 22 August 2021)

Chapter 10: HSTS, CSP, and Pinning

# Configuring HSTS

Web sites that wish to support HSTS do so by emitting the Strict-Transport-Security header on all of their *encrypted* HTTP responses, like so:

    Strict-Transport-Security: max-age=300; includeSubDomains

Assuming that the TLS connection is error free, a compliant browser will activate HSTS for the duration of the retention period specified in the max-age parameter, in seconds. The includeSubDomains parameter indicates that HSTS should be enabled on the host that emitted the header and also on all its subdomains.

> ## Warning
>
> Before deploying HSTS with includeSubDomains enabled, determine if forcing browsers to use encryption on the entire domain name space might have negative consequences on other sites that share the name. If you're not solely responsible for the entire domain name, start a conversation about HSTS with your colleagues. For a stress-free deployment, follow the checklist I outline later in this chapter.

The specification requires user agents to ignore the HSTS header if it is seen on a plaintext connection or on a connection with certificate errors (this includes self-signed certificates). This behavior is intended to prevent *denial of service* (DoS) attacks against plaintext-only sites, which would otherwise be trivial to execute by an active network attacker. In addition, using HSTS on IP addresses is not permitted.

Production-quality HSTS policies usually specify much longer policy duration, certainly in excess of one year. In addition, the preload directive can be attached to give permissions for browser vendors to embed HSTS configuration in order to protect even the first user request to a web site.

    Strict-Transport-Security: max-age=31536000; includeSubDomains; preload

It is possible to revoke HSTS; to do so, set the max-age parameter to zero:

    Strict-Transport-Security: max-age=0

However, the revocation happens only when a browser (one that previously enabled HSTS for the site) visits the site again and updates its configuration. Thus, the success of revocation (and policy adjustment, for that matter) will depend on the frequency of user visits.

HSTS should be configured at the location that is closest to the user. For example, if your web sites are behind a reverse proxy or a web application firewall, configure HSTS and all your HTTP security headers there. In this case, actually, the best practice is to drop any security headers emitted by the origin web servers so that a single consistent policy can be enforced.

Otherwise, configure HSTS at the web server level, which maximizes the chances that all important HTTP responses are covered. Consult your web server's documentation about setting of response headers on error responses; some servers don't do this by default.

Configuring HSTS at the application level may also be good enough, although there are often some HTTP requests that applications don't see, such as redirections and static resources. Whatever location you choose, stick with it. Configuring policies in multiple locations generally only leads to increased maintenance load and inconsistencies over time.

## Ensuring Hostname Coverage

By default, HSTS is enabled only on the hostname that emits the `Strict-Transport-Security` response header. Sites that are deployed across more than one hostname (e.g., *store.example.com* and *accounts.example.com*) should therefore take care to activate HSTS on all of them. Otherwise, it might happen that some users, who visit some hosts but not the ones with the HSTS instructions, are left unprotected.

Some applications use *domain cookies*, which are set on the bare or apex domain name (e.g., *example.com*) and can be used by any subdomain. This technique is typically used with sites that are spread across multiple hostnames but require unified authentication and session management. In this case, it is even more important to enable HSTS on all deployed hostnames, including the apex. You don't want to leave a loophole that might be exploited for attacks.

Even sites that use only one hostname need to consider this problem, because it is very likely that their users will sometimes access the site without the prefix (e.g., *example.com*) and sometimes with (e.g., *www.example.com*). Because we don't control inbound links, we have to take extra care when configuring HSTS and enable it on all hostnames.

> ### Warning
>
> A common mistake is to forget to configure HSTS on redirections. For example, even though your web site might use the hostname variant with the *www* prefix, some of your users might arrive via a link or bookmark that uses the apex (e.g., *example.com*). If you don't have HSTS configured on the apex, users who arrive that way will continue to be vulnerable to SSL stripping attacks, despite HSTS on the main domain name. For best results, enumerate all paths that lead to your web site, and ensure you have HSTS on all of them.

## Cookie Security

Because HSTS enforces encryption on all connections to a particular web site, you might think that even insecure cookies remain safe against an active network attacker. Unfortunately, the cookie specification is very permissive and creates opportunities for additional attack vectors, such as:

**Attacks via made-up hostnames**

Cookies are typically set for a particular hostname and all its subdomains. At the same time, an active network attacker can manipulate the DNS at will and create arbitrary hostnames under the same domain name as the target web site. Thus, if you set a cookie for *www.example.com*, the attacker can steal it by forcing and intercepting access to *madeup.www.example.com*. If the cookie is insecure, plaintext access will do. If the cookie is secure, the attacker can present a self-signed certificate and hope that the user will click through.

**Cookie injection**

The cookie specification historically doesn't use a separate namespace for secure cookies. What this means is that a cookie set from a plaintext connection can overwrite an existing secure cookie. In practice, this means that an active network attacker can inject arbitrary cookies into an otherwise secure application.

In the case of domain cookies, the attacker can inject a cookie from an existing sibling hostname (e.g., `blog.example.com`). Otherwise, an active network attacker can make up an arbitrary hostname and inject from it.

These problems can largely be mitigated with the use of the `includeSubDomains` parameter, which activates HSTS on the delivering hostname and all its subdomains. When domain cookies are used, the only secure approach is to activate HSTS on the apex domain name and thus on the entire domain namespace. Modern browsers continue to improve cookie security and add useful new features. As a result, cookie security has greatly improved in recent years. For more information, refer to the section called "Cookie Manipulation" in Chapter 6.

# Attacking HSTS

HSTS greatly improves our ability to secure web sites, but there are several edge cases that you need to be aware of. Consider the following situations.

**First access**

Because HSTS is activated via an HTTP response header, it does not provide security on the first access. This is not ideal, but the chances that the attacker will catch a victim on the first visit are usually small. The lack of security on the first access is mitigated by browsers embedding (or *preloading*) a list of sites that are known to support HSTS.

### HSTS cache eviction

The HSTS standard mandates that a policy is stored until expiration, but what actually happens is up to the client developers. For example, Firefox is known to limit the HSTS cache to only 1,024 entries, putting heavy users at risk.[4] Even worse, the addition of the HSTS cache partition led to an explosion of entries, quickly affecting most users until the problem was fixed in Firefox 91.[5]

### Short retention duration

HSTS works best when deployed with a long retention period (e.g., at least a year). That way, users are protected for the duration of their first session but also on their subsequent visits to the web site. If the retention period is short and the users don't visit again before it expires, their next access will not be protected.

### Clock attacks

Users whose computers are configured to automatically update their clocks using *Network Time Protocol* (NTP) without authentication could be exploited by a network attacker who can subvert the NTP messages. Setting the computer's clock to a time in the future will cause a site's HSTS policy to lapse, allowing the victim's next visit to be insecure. This attack is easier to carry out because browsers tend to limit maximum HSTS policy duration to about two years. In addition, browsers also often disable security mechanisms once too much time has passed, and a clock-attack may trigger that prematurely.

The danger of this attack vector depends on the NTP access frequency. This will typically be once or twice a day. According to research published in October 2014, operating systems range from easy to difficult to attack. Some, like Fedora, synchronize their clocks every minute, making them an easy target for the attacker. Others, like OS X, synchronize less frequently (minutes), but are still a relatively easy target. Windows seems the most secure of all; even though it too uses NTP without authentication, it synchronizes only once a week and has built-in defense measures to prevent very large time changes.[6]

### Response header injection

Response header injection is a web application vulnerability that enables the attacker to inject arbitrary response headers into the victim's traffic. If such a vulnerability is present in an application, an attacker can inject a forged `Strict-Transport-Security` header that disables HSTS. Against an application that does not use HSTS, this attack could be used to enable it and potentially execute a DoS attack.

---

[4] Breaking Out HSTS (and HPKP) on Firefox, IE/Edge and (possibly) Chrome [fsty.uk/t551] (Telefónica Tech, 11 December 2017)

[5] Analysis of HSTS Caches of Different Browsers [fsty.uk/t552] (Florian Bausch, 6 May 2021)

[6] Bypassing HTTP Strict Transport Security [fsty.uk/t553] (Jose Selvi, October 2014)

---

Chapter 10: HSTS, CSP, and Pinning

When this attack is delivered against an application that already uses HSTS, the outbound response headers will include two copies of the `Strict-Transport-Security` header. The attacker's header will be used if it ends up being first in the response.

**TLS truncation**

Although the TLS protocol is not vulnerable to truncation attacks, browsers' implementations may be. A skilled active network attacker can use a special technique to intercept a TLS connection and truncate it after the first digit of the `max-age` parameter. If successful, such an attack can reduce the HSTS duration to, at most, nine seconds. This is a *cookie cutter attack*, which I discuss in the section called "Cookie Cutting" in Chapter 7.

**Mixed content issues**

The designers of HSTS chose not to fully address mixed content issues, most likely because it's a hard problem and because browser vendors tend to have different ideas about dealing with it. As a result, HSTS includes only non-normative advice against allowing mixed content in Section 12.4 ("Disallow Mixed Security Context Loads").

Still, HSTS provides a partial solution because plaintext requests for the same hostname (where HSTS is active) are not allowed. To address third-party mixed content, deploy *Content Security Policy* (CSP), which can be used to allow only HTTPS requests from a given page.

**Hostname and port sharing**

HSTS is activated on an entire hostname and across all ports. This approach does not work very well in shared hosting situations in which multiple parties are able to control a site's response headers. In such situations, care should be taken to screen all responses to ensure that the correct HSTS header is sent (or that no HSTS header is sent at all).

# Browser Support

There is currently very good support for HSTS in desktop browsers thanks to early adoption by Chrome and Firefox in 2010 and 2011, respectively. Safari joined them with the OS X 10.9 release in late 2013. Internet Explorer 11 added support in June 2015 for Windows 7 and 8.1 platforms. Support for HSTS has since become effectively mandatory in all new browsers and even some command-line clients support it.

Most browsers ship with a list of sites that are known to support HSTS, and that allows them to make even the first connection to a site fully secure. Having an embedded store of web sites that are known to support HSTS also addresses a variety of other potential attacks. Initially, such lists were compiled manually or via remote scanning. After a while, Google started a central preload registration service called *hstspreload.org* for everyone to use.

Table 10.1. Browser support for HTTP Strict Transport Security

| Browser | HSTS Support | Since | Preloading |
|---|---|---|---|
| Chrome | Yes | v4.0.249.78; January 2010[a] | Yes |
| Firefox | Yes | v4; March 2011[b] | Yes (v17+) |
| Internet Explorer | Yes | v11 (Windows 7 and 8.1); June 2015[c] | Yes |
| Opera | Yes | v12 (Presto/2.10.239); June 2012[d] | Yes (v15+) |
| Safari | Yes | v7 (OS X 10.9 Mavericks); October 2013 | Yes |

[a] Stable Channel Update [fsty.uk/t554] (Chrome Releases blog, 25 January 2010)

[b] Firefox 4 release notes [fsty.uk/t555] (Mozilla, 22 March 2011)

[c] HTTP Strict Transport Security comes to Internet Explorer 11 on Windows 8.1 and Windows 7 [fsty.uk/t556] (Microsoft Edge Dev Blog, 9 June 2015)

[d] Web specifications support in Opera Presto 2.10 [fsty.uk/t557] (Opera, retrieved 19 April 2014)

# Deployment Checklist

Even though HSTS is relatively simple, deploying it can be challenging in complex environments. Unless you know exactly what you're dealing with and have full control, I recommend deploying HSTS via a series of small steps. The idea is to configure everything right from the start while using a very short policy duration value, making it possible to recover quickly in case of a problem.

To get started, follow these steps:

1. Compile a list of all domain names on which you will enable HSTS. It is crucial that your list includes all domain names exposed to your users, including those used only for redirections, for links from email messages, and such.

2. Enumerate all subdomains on all the domain names. This is best done by inspecting your DNS configuration (zone files), which is the definitive source of truth. Using the list, identify people and departments responsible for each web site and talk to them; build a consensus about your move to HSTS before any changes are made.

3. Plan how you're going to monitor the progress of your deployment. Use whatever information you have at your disposal—for example, web site access logs, revenue information, that sort of thing. If you're dealing with web sites, there is an experimental technology called *Network Error Logging* (NEL) that can be used to collect failure reports from browsers. NEL can be enabled on apex domain names and activated across all domains.

4. Ensure that HTTPS is fully operational and correctly configured throughout.

5. Redirect all HTTP (port 80) traffic to HTTPS (port 443) while keeping the hostnames the same. This will ensure that your users always receive the HSTS instructions on their first visit. For best performance, use permanent redirection.

6. Deploy the HSTS configuration on all intended hosts using a short duration period, such as 300 seconds. This will allow you to recover quickly if you forget to upgrade an important plaintext-only site. The `includeSubDomains` directive should also be set. Do not use the `preload` directive at this time; you don't want someone to jump the gun and preload your web sites before you're ready.

7. For extra points, modify your web sites that are not hosted at the apex domain names (e.g., *blog.example.com*) so that they reference at least one resource hosted at the apex domain name. This will ensure that HSTS is fully enabled on the entire domain namespace, even if your users never visit the apex domain name directly.

At this point, most of the hard work is hopefully behind you. Now it's time to monitor the situation carefully to see if something breaks.

After a period of time, when you establish that your deployment is progressing well, start to increase the policy retention duration. It's best to do this slowly, from minutes to hours, then days, then weeks. At some point, when you're ready to commit, move to preload all your domain names:

1. Increase the policy retention duration to a long-term value—for example, 12 months (about 31,536,000 seconds). This is usually long enough to give you good protection and it satisfies the preloading requirements.

2. Add the `preload` directive to your configuration on all domains in order to give permission for preloading.

3. Finally, submit your domain names for preloading at *hstspreload.org*.

## What If You Can't Activate HSTS on the Entire Domain Name?

For best results, HSTS should be enabled on the main domain name and all its subdomains. Unfortunately, this might not always be possible. Especially if you're working with a large existing infrastructure, it might be some time until you are able to migrate all the services to HTTPS.

When you can't do everything, do what you can. Even the worst HSTS configuration is better than none. Further, if your web site is deployed on a hostname with a *www* prefix, it should be safe to use `includeSubDomains`. There are usually no further subdomains from that name, but enabling HSTS on the theoretical subdomains usually improves cookie security.

Still, tread carefully. Because HSTS policies do not include the names of the hostnames to which they apply, it's possible to inadvertently activate HSTS from the wrong place. A misguided attempt to do good by one of your developers can have serious consequences. This type of problem is best prevented with a reverse proxy where all policies can be enforced centrally.

When deploying HSTS without any subdomain coverage, the risks described in the section called "Cookie Security" apply.

## Privacy Implications

The nature of HSTS dictates that browsers use a persistent store to keep track of the HSTS sites they visit. When a user encounters an HSTS site for the first time, an entry is added to the browser's HSTS database. This fact makes it possible to test if someone has visited a particular site before—just ask them to follow a plaintext link to the site. If they visit the link, they had never been to that site before. However, if they had visited that site before, HSTS will kick in, rewrite the link, and redirect the browser to the HTTPS variant instead.

In essence, a HSTS policy can be used to store one bit of information in a browser. One bit does not sound like much, but, when used with a wildcard certificate, an adversary could create as many different hostnames as they needed, each with a separate HSTS policy, and each carrying one bit of information.[7]

This is not an easy problem to fix, but browsers are aware of this weakness and are improving mitigation techniques over time.[8]

## Content Security Policy

*Content Security Policy* (CSP) is a declarative security mechanism that allows web site operators to control the behavior of compliant user agents (typically browsers). By controlling what features are enabled and where content is downloaded from, web sites can reduce their attack surface.

The main goal of CSP is defense against *Cross-Site Scripting* (XSS) attacks. For example, CSP can be used to completely disable inline JavaScript and control where external code is loaded from. It can also disable dynamic code evaluation. With all of those attack vectors disabled, attacking with XSS becomes much more difficult. Because this book is not about XSS, we're going to focus only on the features that can improve how web sites deploy encryption. In particular, we're interested in the aspects of CSP that enable us to prevent loading of plaintext resources.

CSP originated at Mozilla, which experimented with the concept over several years, first calling it *content restrictions*[9] and later Content Security Policy.[10] The first version of CSP

---

[7] The Double-Edged Sword of HSTS Persistence and Privacy [fsty.uk/t558] (Leviathan Security Group, 4 April 2012)

[8] Privacy-preserving HSTS [fsty.uk/t559] (WHATWG / Fetch, retrieved 22 August 2021)

[9] Content Restrictions [fsty.uk/t560] (Gervase Markham, last update 20 March 2007)

[10] Content Security Policy [fsty.uk/t561] (Mozilla's CSP Archive, last updated in 2011)

---

was released in November 2012 and has continued to evolve since; it's currently in its third incarnation.[11]

A web site that wishes to enable CSP sets the desired policy by using the Content-Security-Policy response header. Actually, it's possible to specify multiple policy headers and also embed policies in the HTML. Browsers evaluate each policy separately.[12] To give you an idea of what policies look like, consider this example adapted from the specification:

```
Content-Security-Policy: default-src 'self'; img-src *;
                         object-src *.cdn.example.com;
                         script-src scripts.example.com
```

This policy allows resources to be loaded only from the page's own origin by default, but allows images to be loaded from any URI, plug-in content only from the specified CDN addresses, and external scripts only from *scripts.example.com*.

Unlike with HSTS, CSP policies are not persistent; they're used only on the pages that reference them and are then promptly forgotten. Thus, CSP is much less risky to use. If an error is made, the policy can be updated with immediate effect. There is also no danger of persistent denial of service attacks stemming from injected response headers.

## Preventing Mixed Content Issues

Mixed content issues arise when a secure web page relies on resources (e.g., images and scripts) that are retrieved over plaintext connections. Browsers improved their handling of this problem in recent years, but their approach is generally still lax. For example, browsers tend to allow *passive mixed content*, typically images. Not unexpectedly, there are also differences in the handling among browsers. You'll find a detailed discussion of mixed content issues in the section called "Mixed Content" in Chapter 6.

Because CSP enables us to control where content comes from, we can use it to instruct compliant browsers to use only secure protocols. With modern browsers, this is as simple as this:

```
Content-Security-Policy: upgrade-insecure-requests
```

If you come across a recommendation to use block-all-mixed-content, that approach may also work, but this extension has been deprecated and may be removed in the future.

---

[11] Content Security Policy Level 3 [fsty.uk/t562] (W3C Working Draft, retrieved 22 August 2021)

[12] You might see other header names mentioned in blog posts, for example, X-Content-Security-Policy and X-Webkit-CSP. Those headers were used in the early days of CSP, when the functionality was largely experimental. The only header name relevant today is the official one.

**Note**

As always, when deploying a new security feature, it's a good idea to first try it in a report-only policy. This is especially easy with CSP, which supports multiple policies on the same page. If you already have one main enforcing configuration, you can add new features in a separate report-only policy. In this way you'll receive violation reports for every plaintext link browsers encounter on your site.

The old-fashioned way to use CSP to address mixed content issues is to craft policies that only allow encrypted protocols. This approach takes more effort, but it works with older browsers. Consider the following CSP policy as a starting point:

```
Content-Security-Policy: default-src https: 'unsafe-inline' 'unsafe-eval';
                         connect-src https: wss:
```

The policy includes three main elements:

- The `default-src` directive establishes that the page can load content from anywhere (any host and any port), provided it's done securely (`https` or `wss`).

- The `'unsafe-inline'` and `'unsafe-eval'` expressions re-enable inline JavaScript and dynamic code evaluation, which are disabled by default by CSP. Ideally, you wouldn't want to have these expressions in a policy, but without them most existing applications break.

- The `connect-src` directive controls content locations used by script interfaces, such as XMLHttpRequest, WebSockets, EventSource, and so on.

Once you establish that this initial policy is working for you, consider tightening JavaScript execution (by removing the `'unsafe-inline'` and `'unsafe-eval'` expressions) and replacing generic source restrictions with more specific hosts (e.g., `https://cdn.example.com` instead of `https:`).

In addition to preventing mixed content, you may also be interested in preventing the page from submitting forms to plaintext URLs; this can be achieved using the `form-action` directive:

```
Content-Security-Policy: form-action https:
```

# Policy Testing

A nice thing about CSP is that it is able to enforce one policy while testing others in parallel. This means that you are even able to deploy testing policies in production, which tend to be much more complex than development environments.

The `Content-Security-Policy-Report-Only` response header can be used to create a test policy:

```
Content-Security-Policy-Report-Only: default-src 'self'
```

If a report-only policy fails, nothing is blocked, but reporting should be configured so that the failure can be communicated back to the originating web site.

## Reporting

The reporting feature of CSP makes it possible to monitor the performance of your policies and receive real-time reports on any issues that arise. This feature, which makes development much easier, is also very comforting because it helps you know that your efforts to secure your web sites didn't actually break anything.

To enable reporting, use the `report-uri` directive:

```
Content-Security-Policy: default-src 'self';
                         report-uri http://example.org/csp-report.cgi
```

With that, CSP policy violations will be submitted to the specified URI, using the POST request method and the report data in the request body. For example:

```
{
  "csp-report": {
    "document-uri": "http://example.org/page.html",
    "referrer": "http://evil.example.com/haxor.html",
    "blocked-uri": "http://evil.example.com/image.png",
    "violated-directive": "default-src 'self'",
    "original-policy": "default-src 'self'; report-uri http://example.org↵
/csp-report.cgi"
  }
}
```

## Pinning

*Pinning* is a security technique that can be used to associate a service with one or more cryptographic identities—for example, certificates and public keys. The best way to think about it is as two-factor authentication: you rely on some primary mechanism for security, but you want to do just a little bit better than that. Take public certificates, for example. Because it is difficult to establish trust among parties that haven't met, especially when their numbers are in the billions, we use third parties as intermediaries.

This evidently works very well, but, you lose some control in the process. Pinning, when done well, can be used to get some of that control back. But it is a controversial technique because it's difficult to get right and easy to break things in the process. Let's take a better look at some of its advantages and disadvantages.

### Attack surface reduction

The dominant TLS authentication model in use today relies on public CAs, whose job is to issue certificates to domain name owners but not to other random people. In turn, user agents trust all CA-issued certificates unconditionally. Traditionally, this model suffered from an enormous flaw, which is that a domain owner's authorization is not required for certificate issuance. As a consequence, any CA can issue a certificate for any domain name. Given that there are hundreds of CAs and possibly thousands of entities who influence certificate issuance in one way or another, the attack surface is huge. Today, we have *Certification Authority Authorization* (CAA), but it's an operational control that certificates have to implement and not something that's technically enforced.

With pinning, owners can use cryptographic pins for public key material they control, ensuring that even any fraudulent certificates can still be distinguished from the genuine (endorsed) certificates. This security improvement also works against other attack vectors that enable attackers to get valid certificates—for example, BGP and DNS hijacking.

### Defense against reverse engineering

If you're developing native applications that communicate with some backend, you often don't want to make it easy for others to look at the traffic that's leaving the application. If a custom root certificate is added to a device (e.g., after jailbreaking), the communication with your backend can be intercepted and captured. With pinning in place, your application can distinguish interception certificates from your own, thus making reverse engineering of your APIs more difficult.

There are other useful applications for pinning outside the main use cases. For example, the SSH protocol creates a pin for a server's key when it encounters it for the first time. This approach is known as *trust on first use* (TOFU). Similarly, DANE (discussed later in this chapter) supports a variety of pinning approaches and can even be used for authentication when DNSSEC is already in place.

## Should You Use Pinning?

Pinning is a powerful technique for attack surface reduction, but it does not come for free. To deploy it you need a good understanding of the tradeoffs, and a mature organization that can deal with the operational challenges. The obvious problem is that pinning ensures that TLS connections are established only to the pinned identities. What happens if you lose those identities, for whatever reason?

The fear of the self-inflicted denial of service is possibly the reason that pinning has been slow to take off. Simply said, for most, the disadvantages outweigh the advantages. However, if you believe that you might be attacked via a fraudulently issued certificate (e.g., you're running a high-profile web site), then pinning is the only way to defend yourself. For everyone else, it's probably not worth the effort.

In addition, there's a strong case to make for techniques that provide similar security benefits but are easier to deploy. In particular, when you control both the client and server ends, you don't actually have to resort to pinning to increase your security. You can use one of the following two easier approaches instead.

**Private CA infrastructure**

If your clients will ever only talk to your own backends, it's conceptually easy to avoid public certificates altogether. Instead, you can create your own private CAs and issue your own certificates. With this approach, it's your PKI, and you will have full control. There won't be a danger that public certificates will be mistaken for yours (because you won't trust any of them) and, as a bonus, you will be insulated from whatever changes are happening in the public PKI space.

This option used to be much more difficult in the past, when you had to manage your own private CAs. These days, the major cloud providers such as AWS and GCP provide affordable private CA services. A robust approach would be to run one private CA in each of these, plus create a third private CA in-house for disaster recovery purposes.

**DNSSEC and DANE**

If you're already using DNSSEC or if you don't fall into the camp that strongly opposes it, DANE comes with comprehensive pinning support. In this case, in fact, you don't even need to create public CAs; you can just generate some self-signed certificates and endorse them via DNS. You may still want to use a private CA so that you are able to create a stable set of intermediaries and reusable pins. The advantage of this approach is that if any problems arise, you can recover from them simply by updating your DNS infrastructure.

If you choose to pursue this direction, you will need to resolve DNSSEC yourself. In fact, the best approach would be to bypass any DNS resolution at all and instead use your own *DNS over HTTP* (DoH) or *DNS over TLS* (DoT) resolvers.

In the end, the question is not whether you need pinning, but whether you have sufficient security. If you do, you don't need to pin. Otherwise, a small operation may use certificates issued from a private CA, but if your team is a part of a large organization, pinning may make sense so that the attack surface is reduced. It's the same with DNSSEC and DANE; you can use it with public and private infrastructures alike. I would recommend that you prototype a variety of threat models, from least secure to the most secure, understand all of them, and then decide.

# What to Pin?

Pinning can be used with several cryptographic elements; the usual candidates are certificates and public keys. For example, one approach is to keep a list of one or more certificates you expect to see for a particular site; every time you visit the site, you compare the certificate you get against your stored list. With this approach, fraudulent certificates are easily detected. Because certificates don't change, it is even easier to keep track of them via their hashes (e.g., SHA256), which are much easier to handle.

In practice, public key pinning may be more practical because it's possible to get a new certificate with the same public key. This may be useful, for example, if your CA is forced to revoke its certificate for whatever reason. If you pinned to the server's public key, the new certificate will just work. Protocols that do not rely on certificates have to pin to public keys.

When it comes to TLS and X.509 certificates, pinning is commonly done using the SubjectPublicKeyInfo (SPKI) field.[13] This field contains the public key itself, as well as additional metadata that identifies the algorithm:

```
SubjectPublicKeyInfo  ::=  SEQUENCE  {
    algorithm           AlgorithmIdentifier,
    subjectPublicKey    BIT STRING  }
```

If you want to examine the contents of the SPKI field for a given certificate, use this command:

```
$ openssl x509 -in server.crt -noout -text
[...]
Subject Public Key Info:
            Public Key Algorithm: rsaEncryption
                Public-Key: (2048 bit)
                Modulus:
                    00:b8:0e:05:25:f8:81:e9:e7:ba:21:40:5f:d7:d4:
                    09:5c:8c:d4:e9:44:e7:c0:04:5b:7f:6e:16:8a:01:
                    37:2b:b9:ed:b6:09:cd:1f:55:d5:b8:ee:79:13:ae:
                    e7:1d:6a:ec:01:7c:02:5a:10:af:f9:68:28:ff:d5:
                    61:b0:37:f8:a6:b2:87:42:90:3c:70:19:40:67:49:
                    99:1d:3c:44:3e:16:4e:9a:06:e4:06:66:36:2f:23:
                    39:16:91:cf:92:56:57:1d:30:db:71:5a:68:a2:c3:
                    d5:07:23:e4:90:8e:9e:fb:97:ad:89:d5:31:3f:c6:
                    32:d0:04:17:5c:80:9b:0c:6d:9b:2a:b2:f9:39:ac:
                    85:75:84:82:64:23:9a:7d:c4:96:57:1e:7b:bf:27:
                    2e:48:2d:9e:74:90:32:c1:d8:91:54:12:af:5a:bb:
                    01:20:15:0e:ff:7b:57:83:9d:c2:fe:59:ce:ea:22:
                    6b:77:75:27:01:25:17:e1:41:31:4c:7f:a8:eb:0e:
                    8c:b9:18:b2:9a:cc:74:5e:36:1f:8f:a1:f4:71:a9:
```

---

[13] More information on the structure of X.509 certificates is available in the section called "Certificates" in Chapter 4.

```
                ff:72:e6:a0:91:f0:90:b2:5a:06:57:79:b6:1e:97:
                98:6b:5c:3a:a9:6a:be:84:bc:86:75:cb:81:6d:28:
                68:c0:e5:d5:3e:c5:f0:7d:85:27:ae:ce:7a:b7:41:
                ce:f9
        Exponent: 65537 (0x10001)
```

To generate a SPKI hash, first extract the field from the certificate into its own file:

```
$ openssl x509 -in server.crt -noout -pubkey | \
    openssl asn1parse -inform PEM -noout -out server.spki
```

You can then, for example, calculate a SHA256 hash of it and encode it using Base64 encoding:

```
$ openssl dgst -sha256 -binary server.spki | base64
zB8EXAKscl3P+4a5lFszGaEniLrNsw0Q1ZGwD+TzADg=
```

## Where to Pin?

So we know that we pin certificates or public keys, but where exactly? In PKI we deal with certificate chains, which means that we have a leaf, followed by one or more certificates, followed by a root. So we can have a discussion of which of these certificates we should pin. Many of these options are very tempting because, on the surface, they can make a complex job easier. But in fact, most of the options are traps that can lead to an unfortunate outcome.

So before we proceed, let's start with the first rule of pining: *only pin to the key material you control*. This one simple rule will save you from a ton of potential misery if you make the wrong decision.

A good example of following this rule is when you pin to server public keys. This approach gives you the best security because you have full control over the distribution of those keys. Sure, the servers are exposed on the public networks and the keys can be compromised, but that's why you'll have backup keys to recover.

However, pinning leaves is a hassle. They can be compromised, and it's also a good practice to continuously rotate your key material in order to start from a clean slate in case there had been a compromise you were not aware of.

For this reason, some architects start to look at pinning elsewhere in the chain. The thinking goes something like this. If we pin to the CA's intermediate, in the future we will be able to get a new server certificate with the same pin. We won't have to bother with pin rotation and so forth. If you're not sure about what intermediates to pin to, you can seemingly choose to pin to the CA's roots, in which all the certificates would work for you. Or would they? Consider the following problems:

---

### CAs own multiple roots

When you start to look into how PKI works, you will realize that CAs have many roots. These roots come and go, due to need, age, or acquisitions. If you want to pin to a CA, then you need to be absolutely sure that you know about all of its roots. To be fair, this has gotten a bit easier because of CT and CCADB, but it's still not straightforward.

### Cross-signing

Then we have the fact that CAs usually sign roots belonging to other CAs. These days, for example, it's the only way to start a new CA. What this means is that the chain you configure in your server may not necessarily be the chain that's used. If you pin one root, you may end up in a situation where clients decide to build a path to another root. To solve this problem you'll need to find all the alternative roots and pin them as well. In the end, you may end up allowing a large number of CAs.

### Inadequate path-building

In fact, the problem with path-building is that virtually all operating systems and libraries return one path they think will work. So there may be several working paths from their perspective, but only one from yours, with the pinning taken into account. To pin reliably, you need to implement your own path-building that's aware of the pinning constraints.

### Revocation

You should work under the assumption that any certificate can and will be revoked. This is the reality thanks to technical issues, security problems, or simply mistakes. There have been cases where CAs have mistakenly revoked their own perfectly fine intermediates, for example. Then there is the constant change in the PKI ecosystem where what is good today may not be considered such tomorrow. There was a point in the past when we thought that CAs were too important to fail, but, as the demise of Symantec showed, that's definitely not true.

All of this is not to say that it's impossible to get pinning elsewhere in the chain right. We know that there are a handful of organizations who are definitely using it. But those organizations have chosen to invest in the long-term activities of fully understanding all the aspects of pinning and staying on top of new developments. In the end, it's a sizable effort that makes pinning to server certificates small in comparison.

Even CAs don't want you to pin to their certificates. Historically, many of them have been burnt by the pinning mistakes made by their important customers, some of which were important elements of the security ecosystem. For example, an article from DigiCert explicitly tells its customers to avoid pinning.[14]

---

[14] Stop Certificate Pinning [fsty.uk/t563] (DigiCert, 22 July 2020)

---

Chapter 10: HSTS, CSP, and Pinning

On top of this, only pinning to server certificates gives you strong technical controls. If you pin to CAs, either via their intermediates or roots, you are de facto allowing them to issue certificates for your domain names. So you may not get as much security as you'd like.

## How to Pin

If the discussion about the challenges you may be facing with public key pinning hasn't scared you off, in this section I am going to outline a set of best practices that you should follow if you choose to proceed:

1. Start by building an inventory of application releases and embedded public key pins, as well as a telemetry platform that enables you to track what applications are still running. This step will give you the necessary situational awareness.

2. You really want to deploy only applications that can update both their trusted roots and the pins without requiring a full software update. Having a mechanism for this will enable you to react quickly and recover from small issues easily. Without an update mechanism you may be forever locked into using particular public keys (if your users don't update), which may end up being fatal in the case of a security compromise.

3. Similarly, you'll also want a reporting mechanism that will alert you about pinning failures.

4. Choose your redundancy number. For example, three is a good number. You could use two public CAs as well as one private CA. An update mechanism ensures you are not locked into any one CA.

5. Get all the certificates issued. Don't expect that you will be able to get a certificate issued at a time of need. There are many things that can go wrong with that approach, and chances are that some will. In fact, this is the second rule of pinning: you don't actually control the public key material unless you have a valid certificate attached to it.

6. Have only one set of public keys online, keeping the rest as backup.

7. Rotate the online keys frequently, promoting to backup keys online, and getting a new set of backups from the next CA in line. With this setup, if you issue a new set of certificates and public keys every six months, you will have three sets of keys at any point that you can use: former online, current online, and the backup.

8. Ensure that the pins are advertised and received by all your applications while leaving a healthy safety margin to account for those users who are not active all the time. Inevitably, connectivity from some users will fail, at which point you have two options: tell them to update to a later version or install an update of some sort or simply drop the pinning requirement for very old installations.

9. Monitor the health of all certificates so that you're able to replace them if they are revoked for any reason.

10. Implement the pinning logic in your applications. My advice would be to start slowly, first by checking the pins without enforcing them, and later by having a variety of safety measures you can invoke if things go wrong.

As you can see, there is an entire platform you'll need to build in order to support pinning. What people normally refer to as *pinning*—the actual checking on access if a certain certificate chain matches the expectations—is only a small part. Also, that part is usually supported in popular HTTP libraries and even on platforms. Android and iOS support pinning natively these days. Alternatively, use the open source TrustKit, which is available[15] for both platforms[16] and has the benefit of supporting reporting.

## Static Browser Public Key Pinning

Google started to experiment with public key pinning with Chrome 12,[17] when it shipped a user interface that allows for custom HSTS and pinning configuration.[18] Then, in Chrome 13, it added embedded pins for most of its own web sites.[19]

Behind the scenes, the same mechanism is used for both HSTS preloading and pinning; the required information is hardcoded in the browser itself. Because Chrome is based on the open source Chromium browser, the source file containing this information is available to view.[20]

The policy file contains a single JSON structure with two lists: (1) web sites that support HSTS or pinning and (2) *pinsets* to define acceptable public keys for them.

Each web site entry carries information about its HSTS configuration and the desired pinset:

```
{
    "name": "gmail.com",
    "policy": "google",
    "mode": "force-https",
    "pins": "google"
}
```

A pinset is a collection of allowed SPKI hashes; it uses the names of certificates that are not in the file but are shipped with the browser:

---

[15] TrustKit for iOS, macOS, tvOS, and watchOS [fsty.uk/t564] (Data Theorem, retrieved 25 August 2021)

[16] TrustKit for Android [fsty.uk/t565] (Data Theorem, retrieved 25 August 2021)

[17] New Chromium security features, June 2011 [fsty.uk/t566] (The Chromium Blog, 14 June 2011)

[18] The present versions of Chrome still include this user interface; it can be accessed via `chrome://net-internals/#hsts`.

[19] Public key pinning [fsty.uk/t567] (Adam Langley, 4 May 2011)

[20] `transport_security_state_static.json` [fsty.uk/t568] (Chromium source code, retrieved 25 August 2021)

---

```
{
    "name": "google",
    "static_spki_hashes": [
      "GoogleBackup2048",
      "GTSCA101",
      "GTSRootR1",
      "GTSRootR2",
      "GTSRootR3",
      "GTSRootR4",
      "GlobalSignRootCA_R2"
    ],
    "bad_static_spki_hashes": [
      "GlobalSignExtendedValidationCA",
      "GlobalSignExtendedValidationCA_G2",
      "GlobalSignExtendedValidationCA_SHA256_G2"
    ],
    "report_uri": "http://clients3.google.com/cert_upload_json"
}
```

This pinset approach supports allowed and disallowed pins; a certificate chain is accepted if it contains at least one desired public key and doesn't contain any public keys that are on the deny list.

As you can see, this all seems very straightforward. Chrome allows other organizations to use static pinning, and a handful of them do. If you peek in the configuration file, you will find several big names you know and even some you won't have heard about. The number of organizations using pinning is very small, in contrast to the tens of thousands using the less-dangerous HSTS.

### Warning

To allow users to intercept their own traffic, browsers never enforced pinning on certificates issued from manually added root certificates. On the one hand, this allows for local debugging (e.g., using local developer proxies) and content inspection by antivirus products; on the other, it also allows for transparent corporate traffic interception. It has been reported that some malware authors install custom certificates to perform active network attacks; such certificates would also bypass pin validation.[21]

Chrome includes a reporting mechanism that is used to report pin validation failures to Google. We know this because Chrome's pinning detected several PKI incidents involving creation of misissued certificates for Google's properties. You can read about these incidents in Chapter 5, *Attacks against PKI*. In the early days this mechanism was available only for

---

[21] New Man-in-the-Middle attacks leveraging rogue DNS [fsty.uk/t569] (Don Jackson, PhishLabs, 26 March 2014)

Google's own use, but it's now available to everyone via the optional `report_uri` property in the JSON file.

Firefox 32, released in September 2014, added support for hardcoded public key pinning, which is similar to the mechanism already used in Chrome.[22] Firefox on Android added support for this type of pinning in version 34. Static pinning is also known to be supported in Microsoft's new Edge browser based on Chromium.

## Microsoft's Enterprise Certificate Pinning

In 2017, Windows 10 received an update that enabled *Enterprise Certificate Pinning*. Organizations can use this new feature to create their own pinning rules and push them, via group policies, to all their users. The capabilities of this tool are what you would expect, enabling pinning, logging, and different remediation policies.[23] The main advantage of this approach is the flexibility to update the rules as needed. The downside, of course, is that the pinning protects only Windows 10 users. However, even with a diverse user base, the flexibility of the deployment can allow an organization to experiment with public key pinning (e.g., using logging only) before deploying to browsers.

## Public Key Pinning Extension for HTTP

*Public Key Pinning Extension for HTTP* (HPKP)[24] is a standard for public key pinning for HTTP user agents. This work came out of Google's own pinning efforts in Chrome, chiefly because manually maintaining a list of pinned sites (as Google currently does for the Chrome browser) doesn't scale. Unfortunately, even though HPKP eventually made it into Chrome and Firefox, browser vendors reversed direction and removed support. Chrome led the way in late 2017.[25] At the time of writing, HPKP is dead and there are no signs that the situation will change.

The signs about the imminent death of HPKP were obvious pretty much straightaway; I wrote about it in as early as 2016.[26] The outcome was the result of several factors:

**HPKP is very low level**

> With HPKP you could deploy any type of pinning you wanted—for example, choosing the number of active and backup pins and choosing whether to pin to the leaf certificates or any of the intermediates or root CAs. This approach is great for those who understand PKI well and know what they're doing. However, it turns out that

---

[22] Public key pinning released in Firefox [fsty.uk/t570] (Mozilla Security blog, 2 September 2014)

[23] Enterprise Certificate Pinning [fsty.uk/t571] (Microsoft Windows IT Center, May 2017)

[24] RFC 7469: Public Key Pinning Extension for HTTP [fsty.uk/t572] (Evans et al., April 2015)

[25] Intent to Deprecate and Remove: Public Key Pinning [fsty.uk/t573] (Chris Palmer, 27 October 2017)

[26] Is HTTP Public Key Pinning Dead? [fsty.uk/t574] (Ivan Ristić, 6 September 2016)

making it easy to pin allowed even those who didn't want to put the required level of thought into it to use it. As a result, many people started to get it wrong.

**No recovery**

Unusually, HPKP ended up without any sort of safety net in case of botched pinning. This meant that all those people who got it wrong and bricked their web sites couldn't do anything to recover. The only way out was waiting for the policies to expire.

**Easy to activate**

To make things worse, HPKP was very easy to activate. At first thought this may come across as good, but in fact it opened the door to what is now usually referred to as the RansomPKP attack:[27] someone could break into your servers or otherwise compromise your infrastructure to configure pins that you don't have access to. The only way to restore access to your web sites would be to pay the attackers a ransom and get the public keys from them.

It didn't have to be this way. Even with the poor first specification, HPKP could have been saved. For example, a revocation mechanism could have been added.[28] Additional measures could have been taken to ensure that activation is delayed or restricted in some other way.[29] Unfortunately, that was a direction browser vendors didn't want to take. For them, there was no upside, only downsides. And that was the end of HPKP.

## Configuring HPKP

HPKP is conceptually very similar to HSTS. If you haven't already read the section on HSTS, I propose that you do so now for a longer discussion of various positives and negatives inherent in the approach. Otherwise, here's a quick overview of the common features:

- HPKP is set at the HTTP level, using the Public-Key-Pins (PKP) response header.

- Policy retention period is set with the max-age parameter, which specifies duration in seconds.

- Pinning can be extended to subdomains if the includeSubDomains parameter is used.

- The PKP header can be used only over a secure encryption without any errors; if multiple headers are seen, only the first one is processed.

- When a new PKP header is received, the information in it overwrites previously stored pins and metadata.

Pins are created by specifying the hashing algorithm and an SPKI fingerprint computed using that algorithm. For example:

---

[27] Abusing Bleeding Edge Web Standards for AppSec Glory [fsty.uk/t575] (Zadegan and Lester, 3 August 2016)

[28] Fixing HPKP with Pin Revocation [fsty.uk/t576] (Ivan Ristić, 5 September 2017)

[29] Fixing HPKP with Certificate Constraints [fsty.uk/t577] (Ivan Ristić, 19 September 2017)

---

```
Public-Key-Pins: max-age=2592000;
        pin-sha256="E9CZ9INDbd+2eRQozYqqbQ2yXLVKB9+xcprMF+44U1g=";
        pin-sha256="LPJNul+wow4m6DsqxbninhsWHlwfpOJecwQzYpOLmCQ="
```

The only hashing algorithm supported at the moment is SHA256; the sha256 identifier is used when configuring the pins. The fingerprints are encoded using Base64 encoding.

To enable pinning, you must specify the policy retention period and provide at least two pins. One of the pins must be present in the chain used for the connection over which the pins were received. The other pin *must not* be present. Because pinning is a potentially dangerous operation (it's easy to make a mistake and perform a self-inflicted denial of service attack), the second pin is required as a backup. The recommended practice was to have a backup certificate from a different CA and to keep it offline, with periodic testing and rotation. The idea was to make sure that the backup certificate worked when you needed it the most.

## Reporting

Unlike HSTS, but similarly to CSP, HPKP specifies a mechanism for user agents to report pin-validation failures. This feature is activated using the report-uri parameter, which should contain the endpoint to which the report will be submitted.

```
Public-Key-Pins: max-age=2592000;
        pin-sha256="E9CZ9INDbd+2eRQozYqqbQ2yXLVKB9+xcprMF+44U1g=";
        pin-sha256="LPJNul+wow4m6DsqxbninhsWHlwfpOJecwQzYpOLmCQ=";
        report-uri="http://example.com/pkp-report"
```

The report is submitted using a POST HTTP request, which includes a JSON structure in the request body. For example (taken from a draft version of the HPKP specification):

```
{
  "date-time": "2014-04-06T13:00:50Z",
  "hostname": "www.example.com",
  "port": 443,
  "effective-expiration-date": "2014-05-01T12:40:50Z"
  "include-subdomains": false,
  "served-certificate-chain": [
    "-----BEGIN CERTIFICATE-----\n
    MIIEBDCCAuygAwIBAgIDAjppMAOGCSqGSIb3DQEBBQUAMEIxCzAJBgNVBAYTAlVT\n
    ...
    HFa9llF7b1cq26KqltyMdMKVvvBulRP/F/A8rLIQjcxz++iPAsbw+zOzlTvjwsto\n
    WHPbqCRiOwY1nQ2pM714A5AuTHhdUDqB1O6gyHA43LL5Z/qHQF1hwFGPa4NrzQU6\n
    yuGnBXj8ytqUOCwIPX4WecigUCAkVDNx\n
    -----END CERTIFICATE-----",
    ...
  ],
```

```
"validated-certificate-chain": [
  "-----BEGIN CERTIFICATE-----\n
  MIIEBDCCAuygAwIBAgIDAjppMAOGCSqGSIb3DQEBBQUAMEIxCzAJBgNVBAYTAlVT\n
  ...
  HFa9llF7b1cq26KqltyMdMKVvvBulRP/F/A8rLIQjcxz++iPAsbw+zOzlTvjwsto\n
  WHPbqCRiOwY1nQ2pM714A5AuTHhdUDqB1O6gyHA43LL5Z/qHQF1hwFGPa4NrzQU6\n
  yuGnBXj8ytqUoCwIPX4WecigUCAkVDNx\n
  -----END CERTIFICATE-----",
  ...
],
"known-pins": [
  "pin-sha256=\"d6qzRu9zOECb9OUez27xWltNsjOe1Md7GkYYkVoZWmM=\"",
  "pin-sha256=\"E9CZ9INDbd+2eRQozYqqbQ2yXLVKB9+xcprMF+44U1g=\""
]
}
```

## Deployment without Enforcement

Reports are especially useful when HPKP is deployed without enforcement. This can be achieved using the Public-Key-Pins-Report-Only response header. This approach allows organizations to deploy pinning without fear of failure, ensure that it is configured correctly, and only later move to enforcement. Depending on their risk profile, some organizations would choose to never enable enforcement; knowing that you are being attacked is often as useful as preventing the attack.

# DANE

*DNS-based Authentication of Named Entities* (DANE)[30] is a standard that can be used to associate a domain name with one or more cryptographic identities. The idea is that domain name owners, who already have control over their DNS configuration, can use the DNS infrastructure to distribute information needed for robust TLS authentication. DANE is straightforward and relatively easy to deploy but is not complete by itself. Instead, it assumes and builds upon DNS integrity provided by DNSSEC (*Domain Name System Security Extensions*).

DNSSEC extends the standard DNS, which does not provide transport security, with an architecture that supports authentication using digital signatures. With authentication in place, it's possible to cryptographically verify that the DNS information we obtain came from the domain owner. DNSSEC is quite controversial. It's been in development for more than a decade, and its adoption has been slow, with strong opinions from people who see it as an important next step, as well as those who have already decided that it's a dead end.

---

[30] RFC 6698: The DNS-Based Authentication of Named Entities (DANE) Transport Layer Security (TLS) Protocol: TLSA [fsty.uk/t578] (Hoffman and Schlyter, August 2012)

---

Today, it's generally possible to deploy DNSSEC with DANE to secure server-to-server communication (e.g., SMTP), but there is very little, if any, client-side support. Of the major browsers, Chrome experimented with DANE back in 2011 (in Chrome 14) but eventually removed support, citing lack of use.[31] Clearly, browsers not wanting to adopt DNSSEC is a major obstacle to wider adoption. On the technical side, DNSSEC also faces a problem in that it requires client resolvers that understand it, as well as middleboxes that allow the additional DNS resource records it needs to pass through. In the context of TLS, one possibility is to use a special protocol extension to carry DNSSEC information, which would enable authentication to take place even if a full transport infrastructure is not in place. After years of discussions, an experimental RFC for that was released in August 2021.[32]

## DANE Use Cases

In our current model for TLS authentication, we rely on a two-step approach: (1) first we have a group of certification authorities that we trust to issue certificates only to authorized parties (e.g., domain name owners), then, whenever a site is accessed, (2) user agents (e.g., browsers) check that the certificates are correct for the intended names. This split model is required because authentication of distant parties (e.g., people who have never met) is very tricky to get right, especially at scale. With a set of trusted intermediaries, the complexities are manageable. This system is designed under the assumption that the information obtained by end users from the DNS cannot be trusted; this is the active network attacker threat model.

With DNSSEC, we get a communication channel that ensures that the information we receive comes from domain name owners; this means that we don't necessarily need third parties (CAs) to vouch for them any more. This opens up several interesting use cases:

**Secure deployment of self-signed certificates**
Self-signed certificates are insecure because there is no way for a user to differentiate them from self-signed certificates that an active network attacker might use. In other words, all self-signed certificates look the same. But we can use a secure DNS to pin the certificate, thus allowing user agents to trust the right self-signed certificates and reject others.

**Secure deployment of private roots**
If you can securely pin the server certificate, then you can just as well pin any other certificate in the chain. That means that you can create your own root certificate and make users agents trust it—but only for the sites you own. This is a variation of the previous use case and largely of interest to those who have many sites. Rather than

---

[31] DNSSEC authenticated HTTPS in Chrome [fsty.uk/t579] (Adam Langley, 16 June 2011)
[32] RFC 9102: TLS DNSSEC Chain Extension [fsty.uk/t580] (Dukhovni et al., August 2021)

pin individual certificates (of which there are many, and they need to be frequently rotated), you create one root and pin it only once on all sites.

**Certificate and public key pinning**

DANE is not necessarily about displacing the current trust architecture. You can as easily pin CA-issued certificates and public CA roots. By doing this, you will be reducing the attack surface and effectively deciding which CAs are allowed to issue certificates for your properties.

# Implementation

DANE introduces a new DNS entry type, called *TLSA Resource Record* (TLSA RR, or just TLSA), which is used to carry certificate associations. TLSA consists of four fields: (1) *Certificate Usage* to specify which part of a certificate chain should be pinned and how the validation should be performed; (2) a *Selector* to specify what element is used for pinning; (3) a *Matching Type* to choose between an exact match or hashing; and (4) *Certificate Association Data*, which carries the actual raw data used for matching. Different combinations of these four fields are used to deploy different pinning types.

## Certificate Usage

The *Certificate Usage* field can have four different values. In the original RFC, the values are simply digits from 0 to 3. A subsequent RFC added acronyms to make it easier to remember the correct values.[33]

**CA constraint (0; PKIX-TA)**

Creates a pin for a CA, whose matching certificate must be found anywhere in the chain. PKIX validation is performed as usual, and the root must come from a trusted CA.

**Service certificate constraint (1; PKIX-EE)**

Creates an end-entity pin, whose certificate must be presented at the first position in the chain. PKIX validation is performed as usual, and the root must come from a trusted CA.

**Trust anchor assertion (2; DANE-TA)**

Creates a trust anchor pin for a CA certificate (root or intermediate) that must be present in the trust chain. PKIX validation is performed as usual, but user agents must trust the pinned CA certificate. This option allows for certificates that are not issued by public CAs.

---

[33] RFC 7218: Adding Acronyms to Simplify Conversations about DANE [fsty.uk/t581] (Gudmundsson, April 2014)

**Domain-issued certificate (3; DANE-EE)**

Creates an end-entity pin, whose certificate must be presented at the first position in the chain. There is no PKIX validation, and the pinned certificate is assumed to be trusted.

## Selector

The *Selector* field specifies how the association is presented. This allows us to create an association with a certificate (0; Cert) or with the SubjectPublicKeyInfo field (1; SPKI).

## Matching Type

The *Matching Type* field specifies if the matching is by direct comparison (0; Full) or via hashing (1 and 2, meaning SHA2-256 and SHA2-512, respectively). Support for SHA256 is required; support for SHA512 is recommended. Although direct comparison is supported, matching using hashing is the preferred approach. Hashes take up much less space than certificates.

## Certificate Association Data

The *Certificate Association Data* field contains the raw data that is used for the association. Its contents are determined by the values of the other three fields in the TLSA record. The certificate, which is always the starting point of an association, is assumed to be in DER format.

# Deployment

Leaving DNSSEC configuration and signing aside (only because it is out of scope of this book), DANE is pretty easy to deploy. All you need to do is add a new TLSA record under the correct name. The name is not just the domain name you wish to secure; it's a combination of three segments separated by dots:

- The first segment is the port on which the service is running, prefixed with an underscore. For example, _443 for HTTPS and _25 for SMTP.

- The second segment is the protocol, also prefixed with an underscore. Three protocols are supported: UDP, TCP, and SCTP. For HTTPS, the segment will be _tcp.

- The third segment is the fully qualified domain name for which you wish to create an association. For example, www.example.com.

In the following example, an association is created between a domain name and the public key of a CA (Certificate Usage is 0), identified by the SubjectPublicKeyInfo field (Selector is 1) via its hex-encoded SHA256 hash (Matching Type is 1):

```
_443._tcp.www.example.com. IN TLSA (
    0 1 1 d2abde240d7cd3ee6b4b28c54df034b9
          7983a1d16e8a410e4561cb106618e971 )
```

DANE is activated by adding one or more TLSA records to the desired domain name. If at least one association is present, user agents are required to establish a match; otherwise they must abort the TLS handshake. If there are no associations, then the user agent can process the TLS connection as it would normally.

Because multiple associations (TLSA records) can be configured for a domain name, it's possible to have one or more backup associations. It's also possible to rotate associations without any downtime. Unlike other pinning techniques, DANE does not specify a memory effect, but there is one built into DNS itself: the *time to live* (TTL) value, which is the duration for which a record can be cached. The lack of explicit memory effect is DANE's strength; mistakes are easy to correct by reconfiguring DNS. When deploying, especially initially, it's best to use the shortest TTL possible.

In recent years, there has been a push toward automation of certificate renewal in combination with reduced validity periods. Three months is the new default. Although this is good for security, it becomes a challenge to keep the certificates in sync with the DANE configuration.

## Other Pinning Proposals

During the period when pinning was still seen as a feasible approach, there were other proposals submitted to the community that didn't gain traction. I am including them here for completeness.

**Trust Assertions for Certificate Keys (TACK)**
TACK[34] is a proposal for public key pinning that aims to be independent of both public CAs and DNS. The idea is that site operators create their own cryptographic identities and signing keys (known as *TACK Signing Keys*, or *TSKs*). Once a user agent recognizes a TSK for a particular site, that key can be used to revoke old server keys, issue new ones, and so on. In other words, a TSK is conceptually similar to deploying a private CA.

**TLS Server Identity Pinning with Tickets**
Experimental RFC 8627[35] proposes a pinning approach for TLS 1.3 that introduces *pinning tickets*. After the first connection to a server is established, a client requests a pinning ticket from the server. On subsequent connections, the server must prove that it can decrypt the previously issued ticket. Compared to TACK, RFC 8627

---

[34] Trust Assertions for Certificate Keys [fsty.uk/t582] (Marlinspike and Perrin, January 2013)
[35] RFC 8627: TLS Server Identity Pinning with Tickets [fsty.uk/t583] (Sheffer and Migault, October 2019)

proposes a mechanism that's operationally simpler and works as a second factor on top of the public infrastructure.

# 11 Configuration Guide

This chapter is where everything comes together; it tells you everything you need to know, at a practical level, to securely deploy TLS servers and web applications. In many ways, this chapter is the map for the entire book. If you've read through the chapters in order, you're ready. If you've come to this chapter first because you want answers quickly, refer to earlier chapters for more information as you need it.

## Private Keys and Certificates

Private keys are the cornerstone of TLS security, but also the easiest thing to get right. After all, CAs won't be willing to issue certificates against weak keys. But despite our focus on key sizes, the weakest link is usually key management, or the job of keeping the private keys private. We'll touch upon that in this section. Equally important are certificates, which build upon the keys with important metadata, such as the permission to associate a certificate with a particular domain name.

## Use Strong Private Keys

For the certificate private key, you have a choice of RSA or ECDSA algorithms. The easy option is to use RSA keys because they are universally supported. But at 2,048 bits, which is the current minimum, RSA keys offer less security and worse performance than ECDSA keys.

At the same time, ECDSA is the algorithm of the future and RSA is slowly being left behind. A 256-bit ECDSA key provides 128 bits of security versus only 112 bits for a 2,048-bit RSA key. At these sizes, in addition to providing better security, ECDSA is also significantly faster.

By now, ECDSA is very widely supported and the devices that don't support it are very rare and probably support only obsolete security protocols. If you're still concerned about interoperability, it's possible to deploy services with dual certificates, thus supporting RSA and ECDSA keys simultaneously. The only disadvantage of this setup is the increased maintenance overhead. Some managed providers do this automatically and thus make it trivial.

## Secure Your Private Keys

Although we spend the most time obsessing about key size, issues surrounding key management are more likely to have a real impact on your security. There is ample evidence to suggest that the most successful attacks bypass encryption rather than break it. If someone can break into your server and steal your private key or otherwise compel you to disclose the key, why would they bother with brute-force attacks against cryptography?

**Keep your private keys private**

Treat your private keys as an important asset, restricting access to the smallest possible group of employees while still keeping the arrangements practical. Some CAs offer to generate private keys for you, but they should know better. The hint is in the name: private keys should stay private, without exception.

**Think about random number generation**

The security of encryption keys depends on the quality of the random number generator (RNG) of the computer on which the keys are generated. Keys are often created on servers right after installation and rebooting, but at that point the server might not have sufficient entropy to generate a strong key. It's better to generate all your keys in one (offline) location, where you can ensure that a strong RNG is in place.

**Password protect your keys**

Your keys should have a passphrase on them from the moment they are created. This helps reduce the attack surface if your backup system is compromised. It also helps prevent leakage of the key material when copying keys from one computer to another (directly or using USB sticks); it's getting increasingly difficult to safely delete data from modern file systems.

**Don't share keys among unrelated servers and applications**

Sharing keys is dangerous: if one system is broken into, its compromised key could be used to attack other systems that use the same key, even if they use different certificates. Different keys allow you to establish strong internal access controls, giving access to the keys only to those who need them.

**Change keys regularly**

Treat private keys as a liability. Keep track of when the keys were created to ensure they don't remain in use for too long. You *must* change them after a security incident and when a key member of your staff leaves, and you should change them when obtaining a new certificate. When you generate a new key, you remove the old key as an attack vector. This is especially true for systems that do not use or support forward secrecy. In this case, your key can be used to decrypt all previous communications, if your adversary has recorded them. By deleting the key safely, you ensure that it can't be used against you.

Your default should be to generate a new private key with every certificate renewal. Systems with valuable assets that do not use forward secrecy (which is not advisable) should have their keys changed at least quarterly.

**Store keys safely**

Keep a copy of your keys in a safe location. Losing a server key is usually not a big deal because you can always generate a new one, but it's a different story altogether with keys used for intermediate and private CAs and keys that are used for public key pinning.

Generating and keeping private keys in tamper-resistant hardware is the safest approach you can take, if you can afford it. Such tools are known as *Hardware Security Modules* (HSMs). If you use such a device, private keys never leave the HSM and, in fact, can't be extracted. These days, HSMs are even available as a service. They don't provide the same level of security as tools that you might be able to host in your data centers, but they're a great improvement nevertheless.

# Choose the Right Certification Authority

For a small site that needs only a simple domain-validated certificate, virtually any CA will suffice. You can do what I do—just buy the cheapest certificate you can find. Or, if you can automate certificate renewal, just get your certificates for free from Let's Encrypt and other similar providers. After all, any public CA can issue a certificate for your web site without asking you; what's the point of paying more if you don't have to? If you have complex requirements, you may want to explore the commercial options, at which point you should take your time and select a CA that meets your requirements.

**Features**

At a minimum, you will want to work with a CA that supports both RSA and ECDSA certificate keys. If you care about revocation, your chosen CA must support OCSP certificate revocation checking backed by robust network availability and performance.

We now finally have end user standards for automated certificate issuance (*Automatic Certificate Management Environment*, or ACME for short), and you should use them wherever possible. For this, you'll need a CA that supports automation.

**Focus and expertise**

PKI is a field that requires deep expertise and dedication; it's easy to make a big mistake. If you're going to be relying on a CA for a critical function, you may as well choose an organization that's serious about it. This is not quite easy to quantify, but you should examine the CA's history, staff, and business direction. It's best to work with CAs for which certificate issuance is the core part of their business.

**Service**

At the end of the day, it's all about the service. The certificate business is getting more complicated by the day. If you don't have experts on your staff, perhaps you should work with a CA on which you can rely. Costs matter, but so do the management interfaces and the quality of the support. Determine what level of support you will require from your CA, and choose an organization that will be able to provide it when you need it.

You should be aware that if you're getting your certificates from only one CA, they are your single point of failure. If your deployments are sufficiently important to justify the additional effort, consider getting your certificates from two different CAs at the same time. With overlapping certificate lifetimes, you will always have a backup certificate to use if the primary fails for whatever reason.

## Prevent Certificate Warnings

Certificate warnings are not unusual and happen for a number of reasons, but all of them can be prevented. The world of technology is confusing enough; you shouldn't add to the cognitive load your users are already experiencing. If you don't pay attention, you will confuse them and weaken their confidence in your technical abilities. In addition, for web sites that disable certificate warnings via *HTTP Strict Transport Security* (HSTS), misconfigured certificates lead to immediate breakage.

Getting certificates right is not very difficult, especially when compared to everything else you need to do to ensure security. With correct initial configuration, renewal automation, and monitoring, you will ensure a smooth experience for your users.

You should pay attention to ensure you have valid certificates for all different domain names and subdomains. As a rule of thumb, keep track of every DNS name that points to your properties and get certificates for all of them. For example, if your main web site is at *www.example.com*, the domain name *example.com* should also have a valid certificate, even though this variant will be configured only to redirect your users to the main location. It's easy to use just one certificate for all of this.

## Control Key and Certificate Sharing

In PKI, private keys and certificates can be shared among properties. This practice is not necessarily insecure, but only if it's done in a way that's understood. For best results, don't share. Don't use the same certificate on multiple properties; don't even put different hostnames on the same certificate. With this approach, each property will be independently secured.

The main issue with sharing is that if one property is compromised, the other ones in the same group also follow. There are situations in which this is not a problem. For example, if you have a group of properties that are all managed by the same team and are all part of the same system, sharing is not necessarily bad. On the other hand, multiple teams and multiple distinct properties sharing certificates is always bad.

Wildcard certificates have their place. For example, they are best used by a single property when you need to support an arbitrary number of subdomains, usually one per customer. Avoid them otherwise.

## Think Chains, Not Certificates

Although we spend a lot of time talking about server certificates, in practice we need complete and valid *certificate chains* to establish secure connections. Because this is something server operators have to configure manually, mistakes are rife. Most commonly, you will see TLS servers with just the leaf certificate or a set of certificates that don't actually form a valid chain.

An invalid certificate chain may render the server certificate invalid, causing a browser warning. To make things worse, this problem is often difficult to diagnose because some browsers try hard to fix it and others don't. This is a good example of a problem that should be diagnosed by an independent assessment tool.

## Deploy Certification Authority Authorization

*Certification Authority Authorization* (CAA) is a relatively recent security standard that enables you to restrict what CAs are allowed to issue certificates for your properties. CAA is delivered via DNS. When a new certificate is requested, the CA must look for a CAA policy on the affected hosts and verify that they have permission to proceed. If they don't, the issuance fails.

```
example.com.  CAA     0 issue "digicert.com"
example.com.  CAA     0 issue "globalsign.com"
example.com.  CAA     0 issue "letsencrypt.org"
example.com.  CAA     0 issue "sectigo.com"
```

CAA is a very useful addition to the defense arsenal. Even a policy that allows many CAs is helpful as a way of reducing the attack surface, compared to the default, which allows all CAs. Deploying CAA may be difficult in complex environments because a policy set on the domain name applies to all subdomains.

---

## Automate Certificate Renewal

When it comes to certificate lifetimes, renew yearly if you're still doing this work by hand. Aim to automate certificate renewal, then switch to quarterly issuance. Because it is currently impossible to revoke compromised certificates reliably, certificates with shorter lifespans are effectively more secure.

Don't leave it until the last moment to initiate the renewal. In fact, it's better if you start much earlier, about a month before the current certificate expires. Doing so will provide you with a margin of safety should the new issuance fail for whatever reason. Many things can go wrong, among them issues with the CA itself or issues with the CAA configuration.

For best results, deploy new certificates to production about two weeks after they are issued. This practice (1) helps avoid certificate warnings for some users who don't have the correct time on their computers and also (2) avoids failed revocation checks with CAs that need extra time to propagate their new certificates to their OCSP responders.

## Use Certificate Transparency Monitoring

Since 2018, all public certificates are recorded via *Certificate Transparency* (CT), a Google-led effort to improve transparency of the PKI. There are specialized monitoring services that observe all recorded certificates and make it possible to find all certificates issued for your properties. CT monitoring is an excellent and very cost-effective way to understand issuance in complex environments (in terms of who is doing what and where), enforce policy, and catch unexpected certificates or misissuance.

# Configuration

When it comes to protocol configuration, your choices are likely to be influenced by a combination of security, interoperability, and regulatory requirements. In the ideal world, focusing on security alone, you would allow only TLS 1.3 and disable all other protocol versions. But that works only in well-understood environments; although modern browsers support TLS 1.3, many other products and tools still don't.

## Use Secure Protocols

A web site intended for public use needs to support TLS 1.3 and TLS 1.2 at minimum. You can still use TLS 1.1 and TLS 1.0 if you need to reach a wide audience. The remaining protocols, SSL 3 and SSL 2, are both obsolete and insecure. Let's consider each protocol in turn:

- SSL 2 is completely broken and must not be used. This is the first ever protocol version and is so bad that it can be used to attack even well-configured servers that use overlapping certificates or private keys (the so-called DROWN attack).

- SSL 3 is better, but still insecure when used with HTTP because of the POODLE attack. It's also very weak when used with other protocols. It's obsolete and lacks essential security capabilities. Don't use.

- TLS 1.0 is a legacy protocol that lacks essential security capabilities. Modern clients no longer support this protocol version, but there are still old clients out there that need it. TLS 1.0 is vulnerable to the BEAST attack, although most browsers have deployed mitigations as a workaround.

- TLS 1.1 is also a legacy protocol that lacks modern capabilities. It's usually not needed at all, because all clients that support it also have support for TLS 1.2.

- TLS 1.2 is a relatively modern protocol that can provide good security, but it supports both bad and good cryptographic primitives. It can be used securely, but doing so requires more effort. This protocol version is necessary in order to support a wide range of customers.

- TLS 1.3 is a completely reworked revision of TLS. It's secure by default and requires no further configuration effort. This protocol version, which modern browsers support, should be what protects most of your network communication.

If you need to support older clients and wish to enable TLS 1.0, base your decisions on evidence, not fear. These protocols are seen as not secure enough; for example, the PCI DSS standard no longer allows them.

## Use Forward Secrecy

*Forward secrecy* (also known as *perfect forward secrecy*) is a feature of cryptographic protocols that ensures that every communication (connection) to the server uses a different and unique set of encryption keys. These keys are called *ephemeral* because they are discarded when they are no longer needed. Ephemeral connection keys do not depend on any long-term keys—for example, the server key. When there is no forward secrecy, an adversary who can record your network traffic and later obtain the server key can also decrypt all past communications.

SSL and TLS initially used only the RSA key exchange that doesn't support forward secrecy. To fix that, the ephemeral *Diffie-Hellman* (DHE) and *Elliptic Curve Diffie-Hellman* (ECDHE) key exchanges were added over time, along with some protocol improvements in TLS 1.3. Don't be confused by the fact that RSA can be used for key exchange and authentication; there is nothing wrong with the latter. For as long as you continue to use RSA private keys, the string RSA will remain in the suite name.

In TLS 1.2 and earlier protocol releases, the key exchange (and thus forward secrecy) is controlled via cipher suite configuration. Therefore, you want to ensure that all enabled suites embed the keywords DHE and ECDHE. From TLS 1.3, all suites incorporate forward secrecy and the RSA key exchange is no longer supported.

## Use a Strong Key Exchange

In recent years, the DHE key exchange fell out of fashion; many modern clients no longer support it. As a result, there is only one widely supported secure option for the key exchange, and that's ECDHE. Although DHE suites do have some issues, they are not likely to be a problem in practice if used only as fallback. You shouldn't use the RSA key exchange (not to be confused with RSA keys) because in that case you lose forward security.

For key exchange to be secure, ECDHE and DHE have to be used with secure parameters. For ECDHE, the parameters are called *named curves* and only two are practical: X25519 and P-256 (also known as sec256r1). For DHE (if using), ensure the parameters provide 2,048 bits of security. Some server software provides secure DHE parameters out of the box; with others, you'll have to provide your own.

## Prioritize the Best Cipher Suites

In TLS, servers are in the best position to determine the most secure communication option to use with the connecting clients. That's because the first step of the TLS handshake involves a client sending a list of supported features. What remains is for the server to choose what feature to proceed with.

Unfortunately, many platforms don't actively choose the best option, instead resorting to choosing the first one offered by clients. For the best results, check what your platform does and enable server preference wherever possible. In general, avoid platforms that don't support server preference enforcement as it may not be possible to configure them securely in a general case.

## Use Secure Cipher Suites

In TLS, cipher suites are the most visible aspect of server configuration. Usually a lot of effort goes into understanding what options are available, secure, and required to achieve secure communication. Determining what cipher suites to use has traditionally been difficult; over time, the TLS protocol accumulated a very large number of suites, most of which are considered insecure or inadequate today.

On the positive side, TLS 1.3, the most recent incarnation of the TLS protocol, supports only a handful of suites, and all of them are secure. If you base your configuration on this protocol version, all connections with clients that also support it will be secure with ease. You should lead with the following three suites (which are usually enabled by default anyway):

```
TLS_AES_128_GCM_SHA256
TLS_CHACHA20_POLY1305_SHA256
TLS_AES_256_GCM_SHA384
```

When it comes to TLS 1.2, you should rely on cipher suites that provide strong key exchange, forward secrecy, and AEAD (*authenticated encryption with associated data*) encryption of 128 bits. Also use AES and ChaCha20 encryption algorithms. Your configuration can continue to utilize non-AEAD suites, but only to support very old clients, if that's necessary. Don't use anything else unless you're a cryptographer and know what you're doing.

The preceding recommendations, translated to specific suites, yields the following:

```
TLS_ECDHE_ECDSA_WITH_AES_128_GCM_SHA256
TLS_ECDHE_ECDSA_WITH_CHACHA20_POLY1305_SHA256
TLS_ECDHE_ECDSA_WITH_AES_256_GCM_SHA384
TLS_ECDHE_ECDSA_WITH_AES_128_CBC_SHA
TLS_ECDHE_ECDSA_WITH_AES_256_CBC_SHA
TLS_ECDHE_ECDSA_WITH_AES_128_CBC_SHA256
TLS_ECDHE_ECDSA_WITH_AES_256_CBC_SHA384
TLS_ECDHE_RSA_WITH_AES_128_GCM_SHA256
TLS_ECDHE_RSA_WITH_CHACHA20_POLY1305_SHA256
TLS_ECDHE_RSA_WITH_AES_256_GCM_SHA384
TLS_ECDHE_RSA_WITH_AES_128_CBC_SHA
TLS_ECDHE_RSA_WITH_AES_256_CBC_SHA
TLS_ECDHE_RSA_WITH_AES_128_CBC_SHA256
TLS_ECDHE_RSA_WITH_AES_256_CBC_SHA384
TLS_DHE_RSA_WITH_AES_128_GCM_SHA256
TLS_DHE_RSA_WITH_CHACHA20_POLY1305_SHA256
TLS_DHE_RSA_WITH_AES_256_GCM_SHA384
TLS_DHE_RSA_WITH_AES_128_CBC_SHA
TLS_DHE_RSA_WITH_AES_256_CBC_SHA
TLS_DHE_RSA_WITH_AES_128_CBC_SHA256
TLS_DHE_RSA_WITH_AES_256_CBC_SHA256
```

This configuration is designed with both security and performance in mind. It supports both ECDSA and RSA keys, with priority given to the former, which is faster. It also includes more suites than strictly necessary in order to support a wider range of clients.

If you're using OpenSSL, the following configuration is exactly the same but uses the nonstandard suite names that OpenSSL will understand:

```
ECDHE-ECDSA-AES128-GCM-SHA256
ECDHE-ECDSA-CHACHA20-POLY1305
ECDHE-ECDSA-AES256-GCM-SHA384
```

```
ECDHE-ECDSA-AES128-SHA
ECDHE-ECDSA-AES256-SHA
ECDHE-ECDSA-AES128-SHA256
ECDHE-ECDSA-AES256-SHA384
ECDHE-RSA-AES128-GCM-SHA256
ECDHE-RSA-CHACHA20-POLY1305
ECDHE-RSA-AES256-GCM-SHA384
ECDHE-RSA-AES128-SHA
ECDHE-RSA-AES256-SHA
ECDHE-RSA-AES128-SHA256
ECDHE-RSA-AES256-SHA384
DHE-RSA-AES128-GCM-SHA256
DHE-RSA-CHACHA20-POLY1305
DHE-RSA-AES256-GCM-SHA384
DHE-RSA-AES128-SHA
DHE-RSA-AES256-SHA
DHE-RSA-AES128-SHA256
DHE-RSA-AES256-SHA256
```

I recommend that you always configure OpenSSL with an explicit list of desired suites, as indicated earlier. This approach is the simplest and provides great visibility into exactly what is enabled. With OpenSSL, it's also possible to use the legacy, keyword-based configuration approach, but that approach leads to opaque configurations that are difficult to understand and often end up doing the wrong thing.

## Ensure Ticket Keys Are Rotated

In TLS, session resumption is implemented using one of two approaches. The original approach is to have the server keep the state in persistent storage somewhere. Later, session tickets were added, and they work like HTTP cookies do. The session state is packaged into a binary blob, encrypted, and sent back to the client to keep and send back to the server later.

When session tickets are used, the security of all connections depends on the main ticket key. This key is used to safely encrypt and decrypt session tickets. The security of the ticket key is an area in which current server software doesn't provide adequate controls. Most applications that rely on OpenSSL use implicit ticket keys that are created on server startup and stay the same for the duration of the process. If the process stays up for weeks and months, so does the ticket key. Backdooring applications is easy; you can inject a static, never-changing ticket key to give you the ability to decrypt all communication. The most secure deployments of TLS configure ticket keys explicitly and rotate them on a predetermined schedule—for example, daily.

Session ticket security is very important to get right if you're deploying TLS 1.2. In this situation, knowing the ticket key is all you need to decrypt past communications. TLS 1.3

brought some much-needed improvement in this area. This updated protocol version uses session tickets for authentication, but has an option (enforced by all modern browsers) to perform an ephemeral Diffie-Hellman handshake on all resumed connections. The end result is that knowing the ticket key is no longer sufficient for passive decryption, making it a much smaller attack vector.

# Mitigate Known Problems

There was a period of time when it was common to learn about new protocol issues, but that now appears to be behind us. The problems were exhausted and largely fixed. Then TLS 1.3 came along, which made things much better still. Critical issues at the protocol level are not so common today, but it's generally accepted that security deteriorates over time. For that reason, it's a good practice to be aware of what's going on. At this point in time, the most likely problems you will encounter are implementation issues in libraries and server software. Apply patches promptly when they become available.

# Supporting Legacy Platforms

Sometimes you'll find yourself needing to support legacy clients that don't have the latest and greatest security features. In this case, you will need to reach out for, and enable, certain components that are not ideal but are still acceptable for use in exceptional situations. It could be that the risk of the exploitation is low or that the service is not that valuable, or perhaps you have mitigation measures in place. If you are in this situation, this section is for you; I will outline here some of those imperfect but palatable legacy features.

The good news is that it's generally possible to deploy strong and weak elements at the same time, relying on the TLS negotiation features and server configuration to ensure that individual connections use the best commonly supported features. This means that those weak elements in your configuration will be used only as a last resort.

> ### Note
>
> If you have to resort to using some of these weak encryption components in production, consider splitting your systems into those that are well-configured and those that are intended to serve your legacy clients. Structuring your deployments like that will help you minimize the risk.

### RSA private keys

The ECDSA algorithm is gaining in popularity on account of its speed, but you will often find that it's not supported by some old clients. In this case, fall back to the RSA algorithm. If you care about performance, deploy with two certificates, using both ECDSA and RSA at the same time.

---

### TLS 1.1, TLS 1.0, SSL 3, and SSL 2

Legacy clients won't support TLS 1.2, so you may need to enable TLS 1.0 for them. This is not terrible and you may find that my recommended suite configuration works for you. If you're considering SSL 3, then you should carefully study the weaknesses of this protocol and determine if its use is acceptable in your situation. SSL 2 cannot be used securely—and it's worse than no encryption because this protocol version can be used to exploit secure servers (via DROWN). Nobody cares about TLS 1.1.

### Weak Diffie-Hellman key exchange

There are some old clients (e.g., Java before version 8) that can't use the DH key exchange at 2,048 bits, which is the recommended strength today. You may consider dropping the strength to 1,024 bits to accommodate these clients. If you do, you must generate a unique set of DH parameters on each server. You must not use any of the predefined well-known groups because they can be exploited via a precomputation attack. Anything below 1,024 bits is very easy to exploit.

You need to be aware that if you reduce the DH strength, it will affect both modern and legacy clients. This is one aspect of TLS configuration that cannot be negotiated on a per connection basis. The best approach is to have separate systems for modern and legacy customers. If you can't do that, preferring the ECDHE key exchange (as in my recommended configuration) will ensure that modern clients all use ECDHE and never attempt DHE.

### Weak cipher suites

Very old clients were never capable of great encryption—for example, often not supporting DHE and ECDHE key exchange or the AES encryption algorithm. This is effectively the situation with Windows XP and some early Android platforms. Therefore, to communicate with those platforms you'll have to support the plain old RSA key exchange that doesn't provide forward security. And for Windows XP, you'll need to support 3DES (slow and on the way down, but not entirely out, strictly speaking). Here are some last-resort suites to place at the end of your prioritized list of suites if there is no other way:

```
TLS_RSA_WITH_AES_128_CBC_SHA
TLS_RSA_WITH_AES_256_CBC_SHA
TLS_RSA_WITH_3DES_EDE_CBC_SHA
```

# HTTP and Application Security

Although SSL and TLS were designed so that they can secure any connection-oriented protocol, the immediate need was to protect HTTP. To this day, web site encryption remains the most common TLS use case. Over the years, the Web has evolved from a simple document distribution system into a complex application delivery platform. This complexity creates additional attack vectors and requires more effort to secure.

## Encrypt Everything

There is no longer any excuse not to encrypt everything by default. A long time ago there was—*maybe*—but not any longer. The first barrier fell with the increase of CPU power, which removed encryption as a bottleneck. More recently, several things happened to make encryption widely adopted. First, there was the rise of Let's Encrypt, which started to offer free certificates and automated issuance. Second, browsers started to mark plaintext content as insecure and search engines started to favor encrypted content.

*Mixed content* is the name we use to refer to web pages that are themselves encrypted but rely on resources that are not. For example, an HTML page could be fetching audio or visual files without encryption. The original excuse—that heavy content can't be delivered encrypted—no longer applies, and today we need to deal with the legacy. Browsers have been restricting mixed content for a while. The long-term direction is not only that all content within a page must be encrypted, but also that the related actions (e.g., downloads) must be as well.

## Secure Cookies

In HTTP, cookies are a weak link and need additional attention. You could have a web site that is 100% encrypted and yet remains insecure because of how its cookies are configured.

**Mark cookies secure**

Cookies will by default span HTTP and HTTPS contexts, which is why they need to be explicitly marked as secure for browsers to know to avoid plaintext.

**Mark cookies as HttpOnly**

If a web site uses cookies that need not be accessed from the browser itself, they should be marked as HttpOnly. This is a defense-in-depth technique that aims to minimize the attack surface.

**Use cookie name prefixes**

Cookie prefixes are a new security measure that is now supported by browsers and being added to the main cookie specification (RFC 6265bis). Cookies with names that start with prefixes __Host- and __Secure- are given special powers that address a variety of problems that existed for years. All cookies should be transitioned to use these prefixes.

For best results, consider adding cryptographic integrity validation or even encryption to your cookies. These techniques are useful with cookies that include some application data. Encryption can help if the data inadvertently includes something that the user doesn't already know. Integrity validation will prevent tampering. With these kinds of cookies, it's also a good practice to bond the cookies to the context in which they were issued—for example, to the specific user account.

## Use Strict Transport Security

For proper security of the transport layer, you must indicate your preference for encrypted content. *HTTP Strict Transport Security* (HSTS) is a standard that allows web sites to request strict handling of encryption. Web sites signal their policies via an HTTP response header for enforcement in compliant browsers. Once HSTS is deployed, compliant browsers will switch to always using TLS when communicating with the web site. This addresses a number of issues that are otherwise difficult to enforce: (1) users who have plaintext bookmarks and follow plaintext links, (2) insecure cookies, (3) HTTPS stripping attacks, and (4) mixed-content issues within the same site.

In addition, and perhaps more importantly, HSTS fixes handling of invalid certificates. Without HSTS, when browsers encounter invalid certificates, they allow their users to proceed to the site. Many users can't differentiate between attacks and configuration issues and decide to proceed, which makes them susceptible to active network attacks. With HSTS, certificate validation failures are final and can't be bypassed. That brings TLS back to how it should have been implemented in the first place.

All web sites should deploy HSTS to fix legacy browser issues in how encryption is handled. In fact, deploying HSTS is probably the single most important improvement you can make. The following configuration enables HSTS on the current domain and all subdomains, with a policy duration of one full year:

```
Strict-Transport-Security: max-age=31536000; includeSubDomains; preload
```

For best results, consider adding your properties to the HSTS preload list. With that, browsers and other clients can ship with a full list of encryption-properties, which means that even first access to those sites can enforce encryption.

> ### Warning
>
> Unless you have full control over your infrastructure, it's best to deploy HSTS incrementally, starting with a short policy duration (e.g., 300 seconds) and no preloading. The fact that HSTS has a memory effect, combined with its potential effect on subdomains, can lead to problems in complex environments. With incremental deployments, problems are discovered while they're still easy to fix. Request preloading as the last deployment step, and after you activate sufficiently long policy duration.

HSTS is not the only technology that can help with enforcing encryption. Although much more recent and with a lot of catching up to do, there are also the *HTTPS DNS resource records*, which build on the DNS infrastructure to carry various metadata, including signaling of support for encryption.

## Deploy Content Security Policy

*Content Security Policy* (CSP) is a mechanism that allows web sites to control how resources embedded in HTML pages are retrieved and over what protocols. As with HSTS, web sites signal their policies via an HTTP response header for enforcement in compliant browsers. Although CSP was originally primarily designed as a way of combating XSS, it has an important application for web site encryption; that is, it can be used to prevent third-party mixed content by rejecting plaintext links that might be present in the page via the following command:

```
Content-Security-Policy: upgrade-insecure-requests
```

## Disable Caching

Encryption at the network level prevents network attacks, but TLS doesn't provide end-to-end encryption. Each party involved in the communication has access to the plaintext. Caching is commonly used with HTTP to improve performance, so, for example, browsers may choose to store decrypted data in persistent storage. Intermediate proxy services (e.g., content delivery networks) may choose to not only cache sensitive data, but even share it with other users in some situations.

With the increase of cloud-based application delivery platforms and content delivery networks, it's never been more important to very carefully mark all sensitive content as private. The most secure option is to indicate that the content is private and that it must not be cached:

```
Cache-Control: private, no-store
```

With this setting, neither intermediate devices nor browsers will be allowed to cache the served content.

## Be Aware of Issues with HTTP Compression

In 2012, the CRIME attack showed how data compression can be used to compromise network encryption, and TLS in particular. This discovery eventually led to the removal of compression from TLS. The following year, TIME and BREACH attack variations focused on retrieving secrets from compressed HTTP response content. Unlike TLS compression, HTTP compression has a huge performance and financial impact and the world decided to leave it on, along with the security issue.

TIME and BREACH attacks can target any sensitive data embedded in a HTML page, which is why there isn't a generic mitigation technique. In practice, most attacks would target CSRF tokens, which would give attackers the ability to carry out some activity on a web site under the identity of the attacked user. For best security, ensure that CSRF tokens are masked. In addition, web sites should generally be looking at adopting same-site cookies, another recent security measure designed to improve cookie security, this time against CSRF attacks.

## Understand and Acknowledge Third-Party Trust

When everything else is properly configured and secured, we still can't escape the fact that many web sites have to rely on services provided by third parties. It could be that some JavaScript libraries are hosted on a content delivery network or that ads are supplied by an ad delivery network or that there are genuine services (e.g., chat widgets) supplied by others.

These third parties are effectively a backdoor that can be used to break your web site. The bigger the service, the more attractive it is. For example, Google Analytics is known to provide its service to half the Internet; what if its code is compromised?

This is not an easy problem to solve. Although it would be ideal to self-host all resources and have full control over everything, in practice that's not quite possible because we don't have infinite budgets to do everything ourselves. What we should do, however, is evaluate every third-party dependency from a security perspective and ask ourselves if keeping it is worth the risk.

A technology called *Subresource Integrity* (SRI) can be used to secure resources that are hosted by third parties and that don't change. SRI works by embedding cryptographic hashes of included references, which browsers check every time the resource is retrieved.

# Performance

Everybody worries about security, but they worry about performance even more. What use is a secure service that people can't or don't want to use? Properly configured, TLS is plenty fast. With little effort, the performance will be good enough. In some cases, it's even possible to deploy TLS with virtually no performance overhead. In this section, we'll look at how you can achieve best-in-class performance with some additional effort.

## Don't Use Too Much Security

We all like security, but it's possible to have too much of it. If you go overboard and choose cryptographic primitives that are too strong, your security won't be better in any meaningful way, but your services will nevertheless be slower, and sometimes significantly so. Most sites should aim to use elements that provide 128 bits of security. We make an exception for DHE, which, at 2,048 bits, provides 112 bits of security. That's close enough. You will virtually always use ECDHE anyway, which provides a full 128 bits of security.

The next step up is to use primitives that offer 256 bits of security. This is something you might decide to do if you think quantum computing is a realistic threat.

## Enable Session Resumption

In TLS terminology, when a client and server have a successful handshake, they establish a session. Handshakes involve a fair amount of computation, which is why cryptographic protocols focused on performance also incorporate so-called session caching that makes it possible to continue to use the results of one handshake over a period of time, typically for up to a day. This is called *session caching* or *session resumption*.

Session resumption is an essential performance optimization that ensures smooth operation, even for web sites that don't need to scale. Servers that don't use it or don't use it well are going to perform significantly slower.

## Optimize Connection Management

In the early days, slow cryptographic operations were the main bottleneck introduced by encryption. Since then, CPU speed has improved, so much so that most sites don't worry about its overhead. The main overhead of TLS now lies with the increased latency of the handshake. The best way to improve TLS performance is to find ways to avoid handshakes.

**Keep connections open**

The best approach to avoiding TLS handshakes is to keep existing connections open for an extended period of time and reuse them for subsequent user requests. In HTTP, this feature is known as *keep-alives*, and using it is a simple matter of web server reconfiguration.

**Use TLS 1.3**

The complete redesign of TLS in version 1.3 to improve security was also a good opportunity to improve its performance. As a result, this protocol version reduces full handshake latency by half, compared to the standard handshake in earlier protocol revisions. TLS 1.3 also introduces a special 0-RTT (*zero round-trip time*) mode, in which TLS adds no additional latency over TCP. Your servers will fly with this mode enabled, but with the caveat that using it opens you up to replay attacks. As a result, this mode is not appropriate for use with all applications.

**Use modern HTTP protocols**

There was a very fast pace of HTTP protocol evolution recently. After HTTP/1.1, there was a long period of no activity, but then we got HTTP/2 and soon thereafter

HTTP/3. These two releases didn't really change HTTP itself but focused on connection management and the underlying transport mechanism, including encryption via QUIC.

**Use content delivery networks**

*Content delivery networks* (CDNs) can be very effective at improving network performance, provided they are designed to reduce the network latency of new connections to origin servers. Normally, when you open a connection to a remote server, you need to exchange some packets with it for the handshake to complete. At best, you need to send your handshake request and receive the server's response before you can start sending application data. The further the server, the worse the latency. CDNs, by definition, are going to be close to you, which means that the latency between you and them is going to be small. CDNs that keep connections to origin servers open won't have to open new connections all the time, leading to potentially substantial performance improvements.

# Enable Caching of Nonsensitive Content

An earlier section in this guide recommended that you disable HTTP caching by default. Although that's the most secure option, not all properties require the same level of security. HTTPS is commonly used for all web sites today, even when the content on them is not sensitive. In that case, you want to selectively enable caching in order to improve performance.

The first step might be to enable caching at the browser level by indicating that the content is private:

```
Cache-Control: private
```

If you have a content delivery network in place and want to utilize its caching abilities, indicate that the content is public:

```
Cache-Control: public
```

In both situations, you can use other HTTP caching configuration options to control how the caching is to be done.

# Use Fast Cryptographic Primitives

Measured server-side, the overhead of cryptography tends to be very low and there aren't many opportunities for performance improvements. In fact, my recommended configuration is also the fastest as it prefers ECDSA, ECDHE, and AES with reasonable key sizes. These days, to deploy fast TLS, you generally (1) deploy with ECDSA keys and (2) double-check that your servers support hardware-accelerated TLS.

However, things change somewhat if we look at the performance from the client perspective. Recently there's been an explosion in the adoption of mobile devices, which use different processors and have different performance characteristics. What's good for your servers may not be what's good for mobile phones. So which do you want to optimize?

In practice, some organizations are choosing to take a performance hit on their servers in order to provide a better end user experience. In practice, this means that they choose to negotiate ChaCha20 suites with mobile devices because they are not only several times faster, but also consume less battery. But how do we know which clients are mobile devices?

The trick is to use something called an *equal preference cipher suites configuration*. Normally, we want our servers to select the best possible cipher suite, so naturally that would be something with AES-GCM. But with mobile devices we want ChaCha20. BoringSSL was the first to introduce a feature in which the client's list of suites is analyzed to determine if it prefers ChaCha20 over AES. Only if it did would the server select a ChaCha20 suite over an AES-GCM one. This feature is now also available in OpenSSL.

# Validate and Monitor

Configuring TLS, especially for use on web sites, has become increasingly complex in recent years. There are so many options to choose that you're virtually guaranteed to get something wrong when you first try. Moreover, things change—sometimes accidentally, sometimes silently through software upgrades. For that reason, we recommend that you find a reliable configuration assessment tool that you trust. Use it periodically to ensure that you stay secure.

Several modern browser technologies come with reporting facilities, which can give you real-time insight into problems that your users are experiencing. CSP supports reporting and even a report-only mode without policy enforcement. A more recent technology, called *Network Error Logging* (NEL), provides reporting for a wide variety of network problems, including TLS and PKI.[1]

---

[1] There is also the Expect-CT HTTP response header, which was designed to support early opt-in into CT before this technology became de facto required. With Expect-CT reporting, it's possible to get a full certificate chain that's not CT compliant. Although this feature is very useful, it is most likely that Expect-CT will be deprecated, now that pre-CT public certificates have all expired.

# 12 OpenSSL Command Line

OpenSSL is the world's most widely used implementation of the *Transport Layer Security* (TLS) protocol. At the core, it's also a robust and a high-performing cryptographic library with support for a wide range of cryptographic primitives. In addition to the library code, OpenSSL provides a set of command-line tools that serve a variety of purposes, including support for common PKI operations and TLS testing.

OpenSSL is a de facto standard in this space and comes with a long history. The code initially began its life in 1995 under the name SSLeay,[1] when it was developed by Eric A. Young and Tim J. Hudson. OpenSSL as a separate project was born in 1998, when Eric and Tim decided to begin working on a commercial SSL/TLS toolkit called BSAFE SSL-C. A community of developers picked up the project and continued to maintain it.

Today, OpenSSL is ubiquitous on the server side and in many client programs. The command-line tools are also the most common choice for key and certificate management. When it comes to browsers, OpenSSL also has a substantial market share, albeit via Google's fork, called *BoringSSL*.

OpenSSL used to be dual-licensed under OpenSSL and SSLeay licenses. Both are BSD-like, with an advertising clause. With version 3.0, released in September 2021, OpenSSL simplified its licensing by moving to Apache License v2.0.

## Getting Started

If you're using one of the Unix platforms, getting started with OpenSSL should be easy; you're virtually guaranteed to have it already installed on your system. Still, things could go wrong. For example, you could have a version that's just not right, or there could be other tools (e.g., LibreSSL) configured to respond when OpenSSL is invoked. For this reason, it's best to first check what you have installed and resort to using a custom installation only if absolutely necessary. Another option is to look for a packaging platform. For example, for

---

[1] The letters "eay" in the name SSLeay are Eric A. Young's initials.

OS X you could use Brew or MacPorts. As always, compiling something from scratch once is rarely a problem; maintaining that piece of software indefinitely is.

In this chapter, I assume that you're using a Unix platform because that's the natural environment for OpenSSL. On Windows, it's less common to compile software from scratch because the tooling is not readily available. You can still compile OpenSSL yourself, but it might take more work. Alternatively, you can consider downloading the binaries from the Shining Light Productions web site.[2] If you're downloading binaries from multiple web sites, you need to ensure that they're not compiled under different versions of OpenSSL. If they are, you might experience crashes that are difficult to troubleshoot. The best approach is to use a single bundle of programs that includes everything that you need. For example, if you want to run Apache on Windows, you can get your binaries from the Apache Lounge web site.[3]

## Determine OpenSSL Version and Configuration

Before you do any work, you should know which OpenSSL version you'll be using. TLS and PKI continue to develop at a fairly rapid pace, and you may find that what you can do is limited if your version of OpenSSL doesn't support them. Here's what I get for version information with openssl version on Ubuntu 20.04 LTS, which is the system that I'll be using for the examples in this chapter:

```
$ openssl version
OpenSSL 1.1.1f  31 Mar 2020
```

At the time of writing, OpenSSL 1.1.1 is the dominant branch used in production and has all the nice features. On older systems, you may find a release from the 1.1.0 branch, which is fine because it can be used securely with TLS 1.2, but it won't support modern features, such as TLS 1.3. In the other direction is OpenSSL 3.0, which introduces a major update of the libraries, with substantial architectural changes and a switch to the Apache License 2.0 for better interoperability with other programs and libraries. The command-line tooling, which is what I am covering in this chapter and the next, should be pretty much the same. That said, every release—and especially the major ones—is very likely to change the tools' behavior, often in subtle ways. When you're changing from one branch to another, it's worth going through the change documentation to understand what the differences might be.

> ### Note
>
> Although you wouldn't know it from looking at the version number, various operating systems often don't actually ship the exact official OpenSSL releases.

---

[2] Win32/Win64 OpenSSL [fsty.uk/t584] (Shining Light Productions, retrieved 19 July 2020)

[3] Apache 2.4 VS16 Windows Binaries and Modules [fsty.uk/t585] (Apache Lounge, retrieved 18 September 2021)

---

Chapter 12: OpenSSL Command Line

> More often than not, they contain forks that are either customized for a specific platform or patched to address various known issues. However, the version number generally stays the same, and there is no indication that the code is a fork of the original project that may have different capabilities. Keep this in mind if you notice something unexpected.

To get complete version information, use the -a switch:

```
$ openssl version -a
OpenSSL 1.1.1f  31 Mar 2020
built on: Mon Apr 20 11:53:50 2020 UTC
platform: debian-amd64
options:  bn(64,64) rc4(16x,int) des(int) blowfish(ptr)
compiler: gcc -fPIC -pthread -m64 -Wa,--noexecstack -Wall -Wa,--noexecstack -g -O2 ↵
-fdebug-prefix-map=/build/openssl-P_ODHM/openssl-1.1.1f=. -fstack-protector-strong ↵
-Wformat -Werror=format-security -DOPENSSL_TLS_SECURITY_LEVEL=2 -DOPENSSL_USE↵
_NODELETE -DL_ENDIAN -DOPENSSL_PIC -DOPENSSL_CPUID_OBJ -DOPENSSL_IA32_SSE2 ↵
-DOPENSSL_BN_ASM_MONT -DOPENSSL_BN_ASM_MONT5 -DOPENSSL_BN_ASM_GF2m -DSHA1_ASM ↵
-DSHA256_ASM -DSHA512_ASM -DKECCAK1600_ASM -DRC4_ASM -DMD5_ASM -DAESNI_ASM -DVPAES↵
_ASM -DGHASH_ASM -DECP_NISTZ256_ASM -DX25519_ASM -DPOLY1305_ASM -DNDEBUG ↵
-Wdate-time -D_FORTIFY_SOURCE=2
OPENSSLDIR: "/usr/lib/ssl"
ENGINESDIR: "/usr/lib/x86_64-linux-gnu/engines-1.1"
Seeding source: os-specific
```

I don't suppose that you would find this output very interesting initially, but it's useful to know where you can find out how your OpenSSL was compiled. Of special interest is the OPENSSLDIR setting, which in my example points to /usr/lib/ssl; it will tell you where OpenSSL looks for its default configuration and root certificates. On my system, that location is essentially an alias for /etc/ssl, Ubuntu's main location for PKI-related files:

```
lrwxrwxrwx  1 root root   14 Apr 20 11:53 certs -> /etc/ssl/certs
drwxr-xr-x  2 root root 4096 May 14 21:38 misc
lrwxrwxrwx  1 root root   20 Apr 20 11:53 openssl.cnf -> /etc/ssl/openssl.cnf
lrwxrwxrwx  1 root root   16 Apr 20 11:53 private -> /etc/ssl/private
```

The misc/ folder contains a few supplementary scripts, the most interesting of which are the scripts that allow you to implement a private *certification authority* (CA). You may or may not end up using it, but later in this chapter I will show you how to do the equivalent work from scratch.

# Building OpenSSL

In most cases, you will be using the system-supplied version of OpenSSL, but sometimes there are good reasons to use a newer or indeed an older version. For example, if you have an older system, it may be stuck with a version of OpenSSL that does not support TLS 1.3.

---

On the other side, newer OpenSSL versions might not support SSL 2 or SSL 3. Although this is the right thing to do in a general case, you'll need support for these older features if your job is to test systems for security.

You can start by downloading the most recent version of OpenSSL (in my case, 1.1.1g):

```
$ wget https://www.openssl.org/source/openssl-1.1.1g.tar.gz
```

The next step is to configure OpenSSL before compilation. For this, you will usually use the `config` script, which first attempts to guess your architecture and then runs through the configuration process:

```
$ ./config \
--prefix=/opt/openssl \
--openssldir=/opt/openssl \
no-shared \
-DOPENSSL_TLS_SECURITY_LEVEL=2 \
enable-ec_nistp_64_gcc_128
```

The automated architecture detection can sometimes fail (e.g., with older versions of OpenSSL on OS X), in which case you should instead invoke the `Configure` script with the explicit architecture string. The configuration syntax is otherwise the same.

Unless you're sure you want to do otherwise, it is essential to use the `--prefix` option to install OpenSSL to a private location that doesn't clash with the system-provided version. Getting this wrong may break your server. The other important option is `no-shared`, which forces static linking and makes self-contained command-line tools. If you don't use this option, you'll need to play with your `LD_LIBRARY_PATH` configuration to get your tools to work.

When compiling OpenSSL 1.1.0 or later, the `OPENSSL_TLS_SECURITY_LEVEL` option configures the default security level, which establishes default minimum security requirements for all library users. It's very useful to set this value at compile time as it can be used to prevent configuration mistakes. I discuss security levels in more detail later in this chapter.

The `enable-ec_nistp_64_gcc_128` parameter activates optimized versions of certain frequently used elliptic curves. This optimization depends on a compiler feature that can't be automatically detected, which is why it's disabled by default. The complete set of configuration options is available on the OpenSSL wiki.[4]

> **Note**
>
> When compiling software, it's important to be familiar with the default configuration of your compiler. System-provided packages are usually compiled using

---

[4] Compilation and Installation [fsty.uk/t586] (OpenSSL, retrieved 12 August 2020)

various hardening options, but if you compile some software yourself there is no guarantee that the same options will be used.[5]

If you're compiling a version before 1.1.0, you'll need to build the dependencies first:

```
$ make depend
```

OpenSSL 1.1.0 and above will do this automatically, so you can proceed to build the main package with the following:

```
$ make
$ make test
$ sudo make install
```

You'll get the following in /opt/openssl:

```
drwxr-xr-x 2 root root  4096 Jun  3 08:49 bin
drwxr-xr-x 2 root root  4096 Jun  3 08:49 certs
drwxr-xr-x 3 root root  4096 Jun  3 08:49 include
drwxr-xr-x 4 root root  4096 Jun  3 08:49 lib
drwxr-xr-x 6 root root  4096 Jun  3 08:48 man
drwxr-xr-x 2 root root  4096 Jun  3 08:49 misc
-rw-r--r-- 1 root root 10835 Jun  3 08:49 openssl.cnf
drwxr-xr-x 2 root root  4096 Jun  3 08:49 private
```

The private/ folder is empty, but that's normal; you do not yet have any private keys. On the other hand, you'll probably be surprised to learn that the certs/ folder is empty too. OpenSSL does not include any root certificates; maintaining a trust store is considered outside the scope of the project. Luckily, your operating system probably already comes with a trust store that you can use immediately. The following worked on my server:

```
$ cd /opt/openssl
$ sudo rmdir certs
$ sudo ln -s /etc/ssl/certs
```

## Examine Available Commands

OpenSSL is a cryptographic toolkit that consists of many different utilities. I counted 48 in my version. If there was ever an appropriate time to use the phrase *Swiss Army knife of cryptography*, this is it. Even though you'll use only a handful of the utilities, you should familiarize yourself with everything that's available because you never know what you might need in the future.

To get an idea of what is on offer, simply request help:

---

[5] Hardening [fsty.uk/t587] (Debian, 3 August 2020)

```
$ openssl help
```

The first part of the help output lists all available utilities. To get more information about a particular utility, use the man command followed by the name of the utility. For example, man ciphers will give you detailed information on how cipher suites are configured. However, man openssl-ciphers should also work:

```
Standard commands
asn1parse       ca              ciphers         cms
crl             crl2pkcs7       dgst            dhparam
dsa             dsaparam        ec              ecparam
enc             engine          errstr          gendsa
genpkey         genrsa          help            list
nseq            ocsp            passwd          pkcs12
pkcs7           pkcs8           pkey            pkeyparam
pkeyutl         prime           rand            rehash
req             rsa             rsautl          s_client
s_server        s_time          sess_id         smime
speed           spkac           srp             storeutl
ts              verify          version         x509
```

The help output doesn't actually end there, but the rest is somewhat less interesting. In the second part, you get the list of message digest commands:

```
Message Digest commands (see the `dgst' command for more details)
blake2b512      blake2s256      gost            md4
md5             rmd160          sha1            sha224
sha256          sha3-224        sha3-256        sha3-384
sha3-512        sha384          sha512          sha512-224
sha512-256      shake128        shake256        sm3
```

And then in the third part, you'll see the list of all cipher commands:

```
Cipher commands (see the `enc' command for more details)
aes-128-cbc     aes-128-ecb     aes-192-cbc     aes-192-ecb
aes-256-cbc     aes-256-ecb     aria-128-cbc    aria-128-cfb
aria-128-cfb1   aria-128-cfb8   aria-128-ctr    aria-128-ecb
aria-128-ofb    aria-192-cbc    aria-192-cfb    aria-192-cfb1
aria-192-cfb8   aria-192-ctr    aria-192-ecb    aria-192-ofb
aria-256-cbc    aria-256-cfb    aria-256-cfb1   aria-256-cfb8
aria-256-ctr    aria-256-ecb    aria-256-ofb    base64
bf              bf-cbc          bf-cfb          bf-ecb
bf-ofb          camellia-128-cbc camellia-128-ecb camellia-192-cbc
camellia-192-ecb camellia-256-cbc camellia-256-ecb cast
cast-cbc        cast5-cbc       cast5-cfb       cast5-ecb
cast5-ofb       des             des-cbc         des-cfb
des-ecb         des-ede         des-ede-cbc     des-ede-cfb
des-ede-ofb     des-ede3        des-ede3-cbc    des-ede3-cfb
```

| des-ede3-ofb | des-ofb | des3 | desx |
| rc2 | rc2-40-cbc | rc2-64-cbc | rc2-cbc |
| rc2-cfb | rc2-ecb | rc2-ofb | rc4 |
| rc4-40 | seed | seed-cbc | seed-cfb |
| seed-ecb | seed-ofb | sm4-cbc | sm4-cfb |
| sm4-ctr | sm4-ecb | sm4-ofb | |

# Building a Trust Store

OpenSSL does not come with a collection of trusted root certificates (also known as a *root store* or a *trust store*), so if you're installing from scratch you'll have to find them somewhere else. One possibility is to use the trust store built into your operating system, as I've shown earlier. This choice is usually fine, but the built-in trust stores may not always be up to date. Also, in a mixed environment there could be meaningful differences between the default stores in a variety of systems. A consistent and possibly better choice—but one that involves more work—is to reuse Mozilla's work. Mozilla put a lot of effort into maintaining a transparent and up-to-date root store for use in Firefox.[6]

Because it's open source, Mozilla keeps the trust store in the source code repository:

```
https://hg.mozilla.org/releases/mozilla-beta/file/tip/security/nss/lib/ckfw↵
/builtins/certdata.txt
```

Unfortunately, its certificate collection is in a proprietary format, which is not of much use to others as is. If you don't mind getting the collection via a third party, the Curl project provides a regularly updated conversion in *Privacy-Enhanced Mail* (PEM) format, which you can use directly:

```
http://curl.haxx.se/docs/caextract.html
```

If you'd rather work directly with Mozilla, you can convert its data using the same tool that the Curl project is using. You'll find more information about it in the following section.

> **Note**
>
> If you have an itch to write your own conversion script, note that Mozilla's root certificate file is not a simple list of certificates. Although most of the certificates are those that are considered trusted, there are also some that are explicitly disallowed. Additionally, some certificates may only be considered trusted for certain types of usage. The Perl script I describe here is smart enough to know the difference.

At this point, what you have is a root store with all trusted certificates in the same file. This will work fine if you're only going to be using it with, say, the s_client tool. In that case, all

---

[6] Mozilla CA Certificate Store [fsty.uk/t588] (Mozilla; 9 August 2020)

you need to do is point the -CAfile switch to your root store. Replacing the root store on a server will require more work, depending on what operating system is used.

On Ubuntu, for example, you'll need to replace the contents of the /etc/ssl/certs folder. Ubuntu ships with a tool called update-ca-certificates that might work. Alternatively, you could make the changes manually by replicating the structure of the existing data. From the looks of it, that folder contains the trusted certificates as individual files, as well as all of them in a single file called ca-certificates.crt. You will also observe some symbolic links; they are created by the OpenSSL's rehash or c_rehash tools. The drawback of any manual changes is that they may be overwritten when the system is updated.

## Manual Conversion

To convert Mozilla's root store, the Curl project uses a Perl script originally written by Guenter Knauf. This script is part of the Curl project, but you can download it directly by following this link:

https://raw.githubusercontent.com/curl/curl/master/lib/mk-ca-bundle.pl

After you download and run the script, it will fetch the certificate data from Mozilla and convert it to the PEM format:

```
$ ./mk-ca-bundle.pl
SHA256 of old file: 0
Downloading certdata.txt ...
Get certdata with curl!
[...]
Downloaded certdata.txt
SHA256 of new file: cc6408bd4be7fbfb8699bdb40ccb7f6de5780d681d87785ea362646e4dad5e8↵
e
Processing 'certdata.txt' ...
Done (138 CA certs processed, 30 skipped).
```

If you keep previously downloaded certificate data around, the script will use it to determine what changed and process only the updates.

# Key and Certificate Management

Most users turn to OpenSSL because they wish to configure and run a web server that supports SSL. That process consists of three steps: (1) generate a private key, (2) create a *Certificate Signing Request* (CSR) and send it to a CA, and (3) install the CA-provided certificate in your web server. These steps (and a few others) are covered in this section.

# Key Generation

The first step in preparing to run a TLS server is to generate a private key. Before you begin, you must make several decisions:

**Key algorithm**

OpenSSL supports RSA, DSA, ECDSA, and EdDSA key algorithms, but not all of them are useful in practice. For example, DSA is obsolete and EdDSA is not yet widely supported. That leaves us with RSA and ECDSA algorithms to use in our certificates.

**Key size**

The default key sizes might not be secure, which is why you should always explicitly configure key size. For example, the default for RSA keys used to be 512 bits, which is insecure. If you used a 512-bit key on your server today, an intruder could take your certificate and use brute force to recover your private key, after which she could impersonate your web site. Today, 2,048-bit RSA keys are considered secure, or 256 bits for ECDSA.

**Passphrase**

Using a passphrase with a key is optional, but strongly recommended. Protected keys can be safely stored, transported, and backed up. On the other hand, such keys are inconvenient, because they can't be used without their passphrases. For example, you might be asked to enter the passphrase every time you wish to restart your web server. For most, this is either too inconvenient or has unacceptable availability implications. In addition, using protected keys in production does not actually increase the security much, if at all. This is because, once activated, private keys are kept unprotected in program memory; an attacker who can get to the server can get the keys from there with just a little more effort. Thus, passphrases should be viewed only as a mechanism for protecting private keys when they are not installed on production systems. In other words, it's all right to keep passphrases on production systems, next to the keys. If you need better security in production, you should invest in a hardware solution.[7]

To generate an RSA key, use the following genpkey command:

```
$ openssl genpkey -out fd.key \
-algorithm RSA \
-pkeyopt rsa_keygen_bits:2048 \
-aes-128-cbc
```

---

[7] A small number of organizations will have very strict security requirements that require the private keys to be protected at any cost. For them, the solution is to invest in a *Hardware Security Module* (HSM), which is a type of product specifically designed to make key extraction impossible, even with physical access to the server. To make this work, HSMs not only generate and store keys, but also perform all necessary operations (e.g., signature generation). HSMs are typically very expensive.

---

```
..........................................+++++
...........................................................+++++
Enter PEM pass phrase: ************
Verifying - Enter PEM pass phrase: ************
```

Here, I specified that the key be protected with AES-128. You can also use AES-256 (with the -aes-256-cbc switch), but it's best to stay away from the other algorithms (e.g., DES, 3DES, and SEED).

> ### Warning
>
> By default, OpenSSL will set the public exponent of new RSA keys to 65,537. This is what's known as a *short public exponent*, and it significantly improves the performance of RSA verification. You may come across advice to choose 3 as your public exponent and make verification even faster. Although that's true, there are some unpleasant historical weaknesses associated with the use of 3 as a public exponent, which is why you should stick with 65,537. This choice provides a safety margin that's been proven effective in the past.

When you use the genpkey command, the generated private keys are stored in PKCS #8 format,[8] which is just text and doesn't look like much:

```
$ cat fd.key
-----BEGIN ENCRYPTED PRIVATE KEY-----
MIIFLTBXBgkqhkiG9w0BBQ0wSjApBgkqhkiG9w0BBQwwHAQInW7GrFjUhUcCAggA
MAwGCCqGSIb3DQIJBQAwHQYJYIZIAWUDBAEqBBBn8AErtRKB9p7ii1+g2OhWBIIE
OMnC2dwGznZqpTMXOMYekzyxe4dKlJiIsVr1hgwmjFifzEBs/KvHBV3eIe9wDAzq
[21 lines removed...]
IfveVZzM6PLbDaysxX6jEgi4xVbqWugd9h3eAPeBv9Z5iZ/bZq5hMbt37ElA2Rnh
RfmWSzlASjQi4XAHVLCs6XmULCda6QGvyB7WXxuzbhOv3C6BPXR49z6S1MFvOyDA
2oaXkfS+Ip3x2svgFJj/VpYZHUHwRCzXcDl/CdVg9fxwxcYHuJDH16Qfue/LRtiJ
hqr4fHrnbbk+MZpDaU+h4shLRBg2dONdUEzhPkpdOOkF
-----END ENCRYPTED PRIVATE KEY-----
```

However, a private key isn't just a blob of random data, even though that's what it looks like at a glance. You can see a key's structure using the following rsa command:

```
$ openssl pkey -in fd.key -text -noout
Enter pass phrase for fd.key: ****************
RSA Private-Key: (2048 bit, 2 primes)
modulus:
```

---

[8] You will often see advice to generate private keys using the genrsa command. Indeed, the earlier versions of this very book used this command in the examples. However, genrsa is a legacy command and should no longer be used. There is an entire new family of commands that deal with private keys in a unified manner (i.e., one command for all private key operations, no matter the algorithm). You should also be aware that genrsa outputs keys in a legacy format. Here's how to tell them apart: if you see BEGIN ENCRYPTED PRIVATE KEY at the top of the file, you're dealing with PKCS #8, which is the new format. If you see BEGIN RSA PRIVATE KEY, that's the legacy format.

```
    00:be:79:08:22:1a:bc:78:3c:17:34:4a:d3:5f:2b:
    [...]
publicExponent: 65537 (0x10001)
privateExponent:
    10:20:95:54:b5:e8:d1:51:5d:31:9b:48:4c:5d:90:
    [...]
prime1:
    00:f5:3f:74:cf:ef:8f:93:e9:54:b3:79:a1:f2:91:
    5a:7e:15:13:26:f7:f9:d7:a8:f3:f9:6b:2b:90:93:
    57:54:cc:84:c9:ea:6f:9f:39:ad:ad:60:4c:f0:68:
    16:db:1a:49:51:56:87:f1:70:ae:c9:42:89:2a:38:
    55:3e:17:a0:78:a7:52:49:10:79:cf:99:ae:53:c8:
    e0:60:5d:7e:91:26:86:3b:79:d2:70:c0:39:38:dd:
    ed:ee:75:c0:15:c6:30:51:00:a8:93:f3:8b:25:01:
    04:25:72:fc:9c:e9:73:d0:93:11:2d:82:e2:e3:d0:
    66:c0:36:2f:b6:de:de:0d:47
prime2:
    00:c6:d2:ce:66:b5:35:6b:35:d7:bb:b0:e3:f4:2d:
    [...]
exponent1:
    00:e9:2e:e9:b9:5f:f5:2b:54:fa:c5:1f:4c:7d:5f:
    [...]
exponent2:
    00:83:ea:bc:ad:a2:cf:a5:a9:9c:d0:d8:85:f6:ae:
    [...]
coefficient:
    68:18:a7:4f:aa:86:a7:e0:92:49:76:8d:24:65:fa:
    [...]
```

If you need to have just the public part of a key separately, you can do that with the following rsa command:

```
$ openssl pkey -in fd.key -pubout -out fd-public.key
Enter pass phrase for fd.key: ****************
```

If you look into the newly generated file, you'll see that the markers clearly indicate that the contained information is indeed public:

```
$ cat fd-public.key
-----BEGIN PUBLIC KEY-----
MIIBIjANBgkqhkiG9w0BAQEFAAOCAQ8AMIIBCgKCAQEAvnkIIhq8eDwXNErTXytD
U1JGrYUgFsN8IgFVMJmAuY15dBvSCO+6y9FAOH08utJVtHScyWeOlo1uoOTQ3RWr
Pe7W3O2SaW2gIby2cwzGf/FBExZ+BCNXkN5z8Kd38PXDLt8ar+7MJ3vrb/sW7zs2
v+rtfRar2RmhDPpVvI6sugCeHrvYDGdA/gIZAMMg3pVFivPpHnTH4AR7rTzWCWlb
nCB3z2FVYpvumrY8TvIo5OioD2I+TQyvlxDRo14QWxIdZxvPcCUxXMN9MC8fBtLu
IlllDmah8JzF2CF5IxVgVhi7hyTtSQfKsK91tAvN3OF9qkZNEpjNX37M5duHUVPb
tQIDAQAB
-----END PUBLIC KEY-----
```

It's good practice to verify that the output contains what you're expecting. For example, if you forget to include the -pubout switch on the command line, the output will contain your private key instead of the public key.

The process is similar for ECDSA keys, except that it isn't possible to create keys of arbitrary sizes. Instead, for each key you select a *named curve*, which controls key size, but it controls other EC parameters as well. The following example creates a 256-bit ECDSA key using the P-256 (or secp256r1) named curve:

```
$ openssl genpkey -out fd.key \
-algorithm EC  \
-pkeyopt ec_paramgen_curve:P-256 \
-aes-128-cbc
Enter PEM pass phrase: ****************
Verifying - Enter PEM pass phrase: ****************
```

OpenSSL supports many named curves, but for web server keys, you're generally (still) limited to only two curves that are widely supported: P-256 (also known as secp256r1 or prime256v1) and P-384 (secp384r1). Of these two, P-256 is sufficiently secure and provides better performance. If you're curious to see a list of all named curves supported by OpenSSL, you can get it using the ecparam command and the -list_curves switch.

The recent additions x25519, x448, ed25519, and ed448 are also supported, but they are different types of curves and have to be specified using the -algorithm switch—for example:

```
$ openssl genpkey -algorithm ed25519
-----BEGIN PRIVATE KEY-----
MC4CAQAwBQYDK2VwBCIEIF6K3m4WM7/yMA9COn6HYyx7PjJCIzY7bnBoKupYgdTL
-----END PRIVATE KEY-----
```

## Creating Certificate Signing Requests

Once you have a private key, you can proceed to create a *Certificate Signing Request* (CSR). This is a formal request asking a CA to sign a certificate, and it contains the public key of the entity requesting the certificate and some information about the entity. This data will all be part of the certificate. A CSR is always signed with the private key corresponding to the public key it carries.

CSR creation is usually an interactive process during which you'll be providing the elements of the certificate distinguished name. Read the instructions given by the openssl tool carefully; if you want a field to be empty, you must enter a single dot (.) on the line, rather than just hit Return. If you do the latter, OpenSSL will populate the corresponding CSR field with the default value. (This behavior doesn't make any sense when used with the default OpenSSL configuration, which is what virtually everyone does. It *does* make sense once you realize you can actually change the defaults, either by modifying the OpenSSL configuration or by providing your own configuration files.)

```
$ openssl req -new -key fd.key -out fd.csr
Enter pass phrase for fd.key: ****************
You are about to be asked to enter information that will be incorporated
into your certificate request.
What you are about to enter is what is called a Distinguished Name or a DN.
There are quite a few fields but you can leave some blank
For some fields there will be a default value,
If you enter '.', the field will be left blank.
-----
Country Name (2 letter code) [AU]:GB
State or Province Name (full name) [Some-State]:.
Locality Name (eg, city) []:London
Organization Name (eg, company) [Internet Widgits Pty Ltd]:Feisty Duck Ltd
Organizational Unit Name (eg, section) []:
Common Name (e.g. server FQDN or YOUR name) []:www.feistyduck.com
Email Address []:

Please enter the following 'extra' attributes
to be sent with your certificate request
A challenge password []:
An optional company name []:
```

> **Note**
>
> According to Section 5.4.1 of RFC 2985,[9] *challenge password* is an optional field that was intended for use during certificate revocation as a way of identifying the original entity that had requested the certificate. If entered, the password will be included verbatim in the CSR and communicated to the CA. It's rare to find a CA that relies on this field; all instructions I've seen recommend leaving it alone. Having a challenge password does not increase the security of the CSR in any way. Further, this field should not be confused with the key passphrase, which is a separate feature.

After a CSR is generated, use it to sign your own certificate and/or send it to a public CA and ask it to sign the certificate. Both approaches are described in the following sections. But before you do that, it's a good idea to double-check that the CSR is correct. Here's how:

```
$ openssl req -text -in fd.csr -noout
Certificate Request:
    Data:
        Version: 1 (0x0)
```

---

[9] RFC 2985: PKCS #9: Selected Object Classes and Attribute Types Version 2.0 [fsty.uk/t589] (M. Nystrom and B. Kaliski, November 2000)

```
        Subject: C = GB, L = London, O = Feisty Duck Ltd, CN = www.feistyduck.com
        Subject Public Key Info:
            Public Key Algorithm: id-ecPublicKey
                Public-Key: (256 bit)
                pub:
                    04:8a:d5:de:69:30:c7:77:b0:a0:54:f7:b3:34:9a:
                    96:1c:23:81:e3:9c:0c:81:a6:8a:a5:14:76:f4:4c:
                    b3:10:cb:ee:50:d1:ea:70:e9:7f:8f:75:67:f9:12:
                    83:b0:11:e7:6c:64:de:bc:af:bd:3f:43:da:b8:41:
                    96:75:34:63:85
                ASN1 OID: prime256v1
                NIST CURVE: P-256
        Attributes:
            a0:00
    Signature Algorithm: ecdsa-with-SHA256
        30:44:02:20:52:b9:cf:ca:d1:25:1c:b7:57:65:fb:24:5d:95:
        15:f0:39:79:36:6c:d6:0a:42:6e:26:7c:54:e8:71:17:a5:99:
        02:20:5a:e0:cd:b3:60:ec:2c:fc:29:8c:f9:21:01:08:9a:a3:
        0d:fc:9a:d3:4f:24:fb:23:4f:c6:d7:a2:14:d1:54:f9
```

# Creating CSRs from Existing Certificates

You can save yourself some typing if you're renewing a certificate and don't want to make any changes to the information presented in it. With the following command, you can create a brand-new CSR from an existing certificate:

```
$ openssl x509 -x509toreq -in fd.crt -out fd.csr -signkey fd.key
```

> **Note**
>
> Unless you're using some form of public key pinning and wish to continue using the existing key, it's best practice to generate a new key every time you apply for a new certificate. Key generation is quick and inexpensive and reduces your exposure in case of a compromise that went undetected.

# Unattended CSR Generation

CSR generation doesn't have to be interactive. Using a custom OpenSSL configuration file, you can both automate the process (as explained in this section) and do certain things that are not possible interactively (e.g., how to have multiple domain names in the same certificate, as discussed in subsequent sections).

For example, let's say that we want to automate the generation of a CSR for www.feistyduck.com. We would start by creating a file fd.cnf with the following contents:

```
[req]
prompt = no
```

```
distinguished_name = dn
req_extensions = ext
input_password = PASSPHRASE

[dn]
CN = www.feistyduck.com
emailAddress = webmaster@feistyduck.com
O = Feisty Duck Ltd
L = London
C = GB

[ext]
subjectAltName = DNS:www.feistyduck.com,DNS:feistyduck.com
```

Now you can create the CSR directly from the command line:

```
$ openssl req -new -config fd.cnf -key fd.key -out fd.csr
```

## Signing Your Own Certificates

If you're configuring a TLS server for your own use or for a quick test, sometimes you don't want to go to a CA for a publicly trusted certificate. It's much easier just to use a self-signed certificate.[10]

If you already have a CSR, create a certificate using the following command:

```
$ openssl x509 -req -days 365 -in fd.csr -signkey fd.key -out fd.crt
Signature ok
subject=C = GB, L = London, O = Feisty Duck Ltd, CN = www.feistyduck.com
Getting Private key
Enter pass phrase for fd.key: ****************
```

You don't actually have to create a CSR in a separate step. The following command creates a self-signed certificate starting with a key alone:

```
$ openssl req -new -x509 -days 365 -key fd.key -out fd.crt
```

If you don't wish to be asked any questions, use the -subj switch to provide the certificate subject information on the command line:

```
$ openssl req -new -x509 -days 365 -key fd.key -out fd.crt \
  -subj "/C=GB/L=London/O=Feisty Duck Ltd/CN=www.feistyduck.com"
```

---

[10] To be honest, getting a valid public certificate quickly has become much easier since Let's Encrypt started offering them for free in an automated fashion. We're now seeing the rise of operating systems and even software packages that seamlessly integrate with Let's Encrypt to provide public certificates out of the box. We're not very far from the moment when creating self-signed certificates will be the option that requires more work.

# Creating Certificates Valid for Multiple Hostnames

By default, certificates produced by OpenSSL have only one common name and are valid for only one hostname. Because of this, even if you have related web sites, you are forced to use a separate certificate for each site. In this situation, using a single *multidomain* certificate makes much more sense. Further, even when you're running a single web site, you need to ensure that the certificate is valid for all possible paths that end users can take to reach it. In practice, this means using at least two names, one with the www prefix and one without (e.g., www.feistyduck.com and feistyduck.com).

There are two mechanisms for supporting multiple hostnames in a certificate. The first is to list all desired hostnames using an X.509 extension called *Subject Alternative Name* (SAN). The second is to use wildcards. You can also use a combination of the two approaches when it's more convenient. In practice, for most sites, you can specify a bare domain name and a wildcard to cover all the subdomains (e.g., feistyduck.com and *.feistyduck.com).

> **Warning**
>
> When a certificate contains alternative names, all common names are ignored. Newer certificates produced by CAs may not even include any common names. For that reason, include all desired hostnames on the alternative names list.

First, place the extension information in a separate text file. I'm going to call it fd.ext. In the file, specify the name of the extension (subjectAltName) and list the desired hostnames, as in the following example:

```
subjectAltName = DNS:*.feistyduck.com, DNS:feistyduck.com
```

Then, when using the x509 command to issue a certificate, refer to the file using the -extfile switch:

```
$ openssl x509 -req -days 365 \
-in fd.csr -signkey fd.key -out fd.crt \
-extfile fd.ext
```

The rest of the process is no different from before. But when you examine the generated certificate afterward (see the next section), you'll find that it contains the SAN extension:

```
X509v3 extensions:
    X509v3 Subject Alternative Name:
        DNS:*.feistyduck.com, DNS:feistyduck.com
```

# Examining Certificates

Certificates don't look like much in a text editor, but they contain a great deal of information; you just need to know how to unpack it. The x509 command does just that, so let's use it to look at the self-signed certificates you generated.

In the following example, I use the -text switch to print certificate contents and -noout to reduce clutter by not printing the encoded certificate itself (which is the default behavior):

```
$ openssl x509 -text -in fd.crt -noout
Certificate:
    Data:
        Version: 3 (0x2)
        Serial Number:
            76:bc:fb:f6:06:0e:61:eb:99:5e:83:ea:ef:92:0b:32:4f:fd:3b:51
        Signature Algorithm: ecdsa-with-SHA256
        Issuer: C = GB, L = London, O = Feisty Duck Ltd, CN = www.feistyduck.com
        Validity
            Not Before: Aug 15 09:31:54 2020 GMT
            Not After : Aug 15 09:31:54 2021 GMT
        Subject: C = GB, L = London, O = Feisty Duck Ltd, CN = www.feistyduck.com
        Subject Public Key Info:
            Public Key Algorithm: id-ecPublicKey
                Public-Key: (256 bit)
                pub:
                    04:8a:d5:de:69:30:c7:77:b0:a0:54:f7:b3:34:9a:
                    96:1c:23:81:e3:9c:0c:81:a6:8a:a5:14:76:f4:4c:
                    b3:10:cb:ee:50:d1:ea:70:e9:7f:8f:75:67:f9:12:
                    83:b0:11:e7:6c:64:de:bc:af:bd:3f:43:da:b8:41:
                    96:75:34:63:85
                ASN1 OID: prime256v1
                NIST CURVE: P-256
        X509v3 extensions:
            X509v3 Subject Alternative Name:
                DNS:*.feistyduck.com, DNS:feistyduck.com
    Signature Algorithm: ecdsa-with-SHA256
        30:45:02:20:4d:36:34:cd:e9:3e:df:18:52:e7:74:c4:a1:97:
        91:6a:e7:c1:6d:12:01:63:d1:fd:90:28:32:70:24:5c:be:35:
        02:21:00:bd:02:64:c9:8b:27:8f:79:c7:a4:41:7c:31:2f:98:
        29:3e:db:8c:f3:f1:d7:bb:fa:fe:95:48:be:16:e1:ab:1b
```

Self-signed certificates usually contain only the most basic certificate data, and most of it is self-explanatory. In essence, there's the main body of the certificate, to which a signature is added. By comparison, certificates issued by public CAs are much more interesting, as they contain a number of additional fields (via the X.509 extension mechanism).

# Examining Public Certificates

When you look at a public certificate, in the first part of the output you will find information that is similar to that in self-signed certificates. In fact, the only difference will be that this certificate has a different parent, as indicated by the issuer information.

```
Certificate:
    Data:
        Version: 3 (0x2)
        Serial Number:
            03:5e:50:53:75:08:1a:f2:7d:27:64:4f:d5:6f:1a:02:07:89
        Signature Algorithm: sha256WithRSAEncryption
        Issuer: C = US, O = Let's Encrypt, CN = Let's Encrypt Authority X3
        Validity
            Not Before: Aug  2 23:10:45 2020 GMT
            Not After : Oct 31 23:10:45 2020 GMT
        Subject: CN = www.feistyduck.com
        Subject Public Key Info:
            Public Key Algorithm: rsaEncryption
                RSA Public-Key: (2048 bit)
                Modulus:
                    00:c8:14:4f:33:9a:db:bb:e7:e3:78:93:46:5d:56:
                    a7:bc:58:86:43:dc:ea:c1:01:52:4b:0f:20:b7:38:
                    [...]
                Exponent: 65537 (0x10001)
        X509v3 extensions:
            [...]
```

The main differences are going to be in the X.509 extensions, which contain a great deal of very interesting information. Let's examine what's in the extensions and why it's there, in no particular order.

The *Basic Constraints* extension is used to mark certificates as belonging to a CA, giving them the ability to sign other certificates. Non-CA certificates will either have this extension omitted or will have the value of CA set to FALSE. This extension is critical, which means that all software-consuming certificates must understand its meaning.

```
X509v3 Basic Constraints: critical
    CA:FALSE
```

The *Key Usage* (KU) and *Extended Key Usage* (EKU) extensions restrict what a certificate can be used for. If these extensions are present, then only the listed uses are allowed. If the extensions are not present, there are no use restrictions. What you see in this example is typical for a web server certificate, which, for example, does not allow for code signing:

```
X509v3 Key Usage: critical
    Digital Signature, Key Encipherment
```

```
X509v3 Extended Key Usage:
    TLS Web Server Authentication, TLS Web Client Authentication
```

The *CRL Distribution Points* extension lists the addresses where the CA's *Certificate Revocation List* (CRL) information can be found. This information is important in cases in which certificates need to be revoked. CRLs are CA-signed lists of revoked certificates, published at regular time intervals (e.g., seven days). Let's Encrypt doesn't provide CRLs, so I took the following snippet from another certificate:

```
X509v3 CRL Distribution Points:
    Full Name:
        URI:http://crl.starfieldtech.com/sfs3-20.crl
```

### Note

You might have noticed that the CRL location doesn't use a secure server, and you might be wondering if the link is thus insecure. It is not. Because each CRL is signed by the CA that issued it, clients are able to verify its integrity. In fact, if CRLs were distributed over TLS, browsers might face a chicken-and-egg problem in which they want to verify the revocation status of the certificate used by the server delivering the CRL itself!

The *Certificate Policies* extension is used to indicate the policy under which the certificate was issued. For example, this is where you can expect to find an indication of the type of validation used to ascertain the identity of the owner. *Extended validation* (EV) indicators can be found (as in the example that follows). These indicators are in the form of unique object identifiers (OIDs), some of which are generic and some specific to the issuing CA. In the following example, the OID 2.23.140.1.2.1 indicates a domain-validated certificate. In addition, this extension often contains one or more *Certificate Policy Statement* (CPS) points, which are usually web pages or PDF documents.

```
X509v3 Certificate Policies:
    Policy: 2.23.140.1.2.1
    Policy: 1.3.6.1.4.1.44947.1.1.1
        CPS: http://cps.letsencrypt.org
```

The *Authority Information Access* (AIA) extension usually contains two important pieces of information. First, it lists the address of the CA's *Online Certificate Status Protocol* (OCSP) responder, which can be used to check for certificate revocation in real time. The extension may also contain a link to where the issuer's certificate (the next certificate in the chain) can be found. These days, server certificates are rarely signed directly by trusted root certificates, which means that users must include one or more intermediate certificates in their configuration. Mistakes are easy to make and will invalidate the certificates. Some clients will use the information provided in this extension to fix an incomplete certificate chain, but many clients won't.

```
Authority Information Access:
    OCSP - URI:http://ocsp.int-x3.letsencrypt.org
    CA Issuers - URI:http://cert.int-x3.letsencrypt.org/
```

The *Subject Key Identifier* and *Authority Key Identifier* extensions establish unique subject and authority key identifiers, respectively. The value specified in the Authority Key Identifier extension of a certificate must match the value specified in the Subject Key Identifier extension in the issuing certificate. This information is very useful during the certification path-building process, in which a client is trying to find all possible paths from a leaf (server) certificate to a trusted root. Certification authorities will often use one private key with more than one certificate, and this field allows software to reliably identify which certificate can be matched to which key. In the real world, many certificate chains supplied by servers are invalid, but that fact often goes unnoticed because browsers are able to find alternative trust paths.

```
X509v3 Subject Key Identifier:
    A1:EC:11:C6:E1:E8:F7:E6:98:85:FA:9A:53:F8:B8:F1:D6:88:F9:A3
X509v3 Authority Key Identifier:
    keyid:A8:4A:6A:63:04:7D:DD:BA:E6:D1:39:B7:A6:45:65:EF:F3:A8:EC:A1
```

The *Subject Alternative Name* extension is used to list all the hostnames for which the certificate is valid. This extension used to be optional; if it isn't present, clients fall back to using the information provided in the *common name* (CN), which is part of the *Subject* field. If the extension is present, then the content of the CN field is ignored during validation.

```
X509v3 Subject Alternative Name:
    DNS:www.feistyduck.com, DNS:feistyduck.com
```

Finally, the most recent addition is the *Certificate Transparency* (CT) extension, which is used to carry proof of logging to various public CT logs. Depending on the certificate lifetime, you can expect to see anywhere from two to five *Signed Certificate Timestamps* (SCTs). There isn't a single set of unified requirements for the numbers and types of SCTs that are necessary to recognize a certificate as valid. Technically, it's up to every client to specify what they expect. In practice, Chrome was the first browser to require CT and other clients are likely to follow its lead.[11]

```
CT Precertificate SCTs:
    Signed Certificate Timestamp:
        Version   : v1 (0x0)
        Log ID    : 5E:A7:73:F9:DF:56:C0:E7:B5:36:48:7D:D0:49:E0:32:
                    7A:91:9A:0C:84:A1:12:12:84:18:75:96:81:71:45:58
        Timestamp : Aug  3 00:10:45.300 2020 GMT
        Extensions: none
```

---

[11] Certificate Transparency in Chrome [fsty.uk/t590] (Chromium; retrieved 15 August 2020)

```
Signature : ecdsa-with-SHA256
          30:45:02:21:00:BB:7F:D0:E1:E6:CD:4B:E7:79:30:AE:
          BE:F6:50:4F:36:A4:F6:1D:65:21:1A:05:A9:B3:F0:53:
          BA:FA:AC:6D:FB:02:20:52:23:B9:F9:B6:73:34:7F:3D:
          7F:42:5C:E3:9D:3D:DA:D8:7F:B3:7E:21:0C:27:54:9B:
          DA:E1:3F:0F:8E:09:60
```
[...]

# Key and Certificate Conversion

Private keys and certificates can be stored in a variety of formats, which means that you'll often need to convert them from one format to another. The most common formats are:

**Binary (DER) certificate**

Contains an X.509 certificate in its raw form, using DER ASN.1 encoding.

**ASCII (PEM) certificate(s)**

Contains a base64-encoded DER certificate, with `-----BEGIN CERTIFICATE-----` used as the header and `-----END CERTIFICATE-----` as the footer. Usually seen with only one certificate per file, although some programs allow more than one certificate depending on the context. For example, older Apache web server versions require the server certificate to be alone in one file, with all intermediate certificates together in another.

**Legacy OpenSSL key format**

Contains a private key in its raw form, using DER ASN.1 encoding. Historically, OpenSSL used a format based on PKCS #1. These days, if you use the proper commands (i.e., genpkey), OpenSSL defaults to PKCS #8.

**ASCII (PEM) key**

Contains a base64-encoded DER key, sometimes with additional metadata (e.g., the algorithm used for password protection). The text in the header and footer can differ, depending on what underlying key format is used.

**PKCS #7 certificate(s)**

A complex format designed for the transport of signed or encrypted data, defined in RFC 2315. It's usually seen with `.p7b` and `.p7c` extensions and can include the entire certificate chain as needed. This format is supported by Java's `keytool` utility.

**PKCS #8 key**

The new default format for the private key store. PKCS #8 is defined in RFC 5208. Should you need to convert from PKCS #8 to the legacy format for whatever reason, use the `pkcs8` command.

**PKCS #12 (PFX) key and certificate(s)**

A complex format that can store and protect a server key along with an entire certificate chain. It's commonly seen with `.p12` and `.pfx` extensions. This format is

---

commonly used in Microsoft products, but is also used for client certificates. These days, the PFX name is used as a synonym for PKCS #12, even though PFX referred to a different format a long time ago (an early version of PKCS #12). It's unlikely that you'll encounter the old version anywhere.

## PEM and DER Conversion

Certificate conversion between PEM and DER formats is performed with the x509 tool. To convert a certificate from PEM to DER format:

```
$ openssl x509 -inform PEM -in fd.pem -outform DER -out fd.der
```

To convert a certificate from DER to PEM format:

```
$ openssl x509 -inform DER -in fd.der -outform PEM -out fd.pem
```

The syntax is identical if you need to convert private keys between DER and PEM formats, but different commands are used: rsa for RSA keys, and dsa for DSA keys. If you're dealing with the new PKCS #8 format, use the pkey tool.

## PKCS #12 (PFX) Conversion

One command is all that's needed to convert the key and certificates in PEM format to PKCS #12. The following example converts a key (fd.key), certificate (fd.crt), and intermediate certificates (fd-chain.crt) into an equivalent single PKCS #12 file:

```
$ openssl pkcs12 -export \
    -name "My Certificate" \
    -out fd.p12 \
    -inkey fd.key \
    -in fd.crt \
    -certfile fd-chain.crt
Enter Export Password: ***************
Verifying - Enter Export Password: ***************
```

The reverse conversion isn't as straightforward. You can use a single command, but in that case you'll get the entire contents in a single file:

```
$ openssl pkcs12 -in fd.p12 -out fd.pem -nodes
```

Now, you must open the file fd.pem in your favorite editor and manually split it into individual key, certificate, and intermediate certificate files. While you're doing that, you'll notice additional content provided before each component. For example:

```
Bag Attributes
    localKeyID: E3 11 E4 F1 2C ED 11 66 41 1B B8 83 35 D2 DD 07 FC DE 28 76
```

```
subject=/1.3.6.1.4.1.311.60.2.1.3=GB/2.5.4.15=Private Organization↵
/serialNumber=06694169/C=GB/ST=London/L=London/O=Feisty Duck Ltd↵
/CN=www.feistyduck.com
issuer=/C=US/ST=Arizona/L=Scottsdale/O=Starfield Technologies, Inc./OU=http:/↵
/certificates.starfieldtech.com/repository/CN=Starfield Secure Certification ↵
Authority
-----BEGIN CERTIFICATE-----
MIIF5zCCBM+gAwIBAgIHBG9JXlv9vTANBgkqhkiG9w0BAQUFADCB3DELMAkGA1UE
BhMCVVMxEDAOBgNVBAgTBOFyaXpvbmExEzARBgNVBAcTClNjb3R0c2RhbGUxJTAj
[...]
```

This additional metadata is very handy to quickly identify the certificates. Obviously, you should ensure that the main certificate file contains the leaf server certificate and not something else. Further, you should also ensure that the intermediate certificates are provided in the correct order, with the issuing certificate following the signed one. If you see a self-signed root certificate, feel free to delete it or store it elsewhere; it shouldn't go into the chain.

> **Warning**
>
> The final conversion output shouldn't contain anything apart from the encoded key and certificates. Although some tools are smart enough to ignore what isn't needed, other tools are not. Leaving extra data in PEM files might result in problems that are difficult to troubleshoot.

It's possible to get OpenSSL to split the components for you, but doing so requires multiple invocations of the pkcs12 command (including typing the bundle password each time):

```
$ openssl pkcs12 -in fd.p12 -nocerts -out fd.key -nodes
$ openssl pkcs12 -in fd.p12 -nokeys -clcerts -out fd.crt
$ openssl pkcs12 -in fd.p12 -nokeys -cacerts -out fd-chain.crt
```

This approach won't save you much work. You must still examine each file to ensure that it contains the correct contents and to remove the metadata.

## PKCS #7 Conversion

To convert from PEM to PKCS #7, use the crl2pkcs7 command:

```
$ openssl crl2pkcs7 -nocrl -out fd.p7b -certfile fd.crt -certfile fd-chain.crt
```

To convert from PKCS #7 to PEM, use the pkcs7 command with the -print_certs switch:

```
openssl pkcs7 -in fd.p7b -print_certs -out fd.pem
```

Similar to the conversion from PKCS #12, you must now edit the fd.pem file to clean it up and split it into the desired components.

# Configuration

A common task in TLS server configuration is selecting which cipher suites to use. To communicate securely, TLS needs to decide which cryptographic primitives to use to achieve its goals (e.g., confidentiality). This is done by selecting a suitable cipher suite, which makes a series of decisions about how authentication, key exchange, encryption, and other operations are done. Programs that rely on OpenSSL usually adopt the same approach to suite configuration that OpenSSL uses, simply passing through the configuration options.

Before TLS 1.3, the usual server configuration would include cipher suite configuration and an option for the server to prefer the stronger suites during the negotiation. Because of some differences in the design of TLS 1.3 from earlier protocol versions, OpenSSL decided to configure it differently, increasing the complexity of server configuration. I'll discuss this in the following sections.

Coming up with a good suite configuration can be pretty time consuming, and there are a lot of details to consider. I wrote this section to serve two goals. If you don't want to spend a lot of time learning how to use OpenSSL and how to rank cipher suites, simply use the default configuration I provide. On the other hand, if you prefer to learn the ins and outs of OpenSSL configuration, this section has the answers.

## Obtaining Supported Suites

Let's start this deep dive by first determining which suites are supported by your OpenSSL installation. To do this, invoke the ciphers command with the -v switch and ALL:COMPLEMENTOFALL as a parameter:

```
$ openssl ciphers -v 'ALL:COMPLEMENTOFALL'
```

> **Tip**
>
> From OpenSSL 1.0.0, the ciphers command supports the uppercase -V switch to provide extra-verbose output. In this mode, the output will also contain suite IDs, which are always handy to have. For example, OpenSSL doesn't always use the RFC names for suites; in such cases, you must use the IDs to cross-check. In this section, I use the lowercase -v because the output is easier to show in the book.

At this point you will observe a lot of output, consisting of everything your installation of OpenSSL has to offer. In my case, there were 162 suites in the output. Let's take a look at one line:

```
TLS_AES_256_GCM_SHA384 TLSv1.3 Kx=any Au=any Enc=AESGCM(256) Mac=AEAD
```

Each line of output provides extended information on one suite. From left to right:

1. Suite name

2. Required minimum protocol version[12]

3. Key exchange algorithm

4. Authentication algorithm

5. Encryption algorithm and strength

6. MAC (integrity) algorithm

Traditionally, OpenSSL didn't use official suite names, although it does now for TLS 1.3 suites. As of recently, when you add the `-stdname` switch to the `ciphers` tool, you'll get the official suite names and OpenSSL names at the same time.

> **Note**
>
> You may notice that all TLS 1.3 suites have any under key exchange and authentication. This is because this protocol version moved these two aspects of the handshake out of the cipher suites and into the protocol itself. It also removed all insecure algorithms, so in this context any isn't bad or insecure.

## Understanding Security Levels

In the previous section, we discussed how to get a complete list of supported suites—but that list is deceptive. Just because something is supported doesn't mean it's going to be enabled. Unless you tell it otherwise, the `ciphers` command outputs even the suites that will not be allowed. The trick is to use the `-s` switch, after which the number of suites will go down from 162 to only 77.

Granted, the reduction is in large part due to the removal of PSK and SRP suites, which removes 66 entries (down to 96). The remaining difference of 21 entries is due to the concept called *security level*, which OpenSSL now uses.[13]

Cipher suite configuration is complex, and most people are not experts in cryptography. For example, it's very easy to follow some outdated advice from the Internet and add an insecure element to your configuration. Additionally, there are some aspects of security that cannot be configured via cipher suites and previously couldn't be controlled at all. Security levels therefore are designed to guarantee minimum security requirements, even if incorrect configuration is requested. They are a very useful safety net.

---

[12] Some suites on the list show SSLv3 in the protocol column. This is nothing to worry about. It only means that the suite is compatible with this old (and obsolete) protocol version. Your configuration will not downgrade to SSL 3.0 if these suites are used.

[13] SSL_CTX_get_security_level man page [fsty.uk/t591] (OpenSSL, retrieved 21 August 2020)

Table 12.1. OpenSSL security levels

| Security Level | Meaning |
|---|---|
| Level 0 | No restrictions. Allows all features enabled at compile time. **Insecure.** |
| Level 1 | The security level corresponds to a minimum of 80 bits of security. **Weak.** |
| Level 2 | Security level set to 112 bits of security. |
| Level 3 | Security level set to 128 bits of security. |
| Level 4 | Security level set to 192 bits of security. |
| Level 5 | Security level set to 256 bits of security. |

The most important aspect of security levels is knowing what not to use, and that's the first two levels. Level 0 imposes no restrictions and is potentially insecure (depending on what features were enabled at compile time). You aren't very likely to need this level in practice. Level 1 is slightly better but still allows weak elements. You may need this level for interoperability purposes with legacy systems. Level 1 is the default security level in OpenSSL.

In practice, you should aim to use level 2 as your baseline. This level supports 2,048-bit RSA keys, which most web sites use today. Weak protocols such as SSL 2 and SSL 3 won't be allowed, along with RC4 and SHA1. If you're not using stock OpenSSL, you may find that your distribution already made this choice for you; for example, Ubuntu 20.04 LTS chooses level 2 as the default.

Levels 3 and up are levels you should consider if you have specific security requirements and want to enforce stronger encryption. For example, if you enable level 3, 2,048-bit RSA keys won't be allowed. Because keys stronger than this are quite slow, this choice of security level implicitly restricts you to ECDSA keys.

You can gain a better understanding of security levels by using the -s switch along with the @SECLEVEL keyword as part of your suite configuration. For an example, let's see how the switch from level 3 to level 4 affects one arbitrary suite configuration. At level 3, there are four suites in the output:

```
$ openssl ciphers -v -s -tls1_2 'EECDH+AESGCM @SECLEVEL=3'
ECDHE-ECDSA-AES256-GCM-SHA384 TLSv1.2 Kx=ECDH Au=ECDSA Enc=AESGCM(256) Mac=AEAD
ECDHE-RSA-AES256-GCM-SHA384   TLSv1.2 Kx=ECDH Au=RSA   Enc=AESGCM(256) Mac=AEAD
ECDHE-ECDSA-AES128-GCM-SHA256 TLSv1.2 Kx=ECDH Au=ECDSA Enc=AESGCM(128) Mac=AEAD
ECDHE-RSA-AES128-GCM-SHA256   TLSv1.2 Kx=ECDH Au=RSA   Enc=AESGCM(128) Mac=AEAD
```

However, at level 4 there are only two suites in the output, because the 128-bit suites were removed:

```
$ openssl ciphers -v -s -tls1_2 'EECDH+AESGCM @SECLEVEL=4'
ECDHE-ECDSA-AES256-GCM-SHA384 TLSv1.2 Kx=ECDH Au=ECDSA Enc=AESGCM(256) Mac=AEAD
ECDHE-RSA-AES256-GCM-SHA384   TLSv1.2 Kx=ECDH Au=RSA   Enc=AESGCM(256) Mac=AEAD
```

You may have noticed that the previous example introduces the `-tls1_2` switch, which outputs only suites that can be negotiated with TLS 1.2. This switch, along with `-tls1_3`, `-tls1_1`, `-tls1`, and `-ssl3`, is very useful for removing unwanted output when you're interested in only one protocol.

# Configuring TLS 1.3

If you're working with the `ciphers` tool and you're not familiar with how TLS 1.3 is configured (e.g., you only worked with versions of OpenSSL that did not support this protocol), you may be confused by the fact that no matter what configuration you specify, the TLS 1.3 suites are always listed at the top. This is happening because OpenSSL introduced a separate mechanism for TLS 1.3 suite configuration. At the library level, there are separate function calls for this, and there is a separate approach to use with the command-line tools.

When it comes to the `ciphers` tool, to control TLS 1.3 suites you'll need to use the `-ciphersuites` switch. To illustrate this, let's enable one TLS 1.3 suite and one SEED suite:

```
$ openssl ciphers -v -s -ciphersuites TLS_AES_256_GCM_SHA384 SEED-SHA
TLS_AES_256_GCM_SHA384  TLSv1.3 Kx=any Au=any Enc=AESGCM(256) Mac=AEAD
SEED-SHA                SSLv3   Kx=RSA Au=RSA Enc=SEED(128)   Mac=SHA1
```

When they were adding this new configuration mechanism for TLS 1.3, OpenSSL developers took an opportunity to simplify how suites are configured by removing a variety of tools and keywords that can now be called *legacy suite configuration*. The only supported approach for TLS 1.3 is to provide a colon-separated list of the suites you wish to support, in the order you wish to support them. That's all. For example:

```
$ openssl ciphers -v -s -tls1_3 \
-ciphersuites TLS_AES_128_GCM_SHA256:TLS_AES_256_GCM_SHA384
TLS_AES_128_GCM_SHA256  TLSv1.3 Kx=any Au=any Enc=AESGCM(128) Mac=AEAD
TLS_AES_256_GCM_SHA384  TLSv1.3 Kx=any Au=any Enc=AESGCM(256) Mac=AEAD
```

> **Note**
>
> Even though there is a separate configuration string for TLS 1.3 suites, the configuration is still affected by the security level configuration, which is specified in the legacy configuration string.

How does this new approach to TLS 1.3 configuration affect real life? Depending on your tools, you may now find yourself needing to use two configuration strings where previously there was only one. In the Apache web server, the `SSLCipherSuite` directive has been extended with an optional first parameter, enabling you to target the protocols you wish to configure. So you could do something like this:

```
SSLCipherSuite TLSv1.3 TLS_AES_128_GCM_SHA256
SSLCipherSuite EECDH+AES128+AESGCM
```

The result would be equivalent to the following:

```
TLS_AES_128_GCM_SHA256          TLSv1.3 Kx=any  Au=any  Enc=AESGCM(128) Mac=AEAD
ECDHE-ECDSA-AES128-GCM-SHA256   TLSv1.2 Kx=ECDH Au=ECDSA Enc=AESGCM(128) Mac=AEAD
ECDHE-RSA-AES128-GCM-SHA256     TLSv1.2 Kx=ECDH Au=RSA   Enc=AESGCM(128) Mac=AEAD
```

Not all tools have added support for TLS 1.3 suite configuration. Instead, you always get the OpenSSL defaults. For most users, this is not yet a real problem because all TLS 1.3 suites are strong. But if you want to do something out of the ordinary, perhaps enable the CCM suites that are currently disabled by default, you'll have to resort to using a workaround by changing the OpenSSL defaults via a configuration file, which I will cover in the next section.

## Configuring OpenSSL Defaults

Occasionally, you'll run into a problem trying to configure some applications to use OpenSSL in a certain way, only to be frustrated if there are no configuration options to achieve what you need. In that situation, you can resort to changing the OpenSSL defaults.

On startup, OpenSSL will go through an initialization procedure that attempts to fetch the defaults from the filesystem. This procedure consists of the following steps:

1. Check the OPENSSL_CONF environment variable, which is expected to contain a path to the configuration file. This step is skipped if the binary has the setuid or setguid flag set.

2. Failing that, check the default system-wide location of the configuration directory specified at compile time. OpenSSL will look in this folder for a file called openssl.cnf.

This process ensures that there are a number of options available to control the defaults in a way that solves a particular need. We can change the default configuration of only one program or of all programs that run on the same server.

For the latter use case, use the version tool to determine the location of the default configuration file:

```
$ openssl version -d
OPENSSLDIR: "/usr/lib/ssl"
```

Now that we know how to change the defaults, the question instead becomes what to put into the configuration file. For the syntax of configuration files and detailed information, it's

---

best that you consult the official documentation.[14] However, if you just need to reconfigure the cipher suite configuration, take a look at the following example that does just that:

```
[default_conf]
ssl_conf = ssl_section

[ssl_section]
system_default = system_default_section

[system_default_section]
MinProtocol = TLSv1.2
CipherString = DEFAULT:@SECLEVEL=2
Ciphersuites = TLS_AES_128_GCM_SHA256:TLS_CHACHA20_POLY1305_SHA256
Options = ServerPreference,PrioritizeChaCha
```

This configuration file specifies the minimum supported protocol, security level, legacy cipher suite configuration, and TLS 1.3 suite configuration, and it also enables special ChaCha20 prioritization, which is triggered if OpenSSL detects that client prefers this cipher over AES. For the complete list of available parameters, refer to the official documentation.[15]

## Recommended Suite Configuration

When it comes to cipher suite configuration, the best approach is to avoid legacy keyword-based suite configuration and instead explicitly specify the suites you want to use. By doing this, you don't have to learn about complex keyword behavior, you'll minimize mistakes, and you'll also leave behind a configuration that is self-documenting and easy to understand.

In this section, I will give you my recommendations and explain my reasoning. For simplicity, I'll show the suites as a single ordered list, even though they are configured separately for TLS 1.3 and separately for earlier protocol versions. Here is my recommended default configuration for all TLS services, given as a list of suites in the order of preference:

```
TLS_AES_128_GCM_SHA256
TLS_CHACHA20_POLY1305_SHA256
TLS_AES_256_GCM_SHA384

ECDHE-ECDSA-AES128-GCM-SHA256
ECDHE-ECDSA-CHACHA20-POLY1305
ECDHE-ECDSA-AES256-GCM-SHA384
ECDHE-ECDSA-AES128-SHA
```

---

[14] config man page [fsty.uk/t592] (OpenSSL, retrieved 21 August 2020)

[15] SSL_CONF_cmd man page [fsty.uk/t593] (OpenSSL, retrieved 21 August 2020)

```
ECDHE-ECDSA-AES256-SHA
ECDHE-ECDSA-AES128-SHA256
ECDHE-ECDSA-AES256-SHA384
ECDHE-RSA-AES128-GCM-SHA256
ECDHE-RSA-CHACHA20-POLY1305
ECDHE-RSA-AES256-GCM-SHA384
ECDHE-RSA-AES128-SHA
ECDHE-RSA-AES256-SHA
ECDHE-RSA-AES128-SHA256
ECDHE-RSA-AES256-SHA384
DHE-RSA-AES128-GCM-SHA256
DHE-RSA-CHACHA20-POLY1305
DHE-RSA-AES256-GCM-SHA384
DHE-RSA-AES128-SHA
DHE-RSA-AES256-SHA
DHE-RSA-AES128-SHA256
DHE-RSA-AES256-SHA256
```

This configuration uses only suites that support forward secrecy and provide strong encryption.[16] The preference is for 128-bit suites, which are faster and provide strong security; ECDSA public key encryption, which is faster and more secure than the traditional RSA (at the usual key lengths); ECDHE key exchange, which is faster than DHE; and authenticated encryption, which is faster and more secure than the old CBC mode.

It's possible to have a shorter suite configuration—for example, by removing the 256-bit suites, as well as those that use DHE for the key exchange. However, I have found that having a somewhat diverse collection of suites helps avoid various edge cases with picky clients.

In terms of interoperability, all modern browsers and clients should be able to connect. Some very old clients might not, but we're talking about obsolete platforms—for example, Internet Explorer running on Windows XP. If you really need to support this, you will need to append to the list suites that use obsolete features such as 3DES or the RSA key exchange.

Finally, when it comes to performance, there is one final trick you can employ: tell OpenSSL to use ChaCha20 with clients that prefer this cipher over AES. You will notice that in my configuration, there is always a ChaCha20 suite that follows a 128-bit AES-GCM suite. For most clients, AES-GCM is the right choice, but ChaCha20 is a better option for some mobile clients because they can do it faster.[17] With ChaCha20 prioritization, you can give those mobile clients a better experience (faster loading times).

---

[16] In TLS 1.3, key exchange and authentication are not controlled by cipher suites; negotiation of these aspects has been moved into the protocol. However, because robust forward security is a key feature in TLS 1.3, it's not something we need to worry about when it comes to cipher suite configuration.

[17] Speeding up and Strengthening HTTPS Connections for Chrome on Android [fsty.uk/t594] (Google Security Blog, 24 April 2014)

---

Chapter 12: OpenSSL Command Line

The OpenSSL option for this is called `PrioritizeChaCha`. This feature is a relatively new configuration option, and you will find that not all server software can control it. For example, at the time of writing, Apache can (using `SSLOpenSSLConfCmd`) but Nginx can't. Resorting to changing the OpenSSL defaults, as described in the previous section, should do the trick in the latter situation.

> **Note**
>
> In practice, most systems don't need to be configured to support the best possible performance or mobile client experience. If you enjoy getting your TLS configuration just right, then by all means follow all the advice from this section. Usually, however, you shouldn't spend too much time on the fine-tuning. If you find yourself with a platform that doesn't support TLS 1.3 suite configuration or that isn't able to prioritize ChaCha20, just use the defaults and move on.

## Generating DH Parameters

The DH key exchange has fallen out of fashion, but you may still want to support it in your servers on philosophical grounds. If you do, you may find with some server software (e.g., Nginx) that you need to manually configure the desired DH parameters. This is how:

```
$ openssl dhparam -out dh-2048.pem 2048
```

In practice, only 2,048-bit DH parameters make sense. Anything less is going to be weak or insecure, while anything more is going to slow you down. DH parameters need not be secret. In fact, there are some predefined groups (sometimes called *well-known groups*) that are recommended because they are known to have been securely generated.[18]

Rarely, you may encounter a situation, usually in a legacy environment, in which you need to configure a server with 1,024-bit DH parameters. It's essential that you don't use a well-known group in this case. The issue is that weak DH groups are susceptible to precomputation attacks, which further downgrade their security. If you really must use a 1,024-bit DH parameters, always generate your own unique group using OpenSSL.

## Legacy Suite Configuration

In this section, I'll briefly cover the legacy keyword-based configuration of cipher suites that applies to TLS 1.2 and earlier protocol versions. This section is important largely only if you're interested in how the keyword approach works. Otherwise, you're better off simply specifying the suites you wish to use, as I did with the recommended configuration in the previous section.

---

[18] RFC 7919: Negotiated Finite Field Diffie-Hellman Ephemeral Parameters for TLS [fsty.uk/t595] (D. Gillmor, August 2016)

# Keywords

Cipher suite *keywords* are the basic building blocks of cipher suite configuration. Each suite name (e.g., RC4-SHA) is a keyword that selects exactly one suite.[19] All other keywords select groups of suites according to some criteria. Keyword names are case-sensitive. In this section, I will provide an overview of all cipher suite keywords supported by OpenSSL, one group at a time.

Group keywords are shortcuts that select frequently used cipher suites. For example, HIGH will select only very strong cipher suites.

Table 12.2. Group keywords

| Keyword | Meaning |
| --- | --- |
| DEFAULT | The default cipher list. This is determined at compile time and must be the first cipher string specified. |
| COMPLEMENTOFDEFAULT | The ciphers included in ALL, but not enabled by default. Note that this rule does not cover eNULL, which is not included by ALL (use COMPLEMENTOFALL if necessary). |
| ALL | All cipher suites except the eNULL ciphers, which must be explicitly enabled. |
| COMPLEMENTOFALL | The cipher suites not enabled by ALL, currently eNULL. |
| HIGH | "High"-encryption cipher suites. This currently means those with key lengths larger than 128 bits, and some cipher suites with 128-bit keys. |
| MEDIUM | "Medium"-encryption cipher suites, currently some of those using 128-bit encryption. |
| LOW | "Low"-encryption cipher suites, currently those using 64- or 56-bit encryption algorithms, but excluding export cipher suites. No longer supported. **Insecure.** |
| EXP, EXPORT | Export encryption algorithms. Including 40- and 56-bit algorithms. No longer supported. **Insecure.** |
| EXPORT40 | 40-bit export encryption algorithms. No longer supported. **Insecure.** |
| EXPORT56 | 56-bit export encryption algorithms. No longer supported. **Insecure.** |
| TLSv1.2, TLSv1.0, TLSv1, SSLv3, SSLv2 | Cipher suites that require the specified protocol version. There are two keywords for TLS 1.0 and no keywords for TLS 1.3 and TLS 1.1. These keywords do not affect protocol configuration, just the suites. |

Digest keywords select suites that use a particular digest algorithm. For example, SHA256 selects all suites that rely on SHA256 for integrity validation.

---

[19] With recent OpenSSL releases, you can use the legacy suite names that are specific to OpenSSL, but also the standard suite names.

---

Table 12.3. Digest algorithm keywords

| Keyword | Meaning |
| --- | --- |
| MD5 | Cipher suites using MD5. **Obsolete and insecure.** |
| SHA, SHA1 | Cipher suites using SHA1. |
| SHA256 | Cipher suites using SHA256. |
| SHA384 | Cipher suites using SHA384. |

> **Note**
>
> The digest algorithm keywords select only suites that validate data integrity at the protocol level. TLS 1.2 introduced support for authenticated encryption, which is a mechanism that bundles encryption with integrity validation. When the so-called AEAD (*authenticated encryption with associated Data*) suites are used, the protocol doesn't need to provide additional integrity verification. For this reason, you won't be able to use the digest algorithm keywords to select AEAD suites (currently, those that have GCM in the name). The names of these suites do use SHA256 and SHA384 suffixes, but (confusing as it may be) here they refer to the hash functions used to build the *pseudorandom function* used with the suite.

Authentication keywords select suites based on the authentication method they use. Today, the RSA public key algorithm is still used by the majority of certificates, with ECDSA quickly catching up.

Table 12.4. Authentication keywords

| Keyword | Meaning |
| --- | --- |
| aDH | Cipher suites effectively using DH authentication, i.e., the certificates carry DH keys. Removed in 1.1.0. |
| aDSS, DSS | Cipher suites using DSS authentication, i.e., the certificates carry DSS keys. |
| aECDH | Cipher suites that use ECDH authentication. Removed in 1.1.0. |
| aECDSA, ECDSA | Cipher suites that use ECDSA authentication. |
| aNULL | Cipher suites offering no authentication. This is currently the anonymous DH algorithms. **Insecure.** |
| aRSA | Cipher suites using RSA authentication, i.e., the certificates carry RSA keys. |
| aPSK | Cipher suites using PSK (Pre-Shared Key) authentication. |
| aSRP | Cipher suites using SRP (Secure Remote Password) authentication. |

Key exchange keywords select suites based on the key exchange algorithm. When it comes to ephemeral Diffie-Hellman suites, OpenSSL is inconsistent in naming the suites and the keywords. In the suite names, ephemeral suites tend to have an E at the end of the key exchange algorithm (e.g., ECDHE-RSA-RC4-SHA and DHE-RSA-AES256-SHA), but in the keywords the E is at the beginning (e.g., EECDH and EDH). The preferred names today are DHE and ECDHE; the other keywords are supported for backward compatibility.

Table 12.5. Key exchange keywords

| Keyword | Meaning |
|---|---|
| ADH | Anonymous DH cipher suites. **Insecure.** |
| AECDH | Anonymous ECDH cipher suites. **Insecure.** |
| DHE, EDH | Cipher suites using ephemeral DH key agreement only. |
| ECDHE, EECDH | Cipher suites using ephemeral ECDH. |
| kDHE, kEDH, DH | Cipher suites using ephemeral DH key agreement (includes anonymous DH). |
| kECDHE, kEECDH, ECDH | Cipher suites using ephemeral ECDH key agreement (includes anonymous ECDH). |
| kRSA, RSA | Cipher suites using RSA key exchange. |
| kPSK, kECDHEPSK, kDHEPSK, kRSAPSK | Cipher suites using PSK key exchange. |

Cipher keywords select suites based on the cipher they use.

Table 12.6. Cipher keywords

| Keyword | Meaning |
|---|---|
| AES, AESCCM, AESCCM8, AESGCM | Cipher suites using AES, AES CCM, and AES GCM. |
| ARIA, ARIA128, ARIA256 | Cipher suites using ARIA. |
| CAMELLIA, CAMELLIA128, CAMELLIA256 | Cipher suites using Camellia. **Obsolete.** |
| CHACHA20 | Cipher suites using ChaCha20. |
| eNULL, NULL | Cipher suites that don't use encryption. **Insecure.** |
| IDEA | Cipher suites using IDEA. **Obsolete.** |
| SEED | Cipher suites using SEED. **Obsolete.** |
| 3DES, DES, IDEA, RC2, RC4 | No longer supported by default. **Obsolete and insecure.** |

What remains is a number of suites that do not fit into any other category. The bulk of them are related to the GOST standards, which are relevant for the countries that are part of the Commonwealth of Independent States, formed after the breakup of the Soviet Union. The GOST suites are defined but require the GOST engine to be activated. The GOST engine is not part of the core OpenSSL since version 1.1.0.

Table 12.7. Miscellaneous keywords

| Keyword | Meaning |
|---------|---------|
| @SECLEVEL | Configures the security level, which sets minimum security requirements. |
| @STRENGTH | Sorts the current cipher suite list in order of encryption algorithm key length. |
| aGOST | Cipher suites using GOST R 34.10 (either 2001 or 94) for authentication. Requires a GOST-capable engine. |
| aGOST01 | Cipher suites using GOST R 34.10-2001 authentication. |
| aGOST94 | Cipher suites using GOST R 34.10-94 authentication. **Obsolete.** Use GOST R 34.10-2001 instead. |
| kGOST | Cipher suites using VKO 34.10 key exchange, specified in RFC 4357. |
| GOST94 | Cipher suites using HMAC based on GOST R 34.11-94. |
| GOST89MAC | Cipher suites using GOST 28147-89 MAC instead of HMAC. |
| PSK | Cipher suites using PSK in any capacity. |

## Combining Keywords

In most cases, you'll use keywords by themselves, but it's also possible to combine them to select only suites that meet several requirements, by connecting two or more keywords with the + character. In the following example, we select suites that use the ECDHE key exchange in combination with AES-GCM:

```
$ openssl ciphers -v -s -tls1_2 'EECDH+AESGCM'
ECDHE-ECDSA-AES256-GCM-SHA384   TLSv1.2 Kx=ECDH Au=ECDSA Enc=AESGCM(256) Mac=AEAD
ECDHE-RSA-AES256-GCM-SHA384     TLSv1.2 Kx=ECDH Au=RSA   Enc=AESGCM(256) Mac=AEAD
ECDHE-ECDSA-AES128-GCM-SHA256   TLSv1.2 Kx=ECDH Au=ECDSA Enc=AESGCM(128) Mac=AEAD
ECDHE-RSA-AES128-GCM-SHA256     TLSv1.2 Kx=ECDH Au=RSA   Enc=AESGCM(128) Mac=AEAD
```

## Building Cipher Suite Lists

The key concept in building a cipher suite configuration is that of the *current suite list*. The list always starts empty, without any suites, but every keyword that you add to the configuration string will change the list in some way. By default, new suites are appended to the list. In the following example, the configuration starts with all suites that use the ECDHE key exchange, followed by all suites that use the DHE key exchange:

```
$ openssl ciphers -v 'ECDHE:DHE'
```

The colon character is commonly used to separate keywords, but spaces and commas are equally acceptable. The following command produces the same output as the previous example:

```
$ openssl ciphers -v 'ECDHE DHE'
```

## Keyword Modifiers

Keyword modifiers are characters you can place at the beginning of each keyword in order to change the default action (adding to the list) to something else. The following actions are supported:

**Append**

Add suites to the end of the list. If any of the suites are already on the list, they will remain in their present position. This is the default action, which is invoked when there is no modifier in front of the keyword.

**Delete (-)**

Remove all matching suites from the list, potentially allowing some other keyword to reintroduce them later.

**Permanently delete (!)**

Remove all matching suites from the list and prevent them from being added later by another keyword. This modifier is useful for specifying all the suites you never want to use, making further selection easier and preventing mistakes.

**Move to the end (+)**

Move all matching suites to the end of the list. This works only on existing suites; it never adds new suites to the list. This modifier is useful if you want to keep some weaker suites enabled but prefer the stronger ones. For example, the string AES:+AES256 enables all AES suites but pushes the 256-bit ones to the end.

## Sorting

The @STRENGTH keyword serves a special purpose: it will not introduce or remove any suites, but it will sort them in order of descending cipher strength. Automatic sorting is an interesting idea, but it makes sense only in a perfect world in which cipher suites can actually be compared by cipher strength alone. In most cases, the highest-strength suites are not typically required. You often have them in your configuration only to interoperate with picky clients.

## Handling Errors

There are two types of errors you might experience while working on your configuration. The first is a result of a typo or an attempt to use a keyword that does not exist:

```
$ openssl ciphers -v '@HIGH'
Error in cipher list
140460843755168:error:140E6118:SSL routines:SSL_CIPHER_PROCESS_RULESTR:invalid ↵
command:ssl_ciph.c:1317:
```

The output is cryptic, but it does contain an error message.

Another possibility is that you end up with an empty list of cipher suites, in which case you might see something similar to the following:

```
$ openssl ciphers -v 'SHA512'
Error in cipher list
140202299557536:error:1410D0B9:SSL routines:SSL_CTX_set_cipher_list:no cipher
match:ssl_lib.c:1312:
```

# Performance

As you're probably aware, computation speed is a significant limiting factor for any cryptographic operation. OpenSSL comes with a built-in benchmarking tool that you can use to get an idea about a system's capabilities and limits. You can invoke the benchmark using the speed command.

If you invoke speed without any parameters, OpenSSL produces a lot of output, little of which will be of interest. A better approach is to test only those algorithms that are directly relevant to you. For example, for usage in a secure web server, you might care about the performance of RSA and ECDSA and will do something like this:

```
$ openssl speed rsa ecdsa
```

The first part of the resulting output consists of the OpenSSL version number and compile-time configuration. This information is useful for record-keeping and if you're testing different versions of OpenSSL:

```
OpenSSL 1.1.1f  31 Mar 2020
built on: Mon Apr 20 11:53:50 2020 UTC
options:bn(64,64) rc4(16x,int) des(int) aes(partial) blowfish(ptr)
compiler: gcc -fPIC -pthread -m64 -Wa,--noexecstack -Wall -Wa,--noexecstack -g -O2
-fdebug-prefix-map=/build/openssl-P_ODHM/openssl-1.1.1f=. -fstack-protector-strong
-Wformat -Werror=format-security -DOPENSSL_TLS_SECURITY_LEVEL=2 -DOPENSSL_USE
_NODELETE -DL_ENDIAN -DOPENSSL_PIC -DOPENSSL_CPUID_OBJ -DOPENSSL_IA32_SSE2
-DOPENSSL_BN_ASM_MONT -DOPENSSL_BN_ASM_MONT5 -DOPENSSL_BN_ASM_GF2m -DSHA1_ASM
-DSHA256_ASM -DSHA512_ASM -DKECCAK1600_ASM -DRC4_ASM -DMD5_ASM -DAESNI_ASM -DVPAES
_ASM -DGHASH_ASM -DECP_NISTZ256_ASM -DX25519_ASM -DPOLY1305_ASM -DNDEBUG
-Wdate-time -D_FORTIFY_SOURCE=2
```

The rest of the output contains the benchmark results. Let's first take a look at the RSA key operations:

```
              sign      verify    sign/s   verify/s
rsa   512 bits 0.000073s 0.000005s 13736.4  187091.4
rsa  1024 bits 0.000207s 0.000014s  4828.4   71797.6
rsa  2048 bits 0.000991s 0.000045s  1009.1   22220.4
rsa  3072 bits 0.004796s 0.000096s   208.5   10463.5
```

```
rsa  4096 bits  0.011073s  0.000165s   90.3   6054.5
rsa  7680 bits  0.090541s  0.000565s   11.0   1769.7
rsa 15360 bits  0.521500s  0.002204s    1.9    453.7
```

RSA is most commonly used at 2,048 bits. In my results, one CPU of the tested server can perform about 1,000 sign (server) operations and 22,000 verify (client) operations every second. As for ECDSA, it's typically only used at 256 bits. We can see that at this length, ECDSA can do 10 times as many signatures. On the other hand, it's slower when it comes to the verifications, at barely 6,500 operations per second:

```
                         sign    verify   sign/s   verify/s
256 bits ecdsa (nistp256)  0.0000s  0.0002s  20508.1  6566.2
384 bits ecdsa (nistp384)  0.0017s  0.0013s   580.4   755.0
521 bits ecdsa (nistp521)  0.0006s  0.0012s  1711.5   840.8
```

In practice, you care more about the sign operations because servers are designed to provide services to a great many clients. The clients, on the other hand, are typically communicating with only a small number of servers at the same time. The fact that ECDSA is slower in this scenario doesn't matter much.

What's this output of speed useful for? You should be able to compare how compile-time options affect speed or how different versions of OpenSSL compare on the same platform. If you're thinking of switching servers, benchmarking OpenSSL can give you an idea of the differences in computing power. You can also verify that the hardware acceleration is in place.

Using the benchmark results to estimate deployment performance is not straightforward because of the great number of factors that influence performance in real life. Further, many of those factors lie outside TLS (e.g., HTTP keep-alive settings, caching, etc.). At best, you can use these numbers only for a rough estimate.

But before you can do that, you need to consider something else. By default, the speed command will use only a single process. Most servers have multiple cores, so to find out how many TLS operations are supported by the entire server, you must instruct speed to use several instances in parallel. You can achieve this with the -multi switch. My server has two cores, so that's what I'm going to specify:

```
$ openssl speed -multi 2 rsa
[...]
                sign      verify    sign/s    verify/s
rsa   512 bits  0.000037s  0.000003s  27196.5  367409.6
rsa  1024 bits  0.000106s  0.000007s   9467.8  144188.0
rsa  2048 bits  0.000503s  0.000023s   1988.1   43838.4
rsa  3072 bits  0.002415s  0.000050s    414.1   20152.2
rsa  4096 bits  0.005589s  0.000084s    178.9   11880.8
rsa  7680 bits  0.045659s  0.000285s     21.9    3506.1
rsa 15360 bits  0.264904s  0.001130s      3.8     884.8
```

As expected, the performance is about two times better. I'm again looking at how many RSA signatures can be completed per second, because this is the most CPU-intensive cryptographic operation performed on a server and is thus always the first bottleneck. The result of 1,988 signatures/second (with a 2,048-bit key) tells us that this small server will most definitely handle hundreds of brand-new TLS connections per second. (We have to assume that the server will do other things, not only TLS handshakes.) In my case, that's sufficient—with a very healthy safety margin. Because I also have session resumption enabled on the server—and that bypasses public encryption—I know that the performance will be even better.

When testing speed, it's important to always enable hardware acceleration using the -evp switch. If you don't, the results can be vastly different. As an illustration, take a look at the performance differences on a server that supports AES-NI hardware acceleration. I got the following with a software-only implementation:

```
$ openssl speed aes-128-cbc
[...]
The 'numbers' are in 1000s of bytes per second processed.
type              16 bytes     64 bytes     256 bytes    1024 bytes   8192 bytes
aes-128 cbc       131377.50k   135401.41k   134796.12k   133931.35k   134778.95k
```

The performance is more than three times better with hardware acceleration:

```
$ openssl speed -evp aes-128-cbc
[...]
The 'numbers' are in 1000s of bytes per second processed.
type              16 bytes     64 bytes     256 bytes    1024 bytes   8192 bytes
aes-128-cbc       421949.23k   451223.42k   460066.13k   463651.84k   462883.50k
```

When you're looking at the speed of cryptographic operations, you should focus on the primitives you will actually deploy. For example, CBC is obsolete, so you want to use AES in GCM mode instead. And here we see how the GCM performance is three to four times better:

```
$ openssl speed -evp aes-128-gcm
[...]
The 'numbers' are in 1000s of bytes per second processed.
type              16 bytes     64 bytes     256 bytes    1024 bytes   8192 bytes
aes-128-gcm       219599.85k   588822.40k   1313242.97k  1680529.75k  1989388.97k
```

Then there is ChaCha20-Poly1305, which is a relatively recent addition. Its performance can't compete with hardware-accelerated AES, but it doesn't need to; this authenticated cipher is designed to be fast on mobile phones. Compare its speed to nonaccelerated AES-128-CBC instead.

```
$ openssl speed -evp chacha20-poly1305
[...]
```

```
The 'numbers' are in 1000s of bytes per second processed.
type                16 bytes     64 bytes     256 bytes    1024 bytes   8192 bytes
chacha20-poly1305   148729.65k   273026.35k   590953.90k   1027021.82k  1092427.78k
```

> **Note**
>
> Starting with OpenSSL 3.0, hardware acceleration is always used when supported
> by the CPU, irrespective of the presence or absence of the -evp switch.

# Creating a Private Certification Authority

If you want to set up your own CA, everything you need is already included in OpenSSL.
The user interface is purely command line–based and thus not very user friendly, but that's
possibly for the better. Going through the process is very educational, because it forces you
to think about every aspect, even the smallest details.

The educational aspect of setting a private CA is the main reason why I would recommend
doing it, but there are others. An OpenSSL-based CA, crude as it might be, can well serve
the needs of an individual or a small group. For example, it's much better to use a private
CA in a development environment than to use self-signed certificates everywhere. Similarly,
client certificates—which provide two-factor authentication—can significantly increase the
security of your sensitive web applications.

The biggest challenge in running a private CA is not setting everything up but keeping the
infrastructure secure. For example, the root key must be kept offline because all security
depends on it. On the other hand, CRLs and OCSP responder certificates must be refreshed
on a regular basis, which requires bringing the root online.

> **Note**
>
> Before you begin to properly read this section, I recommend first going through
> Chapter 4, *Public Key Infrastructure*, which will give you a good background in
> certificate structure and the operation of certification authorities.

As you go through this section you will create two configuration files: one to control
the root CA (root-ca.conf) and another to control the subordinate CA (sub-ca.conf).
Although you should be able to do everything from scratch just by following my instructions, you can also download the configuration file templates from my GitHub account.[20]
The latter option will save you some time, but the former approach will give you a better
understanding of the work involved.

---

[20] OpenSSL CA configuration templates [fsty.uk/t596] (Bulletproof TLS and PKI GitHub repository, retrieved 20 October 2021)

# Features and Limitations

In the rest of this section, we're going to create a private CA that's similar in structure to public CAs. There's going to be one root CA from which other subordinate CAs can be created. We'll provide revocation information via CRLs and OCSP responders. To keep the root CA offline, OCSP responders are going to have their own identities. This isn't the simplest private CA you could have, but it's one that can be secured properly. As a bonus, the subordinate CA will be *technically constrained*, which means that it will be allowed to issue certificates only for the allowed hostnames.

After the setup is complete, the root certificate will have to be securely distributed to all intended clients. Once the root is in place, you can begin issuing client and server certificates. The main limitation of this setup is that the OCSP responder is chiefly designed for testing and can be used only for lighter loads.

# Creating a Root CA

Creating a new CA involves several steps: configuration, creation of a directory structure and initialization of the key files, and finally generation of the root key and certificate. This section describes the process as well as the common CA operations.

## Root CA Configuration

Before we can actually create a CA, we need to prepare a configuration file (root-ca.conf) that will tell OpenSSL exactly how we want things set up. Configuration files aren't needed most of the time, during normal usage, but they are essential when it comes to complex operations, such as root CA creation. OpenSSL configuration files are powerful; before you proceed I suggest that you familiarize yourself with their capabilities (man config on the command line).

The first part of the configuration file contains some basic CA information, such as the name and the base URL, and the components of the CA's distinguished name. Because the syntax is flexible, information needs to be provided only once:

```
[default]
name                    = root-ca
domain_suffix           = example.com
aia_url                 = http://$name.$domain_suffix/$name.crt
crl_url                 = http://$name.$domain_suffix/$name.crl
ocsp_url                = http://ocsp.$name.$domain_suffix:9080
default_ca              = ca_default
name_opt                = utf8,esc_ctrl,multiline,lname,align

[ca_dn]
```

```
countryName              = "GB"
organizationName         = "Example"
commonName               = "Root CA"
```

The second part directly controls the CA's operation. For full information on each setting, consult the documentation for the ca command (man ca on the command line). Most of the settings are self-explanatory; we mostly tell OpenSSL where we want to keep our files. Because this root CA is going to be used only for the issuance of subordinate CAs, I chose to have the certificates valid for 10 years. For the signature algorithm, the secure SHA256 is used by default.

The default policy (policy_c_o_match) is configured so that all certificates issued from this CA have the countryName and organizationName fields that match that of the CA. This wouldn't be normally done by a public CA, but it's appropriate for a private CA:

```
[ca_default]
home                     = .
database                 = $home/db/index
serial                   = $home/db/serial
crlnumber                = $home/db/crlnumber
certificate              = $home/$name.crt
private_key              = $home/private/$name.key
RANDFILE                 = $home/private/random
new_certs_dir            = $home/certs
unique_subject           = no
copy_extensions          = none
default_days             = 3650
default_crl_days         = 365
default_md               = sha256
policy                   = policy_c_o_match

[policy_c_o_match]
countryName              = match
stateOrProvinceName      = optional
organizationName         = match
organizationalUnitName   = optional
commonName               = supplied
emailAddress             = optional
```

The third part contains the configuration for the req command, which is going to be used only once, during the creation of the self-signed root certificate. The most important parts are in the extensions: the basicConstraints extension indicates that the certificate is a CA, and keyUsage contains the appropriate settings for this scenario:

```
[req]
default_bits             = 4096
encrypt_key              = yes
```

```
default_md              = sha256
utf8                    = yes
string_mask             = utf8only
prompt                  = no
distinguished_name      = ca_dn
req_extensions          = ca_ext

[ca_ext]
basicConstraints        = critical,CA:true
keyUsage                = critical,keyCertSign,cRLSign
subjectKeyIdentifier    = hash
```

The fourth part of the configuration file contains information that will be used during the construction of certificates issued by the root CA. All certificates will be CAs, as indicated by the basicConstraints extension, but we set pathlen to zero, which means that further subordinate CAs are not allowed.

All subordinate CAs are going to be constrained, which means that the certificates they issue will be valid only for a subset of domain names and restricted uses. First, the extendedKeyUsage extension specifies only clientAuth and serverAuth, which is TLS client and server authentication. Second, the nameConstraints extension limits the allowed hostnames only to *example.com* and *example.org* domain names. In theory, this setup enables you to give control over the subordinate CAs to someone else but still be safe in knowing that they can't issue certificates for arbitrary hostnames. If you wanted, you could restrict each subordinate CA to a small domain namespace. The requirement to exclude the two IP address ranges comes from the CA/Browser Forum's Baseline Requirements, which have a definition for technically constrained subordinate CAs.[21]

In practice, name constraints are not entirely practical, because some major platforms don't currently recognize the nameConstraints extension. If you mark this extension as critical, such platforms will reject your certificates. You won't have such problems if you don't mark it as critical (as in the example), but then some other platforms won't enforce it.

```
[sub_ca_ext]
authorityInfoAccess     = @issuer_info
authorityKeyIdentifier  = keyid:always
basicConstraints        = critical,CA:true,pathlen:0
crlDistributionPoints   = @crl_info
extendedKeyUsage        = clientAuth,serverAuth
keyUsage                = critical,keyCertSign,cRLSign
nameConstraints         = @name_constraints
subjectKeyIdentifier    = hash

[crl_info]
```

---

[21] Baseline Requirements [fsty.uk/t54] (The CA/Browser Forum, retrieved 9 July 2014)

```
URI.0                   = $crl_url

[issuer_info]
caIssuers;URI.0         = $aia_url
OCSP;URI.0              = $ocsp_url

[name_constraints]
permitted;DNS.0=example.com
permitted;DNS.1=example.org
excluded;IP.0=0.0.0.0/0.0.0.0
excluded;IP.1=0:0:0:0:0:0:0:0/0:0:0:0:0:0:0:0
```

The fifth and final part of the configuration specifies the extensions to be used with the certificate for OCSP response signing. In order to be able to run an OCSP responder, we generate a special certificate and delegate the OCSP signing capability to it. This certificate is not a CA, which you can see from the extensions:

```
[ocsp_ext]
authorityKeyIdentifier  = keyid:always
basicConstraints        = critical,CA:false
extendedKeyUsage        = OCSPSigning
keyUsage                = critical,digitalSignature
subjectKeyIdentifier    = hash
```

## Root CA Directory Structure

The next step is to create the directory structure specified in the previous section and initialize some of the files that will be used during the CA operation:

```
$ mkdir root-ca
$ cd root-ca
$ mkdir certs db private
$ chmod 700 private
$ touch db/index
$ openssl rand -hex 16 > db/serial
$ echo 1001 > db/crlnumber
```

The following subdirectories are used:

**certs/**

>   Certificate storage; new certificates will be placed here as they are issued.

**db/**

>   This directory is used for the certificate database (index) and the files that hold the next certificate and CRL serial numbers. OpenSSL will create some additional files as needed.

**private/**

This directory will store the private keys, one for the CA and the other for the OCSP responder. It's important that no other user has access to it. (In fact, if you're going to be serious about the CA, the machine on which the root material is stored should have only a minimal number of user accounts.)

> **Note**
>
> When creating a new CA certificate, it's important to initialize the certificate serial numbers with a random number generator, as I do in this section. This is very useful if you ever end up creating and deploying multiple CA certificates with the same distinguished name (common if you make a mistake and need to start over); conflicts will be avoided, because the certificates will have different serial numbers.

## Root CA Generation

We take two steps to create the root CA. First, we generate the key and the CSR. All the necessary information will be picked up from the configuration file when we use the `-config` switch:

```
$ openssl req -new \
    -config root-ca.conf \
    -out root-ca.csr \
    -keyout private/root-ca.key
```

In the second step, we create a self-signed certificate. The `-extensions` switch points to the ca_ext section in the configuration file, which activates the extensions that are appropriate for a root CA:

```
$ openssl ca -selfsign \
    -config root-ca.conf \
    -in root-ca.csr \
    -out root-ca.crt \
    -extensions ca_ext
```

## Structure of the Database File

The database in `db/index` is a plaintext file that contains certificate information, one certificate per line. Immediately after the root CA creation, it should contain only one line:

```
V    240706115345Z          1001    unknown    /C=GB/O=Example/CN=Root CA
```

Each line contains six values separated by tabs:

1. Status flag (V for valid, R for revoked, E for expired)

---

2.  Expiration date (in YYMMDDHHMMSSZ format)

3.  Revocation date or empty if not revoked

4.  Serial number (hexadecimal)

5.  File location or unknown if not known

6.  Distinguished name

## Root CA Operations

To generate a CRL from the new CA, use the `-gencrl` switch of the `ca` command:

```
$ openssl ca -gencrl \
    -config root-ca.conf \
    -out root-ca.crl
```

To issue a certificate, invoke the `ca` command with the desired parameters. It's important that the `-extensions` switch points to the correct section in the configuration file (e.g., you don't want to create another root CA).

```
$ openssl ca \
    -config root-ca.conf \
    -in sub-ca.csr \
    -out sub-ca.crt \
    -extensions sub_ca_ext
```

To revoke a certificate, use the `-revoke` switch of the `ca` command; you'll need to have a copy of the certificate you wish to revoke. Because all certificates are stored in the `certs/` directory, you only need to know the serial number. If you have a distinguished name, you can look for the serial number in the database.

Choose the correct reason for the value in the `-crl_reason` switch. The value can be one of the following: `unspecified`, `keyCompromise`, `CACompromise`, `affiliationChanged`, `superseded`, `cessationOfOperation`, `certificateHold`, and `removeFromCRL`.

```
$ openssl ca \
    -config root-ca.conf \
    -revoke certs/1002.pem \
    -crl_reason keyCompromise
```

## Create a Certificate for OCSP Signing

First, we create a key and CSR for the OCSP responder. These two operations are done as for any non-CA certificate, which is why we don't specify a configuration file:

```
$ openssl req -new \
    -newkey rsa:2048 \
```

```
-subj "/C=GB/O=Example/CN=OCSP Root Responder" \
-keyout private/root-ocsp.key \
-out root-ocsp.csr
```

Second, use the root CA to issue a certificate. The value of the -extensions switch specifies ocsp_ext, which ensures that extensions appropriate for OCSP signing are set. I reduced the lifetime of the new certificate to 365 days (from the default of 3,650). Because these OCSP certificates don't contain revocation information, they can't be revoked. For that reason, you want to keep the lifetime as short as possible. A good choice is 30 days, provided you are prepared to generate a fresh certificate that often:

```
$ openssl ca \
    -config root-ca.conf \
    -in root-ocsp.csr \
    -out root-ocsp.crt \
    -extensions ocsp_ext \
    -days 30
```

Now you have everything ready to start the OCSP responder. For testing, you can do it from the same machine on which the root CA resides. However, for production you must move the OCSP responder key and certificate elsewhere:

```
$ openssl ocsp \
    -port 9080
    -index db/index \
    -rsigner root-ocsp.crt \
    -rkey private/root-ocsp.key \
    -CA root-ca.crt \
    -text
```

You can test the operation of the OCSP responder using the following command line:

```
$ openssl ocsp \
    -issuer root-ca.crt \
    -CAfile root-ca.crt \
    -cert root-ocsp.crt \
    -url http://127.0.0.1:9080
```

In the output, verify OK means that the signatures were correctly verified, and good means that the certificate hasn't been revoked.

```
Response verify OK
root-ocsp.crt: good
        This Update: Jul  9 18:45:34 2014 GMT
```

# Creating a Subordinate CA

The process of subordinate CA generation largely mirrors the root CA process. In this section, I will only highlight the differences where appropriate. For everything else, refer to the previous section.

## Subordinate CA Configuration

To generate a configuration file (sub-ca.conf) for the subordinate CA, start with the file we used for the root CA and make the changes listed in this section. We'll change the name to sub-ca and use a different distinguished name. We'll put the OCSP responder on a different port, but only because the ocsp command doesn't understand virtual hosts. If you used a proper web server for the OCSP responder, you could avoid using special ports altogether. The default lifetime of new certificates will be 365 days, and we'll generate a fresh CRL once every 30 days.

The change of copy_extensions to copy means that extensions from the CSR will be copied into the certificate, but only if they are not already set in our configuration. With this change, whoever is preparing the CSR can put the required alternative names in it, and the information from there will be picked up and placed in the certificate. This feature is somewhat dangerous (you're allowing someone else to have limited direct control over what goes into a certificate), but I think it's fine for smaller environments:

```
[default]
name                    = sub-ca
ocsp_url                = http://ocsp.$name.$domain_suffix:9081

[ca_dn]
countryName             = "GB"
organizationName        = "Example"
commonName              = "Sub CA"

[ca_default]
default_days            = 365
default_crl_days        = 30
copy_extensions         = copy
```

At the end of the configuration file, we'll add two new profiles, one each for client and server certificates. The only difference is in the keyUsage and extendedKeyUsage extensions. Note that we specify the basicConstraints extension but set it to false. We're doing this because we're copying extensions from the CSR. If we left this extension out, we might end up using one specified in the CSR:

```
[server_ext]
authorityInfoAccess     = @issuer_info
```

```
authorityKeyIdentifier    = keyid:always
basicConstraints          = critical,CA:false
crlDistributionPoints     = @crl_info
extendedKeyUsage          = clientAuth,serverAuth
keyUsage                  = critical,digitalSignature,keyEncipherment
subjectKeyIdentifier      = hash

[client_ext]
authorityInfoAccess       = @issuer_info
authorityKeyIdentifier    = keyid:always
basicConstraints          = critical,CA:false
crlDistributionPoints     = @crl_info
extendedKeyUsage          = clientAuth
keyUsage                  = critical,digitalSignature
subjectKeyIdentifier      = hash
```

After you're happy with the configuration file, create a directory structure following the same process as for the root CA. Just use a different directory name, for example, sub-ca.

## Subordinate CA Generation

As before, we take two steps to create the subordinate CA. First, we generate the key and the CSR. All the necessary information will be picked up from the configuration file when we use the -config switch.

```
$ openssl req -new \
    -config sub-ca.conf \
    -out sub-ca.csr \
    -keyout private/sub-ca.key
```

In the second step, we get the root CA to issue a certificate. The -extensions switch points to the sub_ca_ext section in the configuration file, which activates the extensions that are appropriate for the subordinate CA.

```
$ openssl ca \
    -config root-ca.conf \
    -in sub-ca.csr \
    -out sub-ca.crt \
    -extensions sub_ca_ext
```

## Subordinate CA Operations

To issue a server certificate, process a CSR while specifying server_ext in the -extensions switch:

```
$ openssl ca \
    -config sub-ca.conf \
```

```
-in server.csr \
-out server.crt \
-extensions server_ext
```

To issue a client certificate, process a CSR while specifying `client_ext` in the `-extensions` switch:

```
$ openssl ca \
    -config sub-ca.conf \
    -in client.csr \
    -out client.crt \
    -extensions client_ext
```

> ### Note
>
> When a new certificate is requested, all its information will be presented to you for verification before the operation is completed. You should always ensure that everything is in order, but especially if you're working with a CSR that someone else prepared. Pay special attention to the certificate distinguished name and the `basicConstraints` and `subjectAlternativeName` extensions.

CRL generation and certificate revocation are the same as for the root CA. The only thing different about the OCSP responder is the port; the subordinate CA should use 9081 instead. It's recommended that the responder uses its own certificate, which avoids keeping the subordinate CA on a public server.

# 13 Testing TLS with OpenSSL

Due to the large number of protocol features and implementation quirks, it's sometimes difficult to determine the exact configuration and features of secure servers. Although many tools exist for this purpose, it's often difficult to know exactly how they work, and that sometimes makes it difficult to fully trust their results. Even though I spent years testing secure servers and have access to good tools, when I really want to understand what is going on, I resort to using OpenSSL and Wireshark. I am not saying that you should use OpenSSL for everyday testing; on the contrary, you should find an automated tool that you trust. For online testing, I recommend Hardenize;[1] for offline work, consider testssl.sh.[2] But when you really need to be certain of something, the only way is to get your hands dirty with OpenSSL.

## Custom-Compile OpenSSL for Testing

Using OpenSSL for testing purposes has become more difficult recently because, paradoxically, OpenSSL itself got better. In the aftermath of Heartbleed, the OpenSSL developers undertook a great overhaul, one aspect of which was removal of obsolete cryptography. That is great news for everyone, of course, but does make *our* lives more difficult. To test for a wide variety of conditions, we may need to use two versions: one recent and one old. The recent one is useful to test modern features (e.g., TLS 1.3), but the old one is what you need to test obsolete functionality.

At the time of writing, the new version will most definitely be from the 1.1.1 branch. As for the old, after some research, I settled on OpenSSL 1.0.2g, configured so that the removal of some obsolete features is reverted:

```
$ ./config \
--prefix=/opt/openssl-1.0.2g \
--openssldir=/opt/openssl-1.0.2g \
```

---

[1] Hardenize [fsty.uk/t597] (retrieved 31 August 2020)

[2] testssl.sh [fsty.uk/t598] (retrieved 29 August 2020)

```
no-shared \
enable-ssl2 \
enable-ssl3 \
enable-weak-ssl-ciphers
```

Throughout this chapter, I will refer to these two versions of OpenSSL as *new* and *old*. That's how you'll know which version to use for the testing. Refer to the previous chapter for more information on how to configure and install OpenSSL.

# Connecting to TLS Services

OpenSSL comes with a client tool that you can use to connect to a secure server. The tool is similar to telnet or nc in the sense that it handles the encryption aspect but allows you to fully control the layer that comes next.

To connect to a server, you need to supply a hostname and a port. For example:

```
$ openssl s_client -crlf \
-connect www.feistyduck.com:443 \
-servername www.feistyduck.com
```

Notice that you had to supply the hostname twice. The -connect switch is used to establish the TCP connection, but -servername is used to specify the hostname sent at the TLS level. Starting with OpenSSL 1.1.1, the s_client tool automatically configures the latter. You'll still need to use the -servername switch if (1) you're using an earlier version of OpenSSL, (2) you're connecting to an IP address, or (3) the TLS host needs to be different. Use the -noservername switch to avoid sending hostname information in the TLS handshake.

Once you type the command, you're going to see a lot of diagnostic output (more about that in a moment) followed by an opportunity to type whatever you want. Because we're talking to an HTTP server, the most sensible thing to do is to submit an HTTP request. In the following example, I usc a HEAD request because it instructs the server not to send the response body:

```
HEAD / HTTP/1.0
Host: www.feistyduck.com

HTTP/1.1 200 OK
Date: Mon, 24 Aug 2020 16:38:02 GMT
Server: Apache
Strict-Transport-Security: max-age=31536000; includeSubDomains; preload
Cache-control: no-cache, must-revalidate
Content-Type: text/html;charset=UTF-8
Transfer-Encoding: chunked
Set-Cookie: JSESSIONID=882D48C8842EA82E3F3AFACC4425A695; Path=/; Secure; HttpOnly
Connection: close
```

```
read:errno=0
```

> **Note**
>
> If, when connecting to a remote server in this way, the TLS handshake completes
> but you're getting disconnected after the first HTTP request line, check that you've
> specified the -crlf switch on the command line. This switch ensures that the
> newlines you type are translated to a carriage return plus line feed combo to ensure
> string HTTP compliance.

Now we know that the TLS communication layer is working: we got through to the HTTP
server, submitted a request, and received a response back. Let's go back to the diagnostic
output. The first couple of lines will show the information about the server certificate:

```
CONNECTED(00000003)
depth=2 C = GB, ST = Greater Manchester, L = Salford, O = COMODO CA Limited, CN = ↵
COMODO RSA Certification Authority
verify return:1
depth=1 C = GB, ST = Greater Manchester, L = Salford, O = COMODO CA Limited, CN = ↵
COMODO RSA Domain Validation Secure Server CA
verify return:1
depth=0 OU = Domain Control Validated, OU = PositiveSSL, CN = www.feistyduck.com
verify return:1
```

The next section in the output lists all the certificates presented by the server in the order in
which they were delivered:

```
Certificate chain
 0 s:OU = Domain Control Validated, OU = PositiveSSL, CN = www.feistyduck.com
   i:C = GB, ST = Greater Manchester, L = Salford, O = COMODO CA Limited, CN = ↵
COMODO RSA Domain Validation Secure Server CA
 1 s:C = GB, ST = Greater Manchester, L = Salford, O = COMODO CA Limited, CN = ↵
COMODO RSA Domain Validation Secure Server CA
   i:C = GB, ST = Greater Manchester, L = Salford, O = COMODO CA Limited, CN = ↵
COMODO RSA Certification Authority
```

For each certificate, the first line shows the subject and the second line shows the issuer
information.

This part is very useful when you need to see exactly what certificates are sent; browser
certificate viewers typically display reconstructed certificate chains that can be almost completely different from the presented ones. To determine if the chain is nominally correct, you
might wish to verify that the subjects and issuers match. You start with the leaf (web server)
certificate at the top, and then you go down the list, matching the issuer of the current
certificate to the subject of the next. The last issuer you see can point to some root certificate
that is not in the chain, or—if the self-signed root is included—it can point to itself.

The next item in the output is the server certificate; it's a lot of text, but I'm going to remove most of it for brevity:

```
Server certificate
-----BEGIN CERTIFICATE-----
MIIFUzCCBDugAwIBAgIRAPR/CbWZEksfCIRqxNcesPIwDQYJKoZIhvcNAQELBQAw
gZAxCzAJBgNVBAYTAkdCMRswGQYDVQQIExJHcmVhdGVyIE1hbmNoZXN0ZXIxEDAO
BgNVBAcTB1NhbGZvcmQxGjAYBgNVBAoTEUNPTU9ETyBDQSBMaW1pdGVkMTYwNAYD
[...]
L1MPjFiB5pyvf9jDBxv8TmG4Q6TnDDhw2t2Qil6lhsPAMZ9odP22W3uaLE1y7aB6
zbQXjVsc3E1THfFZWRzDPsU4fN/1iGlbrcAWa2sFfhJXrCDfAowFJ8A1n9jMiNEG
WfQfGgA2ar2xUtsqA7Re6XlXOlwBPuQ=
-----END CERTIFICATE-----
subject=OU = Domain Control Validated, OU = PositiveSSL, CN = www.feistyduck.com
issuer=C = GB, ST = Greater Manchester, L = Salford, O = COMODO CA Limited, CN = ↵
COMODO RSA Domain Validation Secure Server CA
```

> **Note**
>
> By default, the s_client tool shows just the leaf certificate. If you wish to obtain the entire chain, use the -showcerts switch.

If you want to have a better look at the certificate, you'll first need to copy it from the output and store it in a separate file. I'll discuss how to do that in the next section.

The following is a lot of information about the TLS connection, most of which is self-explanatory:

```
---
No client certificate CA names sent
Peer signing digest: SHA512
Peer signature type: RSA
Server Temp Key: ECDH, P-256, 256 bits
---
SSL handshake has read 3624 bytes and written 446 bytes
Verification: OK
---
New, TLSv1.2, Cipher is ECDHE-RSA-AES128-GCM-SHA256
Server public key is 2048 bit
Secure Renegotiation IS supported
Compression: NONE
Expansion: NONE
No ALPN negotiated
SSL-Session:
    Protocol  : TLSv1.2
    Cipher    : ECDHE-RSA-AES128-GCM-SHA256
    Session-ID: 73FC4831AF053C46291C2D8CC90BF7F1D5B12178E488FBB4DC49A302B870E8DE
    Session-ID-ctx:
```

```
        Master-Key: E60DA9C6669C2C7DFFD8A3AD2CD17405CC0B9B69C4184469D779A9BA19A6FD4B3D6↵
02A023BD8B23F8D9A9FF2CBB5DDF7
        PSK identity: None
        PSK identity hint: None
        SRP username: None
        TLS session ticket lifetime hint: 300 (seconds)
        TLS session ticket:
        0000 - 31 95 ff d0 4c 42 dd d0-24 64 03 5c fc 55 1d 17   1...LB..$d.\.U..
        0010 - 05 c4 61 1f b8 ba fd fe-f7 6c 6c e9 ae a2 49 3f   ..a......ll...I?
        0020 - c5 19 d4 e9 69 a5 79 d5-af 13 26 c8 2c e7 f0 01   ....i.y...&.,...
        0030 - 3b 42 d8 c0 29 4c fa 7e-88 aa 8d c8 0b 30 96 ce   ;B..)L.~.....0..
        0040 - 43 40 2c 09 0b aa 2e d5-61 e3 34 7a a3 78 2f 93   C@,.....a.4z.x/.
        0050 - 67 5a b9 96 78 f5 e7 69-b7 b6 2d 8c 00 8f 04 ab   gZ..x..i..-.....
        0060 - 42 1d 26 db 92 ec 2d 2f-ba 1c c6 61 87 64 0e d5   B.&...-/...a.d..
        0070 - f2 ce 20 d0 07 a5 e2 6d-c6 45 50 c2 45 14 a8 ee   .. ....m.EP.E...
        0080 - 59 7c 63 e1 d7 d8 b0 b6-76 21 d2 13 97 eb bd 97   Y|c.....v!......
        0090 - a1 d3 e8 5c 61 da da 2d-85 80 db ae de 56 97 e1   ...\a..-.....V..
        00a0 - e8 7a 25 f9 bf cf b6 18-48 5b b0 03 a5 e6 ec 0a   .z%.....H[......
        00b0 - bf 2f 0d 1a 6b ae 79 10-80 9c cf 4d 66 8f 90 43   ./..k.y....Mf..C
        00c0 - 69 54 32 be 0c 89 57 e8-6d 81 b5 3e 5b cb 5e 8e   iT2...W.m..>[.^.

        Start Time: 1598288068
        Timeout   : 7200 (sec)
        Verify return code: 0 (ok)
        Extended master secret: no
```

The most important information here is the protocol version (TLS 1.2) and cipher suite used (ECDHE-RSA-AES128-GCM-SHA256). Do note that protocol information appears in two locations, which is potentially confusing when different versions are shown. The first location describes the minimum protocol requirement with the negotiated cipher suite, while the second location points to the actual protocol version currently being negotiated. You will see a difference in protocol versions with some older cipher suites—for example:

```
New, TLSv1/SSLv3, Cipher is DHE-RSA-AES128-SHA
```

The selected suite could be used with SSL 3.0, but it's used with TLS 1.2 on this connection:

```
    Protocol  : TLSv1.2
    Cipher    : DHE-RSA-AES128-SHAs
```

You can also determine that the server has issued to you a session ID and a TLS session ticket (a way of resuming sessions without having the server maintain state) and that secure renegotiation is supported.

> **Note**
>
> If you're connecting to a TLS 1.3 server, the output may be different. Sometimes you will observe less information initially, with additional information arriving

later in bursts. This behavior depends on the implementation and reflects the changes in TLS 1.3, which transmits session tickets as separate protocol messages that are sent only after the handshake is complete. Additionally, multiple session tickets are usually sent on the same connection.

# Certificate Verification

Just because you are able to connect to a TLS server, that doesn't mean that the service is configured correctly, even if the server supports all the right protocols and cipher suites. It is equally important that the configured certificate matches the correct DNS names.

By default, the s_client tool reports but otherwise ignores certificate issues. Further, before you begin to trust its judgment you need to be confident that it can recognize a valid certificate when it sees one. This is especially true when you're using a custom-compiled binary.

In the example from the previous section, the verification status code (shown on the penultimate line) was 0, which means that the verification has been successful. If you're connecting to a server that has a valid public certificate but you see status 20 instead, that probably means that trusted roots haven't been correctly configured:

```
Verify return code: 20 (unable to get local issuer certificate)
```

At this point, if you don't wish to fix your OpenSSL installation, you can instead use the -CApath switch to point to the location where the roots are kept. For example:

```
$ openssl s_client -connect www.feistyduck.com:443 -CApath /etc/ssl/certs/
```

If you instead have a single file with the roots in it, use the -CAfile switch:

```
$ openssl s_client -connect www.feistyduck.com:443 \
-CAfile /etc/ssl/certs/ca-certificates.crt
```

Even if you get a successful status code at this point, that doesn't mean that the certificate is correctly configured. That's because the s_client tool doesn't check that the certificate is correct for the given hostname; you have to tell it to do that manually and tell it which hostname to use:

```
$ openssl s_client -connect www.feistyduck.com:443 -verify_hostname ↵
www.feistyduck.com
```

If there is a mismatch, you might see status code 62:

```
Verify return code: 62 (Hostname mismatch)
```

Otherwise, you'll see the familiar status code 0. In the rare instance that you need to verify a certificate that has been issued for an IP address instead of a hostname, you'll need to use the -verify_ip switch for the verification.

# Testing Protocols That Upgrade to TLS

When used with HTTP, TLS wraps the entire plaintext communication channel to form HTTPS. Some other protocols start off as plaintext, but then they upgrade to encryption. If you want to test such a protocol, you'll have to tell OpenSSL which protocol it is so that it can upgrade on your behalf. Provide the protocol information using the -starttls switch. For example:

```
$ openssl s_client -connect gmail-smtp-in.l.google.com:25 -starttls smtp
```

At the time of writing, the supported protocols in recent OpenSSL releases are smtp, pop3, imap, ftp, xmpp, xmpp-server, irc, postgres, mysql, lmtp, nntp, sieve, and ldap. There is less choice with OpenSSL 1.0.2g: smtp, pop3, imap, ftp, and xmpp.

Some protocols require the client to provide their names. For example, for SMTP, OpenSSL will use mail.example.com by default, but you can specify the correct value with the -name switch. If you're testing XMPP, you may need to specify the correct server name; you can do this with the -xmpphost switch.

# Extracting Remote Certificates

When you connect to a remote secure server using s_client, it will dump the server's PEM-encoded certificate to standard output. If you need the certificate for any reason, you can copy it from the scroll-back buffer. If you know in advance you only want to retrieve the certificate, you can use this command line as a shortcut:

```
$ echo | openssl s_client -connect www.feistyduck.com:443 2>&1 | sed --quiet '↵
/-BEGIN CERTIFICATE-/,/-END CERTIFICATE-/p' > feistyduck.crt
```

The purpose of the echo command at the beginning is to separate your shell from s_client. If you don't do that, s_client will wait for your input until the server times out (which may potentially take a very long time).

By default, s_client will print only the leaf certificate; if you want to print the entire chain, give it the -showcerts switch. With that switch enabled, the previous command line will place all the certificates in the same file.

```
$ echo | openssl s_client -showcerts -connect www.feistyduck.com:443 2>&1 | sed ↵
--quiet '/-BEGIN CERTIFICATE-/,/-END CERTIFICATE-/p' > feistyduck.chain
```

Another useful trick is to pipe the output of s_client directly to the x509 tool. The following command shows detailed server information, along with its SHA256 fingerprint:

```
$ echo | openssl s_client -connect www.feistyduck.com:443 2>&1 | openssl x509 ↵
-noout -text -fingerprint -sha256
```

Sometimes you will need to take the certificate fingerprint and use it with other tools. Unfortunately, OpenSSL outputs certificates in a format that shows individual bytes and separates them using colons. This handy command line normalizes certificate fingerprints by removing the colons and converting the hexadecimal characters to lowercase:

```
$ echo | openssl s_client -connect www.feistyduck.com:443 2>&1 | openssl x509 ↵
-noout -fingerprint -sha256 | sed 's/://g' | tr '[:upper:]' '[:lower:]' | sed 's↵
/sha256 fingerprint=//g'
```

> **Note**
>
> Connecting to remote TLS servers and reviewing their certificates is a pretty common operation, but you shouldn't spend your time remembering and typing these long commands. Instead, invest in writing a couple of shell functions that will package this functionality into easy-to-use commands.

## Testing Protocol Support

By default, s_client will try to use the best protocol to talk to the remote server and report the negotiated version in output. As mentioned earlier, you will find the protocol version in the output twice, and you want the line that explicitly talks about the protocol:[3]

```
    Protocol  : TLSv1.2
```

If you need to test support for specific protocol versions, you have two options. You can explicitly choose one protocol to test by supplying one of the -ssl2, -ssl3, -tls1, -tls1_1, -tls1_2, or tls1_3 switches. Naturally, each switch requires support for a specific protocol version in the testing tool. If you want to exclude a particular protocol from the testing, there is a family of switches that disable protocols (e.g., -no_tls_1_2 for TLS 1.2). Sometimes that may be the better approach. Starting with OpenSSL 1.1.0, there are two new options, -min_protocol and -max_protocol, which control the minimum and maximum protocol version, respectively.

For example, here's the output you might get when testing a server that doesn't support a certain protocol version:

---

[3] Do note that when connecting to a TLS 1.3 server, the protocol information may not appear immediately on the connection. Instead, it will be printed when the session ticket is received, which may take a couple of seconds with some servers.

```
$ openssl s_client -connect www.example.com:443 -tls1_2
CONNECTED(00000003)
140455015261856:error:1408F10B:SSL routines:SSL3_GET_RECORD:wrong version ↵
number:s3_pkt.c:340:
---
no peer certificate available
---
No client certificate CA names sent
---
SSL handshake has read 5 bytes and written 7 bytes
---
New, (NONE), Cipher is (NONE)
Secure Renegotiation IS NOT supported
Compression: NONE
Expansion: NONE
SSL-Session:
    Protocol  : TLSv1.2
    Cipher    : 0000
    Session-ID:
    Session-ID-ctx:
    Master-Key:
    Key-Arg   : None
    PSK identity: None
    PSK identity hint: None
    SRP username: None
    Start Time: 1339231204
    Timeout   : 7200 (sec)
    Verify return code: 0 (ok)
---
```

Understanding if a server supports SSL 2.0 may sometimes require more work, due to the fact that this old and very insecure version of the SSL protocol uses a different handshake from that used from SSL 3.0 onward. Although servers that support only SSL 2.0 should now be very rare, to check this eventuality, you'll need to submit a separate check using the -ssl2 switch.

Another protocol difference is that SSL 2.0 servers are sometimes seen without any configured cipher suites. In that case, although SSL 2.0 is supported, technically speaking, any handshake attempts will still fail. You should treat this situation as misconfiguration.

# Testing Cipher Suite Configuration

It's not very likely that you will be spending a lot of time testing cipher suite configuration using OpenSSL on the command line. This is because you can effectively test for only one suite at a time; testing for more than 300 cipher suites that are supported by TLS 1.2

and earlier protocol revisions would take a considerable amount of time. This is a perfect opportunity to use those handy tools that automate the process.

Still, there will be times when you will need to probe servers to determine if they support a particular suite or a cryptographic primitive, or if the preference is correctly configured.

The introduction of TLS 1.3 made testing in this area slightly more complicated, but it's still manageable. Because of the differences between this protocol version and all other revisions, it's usually best to split your tests into two groups. When testing TLS 1.3, always use the -ciphersuites switch in combination with -tls1_3. The usual approach is to specify only one suite to determine if it's supported:

```
$ echo | openssl s_client -connect www.hardenize.com:443 -tls1_3 -ciphersuites TLS↵
_AES_128_GCM_SHA256 2>/dev/null| grep New
New, TLSv1.3, Cipher is TLS_AES_128_GCM_SHA256
```

The output will naturally be different if you pick a suite that is not supported:

```
$ echo | openssl s_client -connect www.hardenize.com:443 -tls1_3 -ciphersuites TLS↵
_AES_128_CCM_SHA256 2>/dev/null | grep New
New, (NONE), Cipher is (NONE)
```

When you're testing the configuration of TLS 1.2 and earlier protocol versions, use the -cipher switch in combination with -no_tls1_3 (assuming you're using a version of OpenSSL that supports TLS 1.3):

```
$ echo | openssl s_client -connect www.hardenize.com:443 -no_tls1_3 -cipher AESGCM ↵
2>/dev/null | grep New
New, TLSv1.2, Cipher is ECDHE-ECDSA-AES128-GCM-SHA256
```

As you can see in the previous example, when testing TLS 1.2 and earlier you don't have to specify only one cipher suite, but in that case you will need to observe what has been negotiated. If you want to probe further, you can always tweak the command line to remove the previously negotiated suite:

```
$ echo | openssl s_client -connect www.hardenize.com:443 -no_tls1_3 -cipher ↵
'AESGCM:!ECDHE-ECDSA-AES128-GCM-SHA256' 2>/dev/null | grep New
New, TLSv1.2, Cipher is ECDHE-ECDSA-AES256-GCM-SHA384
```

Even though you won't be testing for a great many suites manually, there is a quick way to determine if a particular server supports any of the many bad cryptographic primitives. To do this, use your *old* OpenSSL version and list all the bad cipher suite keywords, like this:

```
$ echo | openssl s_client -connect example.com:443 -cipher '3DES DES RC2 RC4 IDEA ↵
SEED CAMELLIA MD5 aNULL eNULL EXPORT LOW' 2>/dev/null | grep New
New, TLSv1/SSLv3, Cipher is DHE-RSA-CAMELLIA256-SHA
```

Another good test is to see if a server supports the RSA key exchange that doesn't support forward secrecy:

```
$ echo | /opt/openssl-1.0.2g/bin/openssl s_client -connect example.com:443 -cipher ↵
kRSA 2>/dev/null | grep New
New, TLSv1/SSLv3, Cipher is AES128-GCM-SHA256
```

Ideally, you'd get a handshake failure here, but it's not terrible if you don't, provided the server uses the RSA key exchange only as a matter of last resort. You can check this by offering suites with forward secrecy as your least preferred option:

```
$ echo | /opt/openssl-1.0.2g/bin/openssl s_client -connect example.com:443 -cipher ↵
'DHE ECDHE kRSA +kECDHE +kDHE' 2>/dev/null | grep New
New, TLSv1/SSLv3, Cipher is ECDHE-RSA-AES128-GCM-SHA256
```

# Testing Cipher Suite Preference

As a general rule, TLS servers should always be configured to enforce their cipher suite preferences, ensuring that they negotiate their preferred cipher suite with every client. This feature is essential with TLS 1.2 and earlier protocol revisions, which support many cipher suites, most of them undesirable. It's a different story with TLS 1.3: it only has a handful of suites available at this time and all of them are secure, so enforcing server preference doesn't matter that much.[4]

> **Note**
>
> Because cipher suite preference doesn't matter much with TLS 1.3, some stacks don't even support it with this protocol, even if they do with earlier protocol versions. Thus, for the best results, you will want to test separately for TLS 1.3 and everything else—or separately for every supported protocol. This is another case in which automation is the better choice.

To test for server suite preference, you first need to have some idea of what suites are supported. For example, you could have the complete list of supported suites. Alternatively, you can probe the server with different suite types—for example, those that use ECDHE versus DHE or RSA key exchange.

With two suites in hand, you need to initiate two connections, first offering one of the suites as your first choice, then the other:

```
$ echo | openssl s_client -connect www.hardenize.com:443 -tls1_3 -ciphersuites ↵
'TLS_AES_128_GCM_SHA256:TLS_AES_256_GCM_SHA384' 2>/dev/null | grep New
```

---

[4] Out of five cipher suites that TLS 1.3 supports, OpenSSL enables only three by default. The remaining two are CCM suites, which are intended for use with embedded systems, in which every little bit of performance and battery life matters. These suites are not worth using for other use cases—especially the CCM_8 suite, which reduces the strength of authentication.

```
New, TLSv1.3, Cipher is TLS_AES_128_GCM_SHA256
zoom:~ ivanr$ echo | openssl s_client -connect www.hardenize.com:443 -tls1_3 ↵
-ciphersuites 'TLS_AES_256_GCM_SHA384:TLS_AES_128_GCM_SHA256' 2>/dev/null | grep ↵
New
New, TLSv1.3, Cipher is TLS_AES_256_GCM_SHA384
```

If you see the same suite negotiated on both connections, that means that the server is configured to actively select negotiated suites. Otherwise, it isn't. The server in the previous example is one of those TLS 1.3 servers that doesn't enforce preference. That very same server does have a preference with TLS 1.2; we can see that it always selects a better suite, even when we push it to the end of our list:

```
$ echo | openssl s_client -connect www.hardenize.com:443 -no_tls1_3 -cipher ↵
'ECDHE+AESGCM RSA' 2>/dev/null | grep New
New, TLSv1.2, Cipher is ECDHE-ECDSA-AES128-GCM-SHA256
$ echo | openssl s_client -connect www.hardenize.com:443 -no_tls1_3 -cipher ↵
'ECDHE+AESGCM RSA +ECDHE' 2>/dev/null | grep New
New, TLSv1.2, Cipher is ECDHE-ECDSA-AES128-GCM-SHA256
```

When it comes to server suite preference testing, the ChaCha20 suites are best avoided. This is because some servers support another type of preference, where they treat AES-GCM and ChaCha20 suites as equal in terms of security and respect client preference as a special case. The idea is that the client will prefer the faster cipher suite, which is typically ChaCha20 for mobile devices and AES-GCM for desktops.

That said, with servers that support this type of preference, you may want to test if it's working correctly. To do that, you'll need to use three supported cipher suites and three tests. The purpose of the first two tests is to establish that the server selects its favorite suite when ChaCha20 is not involved:

```
$ echo | openssl s_client -connect www.hardenize.com:443 -no_tls1_3 -cipher ↵
'ECDHE-RSA-AES128-GCM-SHA256 ECDHE-ECDSA-AES128-GCM-SHA256 ECDHE-ECDSA-CHACHA20-POL↵
Y1305' 2>/dev/null | grep New
New, TLSv1.2, Cipher is ECDHE-ECDSA-AES128-GCM-SHA256
$ echo | openssl s_client -connect www.hardenize.com:443 -no_tls1_3 -cipher ↵
'ECDHE-ECDSA-AES128-GCM-SHA256 ECDHE-RSA-AES128-GCM-SHA256  ECDHE-ECDSA-CHACHA20-PO↵
LY1305' 2>/dev/null | grep New
New, TLSv1.2, Cipher is ECDHE-ECDSA-AES128-GCM-SHA256
```

If you see that the server responds with the same suite in both cases, you can submit another test with a supported ChaCha20 suite first. If you see the server selecting it, you know it's configured to support the client-preferred suite:

```
$ echo | openssl s_client -connect www.hardenize.com:443 -no_tls1_3 -cipher ↵
'ECDHE-ECDSA-CHACHA20-POLY1305 ECDHE-RSA-AES128-GCM-SHA256 ECDHE-ECDSA-AES128-GCM-S↵
```

```
HA256'  2>/dev/null | grep New
New, TLSv1.2, Cipher is ECDHE-ECDSA-CHACHA20-POLY1305
```

# Testing Named Groups

*Named groups* are predefined cryptographic parameters that are used for key exchange. In TLS 1.3, named groups include both elliptic curve (EC) and finite field (DH) parameters. TLS 1.2 and earlier generally use only predefined elliptic curves; the server provides DH parameters on every connection.[5] In a handshake, the client and server have to agree on a common named group over which the key exchange will take place, and it's important that the selected group satisfies desired security requirements.

In practice, there is seldom a need to test servers for named groups. Although there's a fair number of named groups in various RFCs, OpenSSL is probably the only major client to have extensive support. Historically, you could only use NIST's P-256 and P-384 EC groups because these were the only widely supported curves. Relatively recently, X25519 and X448 groups were added as an alternative. Because all these curves are strong, there is little need to spend time thinking about them.

You may find yourself testing named group configuration usually to understand what your web server is doing. For example, you may care about X25519 and want to ensure it's available and preferred. To test for this, use the s_client tool and the -curves switch. For example, here's how to determine if a single named group is supported:

```
$ echo | openssl s_client -connect hardenize.com:443 -curves X25519 2>/dev/null | ↵
grep "Server Temp Key"
Server Temp Key: X25519, 253 bits
```

On success, you will see the named group in the output, because that's the group that was selected for the handshake. On failure, you may see no output, which means that the handshake failed. Alternatively, the server, unable to negotiate an ECDHE suite, may fall back to a DHE suite, indicated by the following output:

```
Server Temp Key: DH, 2048 bits
```

If you need to test for named group preference, you need to offer two or more named groups, with your preferred one last. If you see it negotiated, that will mean that the server actively chooses the group it considers most appropriate. Use colons to separate the groups and be aware that the names are case-sensitive.

---

[5] RFC 7919, which came out in 2016, redefined the elliptic_curves TLS extension to support finite field groups and changed the extension name to supported_groups. Although this extension applies to TLS 1.2, support for it is not widespread.

---

```
$ echo | openssl s_client -connect hardenize.com:443 -curves prime256v1:X25519 ↵
2>/dev/null | grep "Server Temp Key"
Server Temp Key: X25519, 253 bits
```

> **Note**
>
> You can get the complete list of elliptic curves supported by OpenSSL using the
> ecparam tool and the -list_curves switch. To that list, add X25519 and X448.
> Support for finite field groups is currently not available but should arrive with
> OpenSSL 3.0.

# Testing DANE

*DNS-based Authentication of Named Entities* (DANE) is a set of standards that enables you
to endorse the TLS certificates you use via DNS configuration. For this to work, DANE
requires DNS itself to be secure, which means that DNSSEC is necessary. Therefore, DANE
is essentially a mechanism for pinning; only the certificates you approve will be accepted as
valid by DANE-enabled clients. DANE itself is not controversial, but DNSSEC, on which it
relies, is a very divisive topic, with the world split between those who love it and those who
hate it. As a result, DANE is currently not universally supported. It's more commonly used
to secure SMTP servers; there is no support at the browser level.

Supporting DANE adds some complexity to your TLS deployments because of the way DNS
configuration is propagated and cached. Before you use a new certificate you need to ensure
that your new DNS configuration (endorsing that certificate) is fully propagated. Thus, you
would typically first publish your DNS changes, wait for a period time sufficient for the
caches to clear, and only then deploy the certificates.[6]

The testing itself is straightforward; you use the s_client tool while feeding it DANE data.
This is handy because it enables you to test a connection even before making DNS changes.
First, let's see what DANE configuration looks like.

DANE stores configuration in TLSA resource records, using two prefix labels to indicate the
protocol and port:

```
$ host -t TLSA _25._tcp.mail.protonmail.ch
_25._tcp.mail.protonmail.ch has TLSA record 3 1 1 76BB66711DA416433CA890A5B2E5A0533↵
C6006478F7D10A4469A947A CC8399E1
_25._tcp.mail.protonmail.ch has TLSA record 3 1 1 6111A5698D23C89E09C36FF833C1487ED↵
C1B0C841F87C49DAE8F7A09 E11E979E
```

This output contains two endorsements, one per certificate. Having two endorsements is not
unusual. For example, perhaps you might have a service that uses two certificates (e.g., one
with an RSA key and another with an ECDSA key), or you have a backup certificate, or

---

[6] New Adventures in DNSSEC and DANE [fsty.uk/t599] (Jan Schaumann, retrieved 2 October 2020)

you're simply in a transitional period when you're switching certificates. The three numbers at the beginning indicate that the endorsement targets the certificate directly (3) via its public key (1) and a SHA256 hash (1). The rest of the data is the hash itself.

To test, you connect to the SMTP service while providing the DANE data using the -dane_tlsa_domain and -dane_tlsa_rrdata switches:

```
$ openssl s_client -starttls smtp \
-connect mail.protonmail.ch:25 \
-dane_tlsa_domain mail.protonmail.ch \
-dane_tlsa_rrdata "3 1 1 76BB66711DA416433CA890A5B2E5A0533C6006478F7D10A4469A947ACC↵
8399E1"
```

If the verification is successful, you will see something like this in the output:

```
---
SSL handshake has read 5209 bytes and written 433 bytes
Verification: OK
Verified peername: *.protonmail.ch
DANE TLSA 3 1 1 ...8f7d10a4469a947acc8399e1 matched EE certificate at depth 0
---
```

If you'd like to test for validation failure, just break the supplied hash. The result will be similar to the following output:

```
---
SSL handshake has read 5209 bytes and written 433 bytes
Verification error: No matching DANE TLSA records
---
```

For the best results, when testing DANE in this way, always provide all known TLSA records (one per -dane_tlsa_rrdata switch). If you do, services that use multiple certificates simultaneously will check out no matter what certificate is negotiated. For TLS 1.2 and earlier, it's possible to force a particular certificate via a choice of client-supported cipher suites (the -cipher switch). TLS 1.3 suites are different, and for this protocol version you would need to use the -sigalgs switch with a value such as ecdsa_secp256r1_sha256 or rsa_pss_rsae_sha256.

# Testing Session Resumption

When coupled with the -reconnect switch, the s_client command can be used to test session reuse. In this mode, s_client will connect to the target server six times. It will create a new session on the first connection, then try to reuse the same session in the subsequent five connections:

```
$ echo | openssl s_client -connect www.feistyduck.com:443 -reconnect
```

> **Note**
>
> Due to a bug in OpenSSL, at the time of writing session resumption testing doesn't
> work in combination with TLS 1.3. Until the bug is resolved,[7] the best you can do is
> test the earlier protocol versions. Use the -no_tls1_3 switch.

The previous command will produce a sea of output, most of which you won't care about.
The key parts are the information about new and reused sessions. There should be only one
new session at the beginning, indicated by the following line:

```
New, TLSv1.2, Cipher is ECDHE-RSA-AES128-GCM-SHA256
```

This is followed by five session reuses, indicated by lines like this:

```
Reused, TLSv1.2, Cipher is ECDHE-RSA-AES128-GCM-SHA256
```

Most of the time, you don't want to look at all that output and want an answer quickly. You
can get it using the following command line:

```
$ echo | openssl s_client -connect www.feistyduck.com:443 -reconnect 2> /dev/null ↵
| grep 'New\|Reuse'
New, TLSv1.2, Cipher is ECDHE-RSA-AES128-GCM-SHA256
Reused, TLSv1.2, Cipher is ECDHE-RSA-AES128-GCM-SHA256
Reused, TLSv1.2, Cipher is ECDHE-RSA-AES128-GCM-SHA256
Reused, TLSv1.2, Cipher is ECDHE-RSA-AES128-GCM-SHA256
Reused, TLSv1.2, Cipher is ECDHE-RSA-AES128-GCM-SHA256
Reused, TLSv1.2, Cipher is ECDHE-RSA-AES128-GCM-SHA256
```

Here's what the command does:

- The -reconnect switch activates the session reuse mode.
- The 2> /dev/null part hides stderr output, which you don't care about.
- Finally, the piped grep command filters out the rest of the fluff and lets through only
  the lines that you care about.

> **Note**
>
> If you don't want to include session tickets in the test—for example, because not all
> clients support this feature yet—you can disable this method of resumption using
> the -no_ticket switch. This option doesn't apply to TLS 1.3.

[7] s_client -reconnect Option Is Broken with TLSv1.3 [fsty.uk/t600] (OpenSSL, retrieved 31 August 2020)

# Keeping Session State across Connections

If you need better control over resumption, the s_client tool provides options to persist the connection state to a file. On your first connection, use the -sess_out switch to record the state:

```
$ openssl s_client -connect www.feistyduck.com:443 -sess_out sess.pem
```

To view the recorded state, use the sess_id tool:

```
$ openssl sess_id -in sess.pem -noout -text
SSL-Session:
    Protocol  : TLSv1.2
    Cipher    : ECDHE-ECDSA-AES128-GCM-SHA256
    Session-ID: F7384C2C4BE621F66045ECE12A89821FEE789C2E75B78C90C428BE37E0FE4599
    Session-ID-ctx:
    Master-Key: 9D39C582D9AA1618B2F16C7911C4BFFB61D6D1FD578A93B1145FD2B4DBFDE76EB22↵
79BA50AEFFCD95320BEEBC9489FAF
    PSK identity: None
    PSK identity hint: None
    SRP username: None
    TLS session ticket lifetime hint: 64800 (seconds)
    TLS session ticket:
    0000 - a2 d3 e3 04 03 21 85 6d-1a 4f 9c 82 fc 4e 15 e0   .....!.m.O...N..
    0010 - 9b b8 b1 24 0d 95 a3 0a-b8 24 d4 f5 d2 be b8 56   ...$.....$.....V
    0020 - b2 f0 e9 c5 e5 53 31 b5-24 74 96 ba e4 56 32 68   .....S1.$t...V2h
    0030 - fe bb 7a 7f 28 d7 c4 19-6a c5 ca 22 3a a7 2d 45   ..z.(...j..":.-E
    0040 - 52 91 74 f7 a8 fa 75 40-02 b9 84 9c 84 0d a8 06   R.t...u@........
    0050 - c7 a1 65 af 8b 54 19 74-52 e8 c4 f4 47 1c 3f f0   ..e..T.tR...G.?.
    0060 - 46 35 1a 3c a9 a5 73 30-33 b7 20 bd dc 8a b8 f9   F5.<..sO3. .....
    0070 - 79 20 4a de b3 60 83 53-c7 a7 62 e1 a2 9e 55 8c   y J..`.S..b...U.
    0080 - 24 0a f5 4c ab 81 a5 d9-36 ae 52 61 a1 4e b7 99   $..L....6.Ra.N..
    0090 - 20 9e ca 67 49 ea 80 a4-14 ce ac 36 aa 20 0e 53    ..gI......6. .S
    00a0 - d7 9f 14 a6 7c b9 88 4c-6b 69 93 d4 62 fb 02 50   ....|..Lki..b..P

    Start Time: 1602414785
    Timeout   : 300 (sec)
    Verify return code: 20 (unable to get local issuer certificate)
    Extended master secret: no
```

Finally, to connect again using the same session state, use the -sess_in switch:

```
$ openssl s_client -connect www.feistyduck.com:443 -sess_in sess.pem
```

Keeping the state across connections in this way gives you more control and enables you to completely change connection parameters from one connection to another. For example, you could connect to one server on your first attempt, then another server on your second.

---

This may be of use when you need to test if session resumption is correctly implemented on a web server cluster. Manual control of your connections allows you to spread them over time, perhaps testing for session timeouts and ticket key rotation.

# Checking OCSP Revocation

If an OCSP responder is malfunctioning, sometimes it's difficult to understand exactly why. Checking certificate revocation status from the command line is possible, but it's not quite straightforward. You need to perform the following steps:

1. Obtain the certificate that you wish to check for revocation.

2. Obtain the issuing certificate.

3. Determine the URL of the OCSP responder.

4. Submit an OCSP request and observe the response.

For the first two steps, connect to the server with the -showcerts switch specified:

```
$ openssl s_client -connect www.feistyduck.com:443 -showcerts
```

The first certificate in the output will be the one belonging to the server. If the certificate chain is properly configured, the second certificate will be that of the issuer. To confirm, check that the issuer of the first certificate matches the subject of the second:

```
Certificate chain
 0 s:OU = Domain Control Validated, OU = PositiveSSL, CN = www.feistyduck.com
   i:C = GB, ST = Greater Manchester, L = Salford, O = COMODO CA Limited, CN = ↵
COMODO RSA Domain Validation Secure Server CA
-----BEGIN CERTIFICATE-----
MIIFUzCCBDugAwIBAgIRAPR/CbWZEksfCIRqxNcesPIwDQYJKoZIhvcNAQELBQAw
[...]
zbQXjVsc3E1THfFZWRzDPsU4fN/1iGlbrcAWa2sFfhJXrCDfAowFJ8A1n9jMiNEG
WfQfGgA2ar2xUtsqA7Re6XlXOlwBPuQ=
-----END CERTIFICATE-----
 1 s:C = GB, ST = Greater Manchester, L = Salford, O = COMODO CA Limited, CN = ↵
COMODO RSA Domain Validation Secure Server CA
   i:C = GB, ST = Greater Manchester, L = Salford, O = COMODO CA Limited, CN = ↵
COMODO RSA Certification Authority
-----BEGIN CERTIFICATE-----
MIIGCDCCA/CgAwIBAgIQKy5u6tl1NmwUim7bo3yMBzANBgkqhkiG9w0BAQwFADCB
hTELMAkGA1UEBhMCROIxGzAZBgNVBAgTEkdyZWF0ZXIgTWFuY2hlc3RlcjEQMA4G
[...]
```

If the second certificate isn't the right one, check the rest of the chain; some servers don't serve the chain in the correct order. If you can't find the issuer certificate in the chain, you'll have to find it somewhere else. One way to do that is to look for the *Authority Information Access* extension in the leaf certificate:

```
$ openssl x509 -in fd.crt -noout -text
[...]
    Authority Information Access:
        CA Issuers - URI:http://crt.comodoca.com/COMODORSADomainValidationSecureSer↵
verCA.crt
        OCSP - URI:http://ocsp.comodoca.com
```

If the *CA Issuers* information is present, it should contain the URL of the issuer certificate. If the issuer certificate information isn't available, you can try to open the site in a browser, let it reconstruct the chain, and download the issuing certificate from its certificate viewer. If all that fails, you can look for the certificate in your trust store or visit the CA's web site.

If you already have the certificates and just need to know the address of the OCSP responder, use the -ocsp_uri switch with the x509 command as a shortcut:

```
$ openssl x509 -in fd.crt -noout -ocsp_uri
http://ocsp.comodoca.com
```

Now you can submit the OCSP request:

```
$ openssl ocsp -issuer issuer.crt -cert fd.crt -url http://ocsp.comodoca.com ↵
-CAfile issuer.crt
WARNING: no nonce in response
Response verify OK
fd.crt: good
        This Update: Aug 30 22:35:12 2020 GMT
        Next Update: Sep  6 22:35:12 2020 GMT
```

You want to look for two things in the response. First, check that the response itself is valid (Response verify OK in the previous example), and second, check what the response said. When you see good as the status, that means that the certificate hasn't been revoked. The status will be revoked for revoked certificates.

> **Note**
>
> The warning message about the missing nonce is telling you that OpenSSL wanted to use a nonce as a protection against replay attacks, but the server in question did not reply with one. This generally happens because CAs want to improve the performance of their OCSP responders. When they disable the nonce protection (the standard allows it), OCSP responses can be produced (usually in batch), cached, and reused for a period of time.

You may encounter OCSP responders that do not respond successfully to the previous command line. The following suggestions may help in such situations.

---

**Do not request a nonce**

Some servers cannot handle nonce requests and respond with errors. OpenSSL will request a nonce by default. To disable nonces, use the -no_nonce command-line switch.

**Supply a Host request header**

Although most OCSP servers respond to HTTP requests that don't specify the correct hostname in the Host header, some don't. If you encounter an error message that includes an HTTP error code (e.g., 404), try adding the hostname to your OCSP request. You can do this with the help of the -header switch.

With the previous two points in mind, the final command to use is the following:

```
$ openssl ocsp -issuer issuer.crt -cert fd.crt -url http://ocsp.comodoca.com ↵
-CAfile issuer.crt -no_nonce -header Host ocsp.comodoca.com
```

# Testing OCSP Stapling

OCSP stapling is an optional feature that allows a server certificate to be accompanied by an OCSP response that proves its validity. Because the OCSP response is delivered over an already existing connection, the client does not have to fetch it separately.

OCSP stapling is used only if requested by a client, which submits the status_request extension in the handshake request. A server that supports OCSP stapling will respond by including an OCSP response as part of the handshake.

When using the s_client tool, OCSP stapling is requested with the -status switch:

```
$ echo | openssl s_client -connect www.feistyduck.com:443 -status
```

The OCSP-related information will be displayed at the very beginning of the connection output. For example, with a server that does not support stapling you will see this line near the top of the output:

```
CONNECTED(00000003)
OCSP response: no response sent
```

With a server that does support stapling, you will see the entire OCSP response in the output:

```
OCSP Response Data:
    OCSP Response Status: successful (0x0)
    Response Type: Basic OCSP Response
    Version: 1 (0x0)
    Responder Id: 90AF6A3A945A0BD890EA125673DF43B43A28DAE7
    Produced At: Aug 30 22:35:12 2020 GMT
    Responses:
```

```
Certificate ID:
  Hash Algorithm: sha1
  Issuer Name Hash: 7AE13EE8A0C42A2CB428CBE7A605461940E2A1E9
  Issuer Key Hash: 90AF6A3A945A0BD890EA125673DF43B43A28DAE7
  Serial Number: F47F09B599124B1F08846AC4D71EB0F2
Cert Status: good
This Update: Aug 30 22:35:12 2020 GMT
Next Update: Sep  6 22:35:12 2020 GMT

Signature Algorithm: sha256WithRSAEncryption
     1b:9d:be:3e:e6:b2:9a:e6:22:fe:69:cc:55:a9:62:5d:29:79:
     [...]
```

The certificate status good means that the certificate has not been revoked.

# Checking CRL Revocation

Checking certificate verification with a *Certificate Revocation List* (CRL) is even more involved than doing the same via OCSP. The process is as follows:

1. Obtain the certificate you wish to check for revocation.

2. Obtain the issuing certificate.

3. Download and verify the CRL.

4. Look for the certificate serial number in the CRL.

The first steps overlap with OCSP checking; to complete them follow the instructions in the section called "Checking OCSP Revocation".

The location of the CRL is encoded in the server certificate; look for the "X509v3 CRL Distribution Points" section in the text output. For example:

```
$ openssl x509 -in fd.crt -noout -text | grep -A 5 CRL
[...]
                URI:http://crl.comodoca.com/COMODORSADomainValidationSecureServer↵
CA.crl
```

Then fetch the CRL from the CA:

```
$ wget http://crl.comodoca.com/COMODORSADomainValidationSecureServerCA.crl -O ↵
comodo.crl
```

Verify that the CRL is valid (i.e., signed by the issuer certificate):

```
$ openssl crl -in comodo.crl -inform DER -CAfile issuer.crt -noout
verify OK
```

Now, determine the serial number of the certificate you wish to check:

---

```
$ openssl x509 -in fd.crt -noout -serial
serial=F47F09B599124B1F08846AC4D71EB0F2
```

At this point, you can convert the CRL into a human-readable format and inspect it manually:

```
$ openssl crl -in comodo.crl -inform DER -text -noout
Certificate Revocation List (CRL):
        Version 2 (0x1)
        Signature Algorithm: sha256WithRSAEncryption
        Issuer: C = GB, ST = Greater Manchester, L = Salford, O = COMODO CA ↵
Limited, CN = COMODO RSA Domain Validation Secure Server CA
        Last Update: Aug 31 07:52:03 2020 GMT
        Next Update: Sep  7 07:52:03 2020 GMT
        CRL extensions:
            X509v3 Authority Key Identifier:
                keyid:90:AF:6A:3A:94:5A:0B:D8:90:EA:12:56:73:DF:43:B4:3A:28:DA:E7

            X509v3 CRL Number:
                2149
            1.3.6.1.4.1.311.21.4:
200903195203Z    .
Revoked Certificates:
    Serial Number: 70DAB4B3229280F04364BC58DB2AB922
        Revocation Date: May 29 12:18:27 2017 GMT
    Serial Number: 51894D40389CDAB84A7A6F3374E1D893
        Revocation Date: May 30 23:20:55 2017 GMT
    [...]
    Signature Algorithm: sha256WithRSAEncryption
        5a:7c:6e:6e:98:05:c4:24:2b:84:7a:28:6f:45:26:33:6b:88:
        4d:dd:61:22:e4:23:47:76:c7:8a:55:ec:f9:72:29:47:21:73:
        [...]
```

The CRL starts with some metadata, which is followed by a list of revoked certificates, and it ends with a signature (which we verified in the previous step). If the serial number of the server certificate is on the list, that means it had been revoked.

If you don't want to look for the serial number visually (some CRLs can be quite long), grep for it, but be careful that your formatting matches that used by the crl tool. For example:

```
$ openssl crl -in comodo.crl -inform DER -text -noout | grep F47F09B599124B1F08846A↵
C4D71EB0F2
```

# Testing Renegotiation

In TLS, renegotiation is a failed feature that was responsible for several protocol weaknesses, some of which are quite easy to exploit. TLS 1.3 no longer supports renegotiation, but there are still older servers out there that support it with earlier protocol revisions.

The s_client tool has a couple of features that can assist you with manual testing of renegotiation. First of all, when you connect, the tool will report if the remote server supports secure renegotiation. This is because a server that supports secure renegotiation indicates its support for it via a special TLS extension that is exchanged during the handshake phase. When support is available, the output may look like this:

```
New, TLSv1/SSLv3, Cipher is AES256-SHA
Server public key is 2048 bit
Secure Renegotiation IS supported
Compression: NONE
Expansion: NONE
SSL-Session:
    [...]
```

If secure renegotiation is not supported, the output will be slightly different:

```
Secure Renegotiation IS NOT supported
```

> ### Note
>
> Because TLS 1.3 doesn't support renegotiation, the s_client tool will always give a
> negative answer if this protocol version is negotiated. To ensure reliable results, use
> the -no_tls1_3 switch to force negotiation of an earlier protocol version.

Even if the server indicates support for secure renegotiation, you may wish to test whether it also allows clients to initiate renegotiation. *Client-initiated renegotiation* is a protocol feature that doesn't serve any purpose in practice (because the server can always initiate renegotiation when it is needed) and makes the server more susceptible to denial of service attacks.

To initiate renegotiation, after the TLS handshake is complete, type an R character on a line by itself. For example, assuming we're talking to an HTTP server, you can type the first line of a request, initiate renegotiation, and then finish the request. Here's what that looks like when talking to a web server that supports client-initiated renegotiation:

```
GET / HTTP/1.0
R
RENEGOTIATING
depth=2 C = US, O = DigiCert Inc, OU = www.digicert.com, CN = DigiCert High ↵
Assurance EV Root CA
verify return:1
```

```
depth=1 C = US, O = DigiCert Inc, OU = www.digicert.com, CN = DigiCert SHA2 ↵
Extended Validation Server CA
verify return:1
depth=0 businessCategory = Private Organization, jurisdictionC = US, ↵
jurisdictionST = California, serialNumber = C2543436, C = US, ST = California, L = ↵
Mountain View, O = Mozilla Foundation, OU = Cloud Services, CN = addons.mozilla.org
verify return:1
Host: addons.mozilla.org

HTTP/1.1 301 Moved Permanently
Content-Type: text/plain; charset=utf-8
Date: Mon, 31 Aug 2020 12:40:49 GMT
Location: /en-US/firefox/
Strict-Transport-Security: max-age=31536000
Content-Length: 49
Connection: Close

Moved Permanently. Redirecting to /en-US/firefox/closed
```

When renegotiation is taking place, the server will send its certificates to the client again. You can see the verification of the certificate chain in the output. The next line after that continues with the Host request header. Seeing the web server's response is the proof that renegotiation is supported. Because of the various ways the renegotiation issue was addressed in various versions of SSL/TLS libraries, servers that do not support renegotiation may break the connection or may keep it open but refuse to continue to talk over it (which usually results in a timeout).

A server that does not support renegotiation will flatly refuse the second handshake on the connection:

```
HEAD / HTTP/1.0
R
RENEGOTIATING
140003560109728:error:1409E0E5:SSL routines:SSL3_WRITE_BYTES:ssl handshake ↵
failure:s3_pkt.c:592:
```

At the time of writing, the default behavior for OpenSSL is to connect to servers that don't support secure renegotiation; it will also accept both secure and insecure renegotiation, opting for whatever the server is able to do. If renegotiation is successful with a server that doesn't support secure renegotiation, you will know that the server supports insecure client-initiated renegotiation.

> ### Note
>
> The most reliable way to test for insecure renegotiation is to use the method described in this section, but with a version of OpenSSL that was released before the discovery of insecure renegotiation (e.g., 0.9.8k). I mention this because there

is a small number of servers that support both secure and insecure renegotiation. This vulnerability is difficult to detect with modern versions of OpenSSL, which always prefer the secure option.

# Testing for Heartbleed

You can test for Heartbleed manually with OpenSSL or by using one of the tools designed for this purpose. There are now many utilities available, because Heartbleed is very easy to exploit. But, as usual with such tools, there is a question of their accuracy. There is evidence that some tools fail to detect vulnerable servers.[8] Given the seriousness of Heartbleed, it's best to either test manually or by using a tool that gives you full visibility of the process. I am going to describe an approach you can use with only a modified version of OpenSSL.

Some parts of the test don't require modifications to OpenSSL, assuming you have a version that supports the Heartbeat protocol (starting with 1.0.1, but before 1.1.0). For example, to determine if the remote server supports the Heartbeat protocol, use the -tlsextdebug switch to display server extensions when connecting:

```
$ openssl s_client -connect www.feistyduck.com:443 -tlsextdebug
CONNECTED(00000003)
TLS server extension "renegotiation info" (id=65281), len=1
0001 - <SPACES/NULS>
TLS server extension "EC point formats" (id=11), len=4
0000 - 03 00 01 02                                       ....
TLS server extension "session ticket" (id=35), len=0
TLS server extension "heartbeat" (id=15), len=1
0000 - 01
[...]
```

A server that does not return the heartbeat extension is not vulnerable to Heartbleed. To test if a server responds to heartbeat requests, use the -msg switch to request that protocol messages are shown, connect to the server, wait until the handshake completes, then type B and press return:

```
$ openssl s_client -connect www.feistyduck.com:443 -tlsextdebug -msg
[...]
---
B
HEARTBEATING
>>> TLS 1.2  [length 0025], HeartbeatRequest
    01 00 12 00 00 3c 83 1a 9f 1a 5c 84 aa 86 9e 20
    c7 a2 ac d7 6f f0 c9 63 9b d5 85 bf 9a 47 61 27
    d5 22 4c 70 75
```

---

[8] Bugs in Heartbleed detection scripts [fsty.uk/t601] (Shannon Simpson and Adrian Hayter, 14 April 2014)

```
<<< TLS 1.2  [length 0025], HeartbeatResponse
    02 00 12 00 00 3c 83 1a 9f 1a 5c 84 aa 86 9e 20
    c7 a2 ac d7 6f 52 4c ee b3 d8 a1 75 9a 6b bd 74
    f8 60 32 99 1c
read R BLOCK
```

This output shows a complete heartbeat request and response. The second and third bytes in both heartbeat messages specify payload length. We submitted a payload of 18 bytes (12 hexadecimal) and the server responded with a payload of the same size. In both cases there were also additional 16 bytes of padding. The first two bytes in the payload make the sequence number, which OpenSSL uses to match responses to requests. The remaining payload bytes and the padding are just random data.

To detect a vulnerable server, you'll have to prepare a special version of OpenSSL that sends an incorrect payload length. Vulnerable servers take the declared payload length and respond with that many bytes irrespective of the length of the actual payload provided.

At this point, you have to decide if you want to build an invasive test (which exploits the server by retrieving some data from the process) or a noninvasive test. This will depend on your circumstances. If you have permission for your testing activities, use the invasive test. With it, you'll be able to see exactly what is returned, and there won't be room for errors. For example, some versions of GnuTLS support Heartbeat and will respond to requests with incorrect payload length, but they will not actually return server data. A noninvasive test can't reliably diagnose that situation.

The following patch against OpenSSL 1.0.1h creates a noninvasive version of the test:

```
--- t1_lib.c.original    2014-07-04 17:29:35.092000000 +0100
+++ t1_lib.c     2014-07-04 17:31:44.528000000 +0100
@@ -2583,6 +2583,7 @@
 #endif

 #ifndef OPENSSL_NO_HEARTBEATS
+#define PAYLOAD_EXTRA 16
 int
 tls1_process_heartbeat(SSL *s)
        {
@@ -2646,7 +2647,7 @@
                * sequence number */
               n2s(pl, seq);

-              if (payload == 18 && seq == s->tlsext_hb_seq)
+              if ((payload == (18 + PAYLOAD_EXTRA)) && seq == s->tlsext_hb_seq)
                      {
                      s->tlsext_hb_seq++;
                      s->tlsext_hb_pending = 0;
@@ -2705,7 +2706,7 @@
```

```
            /* Message Type */
            *p++ = TLS1_HB_REQUEST;
            /* Payload length (18 bytes here) */
-           s2n(payload, p);
+           s2n(payload + PAYLOAD_EXTRA, p);
            /* Sequence number */
            s2n(s->tlsext_hb_seq, p);
            /* 16 random bytes */
```

To build a noninvasive test, increase payload length by up to 16 bytes, or the length of the padding. When a vulnerable server responds to such a request, it will return the padding but nothing else. To build an invasive test, increase the payload length by, say, 32 bytes. A vulnerable server will respond with a payload of 50 bytes (18 bytes sent by OpenSSL by default, plus your 32 bytes) and send 16 bytes of padding. By increasing the declared length of the payload in this way, a vulnerable server will return up to 64 KB of data. A server not vulnerable to Heartbleed will not respond.

To produce your own Heartbleed testing tool, unpack a fresh copy of OpenSSL source code, edit ssl/t1_lib.c to make the change as in the patch, compile as usual, but don't install. The resulting openssl binary will be placed in the apps/ subdirectory. Because it is statically compiled, you can rename it to something like openssl-heartbleed and move it to its permanent location.

Here's an example of the output you'd get with a vulnerable server that returns 16 bytes of server data (in bold):

```
B
HEARTBEATING
>>> TLS 1.2  [length 0025], HeartbeatRequest
    01 00 32 00 00 7c e8 f5 62 35 03 bb 00 34 19 4d
    57 7e f1 e5 90 6e 71 a9 26 85 96 1c c4 2b eb d5
    93 e2 d7 bb 5f
<<< TLS 1.2  [length 0045], HeartbeatResponse
    02 00 32 00 00 7c e8 f5 62 35 03 bb 00 34 19 4d
    57 7e f1 e5 90 6e 71 a9 26 85 96 1c c4 2b eb d5
    93 e2 d7 bb 5f 6f 81 0f aa dc e0 47 62 3f 7e dc
    60 95 c6 ba df c9 f6 9d 2b c8 66 f8 a5 45 64 0b
    d2 f5 3d a9 ad
read R BLOCK
```

If you want to see more data retrieved in a single response, increase the payload length, recompile, and test again. Alternatively, to retrieve another batch of the same size, use the B command again.

# Determining the Strength of Diffie-Hellman Parameters

Starting from OpenSSL 1.0.2, when you connect to a server, the s_client command prints the strength of the ephemeral Diffie-Hellman key if one is used. Thus, to determine the strength of server's DH parameters, all you need to do is connect to it while offering only suites that use the DH key exchange. For example:

```
$ openssl s_client -connect www.feistyduck.com:443 -cipher kEDH
[...]
---No client certificate CA names sent
Peer signing digest: SHA512
Peer signature type: RSA
Server Temp Key: DH, 2048 bits
---
[...]
```

Servers that support export suites might actually offer even weaker DH parameters. To check for that possibility, connect using your old OpenSSL[9] while offering only export DHE suites:

```
$ openssl s_client -connect www.feistyduck.com:443 -cipher kEDH+EXPORT
```

This command should fail with well-configured servers. Otherwise, you'll probably see the server offering to negotiate insecure 512-bit DH parameters.

---

[9] Support for EXPORT cipher suites was removed in OpenSSL 1.1.0.

# 14 Summary

Congratulations on making it all the way through this book! I hope you've had as much fun reading it as I did writing it. But with so many pages dedicated to the security of TLS, where are we now? Is TLS secure? Or is it irreparably broken and doomed?

As with many other questions, the answer is that it depends on what you expect. It's easy to poke holes in TLS by comparing it with an imaginary alternative that doesn't exist; and it's true, TLS has had many holes, which we've been repairing over the years. However, the success of a security protocol is measured not only in pure technical and security terms but also by its success and usefulness in real life. So, although it's certainly not perfect, TLS has been a great success for the billions of people who use it every day. If anything, the biggest problems in the TLS ecosystem come from the fact that we're not using enough encryption and that, when we do, we don't quite make up our minds if we really want proper security. (Think about certificate warnings.) The weaknesses in TLS are not our biggest problem.

Therefore, we're talking about the security of TLS because it's been so successful; otherwise we would have long ago replaced it with something better. But chances are that even if we replaced TLS with something else, years of steady use would have led us to the same result. It's impossible to achieve perfect security at a global scale. With its diversity, the world moves slowly and prefers avoiding breakage to enhanced security. And you know what? That's fine. It's the cost of participating in the global computer network.

The good news is that TLS itself has been fixed. At some point a couple of years ago, we started to pay more attention to security, especially encryption. This process accelerated during 2013, when we discovered the harsh reality of widespread mass surveillance. The TLS Working Group started to address the discovered issues and fixed a great many of them with the release of TLS 1.3 in 2018. Our next challenge is to deploy it everywhere, after which we can move onto other problems.

# Index

## Symbols

0/n split, 267
0-RTT, **50**, 332
1/n-1 split, 267
64-bit block ciphers, 312

## A

Abstract Syntax Notation One (see ASN.1)
ACME, 126
Active network attack (see MITM)
Advanced Encryption Standard, 8
AEAD (see Authenticated encryption)
AES (see Advanced Encryption Standard)
AIA (see Authority Information Access)
Alert protocol, 42, 80
Alice and Bob, 5
ALPACA, 251
ALPN, 86, 90
ANSSI, 156
Apple, 213
application_layer_protocol_negotiation extension, 86
Application data protocol, 80
Application Layer Protocol Negotiation (see ALPN)
ARP spoofing, 19
ASN.1, **101**, 217
Asymmetric encryption, 12
Authenticated encryption, 26, 78
Authority Information Access, 443
Authority Information Access certificate extension, **104**, 112
Authority Key Identifier certificate extension, 104

## B

Baseline Requirements, 100
Basic Constraints, **104**, 141, 212, 213, 442

Certificate extension, 104
Basic Encoding Rules (see BER)
BEAST, 262-272
BER, 101
BGP route hijacking, 20
Birthday paradox, 312
Bit (see Cryptography strength)
BlackSheep tool, 171
Black Tulip, 147
Bleichenbacher (see Bleichenbacher attack)
Bleichenbacher attack, 315
Block ciphers, 8
    In TLS, 76
    Modes of operation, 10
Brainpool elliptic curves, 87
BREACH, 278
    context hiding, 285
Bullrun, 319

## C

CA (see Certification authority)
CA/Browser Forum, The, 100
CAA (see Certification Authority Authorization)
Captive portals, 207
CBC, 11
    (see also Block ciphers)
    In TLS, 76
    Padding attacks, 287
    Predictable IV, 264
CCM, 78
Certificate, 100-108
    Chains, 106
    Conversion, 421
    Extensions, 103
    Fields, 101
    Intermediary certificates, 106
    Lifecycle, 110
    Lifetimes, 112
    Optimization, 338

---

Hardware acceleration, 347
History, 3
Limitations, 93
Protocol attacks, 253-321
Protocol goals, 2
Random fields, 63
Record, 23, 58
    Buffering, 346
    Overhead, 341
    Size tuning, 346
Session, 60
Session ID, 63
Stream encryption, 75
Working group, 57
TLS_EMPTY_RENEGOTIATION_INFO_SCSV, 90
TLS 1.0, 94, 262
TLS 1.1, 94
TLS 1.2, 57-95
TLS 1.3, 23-55
TLS Authentication Gap (see Insecure renegotiation)
transcript collision attacks, 307
Transport Layer Security (see TLS)
Triple Handshake Attack, 295-301
Truncation attacks, 247
Trust, 99
Trust anchor, 98
Trust Assertions for Certificate Keys (see TACK)
Trust store, 108, 407
Trustwave, 128
TURKTRUST, 156

## U

Unknown Key-Share, 295

## V

Verisign, 135
Virtual host confusion, 251
Voluntary Protocol Downgrade, 241

## W

WAN optimization, 334
Web PKI (see PKI)
Web Proxy Auto-Discovery Protocol, 19, 153
WEP, 289
WoSign
    Removal of trust, 163
WPAD (see Web Proxy Auto-Discovery)

## X

X.509 (see Certificate)

## Z

Zoombie POODLE (see POODLE TLS)

CPSIA information can be obtained
at www.ICGtesting.com
Printed in the USA
LVHW062122210723
753026LV00010B/1461